CATHOLIC CHURCH RECORDS

of the

PACIFIC NORTHWEST

ST. PAUL, OREGON

St. Paul's Mission, Willamette Valley — 1847

Catholic Church Records
of the Pacific Northwest:
St. Paul, Oregon 1839-1898
Volumes I, II and III

Compiled by

Harriet Duncan Munnick

In collaboration with

Mikell Delores Warner

Binford & Mort

Thomas Binford, Publisher

2536 S.E. Eleventh • Portland, Oregon 97202

Catholic Church Records of the Pacific Northwest
St. Paul, Oregon
Volumes I, II, and III
Copyright © 1979 by Binford & Mort, Publishers
Printed in the United States of America
Library of Congress Catalog Card Number: 79-3575
ISBN: 0-8323-0348-8
First Edition 1979

DEDICATION

For Mikell
whose eager pen was
too soon laid by

FOREWORD

Nothing is quite so difficult as piecing together with accuracy and completeness the detailed records of a segment of a significant period of history. The one who undertakes such a task must have an overpowering interest in the project, must be possessed of a profound conviction of the value of the work to present and future generations, must be ready to spend years in painstaking and frustrating research, and must be endowed with an inexhaustible reservoir of dedication and patience.

Harriet D. Munnick, author and compiler of *Catholic Church Records of the Pacific Northwest*, has the happy combination of all of the necessary ingredients to have been able to put together a monumental work which deserves to be on bookshelves not only throughout the Pacific Northwest, but throughout the United States and Canada. It is part of our roots.

The significance of such a work lies in its interpretation of an era then in transition. The record is not only that of the Church but of social change as the nomadic life of natives and adventurers gave way to an order of stability and community building. The important role of the Church in this transition is the underlying theme of the book. It is hoped that herein genealogists, sociologists and historians may each find something of interest in addition to the pure history of a hitherto little documented time and place.

+ Cornelius M. Power
Archbishop of Portland in Oregon

CONTENTS

ILLUSTRATIONS

PREFACE

The earliest Church records of St. Paul are found in the Vancouver Register, Volume I, under the caption "Acts made at the Catholic Mission of the Walamet". Father F.N. Blanchet made two missions to the French settlement of St. Paul, from January 6 to February 3 and from May 13 to June 10, 1839. He carried the records of these missions back to Fort Vancouver to be entered in his permanent register there.

The first St. Paul volume begins with the establishment of the parish in October, 1839. Other volumes continue to the present day, but for the authors' translations and annotations in this work here offered, an arbitrary cut-off date was set at 1898. The pioneer era had largely ended and the composition of the settlement had shifted from French Canadian to American, Irish and German newcomers. Oregon had become a state, with governmental records of the populace to supplement material formerly available through the Church.

The St. Paul Registers are nine by twelve inch books with pages of good quality paper. Ink has faded over the years, but little is entirely illegible. The originals are preserved in the Archives of the Archdiocese, and were made available to the authors through the kindness and courtesy of Archbishop Robert J. Dwyer. Most of the entries are written in French, with the occasional use of English when the communicant was not French Canadian, or of Latin for certain churchly matters.

The work of meticulously checking the translations was cut short by the untimely death of Mikell Warner on January 13, 1973, but little revision of her first careful work has proved necessary. Her "Translator's Notes", appearing in the Vancouver volume, are equally applicable to the present work:

In the interest of conserving space and for ease of reading, numerals are used for dates and ages, whereas the priests almost always wrote them in longhand.

( )   found in the text were used by the priests.

/ /   or brackets enclosing a different type face indicate material and/or information inserted by the compilers.

/?/   indicates a question as to reading - i.e. is unclear, partially illegible or subject to another interpretation.

. . .   means left blank by the priest.

_____means a line drawn by the priest.

"Engage" is used in translation rather than "employee" or "hired man", as being more definitive and having a special meaning in the Fur Companies.

"Metis" and "metisse", meaning mixed-blood, is used rather than the less precise "half-breed", as the former indicated not only Indian-white, but Iroquois-Western Indian, Hawaiian-Indian, and various mixtures of all three.

In the rigid social structure of the Fur Trade, protocol was observed, so we find "Sieur" and "Esquire" designating the gentlemen or Company officers; "Monsieur" and "Monsigneur" the Church hierarchy.

"Dit", meaning nicknamed or called, is confusing. The custom in French Canada of having and using a nickname was common. Sometimes in later years the "dit" came to be used as the surname of a family.

"Qui n'a su signer" (who has not known how to sign) was the format used by the priests, the records themselves being legal documents. In most cases it was true among a largely illiterate people, but sometimes the priest wrote it from force of habit when a person who was witness or godparent *could* sign. Again, many entries were first made as field notes, to be transcribed later into the register, and although the witness may have signed in the field, he was not at hand to sign the transcription.

Among the Indians (excluding Iroquois) and other peoples who did not have surnames, the priests used a patronymic system - i.e. the father's name (Christian or tribal) became the surname of the child. See Index abbreviation notes.

"Flathead" was used for both the Flathead tribe of the mountains and for some of the Chinookan peoples. Context, location and other clues must be considered to determine which is intended.

"Chez", meaning at the house, or place, of, included others than the family, such as orphans, relatives, slaves and hired help. There were often native huts clustered about a home. Inhabitants of these huts might be said to belong "to the house of" the landowner.

The best possible reading has been given to tribal names written by the priests, but this reading is open to other interpretation, as the priests, themselves, were trying to write the sounds they heard of difficult and gutteral native tongues.

The priests' spelling has been used throughout the text. They were not pedantic, often spelling a name in different ways in the same entry or on the same page, and omitting accent and punctuation marks.

[sic] has been used sparingly.

Slave means *a* slave, not the Indian tribe of Canada.

Place names in the text and Annotations - locations, parishes, towns - are in the Pacific Northwest, unless otherwise specified.

Notes regarding Annotations:

The Annotations do not include many names which appear in the text, as little or nothing more than is in the Church records is known. The Annotations supplement, when possible, but do not recapitulate the entries written by the priests. They also indicate where further entries may be found in other parish records.

Material in the Annotations complements and expands what appears in the Church records about persons and places. No documentation appears because of the great number of references involved, but in most cases the source is mentioned or is self-evident. The information is from many and varied sources, such as land records, other parish records, pension files, histories, biographies, Hudson's Bay Company Records, tax rolls, census lists, Army records, and interviews with descendents - to name a few.

Mikell De Lores Wormell Warner

ACKNOWLEDGMENTS

I acknowledge gratefully the help and encouragement of the Most Reverend Cornelius Power, Archbishop of Portland in Oregon, of the late Archbishop Robert J. Dwyer and the Staff of the Chancery of Portland, of the president and membership of the St. Paul Mission Historical Society, and the descendants of the French Canadians whose genealogies are here recorded in the St. Paul Registers. Only by their continued and generous support has it been possible to offer these precious records in translation to historians, genealogists and readers at large.

Harriet D. Munnick

1979

INTRODUCTION

French Prairie, of which St. Paul may be considered the heart, is a level region lying within the big bend of the Willamette River some miles above the falls at Oregon City. It is roughly twenty miles in length and half as much in width, an ancient flood plain with an undeveloped drainage pattern that in early times left the plain deep in silt. Its natural boundaries are the Willamette River on the north and west, the Pudding River on the east, and Lake Labiche, more swamp than lake, on the south. The land was open and fertile. The region was well-known to the engages from years of passing by it on the river, traversing its trails on horse brigades, and camping on its long grassy reaches.

Following the example of Etienne Lucier, Joseph Gervais and Jean Baptiste Desportes, other retired Canadians began to form a loose colony or farm community, beginning about 1830. A newspaper reporter for the Peoria Register and Northwestern Gazetter, after hearing Jason Lee's address in Peoria, Illinois, in 1836, probably voiced the current American opinion of them:

> "They were men who had been in the employ of the Hudson Bay Company, but had taken Indian wives and had settled here to pursue the business of farming. They numbered 15 or 20 families, and had become as uncivilized, nearly, as the savages around them."

By the mid-1830's the Methodists under Jason Lee had established a mission at the upper end of French Prairie, and plans for an Episcopalian pastor at Fort Vancouver were under way, but as yet no Catholic missionary had entered the far western field, to the distress of the French Canadians. About twenty such families of retired Company employees were now settled on the Prairie, a few American loners not connected with the Methodist Mission, and a cluster of Iroquois on the north side of the Willamette along the tributary Yamhill River. At length the heads of these families, taking matters into their own hands, addressed a petition, dated July 3, 1834, to the Bishop of Red River asking that they be supplied with a priest. As all the Canadians were illiterate, they seem to have enlisted the help of an un-named American in setting their thoughts down in writing. No reply came.

A second petition, dated February 23, 1835, brought a reply from Bishop Provencher, addressed to "all the families settled in the Willamette Valley and other Catholics beyond the Rocky Mountains", in care of Chief Factor McLoughlin at Fort Vancouver. In his letter he expressed regret that no priests were available at the time, but promised to send one as soon as possible; he exhorted them to keep the faith, to raise their children "the best way you can", and by setting a Christian example before the natives, to smooth the path for the promised missionary.

The settlers, greatly heartened by the Bishop's promise, sent back a letter of thankfulness and plans, dated March 22, 1836, and carried by the spring brigade.

> Reverend Sir
> We recived youre kinde Letter last fall wich gave us Much pleasure and ease to oure minds for it has been a Long time since we have heard the Likes of it it has Gave us a new heart since we recived youre kinde instructions to us we will do oure Best in deavors to instruct our fammilies to youre wishes still Living in hopes of some Speady Releafe wich we are looking for with eager hearts for the day to Come since we Recived youre kinde Letter we have be Gun to Build and to make some preparations to Recive oure kind father wich we hope that oure Laboure will not be in vaine for you know our sittiwations better than oureselves for Some of us stands in great Neade of youre Assistance as quick as possible We have nothing to Right to you about the Countrey but that the farms are All in a very thriving state and produces fine Crops We have sent theis few Lines to you hoping that it will not trouble you to much for Righting so quick to you but the Countrey is setteling Slowly and oure Children are Learning very fast wich makes us very eager for Youre assistance Wich we hope by Gods helpe will be very Sone. our prayears will be for his safe Arivale We have sent you a list of the families that Are at present in the settelment So no more Preasent from youre humble servants

	Willammeth Settelers		
	Children		Children
Joseph Jarvay	7	Luey Fiourcy	3
Havier Laderout	1	Lamab Erquet	3
Eken Luceay	6	Jion Bt Perroult	2

Peare Belleck	3	Joseph Desport	3
Charles Rondo	3	Andrey Longten	4
Charles Plant	4	John Bt Desportes	8
Pear Depo	1	William Johnson	2
Andrey Pecor	4	Charlo Chata	
Joseph Delar	5	William MCarty	

The Canadians wrote a second letter, dated March 8, 1837, "hoping this will meate you on youre way to oure settlement". They expressed their "Greate Angsitty for youre Arivall", and continued, "But we finde the time very Long Revernd sir you will think us very troublesome But we hope you will exscuse us for We have much neede of some Assistance from you for we have allmost Every Relgion but oure own . . . we have built a bedend to recive the Revernd Gentleman that should please to come wich will be a happy day for us . . ."

The exact site of the log chapel as the Canadians first placed it has never been positively identified. Later writers say "at Fairfield", but as that river port was not established until some twenty years later, the location of the chapel is still moot. Archbishop Blanchet, writing his *Sketches* long afterward, by which time there was indeed a Fairfield, stated that ". . . finding the log church the Canadians had built a few miles below Fairfield in 1836 not properly located, ordered it to be removed and rebuilt on a large prairie, its present beautiful site." He went on to describe the building as "70 feet by 30 feet, built on a prairie on the eastern side of the river, on the road to Champoeg. (It had been moved and was in the process of "rebuilding".) The vicar general took possession of a part of the church at the back of the altar, measuring 12 by 30 feet, which was later divided by an alley of 6 feet to provide accommodation for two bedrooms on one side and a kitchen and dining room on the other. This space behind the altar was perhaps the "bedend" mentioned by the Canadians for the "Revernd Gentleman".

Two priests, Father Francois Norbert Blanchet and Father Modeste Demers, were dispatched from Red River with the west-bound spring Company brigade of 1838, reaching Fort Vancouver late in November. Their instructions from the Bishop of Quebec, Joseph Signay, listed six definite objectives for them to keep in mind: "To withdraw from barbarity and the disorders which it produces, the Indians scattered in that country", "to tender your services to the wicked Christians who have adopted there the vices of the Indians, and live in licentiousness and the forgetfulness of their duties", and to preach the Gospel to learn the Indian languages, to make regular the fur trade or native unions of the Canadians; to establish schools and catechism classes.

Father Blanchet made Fort Vancouver his headquarters until certain questions involving British interests below the Columbia River could be resolved; it was January before he made his first visit to the Prairie. There, in addition to his usual missionary duties of instruction and observance of holy rites, he laid claim to a tract of land in the name of the Church and set aside an acre of ground, "fenced and blessed, for a graveyard, with a high cross in the center". An old Indian man and a young Indian girl were the first to be buried there. The "Old Cemetery", now much reduced in size by road-building and with no stones remaining, was in use until 1875, when the "New Cemetery" was opened on a little hill a short distance to the southeast. The old cemetery continued to be used, however, by families whose earlier members had been interred there. The last recorded burial was that of Julien C. Provost, 1 day old, in 1891. In all, 534 were registered by the Church, and one of an unregenerate buried "outside the fence, at the edge of the woods." Twelve were subsequently moved to family lots in the New Cemetery.

The log chapel seemed to the missionaries crude in the extreme, but in it Father Blanchet held two missions of several weeks each in January and in late spring, 1839. The records of these early Acts of Faith are contained in Volume One of the Vancouver Register. In October of the same year, when certain restrictions concerning the location of the mission had been removed, Father Blanchet took up his residence in the chapel at St. Paul, which was still unfinished after being "removed and rebuilt". He hired a man to fix the loose flooring, put in some partitions and a ceiling, and perhaps to help in mounting the 80-lb. bell that the priest had brought with him "on a platform over the doorway". An old lithograph showing the only known picture of the chapel indicates that the platform over the door was later enclosed to form a conventional belfry tower.

In his 1841 report to his superior in Quebec, Father Blanchet expanded his account of the improvements made in the chapel by adding, "The floor as well as partition are whitened . . . This house is intended for nuns whom they hope to see sooner or later in order to intrust them with the education of the native girls; for the time is not distant when the inhabitants of this fort

(?) will be able to erect for the divine worship a temple worthier of the majesty of the Lord."

Almost as an afterthought to his account of a visit from Captain Charles Wilkes, Father Blanchet noted in his *Sketches*, "A house 62 by 25 feet was raised in March (1841) at St. Paul, to serve as a hall for the people on Sunday and a lodging for the priest." The minutes of the second public meeting of the Willamette settlers leading up to the formation of a provisional government in Oregon record that the meeting was adjourned in February "to meet on the first Tuesday of June, at the New Building, near the Catholic church." Nothing more is heard of the building, but very soon a boys' school comes into view, spurred by a large donation from Joseph LaRoque in Paris, the school to be called "St. Joseph's College" in honor of its benefactor. It appears that the peoples' hall of 1841 had become the college of 1843.

Nor did the priest gain a new apartment, or at least one of them did not (there being several coming and going at various times) for Father Bolduc, writing in 1842, had little good to say about St. Paul as a whole. "There is yet here only an old chapel which will fall at the first gust of wind on the back of the poor priest, who is lodged in the sacristy." He was speaking of Father Langlois, who was now the parish priest.

Neither did the nuns, who arrived in 1844, inherit the old chapel; it was still the parish church, and the Sisters moved at once into their unfinished convent.

St. Joseph's College opened October 17, 1843, with three faculty members and thirty boarders. All the boys were enrolled as "sons of farmers" except one, who was the son of an Indian chief. Although no roster of the pupils is at hand, it is possible to learn the names of some from the Church Register from 1843 to 1849, the life span of the school. The same boys witnessed again and again at burials, sometimes of their own classmates, or at the baptisms of small children. At times they signed their names, at other times the same lads "could not", meaning only that they were not at hand when the priest transcribed his notes into the register. The following list is tentative, suggesting the names of some who apparently attended the school at one time or another:

Pierre Groslouis   Louis Lucier
John Groslouis   Claude Lacourse
Charles Groslouis   Antoine Cloutier
Bartholomie Martineau   Joseph Laderoute
Amable Arcouet   Pierre Charles Kitson
Jean B. Dubreuil   Louis Guilbeau
Andre Palous   Michel Rivet
                                    Andre Hop-hop (Indian)

The years 1844-1846 saw the completion of the building complex of St. Paul Parish. The Jesuits had built a two-story residence on the bluff above Lake Ignatius, now called Connor's Lake, a barn, shop, forge and various smaller buildings. A second story was added to St. Joseph's College. The north wing of the convent was finished and a chapel, 80 by 30 feet, added to the girls' school, now called Ste. Marie de Wallamette. The new brick church and a dwelling for the priest were the crowning endeavors.

No doubt in the archives of the Sisters of Notre Dame du Namur in Belgium there exists a roll of the girls in their school, which endured from 1844 until 1852; lacking such a list, a tentative roll of the boarding pupils in 1850 can be offered. The census taker of that year numbered the houses as he came to them on his rounds, that of the convent being House No. 454, identified by the names of the Sisters there listed. The same house number gives the names of the girls and their ages:

Lizette Wagner		Marie Pressee	9
Esther Belique	10	Rosalie Plouff	10
Victoire Masta	7	Josephte Lavigueur	10
Angelique Plamondon	9	Catherine Brisbois	3
Helene St. Andre			
Angele Poitier			
Catherine Monique	11		

The Church Register adds the deaths of Elizabeth McKay, aged 14½, Catherine McPhail, aged 13, Rosalie Calispell (Kalispel), no age given, and Rose Fenlay, no age given.

The brick church remains basically the same today as when first constructed in 1846, all the

xix

additions and alterations made in later times being mainly those of beautification. The builder, one "McCaddon, living on the Santiam River" dug the clay from pits behind the church, it is said, and burned the bricks on the site. Marguerite Pichet used to say that in childhood she played in the pits where Indian women had puddled the clay with their bare feet. A large bell, weighing about five hundred pounds, was sent from Europe as a gift for the high belfry. Engraved in Latin are the words, "God, thus your praise goes to the ends of the earth. Ps. 47 To Rev. Father Aloysius Vercruysse, S.J." The same bell hangs in the belfry today.

After twenty years the interior of the church was still unfinished. A "Letter to the Editor" of the *Portland Herald*, written by Archbishop Blanchet in 1867 to correct a careless claim by some reporter, adds bits of Church history to complete the picture:

> It is 100 feet long by 45 wide—built in the form of a latin cross—the two lateral chapels exceeding the main walls 15 feet by 15. It has an elegant belfry, which contains a bell weighing over 500 pounds, and carries and shows the sacred sign of Christianity and of our Redemption eighty-four feet from the ground. The walls are twenty-four feet high and very strong. Since that time the inside had remained unfinished. In 1866 the good parishioners of St. Paul, before going to any expense for finishing it, called from Portland Mr. Burton, a man of great experience in brick building. Having examined it thoroughly he declared the whole structure to be good and sound from bottom to top, and would last one hundred years. Consequently the reparations were begun. The roof was shingled anew, the belfry was restored; two rows of columns supporting the roof were placed inside, ten feet from the walls, which were plastered; a back gallery was made for the choir; four rows of pew seats were made, to accommodate a large congregation; the arch roof was ceiled, and all the carpenter work was painted. The sanctuary, the three altars, the pulpit and rail communion, and in a word, everything inside makes the church a beautiful one, when, at the same time, it is now the largest church on the coast. It cost $20,000 in 1846, when labor and material were so dear. The expense in 1866 went over $2,000. The late bazaar at St. Paul, which realized about $800, came in aid to pay the balance.

The 1866 reshingling of the church was the first of four. The second came in the 1890's when much exterior trim was added to the stark brick walls and the belfry was remodelled, the third during the 1930's and the fourth in 1972.

The early unsigned lithograph mentioned above, circa 1850, identifies all the buildings in the original complex. No local memory recalls what became of them beyond the vague recollection that there were two fires. The brick church alone remains. The artist Paul Kane, touring the West in the 1840's, made a small water color of "St-Paul de Wallamette, 1847", showing, with an eye for composition, only two or three other buildings, yet the charming scene of the new church in a setting of delicate April on the Prairie creates an atmosphere far beyond literal verity.

The great migrations of Americans from the Midwest and the East began during the decade of the 1840's and reached a climax in the 1850's, following the expiration of the Joint Occupation Treaty with Great Britain and the passage of Donation Land Acts by the United States. As the homogeneous group of French Canadians were absorbed or dispersed to more remote regions by the immigrant wave, the new composition of the settlement became reflected in the parish register, where Irish, German and pioneer American names came to replace the French names of the original colony at St. Paul.

In 1845 Grand Prairie, as the southern part of the parish was called, was formed into a separate parish to be known as St. Louis. The register of the St. Louis Church begins with entries copied from a notebook kept before the new parish had been formally established.

A second division of the original Willamette Mission was made in 1875 by the formation of the Gervais Parish in the eastern part of the Prairie. The register of St. Gervais and St. Protase opens with the year 1876, although the priest noted that four rites performed at Gervais in the latter part of 1875 had been entered in the St. Louis Register.

Still another division was made by the formation of a parish at Brooks, temporarily, as it proved. The registers of all the parishes remained with the local priest as part of his church library. But time and wear took heavy toll of the aging volumes; over a period of years the Archbishop called in the registers in order that they could be preserved in the Chancery Archives. Local parishes are usually provided with xerox or photostatic copies of the originals. It is the hope of the authors, in compiling these volumes, that the pioneers' history as set down at the time it occurred might thus be made more readily accessible to their descendents, who may sense in it a delayed homecoming to the land their fathers chose, the prairie of grass, swale, river and open sky.

Harriet Duncan Munnick
West Linn, Oregon
1973

ST. PAUL 1839 - 1847
Volume I

[This volume contains some probable 1848 records, January through 21 April. See pp 171 - 173 and annotations]

[There is one page, un-numbered, bound in the front of this volume which contains the following on the first side:]

Jean Gingras was born at St. Michel ....ka *[probably Yamaska]* the 15 April, 1802.

[On the reverse side of the above page.]

Sketch

1st. Monsigneur Blanchet arrived at the Wallamette the 5 January, at the hour of 10 in the morning, 1839, there to make a first mission to the Catholic inhabitants of that place.

2nd. The first Mass in this place was celebrated the next day, the 6 January, 1839. The happiness of the inhabitants was great; during that mission which lasted from 5 January to 3 February, there were 74 baptisms, of which 26 adults; 25 marriages; 1 burial. The cemetery was made and enclosed.

3rd. The second mission took place in the month of May, from 8 May to 10 June, 1839. There were 6 baptisms, of which 2 adults; 2 marriages; 3 burials of baptized Indians.

4th. Monsigneur Blanchet arrived the 12 October, 1839 at the Wallamette, to reside there habitually, the objections of the Company of Hudson's Bay having been lifted. The workman was engaged at 7 shillings 6 pence to prepare a dwelling. The Bell was blessed the 23 December and raised the same day on a platform, Sunday in the presence of the parish.

Benediction of the first stone of the church in brick of St. Paul the 24 May, 1846 - p. 69.

Benediction of the church in brick, under the invocation of St. Paul, the 1 November, 1846 - p. 73.

[F. N. Blanchet numbered in long hand and signed each page of the register used for Volume I on the upper right hand corner. The original numbering is indicated in this text in capital letters. At some later date the pages were re-numbered, the FIRST PAGE becoming p 1 and p 2, the SECOND PAGE becoming p 3 and p 4, etc. The numerals are cited in the index.]

FIRST PAGE F. N. Blanchet, priest, V.G.

p 1   1839

I undersigned Missionary priest of the Columbia, certify that the present register containing 86 pages, has been numbered and signed from the first to the last page, by Us, Vicar General, to serve for the registration of the Acts of Baptisms, Marriages and Burials made in the Catholic Missions of the Columbia, and in particular that of St. Paul of the Wallamette, from the year 1839 in faith of which we have signed.

Catholic Mission of St. Paul of the Wallamette
The 13 October, 1839

F. N. Blanchet, priest, V.G.

At Wallamette

B-1 Pierre Depot	This 13 October, 1839, we priest undersigned have baptized Pierre, born since 4 months of the legitimate marriage of Pierre Depot, farmer of the Wallamette, and of Marguerite Klamak. Godfather, ..., who as well as the father has not known how to sign. F. N. Blanchet, priest, V.G.
B-2 Angelique Desrivieres	This 26 October, 1830 *[1839?]*, we priest undersigned have baptized Angelique, aged 2 years, natural child of Pierre Desrivieres, Assiniboine by nation, and of Manon, infidel Indian woman. Godfather Amable Arcouet who has not known how to sign as well as the father. F. N. Blanchet, priest, V.G.
M-1 Pierre Desrivieres and Marie	This 28 October, 1838, in view of the dispensation of three *[bans]* of marriage granted this day by us Vicar General, between Pierre Desrivieres, Assiniboine by nation, instructed and baptized at Montreal, and now in service of the Honorable Company, on one part, and Marie Manon, of infidel parents, having been probably baptized, on the other part, nor any

Manon	impediment to the said marriage appearing. We priest undersigned, Missionary of the Columbia, have received their mutual Consent of marriage and have given them the nuptial benediction in presence of Amable Arcouet and of Andre Picard witnesses, before whom the said spouses have declared as their legitimate children Marie Louise aged 5 years, Angelique aged 2 years; neither the witnesses nor the spouses have known how to sign.

F. N. Blanchet, priest, V.G.

B-3 Marie Manon	This 28 October, 1839, we priest undersigned have baptized Marie Manon, aged 26 years, born of infidel parents. Godmother, Marguerite Tchinouk, wife of Arcouet.

F. N. Blanchet, priest

p 2

B-4	This 12 November, 1839, we priest undersigned have baptized Isabelle, aged 18 years, natural daughter of the late Jean Baptiste Boucher and of Josephte, infidel Indian woman. Godfather Andre Picard, Godmother Marie Okanogan, who have not known how to sign.

F. N. Blanchet, priest, V.G.

M-2 Joseph Barnabe and Isabelle Boucher	This 12 November, 1839, in view of the dispensation of one ban granted by us Missionary, and the publication of two others, between Joseph Barnabe, domiciled in this place, legitimate son of Francois Barnabe and of Francoise Dagneau, of Montreal, in Canada, on one part, and Isabelle Boucher, domiciled in this place, natural daughter of the late Jean Baptiste Boucher and of Josephte of Colville on the other part, nor having discovered any impediment, we priest undersigned Missionary of the Columbia, have received their mutual consent of marriage and have given them the nuptial benediction in presence of Andree Picard and of Hyacinthe Lavigueur, witnesses, before whom the said spouses have recognized as their legitimate child Adelaide, aged 1 year. The witnesses as well as the spouses have not known how to sign.

F. N. Blanchet, priest, V.G.

B-5 Catherine Kalapoya	This 13 November, 1839, we priest undersigned have baptized at the house of Joseph Delard in danger of death Catherine, aged about 8 or 9 years, Kalapoya by nation. Godmother Lisette Souchouabe, who has not known how to sign.

F. N. Blanchet, priest, V.G. Miss.

S-1 Catherine Kalapoya	This 2 December, 1839, we priest undersigned have buried in the cemetery of the mission of St. Paul of the Wallamette, the body of Catherine, Kalapoya by nation, deceased day before yesterday, aged about 9 years, at the home of Joseph Delard. Present Pierre Delard, who has not known how to sign, and Jean Bte Jeaudoin undersigned.

Jean Bte. Jeaudoin
F. N. Blanchet, priest, V.G.

B-6 Joseph McKarty	This 18 December, 1839, we priest undersigned have baptized at the house of William McCarty, in danger of death, Joseph aged about 14 years, child of his wife with another man before her legitimate present marriage. Godmother the wife of Alexis Aubichon who has not known how to sign.

F. N. Blanchet, priest, V.G.

SECOND PAGE F N B priest V G

p 3

S-2 Joseph McKarty	This 22 December, 1839, we priest undersigned have buried in the cemetery of this mission the body of Joseph, natural son of the wife of William McKarty, deceased yesterday at the age of 14, after having received baptism at home. Present Joseph Despard and Jean Baptiste Jeaudoin, alone undersigned.

[No signature]
F. N. Blanchet, priest, V.G.

B-7 Marie McKeiy	This 25 December, 1839, we priest undersigned have baptized Marie, born the 4 of this month of the legitimate marriage of Thomas McKeiy, Esq., and of Isabelle Montour; Godfather Joseph McLoughlin and Godmother

[McKay,
pronounced
McKy]

Victoire McMullen who has not known how to sign. The father and the godfather have signed with us.

Thomas McKay

Joseph McLoughlin

F. N. Blanchet, priest, V.G.

Blessing
of the
Bell

The 22 December, day of Sunday, 1839, we priest undersigned, missionary of the Columbia, have blessed about one hour after noon, following the form prescribed in the processional of the diocese, a bell under the invocation of Mary, to serve for the use of the chapel of the Mission of St. Paul of the Wallamette; and having been mounted and erected upon the platform prepared for this purpose and resting on the doorway of the said chapel, it has been tolled during all the Te Deum, which has closed the said ceremony; in presence of the parishioners; Jean Baptiste Perrault was godfather and Angele, his wife, was godmother, who have not known how to sign. In faith of which we have signed.

F. N. Blanchet, priest, V.Gen.

Baptisms   7
Marriages   2
Burials   2

p 4

- 1840 -

B-8
Marie
Petit

This 9 January, 1840, we priest undersigned have baptized Marie born day before yesterday of the legitimate marriage of Amable Petit engage of the Company of the Bay of Hudson, and of Susanne Tawakon. Godmother Marie, wife of Charles Tse-te, who has not known how to sign.

F. N. Blanchet, priest, V.G.

B-9
Charles
Petit

This 9 January, 1840, we priest undersigned have baptized under condition Charles aged 3 years, legitimate son of Amable Petit, engage of the Company of the Bay of Hudson, and of Susanne Tawakon. Godfather Charles Tse-te, Iroquois, who has not known how to sign.

F. N. Blanchet, priest, V.G.

S-1
Josephte
Nouette

This 12 January, 1840, we priest undersigned have buried in the cemetery of this mission the body of Josephte, wife of Etienne Lucier, farmer of this place, deceased day before yesterday, aged 40 years. Present Etienne Lucier and Pierre Beleque who have not known how to sign.

F. N. Blanchet, priest, V.G.

S-2
Julien
Dompierre

This 26 January, 1840, we priest undersigned have buried in the cemetery of this place the body of Julien legitimate son of David Dompierre, farmer of this place, and of Marguerite Souliere, deceased day before yesterday, aged 7 months. Present Amable Petit and Hyacinthe Lavigueur, who have not known how to sign.

F. N. Blanchet, priest, V.G.

B-10
Jean Bte
Plante

This 17 January, 1840, we priest undersigned missionary have baptized at home in a state of sickness, Jean Baptiste, aged about 12 years, legitimate son of Charles Plante and of . . . of the mission of St. Paul. Godfather Charles Rondeau who has not known how to sign.

F. N. Blanchet, priest V.G.

B-11
Me Anne
Perrault

This 28 January, 1840, we priest undersigned have baptized Marie Anne aged 17 years, legitimate daughter of Jean Baptiste Perrault and of a Tchinouk woman. Godfather Amable Arcouet, who as well as the father has not known how to sign.

B-12
Me. Anne
Perrault

[A repeat of B-11 with slight additions]

This 28 January, 1840, we priest undersigned have baptized Marie Anne aged 17 years, legitimate daughter of Jean Baptiste Perrault, farmer of this place, and of a Tchinouk woman. Godfather Amable Arcouet who as well as the father and the one baptized have not known how to sign.

F. N. Blanchet, priest, V.G.

THIRD PAGE FNB VG

P 5

M-1

This 29 January, 1840, after the publication of 3 bans of marriage made at

Jn Bte
Deguire
and
Marie
Anne
Perrault

the Sermon of the parish Mass between Jean Baptiste Deguire, domiciled in this place, son of Jean Baptiste Deguire and of Eulalia Bernier of Ste. Genevieve, State of St. Louis, on the one part; and Marie Anne Perrault, domiciled in this place, minor daughter of Jean Baptiste Perrault farmer and of . . . tchinouk by nation on the other part, nor any impediment being discovered, and in view of the consent of the father of the girl, and inquiries made to certify the liberty of the young man, we priest undersigned missionary of the Columbia, have received their mutual consent of marriage and have given them the nuptial benediction in presence of Amable Arcouet, of Joseph Despard and of Jean Baptiste Mollens, witnesses, who as well as the spouses and the father of the bride present have not known how to sign.
F. N. Blanchet, priest, V.G.

S-3
Margte
Clatsope

This 29 January, 1840, we priest undersigned have buried in the cemetery of the Mission of St. Paul of this place the body of Marguerite Clatsope by nation, wife of Joseph Gervais farmer of this place, deceased day before yesterday, aged 25 years. Present Hyacinthe Lavigueur and Andree Picard who have not known how to sign.
F. N. Blanchet, priest, V.G.

B-13
Sophie
Tchinouk

This 3 February, 1840, we priest undersigned have baptized Sophie aged 17 years, tchinouk ny nation. Godfather Charles Rondeau who has not known how to sign.
F. N. Blanchet, priest, V.G.

M-2
Antoine
Masta
and
Sophie
Tchinouk

This 3 February, 1840, seeing the dispensation of two bans of marriage granted by us missionary undersigned and the publication of the third between Antoine Masta, farmer of this place, formerly of the parish of St. Esprit in Canada, on the one part, and Sophie Tchinouk by nation on the other part, nor any impediment appearing, we priest undersigned missionary have received their mutual consent to marriage and have given them the nuptial benediction in presence of Amable Petit and of Charles Rondeau who as well as the spouses have not known how to sign.
F.N. Blanchet, priest, V.G.

p 6
S-4
Alexis
Yamhile

This 12 February, 1840, we priest undersigned have buried in the cemetery of this mission the body of Alexis, baptized in his hut, born Yamhile by nation, deceased day before yesterday, aged 15 years. Present Francois Xavier Laderoute and David Gervais, who have not known how to sign.
F. N. Blanchet, priest

B-14
Pierre
Tchinouk

This 20 February, 1840, we priest undersigned have baptized at the house of Amable Arcouet, in danger of death, Pierre, aged 50 years, Tchinouk by nation. Godfather Amable Arcouet who has not known how to sign.
Mod. Demers, priest

S-5
Pierre
Tchinouk

This 21 February, 1840, we priest undersigned have buried in the cemetery of this mission the body of Pierre, baptized and deceased yesterday, aged 50 years, Tchinouk by nation. Present Amable Arcouet who has not known how to sign.
Mod. Demers, priest

B-15
Lucie
Chalifou

This 23 February, 1840, we priest undersigned have baptized Lucie born since 4 months of the legitimate marriage of Andree Chalifou, farmer of this place, and of Catherine Russie. Godfather Etienne Lucier, Godmother Genevieve St. Martin who have not known how to sign.
F. N. Blanchet, priest

B-16
Abraham
Laframboise

This 1st of March, 1840, we priest undersigned have baptized Abraham born yesterday of the legitimate marriage of Michel Laframboise, clerk in the service of the Company of the Bay of Hudson, and of Emelie Picard. Godfather Francois Xavier Laderoute, godmother Lisette Souchouabe wife of Delard, who have not known how to sign. The father absent.
F. N. Blanchet, priest

B-17

This 3 March, 1840, we priest undersigned have baptized Genevieve born

Genevieve Lonetain — day before yesterday of the legitimate marriage of Andre Lonetain farmer of this place, and Nancy Okinogan. Godfather Joseph Despard, godmother Genevieve St. Martin, who as well as the father have not known how to sign.

F. N. Blanchet, priest

FOURTH PAGE F.N.B. V. Gen.

p 7

B-18 Mgte Lacourse — This 4 March, 1840, we priest undersigned have baptized Marguerite born since 6 days, natural daughter of Pierre Lacourse, in the service of the Company of the Bay of Hudson, and Skoucisse Tchinouk. Godfather Joseph Delard, godmother Lisette Souchaube who have not known how to sign. The father absent.

F. N. Blanchet, priest

S-6 Abraham Laframbois — This 5 March, 1840, we priest undersigned have buried in the cemetery of this parish the body of Abraham deceased yesterday, aged 6 days, legitimate child of Michel Laframboise and of Emelie Picard. Present Andre Picard and his Indian [male] who have not known how to sign.

F. N. Blanchet, priest

B-19 Paul Lussier dit Gariessi — This 8 March, 1840, we priest undersigned have baptized Paul aged 3 years, natural son of Jean Baptiste Lussier dit Gariessi, and of Catherine Delard. Godfather Andre Picard and his wife for godmother, who have not known how to sign. The father absent.

F. N. Blanchet, priest

S-7 Jacques, (Indian) — In the course of the summer, 1839, has been buried, in the absence of the missionary, in the cemetery of this parish, the body of Jacques, baptized in danger of death at the house of Joseph Gervais and died some weeks later. Present Joseph Gervais. He was aged 33 years.

F. N. Blanchet, priest

S-8 Betsy Kalapoya — In the course of the summer, 1840 [1839?] has been buried in the cemetery of this place the body of Betsy, aged 15 years, baptized at the house of Joseph Delard, in danger of death; and died some weeks later, in the absence of the missionary. Present Joseph Delard.

F. N. Blanchet, priest

Baptisms	12
Marriage	1
Burials	8

went to Canada by the express of 21 March, 1840.

p 8

Since the express of the 21 March, 1840

B-20 Margte Crise [Cree] — This 2 April, 1840, we priest undersigned have baptized at the house of Baptiste Aubichon, Marguerite, cripple Crise by nation, at the age of about 36 years. Godfather, Jean Baptiste Aubichon, godmother Marie Tchinouk, wife of Aubichoon, who as well as the one baptized has not known how to sign.

F. N. Blanchet, priest

M-2 Andree Dubois and Margte Crise — This 2 April, 1840, in view of the dispensation of three bans of marriage and that of the Forbidden Times, granted by us priest undersigned missionary, between Andree Dubois, formerly of the parish of Vaudreuil, Lower Canada, and resident and farmer of the Wallamette, on the one part, and Marguerite Cris by nation, on the other part, nor having discovered any impediment, we priest undersigned Missionary of the Columbia, have received their mutual consent of marriage and have given them the nuptial benediction in presence of Thomas Roy and of Jean Baptiste Aubichon, witnesses, before whom the spouses have declared to recognize as their legitimate children Basile Dubois, aged 11 years, and Joseph Crochiere, aged 13 years, child which the said bride had had before of one named Crochiere. The witnesses as well as the spouses have not known how to sign.

F. N. Blanchet, priest, V.G.

B-21 — This 12 April, 1840, we priest undersigned have baptized Adelaide born

Adelaide Rivet	since 4 days of the legitimate marriage of Joseph Rivet, farmer of this place, and of Rose Lacourse. Godfather, Andree Chalifou, godmother Catherine Russie, who as well as the father have not known how to sign. F. N. Blanchet, priest, V.G.
B-22 Philomene Aubichon	This 16 April, 1840, we priest undersigned have baptized Philomene born the 7th of this month of the legitimate marriage of Alexis Aubichon, farmer of this place, and of Marie Anne Tchinouk. Godfather Jean Baptiste Aubichon, godmother Catherine Russie who as well as the father have not known how to sign. F. N. Blanchet, priest, V.G.

FIFTH PAGE F.N.B. V.G.

p 9

B-23 Rose Forcier	This 19 April, 1840, we priest undersigned have supplied the ceremonies of baptism to Rose, born the 1st and baptized privately the 3rd of January last by us undersigned, of the legitimate marriage of Louis Forcier, farmer of this place, and of Catherine Tchinouk. Godfather Joseph Gervais, godmother Julie Gervais who as well as the father have not known how to sign. F. N. Blanchet, priest, V.G.
M-3 Thomas Roy and Marie Lafleur	This 21 April, 1840, in view of the dispensation of one ban granted by us priest undersigned, and the publication of two others between Thomas Roy, domiciled in this place, formerly of Canada, of-age son of Alexis Roy and of Marguerite Isadore, also of Canada, on one part, and Marie Lafleur, domiciled in this place, natural daughter of Francois Lafleur and Marguerite Crise by nation, on the other part; nor having found any impediment to the said marriage, we priest undersigned, missionary of the Columbia, have received their mutual consent of marriage and have given them the nuptial benediction in presence of Andre Dubois and of Joseph Gervais, witnesses, before whom the said spouses have recognized as their lawful child Andre, aged 2 years; the witnesses and spouses have not known how to sign. F. N. Blanchet, priest, V.G.
B-23 [sic] Marie Lafleur	This 27 April, 1840, we priest undersigned have baptized before her marriage Marie, aged 20 years, natural daughter of Francois Lafleur and of Marguerite Crise by nation. Godfather Francois Laderoute, godmother Julie Gervais who have not known how to sign. F. N. Blanchet, priest
B-24 Rosalie Plouffe	This 6 May, 1840, we priest undersigned have baptized Rosalie, born 26 days ago, of the legitimate marriage of Joseph Plouffe, blacksmith, servant, and of Therese Makaino, residents at Vancouver. Godfather Etienne Lussier, godmother Julienne Watiece, who have not known how to sign nor could the father. F. N. Blanchet, priest, V.G.

p 10

B-25
Edouin
Kitson
	ACTS OF FAITH AT NESQUALLY, 1840—MAY—
	This 19 May, 1840, we priest undersigned have baptized Edouin, aged 6 months, born of the legitimate marriage of William Kitson, Esquire, Lieutenant, in charge of Fort Nesquallie, and of Helene McDonald. The undersigned has been godfather. The father has signed with us.
	          [no Kitson Signature]
	          F. N. Blanchet, priest

B-26 Zoe Lahtchedom	This 22 May, 1840, we priest undersigned have baptized Zoe aged 4 years, natural child of Lahtchedom and of Skehoma, Indians of Nesquallie. Godmother Jany, wife of Jean Bte. Ouvre. F. N. Blanchet, priest
B-27 Marie Holhalshate	This 22 May, 1840, we priest undersigned have baptized Marie aged 3 years, natural child of Holhalshate and of . . . godmother Jany, wife of Jn. Bte. Ouvre, who has not known how to sign. F. N. Blanchet, priest, V.G.
B-28 Jn. Bte.	This 22 May, 1840, we priest undersigned have baptized Jean Baptiste aged 2 years, natural child of Holhalshate, Indian and of . . . Godmother

Holhalshate	Jany, wife of Ouvre.
	F. N. Blanchet, priest
B-29 Nathalie Sahewamish	This 22 May, 1840, we priest undersigned have baptized Nathalie aged 5 years, child of chief Sahewamish of Nesquallie. Godmother Jany, wife of Jean Baptiste Ouvre.
	F. N. Blanchet, priest
B-30 Thomas Tchapihk	This 23 May, 1840, we priest undersigned have baptized Thomas Tchapihk, aged about 40 years, in danger of death, Indian of Nesquallie. Godmother Jany wife of Jn. Bte. Ouvre.
	F. N. Blanchet, priest, V.G.
B-31 Genevieve Khouliak	This 23 May, 1840, we priest undersigned have baptized Genevieve Khouliak aged 4 years. Godmother Jany wife of Jean Bte. Ouvre.
	F. N. Blanchet, priest, V.G.

SIXTH PAGE F.N.B. VGen
p 11

B-32 Anne Elisabeth Acock	This 26 May, 1840, we priest undersigned have baptized Anne Elisabeth, aged 5 years, born of the legitimate marriage of John Acock, farmer, engage, and of Susanne Lane. Godmother Helene McDonald, Dame Kitson, who has not known how to sign, nor could the mother. The father absent.
	F. N. Blanchet, priest, V.G.
B-33 Richard Acock	This 26 May, 1840, we priest undersigned have baptized Richard aged 5 months and 28 days born of the legitimate marriage of John Acock, farmer, engage, and of Susanne Lane. Godmother Helene McDonald, Dame Kitson, who as well as the mother has not known how to sign. The father absent.
	F. N. Blanchet, priest, V.G.
B-34 Charles Lahalette	This 26 May, 1840, we priest undersigned have baptized Charles aged 6 months, child of Lahalette from a second wife. Godmother Jany wife of Ouvre.
	F. N. Blanchet, priest, V.G.
B-35 Agathe Lahalette	This 26 May, 1840, we priest undersigned have baptized Agathe aged 3 years, child of Lahalette, Indian Chief, from a second wife. Godmother Jany wife of Jean Bte. Ouvre.
	F. N. Blanchet, priest, V.G.
B-36 Magdeleine Skolokivalitte	This 27 May, 1840, we priest undersigned have baptized Magdeleine, aged 6 years, child of the late Skolokivalitte, Indian, and of . . . Godmother Jany wife of Jean Bte. Ouvre.
	F. N. Blanchet, priest, V.G.
B-37 Mathieu Tsattein	This 27 May, 1840, we priest undersigned have baptized Mathieu aged 2 years child of Tsattein, infidel Indian and of . . . Godmother Jany wife of Jean Bte. Ouvre.
	F. N. Blanchet, priest, V.G.

p 12

B-160 123 Indians	The 31 May, 1840, we priest undersigned have baptized 123 children, of whom 43 girls, and 80 boys, aged from 1 month to 6 or 7 years, all born of infidel parents, catechumens, on the island White Bay's Island *[Whidby]* on the Puget Sound. Godfather Jean Bte. Ouvre, Sunday afternoon.
	F. N. Blanchet, priest
B-256 96 Indians	The 3 June, 1840, we priest undersigned have baptized 96 children, of whom 53 girls and 63 boys, and including an adult in danger of death, aged from 1 month to 6 to 7 years, all born of infidel parents, in the ranks of catechumen, of the nation of the Tkekivamus. Godfather Jean Bte. Ouvre.
	F. N. Blanchet, priest
B-261 Baptized privately 5	The 8 June, 1840, we priest undersigned have baptized privately, in route, 5 Indian children, of whom only one has been brought by the mother to Cowlitz there to receive the ceremonies of baptism.
	F. N. Blanchet, priest

MISSION OF THE WALLAMETTE

B-262
Josephte
Laviguere

This 28 June, 1840, we priest undersigned have baptized Josephte, born the 15 of this month of the legitimate marriage of Hyacinthe Lavigueur, farmer of this place, and of Marguerite Colville. Godfather Pierre Beleque, godmother Catherine Russie who as well as the father have not known how to sign.

F. N. Blanchet, priest

B-263
Lucie
Ducharme

This 28 June, 1840, we priest undersigned have baptized Lucie aged 4 years, natural child of Jean Baptiste Ducharme and a woman of the Flat Heads nation. Godfather Louis Forcier, godmother Catherine Russie who have not known how to sign.

F. N. Blanchet, priest

B-264
Marie
Indian

The 19 June, 1840, we priest undersigned have baptized privately, at the Falls of the Wallamette, en route, a sick child of infidel parents, Indians of that place.

F. N. Blanchet, priest

SEVENTH PAGE F N B

p 13

B-265
Me.
Angelique

This 5 July, 1840, we priest undersigned have baptized Marie Angelique aged about 45 years, born of infidel parents Tchinouks. Godfather David Dompierre, godmother Catherine Russie who have not known how to sign.

F. N. Blanchet, priest

M-4
Joseph
Gervais
and
Me.
Angelique

This 6 July, 1840, in view of the dispensation of 2 bans granted by us missionary undersigned and the publication of the third between Joseph Gervais, farmer of this place, widower of the late Marguerite Clatsop, and Marie Angelique Tchinouk, formerly of Vancouver; nor any impediment being discovered, we priest undersigned, missionary of the Columbia, have received their mutual consent of marriage and have given them the nuptial benediction in presence of Andre Chalifou and Pierre Beleque, witnesses who have not known how to sign, nor could the spouses.

F. N. Blanchet, priest, V.G.

S-9
Jn. Bte.
Depati

This 6 July, 1840, we priest undersigned have buried in the cemetery of this mission the body of Jean Baptiste, natural child of Jean Baptiste Depati, farmer of this place and of . . . , deceased yesterday aged 16 months. Present Charles Rondeau and Pierre Depot who have not known how to sign.

F. N. Blanchet, priest, V.G.

B-266
William
Turner

This 12 July, 1840, we priest undersigned missionary have baptized William, aged 4 years, 9 months and ½, natural child of John Turner, farmer of this place, and of a Cayuse woman, infidel now dead. Godfather William McCarty, Catholic. Godmother Catherine, wife of Aucent. The father as well as the godfather have not signed.

F. N. Blanchet, priest, V.G.

B-267
Archange
Tyelis

This 13 July, 1840, we priest undersigned have baptized Archange aged about 36 years, Indian woman born of infidel parents, Tyelis by nation. Godfather Francois Rivet, godmother Ursule Grolouis who have not signed.

F. N. Blanchet, priest V.G.

p 14

M-5
Pierre
Lacourse
and
Archange
Tyelis

This 13 July, 1840, in view of the dispensation of one ban of marriage granted by us undersigned missionary and the publication of two others between Pierre Lacourse, free man, formerly of Berthier in Canada, on one part and Archange Tyelis by nation on the other part, nor any impediment to the said marriage being discovered, we priest undersigned, missionary of the Columbia have received their mutual consent of marriage and have given them the nuptial benediction in presence of Augustin Rochon, and . . . in presence of whom, the said spouses have acknowledged as their legitimate children Pierre, aged 12 years, Claude aged 8 years, Alexis aged 5 years, Gilbert aged 3 years, and Marguerite aged 3 months. The witnesses and the spouses have not known how to sign.

F. N. Blanchet, priest

B-268
Emelie
Tsassate

This 20 July, 1840, we priest undersigned have baptized Emelie aged about 20 years, born of infidel parents Tsassete by nation. Godfather Andree Picard, godmother Ursule Groslouis who have not known how to sign.

F. N. Blanchet, priest

M-6
Joseph
Lino
and
Emelie
Tsassete

This 20 July, 1840, in view of the dispensation of two bans granted by us priest missionary, and the publication of the third between Joseph Lino, free man, aged about 21 years, born of Catholic parents in Mexico on one part, and Emelie, Indian woman, Tsassete by nation on the other part, nor having discovered any impediment nor opposition to the said marriage, we priest undersigned missionary to the Columbia, have received their mutual consent of marriage and have given them the nuptial benediction in presence of Andree Picard and of Augustin Rochon, witnesses, who as well as the spouses have not known how to sign.

F. N. Blanchet, priest

EIGHTH PAGE F N B priest
p 15
B-269
Me.
Marguerite
Tchinouk

This 10 August, 1840, we priest undersigned have baptized Marie Marguerite, aged 40 years, born of infidel parents, Tchinouks by nation. Godfather Pierre Beleque godmother Genevieve [St.] Martin who has not known how to sign.

F. N. Blanchet, priest, V.G.

M-7
Etienne
Lussier
and
Me.
Marguerite
Tchinouk

This 10 August, 1840, in view of the dispensation of one ban of marriage granted by us priest missionary, and the publication of two others, between Etienne Lussier, farmer of this place, widower of the late Josephte Noete on one part, and Marie Marguerite Tchinouk by nation, on the other part, nor any impediment being discovered, we priest undersigned, missionary, have received their mutual consent of marriage and have given them the nuptial benediction in presence of Joseph Despard and of Pierre Beleque, who with the spouses have not known how to sign.

F. N. Blanchet, priest, V.G.

B-270
Joseph
Shoimes

This 30 August, 1840, we priest undersigned have baptized Joseph born since the 8 of May last of the natural marriage of Shoimes, Flathead, and of Henriette, both infidels. Godmother Ursule Groslouis who has not known how to sign.

F. N. Blanchet, priest

B-271
Genevieve
Kaikekoe

This 30 August, 1840, we priest undersigned have baptized Genevieve aged 1 year and a half, born of the natural marriage of Yalami and of Kaikekoe both infidels. Godmother Ursule Groslouis who has not known how to sign.

F. N. Blanchet, priest

B-272
Amable
Aohy

This 30 August, 1840, we priest undersigned have baptized Amable born since two years of the natural marriage of Aohy and of Shinshint, both infidels. Godfather Amable Petit who has not known how to sign.

F. N. Blanchet, priest

M-8
Louis
Vendal
and
Cecile
McDonald

This 14 September, 1840, in view of the dispensation of 2 bans granted by us priest undersigned, and the publication of the third, between Louis Vendal, servant of the Honorable Company, son of Augustin Vendal and of Josephte Bourivet of Sorel in Canada, on one part, and Cecile, natural daughter of Mr. McDonald and a woman of the country on the other part, nor any impediment being discovered to the said marriage we priest undersigned have received their mutual consent to marriage and have given them the nuptial benediction in presence of Louis Aucent and Joseph Corneiller, witnesses who as well as the spouses have not known how to sign.

F. N. Blanchet, priest miss.

p 16
B-273
James
Warfield

This 14 September, 1840, we priest undersigned have baptized James Warfield, formerly Anabaptist coming from Tenesse, having received publicly his profession of faith, at the age of 29 years. Godfather Jean Baptiste Champagne who has not known how to sign.

F. N. Blanchet, priest

B-274 Lisette Oyer	This 14 September, 1840, we priest undersigned have baptized Lisette aged 22 years, natural daughter of Charles Oyer, and of a woman of the country. Godfather Andree Picard, godmother Ursule Groslouis who have not known how to sign. F. N. Blanchet, priest
B-275 Isabelle Lumbers	This 14 September, 1840, we priest undersigned have baptized Isabelle, aged 7 years, natural daughter of Lumbers and now in care of James Warfield. Godmother Ursule Groslouis who has not known how to sign. F. N. Blanchet, priest
B-276 Marie Warfield	This 14 September, 1840, we priest undersigned have baptized Marie aged 3 years, natural daughter of James Warfield and of Lisette Oyer. Godmother Ursule Groslouis, who has not known how to sign. F. N. Blanchet, priest
B-277 Betsy Warfield	This 14 September, 1840, we priest undersigned have baptized Betsy aged 3 months, natural daughter of James Warfield and of Lisette Oyer. Godmother Ursule Groslouis who has not known how to sign. F. N. Blanchet, priest

NINTH PAGE F.N.B. priest

p 17

M-9 James Warfield and Lisette Oyer	This 14 September, 1840, in view of the dispensation of 3 bans of marriage between James Warfield, formerly of Tenesse which he left years since, on one part, and Lisette Oyer natural daughter of Chalres Oyer and of a woman of the country on the other part, nor any impediment being discovered, we priest undersigned have received their mutual consent of marriage and have given them the nuptial benediction in presence of Jean Baptiste Champagne and of Andre Picard before whom the spouses have declared as legitimate Marie and Betsy, baptized above; the witnesses and the spouses have not signed. F. N. Blanchet, priest
B-278 Paul Kalapoya	This 24 November, 1830 *[September, 1840?]* we priest undersigned have baptized at the house of Charles Rondeau Paul dit Captain, aged 20 years, sick with consumption, born of infidel parents of Kalapoyas nation. Godfather Charles Rondeau who has not known how to sign. F. N. Blanchet, priest
S-10 Paul Kalapoya	This 1st October, 1840, we priest undersigned have buried in the cemetery of this parish the body of Paul dit Captain Kalapoya by nation, deceased yesterday aged about 20 years. Present Charles Rondeau and Augustin Rochon who have not known how to sign. F. N. Blanchet, priest
B-279 Henriette Lonetain	This 4 October, 1840, we priest have baptized Henriette aged 16 years, legitimate daughter of Andree Lonetain, farmer of this place, and of Nancy Okanogan. Godfather Jean Baptiste Dubreuil, godmother Ursule Groslouis, who have not known how to sign. F. N. Blanchet, priest
B-280 Catherine Lonetain	This 4 October, 1840, we priest undersigned have baptized conditionally Catherine, aged about 15 years, legitimate daughter of Andree Lonetain, farmer of this place, and of Nancy Okanogan. Godfather Jean Baptiste Dubreuil, godmother Ursule Groslouis who have not known how to sign. F. N. Blanchet, priest
B-281 Joseph Despard	This 4 October, 1840, we priest undersigned have baptized conditionally Joseph aged about 13 years, legitimate son of Joseph Despard, farmer of this place, and of Lisette Tchinouk. Godfather Jean Baptiste Champagne, godmother Ursule Groslouis who have not known how to sign. F. N. Blanchet, priest

p 18

B-282 Adrienne Lussier	This 4 October, 1840, we priest undersigned have baptized under condition Adrienne aged 18 years, daughter of Etienne Lussier and the late Josephte Nouette. Godfather Pierre Beleque, godmother Genevieve *[St.]* Martin who have not known how to sign. F. N. Blanchet, priest, Vic Gen

B-283 Pelagie Lussier	This 4 October, 1840, we priest undersigned have baptized Pelagie aged about 14 years, legitimate daughter of Etienne Lussier and the late Josephte Nouette. Godfather Jean Baptiste Dubreuil, godmother Marguirite wife of Lussier who have not known how to sign. F. N. Blanchet, priest miss.
B-284 Jean Baptiste Jeaudoin	This 4 October, 1840, we priest undersigned have baptized conditionally Jean Baptiste aged about 20 years, natural son of Jean Baptiste [Charles?] and of a woman of the country now dead. Godfather, Pierre Beleque, godmother Genevieve [St.] Martin who have not known how to sign. F. N. Blanchet, priest miss.
B-285 Ignace Tchinouk	This 3 October, 1840, we priest undersigned have baptized at the house of Pierre Beleque, in danger of death, Ignace, aged about 25 years, Indian of the nation of the Tchinouks, born of infidel parents. Godfather and godmother Pierre Beleque and Genevieve [St.] Martin who have not known how to sign. F. N. Blanchet, priest miss.
B-286 Rose Pika	This 10 October, 1840, we priest undersigned have baptized Rose aged 3 years, natural daughter of Pika, Owyhee by nation, and of a Tchinouk woman, both infidels. Godfather Amable Arquet, godmother Marguerite Tchinouk. F. N. Blanchet, priest
B-287 Francois Pika	This 10 October, 1840, we priest undersigned have baptized Francois aged 1 month and a half, natural son of Pika Owyhee and of a Tchinouk woman, both infidels. Godfather Amable Arquet, godmother Marguerite Tchinouk. F. N. Blanchet, priest

AT VANCOUVER

TENTH PAGE F N B priest miss.

p 19

B-288 Pierre Kinsneau	The 29 November, 1840, we priest undersigned have baptized Pierre, aged 2 years, Indian child born of infidel parents, namely of Kinsneau, chief, and of a Tchinouk woman. Godmother . . . F. N. Blanchet, priest miss.
B-289 Jean Kopa	The 29 November, 1840, we priest undersigned have baptized Jean, aged aged 1 year or 2, born of Kopa, sailor, and of an infidel Indian woman. Godmother . . . F. N. Blanchet, priest miss.
B-290 Jacques Wheststin	This 29 November, 1840, we priest undersigned have baptized Jacques, aged . . . natural son of Wheststin and . . . both infidel Indians. Godmother . . . F. N. Blanchet, priest miss.

AT WALLAMETTE

B-291 Jean Bte Gariessy [Lucier]	This 25 November, 1840, we priest undersigned have baptized Jean Baptiste aged about 25 years, metis, natural son of Joseph Lussier and of a Cree woman; usually called Gariessy. Godfather Augustin Rochon who as well as the baptized has not known how to sign. F. N. Blanchet, priest miss.
B-292 Madeleine Okanogan	The 20 September, 1840, we priest undersigned have baptized Marie [?] aged 2 years, natural child of Joseph Okanogan and of an Okanogan woman, both infidel Indians of Okanogan. Godmother Ursule Groslouis who has not known how to sign. F. N. Blanchet, priest
B-293 Martine Okanogan	The 20 September, 1840, we priest undersigned have baptized Martine aged 3 years, natural child of Joseph Okanogan and of . . . Okanogan, infidel Indians of Okanogan. Godmother Ursule Groslouis who has not known how to sign. F. N. Blanchet, priest
B-294 Zoe	The 20 September, 1840, we priest undersigned have baptized Zoe, born a month ago of the legitimate marriage of Laurent Quintal, farmer of this

Quintal

place, and of Marie Anne Nipissing. Godmother Catherine Russie who has not known how to sign.

F. N. Blanchet, priest

p 20
B-295
Ambroise
Lino

The 29 November, 1840, we priest undersigned have baptized Ambroise born a month ago of the legitimate marriage of Joseph Lino, day laborer of this place, and of Marie . . . Indian. Godparents Francois Rivet and Angelique Gervais who have not known how to sign.

F. N. Blanchet, priest miss.

B-296
Marie
Despard

This 29 November, 1840, we priest undersigned have baptized Marie born the 22 of October of the legitimate marriage of Joseph Despard, farmer of this place, and of Lisette Tchinouk. Godparents Andre Lonetain and Marguerite Lussier who have not known how to sign.

F. N. Blanchet, priest miss.

B-297
Madeleine
Laferte

This 29 November, 1840, we priest undersigned have baptized Madeleine born 3 months ago of the legitimate marriage of Michel Laferte, farmer of this place, and of Josephte Pendoreille. Godfather Etienne Lussier, god-mother Catherine Russie who have not known how to sign.

F. N. Blanchet, priest

S-11
Un-named
of
Roy

This 11 November, 1840, we priest undersigned have buried in the cemetery of this mission the body of an un-named child born, privately baptized and deceased some days after its birth, legitimate son of Thomas Roy and of Marie Lafleur, residents of this mission. Present Etienne Montour and Jean Groslouis who have not signed.

F. N. Blanchet, priest

B-298
David
Gervais

This 24 December, 1840, we priest undersigned have baptized conditionally David, aged 18 years, legitimate son of Joseph Gervais and of an infidel woman now dead, a Tchinouk. Godfather . . .

F. N. Blanchet, priest

B-299
Reine
Perrault

This 24 December, 1840, we priest undersigned have baptized Reine, aged 20 years, legitimate daughter of Jean Baptiste Perrault, farmer of this place, and of Angelique Tchiailis. Godfather . . .

F. N. Blanchet, priest

B-300
Esther
Beleque

This 24 December, 1840, we priest undersigned have baptized Esther, born the 11 of this month of the legitimate marriage of Pierre Beleque, farmer of this place, and of Genevieve St. Martin. Godfather Louis Pichet.

F. N. Blanchet, priest miss.

ELEVENTH PAGE F N B priest miss

p 21
B-301
Ignace
Iroquois

This 30 December 1840, we priest undersigned have baptized at home in danger of death Ignace aged 24 years, natural son of an Iroquois father and of a woman of the country. Godfather Etienne Lussier.

F. N. Blanchet, priest

B-302
John
[Ignace
crossed out]
Anson [in
different hand-
writing]

This 18 December 1840, we priest undersigned have baptized John aged 4 years natural son of an English father ["Anson" above line in different hand-writing] and of a Tchinouk woman, now the wife of Ignace the Iroquois [Helene Chinook, see M 2, p 22a]. Godfather Jos Rivet [name in different writing].

F. N. Blanchet, priest miss.

Baptisms	291	First ceremony
Marriages	9	Bapt of adults
Burials	11	Bapt of infidel children

THE YEAR 1841

B-303
Maria
Montour

This 7 January 1841, we priest undersigned have baptized at home, in danger of death, Maria, aged 10 years, legitimate daughter of Nicholas Montour, farmer of this place, and of Susanne Humperville. Godfather Pierre Depot, godmother Isabelle Montour McKay who have not known how to sign.

F. N. Blanchet, priest miss.

B-304 Andre Setana	This 8 January 1841, we priest undersigned have baptized Andre aged 4 months, natural child of Setana and of Tekawas, infidels, KliKatates. Godfather Andre Dubois. F. N. Blanchet, priest miss.
B-305 Marie Pohait	This 8 January 1841, we priest undersigned have baptized Marie aged 8 months, natural child of Pohait and of Walikley infidels Klikatates. Godfather Andre who ... F. N. Blanchet, priest miss.
B-306 Peter Kalapouya	This 9 January 1841, we priest undersigned have baptized Peter aged 15 years, orphan boy, Kalapouya by nation, in danger of death at the house of Etienne Lussier who acted as godfather. F. N. Blanchet, priest miss.

[When the pages were re-numbered at the bottom of the page at some later date, a mistake was made, so that there is a p 21a and pages 22a and 22b. See note on pagination preceding FIRST PAGE.]

p 21a

B-307 Ignace Indian LaBonte	This 27 January 1841, we priest undersigned have baptized sick at the house of Louis LaBonte, under the name Ignace an Indian aged about 25 years, born of infidel parents. Godfather Louis Labonte who has not known how to sign. F. N. Blanchet, priest miss.

1841

S-1 Adelaide Gervais	This 31 January, 1841, we priest undersigned have buried in the cemetery of this parish the body of Adelaide, legitimate daughter of Joseph Gervais and of the late Marguerite Tchinouk, deceased day before yesterday, aged 3 years. Present Joseph Gervais and Augustin Rochon, who have not known how to sign. F. N. Blanchet, priest
B-308 Catherine Cayuse	This 1st February, 1841, we priest undersigned have baptized Catherine, aged 30 years, born of infidel parents, Kayous by nation. Godfather Pierre Lacourse who has not known how to sign. F. N. Blanchet, priest
M-1 Joseph Gray and Catherine Kayous	This 1st February, 1841, in view of the dispensation of one ban of marriage granted by us and the publication of two others between Joseph Gray, Iroquois, formerly of St. Regis, and domiciled in this place, on one part, and Catherine, baptized, Kayous by nation, on the other part, nor any impediment appearing to the said marriage, we priest undersigned missionary of the Columbia have received their mutual consent of marriage and have given them the nuptial benediction in presence of Pierre Lacourse and Joseph Groslouis, who have not signed. F. N. Blanchet, priest
B-309 Helene St. Andre	This 6 February, 1841, we priest undersigned have baptized Helene, aged about 2 months, legitimate daughter of Pierre St. Andre, servant of the Company, and of Marie Tumwater. Godfather Joseph Despard, Jr., godmother Archange Lacourse, who have not known how to sign. F. N. Blanchet, priest

TWELFTH PAGE N B priest miss.

p 22 a

B-310 Helene Tchinouk	This 1st February, 1841, we priest undersigned have baptized Helene, aged about 20 years, natural daughter of infidel parents Tchinouk by nation. Godmother Archange Lacourse who has not known how to sign. F. N. Blanchet, priest
M-2 Ignace Iroquois and Helene Tchinouk	This 1st February, 1840[1841], in view of the dispensation of two bans of marriage granted by us undersigned, and the publication of the third between Ignace, Iroquois, baptized before in danger of death, and domiciled in this place, and Helene, Tchinouk by nation, on the other part, nor any impediment discovered to the said marriage, we priest undersigned have received their mutual consent to marriage and have given them the

nuptial benediction in presence of Francois Bercier and of Joseph Groslouis who have not signed.

F. N. Blanchet, priest

B-311
Marie
Kalapoya

This 15 February, 1841, we priest undersigned have baptized privately at the house of Jeaudoin a sick child, aged 1 month, natural daughter of infidel parents, Kalapoya by nation. Godfather Andre Picard who has not known how to sign.

F. N. Blanchet, priest

B-312
(Sepult) 1
Charlotte
Kahous

This 19 February, 1841, we priest undersigned have buried in the cemetery of this mission the body of Charlotte, privately baptized at home by Charles in danger of death and deceased the same day, day before yesterday, aged about 16 years, daughter of infidel parents Kahous by nation. Witnesses Charles Rondeau and Joseph GrosLouis.

F. N. Blanchet, priest

S-2
Lisette
Souchouabe

This 20 February, 1841, we priest undersigned have buried in the cemetery of this parish the body of Lisette Souchouabe, legitimate wife of Joseph Delard, deceased yesterday aged 36 years. Present Joseph Gervais and Francois Bernier who have not known how to sign.

F. N. Blanchet, priest

B-313
Francois
Barnabe

This 26 February, 1841, we priest undersigned have baptized Francois born the 4th of this month, of the legitimate marriage of Joseph Barnabe farmer of this place, and of Isabelle Boucher. Godfather Francois Bernier, godmother Marguerite wife of Lavigueur who have not known how to sign.

F. N. Blanchet, priest

p 22 b
B-314
Judith
illegitimate

This 27 February, 1841, we priest undersigned have baptized Judith born the 20th of this month, born illegitimate of Agathe, Indian girl living at the house of Pierre Beleque. Godfather . . .

F. N. Blanchet, priest

B-315
Pierre
Dalcourt

This 27 February, 1840 *[1841]*, we priest undersigned have baptized Pierre born the 10 November last of the legitimate marriage of Jean Baptiste Dalcourt, farmer of this place, and of Agathe Khoosa. Godfather Joseph Corneiller, godmother . . . who have not known how to sign.

F. N. Blanchet, priest

B-316-317
[two
children]
B-318
Me. Anne
Tchinouk

The 8 March, 1841, we priest undersigned have baptized privately at the house of Gendron two children. In testimony of which

F. N. Blanchet, priest

This 8 March, 1841, we priest undersigned have baptized under condition, at the house of old Quesnel, in danger of death, Marie Anne, aged about 36 years, born of infidel parents Tchinouk by nation. Godfather Louis Aussant who has not known how to sign.

F. N. Blanchet, priest

B-319
Antoine
Depati

This 9 March, 1841, we priest undersigned have baptized Antoine born the 16 of February last of the illegitimate union of Jean Baptiste Depati, farmer of this place, and of Jany . . . Indian woman. Godfather Antoine Rivet, godmother Rose Lacourse, who have not known how to sign.

F. N. Blanchet, priest

S-3
Ignace

This 9 March, 1841, we priest undersigned have buried in the cemetery of this place the body of Ignace, baptized the 27th of January last and died at the house of Louis Labonte, aged about 25 years. Present Louis Labonte and Pierre Kayous.

F. N. Blanchet, priest

Bapt-334
15 Indians

This 14 March, 1841, we priest undersigned missionary have baptized at the camp of Indians at the prairie of Lake Wapeto on the Wallamette 14 Indian children, namely: Joseph, aged 6 years, Peter, aged 6 years, Anne, aged 6 years, Joachim, aged 6 months, Madeleine aged 2 years, Barbe aged 5 years, Jean aged 6 years, Madeleine aged 7 years, Marie aged 8 years, Pierre aged 1 year, Marie aged 7 years, Therese aged 4 years, Scholastique aged 8 years, Andre aged 4 years; and an adult in danger of death aged 50 years, under the name of Paul. The missionary was the godfather.

F. N. Blanchet, priest miss.

THIRTEENTH PAGE F N B priest miss.

p 23

B-335
wife
Weremus

The 26 March, 1841, we priest undersigned have baptized privately in urgent danger of death, at the Falls of the Wallamette, under the name of Marie, the wife of the chief Weremus, dead two hours later. The missionary has been the godfather.

F. N. Blanchet, priest miss.

Total sent to Quebec in March, 1841

	By Msr. Blanchet			By Msr. Demers			
Bapt. Mar. Sept. Con.	B	M	S	B	M	S	
443	280			163	1		Indians
67	38			29			Children of whites
36 [sic]	15			11			Adult Indians
12	11			1			Adult whites

Total of March, 1840, to March, 1841

| 510 [sic] 12 11 60 | 318 | 10 | 6 | 192 | 2 | 5 |

Since Jack River the 17 June to 1st March, 1839 sent to Quebec
Indians - Children of Whites - Adult Indians - Adult Whites
Totals, 1839

309	60	9, of which	127	12	2 to the east, and
			182	48	7 to the west of the mountains

Since the month of March, 1839, to the month of March, 1840, sent to Quebec
Indians - Children of Whites Adult Indians Adult Whites

1840	204	35	14	
1839	309	60	9	
1841	510	12	11	60

Grand Total

	1023	107	34	60

p 24

Since the time of the Express March 22 - 1841

B-336
George
LeBreton

This 11 April, 1841, we priest undersigned have received the profession of Faith in the Catholic Church of George LeBreton, son of Peter LeBreton of Newbury, Massachusetts, and of Tabitha Lewis, of Marblehead, United States; and to him have administered at the same time the baptism under condition, in testimony whereof he has signed with us.

George LeBreton

F. N. Blanchet, priest, V.G.

B-337
Paul
Kopalemehou

This 16 April, 1841, by us priest undersigned has been baptized Paul aged 2 years, natural son of Kopa lemehou and of Tepathels, Tchinouk by nation. The missionary acted as godfather.

F. N. Blanchet, priest

B-338
Joseph
Kouiesse

This 17 April, 1841, by us priest undersigned has been baptized in danger of death, at the hut of his father at the Camp of Sand, Joseph, aged 15, natural son of Kouyesset, Kalapoya, and of . . . both infidels. Godfather, the undersigned.

F. N. Blanchet, priest

B-339
Joseph
Kalapoya

This 23 April, 1841, we priest undersigned have baptized at the hut of a Kalapoya Indian, a boy child, in danger of death, aged 10 days. The father absent. The mother sick. Godfather, the undersigned.

F. N. Blanchet, priest miss.

B-340
Marie
Kilimaux

This 23 April, 1841, we priest undersigned have baptized at the hut of her relative, in danger of death, Marie, aged about 18 years, formerly the wife of Cooper, and of the tribe of Kilimaux. Godfather the undersigned.

F. N. Blanchet, priest miss.

10 B-341 Indians	The 2 May, 1841, we priest undersigned have baptized at the Falls of the Wallamette the Indian children following: namely, Madeleine, Marie, Pierre, Catherine, Michel, Madeleine, Barbe, Claire, Marie, Pierre, all less than 7 years. The godfather has been the undersigned. F. N. Blanchet, priest
B-342 Joseph Louis Iroquois	This 27 April, 1841, we priest undersigned have baptized Joseph born a month and a half ago of the legitimate marriage of Louis Frise, Iroquois, and of Louis Kalapoya. Godmother the wife of Charles Iroquois. F. N. Blanchet, priest

FOURTEENTH PAGE F N B priest miss.

p 25

5 B-343 Katlachimano	This 13 May, 1841, we priest undersigned have baptized at the river Tlakemas the following children: namely, Hyacinthe, Joachim, Anne, Charles and Pierre, children of Katlachemano, Indian of this place. Godfather the undersigned. F. N. Blanchet, priest
M-1 Andree Lachapelle and Adrienne Lussier	This 17 May, 1841, in view of the dispensation of two bans of marriage granted by us undersigned, and the publication of the third between Andree Lachapelle, domiciled in this place, son of Andre Lachapelle and of Josephte Vincent, of the Faubourg St. Laurent of Montreal, on one part, and Adrienne Lussier, domiciled in this place, minor daughter of Etienne Lussier, farmer of this place, and of the late Josephte Nouite on the other part, nor any impediment being discovered to the said marriage, and with the consent of the father of the girl, we priest undersigned have received their mutual consent of marriage and have given them the nuptial benediction in presence of Etienne Lucier, father of the bride, and of Pierre Blelque, friend of the groom, who as well as the spouses have not known how to sign. F. N. Blanchet, priest
S-1 Marie Tchailis	This 16 May, 1841, we priest undersigned have buried in the cemetery of this mission Marie, wife of old Quesnel, deceased yesterday, of sickness, at the age of 30 years. Present Pierre Blelque and Etienne Lussier who have not known how to sign. F. N. Blanchet, priest
S-2 Maria Montour	This 21 May, 1841, we priest undersigned have buried in the cemetery of this mission Maria, legitimate daughter of Sieur Narcisse [Nicholas] Montour farmer of this place, and of Susanne Humphreys, deceased yesterday aged 12 years. Present Pierre Beleque and Etienne Lussier who have not known how to sign. F. N. Blanchet, priest

p 26

B-21 Rosalie Tianesse	This 7 June, 1841, we priest undersigned have baptized Rosalie born the 3 of this month, natural child of Baptiste Tianesse and of Marie Sassete, both infidel Indians. Godfather Amable Arquoite who has not known how to sign. F. N. Blanchet, priest
B-22 Catherine of NanKaselias	This 19 June, 1841, we priest undersigned have baptized Catherine aged 41 years, born of infidel Indians of NanKaselias to the north. Godfather Jean Baptiste Aubichon, godmother Marie Tselilet who have not known how to sign. F. N. Blanchet, priest
M-2 Louis Vendal, and Catherine NanKaselias	This 19 June, 1841, in view of the dispensation of three bans of marriage granted by us undersigned, between Louis Vendal, domiciled in this place, formerly of Sorel in Canada, on one part, and Catherine NanKaselias, domiciled in this place, on the other part, nor any opposition or impediment whatsoever being discovered, we missionary priest undersigned have received their mutual consent of marriage and have given them the nuptial benediction in presence of Jean Baptiste Aubichon and of Louis Roy, before whom they have legitimatized the following children who were born before

their marriage, namely: Louis aged 7 years, and Genevieve aged 2 years. The spouses and the witnesses have not known how to sign.

F. N. Blanchet, priest

B-23
Marie
Shokelkouchem

This 20 June, 1841, we priest undersigned have baptized Marie aged 1 month and a half, natural daughter of (Gregoire) Shokelkouchom, Indian, chief of the tribe of Isles de Pierres on the Columbia, and a woman of the country named (Elisabeth) NKomkonnetlik, both infidels. Godfather . . .

F. N. Blanchet, priest

B-24
Francoise

This 20 June, 1841, we priest undersigned have baptized Francoise born the 4th of March last, natural child of Marie Anne . . . Godfather Joseph Gervais, godmother Catherine Russie who have not known how to sign.

F. N. Blanchet, priest

FIFTEENTH PAGE F N B priest miss.
p 27
B-25
Ursule
Azur

This 20 June, 1841, we priest undersigned have baptized Ursule born 10 months ago, natural child of Antoine Azur and of Lisette Kilimaux. Godfather Pierre Jacquet, godmother Genevieve Martin, who have not known how to sign.

F. N. Blanchet, priest

B-26
Isadore
Laderoute

This 18 July, 1841, we priest undersigned have baptized Isadore born 4 days ago of the legitimate marriage of Francois Xavier Laderoute, farmer of this place, and of Julie Gervais. Godfather David Gervais godmother Marie Anne Toupin who have not known how to sign.

See Addendum, end of Vol. I, page 173
F. N. Blanchet, priest

p 28
B-30
Catherine
Delard

This 19 July, 1841, we priest undersigned have baptized Catherine, aged 20 years, legitimate daughter of Joseph Delard, farmer of this place, and of Lisette Soushouabe, now dead. Godmother Marie Okanogan, wife of Andre Picard.

F. N. Blanchet, priest

M-3
Jean Bte
Lussier
and
Catherine
Delard

This 19 July, 1841, in view of the dispensation of two bans and the publication of the third between Jean Baptiste Lussier dit Gariessi, domiciled in this place, on one part, and Catherine Delard, daughter of Joseph Delard, consenting to the said marriage, and farmer of this place, and of the late Lisette Souchouabe, on the other part, nor any impediment being discovered, we priest undersigned have received their mutual consent of marriage and have given them the nuptial benediction in presence of Joseph Delard, father of the bride, of Jean Baptiste Toupin and of Francois Xavier Laderoute friends of the groom, and witnesses before whom the said spouses have legitimatized Paul aged 3 years. The witnesses and the spouses have not known how to sign.

F. N. Blanchet, priest

B-31
Marie
Laguivoise

This 19 July, 1841, we priest undersigned have baptized Marie Laguivoise, aged about 50 years, born of infidel parents Indians of St. Louis, United States. Godfather Joseph Delard, godmother Angelique who have not known how to sign.

F. N. Blanchet, priest

M-4
Jean
Bte
Toupin
and
Marie
Laguivoise

This 19 July, 1841, after the publication of three bans between Jean Baptiste Toupin, farmer of this place, formerly of Maskinonge in Canada, on one part, and Marie Laguivoise, born of infidel parents of the territory of St. Louis, United States, on the other part, nor any impediment being discovered, we priest undersigned have received their mutual consent of marriage and have given them the nuptial benediction in presence of Joseph Delard and of Francois Xavier Laderoute witnesses before whom the spouses have legitimatized the children who were born to them before their marriage, namely, Francois aged 16 years, and Marie Anne aged 14 years. The wife admits to have had of two other alliances previously, Marguerite Vernier, aged 22 years, and Jean Baptiste Dorion, aged 25 years. The witnesses and the spouses have not known how to sign.

F. N. Blanchet, priest miss.

SIXTEENTH PAGE F N B priest miss.

p 29

B-32
Celeste
Jeaudoin

This 25 July, 1841, we priest undersigned have baptized Celeste aged 14 years, natural daughter of Jean Baptiste [Charles] Jeaudoin, and of an Indian woman of the Tchinouk tribe, now dead. Godfather Michel Laframboise, godmother Emelie Picard, his wife.

F. N. Blanchet, priest

B-33
Catherine
Hu

This 25 July, 1841, we priest undersigned have baptized Catherine, aged 14 years, natural daughter of a Canadian named Hu, now dead, and of a Pendoreille woman, now dead. Godfather Francois Rivet, godmother Therese Pendoreille who have not known how to sign.

F. N. Blanchet, priest

B-34
Joseph
Groslouis

This 25 July, 1841, we priest undersigned have baptized under condition Joseph, aged 12 years, natural child of the late Charles Groslouis, Canadian, and of a woman now dead, Pendoreille by nation. Godfather Joseph Gervais, godmother Marie Okanogan who have not known how to sign.

Joseph Groslouis

F. N. Blanchet, priest

B-35
Pierre
Groslouis

This 25 July, 1841, we priest undersigned have baptized Pierre aged 14 years, natural son of the late Charles Groslouis and of a Pendoreille woman now dead. Godfather Joseph Gervais, godmother Marie Okanogan who have not known how to sign.

F. N. Blanchet, priest

B-36
Pierre
Dorion

This 25 July, 1841, we priest undersigned have baptized Pierre aged 5 years, natural child of Jean Baptiste Dorion and of a woman of Walla Walla. Godfather Andree Lachapelle, godmother Adrienne Lussier.

F. N. Blanchet, priest

p 30

B-37
Francois
Toupin

This 25 July, 1841, we priest undersigned have baptized Francois, aged 17 years, natural son of Jean Baptiste Toupin and of Marie Laguivoise. Godfather Andree Lachapelle, godmother Adrienne Lussier.

F. N. Blanchet, priest

B-38
Joseph
Laroque

This 25 July, 1841, we priest undersigned have baptized Joseph born the 17 of this month of the legitimate marriage of Joseph Laroque farmer of this place and of Lisette Walla Walla. Godfather Augustin Rochon, godmother Marguerite Vernier.

F. N. Blanchet, priest

M-5
Jn Bte
Ducharme
and
Catherine
Hu

This 26 July, 1841, after the publication of three bans of marriage between Jean Baptiste Ducharme, formerly of Berthier in Canada and now domiciled in this place, of-age son of Francois Ducharme and of . . . Robillard, on one part, and Catherine Hu, domiciled in this place, daughter of the late Paul Hu, Canadian, and of a Pondoreille woman on the other part; nor any impediment to the said marriage being discovered we priest undersigned have received their mutual consent to marriage and have given them the nuptial benediction in presence of Jean Baptiste Aubichon and of Jean Baptiste Dubreuil, witnesses who as well as the spouses have not known how to sign.

F. N. Blanchet, priest

S-3
Un-named
Tchinouk

This 29 July, 1841, we priest undersigned have buried in the cemetery of this mission the body of an Indian, un-named, baptized privately at home in the extremity, deceased yesterday aged about 50 years. Present Laurent Quintal and Lóuis Boisverd who have not known how to sign.

F. N. Blanchet, priest

B-58 [sic]
Charlotte
Okanogan

This 2 August, 1841, we priest undersigned have baptized Charlotte Okanogan, aged about 36 years, born of infidel parents of Okanogan. Godfather Luc Gagnon who has not known how to sign.

F. N. Blanchet, priest

SEVENTEENTH PAGE F.N.B. priest miss.

p 31

B-59

This 2 August, 1841, we priest undersigned have baptized Julie, aged 22

Julie
Gregoire

years, natural daughter of . . . Gregoire and of a woman of the country of the Carriers. Godfather Jean Gingras who has not known how to sign.

F. N. Blanchet, priest

M-6
Jean
Gingras
and
Charlotte
Okanogan

This 2 August, 1841, in view of the dispensation of one ban granted by us undersigned, and the publication of two others between Jean Gingras, formerly of Petit Maska in Canada and domiciled in this place, on one part; and Charlotte Okanogan, Indian woman of the country of that name, on the other part; nor any impediment being discovered, we priest undersigned have received their mutual consent of marriage and have given them the nuptial benediction in presence of Luc Gagnon and of Joseph Groslouis, witnesses, before whom the said spouses have legitimatized the following children who were born to them before their marriage, namely: Joseph aged 13 years, Jean aged 9 and ½, Narcisse aged 7 years and ½, Angele aged 6 years, and finally Marguerite aged 3 years and ½; the said spouses and the witnesses have not known how to sign.

F. N. Blanchet, priest

M-7
Luc
Gagnon
and
Julie
Gregoire

This 2 August, 1841, in view of the dispensation of one ban granted by us undersigned, and the publication of two others between Luc Gagnon, formerly of Canada and now farmer of this place, on one part; and Julie Gregoire, of age daughter of . . . Gregoire and of an Indian woman of the country of the Carriers; nor any impediment being discovered, we priest undersigned have received their mutual consent of marriage and have given them the nuptial benediction in presence of Jean Gingras and of Joseph Groslouis, witnesses, in presence of whom the spouses have legitimatized the following children who were born to them before their marriage, namely: Emerance aged 4 years and Marguerite aged 2 years. The spouses and the witnesses have not signed.

F. N. Blanchet, priest

p 32
B-60
Paul
adult

This 10 August, 1841, we priest undersigned have baptized Paul, aged about 30 years, Indian sick in danger at his hut. Godfather the undersigned.

F. N. Blanchet, priest

B-61
Reine
Staha

This 15 August, 1841, we priest undersigned have baptized Reine, aged 3 months, natural daughter of Staha and of a woman . . . both infidel Indians. Godmother Reinette Perrault who has not known how to sign.

F. N. Blanchet, priest

B-62
Helene
Bourjeau

This 15 August, 1841, we priest undersigned have baptized Helene born on this day of the legitimate marriage of Sylvain Bourjeau and of Jesephte Tchinouk, domiciled in this place. Godfather Andre Chalifou, godmother Catherine Russie who have not known how to sign.

F. N. Blanchet, priest, V.G.

M-8
Jn Bte
Gobin
and
Mgt
Venier

This 23 August, 1841, in view of the dispensation of two bans of marriage granted by us, and the publication of the third between Jean Baptiste Gobin formerly of St. Michel Grand Maska, Canada, and now farmer of this place, son of Antoine Gobin and of Angelique Gaucher, of Canada, on one part, and Marguerite Venier, domiciled in this place, natural daughter of the late Joseph Venier and of Marguerite Laguivoise on the other part, nor any impediment being discovered, we priest undersigned have received their mutual consent of marriage and have given them the nuptial benediction in presence of Jean Bte. Toupin, step-father of the bride, and of Joseph Delard friend of the groom, and witnesses, who as well as the spouses have not known how to sign.

F. N. Blanchet, priest, V.G.

AT VANCOUVER
B-63
Francois
Jose
Monique

This 2 September, 1841, we priest undersigned have baptized Francois, aged 1 month and ½, illegitimate son of Jose Monique and a woman of the Cascades. Godmother wife of Olivier Couturier *[Marguerite Cassino Chinook]*.

F. N. Blanchet, priest, V.G.

EIGHTEENTH PAGE F.N.B. priest miss.

p 33

B-64 Philomene Owyhee	This 4 September, 1841, by us undersigned priest has been baptized Philomene aged 11 months, illegitimate daughter of natural of an Owyhee and a woman of the country. Godmother . . . F. N. Blanchet, priest miss.
B-65 Thomas Tas-Mikt	This 6 September, 1841, we priest undersigned have baptized Thomas aged 1 month, natural son of Tas-Mikt and of Wohenoa, both infidels, Indians of the Cascades. Godmother wife of the late LeBlanc. F. N. Blanchet, priest, V.G.
B-66 Marie Tchinoik	This 5 September, 1841, we undersigned priest have privately baptized at the village of Vancouver an Indian woman in danger of death and have given her the name of Marie. In testimony of which I have undersigned. F. N. Blanchet, priest miss.
B-67 Agnes Douglas	This 6 September, 1841, we priest undersigned have baptized Agnes born the 12 July last, of the legitimate marriage of James Douglas, Esquire, Chief Factor, and of Dame Amelie Connely, resident at Fort Vancouver. Godfather John McLoughlin, Esquire, Chief Factor, godmother Dame Marguerite McLoughlin, his wife, who has not known how to sign, the father absent; the godfather has signed with us, as well as R. R. Waldron, Esquire, present. John McLoughlin R. R. Waldron, U. States Navy F. N. Blanchet, priest miss.
S-4 Marie Tchinouk	This 8 September, 1841, we priest undersigned have buried in the Catholic cemetery of this place the body of Marie Tchinouk, deceased yesterday, aged about 30 years. Present Jean Heroux and Joseph Groslouis. F. N. Blanchet, priest, V.G.

p 34

B-68 Louise Jamymin Kitson	This 11 September, 1841, we priest undersigned have baptized under condition Louise Jamymin, born the 26 July, 1836, of the legitimate marriage of William Kitson, Esquire, . . . and of Helene McDonald. Godmother Dame Marguerite McLoughlin who has not known how to sign. F. N. Blanchet, priest miss.
B-69 Marguerite McLoughlin	This 11 September, 1841, we priest undersigned have baptized conditionally at the age of about . . . Marguerite wife of John McLoughlin, Esquire, and Governor of the Forts within the Rocky Mountains. Godmother Dame Helene McDonald Kitson, Godfather we, undersigned. F. N. Blanchet, priest miss.
B-70 Marguerite Comeau	This 13 September, 1841, we priest undersigned have baptized Marguerite aged about 12 years, natural daughter of Comeau, Owyhee, and of a woman of the country. Godmother Louise Dominic Farron who has not known how to sign. F. N. Blanchet, priest, V.G.
Cascades 9 B-79	This 18 September, 18[41], we priest undersigned have baptized at the Cascades the Indian children following: 1. Alexandre aged 4 years, orphaned of father, having for mother Tchokiva-menak. 2. Germain aged about 4 years, natural child of the late Tassivik and of a woman of the country. 3. Pierre aged about 3 years, natural child of Kametchan neh tshan, his mother, his father being dead. 4. Laurent aged about 1 year son of Wiwoy nouks and of Stikan. 5. Jerome aged about 2 years, child of Wiwoy nouks and of Stikan. 6. Rose aged about 3 years, daughter of Wiwoy and of Stikan. 7. Francois aged about 4 years, son of Aya-Kilaita and of Wo he he. 8. Jean Baptiste, aged about 5 years, son of . . . now dead, and of Ketane. 9. Genevieve aged about 2 years, natural daughter of Eshkanel and of Lkawala. The godfather has been Laurent Iroquois who has not known how to sign. F. N. Blanchet, priest miss.

NINETEENTH PAGE F.N.Bl. priest miss

p 35

10 B	This 20 September, 1841, we priest undersigned have baptized at the Indian
at the	camp of the Cascades the following children born of infidel Indians,
Cascades	namely:
10 B-89	1. Therese aged about 3 years, legitimate child of Sataheoa and of . . . now

dead, Godfather Laurent Iroquois.

2. Antoine aged about 2 years, legitimate child of Nametsout and of . . . ; Godfather Laurent Iroquois.

3. Madeleine, aged about 6 years, legitimate daughter of Auptenche, her mother, her father dead. Godfather Laurent Iroquois.

4. Mathias, aged about 2 years, legitimate son of Wakekas and of . . . ; Godfather Laurent Iroquois.

5. Etienne, aged about 1 year, legitimate son of Sehetlamakak and of Tawaika; Godfather Laurent Iroquois.

6. Paul, aged about 3 years, legitimate son of Sehetlamakak and of Tataika; Godfather Laurent Iroquois.

7. Barbe, aged about 3 years, legitimate daughter of Pautecand and of Weshta, Indians from above. Godfather Laurent Iroquois.

8. Catherine, aged about 1 year, legitimate daughter of Paute and of Weshta, Indians from above. Godfather Laurent Iroquois.

9. Michel, aged about 2 years, legitimate son of Kallakat and of Tchoks. Godfather Laurent Iroquois.

10. Jeanne, aged about 1 year, legitimate daughter of Kayapessh and of Ehkewesh. Godfather Laurent Iroquois.

In testimony of which I have signed

F. N. Blanchet, priest miss.

Cascades
5 B, S-94

This 21 September, 1841, we priest undersigned missionary have baptized at the encampment of the prairie below the rapids the Indian children of the people of the Cascades, namely:

1. Jacques, aged about 2 months, natural son of Shelaote and of Mattair; Godfather Laurent Iroquois.

2. Catherine, aged about 2 years, natural daughter of Kootche and of Soel; Godfather Laurent Iroquois.

3. Apolline, aged about 3 years, natural child of . . .

4. Magdelein, aged about 2 years, natural child of Tchohira menak and of . . . ; Godfather Laurent Iroquois.

5. Elisabeth, aged about 1 year, natural child of Hiakawaie and of Kaikok-witche; Godfather Laurent Iroquois.

In testimony of which I have signed.

F. N. Blanchet, priest miss.

p 36
Cascades
5 B-99

This 25 September, 1841, we priest undersigned missionary have baptized at the camp of the Indians of the Cascades the following children of the same tribe, namely:

1. Dorothe, aged about 3 years, natural child of Wateselete and of Waimasta; Godfather Laurent Iroquois.

2. Reine, aged about 4 years, natural child of Taikane and of Yawatorusha: Godfather Laurent Iroquois.

3. Claire, aged about 5 years, natural child of Hathatssa and of Kom shapan; Godfather Laurent Iroquois.

4. Philippe, aged 3 years, natural child of Taikane and of Tom-eoh; Godfather Laurent Iroquois.

5. Jean Baptiste, baptized the 26 of the same month, aged about 4 years, natural son of Tchokivak and of Katine; Godfather Laurent Iroquois.

In testimony of which I have signed

F. N. Blanchet, priest miss.

AT VANCOUVER
B-100
Henriette

The 29 September, 1841, we priest undersigned have baptized Henriette born yesterday of the legitimate marriage of Joseph Plouffe, servant, and of

2

737th, & 38th pgs

| Plouffe | Therese Makaino. Godfather Louis Vivet, godmother Henriette Groslouis who have not known how to sign. |

F. N. Blanchet, priest miss.

TWENTIETH PAGE F N B priest miss

p 37

| Tlackamas 9 B-109 | This 5 October, 1841, we priest have baptized at the Indian camp of the Tlackamas the following children of the said tribe:
1. Agathe aged about 3 years, slave of Katamus bought last summer of the Molelis.
2. Elizabeth aged about 2 years, natural child of . . . now dead, and of a Molalis woman.
3. Eleanore aged about 1 year, natural child of . . . and of the same Molalis woman.
4. Marie aged about 3 years, natural child of . . . Molelis by nation and of Kileparta.
5. Sophie aged about 2 years, natural child of Nomassaya and of Talsowas.
6. Marguerite aged about 3 years, orphaned of father and of mother.
7. Ursule aged about 6 years, Walla enik her father, her mother dead.
8. Marie aged about 4 years, orphaned of father and of mother.
9. Marie aged some months, natural child of Kianainays mother Sikossa. The godfather we priest undersigned. |

F. N. Blanchet, priest miss.

| Tlackamas 2 B-112 | The 2 October, 1841, we priest undersigned have baptized in danger of death at the Indian huts of the camp of Tlackamas Joseph adult aged about 40 years, and Marie, wife, adult, aged about 30 years. Godfather we undersigned. |

F. N. Blanchet, priest miss.

| 2 B, S-114 Bapt. privately | The 30 August, 1841, we priest undersigned have baptized privately in route to Cowlitz, and at Cowlitz itself, 1. an Indian child *[boy]*, and 2. an Indian girl in danger of death aged about 15 years. |

F. N. Blanchet, priest miss.

| M-8 David Gervais and Me. Anne Toupin | This 9 November, 1841, in view of the dispensation of two bans of marriage granted by us and the publication of the third between David Gervais, domiciled in this place, minor son of Joseph Gervais, farmer of this place, and of a Tchinouk mother, now dead, on one part; and Marie Anne Toupin, domiciled in this place, minor daughter of Joseph *[Jean Baptiste?]*, farmer of this place, and of Marie Laguivoise, on the other part, nor any impediment being discovered to the said marriage, and with the consent of the parents, we missionary priest have received their mutual consent of marriage and have given them the nuptial benediction in presence of Joseph Gervais, father, and a friend of the groom, of Joseph *[?]* Toupin, father, and of Francois Xavier Laderoute friend of the bride who as well as the spouses has not known how to sign. |

F. N. Blanchet, priest, V.G.

p 38
AT VANCOUVER

| B-115 Apolline Indian | The 12 December, 1841, we priest undersigned have baptized Apolline aged 10 months, legitimate daughter of Manomas and of aye whenitte, both infidel Indians. Godfather we undersigned. |

F. N. Blanchet, priest

| B-116 Marie Lahye *[Lattie]* | This 13 December, 1841, we priest undersigned have baptized Marie aged 4 months, natural daughter of Lahye, Scot, and of a Tchinouk woman, Sikas by name. Godmother Therese wife of Joseph Plouffe. |

F. N. Blanchet, priest

| B-117 Matilde Create | This 13 December, 1841, we priest undersigned have baptized Aimie Matilde aged 6 weeks, natural daughter of William Frederic Create, carpenter, and of a Tchinouk woman. Godmother Dame McLoughlin. |

F. N. Blanchet, priest

| B-118 | The 12 December, 1841, we priest undersigned have baptized Ambroise |

Ambroise Tsinitie	aged, or born yesterday, natural son of Tsinitie and of Temaiteme, both infidel Indians. Godfather Joseph Rochon. F. N. Blanchet, priest
S-5 Matilde Create	This 14 December, 1841, we priest undersigned have buried in the Catholic cemetery of Vancouver Aimie Matilde, natural daughter of William Frederic Create, carpenter, and of a woman of the country, found dead this morning in her bed. Present Augustin Rochon and William Alexandre Create. F. N. Blanchet, priest

TWENTY-FIRST PAGE F N B priest miss

p 39

5 B-123 Indians	The 26 December, 1841, we priest undersigned have baptized 5 Indian children of infidel parents. Godfather Augustin Rochon. F. N. Blanchet, priest

[The above act crossed out, but readable]

S-6 William Kitson	This 28 December, 1841, we priest undersigned have buried in the Catholic cemetery of Fort Vancouver the body of William Kitson, Esquire, husband of Dame Helene McDonald, second lieutenant in the Voltiguers Canadian, and lastly in the service of the Honorable Company of the Bay of Hudson, deceased *[several words crossed out]* the 25 of this month, after a long and painful sickness, at the age of 47 years; in the presence of a great number of friends and in particular of James Douglas, Esquire, Chief Factor, and of F. Barclay, Esquire, Doctor, who have signed with us. *[No signatures]* F. N. Blanchet, priest
S-7 Joseph Rocher	This 28 December, 1841, we priest undersigned have buried in the Catholic cemetery at Vancouver the body of Joseph Rocher, widower of a Tchinouk woman, found dead this morning, after several months of alienation of mind, aged about 40 years. Present James Douglas, Esquire, Chief Factor, and F. Barclay, Esquire, Doctor, undersigned with us. *[No signatures]* F. N. Blanchet, priest

p 40

B-119 Joseph Guilbert	This 29 December, 1841, we priest undersigned have baptized Joseph born 3 days ago, natural son of Guilbert, sailor, and of a Tchinouk woman. Godmother Therese, wife of Joseph Plouffe. F. N. Blanchet, priest
B-120 Marie Indian	This 31 December, 1841, we priest undersigned have baptized privately, in route, in a hut, a little girl of 6 years, in danger of death, born of infidel Indian parents. F. N. Blanchet, priest
B-121 Joseph Laframboise	The 25 December, 1841, we priest undersigned have baptized Joseph, aged 1 month, born of the legitimate marriage of Mr. Michel Laframboise, farmer of this place, and of Emelie Picard. Godfather Andre Lachapelle, godmother Adrienne Lucier who have not known how to sign. F. N. Blanchet, priest
B-122 Jean Bte. Deguire	This 25 December, 1841, we priest undersigned have baptized Jean Baptiste born 8 days ago of the legitimate marriage of Jean Baptiste Deguire, farmer of this place, and of Marie Anne Perreau. Godfather Joseph Despard, godmother Reinette Perrault who have not known how to sign. F. N. Blanchet, priest

- 1842 -

S-9 Marie Indian	This 1st of January, 1842, we priest undersigned have buried in the cemetery of this parish the body of Marie, Indian girl, deceased yesterday a short time after having been privately baptized at the hut of her parents. Present Amable Petit and Joseph Pin who have not known how to sign. F. N. Blanchet, priest,
S-10 Agathe	This 6 January, 1842, we priest undersigned have buried in the cemetery of this parish the body of Agathe, wife of Charles Plante, farmer of this

Plante   place, deceased yesterday morning, aged about 22 years. Present Charles Plante and Joseph Gervais who have not known how to sign.

F. N. Blanchet, priest

TWENTY SECOND PAGE F.N.B. priest miss.

p 41

M-9
Jacques
Servant
and
Josephte
Okanogan

This 8 January, 1842, in view of the dispensation of two bans of marriage granted by us undersigned missionary, and the publication of the third between Jacques Servant, tennant farmer of the Catholic Mission of the Wallamette, of-age son of Jacques Servant and of Josephte Charlebois, of the parish of Vaudreuil in Canada, on one part, and Josephte, born of infidel parents, of the country of Okanogan, on the other part, having probably been baptized, nor any impediment being discovered, we priest undersigned missionary of the Columbia, have received their mutual consent of marriage and have given them the nuptial benediction in presence of Augustin Rochon and of Sylvain Bourgeau, witnesses, before whom the spouses have declared legitimate the following children who were born to them before their marriage, namely, Marie Anne aged 17 years, Marie aged 12 years, Marguerite aged 9 years, Antoine aged 5 years, Angelique aged 3 years, Pierre aged 1 year. The witnesses and the spouses have not known how to sign.

F. N. Blanchet, priest

B-123
Francoise
Depati

This 10 January, 1842, we priest undersigned have baptized Francoise aged 14 years, natural daughter of Jean Baptiste Depati and of a Kalipouya woman. Godfather Charles Rondeau, godmother Josephte wife of Jacques Servant, who have not known how to sign.

F. N. Blanchet, priest

M-10
Ant.
Bonenfant
and
Francoise
Depati

This 10 January, 1842, in view of the dispensation of two bans of marriage granted by us priest undersigned and the publication of the third between Antoine Bonenfant, farmer of this place, of-age son of Antoine Bonenfant and of Marie Anne Pepin of the Grand Maska in Canada, on one part, and Francoise Depati, natural daughter of Jean Baptiste Depati and of a Kalipouya woman, on the other part, nor any impediment being discovered, we priest undersigned have received their mutual consent of marriage and have given them the nuptial benediction in presence of Charles Rondeau, of Pierre Depot, and of Jean Baptiste Depati, witnesses, in presence of whom the said Antoine Bonenfant has recognized as legitimate Antoine aged 11 years, and Martin aged 8 years whom he has had of another woman.

F. N. Blanchet, priest, miss.

p 42

B-124
Leon
Arquoite

This 13 January, 1842, we priest undersigned have baptized Leon born yesterday of the legitimate marriage of Amable Arquoite, farmer of this place, and of Marguerite Tchinouk. Godfather Augustin Rochon who has not known how to sign, as well as the father.

F. N. Blanchet, priest, miss.

B-125
Josephine
Okanagan

The 8 January, 1842, we priest undersigned have baptized Josephte aged about 36 years, born of infidel parents, Indians of Okanagan. Godfather Augustin Rochon, godmother the wife of Andree Picard, who have not known how to sign.

F. N. Blanchet, priest, miss.

B-126
Gregoire
Patetisse

This 27 January, 1842, we priest undersigned have baptized Gregoire born 15 days ago of the natural marriage of Patetisse and of Statch, infidel Skayous. Godmother Catherine Cayuse, wife of Jos. Gray, Iroquois.

F. N. Blanchet, priest

S-11
Gregoire
Patetisse

This 22 January, 1842, we priest undersigned have buried Gregoire, aged 15 days, legitimate son of Patetisse and of Statch, infidels Skayous by nation. Present the father and the uncle of the child.

F. N. Blanchet, priest

TWENTY THIRD PAGE F N B priest miss.

p 43

B-127 Susanne Kohoss	This 7 February, 1842, we priest undersigned have baptized Susanne, Kohoss by nation, aged 24 years. Godfather Amable Arquoite, godmother wife of Aucent who have not known how to sign. F. N. Blanchet, priest
M-11 Charles Plante and Susanne Kohoss	This 7 February, 1842, in view of the dispensation of one ban of marriage granted by us undersigned, and the publication of two others between Charles Plante, farmer of this place, widower of Agathe, on one part, and Susanne Kohoss by nation, on the other part, nor any impediment being discovered, nor opposition, we priest undersigned missionary have received their mutual consent of marriage and have given them the nuptial benediction in presence of Amable Arquoite and of Louise Aucent, witnesses, who have not known how to sign, as well as the spouses. F. N. Blanchet, priest
B-128 Susanne Yengula	This 20 February, 1842, we priest undersigned have baptized Susanne, Indian, aged 6 years, of the nation of Yengula. Godfather Joseph Bonenfant, godmother Francoise Depati, who have not known how to sign. F. N. Blanchet, priest
B-129 Alexis Forcier	This 23 *[February?]*, 1842, we priest undersigned have baptized Alexis born day before yesterday of the legitimate marriage of Louis Forcier farmer of this place, and of Catherine Tchinouk. Godfather, Alexis Aubichon, godmother Marie Anne Tchinouk, who have not known how to sign. F. N. Blanchet, priest
S-12 Pierre Dalcourt	This 24 February, 1842, we priest undersigned have buried in the cemetery of this place the body of Pierre legitimate son of Jean Baptiste Dalcourt, farmer of this place, deceased yesterday, aged 15 months. Present Jean Bte. Dalcourt, and Joseph Corneiller. F. N. Blanchet, priest

p 44

At Champoik 2 B-130	This 6 March, 1842, we priest undersigned have baptized at an Indian hut, Champoik, 1. Marie, aged about 30 years, sick in danger of death, at the hut of Hiyasset, Indian, her husband. 2 Joseph, aged 2 years, born of infidel Indian parents of the nation of the Kalapouia. F. N. Blanchet, priest
At Vancouver 5 B. s. 136	This 22 November, 1842, we priest undersigned missionary have baptized at Fort Vancouver the following Indian children: 1. Agathe, aged 1 month, daughter of chief Kaniseno 2. Jerome, aged 3 years, child of Tsikittakwah 3. Madeleine, aged 6 years, daughter of Kahatchehop 4. Marie Anne, aged 4 years, orphaned of father, her mother called Charlotte 5. Etienne, aged 5 months, natural son of Dick Napui and an infidel named Charlotte. F. N. Blanchet, priest miss.
At Vancouver 3 B. S. 139	This 25 November, 1842, we undersigned priest missionary have baptized at Fort Vancouver the following Indian children: 1. Roch, aged 5 years 2. Marc, aged 3 years 3. Jeanne, aged 2 years F. N. Blanchet, priest miss.
At Vancouver S-13 Moise Caille	The 27 November, 1842, we priest undersigned have buried in the Catholic cemetery of Vancouver the body of Moise, legitimate son of Pascal Caille, engage, and of Louise, his wife, deceased yesterday aged 2 years. Present Pascal Caille and . . . F. N. Blanchet, priest miss.
At Vancouver	This 24 November, 1842, we priest undersigned have baptized at Fort Vancouver Pierre, aged 11 months, natural son of Jacques Servant, engage,

B-140   and of Josephte Okanagan.
Pierre   F. N. Blanchet, priest
Servant

TWENTY FOURTH PAGE F.N.B. priest miss

p 45

B-141   This 6 March, 1842, we priest undersigned have baptized Louis aged 14
Louis   days, born of the legitimate marriage of Joseph Corneiller farmer of this
Corneiller place and of Therese . . . Indian woman. Godfather Francois Bernier,
godmother Celeste Jeaudoin.

F. N. Blanchet, priest miss.

2 B 143   The 6 March, 1842, we priest undersigned have baptized at the hut of chief
1 adult Me. Hiyesset at Champoik his wife, sick in danger of death, and have given
1 child   her the name of Marie; and that of Joseph to an Indian child of the nation
Joseph   of Kalapouia baptized at the same time.

F. N. Blanchet, priest miss.

[This entry is a repeat of 2 B 130 on p. 44

S-14   This 13 March, 1840 *[1842?]* we priest undersigned have buried in the ceme-
Marie   tery of this parish the body of Marie, wife of the Indian Hiyesset, deceased
Indian   the day before yesterday, aged about 30 years.

F. N. Blanchet, priest miss.

List since 21 March 1841 to 21 March 1842
By Mr. Blanchet

	Baptism Total	Adult Baptisms	Children of Christians	Adult Indians	Children of Indians	Total
	143	6	45	13	79	92
By Mr. Demers						
	822	4	16	4	798	802
Total during the year						
	905	10	61	17	877	

By Mr. Blanchet

	Mar.	Burials	1st Com.	entries omitted
	11	14	88-77	3
By Mr. Demers				
	2	7	4-27-23	3
Totals	13	21	115	6

p 46

S-1   Since the 19 March, 1842 - departure of the express
Susanne   This 22 March, 1842, we priest undersigned have buried in the cemetery
Sanders   of this parish the body of Susanne, wife of John Alexandre Sanders, farmer
of this place, deceased yesterday aged about 21 years. Present Thomas Roy
and Amable Petit who have not known how to sign.

F. N. Blanchet, priest

B-1   This 3 April, 1842, we priest undersigned have baptized Jean Baptiste,
JnBte   born the 20 March last, of the legitimate marriage of Charles Rondo, farmer
Rondeau of this place, and of Agathe Depati. Godfather Charles Plante, godmother
Francois Depati.

F. N. Blanchet, priest

M-1   This 4 April, 1842, in view of the dispensation of two bans granted by us
Augustin undersigned, and the publication of the third between Augustin Rochon,
Richon   domiciled in this place, of-age son of Joseph Rochon and of Elisabeth Goyer
and   of Vaudreuil in Canada, on one part; and Celeste Jeaudoin, domiciled in
Celeste   this place, daughter of Charles Jeaudoin farmer of this place and of the
Jeaudoin late Wallalikas Tchinouk, on the other part; nor any impediment being
discovered to the said marriage, we undersigned missionary priest have
received their mutual consent to marriage and have given them the nuptial
benediction in presence of Francois Xavier Laderoute, of Francois Bernier,
and Michel Laframboise, undersigned, friends of the groom, and of Charles
Jeaudoin, father of the bride, who have not known how to sign.

Michel Laframboise, witness

F. N. Blanchet, priest

B-2 Thomas Roy	This 6 April, 1842, we priest undersigned have baptized Thomas born the 23 February last of the legitimate marriage of Thomas Roy farmer of this place and of Marie Lafleur. Godfather Gedeon Senecal, godmother Catherine Lonetain who have not known how to sign. F. N. Blanchet, priest
B-3 Josephte Youtes	This 10 April, 1842, we priest undersigned have baptized Josephte aged 18 years, born of Indian parents, infidels, of the nation of Youtes. Godfather Louis Pichet, godmother Susanne wife of Amable Petit. F. N. Blanchet, priest

TWENTY FIFTY PAGE F N B priest miss

p 47

B-4 Joseph Menard	This 10 April, 1842, we priest undersigned have baptized Joseph aged 3 years, natural child of Pierre Menard and of Josephte Youte. Godfather Louis Pichet who has not known how to sign. F. N. Blanchet, priest
B-5 Pierre Menard	This 10 April, 1842, we priest undersigned have baptized Pierre aged 2 years, natural child of Pierre Menard and of Josephte Youte. Godfather Jean Baptiste Dubreuil who has not known how to sign. F. N. Blanchet, priest
M-2 Pierre Menard and Josephte Youte	This 11 April, 1842, in view of the dispensation of one ban of marriage granted by us, and the publication of two others between Pierre Menard, domiciled in this place, and formerly of Berthier in Canada, of-age son of Louis Menard and of Therese Labonte, on one part; and Josephte, Indian woman of the nation of Youtes, on the other part; nor any impediment being discovered, we priest undersigned have received their mutual consent of marriage and have given them the nuptial benediction in presence of Jacques Servant and of Mahumuhumu, witnesses before whom the two spouses recognize as legitimate the following children, namely: Joseph and Pierre of whom the acts of baptism are found above; the witnesses and the spouses have not known how to sign. F. N. Blanchet, priest
B-6 Catherine Horagan	This 13 April, 1842, we priest undersigned have baptized Catherine born 6 days ago of the legitimate marriage of German Horagan, farmer of this place, and of Nancy Kalapouia. Godfather Joseph Despard, godmother Catherine Lonetain. F. N. Blanchet, priest
B-7 Andre	This 14 April, 1842, we priest undersigned have baptized Andre, Kalapouia Indian, adult, in danger of death, at his hut, Champoik; and further, a boy child of the same nation, 2 years, also under the name Andree; Godmother the wife of Lonetain. F. N. Blanchet, priest

p 48

M-3 Frs. Gendron and Mgte. WallaWalla	This 18 April, 1842, in view of the dispensation of two bans granted by us undersigned, and the publication of the other between Francois Gendron, farmer of this place, of-age son of Toussaint Gendron and of Josephte Tifant, of Canada, on one part; and Marguerite Indian woman of the tribe of WallaWalla after having been previously baptized, on the other part; nor any impediment being discovered, we priest undersigned have received their mutual consent of marriage and have given them the nuptial benediction in presence of Jacques Servant and of Jean Baptiste Dubreuil, witnesses in the presence of whom the said spouses have recognized as their legitimate children Dominic aged 7 years, Lucille aged 4 years, Joseph and Marie Anne twins aged 1 year, and Henriette recently born. The witnesses have not known how to sign. F. N. Blanchet, priest
2 B-8,9	This 27 April, 1842, we priest undersigned missionary have baptized at Tlawillala, the Indian children following: 1. Jean aged 1 year, son of Katomhis and of Setesil both infidels, of the country of Tchehelis. Godfather Laurent Iroquois.

2. Matthieu aged 3 years, son of William Lhaskenemont and of Khekath both infidels, of the village of Kamisneau. Godfather Laurent Iroquois.

F. N. Blanchet, priest miss.

3 B-10, 11, 12   This 3 May, 1842, we priest have baptized the following children at Tlawillala at the Falls of the Wallamette, namely:

1. Irsule aged 1 month, natural daughter of Tjakoak and of . . . of the Cascades;

2. Serassie, aged 3 years, daughter of Shaiko, of the village of Kamisneau, and of the late . . .

3. Antoine aged 1 year, natural son of Hialuhost and of Wopseho; Godfather of the three children Laurent Iroquois.

F. N. Blanchet, priest

[page set in - also numbered 48]

M-3   Dr. Forbes Barclay and Maria Pambrun

[Barclay-   The 12 May, 1842, in view of the dispensation of the publication of three
Pambrun]   bans of marriage granted by us Catholic missionary priest, by virtue of powers received of His Grace Monseigneur the Archbishop of Quebec, between Forbes Barclay, Esquire, member of the Church of Scotland, Doctor, in the service of the Honorable Company of the Bay of Hudson, domiciled at the Fort of Vancouver, on the Columbia River, of-age son of John Barclay, Esquire, Doctor, and of Dame Charlotte Spence of the Shetland Islands, Great Britain, on one part, and Demoiselle Maria Pambrun, member of the Catholic Church, Apostolic and Roman, domiciled at the afore mentioned Fort of Vancouver, minor daughter of the late Pierre Chrysologue Pambrun, in his lifetime Esquire, lieutenant of the Regiment of Her British Majesty, The Voltiguers Canadian, in the service of the Honorable Company of the Bay of Hudson, and of Dame Catherine Umphbrell, formerly domiciled at the Fort of Walla Walla, on the other part; nor any impediment being discovered to the said marriage, with the consent of the mother of the bride, and as Vicar General of His Lordship the Archbishop of Quebec, authorized by him to celebrate mixed marriages between Catholic and Protestant by virtue of a special power, and on the express condition consented to by the said gentleman groom that the children coming from the said marriage will be reared in the Catholic Religion. We priest undersigned have received the mutual consent of marriage of the said spouses in presence of John McLoughlin, Esquire, Magistrate, Chief Factor *[some lines crossed out]* of James Douglas, Esquire, Magistrate, Chief Factor, witnesses, consenting and signing with us, as well as the spouses and several of their friends. *[Several lines crossed out, nul].*

John McLoughlin   Forbes Barclay
C.F.   Maria Pambrun
James Douglas, C.F.
Dugald McTavish, Clr HBCo
David McLoughlin, Clk H.B. Coy
Adolphus Lee Lewes, Clk HB Co.
F. N. Blanchet, priest, V.G.

TWENTY SIXTH PAGE F.N.B. priest miss.

p 49

B-13   This 8 May, 1842, we priest undersigned have baptized Andree born 4
Andre   weeks ago of the legitimate marriage of Andre Chalifou, farmer of this
Chalifou   place, and of Catherine Russie. Godfather Pierre Beleque, godmother Indian wife of Chambreland who have not known how to sign.

F. N. Blanchet, priest, V. Gen.

B-14   This 22 May, 1842, we priest undersigned have baptized Marie born the
Marie   7 February last, of the legitimate marriage of Louis Vendale, farmer of this
Vendale   place and of Catherine of the tribe of Carriers. Godfather Andre Dubois, godmother Marie Lafleur who have not known how to sign.

F. N. Blanchet, priest

B-15   This 23 May, 1842, we priest undersigned have baptized Lisette, aged

Lisette
Indian

about 15 years, Indian of the tribe of Indians above the Grand Dalles; God-father Thomas Roy, godmother . . . who have not known how to sign.
F. N. Blanchet, priest

M-4
Jean
Sanders
and
Lisette
. . .

This 23 May, 1842, in view of the dispensation of two bans of marriage granted by us undersigned, and the publication of the third between Jean Sanders, domiciled in this place, farmer, of-age widower of the late Susanne of the Klou Indian tribe, on one part; and Lisette, domiciled in this place, Indian born above the Grand Dalles, on the other part; nor any impediment being discovered, we undersigned missionary priest have received their mutual consent of marriage and have given them the nuptial benediction in presence of Jean Baptiste Aubichon, Thomas Roi, Andree Picard, Andree Dubois witnesses who as well as the spouses have not known how to sign.
F. N. Blanchet, priest miss.

p 50
S-2
Charlotte
McKarty

This 25 May, 1842, we priest undersigned have buried in the cemetery of this mission the body of Charlotte wife of William McKarty, Irish Catholic and farmer of this place, deceased day before yesterday aged 34 years. Present John Howard and William McKarty, witnesses.
F. N. Blanchet, priest

B-16
Charles
Pichet

This 24 May, 1842, we priest undersigned have baptized Charles born yesterday of the legitimate marriage of Louis Pichette farmer of this place and of Marguerite Bercier. Godfather Andree Chalifoux, godmother Catherine Russie who have not known how to sign.
F. N. Blanchet, priest

B-17
Lucille
Gendron

This 24 May, 1842, we priest undersigned have supplied the ceremonies of baptism to Lucille, formerly privately baptized at home by us under-signed, legitimate daughter of Francois Gendron, tenant-farmer of this place, and of Marguerite Walla Walla. Godfather Jean Baptiste Jeaudoin, godmother Catherine Lonetain.
F. N. Blanchet, priest

B-18
Joseph
Lino

This 12 June, 1842, we priest undersigned have baptized Joseph born 2 months ago of the legitimate marriage of Joseph Lino, tenant-farmer of this place, and of Marie Sassete. Godfather Joseph Gervais, godmother Gervais who have not known how to sign.
F. N. Blanchet, priest

S-3
Madeleine
Joseph

This 18 June, 1842, we priest undersigned have buried in the cemetery of this parish the body of Madeleine, legitimate or natural child of Joseph Okanogan, Indian, and of . . . Present Amable Petit and Pierre Lavelle.
F. N. Blanchet, priest

[Two pages set in between pp 50 and 51, not numbered]
At Vancouver
B-19
Margte
Souchouabe

This 24 June, 1842, we priest undersigned have baptized Marguerite aged about 36 years, born of infidel Indian parents of Caledonia; Godfather John McLoughlin, Esquire, Governor of Vancouver, godmother Marguerite his wife who has not known how to sign. The godfather has signed with us.
John McLoughlin
F. N. Blanchet, priest miss.

M-5
Etienne
Gregoire
and
Margte.
Souchouabe

This 24 June, 1842, in view of the dispensation of three bans of marriage between Etienne Gregoire, servant, engage of the Company, son of Etienne Gregoire and of Marie Savigny of Maskinonge in Canada, on one part, and Marguerite Souchouabe, born of infidel parents, as above explained, on the other part, nor any impediment being discovered, we priest missionary undersigned have received their mutual consent and have given them the nuptial benediction in presence of Monsieur the Governor John McLoughlin undersigned and of Peter Ogden, Esquire, witnesses, before whom the spouses have recognized as their legitimate children Julie aged 23 years, Antoine aged 19 years in October next, Sophie aged 16 years in October next, David aged 13 years, Felix aged 12 years, Etienne aged 8 years, in testimony of which the witnesses have signed with us, the spouses have not known how to sign.

John McLoughlin
Peter Keen [sic] Ogden
F. N. Blanchet, priest miss.

Sepult. 4
Madeleine
Laferte

This 3 July, 1842, we priest undersigned have buried in the cemetery of this mission the body of Madeleine legitimate daughter of Michel Laferte, farmer of this place, and of Josephte Nez-perce, deceased day before yesterday aged 2 years. Present Joseph Gervais and Andree Lonetain who have not known how to sign.

F. N. Blanchet, priest

Affidavit

St. Paul of the Wallamette, the 9 July, 1842

Before me priest missionary has appeared Robert Newell, farmer established on the plain of Twalates, who declares on the Holy Bible that he has known since about 20 years the family of John Larisson to be a very honest family, and since 11 [years] he has known the said John Larisson, that he has hardly six months apart from him, so that he can certify and certifies under oath that he has not known, nor learned nor heard said that he was married anywhere and that he believes him to be free of all engagement, sworn on the Holy Bible after two readings and signed by the said Robert Newell before us undersigned and in the presence of Richard McCarty, undersigned.

Robert Newell   Richard Mcary
F. N. Blanchet, priest miss. V.G.

Affidavit

The day and year herein said, the 9 July, 1842, has appeared before me missionary priest undersigned Richard McCary, American citizen, established more than 6 miles below the Falls of the Wallamette, who declares under oath made on the Holy Bible, that he knows personally since 12 years John Larisson, American citizen, resident of the Wallamette, and that during that space of time, it is outside his knowledge that the said John Larisson had been married anyplace; and that having seen a great number of his fellow citizens of the same place as the said John Larisson, he had not heard said that he was married even before the last 12 years; in testimony of which he has declared these facts under oath and has signed them with confidence in front of me and Robert Newell, undersigned.

Robert Newell   Richard Mcary
F. N. Blanchet, priest miss. V.G.

B-19
John
Larison

This 11 July, 1842, we priest undersigned have baptized John Larison, farmer of this place, at the age of . . . legitimate son of John Larison and of Nancy Galaspa, of the state of Ohio, United States. Godfather George LeBreton.

F. N. Blanchet, priest

M-6
John
Larison
and
Reinette
Perrault

This 11 July, 1842, in view of the dispensation of two bans of marriage granted by us Vicar General undersigned, between John Larison, domiciled and farmer of this place, legitimate son of John Larison and Nancy Galaspa, domiciled in the state of Ohio, United States, on one part, and Reinette Perrault, domiciled in this place, legitimate daughter of Jean Baptiste Perrault, farmer of this place, and of . . . Tchinouk, on the other part; nor any impediment being discovered, with the consent of the father of the bride, and after having assured ourselves by the affidavits under oath of the liberty of the said John Larison, and after having previously baptized him, we missionary priest undersigned have received their mutual consent of marriage and have given them the nuptial benediction in presence of Jean Baptiste Perrault, father, and of Andre Chalifou, friends of the bride, and of Ronert Newell and Richard McKarty, friends of the groom and of several other friends who have signed with us. The bride has not known how to sign.

Robert Newell   John (X) Larison
Richard Mcary   Reinette (X) Perrault
George LeBreton   their marks

John Hord
Charles Roy
F. N. Blanchet, priest

TWENTY SEVENTH PAGE F.N.B. priest miss.

p 51

B-20
Nancy
Pion

This 18 July, 1842, we priest undersigned have baptized Nancy, aged about 18 years, daughter of William Pion and of the late Charlotte Okanogan. Godfather Francois Xavier Laderoute, godmother Julie Gervais who have not known how to sign.

F. N. Blanchet, priest miss.

B-21
Marguerite
Desjarlais

This 18 July, 1842, we priest undersigned have baptized Marguerite aged about 18 years, natural daughter of Thomas Desjarlais and of Marguerite Maskegonne. Godfather Thomas Roi, godmother Marguerite Souchouabe.

F. N. Blanchet, priest miss.

M-7
Alexis
Laprate
and
Nancy
Pion

This 18 July, 1842, in view of the dispensation of the publication of one ban granted by us Vicar General, and the publication of two others between Alexis Laprate, domiciled in this place, son of Louis Laprate and of Angelique Matte, of Berthier, district of Montreal on one part, and Nancy Pion, domiciled in this place, daughter of William Pion and of Charlotte Okinagan, on the other part, nor any impediment being discovered to the said marriage, we priest undersigned have received their mutual consent of marriage and have given them the nuptial benediction in presence of Jean Gingras, step-father of the girl, and of Xavier Laderoute, witnesses who as well as the spouses have not known how to sign.

F. N. Blanchet, priest miss.

M-8
Joseph
Gagnon
and
Margte.
Desjarlais

This 18 July, 1842, in view of the dispensation of two bans of marriage granted by us Vicar General and the publication of the third between Joseph Gagnon, domiciled in this place, son of Louison Gagnon and of Bebe Caron, of St. Cuthbert, district of Montreal, on one part, and Marguerite Desjarlais domiciled in this place, daughter of Thomas Desjarlais and of Marguerite Maskegonne, on the other part, nor any impediment being discovered, we priest undersigned have received their mutual consent of marriage and have given them the nuptial benediction in presence of Andre Dubois and of Luc Gagnon, witnesses who as well as the spouses have not known how to sign.

F. N. Blanchet, priest miss.

p 52

B-22
Frs.
Xavier
Gobin

This 20 July, 1842, we priest undersigned have baptized Francois Xavier born yesterday of the legitimate marriage of Jean Baptiste Gobin, farmer of this place, and of Marguerite Vernier. Godfather Francois Toupin, godmother Pelagie Lussier, who have not known how to sign; the father absent.

F. N. Blanchet, priest miss.

B-23
Hyacinthe
Lavigueur

This 25 July, 1842, we priest undersigned have baptized Hyacinthe born 10 days ago of the legitimate marriage of Hyacinthe Lavigueur farmer of this place and of Marguerite Okanogan. Godfather Andre Chalifou, godmother Angelique St. Martin who have not known how to sign.

F. N. Blanchet, priest miss.

B-24
Josephte
Chaudiere

This 2 August, 1842, we priest undersigned have baptized Josephte aged about 40 years, born of infidel Indian parents of the vicinity of Colville; Godfather Andre Picard, godmother the wife of Picard who have not known how to sign.

F. N. Blanchet, priest miss.

M-9
Joachim
Hubert
and
Josephte
of the

This 2 August, 1842, in view of the dispensation of three bans of marriage granted by us Vicar General between Joachim Hubert, domiciled in this place, son of Ignace Hubert and of Marguerite Charlot Charles, on one part, and Josephte of the Chaudiere born of infidel Indian parents, on the other part, nor any impediment being discovered, we priest undersigned have received their mutual consent of marriage and have given them the

Chaudieres
nuptial benediction in presence of Andre Picard and Joseph Pin, witnesses before whom the said spouses have legitimatized the following children, namely: Andre aged 14 years, Baptiste aged 23 years, Elizabeth aged 9 years, Archange aged 7 years, Adele aged 1 year, Lisette aged 16 years, Josephte Boucher aged 29 years. The spouses as well as the witnesses have not known how to sign.

F. N. Blanchet, priest miss.

TWENTY EIGHTH PAGE F N B priest miss
p 53

B-25
Thomas
McKay
This 14 August, 1842, we priest undersigned have baptized Thomas born 3 weeks ago of Mr. Thomas McKay, farmer on the Columbia, and of Isabelle Montour. Godfather John McLoughlin, Esquire, Chief Factor, godmother Maria Pambrun, Dame Barclay undersigned, the father absent.
[no signatures]
F. N. Blanchet, priest miss.

B-26
Joseph
Azur
This 14 August, 1842, we priest undersigned have baptized Joseph born the 1st of June last of the illegitimate union of Antoine Azur and of Lizette Indian woman. Godfather Joseph Cline, godmother Louise Braconnier who have not known how to sign.
F. N. Blanchet, priest miss.

B-27
Isaac
Dubreuil
This 4 August, 1842, we priest undersigned have baptized Isaac born 3 months ago of the legitimate marriage of Jean Baptiste Dubreuil farmer of this place, and of Marguerite Yolgolta. Godfather Luc Gagnon, godmother Julie Gregoire who have not known how to sign.
F. N. Blanchet, priest miss.

B-28
Jean Bte.
Gobin
This 10 August, 1842, we priest undersigned have baptized Jean Baptiste, illegitimate of Bte. Gobin and of an Indian woman. Godfather Joseph Gervais, *[godmother]* Marie Anne, who have not known how to sign.
F. N. Blanchet, priest miss.

3 B-31
This 22 August, 1842, we priest undersigned have baptized the Indian children
1. Catherine aged 6 months, natural child of infidel Indians of Cowlitz
2. Barbe aged about 7 years, natural child of infidel Indians Tlakatates
3. Anne aged about 6 years, natural child of infidel Indians Tlakatates
Godfather Francois Fagnent, godmother the wife of Plamondon who have not known how to sign.
F. N. Blanchet, priest miss.

p 54
B-32
Antoine
Farron
This 22 August, 1842, we priest undersigned have baptized Antoine born the 30 July last of the legitimate marriage of Dominique Farron farmer of this place, and of Josephte Sohok. Godfather Simon Plamondon, godmother Emelie Desjarlais *[Finlay?]* who have not known how to sign.
F. N. Blanchet, priest miss.

4 B-36
Indian
children
This 27 August, 1842, we priest undersigned, in route to Nesquale, have privately baptized 4 Indian children, at the hut of two rivers, apart from two others who have been previously. In faith of which we have signed.
F. N. Blanchet, priest

B-37
Isadore
St. Martin
This 28 August, 1842, we priest undersigned have baptized Isadore born the 5 November of last year of the legitimate marriage of Andre St. Martin, engage, at Fort Nesqualey, and of Catherine Tawakon. Godfather Isodore Bernier who has not known how to sign.
F. N. Blanchet, priest

B-38
Elyza
Slocum
This 28 August, 1842, we priest undersigned have baptized Elyza aged 5 weeks, born of the illegitimate alliance of Richard Slocum, engage resident at Nesquale, and of an Indian woman of that place. Godfather Andre St. Martin, godmother Catherine Tawakon.
F. N. Blanchet, priest

TWENTY NINTH PAGE F N B priest missre.

p 55

B-39
. . .
Joyal

This 28 August, 1842, we priest undersigned have baptized . . . born 6 days ago of the legitimate marriage of Toussaint Joyal, farmer of Nesqualey, and of . . . Godfather Isadore Bernier who has not known how to sign.
F. N. Blanchet, priest miss.

17 B-56

This 1st September, 1842, we priest undersigned have baptized the following Indian children of Cowlitz, namely:
1. Catherine aged 3 years
2. Maurice aged 4 years
3. Jean aged about 3 years
4. Andre aged about 7 years
5. Louis aged about 3 years
6. Hyacinthe aged about 6 years
7. Philippe aged about 5 years
8. Rose aged about 2 years
9. Antoine aged about 2 years
10. Marguerite aged about 8 years
11. Anne aged about 3 years
12. Genevieve aged about 2 years
13. Simon Kloshi, adult, aged about 40 years, in danger of death at the house of Francois Fagnant, Indian of the Cowlitz. Godfather Francois Fagnant.
15. [sic] Luc, aged 5 years, Kwamelheou by name, born of infidel parents of the Cowlitz. Godfather Thomas, Indian.
16. Marie aged 3 years, Makakshionna by name, born of infidel parents of the Cowlitz. Godfather Thomas, Indian.
17. Martin, aged about 7 years, Skwalhahau by name, of Tchinouk infidel parents. Godfather Thomas, Indian.
F. N. Blanchet, priest miss.

p 56

B-57
Etienne
Poirier

This 4 September, 1842, we priest undersigned have baptized conditionally Etienne aged about 15 years, legitimate son of Basile Poirier, baker at Vancouver, and of . . . Tchinouk. Godfather Francois Fagnant, godmother his wife.
F. N. Blanchet, priest miss.

4 B-61

This 5 September, 1842, we priest undersigned have baptized the following Indian children:
1. Jean Baptiste aged about 6 years
2. Felicite aged about 4 years
3. Marie aged about 3 years
4. Francois aged about 7 years
Godfather and godmother Francois Fagnant and Felicite Indian, his wife who have not known how to sign.
F. N. Blanchet, priest miss.

4 B-65

This 6 September, 1842, we priest undersigned have baptized privately in route 4 Indian children of the Cowlitz to whom I have given pictures of their patron saints.
F. N. Blanchet, priest

B-66

This 9 September, 1842, we priest undersigned have baptized privately in route at the Falls of the Wallamette an Indian child [male].
F. N. Blanchet, priest

B-67
Alexandre
Plourde

This 11 September, 1842, we priest undersigned have baptized Alexandre born 12 days ago of the legitimate marriage of Francois Plourde dit Jacques, farmer of this place and of Susanne Dubois. Godfather Hyacinthe Lavigueur, godmother Angelique Marchelais who as well as the father have not known how to sign.
F. N. Blanchet, priest miss.

B-68

This 11 September, 1842, we priest undersigned have baptized Celeste

| Celeste Petit | born 3 weeks ago of the legitimate marriage of Amable Petit, employed at the mission, and of Susanne Tawakon. Godfather Augustin Rochon, godmother Celeste Jeaudoin who as well as the father have not known how to sign. |

F. N. Blanchet, priest miss.

THIRTIETH PAGE F N B priest miss

p 57

B-69 Joseph Gervais — This 11 September, 1842, we priest undersigned have baptized Joseph born the 31 August last of the legitimate marriage of David Gervais, farmer of this place, and of Marie Anne Toupin. Godfather Joseph Gervais, godmother Angelique Tchinouk who as well as the father have not known how to sign.

F. N. Blanchet, priest miss.

B-70 Alexis Laprate — This 12 September, 1842, we priest undersigned have baptized Alexis born the 15 August last of the legitimate marriage of Alexis Lapratte farmer of this place and of Nancy Pion. Godfather Etienne Gregoire, godmother Marie Okanogan who as well as the father have not known how to sign.

F. N. Blanchet, priest miss.

B-71 Joseph Hubert — This 17 September, 1842, we priest undersigned have baptized Joseph *[born]* 25 days ago of the legitimate marriage of Joachim Hubert farmer of this place, and of Josephte Chaudiere. Godfather Hyacinthe Lavigueur, godmother Isabelle Boucher who as well as the father have not known how to sign.

F. N. Blanchet, priest miss.

M-10 John Hord *[Howard]* and Catherine Lonetain — This 19 September, 1842, in view of the dispensation of two bans of marriage granted by Francois Norbert Blanchet Vicar General, and the publication of the third between John Hord, farmer of this place, of-age widower of . . . Despati, on one part, and Catherine Lonetain, domiciled in this place, minor daughter of Andre Lonetain and of Nancy Okinogan, on the other part, nor any impediment being discovered, we priest undersigned have received their mutual consent of marriage and have given them the nuptial benediction in presence of Pierre Belecque friend of the groom, and Andre Lonetain, father of the bride, witnesses, who as well as the bride have not known how to sign. The groom has signed.

[no signature]

A. Langlois, priest

p 58

B-72 Pierre Delard — This 26 September, 1842, we priest undersigned have baptized Pierre aged 18 years, legitimate son of Joseph Delard and of the late Lisette Marie Okanogan. Godfather Andree Picard, godmother Marie Okanogan who have not known how to sign.

F. N. Blanchet, priest, V.G.

B-73 Jean Picard — This 26 September, 1842, we priest undersigned have baptized Jean aged 14 years, legitimate son of Andre Picard farmer of this place, and of Marie Okanogan. Godfather Joseph Delard, godmother Marie Okanogan who have not known how to sign.

F. N. Blanchet, priest, V.G.

B-74 Joseph Gingras — This 26 September, 1842, we priest undersigned have baptized Joseph aged 14 years, legitimate son of Jean Gingras farmer and of Charlotte Okanogan. Godfather Francois Laderoute, godmother Julie Gervais, who have not known how to sign.

F. N. Blanchet, priest, V.G.

B-75 Henriette Vivet — This 26 September, 1842, we priest undersigned have baptized Henriette aged 13 years, natural daughter of Louis Vivet and of . . . Indian woman. Godfather Pierre Belecque, godmother Catherine Russie who have not known how to sign.

F. N. Blanchet, priest miss.

B-76 Louis — This 26 September, 1842, we priest undersigned have baptized Louis born 4 days ago of the legitimate marriage of Jean Gingras farmer of this place,

Gingras	and of Charlotte Okinagan. Godfather Andre Picard, godmother Marie Okinagan who have not known how to sign.

F. N. Blanchet, priest miss.

B-77 Jacob Indian adult	This 29 September, 1842, we priest undersigned have baptized privately at the home of Joseph Larocque in danger of death, an Indian of the name of Jacob. The ceremonies of baptism have been supplied to him later. Godfather Joseph Larocque who has not known how to sign.

[no priest's signature,
Blanchet's handwriting.]

THIRTY FIRST PAGE F.N.B. priest miss.

p 59

M-11 Thomas Moisan and Henriette Lonetain	The 3 October, 1842, in view of the dispensation of two bans of marriage granted by F. N. Blanchet Vicar General and the publication of the third at the sermon of the parish mass of this place, between Thomas Moisan, farmer domiciled in this parish, of-age son of Ignace Moisan and of Elisabeth Burk of St. Jacques, of Montreal on one part, and Henriette Lonetain, domiciled in this place, minor daughter of Andree Lonetain farmer of this place, and of Nancy Okanogan of this parish, on the other part, nor any impediment being discovered to the said marriage, we undersigned priest missionary have received their mutual consent of marriage and have given them the nuptial benediction in presence of Francois Bernier, of Jean Gingras, of Francois Rivet, friends of the groom, and of Andree Lonetain, father of the bride, who as well as the bride have not known how to sign. The groom has signed with us.

Thomas Moisan
Ant. Langlois, priest

M-12 Moyse Lord and Marie Anne Sanders	The 3 October, 1842, seeing the dispensation of one ban of marriage and the publication of the other two bans, at the sermon of our parish masses between Moyse Lord, domiciled in this parish, of-age son of the late Honore Lord and of the late Marguerite Babin of the parish of St. Luc of Montreal, and Marie Anne Sanders, minor daughter of John A. Sanders farmer, and of the late Catherine Chinook of this parish, nor any impediment appearing, we undersigned missionary priest, having the said dispensation granted by the Reverend Messire F. N. Blanchet Vicar General, and his authorization, have received their mutual consent of marriage and have given them the nuptial benediction in presence of Pierre Depot friend of the groom and of John A. Sanders father of the bride who have all declared not knowing how to sign.

Ant. Langlois, priest

p 60

M-12 [sic] Ls. Rondeau and Henriette Yogalta	The 3 October, 1842, seeing the dispensation of two bans of marriage granted by the Reverend Messire F. N. Blanchet Vicar General, and seeing the publication of the third at the sermon of our parish Mass, between Louis Rondeau, engage of the Company of the Bay of Hudson, of-age son of Joseph Rondeau and of Agathe Dalcour of the parish of Berthier of Montreal on one part, and Henriette, of-age girl, of the Yogalta nation on the other part; nor any impediment being discovered, we undersigned missionary priest have received their mutual consent of marriage and have given them the nuptial benediction in presence of Charles Rondeau friend of the groom and of Marguerite, godmother of the bride, who all have declared not knowing how to sign.

Ant. Langlois, priest m.

Sep 5 of Jacob Indian	This 3 October, 1842, we priest undersigned have buried in the cemetery of this parish the body of Jacob, Indian, deceased the day before yesterday at the age of . . . Present Francois Bercier and Francois Bilodeau who alone has signed with us.

Francois Bilodeau
J. B. Z. Bolduc, priest

B-79	This 3 October, 1842, we priest undersigned have baptized Catherine aged

Catherine Gendron	2 years 4 months and 16 days, legitimate daughter of Joseph Gendron, farmer of this place, and of Louise Chinook. Godfather Pierre Beleque, godmother Catherine Lonetain who have not known how to sign. J. B. Z. Bolduc, priest

THIRTY SECOND PAGE F N B priest miss.

p 61

B-80 Edouard Gendron	This 3 October, 1842, we priest undersigned have baptized Edouard aged 1 year 9 months and 3 days, son of Joseph Gendron farmer of this place and of Louise Chinouk. Godfather Augustin Rochon, godmother Celeste Jeaudoin, who, as well as the father, have not known how to sign. J. B. Z. Bolduc, priest
Sep 6 of Catherine Indian	This 8 October, 1842, we priest undersigned have buried in the cemetery of this parish the body of Catherine Indian, deceased at the age of 7 years and about 6 months, a short time after having been privately baptized. Present Michel Laframboise and Francois Bilodeau who have signed with us. Francois Bilodeau *[no Laframboise signature]* J. B. Z. Bolduc, priest
B-81 Marie *[sic]* Desrivieres	This 8 October, 1842, we priest undersigned have baptized Josette aged 2 days, legitimate daughter of Pierre Desrivieres farmer of this place, and of Marie Chinouk. Godfather Michel Laframboise, godmother Emilie Picard, she as well as the father present has not known how to sign. Michel Laframboise J. B. Z. Bolduc, priest
Sepult 7 of Andree Indian	This 8 October, 1842, we priest undersigned have buried in the cemetery of this parish the body of Andree, Indian, deceased day before yesterday at the hut of his parents, at the age of about 3 years. Present Francois Bercier and Francois Bilodeau who alone has signed with us. Francois Bilodeau J. B. Z. Bolduc, priest
B-82 Genevieve Dorion	This 16 October, 1842, we priest undersigned have baptized Genevieve aged 20 days, legitimate daughter of Jean Baptiste Dorion farmer of this place and of Josephte Nez-Perce. Godfather Antoine Rivet, godmother Emelie Pendant d'Oreilles who have not known how to sign. The father absent. J. B. Z. Bolduc, priest

p 62

B-83 Marie Lafantaisie	This 23 October, 1842, we priest undersigned have baptized Marie aged 16 days, legitimate daughter of Charles Lafantaisie farmer of this place and of Isabel Spokane. Godfather Antoine Rivet; godmother Marie Anne Crie who, as well as the father present have not known how to sign. J. B. Z. Bolduc, priest
B-84 Pierre Lucier	The 30 October, 1842, we priest undersigned have baptized Pierre born the 25 of the present month of the legitimate marriage of Etienne Lucier farmer and of Marguerite Chinouk of this parish. Godfather Francois Bernier, godmother Pelagie Lucier who have not known how to sign. Ant. Langlois, priest
B-85 Therese Rivet	The 2 November, 1842, we priest undersigned have baptized Therese born the day preceding of the legitimate marriage of Joseph Rivet and of Rose Indian of this parish. Godfather Francois Bernier, godmother Emilie, Indian, who have not known how to sign. Ant. Langlois, priest
B-86 Felicite Lachapelle	The 10 November, 1842, we priest undersigned have baptized Felicite, born the day before of the legitimate marriage of Andre Lachapelle farmer and of Adrienne Lucier of this parish. Godfather Francois Bernier, godmother Pelagie Lucier who have not known how to sign. Ant. Langlois, priest

THIRTY THIRD PAGE F N B priest miss.

p 63

B-86 *[sic]*
Adelaide
Depoe

The 11 November, 1842, we priest undersigned have baptized Adelaide born the same day of the legitimate marriage of Pierre Depoe farmer and of Marguerite Tlamak of this parish. Godfather Charles Rondeau, godmother Marie Anne . . . of this parish who have not known how to sign.

Ant. Langlois, priest

B-87
Marie

These last days we priest undersigned have baptized Marie, Indian woman, dangerously ill, of an advanced age and of infidel parents. Godfather the minister undersigned. 11 November, 1842.

Ant. Langlois, priest

B-88
Joseph
Lacourse

The 20 November, 1842, we priest undersigned have baptized Joseph born the 3 of the present month of the legitimate marriage of Pierre Lacourse farmer and of Archange of this parish. Godfather Joseph Gervais, godmother Catherine Russil Chalifou who have not known how to sign.

Ant. Langlois, priest

B-89
Laurent
Quintal

The 27 November, 1842, we priest undersigned have baptized Laurent born 2 days ago of the legitimate marriage of Laurent Quintal farmer and of Marie Anne of this parish. Godfather Louis Boisvert, godmother Genevieve, who have not known how to sign.

A. Langlois, priest

S-8
Marie
Indian

The 27 November, 1842, we priest undersigned have buried in the cemetery of this parish the body of Marie, Indian, baptized and administered the sacraments these days past. Present Gabriel Canai and Pierre Groslouis, undersigned.

Pierre Groslouis
A. Langlois, priest

p 64

S-9
Laurent
Quintal

The 5 December, 1842, we priest undersigned have buried in the cemetery of this parish the body of Laurent Quintal deceased 2 days ago aged 10 days, legitimate child of Laurent Quintal farmer and of Marie Anne of this parish. Present Laurent Quintal, father, and Jean Groslouis who have not known how to sign.

A. Langlois, priest

S-10
Marie
Lafantaisie

The 5 December, 1842, we priest undersigned have buried in the cemetery of this parish the body of Marie, deceased the day before aged 1 month and about 10 days, legitimate child of Charles Lafantaisie farmer and of Elizabeth Canote of this parish. Present Joseph Rivet and Charles Lafantaisie, father, who have not known how to sign.

A. Langlois, priest

S-11
Francoise
Gervais

The 10 December, 1842, we priest undersigned have buried in the cemetery of this parish the body of Francoise deceased 2 days ago aged 10 years and some months, legitimate child of Joseph Gervais and of Marguerite Indian of this parish. Present Pierre Groslouis, undersigned, Francois Poirier and a great number of others, who have not known how to sign or who have not wished to sign.

Pierre Groslouis
A. Langlois, priest

THIRTY FOURTH PAGE F.N.B. priest miss.

p 65

B-90
Magdeleine
Plante

The 19 December, 1842, we priest undersigned have baptized Magdeleine born the 15 of this month, legitimate child of Charles Plante farmer and of Suzanne of this parish. Godfather Louis Laroque, godmother Marie Laroque who have not known how to sign.

A. Langlois, priest

1843

S-12
Suzanne
Plante

The 10 January, 1843, we priest undersigned have buried in the cemetery of this parish the body of Suzanne, deceased 2 days ago aged about 20 years, wife of Charles Plante farmer of this parish. Present Charles Plante, Louis

Aussan and several others who have not known how to sign.

Ant. Langlois, priest

M-13
Jos.
Delard
and
Marie
Toussaint
Poirier

The 16 January, 1843, after the publication of two bans of marriage made at the sermons of our parish Masses, and the dispensation of the third granted by us priest undersigned invested of these powers by Messire Blanchet, first missionary of the locality and Vicar General, between Joseph Delard, farmer, of-age, widower of Elizabeth Shoushwab, of this parish, on one part, and Marie Poirier, minor daughter of Toussaint Poirier farmer and of Catherine Clatsop, both consenting, also of this parish, on the other part. Nor any impediment appearing, we priest undersigned have received their mutual consent and have given them the nuptial benediction in presence of Louis Aussan, friend of the groom, and of Toussaint Poirier, father of the bride, who have not known how to sign.

A. Langlois, priest

p 66
B-91
Joseph
Dalcour

The 22 January, 1843, we priest undersigned have baptized Joseph born the 10 November last of the marriage of Dalcour, farmer, and of Agathe Coos, of this parish. Godfather Joseph Gaspard, godmother Catherine Coss who have not known how to sign.

Ant. Langlois, priest

B-92
Agathe

The 22 January, 1843, we priest undersigned have baptized Agathe, young Indian girl aged about 10 years, living at the house of Charles Plante in this parish. Godfather Charles Plante who has not known how to sign.

Ant. Langlois, priest

S-13
Agathe

The 27 January, 1843, we priest undersigned have buried in the cemetery of this parish the body of Agathe, deceased the day before, aged about 10 years, born of infidel parents and living at the house of Charles Plante, baptized some days ago. Present Louis Labonte and Charles Plante who have not known how to sign.

Ant. Langlois, priest

B-93
Victoire
Despard

This 28 January, 1843, we priest undersigned have baptized Victoire, born the 15 of the present month of the legitimate marriage of Frederic Despard farmer of this place and of Lisette Tchinouk. Godfather Pierre Beleque, godmother Genevieve Martin who have not known how to sign.

F. N. Blanchet, priest

B-94
Josephte
Laurent
Iroquois

This 5 February, 1842 *[sic]*, we priest undersigned have baptized Josephte born 8 days ago of the legitimate marriage of Laurent Iroquois and of Therese Tchinouk. Godfather Amable Petit, godmother Marie Charles Iroquois who have not known how to sign.

F. N. Blanchet, priest

THIRTY FIFTH PAGE F N B priest miss.

p 67
B-95
Catherine
Pierriche

This 5 February, 1843, we priest undersigned have baptized Catherine born the day before yesterday of the *[legitimate crossed out]* natural marriage of Pierre, Indian, and of Agathe, Indian, both infidels. Godfather Louis Aussan, godmother Celeste Jeaudoin Rochon who have not known how to sign.

F. N. Blanchet, priest

B-96
Guillaume
Baker

This 19 February, 1842 *[sic]*, we priest undersigned have baptized Guillaume born 6 months ago, natural child of James Baker and of Betsy, infidel Indian woman of the Cascades. Godfather Davis Gervais, godmother Catherine Russie who have not known how to sign.

F. N. Blanchet, priest

M-14
Francois
Bernier
and
Pelagie
Lucier

The 27 February, 1843, in view of the publication of one ban of marriage and the dispensation of two others granted by Messire F. N. Blanchet Vicar General, between Francois Bernier, joiner, domiciled in this place, of-age son of Francois Bernier, farmer, and of Genevieve Layote of the parish of Maskinonge of Canada, on one part, and Pelagie Lucier, minor daughter of Etienne Lucier, farmer, and of Josephte of this parish, nor any impediment appearing, the father consenting, we missionary priest and authorized as regards the place have received their mutual consent of marriage and have given them the nuptial benediction in presence of Francois Rivet and Pierre Beleque, friend of the groom, of Etienne Lucier, father, and of Andre Lachapelle, brother-in-law of the bride, who as well as the said spouses have declared not knowing how to sign.

Ant. Langlois, priest

p 68
M-15
Gedeon
Senegal
and
Marie
Anne
Grenier

The 27 February, 1843, after the publication of two bans of marriage and the dispensation of the third granted by Messire F. N. Blanchet Vicar General, between Gedeon Senegal, domiciled in this place, of-age son of Jacques Senegal and of Josephte Chrystophe of the parish of la Prairie of the Madeleine in Canada, on one part - and Marie Anne Grenier, domiciled in this place, minor daughter of the late Pierre Grenier and of Therese Spokan, consenting, of this parish on the other part, nor any impediment being discovered, we priest undersigned missionary have received their mutual consent of marriage and have given them the nuptial benediction in presence of Andre Dubois and of Augustin Remond, friends of the groom, of Joseph Corneille and of Moyse Lord, friends of the bride, who as well as the said spouses have declared not knowing how to sign.

A. Langlois, priest

B-97
Marie
Anne
Grenier

This 27 February, 1843, we priest undersigned have baptized under condition Marie Anne aged 17 years, daughter of the late Pierre Grenier and of Therese Spokan. Godfather Augustin Rochon, godmother Celeste Jeaudoin who have not known how to sign.

F. N. Blanchet, priest

B-98
Alexis
Indian

This 24 February, 1843, we priest undersigned have baptized at the house of Francois Xavier Laderoute, under the name Alexis, an Indian child aged 6 years, in danger of death. Godfather Laderoute, godmother Julie Gervais.

F. N. Blanchet, priest

THIRTY SIXTH PAGE F.N.B. priest miss.

p 69
S-14
Alexis

The 26 February, 1843, we priest undersigned have buried in the cemetery of this parish the body of Alexis Indian child born of infidels.

F. N. Blanchet, priest

B-99
Francois
Xavier
Barnabe

The 12 March, 1843, we priest undersigned have baptized Francois Xavier born the 4 of this month of the legitimate marriage of Joseph Barnabe farmer and of Elizabeth Boucher of this parish. Godfather Francois Xavier Laderoute, godmother Victoire M'Malen who have not known how to sign.

Ant. Langlois, priest

B-100
Gedeon
Barnabe

This 12 March, 1843, we priest undersigned have baptized Gedeon born the 4 of this month of the marriage of Joseph Barnabe and of Elizabeth Boucher of this parish. Godfather Augustin Rochon, godmother Julie Gervais who have not known how to sign.

A. Langlois, priest

B-101
Elizabeth
Servant

The 12 March, 1843, we priest undersigned have baptized Elizabeth born the 9 of this month of the marriage of Jacques Servant and of Josephte, Indian. Godfather John Picard, godmother Catherine Lonetain who have not known how to sign.

A. Langlois, priest

B-102
Marie Anne
Larisson

The 12 March, 1843, we priest undersigned have baptized Marie Anne born 1 month ago of the marriage of John Larisson farmer and of Reinette of this parish. Godfather Etienne Lucier, godmother Nancy Lonetain, who have not known how to sign.

Ant. Langlois, priest

p 70

Since the departure of the express 1843

S-1
Basile

The 30 March, 1843, we priest undersigned have buried in the cemetery of this parish the body of Basile, deceased 2 days ago aged 11 years, child

Picard	of Andre Picard and of Marie of this parish. Present among a good number of others, Francois Bilodeau and John Groslouis, undersigned. Francois Bilodeau John Groslouis A. Langlois, priest
B-1 J. Bte. Menard	The 2 April, 1843, we priest undersigned have baptized Jean Baptiste born 2 days ago of the marriage of Francois Menard and of Josephte Snake of this parish. Godfather Charles Jeaudoin, godmother Angelique Gagnon, who have not known how to sign. A. Langlois, priest
S-2 James	The 10 April, 1843, we priest undersigned have buried in the cemetery of this parish the body of James, deceased 2 days ago aged about 2 years and a half of unknown parents. Present Gabriel Awahie and Barthalemi Martineau who have not known how to sign. A. Langlois, priest
B-2 Joseph Beleque	The 15 April, 1843, we priest undersigned have baptized Joseph born the 5 of this month of the legitimate marriage of Pierre Beleque, farmer, and of Genevieve of this parish. Godfather Joseph M'Loughlin junior, godmother Victoire M'Loughlin his wife, who have signed with us. [no signatures] A. Langlois, priest

THIRTY SEVENTH PAGE F N B priest miss.

p 71

S-3 Alexis	The 23 April, 1843, we priest undersigned have buried in the cemetery of this parish an Indian named Alexis living at the house of Etienne Lucier and baptized some days ago, deceased yesterday aged about 18 years. Present Francois Bilodeau and Pierre Groslouis undersigned. Francois Bilodeau Pierre Groslouis A. Langlois, priest
B-3 Marie Graice Hoe	The 23 April, 1843, we priest undersigned have baptized Marie Graice aged about 4 months, child of the marriage of Dominique Hoe farmer and of Betsey, of this vicinity. Godfather Louis Labonte, godmother Marguerite, who have not known how to sign. A. Langlois, priest
B-4 Elizabeth	The 24 April, 1843, we priest undersigned have baptized Elizabeth Chinouk, living in this parish aged about 20 years. Godfather Joseph Tse, and godmother Sophie, who have not known how to sign. A. Langlois, priest
M-1 C. Plante and Elizabeth	The 24 April, 1843, after the publication of one ban of marriage and the dispensation of two others, we priest undersigned, missionary for this country, have received the consent of marriage of Charles Plante, farmer, of-age widower of Susanne of this parish on one part, and Elizabeth Chinook, living also in this parish, on the other part, and have given them the nuptial benediction in presence of Joseph Tse and of John Groslouis who alone has signed. John Groslouis A. Langlois, priest missionary

p 72

B-5 Louis Labonte	This 8 May, 1843, we priest undersigned have baptized Louis aged 24 years, legitimate son of Louis Labonte farmer and of Marguerite Tlatsop. Godfather Andree Chalifou, godmother Catherine . . . who have not known how to sign. F. N. Blanchet, priest
B-6 Caroline Montour	This 8 May, 1843, we priest undersigned have baptized Caroline aged about 21 years, legitimate daughter of Sieur Nicolas Montour farmer, and of Anne Humpherville. Godfather Pierre Depot, godmother Marguerite Tlamath who have not known how to sign. F. N. Blanchet, priest

M-2 Louis Labonte and Caroline Montour	This 5 May, 1843, after the publication of three bans of marriage between Louis Labonte domiciled in this place, of-age son of Louis Labonte farmer and of Marguerite Tlatsop, on one part, and of Caroline Montour, domiciled in this place, of-age daughter of Nicolas Montour, farmer, and of . . . Humpherville on the other part, we missionary priest of the Columbia, no impediment appearing, have received their mutual consent to marriage and have given them the nuptial benediction in presence of Louis Labonte, father, of Andree Chalifou, and of Nicolas Montour, father, of Pierre Depot friend of the bride, who have not known how to sign, except the father of the bride. <div align="center">Nicholas Montour F. N. Blanchet, priest</div>

THIRTY EIGHTH PAGE F N B priest miss
p 73

S-4 . . . Plante	This 25 May, 1843, we priest undersigned have buried in the cemetery of this parish the body of Baptiste, legitimate son of Charles Plante, farmer of this place, and of the late . . . Indian. Present John Groslouis and Andre, Indian. He was aged 16 years. <div align="center">F. N. Blanchet, priest</div>
B-7 Joseph Poirier	This 27 May, 1843, we priest undersigned have baptized Joseph born 8 days ago of the legitimate marriage of Toussaint Poirier farmer of this place, and of Catherine Tlatsop. Godfather Joseph Delard, godmother Marie Poirier. <div align="center">F. N. Blanchet, priest</div>
B-8 Philomene Dompierre	This 28 May, 1843, we priest undersigned have baptized Philomene born 4 days ago of the legitimate marriage of Pierre Davis Dompierre farmer of this place and of Marguerite Souliere. Godfather Augustin Rochon, godmother Celeste Jeaudoin. <div align="center">F. N. Blanchet, priest</div>
B-9 Joseph Beaulieu	This 28 May, 1843, we priest undersigned have baptized Joseph Beaulieu, aged 51 years, servant of the Company. Godfather Amable Petit, godmother Susanne . . . <div align="center">F. N. Blanchet, priest</div>
S-5 Xavier Barnabe	This 2 June, 1843, we priest undersigned have buried in the cemetery of this parish the body of Xavier, legitimate son of Joseph Barnabe, farmer of this place, and of Isabelle Boucher, deceased yesterday, aged 3 months. Present Xavier Laderoute and Joseph Barnabe. <div align="center">F. N. Blanchet, priest</div>

p 74

B-10 Marie	The 29 May [sic] 1843, we priest undersigned have baptized privately, in route to the Falls, an Indian child, Molalis by nation, under the name of Marie. <div align="center">F. N. Blanchet, priest</div>
B-11 Luce Lonetain	This 28 June, 1843, we priest undersigned have baptized Luce, born some days ago of the legitimate marriage of Andree Lonetain, farmer, and of Nancy Okinagan. Godfather John Hord, undersigned, godmother his wife. <div align="center">John Hord F. N. Blanchet, priest</div>
B-12 Paul John Spok.	This 9 July, 1843, we priest undersigned have baptized Paul, aged 1 year, natural son of John Spokan by nation, and of Henriette, both infidels. Godfather Jean Baptiste Dubreuil, godmother Susanne Petit. <div align="center">F. N. Blanchet, priest</div>
B-13 Madeleine Servant	This 10 July, 1843, we priest undersigned have baptized Madeleine aged 18 years, legitimate daughter of Jacques Servant farmer of this place, and of Josephte Okanagan. Godfather . . . <div align="center">F. N. Blanchet, priest</div>
M-3 Charles Jeaudoin	This 10 July, 1843, seeing the dispensation of the publication of one ban, granted by us undersigned, and the publication of two others between Charles Jeaudoin, farmer of this place, of-age son of L . . . Jeaudoin and

and Madeleine Servant	of Marie Anne Laverdure of Varennes, Canada, on one part; and Madeleine Servant, minor daughter of Jacques and of Josephte . . . of this parish, on the other part, nor any impediment appearing, and with the consent of the father of the bride, we priest have received their mutual consent of marriage and have given them the nuptial benediction in presence of Augustin Rochon, of Jacques Servant, father, and of several others who as well as the spouses have not known how to sign. F. N. Blanchet, priest

THIRTY NINTH PAGE F N B priest miss.

p 75

S-6 Barthelimi Martineau	This 19 July, 1843, we priest undersigned have buried in the cemetery of this parish the body of Barthelemi legitimate son of Alexis Martineau and of Betsy Snoday, deceased yesterday aged about 12 years. Present Joseph Crochiere and Isaac Gervais who have not known how to sign. F. N. Blanchet, priest, V.G.
B-14 Amable Koosse	This 20 July, 1843, we priest undersigned have baptized Amable Koosse Indian, aged about 20 years. Godfather Amable Petit. F. N. Blanchet, priest, V.G.
S-7 Amable Koosse	This 21 July, 1843, we priest undersigned have buried in the cemetery of this parish the body of Amable Koosse, Indian, since three years in the service of this mission, deceased yesterday at the age of 20 years. Present Isaac Gervais and Augustin Delard. F. N. Blanchet, priest, V.G.
B-15 Joseph Crochiere	This 27 July, 1843, we priest undersigned have baptized Joseph Crochiere aged 18 years, natural son of . . . Crochiere and of Marguerite Crise, now wife of Andre Dubois. Godfather Joseph Rivet, godmother Rose Lacourse. F. N. Blanchet, priest, V.G.
B-16 Isaac Gervais	This 27 July, 1843, we priest undersigned have baptized Isaac, aged 15 years legitimate son of Joseph Gervais and the late . . . Godfather Antoine Rivet, godmother Emelie Pend Oreille. F. N. Blanchet, priest, V.G.
B-17 Xavier Plante	This 27 July, 1843, we priest undersigned have baptized Xavier, aged 13 years, legitimate son of Charles Plante, farmer, and of the late . . . Godfather Thomas, godmother Marie Lafleur. F. N. Blanchet, priest, V.G.

p 76

B-18 Pierre Lacourse	This 27 July, 1843, we priest undersigned have baptized Pierre aged 15 years, legitimate son of Pierre Lacourse and of Archange Tichelis. Godfather Laurent Quintal, godmother Marie Anne Nipissing. F. N. Blanchet, priest,
B-19 Augustin Delard	This 27 July, 1843, we priest undersigned have baptized Augustin Delard aged 15 years, legitimate son of Joseph Delard and of the late . . . Godfather Louis Pichet, godmother Marguerite Bercier. F. N. Blanchet, priest,
B-20 Joseph Pin	This 27 July, 1843, we priest undersigned have baptized Joseph aged 15 years, legitimate son of Joseph Pin and of Marguerite Pend'Oreille. Godfather Francois Bilodeau, godmother Henriette Vivet. F. N. Blanchet, priest,
B-21 Narcisse Vivet	This 27 July, 1843, we priest undersigned have baptized Narcisse aged 12 years, natural son of Louis Vivet farmer and of the late . . . Godfather Xavier Laderoute, godmother Julie Gervais. F. N. Blanchet, priest,
B-22 Ebnezer Antony Pomeroy	The 1st of August, 1843, we priest undersigned have baptized Ebnezer Antony aged 3 years and 1 month, legitimate child of Walter Pomeroy carpenter and of Jane Teller of the Falls of the Wallamette. The godfather has been the priest himself undersigned and the godmother Catherine Garithy who has not known how to sign. A. Langlois, priest

fORTIETH PAGE F N B priest miss

p 77

B-23 Claude Lacourse	This 27 July, 1843, we priest undersigned have baptized Claude, aged 12 years, legitimate son of Pierre Lacourse, farmer, and of Archange Tihelis. Godfather Joseph Gervais, godmother Angelique his wife. F. N. Blanchet, priest,
B-24 Louis Pichet	The 27 July, 1843, we priest undersigned have baptized Louis aged 11 years, legitimate son of Louis Pichet farmer of this place and of Marguerite Bercier. Godfather Joseph Guertin, godmother Marie Anne Senegal. F. N. Blanchet, priest,
B-25 Noel Lavigueur	The 27 July, 1843, we priest undersigned have baptized Noel aged 13 years legitimate son of Hyacinthe Lavigueur farmer, and of Marguerite of the Chaudieres. Godfather Louis Pichet, godmother Marguerite Bercier. F. N. Blanchet, priest,
B-26 Marie Anne Ouvre	The 27 July, 1843, we priest undersigned have baptized Marie Anne aged 13 years, legitimate son [sic] of Jean Baptis' Ouvre and of the late . . . Godfather Louis Vivet, godmother Marie Anne Toupin. F. N. Blanchet, priest,
B-27 Rose Aussent	The 27 July, 1843, we priest undersigned have baptized Rose aged 14 years, legitimate daughter of Louis Aussent, farmer, and of Catherine Koosse. Godfather Etienne Gregoire, godmother his wife. F. N. Blanchet, priest,
B-28 Virginia Chamberlain	The 29 August, 1843, we priest undersigned have baptized Virginia born the 12 of the legitimate marriage of Adolphe Chamberlain farmer of this parish, and of Julienne. Godfather Olivier Dobin, godmother Julie Gervais, the father alone has signed. Adolphe Chamberlain A. Langlois, priest

p 78

B-29 Ant. Bap privately at the Falls	The 24 August, 1843, an Indian child baptized privately at the Falls, his name is Antoine; the Indian child was given the name of the undersigned. A. Langlois, priest
5 B-34 2 baptisms 3 privately baptized	In the month of August, 1843, I have baptized at the village of Tlackamas two little Indian girls under the name of Marie; privately baptized at the same time at the hut of Old Astekoss three Indian children. F. N. Blanchet, priest,
B-35 Romain Gagnon	This 14 September, 1843, we priest undersigned have baptized Romain born yesterday of the legitimate marriage of Francois Gagnon farmer of this place, and of Angelique . . . Godfather Joseph Gagnon, godmother Marguerite Gerlais [Desjarlais]. F. N. Blanchet, priest,
B-36 Pierre Laferte	The 17 September, 1843, we priest undersigned have baptized Pierre aged 18 days, legitimate child of Michel Laferte farmer, and of Josephte Pen d'Oreille of this parish. Godfather Pierre Beleque, godmother Jeanne Beleque, who have not known how to sign. A. Langlois, priest
Abjuration Walter John Pomeroy	The 20 September, 1843, we priest undersigned have received the abjuration of Methodism and the profession in the Catholic faith of Walter John Pomeroy and have absolved him of the excommunication incurred by the profession of the said error. In presence of Joseph Guertin and Francois Xavier Mathieu alone signed with us. F. X. Mathieu Walter John Pomeroy F. N. Blanchet, priest,
B-37 Walter John Pomeroy	The 20 September, 1843, we priest undersigned have baptized Walter John Pomeroy, carpenter and joiner, of Oregon City, aged 41 years. Godfather Joseph Guertin who has not known how to sign. The baptized has signed. Walter John Pomeroy F. N. Blanchet, priest,

FORTY FIRST PAGE F.N.B. priest miss

p 79

M-4
Walter John
Pomeroy
and Jane
Taylor

The 20 September, 1843, in view of the dispensation of three bans of marriage granted by us undersigned, between Walter John Pomeroy, carpenter and joiner, of Oregon City, widower of Betsy Hays dead since six years, and Jane Taylor, Irishwoman, domiciled in Oregon City, widow of Terna McGarty dead since ten years, on the other part, nor any impediment appearing, we undersigned missionary priest have received their mutual consent of marriage and have given them the nuptial benediction in presence of Joseph Guertin and of F. X. Mathieu witnesses undersigned as well as the groom, the bride has not known how to sign.

F. X. Mathieu   Walter John Pomeroy
                       Jany (X) Taylor
F. N. Blanchet, priest,

B-38
Magdeleine
Portier

This 23 September, 1843, we priest undersigned have baptized Magdeleine, born 7 days ago, natural child of Nicholas Jean Portier, and of a woman of California. Godfather Stanislas Jacquet, godmother Victoire Tchinouk.

F. N. Blanchet, priest,

S-8
Leon
Arquate

The 3 October, 1843, we priest undersigned have buried in the cemetery of this place the body of Leon Arquate, drowned by accident at the Grand Dalles of the Columbia, at the beginning of last July, in the service of the Company of the Bay of Hudson, identified and brought up by his brother Amable Arquaite; at the age of about . . . years. Present Amable Arquaite, Jean Baptiste Dubreuil who have not known how to sign.

F. N. Blanchet, priest,

p 80

B-39
Charlotte
Lapratte

This 8 October, 1843, we priest undersigned have baptized Charlotte born 10 days ago of the legitimate marriage of Alexis Lapratte farmer of this place, and of Nancy Pion. Godfather Jean Gingras, godmother Charlotte Okinagan.

F. N. Blanchet, priest,

B-40
David
Gregoire

The 8 October, 1843, we priest undersigned have baptized David aged about 15 years, natural child of Etienne Gregoire farmer and of Marguerite of this parish. Godfather Luc Gagnon, godmother Adrienne Lucier who have not known how to sign.

A. Langlois, priest

B-41
Susanne
Gaudritche

The 8 October, 1843, we priest undersigned have baptized under condition because of an earlier Protestant baptism, Susanne aged about 14 years, natural daughter of the late . . . Gaudritche and of Helene now the wife of Dobin of this parish. Godfather Louis Aussan, godmother Adrienne Lucier who have not known how to sign.

A. Langlois, priest

B-42
Angelique
Lonetain

The 8 October, 1843, we priest undersigned have baptized Angelique aged about 13 years, natural daughter of Andre Lonetain and of Helene. Godfather Etienne Gregoire, godmother Adrienne Lucier who have not known how to sign.

A. Langlois, priest

B-43
Marie
Servant

The 8 October, 1843, we priest undersigned have baptized Marie Servant aged about 14 years natural daughter of Jacques Servant farmer and of Josephte of this parish. Godfather Louis Pichet, godmother Marguerite Bercier who have not known how to sign.

A. Langlois, priest

FORTY SECOND PAGE F.N.B. priest miss

p 81

B-44
Marie
Sarkina
Canote

The 8 October, 1843, we priest undersigned have baptized Marie Sarkina, widow of the late Canote, aged about 45 years, residing in this parish. Godfather Joseph Gervais, godmother Archange Tihelis who have not known how to sign.

A. Langlois, priest

B-45
Isaac
Arquoit

The 15 October, 1843, we priest undersigned have baptized Isaac aged about 1 month, legitimate child of Amable Arquoit farmer and of Marguerite. Godfather Etienne Gregoire, godmother Marguerite who have not known how to sign.

A. Langlois, priest

B-46
Casimir
[Tianesse?
see B-21,
p 26]

The 15 October, 1843, we priest undersigned have baptized Casimir aged about 10 months, child born of the infidel marriage of Baptiste and of Marie Saste, living at the home of Amable Arquoit. Godfather Amable Arquoit, godmother Marguerite who have not known how to sign.

A. Langlois, priest

B-47
Frederic
Indian

The 10 October, 1843, we priest undersigned have baptized in danger of death, in his hut on the field of Frederic Despard, an old Indian of the nation of Tchinouk, aged about 50 years. Godmother, the wife of Frederic Despard.

F. N. Blanchet, priest,

B-48
Marie

This 10 October, 1843, we priest undersigned have baptized in danger of death, at the house of Charlot Tschte an Indian woman under the name of Marie, aged about 20 years.

F. N. Blanchet, priest,

B-49
Amable

This 10 October, 1843, we priest undersigned have baptized Amable aged some months, son of the infidel marriage of . . . in the service of Charlot Tschte.

F. N. Blanchet, priest,

p 82
B-50
Antoine
Gagnon

The 19 October, 1843, we priest undersigned have baptized under condition Antoine born yesterday of the legitimate marriage of Luc Gagnon farmer and of Julie Gregoire of this parish. Godfather Antoine Gregoire, godmother Rose Aussan who have not known how to sign.

A. Langlois, priest

S-9
Romain
Gagnon

The 14 October, 1843, we priest undersigned have buried in the cemetery of this parish the body of Romain, legitimate son of Francois Gagnon farmer and of . . . deceased yesterday aged 1 month. Present Amable Petit and . . .

F. N. Blanchet, priest,

S-10
Marie
Indian

The 18 October, 1843, we priest undersigned have buried in the cemetery of this parish the body of Marie Indian baptized the 10 of this month at the house of Charles Tschte. Present Amable Petit and . . .

F. N. Blanchet, priest,

B-51
Elizabeth
Aubichon

The 20 October, 1844 *[sic]*, we priest undersigned have baptized Elizabeth born the 17 of March of the legitimate marriage of Alexis Aubichon farmer of this place and of Marie Anne Tchinouk. Godfather Joseph Gervais, godmother Victoire Joseph McLoughlin.

F. N. Blanchet, priest,

B-52
David
Gariesse
[Lucier]

The 20 October, 1843, we priest undersigned have baptized David, aged 5 months, born of the legitimate marriage of Jean Baptiste Gariessi *[Lucier]* farmer of this place and of Catherine Delard. Godfather Joseph Delard, godmother Julie Gervais.

F. N. Blanchet, priest,

FORTY THIRD PAGE F.N.B. priest miss.

p 83
S-11
Eliz.
Plante

The 23 October, 1843, we priest undersigned have buried in the cemetery of this parish the body of Elizabeth, deceased 2 days ago, aged about 14 years, wife of Charles Plante, farmer of this parish. Present Pierre Groslouis and John Groslouis undersigned.

John Groslouis   Pierre Groslouis
A. Langlois, priest

B-53
Josephine
Ignace

This 29 October, 1843, we priest undersigned have baptized Josephine aged 7 months, legitimate daughter of Ignace, Iroquois by his father, and of Helene Tchinouk. Godfather Amable Arquoit, godmother Susanne Goderish who have not known how to sign.

F. N. Blanchet, priest,

B-54 Francois Tlakas	The 1st of November, 1843, we priest undersigned have baptized Francois born 4 days ago of infidel parents, of whom the father calls himself Tlakas and the mother Lisette, living at the house of Antoine Masta. Godfather the said Antoine Masta, godmother Sophie his wife who have not known how to sign. Ant. Langlois, priest
B-55 Louis Toussaint Quintal	The 5 November, 1843, we priest undersigned have baptized Louis Toussaint aged 5 days, legitimate child of Laurent Quintal farmer, and of Marie Anne of this parish. Godfather Andre Lonetain, godmother Julienne Chamberland who have not known how to sign. Ant. Langlois, priest

p 84

M-5 Aug. Remond and Marie Servant	The 6 November, 1843, we priest undersigned have, after the publication of one ban of marriage, having dispensed the two others, have, I say, received the mutual consent of marriage of Augustin Remond farmer domiciled in this parish, of-age son of Toussaint Remond farmer and of the late Marie Bissonnet of the parish of St. Cyprian of Montreal, on one part, and of Marie Servant, minor daughter of Jacques Servant farmer, and of Josephte Aquinagan of this parish, on the other part, nor any impediment appearing, the parents of the said Marie Servant giving consent, we have given them the nuptial benediction in presence of Francois Xavier Mathieu, Jean Baptiste Jeaudoin, Francois Bilodeau and of John Groslouis as well as of several other friends of the said spouses, who have not known how to sign. Of the above witnesses only three signed with us.

F. X. Mathieu   Jean Baptiste Jeaudoin
John Groslouis   Francois Bilodeau
Antoine Langlois, priest miss.
Authorized to marry

S-12 Frs. Tlakas	The 11 November, 1843, buried the body of Francois Tlakes, of infidel parents, aged 15 days, were present John Groslouis and Amable Petit. A. Langlois, priest

FORTY FOURTH PAGE F N B priest miss.

p 85

B-56 John Groslouis	The 12 November, 1843, we priest undersigned have baptized John Groslouis under condition, for having before been by his Protestant Minister formerly; child of the late Charles Groslouis and of a Pen d'Oreille woman also dead, aged about 12 years. Godfather Louis Pichet, godmother Marguerite Bercier, who have not known how to sign. John Groslouis A. Langlois, priest
B-57 Eugenie Depatie	The 12 November, 1843, we priest undersigned have baptized under condition Eugenie, aged about 24 years, daughter of infidel parents, of whom the father is called Wanakske, chief of a tribe at the Falls of the Wallamet, now married by civil act to Jean Baptiste Depatie. Godfather Louis Laroque, godmother . . . Montour, who have not known how to sign. A. Langlois, priest
B-58 Angelique M. Rondeau	The 12 November, 1843, we priest undersigned have baptized under condition, Angelique Marguerite aged about 16 years, natural child of Charles Rondeau farmer and of . . . of this parish. Godfather Pierre Lacourse, godmother Archange Tihelis who have not known how to sign. A. Langlois, priest
B-59 Catherine	The 12 November, 1843, we priest undersigned have baptized Catherine aged about 20 years, of infidel parents, raised by Jean Baptiste Depati. Godfather Louis Laroque, godmother Marie Laroque who have not known how to sign. A. Langlois, priest

p 86

M-6 J. Bte.	The 13 November, 1843, we priest undersigned have after the publication of one ban of marriage made at the sermon of our parish mass and the

Depati and Eugenie Wanakske	dispensation of two other bans granted by Messire Blanchet V.G. between Jean Baptiste Depati farmer domiciled in this parish, of-age son of the late Jean Baptiste Depati and of an infidel woman, of Temiscaming, on one part, and of Eugenie, of-age daughter of the late Wanakske, infidel, as well as his wife, on the other part, nor any impediment appearing and the said Jean Baptiste Depati being certain of the death of a woman with whom he had been married in Canada; that woman called Catherine Ochikapawissa, we, I say, priest undersigned and authorized to ad hoc have received their mutual consent of marriage in presence of Charles Rondeau, son-in-law, and of Francois Rivet who have not known how to sign, of Francois Bilodeau and of Francois Xavier Mathieu, undersigned, friends of the said groom *["of whom only one has signed" crossed out]* who has not known how to sign.

F. Bilodeau
F. X. Mathieu
one line of 7 words ruled nulle and 4 words
above the line correct
Ant. Langlois, priest miss.

B-60 Marie	This 17 November, 1843, we priest undersigned have baptized in a hut, at the place of Frederic Despard an Indian girl in danger of death, aged about 18 years, under the name of Marie.

F. N. Blanchet, priest,

FORTY FIFTH PAGE F.N.B. priest miss.

p 87

B-61 Jos. Matte	The 20 November, 1843, we priest undersigned have baptized Joseph, aged 20 days, natural child of Joseph Matte and of Josephte, newly established in this parish. Godfather Joseph Pin, godmother Susanne Petit, who have not known how to sign.

A. Langlois, priest

B-62 Cecile Lafantaisie	This 21 November, 1843, we priest undersigned have baptized Cecile born yesterday of the legitimate marriage of Charles Lafantaisie farmer, and of Elizabeth Canote, of this parish. Godfather Andre Picard, godmother Lisette Canote.

F. N. Blanchet, priest,

S-13 Marie Indian	This 21 November, 1843, we priest undersigned have buried in the cemetery of this parish the body of Marie Indian woman slave, deceased yesterday, two days after her baptism. Witnesses Amable Petit and Francoix Xavier Laderoute.

F. N. Blanchet, priest,

B-63 Louis Bte. Iroquois *[Tyikwarhi]*	This 3 December, 1843, we priest undersigned have baptized Louis born 20 days ago of the legitimate marriage of Baptiste Iroquois and of Judith of this parish. Godfather Francois Bilodeau, undersigned, godmother Susanne Petit.

F. N. Blanchet, priest,

B-64 Angelique Laroque	The 5 December, 1843, we priest undersigned have baptized Angelique, aged 4 days, legitimate child of Louis Laroque farmer and of Marie Toussaint of this parish. Godfather Jean Baptiste Depati, godmother Marie Laroque who have not known how to sign.

A. Langlois, priest

p 88

B-no number Marie Ducharme	This 6 December, 1843, we priest undersigned have baptized Marie born yesterday of the legitimate marriage of Jean Baptiste Ducharme farmer, and of Catherine Paul of this parish. Godfather Joseph Gagnon, godmother Louise Braconnier, who have not known how to sign.

F. N. Blanchet, priest,

S-14 Frederic Indian	The 2 December, 1843, we priest undersigned have buried in the cemetery of this parish the body of Frederic Indian of the tribe of the Tchinouks, deceased at the house of Jean Baptiste Perrault, aged about 60 years, having been baptized at the house of Frederic Despard, present Jean Bte. Perrault

and Amable Petit.

F. N. Blanchet, priest,

S-15   The 4 December, 1843, we priest undersigned have buried in the cemetery of this parish the body of . . . [remainder blank]

F. N. Blanchet, priest,

S-16
Amable

The 15 December, 1843, we priest undersigned have buried in the cemetery of this place the body of Amable, son, issue of the natural marriage of . . . both infidels, deceased yesterday, aged about 3 months. Present Amable Petit and . . .

F. N. Blanchet, priest,

B-65
Pelagie

This 18 December, 1843, we priest undersigned have baptized Pelagie aged about 36 years, born of infidel parents of the tribe of Tchinouks. Godfather Amable Petit, godmother Susanne Petit.

F. N. Blanchet, priest,

M-7
Plante
. . .
Pelagie

This 18 December, 1843, seeing the dispensation of Forbidden Times and that of the publication of three bans, granted by us priest undersigned between Charles Plant domiciled in this place, widower in the last marriage of the late Lisette, on one part, and Pelagie Tchinouk on the other part, nor any impediment being discovered, we priest undersigned have received their mutual consent of marriage and have given them the nuptial benediction in presence of Amable Petit and of Laurent Iroquois who as well as the spouses have not known how to sign.

F. N. Blanchet, priest,

FORTY SIXTH PAGE F N B priest miss.

p 89

B-66
Lse.
Bte.

The 20 December, 1843, we priest undersigned have baptized Louise born 4 days ago of infidel parents, residents with F. X. Laderoute, the father named Batiste and the mother Catherine. Godfather Francois Xavier Laderoute, godmother Julie Gervais.

A. Langlois, priest

S-17   The 21 December, buried in the cemetery Ignace Indian, resident at the house of J. Bte. Aubichon, baptized ill some months ago. Present Jos. Groslouis and . . .

A. Langlois, priest

B-67
Benoni
Laroque

The 25 December, baptized Benoni aged 4 days, son of the marriage of Joseph Laroque farmer, and Elizabeth WallaWalla. Godfather [repeat] Francois Xavier Laderoute, godmother Catherine Russie.

A. Langlois, priest

B-68
Rosalie
Roi

The ["20" crossed out] 30 December, baptized Rosalie aged 3 days, of the marriage of Thomas Roi farmer and of Marie of this parish. Godfather Joseph Crochiere, godmother Rose Aussan who have not known how to sign.

A. Langlois, priest

1844

M-1
Pierre
P.
Lachance

The 8 January, 1844, after the publication of three bans of marriage between Pierre Pepin dit Lachance, blacksmith, employed for the Catholic mission and working here, of-age son of Guillaume Pepin blacksmith and of Catherine Gendron of Maskinonge of Montreal, on one part, and Susanne Gaudritch, (turn two pages - error) A.L.

[The remainder of this entry will be found on p 92]

p 90

B-1   This 10 January, 1844, baptized Michel, born Indians and resident at the house of Corneille, aged about 10 years.

Ant. Langlois, priest

S-1   The 16 January, buried in the cemetery Michel aged about 10 years, of infidel parents and baptized these days past. Present Courneille and John Groslouis.

A. Langlois, priest

B-2   The 20 January, 1844, baptized Adele aged 3 days of the legitimate mar-

Adele Rivet	riage of Antoine Rivet and of Emilie of this parish. Godfather Joseph Rivet, godmother Rose Lacourse. <div align="right">A. Langlois, priest</div>
B-3 Vincent Abrah. Gilbeau	The 22 January, 1844, we priest undersigned have baptized Vincent Abraham born 2 days ago of the legitimate marriage of Paul Gilbeau farmer, and of Katy of this parish. Godfather Jean Baptiste Dubreuil, god- mother Jeanny St. Martin, who have not known how to sign. <div align="right">A. Langlois, priest</div>
B-4 Antoine	The 28 *[January, 1844]* baptized a child of unknown parents, the mother Indian, living at the house of Dubreuil, aged about 6 months, under the name Antoine. Godfather P. Guilbeau, godmother Jeannie St. Martin. <div align="right">A. Langlois,</div>
S-2 Jacques *[Gagnon]*	The 12 February, 1844, has been buried Jacques Gagnon, deceased yester- day aged 5 years 1 month and 10 days, legitimate child of Francois Gagnon, farmer, and of Angelique Marcellin of this parish. Present Joseph Groslouis and Amable Petit. <div align="right">Joseph Groslouis A. Langlois, priest</div>

FORTY SEVENTH PAGE F N B priest miss
p 91

B-5 Gedeon Forcier	The 23 February, 1844, we priest undersigned have baptized Gedeon aged 15 days, legitimate male child of Louis Forcier, farmer, and of Catherine of this parish. Godfather Amable Arquoit, godmother Marguerite Arquoit who have not known how to sign. <div align="right">A. Langlois, priest</div>
B-6 Catherine Gendron	The 25 February, 1844, - Baptized, Catherine, aged 18 days, legitimate child of Joseph Gendron, farmer, and of Louise. Godfather Augustin Rochon, godmother Catherine Russie who have not known how to sign. <div align="right">A. Langlois, priest</div>
B-7 David Dorion	The 10 March, 1844, we priest undersigned have baptized David, *["aged some weeks and already privately baptized" (A.L.) written above the line]* son of Baptiste Dorion and of Josephte Caious, married in the manner of infidels. Godfather Frs. X. Laderoute, godmother Marie Anne Toupin who have not known how to sign. <div align="right">A. Langlois, priest</div>
S-3 Marg. Crise Dubois	The 13 March, 1844, we priest undersigned have buried in the cemetery of this parish the body of Marguerite Cris, wife of Andre Dubois, farmer of this parish. Present Francois Bilodeau and Pierre Groslouis, under- signed. <div align="right">Francois Bilodeau Pierre Groslouis A. Langlois, priest</div>

p 92

Suzanne Gaudritch	*[This is a continuation of M-1 on page 89]* minor daughter of the late Gaudritch and of Nancy Dobin, consenting, on the other part, nor any impediment appearing, we priest undersigned have given them the bene- diction in presence of Amable Petit, of Paul Guilbeau and of Francois Bilodeau, alone undersigned. *[two pages skipped]* <div align="right">Francois Bilodeau A. Langlois, priest</div>
B-5 Catherine Pichet	The 4 February, 1844, we priest undersigned have baptized Catherine aged about 10 days, child of the legitimate marriage of Louis Pichet farmer and of Marguerite Bercier of this parish. Godfather Hiacynthe Lavigueur, godmother Julienne Chamberland who have not known how to sign. <div align="right">A. Langlois, priest</div>
B-8 Andre Tawakon	The 17 March, 1844, we priest undersigned have baptized Andre aged 21 days, legitimate child of Thomas Tawakon and of Louise Walla Walla, of this parish. Godfather Paul Guilbeau, godmother Susanne Tawakon. <div align="right">A. Langlois, priest</div>

B-9
Ch
Piskel

The 17 March, 1844, we priest undersigned have baptized Charles, aged about 8 months, of the natural marriage of Thomas Piskel, metis, and of Elizabeth, both still infidels, in the service of the Honorable Company of the Bay of Hudson at Fort George. Godfather Alexis Aubichon, godmother Marie Anne Aubichon.

A. Langlois, priest

FORTY EIGHTH PAGE F.N.B. priest missr
p 93

S-4
Toussaint
Racine

The 19 March [1844], buried Toussaint aged 8 years and 4 months, child of Racine formerly of the Company - present Joseph and John Groslouis.

A. Langlois, priest

B-10
Norbert
Bernier

The 25 March, 1844, we priest undersigned have baptized Norbert aged 16 days, legitimate child of Francois Bernier, joiner, and of Pelagie Lucier of this parish. Godfather Francois Xavier Mathieu, godmother Rose Aussan. The godfather alone has known how to sign.

Francois Xavier Mathieu
A. Langlois, priest

S-5
Josephine
Ignace

The 26 March, 1844, we priest undersigned have baptized Josephine, deceased yesterday, legitimate child of Ignace, Iroquois by nation, and of Helene, inhabitants of this place - present John Groslouis, undersigned, and Andre Palous.

John Groslouis
A. Langlois, priest

S-6
Adele
Rivet

The 10 April, [1844] buried Adele Rivet aged about 2 months and a half, child of Antoine Rivet and of Emilie. Present Antoine and Joseph Rivet.

A. Langlois, priest

M-2
F.X.
Mathieu
and
[Rose
Aussent]

p 94

The 15 April, 1844, after the publication of one ban of marriage and the dispensation of two others granted by us Missionary priest authorized of the powers which are given in the same circumstances, between Francois Xavier Mathieu, joiner, domiciled in this parish, of-age son of Francois Xavier Mathieu, farmer, and of Marie Louise Daufin, his father and mother of the parish of St. Louis of Terrebonne, on one part, and Rose Aussan, minor, daughter of Louis Aussant and an infidel woman, I undersigned priest have received their mutual consent with the authorization of the father of the said bride, and have given them the nuptial benediction in presence of Etienne Lucier and of Pierre Beleque, friends of the groom, and of Louis Aussant, father, and of Jean Baptiste Champagne, who have not known how to sign, nor could the said spouses, except the groom.

Francois Xavier Mathieu
Rose (X) Aussan   J. Baptiste (X) Champagne
Louis (X) Aussan   Etienne (X) Lucier
Pierre (X) Belleque
A. Langlois, priest
authorized to marry

B-11
Cath
McKay

The 21 April, 1844, we priest undersigned have baptized Catherine aged 2 weeks, legitimate child of Thomas McKay, farmer, and of Elizabeth Montour, residents on an island of the Columbia River. Godfather Joseph Guertin, godmother Marguerite Gerlais, who have not known how to sign.

A. Langlois, priest

B-12
Catherine
Chalifou

The 25 April, 1844, we priest undersigned have baptized Catherine born the 13 of this month of the legitimate marriage of Andre Chalifou farmer, and of Catherine Russil of this parish. Godfather Laurent Quintal, godmother Marianne, who have not known how to sign.

A. Langlois, priest

FORTY NINTH PAGE F N B priest miss
p 95

M-3
Aug.
Russil

The 29 April, 1844, in view of the publication of one ban of marriage, and the dispensation of two others granted by us, missionary priest, endowed with the power ad hoc, between Augustin Russil farmer domiciled in this

and
Ag.
Taikowari

parish, minor son of the late Augustin Russil old servant of the H. Company of the B. of H. and of an infidel woman of the country on one part, and Agnes, minor daughter of Jean Baptiste Taikwari farmer and of Judith consenting, also of this parish on the other part; nor any impediment appearing except the minority of the groom which is obviated by the consent of the only sister which he has in the country, there being no magistrate to name for him a guardian, we undersigned missionary priest have received their mutual consent of marriage and have given them the nuptial benediction in the presence of Catherine Russil, sister, and of Andre Chalifou, brother-in-law of the groom, and of Jean Baptiste Taikowari, father, and of Judith mother of the bride, who as well as the said spouses have declared not knowing how to sign.

Ant. Langlois, priest missionary

B-13
Jos.
Labonte

The 5 May, 1844, we priest undersigned have baptized Joseph aged 5 days legitimate child of Louis Labonte farmer, and of Caroline Montour of this parish. Godfather Joseph McLoughlin, undersigned, godmother Victoire McMillan who has not known how to sign.

Joseph McLoughlin
A. Langlois, priest

p 96
B-14
Archange
Plouf

The 6 May, 1844, we priest undersigned have baptized Archange born 3 days ago of the legitimate marriage of Joseph Plouf farmer, and of Therese of this parish. Godfather Louis Pichet, godmother Marguerite Bercier who have not known how to sign.

A. Langlois, priest

B-15
Jos.
Bourgeau

The 12 May, 1844, we priest undersigned have baptized Joseph born 3 days ago of the legitimate marriage of Joseph Bourgeau farmer, and of Angele Lafantaisie of this parish. Godfather Louis Aussan, godmother Marguerite Gerlais who have not known how to sign.

A. Langlois, priest

M-6
Pierre
Gauthier
and
Esther
Dalcour

The 20 May, 1844, after the publication of three bans of marriage made at the sermon of our parish Masses between Pierre Gauthier farmer domiciled in this parish, of-age son of Joseph Gauthier farmer, and of Catherine Cartier of the parish of Sorel in Montreal, on one part; and Esther Dalcour, minor daughter of Jean Baptiste Dalcour and of Agathe of this parish, on the other part, nor any impediment appearing, the permission of the father of the said bride having been obtained, we undersigned missionary priest with sufficient powers, have received their mutual consent to marriage and have given them the nuptial benediction in presence of Francois Xavier Mathieux and of Joseph Corneille friends of the groom; of Joseph Despart and of John Young friends of the bride, who as well as the said spouses have declared not knowing how to sign except the said Mathieux.

Francois Xavier Mathieu.
A. Langlois, priest

FIFTIETH PAGE F N B priest miss
p 97
B-16
Frs.
Xavier
Gervais

The 25 May, 1844, we undersigned priest have baptized Francois Xavier Gervais aged about . . . natural child of Joseph Gervais and of Marguerite, now dead. The godfather has been Francois Xavier Laderoute, and the godmother Julie Gervais, his sister, who have not known how to sign.

Francois Xavier Gervais
A. Langlois, priest

B-17
Ch
Rondeau

The 26 May, 1844, we priest undersigned have baptized under condition Charles aged 2 days, legitimate child of Charles Rondeau farmer, and of Agathe Depati of this parish. Godfather Louis Laroc, godmother Marie Toussaint.

A. Langlois, priest

S-7	The 29 May, *[1844]* buried in the cemetery the body of an Indian child, baptized aged about 3½ months.
	A. Langlois, priest
B-18	The 13 May, 1844, I have baptized Germain aged 6 months, son of tami-Swala and of Sattlekive, both infidel Indians. Godfather . . .
	F. N. Blanchet, priest,
p 98 Abjuration of Sophie Carpentier	The 30 May, 1844 we priest undersigned have received the abjuration of Methodism and the profession of the Catholic faith of Sophie Carpentier orphan of a Canadian father and of an Indian woman, and have absolved her from the excommunication incurred by the profession of the said error. Witnesses Paul Guilbeau and Laurent Sauve who have not known how to sign. The bride *[sic]* has made the mark of a cross.
	Sophie (X) Carpentier
	F. N. Blanchet, priest,
B-19 Sophie Carpentier	The 30 May, 1844, we priest undersigned have baptized under condition Sophie, aged about 18 years, daughter of the late Charles Carpentier and of an Indian woman. Godfather Paul Guilbeau, godmother his wife.
	F. N. Blanchet, priest,
M-5 Cesaire Beaudoin and Sophie Carpentier	The 30 May, 1844, in view of the dispensation of three bans of marriage granted by us undersigned between Cesaire Beaudoin, engage of the Company of the Bay of Hudson, of-age son of Joseph Beaudoin and of Cecile Jobin of the parish of the Grand St. Esprit of Montreal on one part, and Sophie Carpentier minor daughter of the late Charles Carpentier, engage of the Company, and of a Snake woman, nor any impediment appearing, and with the consent of her guardian Michel Laframboise, we undersigned priest missionary have received their mutual consent to marriage and have given them the nuptial benediction in presence of Paul Guilbeau and of Laurent Sauve who have not known how to sign as well as the spouses.
	F. N. Blanchet, priest,
S-8 Joseph	The 30 May, 1844, has been buried in the cemetery Joseph aged about 5 years, born of infidel Indian parents.
	A. Langlois, priest,
B-20 Louis Hubert	The 30 May, 1844, we priest undersigned have baptized Louis, aged 10 days, legitimate child of the marriage of Joachim Hubert farmer and Josephte *[des Chaudiere]* of this parish. Godfather Louis Vandel, godmother Cecile Magdeleine *[prob McDonald]* who have not known how to sign.
	A. Langlois, priest,

FIFTY-FIRST PAGE F.N.B. priest miss.

p 99 B-21	The 4 June, baptized Pierre of infidel parents living at the house of Etne Lucier. Godfather Francois Xavier Bernier, godmother the wife of Lucier.
	A. Langlois, priest,
S-9	The 4 June, buried a child of infidel Indian parents, about 3 years.
	A. Langlois, priest
S-10 Helene Ignace	The 11 June, 1844, has been buried in the cemetery the wife of Ignace, metis Iroquois farmer of this parish, baptized under the name of Helene. Present Paul Guilbeau and Ls Pichet who have not known how to sign.
	A. Langlois, priest
S-11 Charles Hord *[Howard]*	The 21 June, has been buried Charles, aged about 15 months deceased the day before, child of John Hord farmer and of Catherine Lonetain.
	A. Langlois, priest
S-12 Janotte	The 22 June, buried Janotte baptized aged about 4 years and of infidel parents. Present Antoine Rivet.
	A. Langlois, priest
S-13 Louis	The 26 June, 1844, we priest undersigned have buried in the cemetery of this parish the body of Louis Vivet, deceased the day before at the house

Vivet	of Etne Lucier, after a short illness, old servant of the Hudson's Bay Company, coming into the country about 23 years ago, and aged about 47 years. Present Narcisse Vivet, his natural son and Andre Picard.
	A. Langlois, priest
p 100	
S-14	The 29 June, buried Pierre aged about 9 years, deceased the day before
Pierre	yesterday, child of the late Pierre Laroque and of Genevieve Toussaint of
Laroque	the other side of the Rocky Mountains. Present Ls. Laroque, and Amable Petit.
	A. Langlois, priest
p 100	
B-22	Benjamin, Indian aged 12 years.
	[no signature]
S-15	The 8 July, has been buried Benjamin, child of infidel parents deceased
Benjamin	yesterday aged about 12 years, living at the house of Frederic Despaty *[Despard]* baptized some days ago.
	A. Langlois, priest
B-23	The 18 July, 1844, we priest undersigned have baptized Basile aged about
Basile	15 years, natural child of Andre Dubois farmer and of the late Marguerite
Dubois	Cree of this parish. Godfather Joseph Cline, godmother Louise Braconnier.
	A. Langlois, priest
B-24	The 18 July, 1844, we priest undersigned have baptized Francois, aged
Francois	25 years, natural child of Francois Dichouquot, formerly engage of the
des	Company of the Bay of Hudson returned to the east of the mountains and
Choquet	of an infidel Indian woman. Godfather Andre Picard, godmother Marie.
	A. Langlois, priest
B-25	The 28 July, 1844, we undersigned priest have baptized Judith, aged 1
Judith	month, natural child of William Kalapoia and of Akliou, both infidels.
William	Godfather Baptiste Iroquois, godmother Marguerite Labonte *[Clatsop]*.
	F. N. Blanchet, priest,

FIFTY-SECOND PAGE F. N. BLANCHET priest miss.

p 101	
B-26	This 28 July, 1844, we priest undersigned have baptized Louise aged 7
Louise	years, natural child of infidel Indians. Godfather Baptiste Iroquois, god-mother Marguerite Labonte.
	F. N. Blanchet, priest,
B-27	This 4 August, 1844, we priest undersigned have baptized Lucie born 3
Lucie	days ago of the legitimate marriage *[of]* Jean Baptiste Perrault farmer, and
Perrault	of Angele Tchinoik, of this place. Godfather Francois Bernier, godmother Genevieve Belique. The father alone has known how to sign.
	Jean Bt. Perrault
	F. N. Blanchet, priest,
2 B-29	The 4 August, 1844, we undersigned priest have baptized Susanne aged 2
Susanne	years, and Leocadie aged 1 month, natural children of Wassanepo and of
and	Nancy, both infidels. Godfather and godmother of Susanne, Amable
Leocadie	Arquoite and Marguerite Tchinouk; godfather and godmother of Leocadie Sylvain Bourgeau and Josephte who have not known how to sign.
	F. N. Blanchet, priest,
B-30	This 11 August, 1844, we priest undersigned have baptized Cecile, born
Cecile	the 6th of this month of the legitimate marriage of Louis Vendale farmer
Vendale	and of Catherine Porteuse. Godfather Louis Vendale the younger, god-mother Cecile McDonnell who as well as the father have not known how to sign.
	F. N. Blanchet, priest,
B-31	This 11 August, 1844, we priest undersigned have baptized Esther aged 14
Esther	days, born of the legitimate marriage of Louis Vendale the younger, farmer,
Vendale	and of Cecile McDonnell. Godfather Louis Vendale the older, godmother Esther Dalcourt, who as well as the father have not known how to sign.
	F. N. Blanchet, priest,

B-32
Melanie
Pady

This 11 August, 1844, we priest undersigned have baptized Melaine, aged 5 weeks, born of the legitimate marriage of Germain Horagan dit Pady, farmer, and of Nancy Atfalate [Tualatin]. Godfather William O'Sullivan, godmother Julie Laderoute, who as well as the father have not known how to sign.

F. N. Blanchet, priest,
[Transcriptions of Mikell Warner end here with her death.]

p 102
M-6
George
Montour
and
Lisette
Canote

The 19 August, 1844, after the publication of three bans of marriage between George Montour, domiciled in this place, of-age son of Nicolas Montour and of Anne Umpherville, of this place, on the one part; and Lisette Canote, domiciled in this place, of-age widow of the late Pierre Martineau, on the other part, nor having discovered any impediment to the said marriage, and of the consent of the parents, we missionary priest have received their mutual consent and have given them the nuptial benediction in the presence of Fabien Malouin and of Antoine Gregoire, of Nicolas Montour, witnesses. The last of whom has signed with us.

Nicolas Montour.
F. N. Blanchet, priest,

S-16
Marie
Deschau-
dieres

The 17 August, 1844, we the undersigned priest have buried in the cemetery of this mission the body of Marie des Chaudieres, wife of Jean Baptiste Lajoie, deceased 4 days ago at the Falls of the Wallamette. Aged 24 years. Present Fabien Malouin and Canote.

F. N. Blanchet, priest,

S-17
Virginie
Chamberland

The 5 September, 1844, we the undersigned priest have buried in the cemetery of this place the body of Virginie, legitimate daughter of Adolphe Chamberland, farmer, and of Julienne Watice, deceased yesterday in the morning, aged 1 year and 3 weeks. Present Adolphe Chamberland and Louis Aussant.

F. N. Blanchet, priest,

S-18

The 5 September, 1844, we the undersigned priest have buried in the cemetery of this place the body of . . . Spanish, deceased yesterday of illness at the age of . . .

F. N. Blanchet, priest,

B-33
Elizabeth

The 10 September, baptized Elizabeth, aged about 20 years and considered as the wife of a protestant who has afterwards received his consent to marriage and to him has given in like manner the same, at her home because she was sick in bed.

A. Langlois, priest

FIFTY THIRD PAGE
p 103
B-34
Antoine

The 7 September, baptized Antoine aged about 15 years, of infidel parents and living at the house of James Baker.

A. Langlois, priest

B-35
Anastasie
Laframboise

The 3 August, 1844, we the undersigned priest have baptized Anastasie, aged 3 weeks, legitimate child of Mr. Michel Laframboise and of Emilie Picard. Godfather Augustin Rochon, godmother Celeste Jeaudoin who could not sign. The father absent.

Mod. Demers, priest

B-36
Francois
Boucher

The 7 October, 1844, we the undersigned priest have baptized Francois born today of the legitimate marriage of Francois Boucher and of Therese Porteuse. Godfather Luc Gagnon, godmother Esther Champagne, who could not sign. The father absent.

Mod. Demers, priest

B-37
Francois
Dubreuil

The 6 October, 1844, we the undersigned priest have baptized Francois aged 8 days, born of the legitimate marriage of Jean Baptiste Dubreuil and of Marguerite Youglta; godfather Pierre Lachance, godmother Susanne Gaderich who could not sign.

Mod. Demers, priest

S-19

The 15 October, 1844, we the undersigned priest have buried in the cemetery of this parish the body of Louis, privately baptized at home in sickness, natural son (part of a line crossed out "of Baptiste Godin") Youta tribe.
F. N. Blanchet, priest,

B-38
Jeanne

The 23 October, 1844, we the undersigned priest have baptized Jeanne aged about 12 years, natural daughter of a Kanak, dead many years and of a Tchinuk woman. Godfather Jean Baptiste Aubichon who could not sign.
J. B. Z. Bolduc, priest

p 104
B-39
Angelique
Payet

The 23 October, 1844, we the undersigned priest have baptized Angelique aged about 14 years, natural daughter of Francois Payet and of a Spokan woman. Godfather Joseph Cornouiller who could not sign.
J. B. Z. Bolduc, priest

B-40
Marguerite
Spokan

The 23 October, 1844, we the undersigned priest have baptized Marguerite, aged about 40 years, born of infidel parents of the Spokan tribe. Godfather David Dompierre who could not sign.
J. B. Z. Bolduc, priest

B-41
F. Xavier
Laderoute

The 10 November, 1844, we the undersigned priest have baptized Francois Xavier, born 3 days ago of the legitimate marriage of Francois Xavier Laderoute and of Julie Gervais, farmer of this parish. Godfather Joseph McLoughlin, godmother Victoire McMillan. The father present. The godfather alone has signed with us.
Joseph McLoughlin
J. B. Z. Bolduc, priest

B-41
Joseph
Hord
[Howard]

The 22 November, 1844, we the undersigned priest have baptized Joseph born yesterday of the legitimate marriage of John Hord and of Catherine Lonetain, farmer of this parish. Godfather Joseph Despard, godmother Angelique Lonetain who could not sign. The father absent.
J. B. Z. Bolduc, priest

S-20
Michel
Indian

The 8 December, 1844, we the undersigned priest have buried in the cemetery of this parish the body of Michel, deceased 3 days ago. Present Amable Petit and Louis Lucier who could not sign.
J. B. Z. Bolduc, priest

B-42
Etienne
Lucier

The 8 December, 1844, we the undersigned priest have baptized Etienne born 3 days ago of the legitimate marriage of Etienne Lucier and of Marguerite Tchinuk. Godfather Augustin Rochon, godmother Celeste Jeaudoin who could not sign.
M. Accolti, S.J.

FIFTY FOURTH PAGE
p 105
S-21
Indian
Louise

The 18 December, 1844, we the undersigned priest have buried in the cemetery of this parish the body of Louise *[sic]*, deceased yesterday at the age of 9 years. Present Amable Petit and Louis Labonte who could not sign.
M. Accolti, S.J.

B-42

The 20 December, 1844, we the undersigned priest have baptized Emilie, adult, in danger of death. Godfather Charles Iroquois - *[Tse-te]*
M. Accolti, S.J.

S-22
Indian
Boy

The 24 December, 1844, we the undersigned priest have buried in the cemetery of this parish the body of a little Indian boy, privately baptized in danger of death by an inhabitant of this parish. Present Amable Petit and Claude Lacourse, the last alone has signed with us.
Claude Lacourse
M. Accolti, S.J.

S-23
Emilie
Indian

The 24 December, 1844, we the undersigned priest have buried in the cemetery of this parish the body of Emilie, deceased the 21 of the same month. Present Amable Petit and Claude Lacourse. The last alone has signed with us.
Claude Lacourse
M. Accolti, S.J.

S-24
Marguerite
Indian

The 24 December, 1844, we the undersigned priest have buried in the cemetery of this parish the body of Marguerite, deceased yesterday, in her lifetime wife of Thomas Smith. Present Amable Petit and Claude Lacourse. The last alone has signed with us.

Claude Lacourse
M. Accolti, S.J.

S-25

The 29 December, 1844, we the undersigned priest have buried in the cemetery of this parish the body of a little Indian boy of whom the name is unknown to us. Present Amable Petit and John Groslouis who alone has signed with us.

[No signature]
J. B. Z. Bolduc, priest

p 106
S-26
Francois
Quesnel

The 29 December, 1844, we the undersigned priest have buried in the cemetery of this parish the body of Francois, deceased day before yesterday at the age of about 65 years. Present John Groslouis and Claude Lacourse who have signed with us.

Claude Lacourse
J. B. Z. Bolduc, priest
1845

S-27
Philomene
Tetreau

The 5 January, 1845, we the undersigned priest have buried in the cemetery of this parish the body of Philomene, deceased yesterday at the age of 5 years and 5 months. Present John Groslouis and Louis Lucier who have signed with us.

John Groslouis
Louis Lucier
J. B. Z. Bolduc, priest

B-44
Joseph
Russie

The 7 January, 1845, we the undersigned priest have baptized Joseph, aged 18 days, legitimate son of Paul Augustin Russie and of Anis [Agnes Tyikwarihi, Norwest]. Godfather Joseph Guertin, godmother Catherine Russie, who could not sign.

J. B. Z. Bolduc, priest

B-45
Julie
Youte

The 20 January, 1845, I undersigned missionary of the Society of Jesus have baptized Julie, aged 15 years, Youte tribe. Godmother Susanne, daughter of TamataWakan Iroquois tribe.

Aloys Vercruysse, S.J.

FIFTY FIFTH PAGE
p 107
M-7
J. Bapt.
Godin
and
Julie
Indian

The 20 January, 1845, I the undersigned missionary of the Society of Jesus, after having published the first ban of marriage and the dispensation of the second and third bans, have received the mutual consent of Jean Baptiste Godin, son of Jaques Godin and of Violette on the one part and of Julie Youte daughter of an Indian man and woman of the Youte tribe on the other part and have given them the nuptial benediction in the presence of Hercule LeBrun and of Amable Petit, witnesses, of whom the second could not sign.

Hercule Lebrun
Aloys Vercruysse, S.J.

B-46
Marie
Rose
Chamberland

The 27 January, 1845, we the undersigned priest have baptized Marie Rose, born yesterday of the legitimate marriage of Adolphe Chamberland and of Julienne Watice. Godfather Joseph Rivet, godmother Rose Lacourse.

J. B. Z. Bolduc, priest

S-28
Marie
Smith

The 2 February, 1845, we the undersigned priest have buried in the cemetery of this parish the body of Marie, deceased since 6 days, in the presence of Amable Petit and of Antoine Cloutier who could not sign.

[No priest's signature]

B-47
[Son]
of
Dorion

The 3 February, 1845, we the undersigned priest have baptized Jean Baptiste, aged about 28 years, natural son of Pierre Dorion and of Marie Aioe. Godfather Paul Guilbeau.

P. DeVos, S.J.

B-48
Angele
Indian

The 3 February, 1845, we the undersigned priest have baptized a little girl, aged near 7 years, born of infidel parents, and have given her the name of Angele. Godmother Marie Aioe, who could not sign.

P. DeVos, S.J.

B-49
Marie
Angelique
Pend d'
Oreille

The 3 February, 1845, we the undersigned priest have baptized Marie Angelique aged about 18 years and born of infidel parents. Godfather Michel Laferte, godmother Sophie Belique, who could not sign.

P. DeVos, S.J.

p 108
B-50
Pierre
Sepiho

The 3 February, 1845, we the undersigned priest have baptized Pierre aged about 30 years, born of infidel parents. Godfather Amable Petit who could not sign.

P. DeVos, S.J.

B-51
Catherine
Tlikatat

The 3 February, 1845, we the undersigned priest have baptized Catherine aged about 17 years born of infidel parents. Godmother Catherine Walla-Walla.

P. DeVos, S.J.

B-52
Josephine
Caius

The 3 February, 1845, we the undersigned priest have baptized Josephine, aged about 22 years, born of infidel parents. Godmother Catherine Walla-Walla who could not sign.

P. DeVos, S.J.

B-53
Marie
unknown

The 3 February, 1845, we the undersigned priest have baptized Marie, born yesterday of unknown parents. Godmother Marie Aioa, who could not sign.

J. B. Z. Bolduc, priest

M-8
J. B.
Couturier
and
Angelique
Pan d'
Oreille

The 3 February, 1845, [some words crossed out] the publication of one ban of marriage and the dispensation of the second and the third (having been granted) between Jean Baptiste Couturier on the one part; and Angelique Pan d'Oreille on the other part, nor having discovered any impediment, we the undersigned priest have received their mutual consent and have given them the nuptial benediction in the presence of Michel Laferte, and Joseph Pin, who could not sign.

P. DeVos, S.J.

M-9
J. B.
Dorion
and
Josephine
Kaius

The 3 February, 1845, the publication of one ban of marriage and the dispensation of the second and third [having been granted] between Jean Baptiste Dorion on the one part, and Josephine Kaius on the other part, nor having discovered any impediment, we the undersigned priest have received their mutual consent and have given them the nuptial benediction in the presence of Paul Guilbeau and Amable Petit, who could not sign.

P. DeVos, S.J.

FIFTY SIXTH PAGE
p 109
M-10
Pierre
Sepiho
and
Catherine
Tlikatat

The 3 February, 1845, in view of the publication of one ban of marriage and the dispensation of the second and third between Pierre Sepiho, Indian, the Yakima [?] on the one part; and Catherine Tlikatat on the other part; nor having discovered any impediment, we the undersigned priest have received their mutual consent and have given them the nuptial benediction in the presence of Paul Guilbeau and of Amable Petit, who could not sign.

P. DeVos, S.J.

S-29
Marie

The 5 February, 1845, we the undersigned priest have buried in the cemetery of this parish the body of Marie, deceased the day before yesterday, aged about 2 days. Present Amable Petit and Antoine Cloutier, who alone has signed with us.   Ant. Cloutier

J. B. Z. Bolduc, priest

S-30
Marie
Rose
Chamberland

The 5 February, 1845, we the undersigned priest have buried in the cemetery of this parish the body of Marie Rose, deceased yesterday at the age of 21 days. Present Amable Petit and Joseph Laderoute, who could not sign.

J. B. Z. Bolduc, priest

B-54 Pierre Pepin dit Lachance	The 8 February, 1845, we the undersigned priest have baptized Pierre, born the 6 of the month of the legitimate marriage of Pierre Lachance of this parish and of Susanne Gaudrich. Godfather Olivier Dobin, godmother Nancy Tlikitat. J. B. Z. Bolduc, priest
S-31 Elizabeth Servant	The 15 February, 1845, we the undersigned priest have buried in the cemetery of this mission the body of Elizabeth, deceased yesterday at the age of 1 year 11 months and 7 days. Present Amable Oetit and Antoine Cloutier who alone has signed with us. Ant. Cloutier J. B. Z. Bolduc, priest

p 110

B-55 Pierre Petit	The 5 February, 1845, we the undersigned priest have baptized Pierre, aged 10 days, born of the legitimate marriage of Amable Petit and of Susanne Tawakon. Godfather Pierre Groslouis, undersigned, godmother Henriette Vivet, who could not sign. *[No signature]* J. B. Z. Bolduc, priest
B-56 Marie Genevieve Dompierre	The 9 February, 1845, we the undersigned priest missionary of the Society of Jesus have baptized Marie Genevieve Dompierre, daughter of David Dompierre and of Marguerite Souliere, metis Cree, born the 24 December of the year 1834. Godfather Jean Pierre Sanders, godmother Genevieve St. Martin. P. DeVos, S.J.
B-57 Marie Sophie Sanders	The 9 February, 1845, we the undersigned priest missionary of the Society of Jesus have baptized Marie Sophie, daughter of Jean Pierre Sanders and of Catherine Tsets Chinouk, born the 25 March of 1834. Godfather David Dompierre, godmother Marguerite Souliere. P. DeVos, S.J.
B-58 Marie Indian	The 1 March, 1845, we priest missionary of the Society of Jesus, have baptized Marie, born of infidel parents, and aged about 2 years. Godfather Etienne Lucier who could not sign. P. [A.] Ravalli, S.J.
S-32 Marie Indian	The 8 March, 1845, we the undersigned priest have buried in the cemetery of this parish the body of Marie, deceased the 6 of this month. Present Claude Lacourse and Antoine Cloutier, who have signed with us. Claude Lacourse Antoine Cloutier Ant Cloutier J. B. Z. Bolduc, priest
B-59 Marie Indian	The 8 March, 1845, we priest missionary of the Society of Jesus have baptized Marie aged about 5 years, born of infidel parents. Godfather Joseph Despard who could not sign. A. Ravalli, S.J.

FIFTY SEVENTH PAGE

p 111

B-60 *[S]* Marie Indian	The 12 March, 1845, we the undersigned priest have buried in the cemetery of this parish the body of Marie, deceased 3 days ago, in the presence of Antoine Cloutier and of Peter Kitson, who have signed with us. Ant Cloutier Peter Kitson J. B. Z. Bolduc, priest
S-33 Jeanne	The 12 March, 1845, we the undersigned priest have buried in the cemetery of this parish the body of Jeanne, deceased yesterday at the age of about 12 years, at the house of Jean Baptiste Aubichon. Present Antoine Cloutier and Joseph Laderoute who have signed with us. Joseph Laderoute Antoine Cloutier J. B. Z. Bolduc, priest

B-61
Gauthier   *[Blank]*
B-62   The 16 March, 1845, we priest of the Society of Jesus undersigned, have
Adrienne   baptized Adrienne born of the legitimate marriage of Andre Lachapelle
Lachapelle   and of Adrienne Lucier. Godfather Louis Lucier, godmother Sophie
                      Belique, who have signed with us.
                                            L. Lucier
                                            S. Belique
                                            J. B. Z. Bolduc, priest
B-63   The 22 March, 1845, we the undersigned priest have baptized Antoine
Antoine   aged about 11 years and a half, natural child of *[Antoine]* Cloutier and of
(Joseph)   Catherine Walla Walla. Godfather Jean Baptiste Zacharie Bolduc, under-
Cloutier   signed.
                                            J. B. Z. Bolduc, priest
B-64   The 23 March, 1845, we priest missionary of the Society of Jesus, have bap-
Michel   tized Michel Saste, aged about 23 years. His godfather has been Laurent
Saste   Sauve and godmother Josette Cotelain.
                                            P. DeVos, S.J.
B-65   The 23 March, 1845, we priest missionary of the Society of Jesus have bap-
Marie   tized Marie Rose Kaihus aged about 20 years. The godparents have been
Rose   Baptiste Delcour and Agathe Kaihus.
Kaihus   P. DeVos, S.J.
p 112
M-11   The 23 March, 1845, after having dispensed of the publication of the
Michel   bans of marriage between Michel Saste on the one part and Marie Rose
Saste   on the other, nor having discovered any impediment, we undersigned
and   priest missionary of the Society of Jesus have received their mutual consent
Marie   and have given them the nuptial benediction in the presence of Laurent
Rose   Sauve and of Baptiste Delcour.
Kaihus   P. DeVos, S.J.
B-66   The 29 February, 1845, we the undersigned priest have baptized Andre,
Andre   natural child of a Kalapuia Indian and a woman of the same tribe. God-
Kalapuia   father Andre St. Martin, godmother . . . wife of Louis Labonte, who have
                      declared unable to sign.
                                            J. B. Z. Bolduc, priest
B-67   The 6 April, 1845, we priest of the Society of Jesus, undersigned, have bap-
Magdeleine   tized Madeleine born the 30 March of the legitimate marriage of Sylvain
Bourgeau   Bourgeau and of Josette (Sok, Tchinouk). Godfather Charles Jeaudoin,
                      godmother Magdeleine Servant, who could not sign.
                                            A. Ravalli, S.J.
B-68   The 6 April, 1845, we priest of the Society of Jesus, undersigned, have
Isabelle   baptized Isabelle, born the 26 March of the legitimate marriage of Pierre
Desrivieres   Desrivieres and of Marie *[Manon]*. Godfather Joseph Klayn *[Klyne]*, god-
                      mother Louise Broquiere *[Braconnier]*, who could not sign.
                                            A. Ravalli, S.J.
B-69   The 10 *[Overwritten]* April, 1845, we the undersigned priest have baptized
                      . . . *[female]* born the 5th of the legitimate marriage of Joseph Gagnon
Gagnon   and of Marguerite Desjarlais. Godfather Luc Gagnon, godmother Marie
                      Desjarlais, who could not sign.
                                            J. B. Z. Bolduc, priest
M-12   The 15 April, 1845, in view of the publication of two bans and the dispensa-
Louis   tion of the third between Louis Bercier, son of the late Pierre Bercier and of
Bercier   Emilie Fenlay on the one part; between Henriette Vivet, natural daughter
and   of the late Louis Vivet and of an infidel Tchinouk mother on the other
Henriette   part, nor having discovered any impediment to marriage, we the under-
Vivet   signed priest have given them the nuptial benediction in the presence of
                      Pierre Belique and of Louis Pichet, who could not sign.
                                            J. B. Z. Bolduc, priest

FIFTY EIGHTH PAGE
p 113

B-70
J Baptiste
Gagnon

The 27 April, 1845, we the undersigned priest of the Society of Jesus have baptized Jean Baptiste born the . . . of the month of the legitimate marriage of Francois Gagnon and of Marguerite Desjarlais [should read Angelique Marcellais]. Godfather Jean Baptiste Ducharme, godmother Louise Brancognee [Braconnier], who could not sign.
A. Ravalli, S.J.

B-71
Louise
Malouin

The 27 April, 1845, we priest of the Society of Jesus, undersigned, have baptized Louise, born the . . . of the month of the legitimate marriage of Fabien Malouin and of Louise [Michel]. Godfather Amable Arquoit, godmother Louise Okania, who could not sign.
A. Ravalli, S.J.

B-72
Philomene
Mathieu

The 1 May, 1845, we priest of the Society of Jesus, undersigned, have baptized Philomene born the 20 April of the legitimate marriage of Francois Xavier Mathieu and of Rose Haussant [Aucent]. Godfather Louis Haussant, godmother Celeste Jeaudoin, who alone has signed with us.
[No signature]
A. Ravalli, S.J.

B-73
J. Baptiste
Sanders

The 4 May, 1845, we priest of the Society of Jesus, undersigned, have baptized Jean Baptiste born the 26 April of the legitimate marriage of Alexandre Sanders and of Louise of the Dalles. Godfather Andre Picard, godmother Marie Konaken [Okanagan], who could not sign.
A. Ravalli, S.J.

S-34

The 7 May, 1845, we priest of the Society of Jesus undersigned, have buried in the cemetery of this mission the body of a child of whom the name is unknown to us. Present Amable Petit and Pierre Kitson who alone has signed with us.
Peter Kitson
A. Ravalli, S.J.

p 114

B-74
Josephine
Saste

The 5 May, 1845, we the undersigned priest missionary of the Society of Jesus have baptized Josephine legitimate daughter of Michel Saste and Marie Rose Kaius, born the 4th of this month. Her godfather has been Laurent Sauve and her godmother Josephine Cotelaine.
P. DeVos, S.J.

S-35
Louise
Okenaken
Gingras

The 9 May, 1845, we the undersigned priest have buried in the cemetery of this mission the body of Louise, in her lifetime wife of Jean Gingras, deceased yesterday. Present Amable Petit and Andre Cloutier, who alone has signed with us.
Antoine Cloutier
J. B. Z. Bolduc, priest

B-75
Marie
Bernier

The 11 May, 1845, we priest of the Society of Jesus, undersigned, have baptized Marie born April 30 of the legitimate marriage of Francois Bernier and of Pelagie Lucier. Godfather Etienne Lucier, godmother Julie Gervais, who could not sign.
A. Ravalli, S.J.

B-76
Paul
Menard

The 18 May, 1845, we priest of the Society of Jesus, undersigned, have baptized Paul born [inserted above line] the 16 [?] of the legitimate marriage of Pierre Menard and of Josephte. Godfather Joseph Barnabe; godmother Isabelle Boucher.
A. Ravalli, S.J.

B-77
Nicholas
Montour

The 19 May, 1845, we priest of the Society of Jesus, undersigned, have baptized Nicolas, born the day before yesterday of the legitimate marriage of George Montour and of Louise Humpherville. Godfather Louis Laroque, godmother Marie Toussaint who could not sign.
A. Ravalli, S.J.

S-36
Nicolas

The 27 [overwritten] May, 1845, we undersigned priest have buried in the cemetery of this parish the body of Nicolas, deceased day before yesterday

Montour	at the age of 9 days. Present Amable Petit and Peter Kitson who alone signed with us.

P. Kitson

J. B. Z. Bolduc, priest

FIFTY NINTH PAGE

p 115

B-78 Marie	The 26 May, 1845, we priest of the Society of Jesus, undersigned, have baptized under the name of Marie an adult woman of the tribe of . . . Godfather Basile Pichereau, who could not sign, no godmother at all. *[No priest's signature]*
M-13 Jean Portier and Marie	The 26 May, 1845, in view of the publication of two bans of marriage and the dispensation of the third, between Jean Portier, of-age son of Jean Portier and of Anne Mauvier, formerly of Bordeaux in France on the one part; between an Indian woman named Marie, coming from California on the other part, nor having discovered any impediment, we priest of the Society of Jesus, undersigned, have received their mutual consent to marriage and have given them the nuptial benediction in the presence of Basile Pichereau and of Stanislaus Jacquet, who could not sign. *[No priest's signature]*
B-79 Marie Anne Indian	The 28 May, 1845, we the undersigned priest have baptized at the house of Jean Baptiste Perrault an Indian girl aged about 20 years in danger of death and have given her the name of Marie Anne. Godfather Jean Baptiste Perrault, who has signed with us. *[No signature]* Mod. Demers, priest
B-80 Joseph Indian	The 5 June, 1845, we the undersigned priest have baptized Joseph, aged about 4 years, born of infidel parents. Godfather Andre St. Martin, godmother Susanne Tawakon, who could not sign. A. Ravalli, S.J.
B-81 Marie Indian	The 5 June, 1845, we the undersigned priest have baptized Marie, born of infidel parents, and aged about 5 years. Godfather Etienne Lucier who could not sign. A. Ravalli, S.J.
B-82 Cagetan Indian	The 5 June, 1845, we the undersigned priest have baptized Cagetan, aged about 5 years, born of infidel parents of the Molelis tribe. Godfather Andre St. Martin, godmother Susanne Tawakon, who could not sign. A. Ravalli, S.J.

p 116

B-83 *[Lavigueur]*	The 8 June, 1845, we priest of the Society of Jesus undersigned, have baptized . . . born . . . of the legitimate marriage of Hyacynthe Lavigueur and of Marguerite des Chaudiere. Godfather . . . A. Ravalli, S.J.
B-84 Marie Anne Bonnenfant	The 17 June, 184 , we the undersigned priest have baptized Marie Anne, born yesterday of the legitimate marriage of Antoine Bonnenfant and of Francoise Depasti. Godfather Pierre Bomnier (Bonin?) godmother Angelique Depasti who as well as the father present could not sign. Mod. Demers, priest
M-14 Joachim Lapherte and Sophie Aubichon	The 23 June, 1845, in view of the publication of two bans of marriage and the dispensation of a third between Joachim Laferte, son of . . . *[The remainder of this entry is blank and is unsigned.]*
B-85 Joseph *[Chechegan]*	The 15 June, 1845, we undersigned priest missionary of the Society of Jesus have baptized Joseph, son of Charles Chechegan and of Marie Therese Calgethphe - Kalispels *[?]*, born the 31 May, 1845. The Godfather has been Joseph Rivet. P. DeVos, S.J.
B-86	The 18 June, 1845, I undersigned priest missionary of the Society of Jesus,

Charles [Chechegan]	have baptized Charles Chechegan, son of Kaimy, Splkan, aged 29 years about, his godfather has been Joseph Rivet and his godmother Rose Lacourse.

P. DeVos, S.J.

[Set in between pp. 116-117 are two pieces of paper, probably field notes, which contain the following Acts:]

I Tiberius "ex Cbus" Soderini, "M. A." *[Missionary Apostolic]* baptized on the 18 June, 1845, Joannem *[Jean]* son of Thomas Lavelle, born the 14 June, 1845. Godfather was Baptiste Dainiei.

I Tiberius "ex Cbus" Soderini, "M. A." baptized on the 18 June, 1845, Cecile daughter of Narcisse Raimon *[Raymond]* born 30 April, 1845. Godfather was Baptiste Sylvestre.

I Tiberius "ex Cbus" Soderini "M. A." baptized on the 18 June, 1845, Angele daughter of Baptiste Bauchemen *[Beauchemin]* born the 28 February, 1836. Godfather was Simeon Gill.

I Tiberius "ex Cbus" Soderini "M. A." baptized on the 18 June, 1845, Angele daughter of Aloys (Louis) Raboin born the 13 June, 1845. Godfather was Hephanny *[Etienne]* Caille.

I Tiberius Soderini M. A. baptized Marie Anne la Rocca *[Laroque]* and joined her in matrimony with Joseph Sebastien la Rocca. Age of the wife 27 years. This day 20 May, 1845. Godfather was Jean Baptiste Sylvestre. Witnesses to the wedding *[undersigned]*

Richard Grant
C. F. [Chief Factor]
HHBC
Alan (X) McDonald

SIXTIETH PAGE
p 117

B-87 Andre Ulschini	The 17 June, 1845, we undersigned priest missionary of the Society of Jesus have baptized Andre Ulschini, son of Neggieme, Pend d'oreille, aged about 27 years, the godfather has been Joseph Rivet and the godmother Rose Lacourse.

P. DeVos, S.J.

B-88 Francois Guilguil- zutlen [?]	The 17 June, 1845, we undersigned priest missionary of the Society of Jesus have baptized Francois son of Goustemni, Chaudiere, aged about 25 years. His godfather has been Joseph Rivet and his godmother Rose Lacourse.

P. DeVos, S.J.

B-89 Marie Therese Calgehpke (Pend d' Oreille)	The 17 June, 1845, we undersigned priest missionary of the Society of Jesus have baptized Marie Therese daughter of GHesengue aged about 23 years. The godfather has been Joseph Rivet and the godmother Rose Lacourse.

P. DeVos, S.J.

M-15 Charles Chechegan and Marie Therese Calgehpke	The 17 June, 1845, we undersigned priest missionary of the Society of Jesus have married according to the ritual of the Roman Catholic Church Charles Chechegan Spokan and Marie Therese Calgehpke Pend d'oreille. The witnesses have been Joseph Rivet and Rose Lacourse.

P. DeVos, S.J.

M-16 Andre Ulschini and Rose Jhepi [?]	The 17 June, 1845, we undersigned priest missionary of the Society of Jesus have married according to the ritual of the Catholic Church, having dispensed the bans, Andre Pend d'oreille and Rose Jhepi (?) Spokan. The witnesses have been Joseph Rivet and Rose Lacourse.

P. DeVos, S.J.

B-90	The 20 June, 1845, we undersigned priest missionary of the Society of Jesus

Louis Montour	have baptized conditionally, Louis Bob Montour, son of Nicolas Montour and of Marguerite Crise, aged about 20 years. His godfather has been Joseph Rivet.

P. DeVos, S.J.

p 118 S-37 Marie Indian	The 26 June, 1845, we the undersigned priest have buried in the cemetery of this parish the body of Marie, deceased 2 days ago. Present Amable Petit and Antoine Cloutier the latter alone has signed with us.

Ant Cloutier
J. B. Z. Bolduc, priest

S-38 Joseph Dalcourt	The 27 June, 1845, we the undersigned priest have buried in the cemetery of this parish the body of Joseph, deceased yesterday at the age of 2 years and 6 months. Present Amable Petit and Claude Lacourse, who alone has signed with us.

Claude Lacourse
J. B. Z. Bolduc, priest

B-91 Susanne Molelis	The 27 June, 1845, we the undersigned priest have baptized Susanne aged about 14 years, in danger of death. Godfather Francois Xavier Laderoute, godmother Susanne Tawakon, who could not sign.

Mod. Demers, priest

S-39 Susanne Molelis	The 1 June [sic], 1845, we the undersigned priest have buried in the cemetery of this parish the body of Susanne, deceased yesterday, in the presence of Claude Lacourse and of Antoine Cloutier who have signed.

Claude Lacourse
Antoine Cloutier
Mod. Demers, priest

B-92 Antoine Laferte	The 6 July, 1845, we the undersigned priest have baptized Antoine, legitimate son of Michel Laferte and of Josephte Pend d'Oreille, aged 18 years. Godfather Andre St. Martin, godmother Susanne Tawakon who could not sign.

Mod. Demers, priest

B-93 Olivier Laferte	The 6 July, 1845, we the undersigned priest have baptized Olivier, son of Michel Laferte and of Josephte Pend d'Oreille, aged 16 years. Godfather Francois Xavier Laderoute, godmother Genevieve St. Martin who could not sign.

Mod. Demers, priest

SIXTY FIRST PAGE

p 119 B-94 Michel Laferte	The 6 July, 1845, we the undersigned priest have baptized Michel, legitimate son of Michel Laferte and of Josephte Pend Oreille, aged 14 years. Godfather Guertin, godmother Marie Grenier, who could not sign.

Mod. Demers, priest

B-95 Joseph Roussin	The 10 July, 1845, we the undersigned priest have baptized Joseph, natural son of . . . Roussin and of Magdeleine Deshoulieres, aged 14 years. Godfather Paul Guilbeau, godmother Catherine Wallawalla, who could not sign.

Mod. Demers, priest

B-96 Jacques Indian	The 6 July, 1845, we the undersigned priest have baptized Jacques, born of infidel parents, aged about 19 years. Godfather Pierre Bellique, godmother Genevieve St. Martin who could not sign.

Mod. Demers, priest

B-97 Louise Okanakan	The 6 July, 1845, we the undersigned priest have baptized Louise, born of infidel parents, aged about 15 years. Godfather Joseph Delard, godmother Marie Okanakan, who could not sign.

Mod. Demers, priest

S-39 Emilie Indian	The 8 July, 1845, we the undersigned priest have buried in the cemetery of this parish the body of an Indian woman baptized privately in danger of death by Etienne Lucier. Present Claude Lacourse and Andre Cloutier, who have signed with us.

Claude Lacourse   A. Cloutier
J. B. Z. Bolduc, priest

S-40   The 11 July, 1845, we the undersigned priest have buried in the cemetery
Julie   of this parish the body of Julie, deceased the 9 of the month, during her
Gervais   life the wife of Francois Xavier Laderoute, farmer of this parish. Present
Claude Lacourse and Antoine Cloutier, who have signed with us.

Claude Lacourse   A. Cloutier

J. B. Z. Bolduc, priest

p 120

B-98   The 15 July, 1845, we the undersigned priest have baptized Joseph Kala-
Joseph   poya, aged 15 years. Godfather Joseph Gervais who could not sign.
Kalapoya   Mod. Demers, priest

B-99   The 6 [written over] July, 1845, we the undersigned priest have baptized
Fabien   Fabien born yesterday of the legitimate marriage of Joseph Rivet and of
Rivet   Rose Lacourse. Godfather Fabien Malouin, godmother Louise Humpher-
ville who could not sign.

Mod. Demers, priest

B-100   The 15 August, 1845, we the undersigned priest have baptized Angelique
Angelique born the 15 of July of the legitimate marriage of Jean Baptiste Gobin and
Gobin   of Marguerite Vagnier. Godfather Joseph Rivet, godmother Marguerite [sic]
his wife who could not sign.

Mod. Demers, priest

M-15   The 28 July, 1845, in view of the publication of one ban and the dispensa-
Jean   tion of the second and of the third, between Jean Gingras widower of Louise
Gingras   Okinakan on the one part and Olive Forcier, daughter of Louis Forcier
and   on the other part, nor having discovered any impediment, we have received
Olive   their mutual consent and have given them the nuptial benediction in the
Forcier   presence of Alexis Aubichon and of Thomas Moisan who as well as the
spouses could not sign.

[No priest's signature]

M-16   The 2- of July, 1845, in view of the dispensation of three bans of marriage,
Antoïne   granted by Messire Demers Vicar General, between Antoine Felix on the
Felix   one part, and Marguerite des Chaudieres, on the other part, nor having
and   discovered any impediment to the marriage, we the undersigned priest
Marguerite have received their mutual consent and have given them the nuptial bene-
des   diction in the presence of Andre St. Martin and Pierre Dubois who as well
Chaudieres as the spouses could not sign. The parties have recognized as their legitimate
children, Antoine aged 8 years, Francois aged 7 years, Marguerite aged 4
years, and Pierre aged 1 year and 1 month.

[No priest's signature]

SIXTY SECOND PAGE

p 121

B-101   The 17 August, 1845, we the undersigned priest have baptized John Corbey
John   (Kirby) born the . . . of the . . . of George Gay and of Louise Tchelelis.
Gay   Godfather John Howard, godmother Catherine Lonetain who could not
sign.

Mod. Demers, priest

[This entry is repeated, with a change in the year, in B-183, p 140.]

B-102   The 18 August, 1845, we the undersigned priest have baptized at the house
Marie   of Francois Xavier Laderoute a little Indian girl in danger of death, aged
Indian   about 6 years and have given her the name of Marie. Godfather Joseph
Laderoute who has signed with us.

Joseph Laderoute

J. B. Z. Bolduc, priest

S-41   The 20 August, 1845, we the undersigned priest have buried in the cemetery
Marie   of this parish the body of . . . baptized privately by . . . at the house of
Snecal   Gedeon Senecal (his or her) father. Present Amable Petit and Antoine
[Senecal] Cloutier who alone could sign with us.

Antoine Cloutier

J. B. Z. Bolduc, priest

S-42   The 1 September, 1845, we the undersigned priest have buried in the ceme-

Rose
Lacourse

tery of this parish the body of Rose Lacourse, in her lifetime the wife of Joseph Rivet, deceased 30 August during the night. Present Peter Kitson and Antoine Cloutier who have signed with us.

Peter Kitson   Antoine Cloutier
Mod. Demers, priest

S-43
Marie
Indian

The 2 September, 1845, we the undersigned priest have buried in the cemetery of this parish the body of Marie, deceased day before yesterday at the house of Francois Xavier Laderoute. Present Amable Petit and Francois Xavier Laderoute who could not sign.

Mod. Demers, priest

p 122
B-103
Paul
Tlamath

The 14 September, 1845, we the undersigned priest have baptized Paul born yesterday of an infidel Tlamath Indian known under the name of Samson (?) and a woman of the same tribe. Godfather Pierre Depot, godmother Marguerite Tlamath who could not sign.

Mod. Demers, priest

S-44

The 15 September, 1845, we the undersigned priest have buried in the cemetery of this parish the body of a woman privately baptized in danger of death by an inhabitant of this place, and deceased at the house of Louis Forcier. Present Antoine Cloutier and Louis Lucier who have signed with us.

Antoine Cloutier   Louis Lucier
J. B. Z. Bolduc, priest

S-45
Esther
Gingras

The 17 September, 1845, we the undersigned priest have buried in the cemetery of this parish the body of Esther, deceased the 15 of this month. Present Peter Kitson and Andree Hophop who have signed with us.

Peter Kitson   Andre Hophop
J. B. Z. Bolduc, priest

B-104
Marie
Uapetiu

The 20 September, 1845, we the undersigned priest have baptized Marie, born of infidel parents and aged about 30 years.

[No priest's signature]

M-17
Edouard
Cameron
and
Marie
Uapetai

The 20 September, 1845, we the undersigned missionary of the Society of Jesus, with the dispensation of three bans, have received the mutual consent of Edouard Cameron, son of John Cameron and of a woman of the tribe of Algonkins, on the one part; and Marie Uapetai of Wallawalla on the other part, as the groom is protestant we have received his mutual consent to the condition that the children coming from this marriage will be reared in the Catholic religion, Apostolic and Roman. The witnesses have been Pierre Dubois and Leonisio Douke, who could not sign.

[No priest's signature]

SIXTY THIRD PAGE

p 123
B-105
Charlotte
Indian

The 22 September, 1845, we the undersigned priest have baptized Charlotte aged about 18 years and in danger of death. Godmother Victoire McMillen who could not sign.

Mod. Demers, priest

S-46
Charlotte
Indian

The 23 September, 1845, we the undersigned priest have buried in the cemetery of this parish the body of Charlotte deceased yesterday at the house of Joseph McLoughlin. Present Peter Kitson and Louis Lucier who have signed with us.

Peter Kitson   Louis Lucier
Mod. Demers, priest

B-106
Philomene
Dorion

The 27 September, 1845, we the undersigned priest have baptized Philomene aged 3 months, born of the legitimate marriage of Jean Baptiste Dorion and of Josephine Kayous. Godfather Pierre Delard, godmother Marie Anne Ouvre who could not sign.

B-107
John

The 3 October, 1845, we the undersigned priest have baptized John born the 1st of March last of the legitimate marriage of George Hannon and of

Hannon	Eliza Jane Evans, both protestants. Godfather Joseph Guertin who could not sign.
	Mod. Demers, priest
B-108	The 19 October, 1845, we the undersigned priest have baptized Francois
Francois	Xavier born the 12 of this month of the legitimate marriage of David Dom-
X	pierre and of Marguerite Souliere. Godfather Jean Baptiste Jeaudoin, under-
Dompierre	signed, godmother Marguerite Servant. The father present has signed with us.
	[No signature]
	Mod. Demers, priest
p 124	
S-47	The 20 October, 1845, we the undersigned priest have buried in the ceme-
Philomene	tery of this parish the body of Philomene, aged 4 months, deceased yesterday
Dorion	child of Jean Baptiste Dorion and of Josephine Kayous, in the presence of Peter Kitson and of Andre Hophop who have signed with us.
	Andre Hophop Peter Kitson
	Mod. Demers, priest
B-109	The 26 October, 1845, we the undersigned priest have baptized Joseph,
Joseph	aged 3 days, born of the legitimate marriage of Antoine Rivet and of Emelie
Rivet	Pend Oreille. Godfather Fabien Malouin, godmother Louise, his wife who could not sign.
	Mod. Demers, priest
B-110	The 27 October, 1845, we the undersigned priest have baptized Louise,
Louise	aged 9 months, child of Kattasso and of Wataike, Tchinouk infidels. God-
[Kattasso]	father Frederic Despard, godmother Louise, his wife, who could not sign.
	Mod. Demers, priest
B-111	The 27 October, 1845, we the undersigned priest have baptized conditional-
J. Baptiste	ly, Jean Baptiste born the 19th of the legitimate marriage of Pierre Belique
Belique	and of Genevieve St. Martin. Godfather Andre St. Martin, godmother Susanne Tawakon, who as well as the father, present, could not sign.
	Mod. Demers, priest
S-48	The 7 November, 1845, we the undersigned priest have buried in the ceme-
	tery of this parish the body of . . . deceased day before yesterday at the
Lafantaisie	age of about 7 years. In the presence of Antoine Cloutier and of Andre Hophop who have signed with us.
	Antoine Cloutier
	Andre Hophop
	J. B. Z. Bolduc, priest
B-112	The 7 November, 1845, we the undersigned priest have baptized Joseph,
Joseph	Indian of The Dalles, aged about 20 (?) and dangerously ill at the house
des	of Louis Vandale, junior, who has been the godfather. No godmother
Dalles	at all.
	J. B. Z. Bolduc, priest

SIXTY FOURTH PAGE

p 125	
S-49	The 9 September, 1845, we the undersigned priest have buried in the ceme-
Joseph	tery of this parish the body of Joseph, Indian of The Dalles, deceased at
des	the house of Louis Vandale, junior, in the presence of Antoine Cloutier
Dalles	and of Peter Kitson who have signed with us.
	Antoine Cloutier
	P. Kitson
	J. B. Z. Bolduc, priest
S-50. 51	The 9 November, 1845, we the undersigned priest have buried in the ceme-
Unknown	tery of this parish the bodies of two little children of the Tchinouk tribe, deceased yesterday at the house of Joseph Despard, of whom the names have not been discovered at all. Present Joseph Despard and Amable Petit who could not sign.
	J. B. Z. Bolduc, priest
B-113	The 9 November, 1845, we the undersigned priest have baptized Emilie,

Emilie Pichet	born the 4th of the month of the legitimate marriage of Louis Pichet and of Marguerite Bercier. Godfather Pierre Belique, godmother Pelagie Lucier, who could not sign. The father present. J. B. Z. Bolduc, priest
B-114 Francois Lafantaisie	The 9 November, 1845, we the undersigned priest have baptized Francois, born the 3 of the month of the legitimate marriage of Charles Lafantaisie and of . . . [Isabelle, Elizabeth] Humpherville. Godfather Pierre Bonin, godmother Angelique Payette who could not sign. The father present. J. B. Z. Bolduc, priest
B-115 Marie Cowlitz	The 9 November, 1845, we the undersigned priest have baptized Marie, born of infidel parents of the Cowlitz, aged about 6 months. Godfather Andre St. Martin, godmother (Marguerite), wife of Louis Labonte, senior, who could not sign. J. B. Z. Bolduc, priest

p 126

B-116 Joseph Tlikatat	The 9 November, 1845, we the undersigned priest have baptized Joseph aged about 18 years and in danger of death at the house of Joseph Gervais. Godfather David Gervais who could not sign. J. B. Z. Bolduc, priest

S-52
Marie
	The 10 November, 1845, we the undersigned priest have buried in the cemetery of this parish the body of Marie, old Tchinouk woman, baptized privately by Etienne Lucier and deceased yesterday. Present Peter Kitson and Antoine Cloutier who have signed with us.
	      P. Kitson [No other signature]
	                           J. B. Z. Bolduc, priest

B-117 Marie St. Martin	The 15 November, 1845, we the undersigned priest have baptized Marie, aged about 24 years, natural daughter of Joseph St. Martin and of an infidel Tchinouk woman. Godfather Andre St. Martin, godmother Genevieve St. Martin, who could not sign. J. B. Z. Bolduc, priest

S-53
Toussaint
Molelis
	The 15 November, 1845, we the undersigned priest have buried in the cemetery of this parish the body of Toussaint, child of the Molelis tribe. Present Peter Kitson and Louis Lucier who have signed with us.
	      P. Kitson L. Lucier
	                           J. B. Z. Bolduc, priest

S-54
Indian
Molelis
	The 22 November, 1845, we the undersigned priest have buried in the cemetery of this parish the body of a little Indian of the Molelis tribe, of whom the name is unknown to us. Present Peter Kitson and Louis Lucier who have signed with us.
	      P. Kitson L. Lucier
	                           J. B. Z. Bolduc, priest

S-55 Joseph des Dalles	The 23 November, 1845, we the undersigned priest have buried in the cemetery of this parish the body of Joseph of The Dalles, deceased yesterday at the house of Joseph Jervais. Present Amable Petit and David Gervais, who could not sign. J. B. Z. Bolduc, priest

SIXTY FIFTH PAGE

p 127

B-118 Francois Matte	The 23 November, 1845, we the undersigned priest have baptized Francois born the 3 of the month of the legitimate marriage of Joseph Matte and of Josephte Serpent [Snake River]. Godfather Francois Raymond, godmother Susanne Gaudrich who could not sign. J. B. Z. Bolduc, priest
B-119 Marie Molelis	The 25 November, 1845, we the undersigned priest have baptized Marie born the 17 of September of infidel parents of the Molelis tribe. Godfather Alexis Villerais, godmother Marguerite Dejarlais. J. B. Z. Bolduc, priest
B-120 Joseph	The 29 November, 1845, we the undersigned priest have baptized at the house of Pierre Lachance an Indian about 8 years under the name of Joseph.

Godfather Pierre Lachance, godmother Susanne Gaudrich, who could not sign with us.

J. B. Z. Bolduc, priest

B-121
F. X.
Moisan

The 17 December, 1845, we the undersigned priest have baptized Francois Xavier born the 15 of the month of the legitimate marriage of Thomas Moisan and of Henriette Lonetain. Godfather Joseph Guertin, godmother Angelique Lonetain who could not sign.

Louis Vercruysse, priest

B-122
Catherine
Nezperce

The 26 December, 1845, we the undersigned priest have baptized Catherine, wife of Robert Newell, in danger of death. No godfather nor godmother at all.

J. B. Z. Bolduc, priest

B-123
(Pierre)

The 28 December, 1845, we the undersigned priest have baptized Pierre, in danger of death at the house of Pierre Belique, aged about 28 years. Godfather Pierre Belique, godmother Genevieve St. Martin, who could not sign.

J. B. Z. Bolduc, priest

p 128
S-56
Elizabeth
Fenlay

The 31 December, 1845, we the undersigned priest have buried in the cemetery of this mission the body of Elisabeth, wife of Hypolittle Brouillet, deceased the day before yesterday in the presence of Peter Kitson and of Pierre Belique who have signed with us.

P. Bellique   *[No Kitson signature]*
J. B. Z. Bolduc, priest

S-57
Indian
unknown

The 31 December, 1845, we the undersigned priest have buried in the cemetery of this mission the body of a young man of the Tchinuk tribe, baptized privately in danger of death by Jean Baptiste Dubreuil and deceased yesterday at the house of Joseph Despard. Present Pierre Bellique and Louis Guilbeau.

P. Bellique
L. Guilbeau
J. B. Z. Bolduc, priest

S-57 (sic)
Joseph
Focilino

The 31 December, 1845, we the undersigned priest have buried in the cemetery of this mission the body of Joseph deceased yesterday at the age of about 6 months. Present Amable Petit and Etienne Gregoire, jr, who alone has signed with us.

[No signature]
J. B. Z. Bolduc, priest

B-124
Joseph
Guilbeau

The 23 December, 1845, we the undersigned priest have baptized Joseph born today of the legitimate marriage of Paul Guilbeau and of Catherine Walla Walla. Godfather Andre St. Martin, godmother Catherine Tawakon, who could not sign.

J. B. Z. Bolduc, priest

[The above entry is cross-hatched out, still readable. No reason given.]

1846

B-124
J. Bts.
Vandal

The 13 March, 1846, we the undersigned priest have baptized Jean Baptiste born the 11 of the month of the legitimate marriage of Louis Vandal and of Cecile McDonald. Godfather Jean Baptiste Aubichon, godmother Marie his wife, who could not sign.

J. B. Z. Bolduc, priest

B-125
Esther
and
Catherine

The 31 January, 1846, we the undersigned priest have baptized Esther, aged 9 years, and Catherine, aged 9 months, daughters of Alkwatkwolki *[?]* and of Holokitsal, Tchinook infidels. Godfather Frederic Despard, godmother Jane St. Martin.

Mod. Demers, priest

SIXTY SIXTH PAGE
p 129
S-58
[Esther
Lefebre]

The 13 January, 1846, we the undersigned priest have buried in the cemetery of this mission the body of Esther, child of the late Louis Lefebre; present Amable Petit and Louis Lucier.

Mod. Demers, priest

B-126
Louise
Pineau

The 15 January, 1846, we the undersigned priest have baptized Louise, aged 3 days, natural daughter of Joseph Pineau and of a Snake woman. Godfather Louis Pichet, godmother (Marie Anne) Nipissing, wife of Quintal.

Mod. Demers, priest

B-127
[Madeleine
Godin]

The 21 January, 1846, we the undersigned priest have baptized Madeleine, aged 5 days, legitimate daughter of Jean Baptiste Godin and of Louise Snake; godfather Alexandre Sanders, godmother Louise his wife.

Mod. Demers, priest

M-18
J. B.
Jeaudoin
and
Isabelle
Hubert

The 2 February, 1846, after the publication of 3 bans of marriage between J. Baptiste Jeaudoin, of-age son of Charles Jeaudoin and of an Indian woman, now dead, on the one part and Isabelle minor daughter of Joachim Hubert and of Josephte, Chaudiere, both of this mission, on the other part, nor having discovered any impediment to the marriage, we the undersigned priest have received their mutual consent, and have given them the nuptial benediction in the presence of Louis Aussan and of Andre Chalifoux.

Mod. Demers, priest

M-19
Nicolas
Portier
and
Marguerite
Laroque

The February [sic], 1846, after the publication of three bans of marriage between Nicolas, of Havre on the one part, and Marguerite, minor daughter of Pierre Laroque and of Marguerite Crise on the other part, nor having discovered any impediment, we the undersigned priest have received their mutual consent to marriage and have given them the nuptial benediction in the presence of . . . Girard and of Etienne Biernise.

Mod. Demers, priest

p 130
M-20
Cyrille
Bertrand
and
Marguerite
Servant

The 2 February, 1846, after the publication of 3 bans of marriage between Cyrille, of-age son of Jean Baptiste Bertrand and of Marguerite Ratelle, on the one part and Marguerite, daughter of Jacques Servant and of Josephte, Okanagan, both of this mission, nor having discovered any impediment we the undersigned priest have received their mutual consent to marriage and have given them the nuptial benediction in the presence of Louis Aussan and of Pierre Bellique who could not sign.

Mod. Demers, priest

B-128
J. B.
Gendron

The 1 February, 1846, we the undersigned priest have baptized J. Baptiste, born the 28 January, legitimate child of Joseph Gendron and Louise, Indian. Godfather Augustin Rochon, godmother Celeste Jeaudoin, who could not sign.

Mod. Demers, priest

B-129
Anne
Gagnon

The 8 February, 1846, we the undersigned priest have baptized Anne, aged 15 days, legitimate daughter of Luc Gagnon and of Julie Gregoire; godfather Joseph Gagnon, godmother Adrienne Lucier, who could not sign.

Mod. Demers, priest

B-130, 131
Aug.
and
Catherine
Skatalkossom

The 10 February, 1846, we the undersigned priest have (baptized) Augustin, aged 5 months, and Catherine, aged 5 days, natural children of Skatalkossom, chief of the Islands of Stones (Iles de pierres) and of Hohtai. Godfather Sifroid Jobin, godmother Catherine Pepin, who could not sign.

Mod. Demers, priest

SIXTY SEVENTH PAGE
p 131
B-132
Pierre
Mokuman

The 11 February, 1846, we the undersigned priest have baptized Pierre, born the 6th, child of Louis Mokuman and of Louise Kayous. Godfather, Augustin, godmother Anne . . . who could not sign.

Mod. Demers, priest

B-133
Louis
Dalcourt

The 11 February, 1846, we the undersigned priest have baptized Louis, born the 1st, legitimate child of Baptiste Dalcourt and of Agathe, Sassete. Godfather Louis Rondeau who could not sign.

Mod. Demers, priest

S-59 [Child of Nashke]	The 17 February, 1846, we the undersigned priest have buried in the cemetery - child of Nashke, present Francois Guilbeau and Simon Gregoire who could not sign. Mod. Demers, priest
B-134 Joseph	The 14 February, 1846, we the undersigned priest have [baptized] Joseph, aged 15 months, natural child of Ponekstitsa and of Wisnainau, infidels, godfather Amable Petit, godmother Catherine Papin, who could not sign. Mod. Demers, priest
B-135 M. Adelle Petit	The 22 January [sic], 1846, we the undersigned priest have baptized Marie Adelle, born the 25 December last, legitimate child of Amable Petit and of Angelique [Amelia] Aubichon; godfather Alexis Aubichon, godmother his wife M. Anne who could not sign. Mod. Demers, priest
S-60 Joseph Indian	The 15 February, 1846, we the undersigned priest have buried in the cemetery the body of Joseph, deceased yesterday, aged about 20 years, present Amable Arquoite and Louis Lucier who could not sign. Mod. Demers, priest
S-61	The 24 February, 1846, we the undersigned priest have buried in the cemetery the body of a little girl, baptized privately—present Amable Arquoite and Louis Lucier who could not sign.
p 132 B-136 Victoire Vassal	The 30 March, 1846, we the undersigned priest have baptized Victoire, aged 2 days, natural daughter of Louis Vassal and of an Indian woman. Godfather Helie Giguere, godmother Victoire Cornoyer who could not sign. Mod. Demers, priest
B-137 Marie Chamberland	The 29 March, 1846, we the undersigned priest have baptized Marie, born the day before, legitimate daughter of Adolphe Chamberland and of Julienne Watiece; godfather Andre Arquoite, godmother Jane St. Martin, who could not sign. Mod. Demers, priest
B-138 Joseph [Francois Tahikwarhi Norwest]	The 17 April, 1846, we the undersigned priest have baptized Joseph, born the 11, natural child of Jean Baptiste Tahkwarihi, and of Josephte, Wallawalla: godfather Amable Petit who could not sign. Mod. Demers, priest
B-139 Jean Boucher	The 11 April [May cross-hatched out], 1846, we the undersigned priest have baptized Jean, aged 20 years, natural child of Wakan Boucher and of Nancy McDougal; godfather Fabien Malouin, godmother Louise, his wife who could not sign. Mod. Demers, priest
S-62 Henriette Plouff [crossed out] [Yogalta]	The 26 April, 1846, we the undersigned priest have (baptized crossed out) buried in the cemetery the body of Henriette [Yogalta], wife of Louis Rondeau, deceased the day before; present Amable Petit, Louis Aussan who could not sign. Mod. Demers, priest
S-63 [Cecile]	The 18 April, 1846, we the undersigned priest have buried in the cemetery the body of Cecile, Indian girl, aged 17 months, deceased the day before; present Amable Petit, Pierre Bellique who could not sign. Mod. Demers, priest

+ see page 69

SIXTY EIGHTH PAGE

p 133 B-140 Julie Montour	The 13 May, 1846, we the undersigned priest have baptized Julie, born the 10th, legitimate daughter of George Montour and of Louise Humpherville. Godfather Antoine Rivet, godmother Isabelle Montour, who could not sign. Mod. Demers, priest

S-64
Susanne
Humphuys
[Humpherville]

The 20 May, 1846, we the undersigned priest have buried in the cemetery the body of Susanne Humphreys, wife of Nicolas Montour, aged 55 years and deceased 2 days ago; present Amable Petit and Antoine Rivet, who could not sign.

Mod. Demers, priest

S-65
Francois
Chaudiere

The 24 May, 1846, we the undersigned priest have buried in the cemetery the body of Francois, Chaudiere Indian, deceased the day before. Present Louis Guilbeau and Michel Rivet, who could not sign.

Mod. Demers, priest

B-141
Jacques
Kalapoya

The 16 May, 1846, we the undersigned priest have baptized Jacques, Kalapoya, aged about 18 years; godfather Jean Baptiste Boisvert, godmother Louise his wife, who could not sign.

Mod. Demers, priest

S-66
Jacques
Kalapoya

The 19 May, 1846, we the undersigned priest have buried in the cemetery Jacques, deceased 2 days ago, aged about 18 years; present Louis Pichet and Louis Aussan, who could not sign.

Mod. Demers, priest

B-142
Cecile
Peltier
[sic,
Gauthier?]

The 17 May, 1846, we the undersigned priest have baptized Cecile, born yesterday, legitimate daughter of Pierre *[Gauthier?]* and of Esther Dalcourt; godfather Louis Vanda, godmother Cecile McDonnel, who could not sign.

Mod. Demers, priest

p 134
S-67
Andre
Picard

The 11 May, 1846, we the undersigned priest have buried in the cemetery the body of Andre Picard, aged about 65 years, deceased 2 days ago; present Louis and Louis Aussan, who could not sign.

Mod. Demers, priest

B-143
Lo. Jean
Cameron

The 31 May, 1846, we the undersigned priest have baptized Louis Jean, born the 22nd, legitimate son of Edouard Cameron and of Marie Wallawalla; godfather Antoine Gregoire, godmother Julie Gregoire, who could not sign.

Mod. Demers, priest

B-144
Mgte
Liard

The 9 May, 1846, we the undersigned priest have baptized Marguerite, born the 5th of October last, legitimate daughter of F. Xavier Lyard and of Marie Anne Nezperce; godfather Paul Guilbeau, godmother Katy his wife, who could not sign.

Mod. Demers, priest

B-145
Mgte
Laroque

The 7 May, 1846, we the undersigned priest have baptized Marguerite aged 15 days, legitimate daughter of Louis Laroque and of . . . ; Godfather Antoine Morais, godmother Marguerite Laroque who could not sign.

Mod. Demers, priest

B-146
Louis
Chalifoux

The 10 May, 1846, we the undersigned priest have baptized Louis born yesterday, legitimate child of Andre Chalifoux and of Catherine Russie; godfather Louis Pichet, godmother Marguerite Bercier, who could not sign.

Mod. Demers, priest

B-147
Mgte
Arquoite

The 10 May, 1846, we the undersigned priest have baptized Marguerite, born the 29 April, legitimate daughter of Andre Arquoite and of Marguerite, Tchinook; godfather Adolphe Chamberland, godmother Louise, wife of Caille.

Mod. Demers, priest

[Page set in]
Benediction
of the first
stone of the
church

The 24 May, 1846, we undersigned, Vicar General of the Apostolic Vicarate of Oregon, assisted by Reverend J. B. Z. Bolduc, undersigned, have solemnly blessed a corner-brick, for want of a stone, following the form prescribed in the Processional, and we have placed it at the right corner of the left-hand side of the altar, outside, at about 4 feet from the earth. In the inside of the same corner, at the same height, has also been deposited a box in sheet iron coated with tin *[fer-blanc]*, containing an act from our hand, a list of those who have struck the brick to contribute to the masonry; a medal, a small

135th, & 136th pgs

piece of money . . .

[No Bolduc signature]
Mod. Demers, V.G.O.

SIXTY NINTH PAGE
p 135

B-148
Henriette

The 20 May, 1846, we the undersigned priest have baptized Henriette, born yesterday, legitimate daughter of Joseph Ducharme and of Catherine Hu; godfather Joseph Crochiere, godmother Josephte Quesnel, who could not sign.

Mod. Demers, priest

S-68 +

The 16 February, 1846, we the undersigned priest have buried in the cemetery the body of a child, privately baptized; present Amable Arquoite and Louis Lucier.

Mod. Demers, priest

M-20
Et.
Bernise
and
Angelique
Rondeau
words
crossed out
nul
M. D.

The 20 April, 1846, after the publication of 2 bans of marriage, and the dispensation of the third [inserted above the line], between Etienne Bernise, French, on the one part, and Angelique, minor daughter of Charles Rondeau and of Louise Belaire (some words scratched out) on the other part, nor having discovered any impediment, we the undersigned priest have received their mutual consent to marriage and have given them the nuptial benediction in the presence of Pierre Bellique and Louis Vendal, who could not sign as well as the spouses. [Words written] between lines good.

Mod. Demers, priest

M-21
Felix
Giguere
and
Victoire
Cornoyer

The 20 April, 1846, after the publication of 3 bans of marriage between Felix, of-age son of Louis Giguere and of Josephte Lessard, of the Riviere du loup, in Canada, on the one part, and Victoire, minor daughter of Joseph Cornoyer and of Therese Okanagan, on the other part, no impediment having been discovered, we the undersigned priest have received their mutual consent to marriage and have given them the nuptial benediction in the presence of Pierre Bellique and of Louis Vendal, who could not sign as well as the said spouses.

Mod. Demers, priest

+ see the reverse of the page (136)

B
Pierre
Lor

The 20 May, 1846, we the undersigned priest have baptized [Pierre], aged 3 days, legitimate son of Moyse Lor and of Marie Anne Sanders, godfather Gedeon Senecal, godmother Marie Anne Grenier, who could not sign.

Mod. Demers, priest

p 136
S-69
[Child
of
Felix]

The 3 June, 1846, we the undersigned priest have buried in the cemetery the body of . . . aged 1 year, deceased the day before, child of Antoine Felix and of Marguerite Chaudiere; present Amable Petit and Simon Gregoire who could not sign.

Mod. Demers, priest

B-169
Therese
Dubreuil

The 14 June, 1846, we the undersigned priest have baptized Therese, born the 7th, legitimate daughter of Jean Baptiste Dubreuil and of Marguerite Yougolta; godfather Pierre Bellique, godmother Jane St. Martin, who could not sign.

Mod. Demers, priest

B-170
Susanne
Indian

The 20 June, 1846, we the undersigned priest have [baptized] Susanne, aged 15 months, child of Tlikatat infidel parents; godfather Paul Guilbeau, godmother Katy, his wife, who could not sign.

Mod. Demers, priest

B-171
Louise
Anderson

The 24 June, 1846, we the undersigned priest have baptized Louise, aged 15 months, child born of the civil marriage of Anderson, metis Kanak [mixed-blood Hawaiian] and of Angelique Carpentier; godfather Cesaire Beaudoin, godmother Sophie Carpentier, who could not sign.

Mod. Demers, priest

+

B-172	The 31 May, 1846, we the undersigned priest have baptized Jane, born
Jane	the 7 February, 1842, godfather Pierre Bellique, godmother Jany St.
B-173	Martin; Helen, born the 2 April, 1844, godfather Adolphe Chamberland,
Helene	godmother Marie St. Martin; Marie Anne, born the 22 March, 1845, god-
B-174	father F. Xavier Laderoute, godmother Victoire McMullen; daughters of
M. Anne	Benjamin Williams and of Anne . . . , the said godfathers and godmothers
[Williams]	could not sign.

Mod. Demers, priest

SEVENTIETH PAGE
p 137

B-175	The 26 June, 1854, we the undersigned priest have baptized Calliste, born
[Calliste	yesterday, legitimate child of Jean Jeanguay [Gingras] and of Olive . . .
Gingras]	

[The above entry is cross-hatched out and unfinished, evidently out of sequence, as see date of year. The remainder of the page is blank.]

p 138

B-175	The 7 July, 1846, we the undersigned priest have baptized Genevieve, aged
Genevieve	11 days, legitimate daughter of Pierre the Iroquois, and of . . . Flat Head,
Iroquoise	godfather Augustin Garant, godmother Therese Tchinouk, who could
	not sign.

Mod. Demers, priest

B-176	The 4 July, 1846, we the undersigned priest have baptized Julien, born
Julien	the 28 June last, [three words crossed out, which read "of an unknown
Laderoute	father", written above the line] of the legitimate marriage of Francois
	Xavier Laderoute and of Marie Anne Ouvre; godfather Augustin Rochon,
	godmother Celeste Jeaudoin who could not sign. 7 words between the lines
	good, three effaced nul, by subsequent legitimation made by us under-
	signed.

Cenas, priest
Mod. Demers, priest

The original record by Modeste Demers was changed by F. Cenas who came to Oregon in 1851.

B-177	The 7 July, 1846, we the undersigned priest have baptized Joseph, born
Joseph	this day, legitimate child of Joseph Kling [Klyne] and of Louise . . .
Kling	[Braconnier]; godfather Andre Plourde, godmother Victoire Cornoyer,
[Klyne]	who could not sign.

Mod. Demers, priest

S-70	The 22 July, 1846, we the undersigned priest have buried in the cemetery
Francois	the body of Francois, aged 9, deceased yesterday, son of Antoine Felix
Felix	and of Marguerite Chaudiere; and also the body of a Kalapoya woman,
[and]	privately baptized, aged about 30 years; in the presence of Amable Petit
S-71	and of Andre Hophop who could not sign.

Mod. Demers, priest

B-178	The 28 July, 1846, we the undersigned priest have baptized Julien, born
Julien	day before yesterday, legitimate child of Pierre Pepin and of Susanne
Pepin	Gaderick [Goodrich]; godfather Adolphe Chamberland, godmother
	Julienne Watiece who could not sign.

Mod. Demers, priest

M-22	The 27 July, 1846, after the publication of 3 bans of marriage between
Benenso	Benenso Alipas, of-age son of Matheo Alipas and of Isabelle Borondo,
Alipas	Spanish, on the one part, and Louise, Okanagan, on the other part, nor
and	any impediment having been discovered, we the undersigned priest have
Louise	received their mutual consent to marriage and have given them the nuptial
[Okanagan]	benediction in the presence of Jacques Servant and of Peter Kitson who
	could not sign.

Mod. Demers, priest

[Also set in with the Soderini baptisms:]

I, Tiberius Soderini, M.A., baptized Marie Anne la Rocca and joined her in matrimony with Joseph Sebastian la Rocca (the age of the wife 27 years). This day 20 May, 1845. Godfather was Jean Baptiste Sylvestre. Witnesses to the wedding

Richard (Grant)
Chief Factor
HHBC
Alan (X) McDonald

SEVENTY FIRST PAGE
p 139

B-179 Sophie illegit- imate	The 27 July, 1846, we the undersigned priest have supplied the ceremonies of Baptism to Sophie, privately baptized by us, aged 4 months, born illegitimate of Louise, Okanagan, named above, and of an unknown father. Godmother Marie, widow of Picard, who could not sign. Mod. Demers, priest

p 140

S-72
[Child
of
Senecal]
The 2 August, 1846, we the undersigned priest have buried the body of a child of Gedeon Senecal, privately baptized at birth by . . . in the presence of Amable Petit and of Michel Rivet, who could not sign.
Mod. Demers, priest

B-181
Charlotte
Wallawalla
The 11 August, 1846, we the undersigned priest have baptized Charlotte, aged about 36 years, Wallawalla; godfather Paul Guilbeau, godmother Katy, his wife.
Mod. Demers, priest

B-182
Charlotte
Okanagan
The 17 August, 1846, we the undersigned priest have baptized Charlotte, Okanagan, aged about 70 years; godfather Jean Gingras, godmother Olive Forcier who could not sign.
Mod. Demers, priest

B-183
John
Gay
The 17 August, 1846, we the undersigned priest have baptized John, born the 6th, child of George Gay and of Louise Tchelis; godfather John Howard, godmother Catherine Lonetain, who could not sign.
Mod. Demers, priest

S-73
J. B.
Lajoie
The 18 August, 1846, we the undersigned priest have buried in the cemetery the body of Jean Baptiste Lajoie, husband of Marie, Pend Oreille, aged 46 years, deceased the day before yesterday, in the presence of Jean Baptiste Dubreuil and of Andre St. Martin, who could not sign.
Mod. Demers, priest

S-74
Thomas
Waticie
The 20 August, 1846, we the undersigned priest have buried in the cemetery the body of Thomas, aged . . . years, natural child of Thomas Waticie and of a Snake woman; in the presence of Jean Baptiste Dubreuil and of Adolphe Chamberland who could not sign.
Mod. Demers, priest

B-184
Angelique
Gobin
The 15 August, 1846, we the undersigned priest have baptized Angelique, [born] the 16 of July last, daughter of Baptiste Gobin and of Marguerite Vagnier [Vernier]; godfather Antoine Rivet, godmother Mary his wife, who could not sign.
Mod. Demers, priest

SEVENTY SECOND PAGE
p 141

B-184
[sic]
Mgte
Bireng
The 23 August, 1846, we the undersigned priest have baptized Marguerite, aged 24 days, natural daughter of Jean Baptiste Birings [?], Spaniard, and of a Wallawalla woman; godfather Cesaire Beaudoin, godmother Sophie Carpentier who could not sign.
Mod. Demers, priest

B-185
Susanne
Indian
The 29 August, 1846, we the undersigned priest have [baptized] Susanne, aged 7 days, Indian child. Godfather Charles Tsehte, godmother Susanne Tawakon - who could not sign.
Mod. Demers, priest

S-75
[Marie
The 30 August, 1846, we the undersigned priest have buried in the cemetery the body of a Kalapoya woman, privately baptized by Joseph McLoughlin,

Kalapoya] — under the name of Marie; in the presence of Amable Petit and of Michel Lucier who could not sign.

Mod. Demers, priest

M-23
P. Delard
and
Josephte
Lapierre

The 3 August, 1846, after the publication of 3 bans of marriage between Pierre, of-age son of Joseph Delard and of Susanne, Shushap, on the one part, and Josephte, minor daughter of Joseph Lapierre and Susanne Okanagan, on the other part, nor having discovered any impediment, we the undersigned priest have received their mutual consent to marriage and have given them the nuptial benediction in the presence of Louis Aussan and of Andre Lonetain who as well as the spouses could not sign.

Mod. Demers, priest

B-185
Angelique
Gobin

The 15 August, 1846, we the undersigned priest have baptized Angelique, born the 16 July last, legitimate daughter of Baptiste Gobin, and of Marguerite Vagnier; godfather Antoine Rivet, godmother Mary, his wife, who could not sign.

Mod. Demers, priest

[The above entry is a repeat of B-184 on page 140]

p 142

B-186
Emilie
Saste

The 8 September, 1846, we the undersigned priest have baptized Emilie, Saste, aged about 15 years; godfather Joseph Cornoyer, godmother Therese his wife, who could not sign.

Mod. Demers, priest

S-76
[Charlotte
Wallawalla]

The 12 September, 1846, we the undersigned priest have buried in the cemetery the body of Charlotte Wallawalla, aged about 36 years, deceased yesterday, in the presence of Amable and of Pierre Bonin who could not sign.

Mod. Demers, priest

B-187
Thomas
Waticie

The 14 September, 1846, has been baptized by the Reverend Louis S.J. *[Vercruysse?]*, Thomas, natural son of . . . *[Watice]*, Iroquois and of a Tchinook Woman; godfather Adolphe Chamberland, godmother Julienne Watiece.

B-188
Marie
[Serpente]

In this manner Marie, Snake *[Serpente]* woman, aged about 30 years; same godfather and same godmother -

M-24
Thomas
Watiese
and
Marie
Serpente

Of whom, Thomas and Marie, the Reverend Father Louis S.J. considering dispensation of bans, has received the mutual consent to marriage and has given them the nuptial benediction in the presence of Adolphe Chamberland and of Joseph Plouff who could not sign. We undersigned certify the truth of this rite.

Mod. Demers, priest

M-25
Jean
Boucher
and
Isabelle
Mainville

The 7 September, 1846, after the publication of three bans of marriage between Jean, of-age son of Wakan Boucher and of Nancy McDougal, on the one part, and Isabelle, minor daughter of Francoise Mainville and of a Sauteuse woman, on the other part, nor having discovered any impediment, we the undersigned priest have received their mutual consent to marriage and have given them the nuptial benediction in the presence of Fabien Malouin and of Francois Boucher, who, as well as the said spouses could not sign. *

Mod. Demers, priest

* see October 8 *[?]*

SEVENTY THIRD PAGE

p 143

B-189
Philomene
Tawakon

The 25 October, 1846, we the undersigned priest have baptized Philomene, aged 6 days, legitimate daughter of Thomas Tawakon and of Louise Wallawalla; godfather Augustin Rochon, godmother Celeste Jeaudoin who could not sign.

Mod. Demers, priest

B-190
Emilie

The 8 September, 1846, we the undersigned priest have baptized Emilie, aged about 15 years, Koos tribe; godfather Joseph Cornoyer, godmother

Koos	Therese his wife, who could not sign.
	Mod. Demers, priest
B-191 Angele Okanagan	The 27 September, 1846, we the undersigned priest have baptized Angele, Okanagan, dangerously ill, aged 20 years; godfather Andre Lonetain who could not sign.
	Mod. Demers, priest
B-192 Joseph [Kalapoya]	The 5 September, 1846, we the undersigned priest have baptized Joseph, Kalapoya, in danger of death, aged about 16 years, godfather Joseph Gervais who could not sign.
	Mod. Demers, priest
B-193 Basile Plourde	The 21 September, 1846, we the undersigned priest have baptized Basile, born 2 days ago, legitimate son of Francois Plourde and of . . . (Susanne Dubois); godfather Basile Dubois, godmother Louise Humpherville who could not sign.
	Mod. Demers, priest
S- Rose Chalifou	The 12 October, 1846, we the undersigned priest have buried in the cemetery the body of Rose, aged 12 years and a half, deceased 2 days ago, Legitimate daughter of Andre Chalifou and of Catherine Russie, present Francois Bernier and Louis Pichet who could not sign.
	Mod. Demers, priest
Consecration of the Church	The 1 November, 1846, we the undersigned Vicar General of the Apostolic Vicarate of Oregon, have in public blessed, following the form of the Processional, a church built of brick, under the patronage of the Apostle St. Paul, to celebrate there the Sacred Sacrifice of the Mass, there to preach the word, there to administer the Sacraments, assisted by the Reverends Jean Baptiste Zepherin Bolduc and Michel Accolti, Jesuit, who have signed with us, and in the presence of a great crowd of people.
	[No signatures] Mod. Demers, V.G.O.
p 144 S-77 Joseph Lilouais	The 4 November, 1846, we the undersigned priest have buried in the cemetery the body of Joseph, aged 9 years, deceased 2 days ago, Lilouais tribe; present Amable Petit and Charles Petit who could not sign.
	Mod. Demers, priest
M-26 [Cuthbert Lambert and Marie Okanagan]	The 9 November, 1846, ["we the undersigned priest" crossed out] after the publication of two bans of marriage and in view of the dispensation of the third, granted by us, between Cuthbert Lambert dit Robillard, of-age son . . . (two lines blank) and Marie, Okanagan, widow of the late Andre Picard, on the other part, nor having discovered any impediment, we the undersigned priest have received their mutual consent to marriage and have given them the nuptial benediction in the presence of Pierre Lacourse and of Pierre Bonin, who, as well as the spouses, could not sign.
	Mod. Demers, priest
S-78 H Lavigueur	The 12 November, 1846, we the undersigned priest have buried in the cemetery the body of Hyacinthe Lavigueur, husband of Marguerite, Chaudiere, deceased the 10th; present Louis Pichet and Andre Chalifoux who could not sign.
	Mod. Demers, priest
B-194 Martha Stimemon	The 28 November, 1846, we the undersigned priest have baptized Martha, aged 15 months, legitimate daughter of Christophe Stimemon, and of Catherine Brons; the godfather has been ourself.
	Mod. Demers, priest
M-27 Jos. Rivet and M. Anne Despard	The 16 November, 1846, after the publication of three bans of marriage between Joseph Rivet, widower of Rose Lacourse, on the one part, and Marie Anne, minor daughter of Frederic Despard and of Louise Tchinook, on the other part, nor having discovered any impediment, we the undersigned priest have received their mutual consent to marriage and have given them the nuptial benediction in the presence of Pierre Bellique and of Antoine Rivet, who as well as the said spouses could not sign.
	Mod. Demers, priest

SEVENTY FOURTH PAGE

p 145

S-79 Marie Jobin	The 2 December, 1846, we the undersigned priest have buried in the cemetery the body of Marie, aged 3 *[days]*, privately baptized at birth and died immediately after, legitimate daughter of Sigfroid Jobin and of Catherine Pepin; present Amable Petit and Peter Kitson who could not sign.

Mod. Demers, priest

B-195 *[Paul Garant]*	The 12 December, 1846, we the undersigned priest have baptized Pau . . . , born this day, legitimate child of Augustin Garant and of Lucie Cowlitch; godfather Andre St. Martin, godmother Catherine Tawakon who could not sign.

Mod. Demers, priest

B-196 Joseph Kalapoya	The 20 December, 1846, we the undersigned priest have baptized Joseph, aged 10 days, Kalapoya; godfather Pierre Pepin, godmother Susanne Gaderick *[Goodrich]* who could not sign.

Mod. Demers, priest

B-197 Marie illegi- timate	The 20 December, 1846, we the undersigned priest have baptized Marie, aged 3 days, born illegitimate of Louise, woman of the Cascades, baptized; godfather Louis Monie *[Monique]*, godmother Charlotte his wife who could not sign.

Mod. Demers, priest

S-80 *[Paul]* Garant	The 23 December, 1846, we the undersigned priest have buried in the cemetery the body of Paul, aged 12 days, child of Augustin Garant and of Lucie Kowlitsh; present Amable Petit and Michel Lucier who could not sign.

Mod. Demers, priest

p 146

S-81 *[Child of Rivet]*	The 27 December, 1846, we the undersigned priest have buried in the cemetery the body of . . . deceased the day before child of Antoine Rivet and of Mary PendOreil;
S-82 *[Marguerite Gingras]*	The same day has also been buried by us the body of Marguerite * deceased the day before, daughter of Jean Gingras and of the late Charlotte, Okanagan, present Amable Petit and Charles Petit, who could not sign. * aged 9 years (good), *[meaning the addition outside the body of the entry was accounted for by the signer.]*

Mod. Demers, priest

B-198 Augustin Russie	The 27 December, 1846, we the undersigned priest have baptized Augustin, born the 17th, legitimate child of Augustin Russie and of Agnes Tahikwarihi; godfather Paul Guilbeau, godmother Marie Anne Tahikwarihi who could not sign.

Mod. Demers, priest

S-83 Jos.	The 4 November, 1846, we the undersigned priest have buried in the cemetery of this mission the body of Joseph deceased yesterday at the College of St. Joseph at the age of about 8 years, in the presence of Amable Petit and of Andre St. Martin who could not sign.

J. B. Z. Bolduc, priest

SEVENTY FIFTH PAGE

1847

p 147

B-1 Profession of Faith of Mary Smith	The 3 January, 1847, we the undersigned priest, we have gone to the house of Mr. James McGinness, and have received the abjuration of Mary Smith, his wife, of the Methodist belief, and she has made in our hands, of her own choice, public profession of the Faith of the Catholic Religion, Apostolic and Roman; in the presence of James McGinnis and of Thomas Smith, who could not sign with us, nor could the professed, dangerously ill.

Mod. Demers, priest

B-2 Mary Smith	The 3 January, 1847, we the undersigned priest have baptized in danger of death Mary, born Smith, wife of James McGinniss, aged 27 years. The godfather has been ourself.

Mod. Demers, priest

S-1 Mary Smith	The 8 January, 1847, we the undersigned priest have buried in the cemetery the body of Mary Smith, aged 27 years, deceased day before yesterday, during her life wife of James McGinniss, in the presence of Thomas Smith and of Amable Petit who could not sign. Mod. Demers, priest
B-3 Angele Okanagan	The 7 January, 1847, we the undersigned priest have baptized Angele, aged 1 month, natural daughter of Joseph, Okanagan, and a woman of the same nation; Godfather Antoine Rivet, godmother Mary, his wife who could not sign. Mod. Demers, priest
S-2 Isabelle Kalapoya	The 12 January, 1847, we the undersigned priest have buried in the cemetery the body of Isabelle aged 3 years, deceased 2 days before, natural daughter of Nanteyakka and of Hilste, Kalapoya infidels; present Joseph Laderoute and Pierre Bellique who could not sign. Mod. Demers, priest
p 148 S-3 Henriette Plouff	The 14 January, 1847, we the undersigned priest have buried in the cemetery the body of Henriette, aged 6 years, deceased the day before, legitimate daughter of Joseph Plouff and of Therese Okanagan; present Baptiste Bouchard and Amable Petit who could not sign. Mod. Demers, priest
M-1 Fr. Toupin and Angelique Lonetain	The 25 January, 1847, in view of the dispensation of one ban granted by us, and the publication of the other two bans of marriage between Francois, of-age son of Jean Baptiste Toupin and of Marie, Aioise [Iowa] tribe, on one part, and Angelique, minor daughter of Andre Lonetain, and of Elizabeth [Nancy] Okanagan, on the other part, nor having discovered any impediment, we the undersigned priest have received their mutual consent to marriage and have given them the nuptial benediction in the presence of Joseph Delard and of Peter Kitson who, as well as the said spouses, could not sign. Mod. Demers, priest

SEVENTY SIXTH PAGE

p 149 M-2 Gedeon Gravelle and Nancy Pin	The 1 February, 1847, after the publication of 3 bans of marriage between Gedeon, of-age son of Vincent Gravelle and of the late Adelaide Bellaire, of the parish of Ste. Rose, diocese of Montreal in Canada, on the one part, and Nancy, minor daughter of Joseph Pin and of Marguerite, Chaudiere, on the other part; nor having discovered any impediment, we the undersigned priest have received their mutual consent to marriage and have given them the nuptial benediction in the presence of Louis Pichet and of Andre Chalifoux, who, as well as the said spouses, could not sign. Mod. Demers, priest
B-4 F. Xavier Beaudoin	The 2 February, 1847, we the undersigned priest have baptized Francois Xavier, born yesterday, legitimate child of Cesaire Beaudoin and of Sophie Carpentier; godfather Sigfroid Jobin, godmother Catherine Pepin who could not sign. Mod. Demers, priest
S-4 Patrick Rowland	The 11 February, 1847, has been buried, outside the cemetery and without the presence of a priest at the edge of the woods, opposite the Church of St. Paul. (No signature)
B-5 Christine Jeaudoin	The 14 February, 1847, we the undersigned priest have supplied the ceremonies of Baptism to Christine, aged 1 month, legitimate daughter of Baptiste Jeaudoin and of Isabelle Hubert; godfather Pierre Bellique, godmother Celeste Jeaudoin who could not sign. Mod. Demers, priest
B-6 Joseph	The 22 February, 1847, we the undersigned priest have baptized Joseph, born the 19 of the month, legitimate child of Augustin Raymond and of

Raymond — Marie Servant; godfather Louis Pichet, godmother Angelique Servant who could not sign.

Mod. Demers, priest

p 150
S-5
Alexis
Lacourse

The 24 February, 1847, we the undersigned priest have buried in the cemetery the body of Alexis, aged 12 years, deceased the day before, legitimate child of Pierre Lacourse and of Archange Tchinook, present Amable [Petit] and Cuthbert Lambert who could not sign.

Mod. Demers, priest

B-7
Profession
of
Faith
of
Nimrod
O'Kelly

The 28 February, 1847, we the undersigned priest have received the abjuration of the protestant religion of Nimrod O'Kelly, who, of his own choice, has made between our hands public profession of the Faith in Our Holy Mother Catholic Church Apostolic and Roman, in the presence of Joseph Gervais and of Paul Guilbeau and of several other persons who could not sign; the said O'Kelly has signed with us.

[No signature]

Mod. Demers, priest

B-8
Nimrod
O'Kelly

The 28 February, 1847, we the undersigned priest have baptized Nimrod O'Kelly, aged 59 years, son of . . . , godparents Joseph Gervais, Catherine Pepin, who could not sign. The baptized has signed with us.

[No signature]

Mod. Demers, priest

S-6
Philippe
Degre

The 29 (sic) February, 1847, we the undersigned priest have buried in the cemetery the body of Philippe Degre, in former times of Sorel in Canada, aged about 108 years; present Louis Pichet and Andre Chalifoux who could not sign.

Mod. Demers, priest

Mon Dieu Mon Dieu

SEVENTY SEVENTH PAGE
p 151
B-9
(Michel
Saste)

The 4 March, 1847, we the undersigned priest have baptized Michel, born this day, legitimate son of Michel, Tsaste, and of Marie, of the same tribe; godfather Laurent Sauve, godmother Josephte, his wife, who could not sign.

Mod. Demers, priest

S-7
(Child
of
Watice)

The 8 March, 1846 (?), we the undersigned priest have buried in the cemetery the body of . . . , child of Thomas Watiecie, and of Marie, Snake . . . in the presence of Amable Petit and of Adolphe Chamberland who could not sign.

Mod. Demers, priest

S-8
Francois
Labonte

The 11 March, 1847, we the undersigned priest have buried in the cemetery the body of Francois, privately baptized and died at birth 2 days ago, legitimate son of Louis Labonte and of Caroline Montour; present Amable Petit and Charles Petit who could not sign.

Mod. Demers, priest

S-9
B
Lavigueur

The 11 March, 1847, we the undersigned priest have buried in the cemetery the body of Jean Baptiste, aged 15 years, deceased 2 days ago, legitimate son of the late Hyacinthe Lavigueur and of Marguerite, Chaudiere; present Amable Petit and Louis Leclerc who could not sign.

Mod. Demers, priest

S-10
Angelique
Payet

The 26 March, 1847, we the undersigned priest have buried in the cemetery the body of Angelique, aged 17 years, deceased the day before, natural daughter of Francois Payet and of a Pendoreil woman; present Pierre Dubois and Amable Petit who could not sign.

Mod. Demers, priest

S-11
Charles
Brouillet

The 27 March, 1847, we the undersigned priest have buried in the cemetery the body of Charles, aged 8 years, deceased the day before, legitimate son of Hyppolite Brouillet and of the late . . . Finlay; present Charles Lafantaisie and Amable Petit, who could not sign.

Mod. Demers, priest

p 152
[The body of this page has nothing written on it. A sheet of paper is pasted on, evidently Acts made in the field. The parentheses are those of DeVos.]

B-10 Pierre Makeman	The 20 of the month of May, 1847, we undersigned have baptized (at Fort Wallawalla) Louis son of Pierre Mackeman of the nation Epissinghue (Canada) and of a Tchinouck mother, born at Fort Vancouver aged 32 years about. His godparents have been Augustin Lambert and Catherine Pichet. P. DeVos, S.J.
B-11 Elizabeth Winnix	The 20 of the month of May, 1847, we undersigned have baptized (at Fort Wallawalla) Elizabeth Winnix, born of a Wallawalla father and of a Cayhous mother, aged 30 years about. Her godfather has been Augustin Lambert and Catherine Pichet her godmother. P. DeVos, S.J.
M-2 (Louis Makeman and Elizabeth Winnix)	The 20 of the month of May, 1847, we undersigned have married according to the rites of the Catholic Church (at Fort Wallawalla) Louis Mackeman and Elizabeth Winnix, in the presence of Augustin Lambert and of Catherine Pichet.

Augustin (X) Lambert
Catherine (X) Pichet   Louis (X) Mackman
Elizabeth (X) Winnix
P. DeVos, S.J.

SEVENTY EIGHTH PAGE
p 153

S-12 Thomas Indian	The 9 April, 1847, we the undersigned priest have buried in the cemetery the body of Thomas, aged about 30 years, Tsaste, deceased the day before
S-13 Joseph Beaudoin	At the same time also has been buried the body of Joseph, aged 2 years, deceased the day before, legitimate son of Cesaire Beaudoin and of Sophie Carpentier; present Amable Petit and Andre St. Martin who could not sign. Mod. Demers, priest
B-12 Michel Saste	The 15 April, 1847, we the undersigned priest have baptized Michel born (this) day, legitimate son of Michel, Saste, and of Rose, of the same tribe; godfather Laurent Sauve, godmother Josephte his wife, who could not sign. Mod. Demers, priest
B-13 Isabelle Boucher	The 16 April, 1847, we the undersigned priest have baptized Isabelle, born the 9 of this month, legitimate daughter of Francois Boucher and of Therese, Porteuse; godfather Jean Boucher, godmother Isabelle Mainville who could not sign. Mod. Demers, priest
S-14 Michel Saste	The 27 April, 1847, we the undersigned priest have buried in the cemetery the body of Michel, aged 12 days, deceased the day before, child of Michel Saste and of Rose Saste; present Michel Lucier and Louis Guilbeau who could not sign. Mod. Demers, priest

[The remainder of the page is blank. Pasted to the page is a small piece of blue paper, evidently field notes, not entered, but numbered. One would assume the year 1847.]
(The top of the page torn - then]

. . . deceased the day before - present Amable Petit and Peter Kitson -

S-15	Wednesday of the same week burial of an Indian died at the house of Plante, privately baptized by himself. Present Michel Lucier and Peter Kitson
S-16	The 16 April burial of the wife of Bap. Aubichon, deceased the 14. Present Andre Dubois and Amable Petit
B-14	Same day Baptism of Fr. Xavier child of J. Servant and of Josephte Okanagan. Godfather A [?] Jeaudoin, godmother Pelagie Lucier. Father present
B-15	Same day. Baptism of Thomas, child of C. Rondeau and of Catherine Depati, born the 4 April. Godfather Thomas Moisan, godmother Henriette Lonetain. Father present.
B-16	May 21 Baptized Francois Barbu Molelis see below [?]

M-3	24 married Ant. Laferte and Nancy *[?]* Wallawalla 24 May - witnesses Paul Guilbeau Michel Lucier, undersigned.
S-17	27 (?) burial of Jos. Bellique aged 5 years
B-17	1 June Baptism of Francois at the house of Bellique
B-18	Baptism of Pierre
B-19	Baptism of Joseph
	Godfather for the three, Bellique; godmother his wife.
B no#	3 *[June?]* Bap. of the child of Monmouton; Godfather P. Chamberland, godmother Julienne
B-20	13 *[June?]* Bapt. of William, child of J. Lusignan, aged 1 and ½ months Godfather Felix, Indian; godmother Aline Larose (?)
B-21	18 *[June?]* Baptism of child of L. Pichet and of Marguerite Bercier, born the 16. Godfather P. Lacourse, godmother Archange, his wife.
S-18	20 *[June ?]* Burial of Marguerite, wife of Pierre Laroque deceased day before yesterday Present Amable Petit and Jean Portier

p 154

B-22 Profession of W. E. Golder	The 2 May, 1847, we the undersigned priest have received the abjuration of William E. Golder, formerly of Pennsylvania, United States, of the presbyterian religion and he has made between our hands, of his own choice, public profession of the Catholic Religion, Apostolic and Roman, in the presence of Fabien Malouin and of Paul Guilbeau who could not sign, the said Golder has signed with us.

[No signature]
Mod. Demers, priest

B-23 W. E. Golder	The 2 May, 1847, we the undersigned priest have baptized conditionally William E. Golder, aged 25, formerly of Pennsylvania; godfather Fabien Malouin, godmother Louise his wife, who could not sign. The baptized has signed with us.

[No signature]
Mod. Demers, priest

M-4 Charles Tschte and . . . Kalapoya	The 2 May, 1847, after the publication of 2 bans of marriage and the dispensation of the third granted by us, between Charles Tschte, Iroquois, widower, on the one part, and . . . , Kalapoya, on the other part, nor having discovered any impediment, we the undersigned priest have received their mutual consent to marriage and have given them the nuptial benediction in the presence of Louis Monic and of Simon Gregoire who as well as the said spouses could not sign.

Mod. Demers, priest

B-24 Kalpoya	The 10 May, 1847, we the undersigned priest have baptized . . . , Kalapoya, aged about 16 years, godfather Louis Monic, godmother Charlotte his wife who could not sign.

Mod. Demers, priest

B-25 Susanne Oulpahat	The 20 May, 1847, we the undersigned priest have baptized Susanne, aged 15 months, natural daughter Oulpahat and of Sipanouai, infidel Tlikatats; godmother Katy, wife of Paul Guilbeau, who could not sign.

Mod. Demers, priest

SEVENTY NINTH PAGE

p 155

B-26 Rachel	The 6 June, 1847, we the undersigned priest, of the Society of Jesus, have baptized Rachel . . . , daughter of . . . ; godfather Andre Chalifoux, godmother Catherine Russie who could not sign.

[No signature of priest]

M-5 Louis Leclerc and Rachel	The 6 June, 1847, after the publication of o ban of marriage and the dispensation of 2 others granted by us, between Xavier (sic) Leclerc, of-age son of Joseph Leclerc and of Aloise Bourret, of the parish of St. [?] Montreal, on the one part, and Rachel . . . , nor having discovered any impediment, we the undersigned priest have received their mutual consent to marriage and have given them the nuptial benediction in the presence of Louis Pichet

and of Michel Laferte, who as well as the said spouses could not sign.

[No signature of priest]

M-6
J. B.
Soletroani
and
Marie
Pendoreil

The 21 June, 1847, after the publication of three bans of marriage between Jean Baptiste, of-age son of the late Ignace, Iroquois, and of a Flat Head woman, on the one part, and Marie, widow of the late Jean Baptiste Lajoie, Pendoreil, on the one part (sic), nor having discovered any impediment, we the undersigned priest have received their mutual consent to marriage and have given them the nuptial benediction in the presence of Paul Guilbeau and of Michel Laferte who as well as the spouses could not sign.

Mod. Demers, priest

p 156
S-19
Isabelle
Mainville

The 5 July, 1847, we the undersigned priest have buried in the cemetery the body of Isabelle, deceased yesterday, wife in her lifetime of Jean Boucher, aged about 25 years; present Amable Petit and Francois Boucher who could not sign.

Mod. Demers, priest

B-27
F. Xavier
Liard

The 10 July, 1847, we the undersigned priest have baptized Francois Xavier, born the 5 of May last, illegitimate child of Stanislaus Liard and of an Okanagan woman. Godfather Francois Liard, godmother Marie Anne, his wife who could not sign.

Mod. Demers, priest

B-28
[Catherine
Umpqua]

The 19 of July, 1847, we the undersigned priest have baptized *[Catherine]* Ampkwa *[Umpqua]* aged about 15 years; godfather Laurent, Iroquois, godmother Therese, his wife who could not sign.

Mod. Demers, priest

M-7
Nota
and
[Catherine]
Ampkwa

The 19 July, 1847, after the publication of 1 ban of marriage and the dispensation of 2 others granted by us, between Louis Nota, formerly of the village called Two Mountains in Canada, widower of the late Kwakweltosion, Susanne, on the one part, and . . . Ampkwa, nor having discovered any impediment, we the undersigned priest have received their mutual consent to marriage and have given them the nuptial benediction in the presence of Laurent, Iroquois, and of Sigfroid Jobin who as well as the said spouses could not sign.

Mod. Demers, priest

S-20
Josephte
Humpherville

The 22 July, 1847, we the undersigned priest have buried in the cemetery the body of Josephte, deceased 2 days ago, aged 10 years, daughter of the late Canote and of Marie Sanpoil; present Pierre Dubois and Amable Petit who could not sign.

Mod. Demers, priest

EIGHTIETH PAGE
p 157
B-29
Pierre
Indian

The 25 July, 1847, we the undersigned priest have baptized Pierre, aged 10 days, child of infidel Kalapoyas. Godfather Louis Forcier, godmother, wife of Caille, who could not sign.

Mod. Demers, priest

B-30
M. Magdelen
Fistgerald
[Fitzgerald]

The 1 August, 1847, we the undersigned priest have baptized Mary Magdelen, born the 30 January last, legitimate daughter of Thomas Fistgerald and of Eldridge Pamilea *[should be reversed]*; godfather Pierre Haquet, godmother his wife who could not sign.

Mod. Demers, priest

S-21
Louise
Nez percez

The 1 August, 1847, we the undersigned priest have buried in the cemetery the body of Louise, Nez Percez, aged 23 years, wife in her lifetime of Louis Nipissing; present Augustin Rochon and Amable Petie, who could not sign.

Mod. Demers, priest

S-22
Louis
Nipissing

The 5 August, 1847, we the undersigned priest have buried in the cemetery the body of Louis, aged 18 months, died yesterday, son of Louis Nipissing and the late Louise Nezpercez; in the presence of Amable Petie and of Charles Petie who could not sign.

Mod. Demers, priest

B-31 Nancy Okanagan	The 9 August, 1847, we the undersigned priest have baptized Nancy, Oka-nagan, aged about 23 years, godfather Cuthbert Lambert, godmother Marie, his wife who could not sign. Mod. Demers, priest
p 158 B-32 Henriette Pendoreille	The 9 August, 1847, we the undersigned priest have baptized Henriette, aged about 20 years, Pendoreil; godfather Michel Laferte, godmother his wife, who could not sign. Mod. Demers, priest
B-33 Skwaleh	The 9 August, 1847, we the undersigned priest have baptized . . . , Skwaleh, aged about 20 years; godfather Laurent Sauve, godmother Josephte his wife, who could not sign. Mod. Demers, priest
M-8 Stanislaus Liard [and Nancy Okanagan]	The 9 August, 1847, after the publication of 1 ban of marriage and the dispensation of 2 others granted by us, between Stanislaus, son of Baptiste, now dead, and Marguerite Tamarle (Samarle?), also dead, of St. Jacques of Montreal on the one part, and Nancy, Okanagan, nor having discovered any impediment, we the undersigned priest have received their mutual consent to marriage and have given them the nuptial benediction in the presence of Francois Xavier Liard and of Cuthbert Lambert who as well as the spouses could not sign * [An addition written mostly in the margin of the page] * before which witnesses the said spouses have recognized to legiti-mate their children Francois Xavier, born the 5 May last. [added later, good] Mod. Demers, priest
M-9 Octave Collet and Skwaleh	The 9 August, 1847, after the publication of 1 ban of marriage and the dispensation of 2 others, granted by us, between Octave Collet, of Oage son of the late Joseph Collet and of the late Charlotte Picard, of St. Roch of Quebec on the one part, and . . . Skwaleh, nor having discovered any impediment, we the undersigned priest have received their mutual consent to marriage and have given them the nuptial benediction in the presence of Joseph Baron and of Laurent Sauve who as well as the spouses could not sign. Mod. Demers, priest
M-10 Baptiste Tahekwarihi and Henriette [Pend d' Oreille]	The 9 August, 1847, after the publication of 1 ban of marriage and the dispensation of 2 others granted by us, between Baptiste Tahikwarihi, Iroquois, widower of the late Marie Anne, Wallawalla, on the one part, and Henriette Pendoreil, on the other part, nor having discovered any impediment, we the undersigned priest have received their mutual consent to marriage and have given them the nuptial benediction in the presence of Michel Laferte and of Antoine Laferte who as well as the spouses could not sign. Mod. Demers, priest

(There are several blank pages. Then facing the —)

EIGHTY FIFTH PAGE

p 166

Indians baptized at Nesqually

1. Marie Lachesmiere	baptized	in Sept. 1839	aged 2 years
2. Etienne Luhalette	,,	,,	,, 1 year
3. Nathalie Sahewamish	,,	22 May 1840	aged 5 years
4. Zoe Lahtcheclam	,,	,,	,, 4 years
5. Marie Holholshate	,,	,,	,, 3 years
6. Jean Bte Holholshate	,,	,,	,, 1 year
7. Genevieve Khouliads	,,	the 23	,, 4 years
8. Thomas Tchapihk	,,	,,	,, 40 years -sick
9. Charles Lahalette	,,	the 26	,, ½ year
10. Agathe Luhalette	,,	,,	,, 3 years
11. Magdeleine Skolokwalitte	,,	the 27	,, 6 years
12. Mathieu Tsattem	,,	,,	,, 2 years

(Several blank pages)

p 169

| B-34
*[Louis
Monique]* | The 26 August, 1847, we the undersigned priest have baptized Louis legitimate child of Louis Monique and of Charlotte. The godfather has been Cesaire Beaudoin and the godmother Celeste Jeaudoin who alone has signed with us. |

Celeste Jeaudoin
Veyret

| B-35
*[Louis
Dompierre]* | The 8 September, we the undersigned priest have baptized Louis, legitimate child of David Dompierre and of Marguerite Deshulieres. Godfather Joseph Roussin, godmother Marie Dompierre who could not sign. |
| B-36
*[Louis
Indian]* | The 9 September, 1847, we the undersigned priest have baptized Louis born of infidel parents, this child was aged 2 months. The godmother has been Catherine, wife of Paul Guilbeau, who has not signed. |

Veyret

p 170

[A note on the upper corner of p. 170]

Mission of the Wallamette
in 1839 and 40
Sowed

	July, 1840 Harvested
20 autumn wheat	294
15m spring wheat	136
20m peas	60
6 oats	100
26 sweet potatoes	50

[There is a small ruled page set in that seems to be some sort of census or enumeration, indecipherable.]

p 171

[The last two pages, very worn and stained, seem to be field notes only, covering the time from September, 1847, to April, 1848. The months between were times of great turmoil: the Whitman Massacre had taken place late in November, an epidemic seems to have been widespread, judging from the number of burials recorded, and Father Demerse was preparing to leave for Rome. Various other priests filled in at St. Paul, and their field notes apparently failed to be transcribed into the register. The new Register, St. Paul II, overlaps by some months; the "2½ blank pages" following p 3 were doubtless left for the transcription of the field notes. Only the entry for the death of Lavigueur's wife was transcribed, however.]

5 December *[1847]* I have baptized an adult Indian at the home of Monique. I have called him Joseph. The godfather has been Louis Monique.

5 December I have buried a small child (male) of Solomon Pelletier

6 December *[?]* I have baptized a little Kinagalle *[?]* relative of the wife of Onktam. He has been called Nicolas. The godfather has been Petit.

8 December I have buried the daughter of Vandale

9 December I have buried the wife of Tshem Boucher

15 d. I have buried the little son of Francois Wakan Boucher

20 d. I have buried Nicolas, small Okanogan baptized 6.

20 D. I have buried the child *[male?]* of a Spaniard Benon Alipsa. Privately baptized by Michel Laframboise

21 D. One has buried the wife of Solomon Peletier

22 D. I have buried the little daughter of Joseph (Spokane) employed at Michel Rivet

29 D. One has buried the wife of Guilbeau

[1848]

1 January I have buried the little boy of Rossi

2   ”   I have baptized Marguerite, Indian, working at the house of Lacourse. The godfather has been Claude Lacourse

3 — I have baptized Marie (Indian) wife of Wagui employed at Arquet

4 January I have buried Marguerite (Indian) house of Lacourse

7   "   I have buried a little boy of Dubois

8   "   I have buried Marie (Indian) living at the house of Arquet

10   "   I have buried the wife of Liard

11 *[January]* I have buried a little Indian *[boy]* from the house of Charles Plante

11 Jan. I have buried a little child *[boy]* of 1 day of F. X. Liard privately baptized by his father

12 I have buried the wife of Forcier *[?]*

12 I have buried a child *[boy]* of Cosgrove

14 I have buried the little Xavier Liard

15 I have baptized Marie Anne daughter of Gedeon Gravelle and of Nancee - godfather has been the grandfather

p 172
16 I have buried Suzanne Godin

20 I have buried a little Indian *[boy]* privately baptized at the house of Thomas and baptized yesterday by Mgr. Demers

21 I have buried the little Gai-hord

21 I have buried the little daughter of Arquet

31 I have buried a little girl of 2 years of Forcier

31 I have buried the little Kopper *[male]* baptized a little before by Mons. Rousseau

1 February *[1848]* I have buried John Sauve

17 I have buried Noel Lavigueur

20 Msr. Rousseau has baptized Joseph Sifroid son of Sifroid Jobin and of Catherine Lachance, the godfather has been Pierre Lachance and the godmother Suzanne Gaudriche

24 At the house of *[a word crossed out]* I have buried an Indian *[female]* of the household of Arquet privately baptized the day before by him

27 I have baptized an Indian *[male]*, Okanogan relative of the wife of Lontain. One has given him the name of Joseph. His godfather has been Joseph the Carefree *[Sans Souci]*

4. March I have buried the little Patrick Rowling, son Pade *[Paddy]*

9 March I have buried an Indian *[male]* employed at Forcier, privately baptized by him the day before

11 I have supplied the ceremonies of Baptism for the little Abraham Leclair privately baptized the same day by the wife of Chalifoux. The place *[?]* of godfather has been Pichet, his wife the godmother

23 March I have baptized a little girl aged 2 years daughter of a mixed-blood Wayi *[Owyhee]*, interpreter of the Army, living at the house of Plante. I have called her Elisabeth. The godfather has been Plante.

27 I have buried a child of 9 years boy or girl of Michel Shaste

31 I have buried the little Elisabeth aged 2 or 5 years daughter of Mongo

1 April One has buried the wife of Lavigueur

2 April I have baptized an Indian at the house of Barnier I have called him Louis of the name of his godfather Louis Hercule Lebrun

Page 173
21 April I have buried Louis died the day before at the house of Barnier and baptized 2 April

March 15 (very nearly) Mr. Rousseau has baptized Sarah daughter of Louis Labonte, jr. and of Caroline Montour. The godfather Joseph McLoughlin, the godmother Victoire McMullin.

March 25 Marie Anne, daughter of Joseph Bourgeau and of Angele Lafantaisie. The godfather Charles Lafantaisie and the godmother Marie Anne Grenier.

End of Volume I
St. Paul
1839-1847

B-27 Charles . . . Iroqs. /Tyikwarhi/	This 18 July, 1841, we priest undersigned have baptized Charles, aged 1 year, born of the legitimate marriage of Jn. Baptiste Iroquois and of Judith Walla Walla. Godfather Charlot Iroquois, godmother Archange Scoucisse, who have not known how to sign. F.N. Blanchet, priest
B-28 Josephte illegitimate	This 5 July, 1841, we priest undersigned have baptized Josephte, illegitimate of an Indian girl in service at the house of Frederic Despard. Godfather Joseph Despard, who has not known how to sign. F.N. Blanchet, priest
B-29 Clarice Rivet	This 27 June /sic/, 1841, we priest undersigned have baptized Clarice born the 21 of this month of the legitimate marriage of Antoine Rivet, farmer of this place, and of Emelie Pendioreille. Godfather Francois Bernier, godmother Pelagie Lussier who have not known how to sign. F.N. Blanchet, priest

INDEX
ST. PAUL PARISH
1839-1847

INDEX (abbreviations used)

Page numbers listed in this index are those of the original ledger. See note regarding page numbering at top of first page of translations.

adj - abjuration
aff - affidavit
B - baptism
fa - father
G - guardian
H - "chez" (house of, place of)
L - legitimatized
M - married
mo - mother
PS - priest's signature (or mention of)
S - burial
S-fa - step-father
sig - person's own signature
V - widow or widower
W - witness or godparent

Place names are listed alphabetically with the exception of towns in Canada, which are under "Canada".

Index 1

B-72, p 113
Mathlomat - see Tumwater
Matte, Angelique
  mo, M-7, p 51
Matte, Francois
  B-118, p 127
Matte, Joseph I
  (and Angelique Snake)
  fa, B-61, p 87
  fa, B-118, p 127
Matte, Joseph II
  B-61, p 87
Mauvier, Anne
  mo, M-13, p 115
Menard, Francois *[Pierre I]*
  (and Josephte Snake)
  fa, B-1, p 70
Menard, Jean Baptiste
  B-1, p 70
Menard, Joseph
  B-4, L, M-2, p 47
Menard, Louis
  fa, M-2, p 47
Menard, Paul
  B-76, p 114
Menard, Pierre I
  M-2, p 47 (to Josephte Youte)
  fa, B-4, B-5, p 47
  fa, B-76, p 114
Menard, Pierre II
  B-5, L, M-2, p 47
Mexico
  M-6, p 14
Moisan, Francois Xavier
  B-121, p 127
Moisan, Ignace
  fa, M-11, p 59
Moisan, Thomas
  M-11, p 59 (to Henriette Lonetain)
  W, M-15, p 120
  fa, B-121, p 127
  W, B-15, p 153
Mokuman see Mackeman
Molala, tribe
  9 B-109, p 37
  B-10, p 74
  B-82, p 115
  B-91, S-39, p 118
  S-53, S-54, p 126
  B-119, p 127
  B-16, p 153
Molelis - see Molala
Mollens, Jean Baptiste
  W, M-1, p 5
Molleur - see Mollens
Monique, Francois
  B-63, p 32
Monique, Jose (Iroquois (?)
  (and a woman of the Cascades)

fa, B-63, p 32
Monique, Louis I (Oskanha)
  (and Charlotte . . .)
  W, B-197, p 145
  W, M-4, B-24, p 154
  fa, B-34, p 169
  W, H, B, p 171
Monique, Louis II
  B-34, p 169
Monmouton
  B-no #, p 153
Montour, Caroline
  B-6, p 72
  M-2, p 72 (to Louis Labonte II)
  mo, B-13, p 95
  W, B-66, p 112
  mo, S-8, p 151
  mo, B-, p 173
Montour, Etienne
  W, S-11, p 20
Montour, George
  M-6, p 102 (to Lisette *[Louise]* Canote
  Humpherville)
  fa, B-77, S-36, p 114
  fa, B-140, p 133
Montour, Isabelle
  (and Thomas McKay I)
  mo, B-7, p 3
  W, B-303, p 21
  mo, B-25, p 53
  mo, B-11, p 94
  W, B-140, p 133
Montour, Julie
  B-140, p 133
Montour, Louis Bob
  B-90, p 117
Montour, Maria
  B-303, p 21
  S-2, p 25
Montour, Nicholas
  (and Susanne Humpherville)
  fa, B-303, p 23
  fa, S-2, p 25
  fa, B-6, M-2, p 72
  W, fa, M-6, p 102
  fa, B-90, p 117 (mo Marguerite Cree)
  V, S-64, p 133
Montour, Nicholas (son of George)
  B-77, S-36, p 114
Monois (?), Antoine
  W, B-145, p 134
Nancy, of The Dalles
  (and 1. "a Frenchman"
  2. . . . . Goodrich
  3. Jean Baptiste Dobin)
  mo, B-41, p 80
  mo, M-71, p 89-92
NanKaselais - see Porteuse, Catherine
Napuis, Dick

mo, S-81, p 146 (Mary?)
W, B-3, p 147
Pend d'Oreille, Henriette
  B-32, p 158
  M-10, p 158 (to Jean Baptiste Norwest)
Pend d'Oreille, Josephte
  (and Michel Laferte)
  mo, B-297, p 20
  mo, S-4, betw 50-51
  mo, B-36, p 78
  mo, B-92, B-93, p 118
  mo, B-94, p 119
  W, B-32, p 158
Pend d'Oreille, Marguerite
  (and Joseph Pin I)
  mo, B-20, p 76
  mo, M-2, p 149
Pend d'Oreille, Marie
  (V of Jean Baptiste Lajoie)
  M-6, p 155 (to Jean B. Soletroani
    Iroquois)
Pend d'Oreille, Marie Angelique
  B-49, p 107 (prob)
  M-8, p 108 (to Jean Baptiste Couturier)
Pend d'Oreille, Marie Therese
  (see Calgethpke)
Pend d'Oreille, Therese [Flathead]
  (and Francois Rivet)
  W, B-33, p 29
Pennsylvania, U.S.A.
  B-22, B-23, p 154
Pepin, Catherine (dit Lachance)
  (and Sigfroid Jobin)
  W, B-130-131, p 130
  W, B-134, p 131
  mo, S-79, p 145
  W, B-4, p 149
  W, B-6, p 150
  mo, B, p 172
Pepin, Guillaume
  fa, M-1, p 89
Pepin, Julien
  B-178, p 138
Pepin, Marie
  mo, M-10, p 41
Pepin, Pierre I, dit Lachance
  M-71, p 89 (to Suzanne Goodrich)
  W, B-37, p 103
  fa, B-54, p 109
  H, W, B-120, p 127
  fa, B-178, p 138
  W, B-196, p 145
  W, B, p 172
Pepin, Pierre II, dit Lachance
  B-54, p 109
Perrault, Jean Baptiste
  (and Angele Chinook [Chehalis])
  W, Blessing of the bell, p 3
  fa, B-11, B-12, p 4

fa, M-1, p 5
fa, B-299, p 20
W, fa, M-6, betw 50-51
H, W, S-14, p 88
fa, B-27, p 101
H, W, B-79, p 115
Perrault, Louise [Lucie]
  B-27, p 101
Perrault, Marie Anne
  B-11, B-12, p 4
  M-1, p 5 (to Jean Baptiste Deguire)
  mo, B-122, p 40
Perrault, Reine (Reinette)
  B-299, p 20
  W, B-61, p 32
  W, B-122, p 40
  M-6, betw 50-51 (to John Larison)
  mo, B-102, p 69
Peter - see Desrivieres
Petit, Amable II
  And Angelique (Emelie) Aubichon
  fa, B-135, p 131
Petit, Amable I
  (and Susanne Tawakon)
  fa, B-8, B-9, p 4
  W, S-2, p 4
  W, M-2, p 5
  W, B-272, p 15
  W, S-9, p 40
  W, S-1, p 46
  W, S-3, p 50
  fa, B-68, p 56
  W, B-94, p 66
  W, B-9, p 73
  W, B-14, p 75
  W, S-9, S-10, p 82
  W, S-12, p 84
  W, S-13, p 87
  W, S-14, S-16, B-65, M-7, p 88
  W, M-71, P 89-92
  W, S-2, p 90
  W, S-20, p 104
  W, S-21 through S-25, p 105
  W, M-7, S-28, p 107
  W, B-50, M-9, p 108
  W, M-10, S-29 through S-31, p 109
  fa, B-55, p 110
  W, S-34, p 111
  W, S-35, S-36, p 114
  W, S-37, S-38, p 118
  W, S-41, S-43, p 121
  W, S-50, S-51, p 125
  W, S-55, p 126
  W, S-57, p 128
  W, S-58, p 129
  W, B-134, p 131
  W, B-138, S-62, S-63, p 132
  W, S-64, p 133
  W, S-69, p 136

mo, B-13, p 153
Portier, Jean
  fa, M-13, p 115
Portier, Magdeleine
  B-38, p 79
Portier, Nicholas
  M-19, p 129 (to Marguerite Laroque)
Portier, Nicholas Jean
  (and a woman of California)
  fa, B-38, p 79
  M-13, p 115 (to Marie . . .)
  W, S-18, p 153
Puget Sound
  B-160, p 12
Quesnel, Francois ["old"]
  H, B-318, p 22b
  V, S-1, p 25 (of Marie Chehalis)
  S-26, p 106
Quesnel, Josephte
  W, B-148, p 135
Quintal, Laurent I
  (and Marie Anne Nipissing)
  fa, B-294, p 19
  W, S-3, p 30
  fa, B-89, p 63
  W, fa, S-9, p 64
  W, B-18, p 76
  fa, B-55, p 83
  W, B-12, p 94
Quintal, Laurent II
  B-89, p 63
  S-9, p 64
Quintal, Louis Toussaint
  B-55, p 83
Quintal, Zoe
  B-294, p 19
Raboin, Angele
  B, Soderini, betw 116-117
Raboin, Louis
  fa, B, Soderini, betw 116-117
Rachel, . . .
  B-26, M-5, p 155 (to Louis Leclerc)
Racine, . . .
  fa, S-4, p 93
Racine, Toussaint
  S-4, p 93
Ratelle, Marguerite
  mo, M-20, p 130
Ravalli, Anthony, S.J.
  PS, p 110, 112 to 116
Raymond, Augustin
  W, M-15, p 68
  M-5, p 84 (to Marie Servant)
  fa, B-6, p 149
Raymond, Cecile
  B-Soderini, betw 116-117
Raymond, Francois
  W, B-118, p 127
Raymond, Joseph

B-6, p 149
Raymond, Narcisse
  fa, B-Soderini, betw 116-117
Raymond, Toussaint
  fa, M-5, p 84
Remond - see Raymond
Rivet, . . .
  S-81, p 146
Rivet, Adele
  B-2, p 90
  S-6, p 93
Rivet, Adelaide
  B-21, p 8
Rivet, Antoine
  (and Emelie Pend d'Oreille)
  W, B-319, p 22b
  fa, B-29, p 27
  W, B-82, p 61
  W, B-83, p 62
  W, B-16, p 75
  fa, B-2, p 90
  W, fa, S-6, p 93
  W, S-12, p 99
  fa, B-109, p 124
  W, B-140, S-64, p 133
  W, B-184, p 140
  W, M-27, p 144
  fa, S-81, p 146
  W, B-3, p 147
Rivet, Clarice
  B-29, p 27
Rivet, Fabien
  B-99, p 120
Rivet, Francois
  (and Therese Flathead [Pend d'Oreille])
  W, B-267, p 1
  W, B-295, p 20
  W, B-33, p 29
  W, M-11, p 59
  W, M-14, p 67
  W, M-6, p 86
Rivet, Joseph
  B-109, p 124
Rivet, Joseph
  (and Rose Lacourse)
  fa, B-21, p 8
  W, B-302, p 21
  fa, B-85, p 62
  W, S-10, p 64
  W, B-15, p 75
  W, B-2, p 90
  W, B-46, p 107
  W, B-85, B-86, p 116
  W, B-87, B-88, B-89, M-15, M-16, p 117
  fa, B-99; W, B-100, p 120
  V, S-42, p 121
  M-27, p 144 (to Marie Anne Despard)
Rivet, Michel
  W, S-65, p 133

B-194, p 144
Sylvestre, Jean Baptiste
  W, B, M, Soderini, betw 116-117
Tamarle, Marguerite
  mo, M-8, p 158
Tami-swala
  fa, B-18, p 97
Tanakon, Susanne *[Tawakon]*
  W, B-8, p 92
Tas-Mikt, Thomas
  B-65, p 33
Tassivik
  9, B-79, p 34
Tawakon, Andre
  B-8, p 92
Tawakon, Catherine
  (and Andre St. Martin)
  mo, B-37; W, B-38, p 54
  W, B-124
  W, B-195, p 145
Tawakon, Philomene
  B-189, p 143
Tawakon, Susanne
  (and Amable Petit)
  mo, B-8, B-9, p 4
  W, B-3, p 46
  mo, B-68, p 56
  W, B-9, p 73 (prob)
  W, B-12, p 74
  W, B-61, B-63, p 87
  W, B-65, p 88
  mo, B-55, p 110
  W, B-80, p 115
  W, B-91, B-92, p 118
  W, B-111, p 124
  W, B-185, p 141
Tawakon, Thomas
  (and Louise Walla Walla)
  fa, B-8, p 92
  fa, B-189, p 143
Taylor, Jane
  mo, B-22, p 76
  M-4, p 79 (to Walter John Pomeroy)
Tchilis - see Chehalis
Tchapihk, Thomas
  B-30, p 10
  B, p 166
Tchinook see Chinook
Tchokiva menak
  B-79, p 34
Tckawas, Klikitat
  mo, B-304, p 21
Teller - see Raylor
Tennessee, U.S.A.
  B-273, p 16
  M-9, p 17
Tepathels, Chinook
  mo, B-337, p 24
Tetana, Klikitat *[Sekana?]*

fa, B-304, p 21
Tetana, Andre Klikitat
  B-304, p 21
Tete-plate - see Flathead
Tianesse, Baptiste
  (and Marie Sapete)
  fa, B-21, p 26
Tianesse, Rosalie
  B-21, p 26
Tifant, Josephte
  mo, M-3, p 48
Tjokoak
  3 B-10, 11, 12, p 48
Tkekivamus, tribe
  B-256, p 12
Tlackamus - see Clackamas
Tlakas, Indian
  (and Lizette . . .)
  fa, B-54, p 83
Tlakas, Francois
  B-54, p 83
  S-12, p 84
Tlamak - see Klamath
Tlawillala, at
  2 B-8, 9; 3 B-10, 11, 12, p 48
Tobin - see Jobin
Toupin, Francois
  L, M-4, p 28
  B-37, p 30
  W, B-22, p 52
  M-1, p 148 (to Angelique Lonetain)
Toupin, Jean Baptiste
  W, M-3, p 28
  M-4, p 28 (to Marie Dorion)
  fa, B-37, p 30
  S-fa, M-8, p 32
  fa, W, M-8, p 37 *[as Joseph?]*
  fa, M-1, p 148
Toupin, Joseph *[Jean Baptiste?]*
  fa, W, M-8, p 37
Toupin, Marie Anne
  W, B-26, p 27
  L, M-4, p 28
  M-8, p 37 (to David Gervais)
  mo, B-69, p 57
  W, B-26, p 77
  W, B-7, p 91
Toussaint, Genevieve
  (and Pierre Laroque I)
  mo, S-14, p 100
Toussaint, Marie
  (and Louis Laroque)
  mo, B-64, p 87
  W, B-17, p 97
  W, B-77, p 114
  mo, B-145, p 134
Tsapete, Emelie
  B-268, M-6, p 14 (to Joseph Leno)
  mo, B-18, p 50

CATHOLIC CHURCH RECORDS

of the

PACIFIC NORTHWEST

St. Paul, Oregon

Vol. II

[2 blue pages set-in in the beginning of the volume.]
[The first:]

St. Paul, Marion Co., Oregon, Nov. 21, 1864 (probably)

School district No.
Bill of the expenses of the building of a new school house for the said district.

1. the buying of a wrecked house	$60.00
2. the taking down and putting up of the same	100.00
3. 10 windows - at $3.00 a pair	30.00
4. 600 feet of sealing $10.00	
1200 feet of weatherboard $10.00	20.00
5. 2½ barels of nails at 8 cts.	20.00
6. ½ gross of screws and a lock	2.00
7. 2500 of shingles at $3.00 and 13 joists $7.50 25 long 2 by 10	15.00

Extras

1. 8 wagonloads at $2.00	16.00
2. 1 top cheminey	2.50
3. 1 large platform	4.00
4. 2 large benches	2.00
5. the puting of an extra sealing	6.00
1 large stove	*- 12.00
	289.50

The second:

St. Paul 10 Jan. 1846
Agreement between Chs. Petit, natural father, and Frs. Brouillard foster-father of Felicite, daughter of the late Olive Forcier, wife of the said Frs. Brouillard: done at the house of the Pastor J. F. I. Malo, priest.

It is understood:
First that the child will be put *[to live]* at the house of Amable Petit, grandfather of the child, as the charge of Chs. Petit, father of the child,

Second that if the child is not well treated with regard to nourishment, clothing and education Frs. Brouillard foster-father of the child will have the right to take her back with the condition that he raise her well in his turn.

Signed
Charles Petit

Witnesses   J. F. Malo, priest   Francois (X) Brouillard
                Narcisse (X) Gingras

[Another set-in page:]
Copy

This English copy of the Act of Marriage must be sent within 30 days to the Register or Clerk of the County-Seat of each County (here, Salem) with one dollar for the Clerk. In virtue of a law of the State passed Oct. 1862, and in force 15 Jan. '63. There is a fine of $5.00 for each day late after the 30 days granted by the law have passed away.

State of Oregon
County of Marion
       This is to certify that the undersigned Priest of the church of St. Paul, in aforesaid County, by authority of a license, bearing date the . . . th day of . . . A.D. 1863 and issued by the County Clerk of the County of Marion did on the . . . th day of . . . A.D. 186 . . . in the said church of St. Paul in the county and State aforesaid, join in lawful wedlock Peter so and so, and Catherine dito (both of the said County of Marion) with their mutual assent in the presence of P. and fn witnesses

J. F. Malo, priest
of St. Paul Church

[The pages in this volume are numbered on each side of each page:]
p 1

B-1 Leocadie Marie Bernier	The 27 August, 1847, we the undersigned priest have baptized Leocadie Marie *[born]* two days ago of the legitimate marriage of Francois Bernier and of Pelagie Lucier, godfather Louis Pichet, godmother Marguerite Bercier who could not sign.

McCormick

S-1
Jean
Laprade

The 31 *[sic]* September, 1847, we the undersigned priest have buried in the cemetery of this parish the body of Jean, aged 7 months, legitimate child of Alexis Laprade and of Nancy Pion. Present Amable Petit, Louis Nota who could not sign.

Mod. Demers, priest

Profession
of faith
of Marie
Tlamath

The 5 September, 1847, Mary, Indian woman of Wallamet has abjured before us the undersigned the Methodist religion; and we have received her public profession of faith in the Catholic Religion, Apostolic and Roman; in the presence of Pierre Bellique and of Jean Baptiste Dubreuil who could not sign.

Mod. Demers, priest

B-2
Marie
Tlamath

The 5 September, 1847, we the undersigned priest have baptized conditionally Mary, Tlamath tribe, aged about 26 years; godfather Pierre Bellique, Godmother Jany St. Martin who could not sign.

Mod. Demers, priest

B-3
Marie

The 19 September, 1847, we the undersigned priest have baptized Marie, born the day before of infidel parents. The godfather has been Andre Plourde, the godmother Marie.

A. Langlois, priest

p 2
B-4
[Calboro]
[Scarborough?]

The 16 September, 1847, we undersigned have baptized Jean Calbero, aged 2 or 3 years, son of Calbeto, Captain of a ship. Godfather Joseph Gervais, godmother Marie St. Martin all of the parish of St. Paul.

Pretot, priest

B-5
*[Marguerite
Laframboise]*

The 19 September, 1847, we undersigned have baptized Marguerite Laframboise daughter of *[Francois]* Laframboise of Vancouver. The godfather has been Amable Arquoitte and the godmother Marguerite Arquoitee, both of the parish of St. Paul

Pretot, priest

S-2
Marie
Indian

The 23 September, 1847, we the undersigned priest have buried in the cemetery of this parish the body of Marie, young girl about 12 years, of infidel parents and baptized some days ago on her death bed at the house of Jean Bte Aubichon. Present at the burial Charles Groslouis, Antoine Cloutier and others -

A. Langlois, priest

B-6

The 2 October, 1847, we undersigned priest have baptized . . . Godfather Laurent, Iroquois, godmother his wife, Therese.

Mod. Demers, priest

B-7
Joseph
Bourgeau

The 24 October, 1847, we the undersigned priest have baptized Joseph, born yesterday of the legitimate marriage of Silvain Bourgeau and of Josephte, Indian; godfather, Joseph Bourgeau, godmother Angele Lafantaisie.

Mod. Demers, priest

B-8
Paul
Chamberland

The 6 October, 1847, we undersigned have baptized Paul, born 2 days ago, legitimate child of Adolphe Chamberland and of Julienne Waticie; godfather Paul Guilbeau, godmother Katy, his wife, who could not sign.

F. Norbert, Archbishop of
Oregon City

[Note the skip in dates from October, 1847, to May, 1848. Evidently the field notes on the final three pages of Book One cover this time, never written up in register.]

1848

B-9

The 1 May has been baptized Louis Vassal, dangerously ill, aged about

Ls.
Vassal
p 3
B-10
Mathilde
Rivet

25 years.

A. Langlois, priest

The 9 May, 1848, we the undersigned priest have baptized Mathilde, born the day before of the legitimate marriage of Joseph Rivet, farmer, and of Marie Anne Despart of this parish. Godfather Mr. Portus, godmother Sophie Gregoire. The godfather alone has undersigned.
Willm Porteus
A. Langlois, priest

B-11
Marie

The 2 August, 1848, we the undersigned priest have baptized at the house of Amable Arquoit an Indian woman in danger of death and have given her the name of Marie. Not any godfather or godmother at all.
J. B. Z. Bolduc, priest

S-3
Marie

The 3[August crossed out] February [?], 1848, we the undersigned priest have buried in the cemetery of this parish the body of Marie, Indian woman baptized yesterday in the presence of Amable Petit who could not sign.
F. Veyret, priest

[B no #]
[Paul]
[Manot]

The 5 [August crossed out] February [?], 1848, we the undersigned priest have given baptism to an Indian child about 2 years, son of Manot, Indian of Lacamaye. We have given him the name of Paul; godfather has been Andre.
F. Veyret, priest

B-12
Celeste
Jeaudoin

The 9 [August crossed out] February [?], 1848, we the undersigned priest have given baptism to a child born yesterday of Elisabeth Hubert and of Baptiste Jodoin. We have given her the name of Celeste. The godfather has been Augustin Rocham and the godmother Rose Ossand.
F. Veyret, priest

B-13
[Pierre
Indian
Child]

The 10 February [?], 1848, we the undersigned priest have given baptism to an Indian child about 2 years. We have given him the name Pierre, the godfather has been Jacques Servant, the godmother, his wife Josephte.
Veyret, priest

[There are here 2½ blank pages. These were apparently meant for entries from the field notes on pages 171-173, Book I, but never transcribed except for S-4 and S-5)
1848

p 4
S-4
Marguerite
widow
of
H.
Lavigueur

The 1 April, 1848, we the undersigned priest have buried in the cemetery of this mission the body of Marguerite widow of the late Lavigueur deceased day before yesterday at her usual dwelling, in the presence of Amable Petit and of Cuthbert Lambert, who could not sign.
J. B. Z. Bolduc, priest

B-14

The 2 April, 1848, we the undersigned priest have baptized a young Indian, about 17 years, under the name of Louis. The godfather has been Louis Lebrun.
Veyret, priest

B-15

The 13 April, 1848, we the undersigned priest have baptized Magdeleine legitimate daughter of Thomas Georges and of Josette, Indian, born 6 days ago. The godfather has been Brulle.
Ls. P. G. Rousseau, priest

S-5

The 21 April, 1848, we the undersigned priest have buried in the cemetery of this mission the body of Louis, young Indian deceased Yesterday, at the house of Bernier, Francois.
Veyret, priest

S-6
Charles
Jeaudoin

The 2 May, 1848, we the undersigned priest have buried in the cemetery of this mission the body of Charles Jeaudoin, deceased day before yesterday, in the presence of Amable Petit and of Augustin Rochon, who could not sign.
J. B. Z. Bolduc, priest

S-7

The 5 May, 1848, we the undersigned priest have buried in the cemetery of this mission the body of . . . , young Indian living at the house of Alexis

Aubichon, deceased yesterday in the presence of Alexis Aubichon and of Amable Petit, who could not sign.

F. Veyret, priest

S-8

The 7 May, 1848, we the undersigned priest have buried in the cemetery of this mission the body of Thomas deceased day before yesterday at the house of Joseph McLoughlin, aged about 28 years, in the presence of Paul Guilbeau and of Amable Petit, who could not sign.

J. B. Z. Bolduc, priest

p 5
S-9

The 9 May has been buried in the cemetery of this parish the body of . . . deceased the day before, legitimate child of Thomas, Christian for some time and also dead. Present Charles Petit and McBeen.

A. Langlois, priest

S-10
Elisabeth
McKay

The 16 May, 1848, we the undersigned priest have buried in the cemetery of this mission the body of Elisabeth deceased day before yesterday at the place of the Sisters of Notre Dame at the age of about 14 years and 6 months, in the presence of Amable Petit and of Augustin Garant who could not sign.

J. B. Z. Bolduc, priest

B-16
Marie
Philomene
Chalifoux

The 16 May, 1848, we the undersigned priest have baptized Marie Philomene born today of the Legitimate marriage of Andre Chalifoux and of Catherine Russie. Godfather David Mongrain, godmother . . . Pelletier who could not sign.

J. B. Z. Bolduc, priest

B-17
Archange
Shohoanni

The 19 May, 1848, we the undersigned priest have baptized Archange born yesterday of the legitimate marriage of Jean Baptiste Shohoanni and of Marie Pend'Oreille woman. The godfather has been Augustin Raymond and the godmother Marie Servant who could not sign.

J. B. Z. Bolduc, priest

S-11
Sara
Labonte

The 20 May, 1848, we the undersigned priest have buried in the cemetery of this mission the body of Sara, deceased day before yesterday at the age of 2 months, in the presence of Sieur Joseph McLoughlin and of Amable Petit, the first alone has signed with us.

Joseph McLoughlin
A. Langlois, priest

B-18
Profession
of faith
of
Cecelia
Lauson
[Lawson]

The 20 May, 1848, we the undersigned priest have received the profession of faith of Cecelia Lauson, wife of James McKay, who has renounced the sect which she had professed until this day, to embrace and profess publicly the Catholic Religion, Apostolic and Roman. The Reverends Achille Lebas; Antoine Langlois have been witnesses and have signed with us.

(No signatures)
F. N. Archbishop of
Oregon City

p 6
B-19
Cecelia
Lauson

The 20 May, 1848, we undersigned have baptized Cecelia, aged about 25 years. Godmother Mary Cosgrove, who could not sign.

F. N. Archbishop
of Oregon City

S-12
Josephte
wife of
L. Sauve

The . . . 1848, we the undersigned priest have buried in the cemetery of this mission the body of Josephte [Tsik], deceased the day before yesterday, in the presence of Jean Baptiste Dalcourt and of Amable Petit who could not sign.

A. Langlois, priest

B-20

The 20 June, 1848, we the undersigned priest have baptized an Indian woman sheltered at the house of Charles Plante for many years, and dangerously ill.

A. Langlois, priest

B-21
[Hubert]

The 24 June, 1848, we the undersigned priest have baptized the young man living at the house of Laurent Sauve, of infidel parents towards California, aged about 17 or 18 years and known under the name of Hubert. This name

has also been his baptismal name. The godfather has been Laurent Sauve.
A. Langlois, priest

B-22
Joseph
dit
Jacques

The 24 June, 1848, we the undersigned priest have baptized Joseph, young man aged about 18 years, of infidel parents, and sheltered at the house of Michel Laframboise since 10 years. The godfather has been Cezaire Beaudouin.
A. Langlois, priest

B-23
Joseph
Thomas
dit
Brule

The 24 June, 1848, we the undersigned priest have baptized Joseph, young man about 18 or 19 years, (metis) of a Canadian Iroquois now dead a long time and of the woman of the name . . . Brule. The godfather has been Pierre Bellique.
A. Langlois, priest

p 7
B-24
Joseph
Smith

The 24 June, 1848, we the undersigned priest have baptized Joseph, young man residing at the house of Robillard, aged about 17 or 18 years of infidel parents. The godfather has been . . . Robillard, the godmother . . .
A. Langlois, priest

B-25
Marie
Anne
Bastien

The 28 June, 1848, we the undersigned priest have baptized conditionally Marie Anne, aged 15 years at least. Raised at the Methodist Mission, she had for her father one named Bastien, whom she has not known, and for mother an infidel woman of the Saste tribe. The godfather has been Amable Petit; the godmother Marguerite Cosgrow. [Cosgrove] Abjuration made the same day.
A. Langlois, priest

B-26
Pierre
P.
Pierriche

The 29 June, 1848, we the undersigned priest have baptized Pierre Paul Pierriche, Indian, aged about 22 years, raised amidst the Canadians. God-father Pierre Bellique, godmother Genevieve St. Martin.
A. Langlois, priest

B-27
Agathe
Pierriche

The 29 June, 1848, we the undersigned priest have baptized Agathe, aged about 18 years, of infidel parents, already wife of one Pierriche by name, since 4 or 5 years. The godfather has been Frederic Despart, the godmother Genevieve St. Martin.
A. Langlois, priest

M-1
Pierre
P.
Pierriche
and
Agathe

The 29 June, 1848, we the undersigned priest have received the mutual consent to marriage and we have given the nuptial benediction to one named Pierre P. Pierriche and Agathe, both Indians, baptized the same day, and already allied since 4 or 5 years in the Indian manner, the publication of the bans of marriage having been dispensed by Monsgr. the Archbishop of Oregon City. The witnesses have been Pierre Bellique and Frederic Despart. The said spouses recognize as their legitimate child Pierre aged 2 years.
A. Langlois, priest missionary
officiating in this place.

p. 8
B-28
Catherine
Atalo

The 2 July, 1848, we the undersigned priest have baptized Catherine, aged about 20 and some years, of infidel Chinouk tribe; the godfather has been Amable Petit, the godmother Suzanne, his wife.
A. Langlois, priest

M-2
Ls
Vassal
and
Catherine
Indian

The 2 July, 1848, we the undersigned priest, officiating in this place have received the mutual consent to marriage of Louis Vassal domiciled at the Grande Prairie near St. Louis, adult recently baptized, aged about 22 years and of Catherine baptized the same day, of infidel parents and already married or allied to the said bridegroom since several years in the manner of the infidels of the country, and have given them the nuptial benediction in the presence of Amable Petit and . . . The said spouses recognize as their legitimate children Victoire, aged 2 years, and Flore aged 3 months.
A. Langlois, priest

S-13

The 6 July, died the Indian [female] baptized at the house of C. Plante, buried in the cemetery [in] presence of Amable and of Charles Petit.
A. Langlois, priest

p 9
M-3
Simon
Plamondon
and
M. L. H.
Pelletier

The 10 July, 1848, in view of the publication of 1 ban of marriage and the dispensation of 2 others granted by us Archbishop undersigned, between Simon Plamondon, farmer, domiciled at St. Francois Xavier of the Cowlitz, of-age, widower of Felicite of Launais *[some words crossed out]*, on the one part and Marie Louise Henriette Pelletier, of-age daughter of the late Jean Baptiste Pelletier and of the late Rose Blanchet, the father and mother of the parish of St. Francois of the River du Sud Province of Lower Canada (Quebec) on the other part; nor having discovered any impediment, the dispensation of publication in the parish of the said groom having also been granted because of the inconveniences of communication, in special prayers We Archbishop undersigned have received their mutual consent to marriage and have given them the nuptial benediction in the presence of Andre Chalifou, L. Pichet, P. Bellique and Soulange Pelletier.

Solanges Peltier   Marie Louise
Frs. (X) Bernier   Henriette Pelletier
Pierre (X) Bellique
Ls (X) Pichet   Simon (X) Plamondon
A (X) Chalifou

F.N. Archbishop of Oregon City

B-29
Narcisse
Tellier

The 10 July, 1848, we the undersigned have baptized Narcisse born the day before of the legitimate marriage of Louis Tellier and of Angelique, Pendoreille, of St. Paul. Godfather Augustin Raimond, godmother Marie Servant.

F. N. Archbishop of Oregon City

B-30
Louise
Soulanges
Pichet

The 16 July, 1848, we undersigned have baptized Louise Soulanges, born yesterday of the legitimate marriage of Louis Pichet, farmer and of Marguerite Bercier, of St. Paul. Godfather Hercule Lebrun, godmother Soulanges Peltier.

F. N. Archbishop of Oregon City

M-4
Amable
Arquoite
and
Marie
Anne
Norwest

The 17 July, 1848, in view of the dispensation of publication of 1 ban of marriage granted by Us undersigned and the publication of 2 others between Amable Arquoite, domiciled in this place, minor son of Amable Arquoite, farmer, and of Marguerite Tchinouk of St. Paul, on the one part, and Marie Anne Norwest, domiciled in this place, minor daughter of Jean Baptiste Norwest, farmer, and of the late Judith, also of St. Paul, on the other part; nor having discovered any impediment, and with the consent of the parents, We have received their mutual consent to marriage and have given them the nuptial benediction in the presence of Alexis Aubichon and of Michel Laframboise and of many other relatives and friends.

F. N. Archbishop of Oregon City

p. 10
B-31
Eulalie
Deguire

The 23 July, 1848, we the undersigned priest have Baptized Eulalie, born the day before of the legitimate marriage of Jean Baptiste Deguire and of Marie Anne Perrault, domiciled in this parish on the other side of the Wallamet River. The godfather has been John Larisson and the godmother Reine Oerrault.

Ant. Langlois, priest

M-5
James
Boucher
and
Rosalie
Plouf

The 24 July, 1848, after the publication of three bans of marriage made at the sermons of our parish Mass between James *[one word crossed out]* Boucher, farmer, domiciled in this parish, of-age son of Wakan Boucher and of Nancy McDougal, employed in the service of the Hudson's Bay Company, in the country of the Carriers, on the one part and Rosalie Plouf, minor daughter of the late Plouf *[Antoine]* and of a woman of the Chaudieres on the other part, nor having discovered any impediment, we the undersigned priest have received their mutual consent to marriage and have given them the nuptial benediction in the presence of Fabien Malouin and of John Young, friends of the groom, of Joseph Plouf, as guardian of the girl, consenting, and of Angelique Dubois, friend of the bride who, as well as the

**B-32
Evariste
Saste**

said spouses could not sign. 1 word effaced nul, 1 word above the line good. The 24 July, 1848, we the undersigned priest have baptized Evariste born the same day of the legitimate marriage of Michel Saste and of Rose, both living among the Canadians of the locality, but of an infidel tribe. Godfather Laurent Sauve, godmother Agathe Champagne.

A. Langlois

**p 11
M-6
Joseph
Brule
and
Maranda**

The 7 August, 1848, in view of the publication of 1 ban of marriage and the dispensation of 2 other bans granted by Mnsr. the Archbishop of Oregon City between Joseph Brule, minor son of the late Jacques Iroquois and of Marguerite Brule of this parish on the one part; and Marie Anne Maranda dit Le Frise and of . . . of this parish on the other part, nor having discovered any impediment, we the undersigned priest, missionary of this place, have received their mutual consent to marriage and have given them the nuptial benediction in the presence of Jean Baptiste Brule foster-father and step-father of the groom, consenting as well as the mother, and of Louis Maranda, dit Le Frise, father of the bride, consenting. All having declared not able to sign.

A. Langlois, priest

**M-7
Hercule
Lebrun
and
M. A.
Ouvrie**

The 18 September, 1848, in view of the dispensation of two *[bans]* granted by Us and the publication of the third between Hercule Lebrun, landowner *[proprietaire]* of this place, of-age son of the late Charles Lebrun and of Marie Anne Lemire of St. Joseph Maskinenge, Canada, on the one part, and Marie Anne Ouvre, minor daughter of the late Jean Baptiste Ouvre and a woman of the Cowlitz on the other part, nor having discovered any impediment, We undersigned have received their mutual consent to marriage and have given them the nuptial benediction in the presence of Joseph Gervais and of Andre Chalifou, witnesses who could not sign. The spouses have signed.

[no signatures]
F. N. Archbishop of Oregon City

**B-33
Elise
Gervais**

The 17 September, 1848, we the undersigned priest have given baptism to a child born in April 1847 of Baptiste Gervet and of Marie Ussi *[Lucier]*. We have given her the name of Elise. The godfather has been Louis Pichet, the godmother Marguerite Russie.

Veyret, priest

**B-34
Marie**

The 24 September, 1848, we the undersigned priest have given baptism to an Indian woman, widow of one Wagui, coming from Fort Vancouver, at the house of Plante. We have given her the name of Marie. The godfather has been the elder Plante.

Veyret, priest

**p 12
B-35
Marcelle
Reimond**

The 1 October, 1848, we the undersigned priest have given baptism conditionally to a child of Augustin Reimond, farmer at St. Paul and of Marie his wife, born the 29 February 1848. We have given him the name of Marcelle. The godfather has been Louis Bergevin and the godmother Magdeleine Servant.

Veyret, priest

**B-36
Nicolas
Andreson**

The 1 October, 1848, we the undersigned priest have given baptism conditionally to a child born of John Andreson living at St. Paul and of Elisabeth his wife, 8 or 9 months ago. We have given him the name of Nicolas. The godfather has been Antoine Rivet, the godmother Catherine the wife of Hord.

Veyret, priest

**B-37
Marie**

The 2 October, 1848, we the undersigned priest have given at the house of Dompierre, resident of St. Paul, baptism to an Indian child. Her name has been Marie, her godfather Dompierre, her godmother the wife of Dompierre.

Veyret, priest

B-38
Jean

The 6 October, 1848, we undersigned have given baptism to an Indian *[male]* in danger *[of death]* living at the house of Bellique. We have given him the name of Jean. The godfather has been Pierre Bellique, the godmother the wife of Pierre Bellique.

Veyret, priest

M-8
Edouard
Dupuis
and
Marguerite
Anne
Dickerson

On the 9th day of October, 1848, I the undersigned married in the city of Champoeg Edouard Dupuis to Marguerite Anne Dickerson in the presence of the undersigned witnesses.

Patrick J. McCormick *[priest]*
Edward Depuis *[sic]*
Margaret Anne Dickerson
David McLoughlin
F. X. Mathieu

B-39
Guillaume
Canada

The 22 October, 1848, we the undersigned priest have given baptism to a child of Baine Canada and of . . . Here living at St. Paul. We have given him the name of Guillaume *[William]*. The godfather has been Thomas and the godmother . . . wife *[Indecipherable]*.

Veyret, priest

p 13
B-40
Marie
Andreson

The 29 October, 1848, we undersigned have given baptism to a little child born 6 weeks ago of Peter Andreson and of Angelique Carpentier living in the camp of the Americans above St. Louis. We have given her the name of Marie. The godfather has been Amable Petit, the godmother the wife of Petit.

Veyret, priest

M-9
Louis
Bergevin
and
Magdeleine
Servant

The 23 October, 1848, we the undersigned priest, after the publication of 2 bans made two consecutive Sundays, the third having been dispensed, and not having discovered any impediment, have received the mutual consent to marriage of Louis Bergevin, landowner at St. Paul, son of Jean *[?]* Charles Bergevin and of Marie Giroux living at St. Martin *[one word indecipherable]* canada, on the one part - and of Magdeliene Servant, widow of the late Jodoin, daughter Jacques Servant and of Josette enguinangen (Okanagan) in the presence of M. M. Dubreuil, Adolphe Chamberlan, Louis Assan, Lamber, Antoine Lucier.

Veyret, priest

S-14
Jean
Indian

The 28 October, 1848, we the undersigned priest have buried in the cemetery of this mission the body of Jean Indian deceased yesterday at the house of Pierre Bellique, aged about 30 years, in the presence of Amable Petit and of Pierre Bellique.

Veyret, priest

M-10
Paul
Guilbeau
and
Francaise

The 6 November, 1848, the publication of three bans having been made, we the undersigned received the mutual consent to marriage of Paul Guilbeau, land-owner at St. Paul, Wallamette, widower of the late Marguerite of Walla walla on the one part; and of Francaise of Wallawalla, widow of the late Tomwokon, in the presence of M. M. Dubreuil, Chanberlan, Fabien Malouis, B. Dalcour.

F. N. Archbishop of Oregon City

B-41
Cyrille
Bertrand

The 12 November, 1848, We undersigned have given baptism to Cyrille born yesterday, son of Cyrille Bertrand and of Marguerite Servant. We have given him the name of Cyrille. The godfather has been Jacques Servant and the godmother Ann Cosgrow.

F. N. Archbishop of Oregon City

P 14
B-42
Julie
Pepin

The 15 November, 1848, we undersigned have given baptism to a daughter born Yesterday of Pierre Pepin and of Suzanne Gaudrich, living at St. Paul. We have given her the name of Julie. The godfather has been J. B. Dubreuil, the godmother Genevieve, wife of Bellique.

Veyret, priest

S-15

The 16 November, 1848, we undersigned have buried in the cemetery of

Celeste Jaudoin	this parish the body of Celeste Jaudoin aged 2 months in the presence of Augustin Rochond and of Amable Petit.
	Veyret, priest
B-43 J. B. Plouf dit Carillon	The 17 November, 1848, we the undersigned priest have given baptism to a child born the 15 November, of Joseph Plouf dit Carillon and of Therese. We have given him the name of Jean Baptiste. The godfather has been J. B. Jodoin, the godmother Celeste, wife of Rochon.
	Veyret, priest
S-16 Marie	The 18 November, 1848, we the undersigned priest have buried in the cemetery of this parish the body of Marie, Indian, deceased yesterday at the house of Plante, in the presence of Amable Petit.
	Veyret, priest
B-44 Honore King	The 19 November, 1848, we undersigned have given baptism to a child born day before yesterday of Honore King and of Marianne . . . , living at St. Paul. We have given him the name of Honore. The godfather has been Joseph Laferte, the godmother Catherine Longtain.
	Veyret, priest
S-17 Son of Gedeon Senecal	The 20 November, 1848, we the undersigned have buried a child of Gedeon Senecal and of Marianne Grenier, baptized privately the day before by his father. In the present of Amable Petit.
	Veyret, priest
B-45 Suzanne Beaudoin	The 22 November, 1848, we the undersigned have supplied the ceremonies of Baptism for Suzanne born yesterday of the legitimate marriage of Cezaire Beaudoin and of Sophie Carpentier, and privately baptized by Amable Petit. The godfather Sauve, the godmother Suzanne wife of Petit.
	Veyret, priest
P 15 S-18 Marguerite Servant wife of Bertrand	The 30 November, 1848, we the undersigned priest of this parish have buried in the cemetery of this parish the body of Marguerite Servant, wife of . . . Bertrand, deceased the day before yesterday, in the presence of Louis Pichet and Amable Petit.
	Veyret, priest
S-19 Joseph McLoughlin	The 23 December, 1848, we the undersigned priest, parish priest of St. Paul, have buried in the cemetery of this parish the body of Joseph McLoughlin, aged about 38 years, deceased the 14 of the month, in the presence of Monsieur J.B.Z. Bolduc and Amable Petit, and so forth.
	L. A. LeBas priest, Miss. Apost.
S-20 Amable Petit	The 26 December, 1848, we the undersigned priest, parish priest of St. Paul, have buried in the cemetery of this parish the body of Amable, son of Amable Petit, deceased the 24 of the month in the presence of Amable Petit.
	L. A. LeBas priest, miss. apost.
B-46 Joseph Biscornet	The 27 December, 1848, we the undersigned priest, parish priest of St. Paul have baptized Joseph, legitimate son of Pascal Biscornet and of Louise, domiciled at the Bute de Sable; the godfather has been Amable Arquot and the godmother Rose Haussent wife of Mathieu.
	L. A. LeBas priest, miss. apost.
	1849
S-1 Angelique Servant	The 7 January, 1849, we the undersigned priest, parish priest of St. Paul, have buried in the cemetery of this parish the body of Angelique Servant, aged 11 years, daughter of Jacques Servant, deceased yesterday, in the presence of Amable Petit and etc.
	L. A. LeBas priest, miss. apost.
M-1 Antoine Lucier	The 8 January, 1849, we the undersigned priest, parish priest of St. Paul, after the publication of three bans, namely, the 1st, the 6th and the 9th of January, without having found any impediment, have received the mutual

and
Julie
Aubichon

consent to marriage of Antoine Lucier, living in this parish, son of the late Antoine Lucier and of Charlotte Desnoyer of Canada, and of Julie Aubichon, minor daughter of Alexis Aubichon and of Marianne, living at the Bute de Sable at the house of her father, in the presence of Messires Etienne Lucier, uncle of the groom, living in the parish of St. Louis, and so on -

L. A. LeBas,
priest, miss. apost.

p 16
B-1
Hugue
Cosgrow

The 11 January, 1849, we the undersigned priest, parish priest of St. Paul, have baptized Hugue Claude, legitimate son of Hugue Cosgrow and of Mary Roster of this parish. The godfather has been Thomas Hunt and the godmother Cecile Lauson Madame McKay, born yesterday.

L. A. LeBas
priest, miss. apost.

S-2
Pierre
Indian

The 13 January, 1849, we the undersigned priest, Director of St. Joseph's College, have buried in the cemetery of this parish the body of Pierre, aged about 2 years and a half, Indian child, deceased yesterday at the house of Remond, in the presence of Amable Petit, etc.

Veyret, priest

S-3
Angelique
Couturier

The 14 January, 1849, we the undersigned priest, parish priest of St. Paul, have buried the body of Marie, legitimate daughter of the late Baptiste Coururier and of Angelique, in the cemetery of this parish, aged 3 years, deceased yesterday at the house of Jean Baptiste Sotshohoanni, dit Ignace, in the presence of Amable Petit and Jean Baptiste Nordwest, etc.

L. A. LeBas,
priest, Miss. apost.

B-2
Marie
Bellandgio
Alipas

The 21 January, 1849, we the undersigned priest, parish-priest of St. Paul, have baptized Marie, legitimate daughter of Bellandgio, Spaniard of nationality, and of Louise, born the 29 of last month at Champoag of this parish. The godfather has been Joseph Picard and the godmother Marie Servant Madame Raimond, both of this parish.

L. A. LeBas,
priest, miss. apost.

B-3
Thomas
Spokan

The 27 January, 1849, we the undersigned priest, parish priest of St. Paul, have baptized Thomas Spokan Indian aged about 20 years, in danger of death, at the house of Michel Laframboise. The godfather has been Joseph Smit, baptized Indian, and Emelie Picard, wife of Michel Laframboise, both of this parish.

L. A. LeBas,
priest, miss. apost.

S-4
Thomas
Spokan

We the undersigned priest, parish priest of St. Paul, today, 30 January, 1849, have buried in the cemetery of this parish the body of Thomas Spokan, Indian deceased yesterday at the house of Michel Laframboise, in the presence of Amable Petit, etc.

L. A. LeBas,
priest, miss. apost.

p 17
M-2
Thanier
Liard
and
Celeste
Rochbrune

The 5 February, 1849, we undersigned priest, parish priest of St. Paul, after the publication of two bans made at the sermon of the parish Mass, in this church as well as that of St. Louis, the 28 January and the 4 February, the parties having obtained dispensation of the third ban in the two churches, without having found any impediment, we received the mutual consent to marriage of Thanier Liard, widower in his first marriage of Catherine, living in this parish and of Celeste minor daughter of Joseph Rochbrune and of Louise, living at the house of her father, in the parish of St. Louis, in the presence of the father of the girl and also in the presence of Messires Hercule Lebrun and of Xavier Liard, the last brother of the groom, inhabitants of this parish, besides Pierre Lacourse and many others, some have signed, the others have made their cross.

Hercule Lebrun mark of the bride Celeste
(X)
mark of the father
mark of Pierre Lacourse (X)
(X)
L. A. LeBas
priest, miss. apost.

S-5
Child of
Silvain
Bourgeau

The 8 February, 1849, we the undersigned priest, Director of St. Joseph's College, have buried in the cemetery of this parish the body of a child privately baptized by Louis Assent and deceased yesterday, legitimate son of Silvain Bourgeau, in the presence of Amable Petit, etc.

Veyret, priest

S-6
Cyrille
Bertrand

The 19 February, 1849, we the undersigned priest, parish priest at St. Paul, have buried in the cemetery of this parish the body of Cyrille, legitimate son of Syrille Bertrand and the late Marguerite Servant, deceased yesterday, aged 3 months and 8 days, in the presence of Amable Petit.

L. A. LeBas
priest, miss. apost.

B-4
Francois
St. Martin

The 22 February, 1849, we the undersigned priest, parish priest officiating at St. Paul, have baptized Francois legitimate son of Andre St. Martin and of Catherine, his wife, born this day; the godfather Amable Petit, the godmother Marguerite Lucier, all of this parish.

L. A. LeBas,
priest, miss. apost.

B-5
Paul
Russie

The 10 March, 1849, we the undersigned priest, parish priest officiating at St. Paul, have baptized Paul, legitimate son of Auguste Russie and of Anne Nordwest, his wife, born today; the godfather Andre Chalifoux, the godmother Catherine Russie, all of this parish.

L. A. LeBas,
priest, miss. apost.

p 18
B-6
Louise
Indian

The 10 March, 1849, we the undersigned priest, parish priest officiating at St. Paul, have baptized Louise, daughter of an Indian, Okinagan, aged about 5 years, the godfather Andre Chalifoux, the godmother Catherine Russie, all of this parish.

L. A. LeBas,
priest, miss. apost.

B-7
Louis
Indian

The 10 March, 1849, we the undersigned priest, parish priest officiating at St. Paul, have baptized Louis, brother of the above mentioned Louise; the godfather Amable Petit, the godmother Marie Madame Robillard, all of this parish.

L. A. LeBas,
priest, miss. apost.

B-8
Josette
Calapouias

The 28 March, 1849, we the undersigned priest, parish priest officiating at St. Paul, have baptized Josette born day before yesterday of the legitimate marriage of Paul Pierre Calapouias and of Agate, his wife. The godfather Amable Petit, the godmother Genevieve, wife of Pierre Bellique, all living in this parish.

L. A. LeBas,
priest, miss. apost.

B-9
J. Baptiste
Pawauaitit

The 1 April, 1849, we the undersigned priest, parish priest officiating at St. Paul, have baptized Jean Baptiste Pawouaitit, aged about 45 years, of the tribe of Yiakmas, born of Indian parents, in the presence of Casimir Chirous, Reverend Father P. Oblate of Marie Immaculate.

L. A. LeBas,
priest, miss. apost.
C. Chirous, OMI

Benediction
of the

The 3 April, 1849, we the undersigned parish priest officiating at St. Paul, have, with the authorization of Monseigneur the Archbishop of Oregon

Cemetery	City, made the benediction of a cemetery reserved to the Sisters of Notre Dame in the interior of their garden in the above day and year, assisted by Monsieur Veyret, Superior of the College of St. Joseph, bursar of the same school, and of the Rd. P. Chirouse, Oblate of Mary Immaculate.

L. A. LeBas, M. P.

priest, miss. apost.

p. 19	
S-7	The 4 April, 1849, we the undersigned parish priest officiating at St. Paul,
Sister	have inhumed in the cemetery of the Sisters of Notre Dame the Reverend
Renilde	Sister Renilde, aged 30 years and 4 months, deceased the 1st of this month,
of	after 5 years and a half of profession, legitimate daughter of Everard Joseph
Notre	Goemare and of Marie Therese Telborg of Wattenen in Belgium, in the
Dame	presence of Monsieur Patrick McCormick, Reverend parish priest officiating
Melanie	at St. John of Oregon City, of Manseiur Francois Veyret, Superior of the
Goemare	College of St. Joseph of St. Paul of Wallamette, and of many other ecclesiastics.
	(Melanie her name in the family.)

L. A. LeBas

priest, miss. apost.

Veyret

B-10	The 10 April, 1849, we the undersigned parish priest officiating at St. Paul
Xavier	have baptized Xavier, legitimate son of Xavier Liard and of . . . his wife,
Liard	born today; the godfather Culbert Lambert, called Robillard, the godmother Agathe, all of this parish.

L. A. LeBas, priest, miss. apost.

S-8	The 12 April, 1849, we priest officiating at St. Paul, undersigned, have
Xavier	buried in the cemetery of this parish the body of Xavier Liard legitimate
Liard	son of Xavier and of . . . of this parish, born on the 10th and deceased the 12th of this month, in the presence of Amable Petit.

L. A. LeBas, priest, miss.apost.

B-11	The 22 April, 1849, we the undersigned parish priest officiating at St. Paul
Paul	have baptized Paul George, son of George Gay and of Louise Hare his wife,
Gay	born the 17th of February last, the godfather Louis Labonte, the godmother Caroline Montour his wife, of this parish.

L. A. LeBas, priest, Miss. Apost.

B-12	The 30 April, 1849, we the undersigned priest have baptized Pierre, young
Pierre	boy born of infidel parents, the godfather has been Jean Baptiste Dubreuil
Indian	who could not sign with us. No godmother at all.

J. B. Z. Bolduc, priest

S-9	The May 1, 1849, we the undersigned parish priest of St. Paul have buried
Marianne	in the parish cemetery the body of Marianne, legitimate daughter of Joseph
Bourgeau	Bourgeau and of Angele Lafantaisie, deceased yesterday at the age of 1 year. Present Amable Petit.

L. A. LeBas, priest, miss. apost.

p 20	
B-13	The 13 May, 1849, we the undersigned priest have baptized Jean, son of
Jean	James Coleman and of Fany Murry, aged about 9 months. The godfather
Colman	has been Miles McDonald and the godmother Mary Cosgrove.

J. B. Z. Bolduc, priest

B-14	The 13 May, 1849, we the undersigned priest have baptized Catherine
Catherine	Anne, daughter of James Coleman and of Fany Murry, aged about 2 years.
Anne	The godfather has been Hughes Cosgrove and the godmother Anne Cos-
Colman	grove.

J. B. Z. Bolduc, priest

B-15	The 14 May, 1849, we the undersigned parish priest of St. Paul have bap-
Philomene	tized a Tsikane Indian of the Grand Dalles, aged about 16 years, to whom
Tsikane	has been given the name Philomene, the godfather Pierre Pepin, called Lachance, the godmother Susanne Gaudriche, his wife, all of this parish.

L. A. LeBas, priest, miss. apost.

M-3
Louis
Forssier
and
Philomene
Tsikane

The 14 February [May] 1849, we the undersigned parish priest of St. Paul, after the publication of one ban made at the sermon of the parish Mass of this church the 13th of this month, the parties having obtained the dispensation of the publication of the two other bans, without having found any impediment, have received their mutual consent to marriage of Louis Forssier, widower of Catherine, living in this parish, and of Philomene Tsikane, Indian of the Grand Dalles, living also in this parish, in the presence of Olivier Daubin and of Pierre Pepin called Lachance, of this parish.
L. A. LeBas, priest, miss. apost.

B-16
Aurelie
Bonin

The 20 May, 1849, we the undersigned parish priest of St. Paul have baptized Aurelie legitimate daughter of Pierre Bonin and of Louise Rondo his wife, born the 17th of this month, the godfather Pierre Lachance, the godmother Archange, of this parish.
L. A. LeBas, priest, miss. apost.

S-10
Olivier
Rochbrune

The 22 May, 1849, we the undersigned parish priest of St. Paul have buried in the cemetery of this parish the body of Olivier, legitimate son of Joseph Rochbrune and of Lizette, deceased yesterday at the age of about 6 in the presence of Thamis Liard, his (Joseph's) brother-in-law.
L.A. LeBas, priest, miss. apost.

p 21
S-11
Hilaire
Guilbeau

The 26 June, 1849, we undersigned priest, parish priest officiating at St. Paul, have buried in the cemetery of this parish the body of Hilaire Guilbeau, deceased the 24 of the current month, in the presence of Andre Chalifou and of Pierre Pepin, dit Lachance.
L. A. LeBas
priest, miss., apost.

S-12
Therese
Tchinouk

The 28 June, 1849, we undersigned priest, parish priest officiating at St. Paul, have buried in the cemetery of this parish the body of Therese Tchinouk, aged about 8 years, deceased yesterday at the home of Etienne Lucier, in the presence of Michel Lucier and of Charles Petit.
L. A. LeBas
priest, miss., apost.

B-17
J Baptiste
Indian

The 8 July, 1849, we undersigned missionary priest officiating at this mission have baptized Jean Baptiste, aged about 1 year, born of infidel parents. The godfather has been Jean Baptiste Tyikwarhi [Norwest] and the godmother Henriette his wife, who could not sign.
J. B. Z. Bolduc, priest, miss.

M-4
Dd.
Mongrain
and
Catherine
Lafantaisie
widow
Dupre

The 17 July, 1849, we priest undersigned officiating at this mission, have received the mutual consent to marriage and have given the nuptial benediction, after the publication of one ban and the dispensation of two others, by us granted, to David Mongrain, domiciled in this mission, and Catherine Lafantaisie, widow Dupre, of the mission of St. Louis, nobody having discovered an impediment. The witnesses have been Andre Chalifoux and Thomas Roy who as well as the two parties could not sign.
J. B. Z. Bolduc, priest, miss.

B-18
J Baptiste
Baulez

The 22 July, 1849, we priest missionary undersigned have baptized Jean Baptiste born the 14 of this month of the legitimate marriage of Joseph Baulez and of Marianne Louis. The godfather has been Francois Guilbeau and the godmother Celeste Rochon who have signed with us. The father present.
Celeste Jeaudoin
[no other signature]
J. B. Z. Bolduc, priest

p 22
B-19
Magdeleine
Okinakan

The 25 July, 1849, we priest missionary undersigned have baptized Magdeleine born of infidel parents of the nation of Okinakan (Okanagan) and aged about 40 years. The godfather has been Jacques Servant and the godmother Madgeleine his wife, who could not sign.
J. B. Z. Bolduc, priest, miss.

S-13
Rosalie
Indian
Calispel

The 11 of August, 1849, we priest undersigned have buried in the cemetery of this mission the body of Rosalie deceased yesterday at the Sisters of Notre Dame, in the presence of William Leclaire, Soudiadre *[sub-deacon]* and of Charles Petit, of whom has signed with us.

G. Leclaire, S D

J. B. Z. Bolduc, priest

B-19 *[sic]*
Josephte
Norta

The 12 August, 1849, we priest undersigned have baptized Josephte born of the legitimate marriage of Louis Norta and of Catherine, aged about 6 months, the godfather has been Louis Bergevin and the godmother Celeste Jeaudoin, who alone has signed with us.

Celeste Jeaudoin

J. B. Z. Bolduc, priest

B-20
Clarisse
Matthieu

The 19 August, 1849, we priest undersigned have baptized Clarisse born of the legitimate marriage of Francois Xavier Matthieu and of Rose Haussant, aged 3 days. The godfather has been Thomas Bernier and the godmother Pelagie L'Hussier (Lucier) who could not sign.

J. B. Z. Bolduc, priest

B-21
Celeste
Jeaudoin

The 23 August, 1849, we priest undersigned have baptized Celeste born day before yesterday of the legitimate marriage of Jean Baptiste Jeaudoin and of Elisabeth Hubert. The godfather has been Louis Bergevin and the godmother Magdelaine Servant his wife who could not sign.

J. B. Z. Bolduc, priest

B-22
J Baptiste
Raby

The 29 August, 1849, we priest undersigned have baptized Jean Baptiste born the 23rd of the legitimate marriage of Abraham Raby and of Louise. The godfather has been Alexis Aubichon and the godmother . . .

J. B. Z. Bolduc, priest

p 23
B-23
Marie
Howard

The 30 September, we priest undersigned have baptized Marie born the 27 of the same month of the legitimate marriage of John Howard and of Catherine Lonetain. The godfather has been Andre Lonetain and the godmother Nancy, his wife who could not sign with us.

J. B. Z. Bolduc, priest

B-24
Augustin
Indian
Tlikatat

The 1 October, 1849, we priest undersigned have baptized Augustin born of infidel parents and aged about 3 months. The godmother has been Celeste Jeaudoin who has signed with us.

Celeste Jeaudoins

J. B. Z. Bolduc, priest

S-14
Catherine
McPheal

The 13 October, 1849, we priest undersigned have buried the body of Catherine McPheal deceased the 10th at the Sisters of Notre Dame, at the age of about 13 years, have been present Amable Petit and Francois Bolduc who have not known how to sign.

J. B. Z. Bolduc, priest

S-15
David
Donpierre

The 19 October, 1849, we priest undersigned have buried in the cemetery of this mission the body of David Donpierre deceased day before yesterday, in presence of Andre Chalifoux and of Louis Pichet who have not known how to sign.

J. B. Z. Bolduc, priest

B-25
Aloys
Gravelle

The 25 October, 1849, we priest undersigned have baptized Aloys born the 20th of the 20th of the legitimate marriage of Gédéon Gravelle and of Nancy Pin. The godfather has been Amable *["Joseph" overwritten]* Petit and Marguerite wife of Etienne Lussier who have not known how to sign.

J. B. Z. Bolduc, priest

B-36 *[sic]*
Rose
Laframboise

The 10 November, 1849, we priest undersigned have baptized Rose, born the 4th of this month of the legitimate marriage of Michel Laframboise and of Emélie Picard his wife, the godfather Francois Xavier Mathieu, the godmother Rose Ossent his wife, all of this parish.

L. A. LeBas,

pr. miss. apost.

S-16

The 11 November, 1849, we priest undersigned have buried in the cemetery

Rose
Fenlay

of this mission the body of Rose deceased yesterday at the house of the Sisters of Notre Dame, in presence of Francois Bolduc and of Amable Petit who have not known how to sign.

J. B. Z. Bolduc, priest

p. 24
B-37
Joseph
Raby

The 20 November, 1849, we priest undersigned have baptized Joseph born of the legitimate marriage of Abraham Raby and of Catherine of the Chinouck nation. Godfather Alexis Aubichon, godmother Marie Anne his wife who have not known how to sign.

J. B. Z. Bolduc, priest

B-38
Joseph
Laferté

The 6 December, 1849, we priest undersigned have baptized Joseph born the 4th of this month of the legitimate marriage of Joseph Laferté and of Sophie Aubichon his wife, the godfather Alexis Aubichon, the godmother Marianne Walès his wife, all of this parish.

L. A. LeBas,
priest, miss, apost.

B-39
Wm
McKay

The 30 December, 1849, we priest undersigned have baptized William born today of the legitimate marriage of James McKay and of Cecilia Lauson. The godfather has been Peter Miles McDonald and the godmother . . . Colman, who have not known how to sign with us.

J. B. Z. Bolduc, priest

B-40
Hubert
Petit

The 30 December, 1849, we priest undersigned have baptized Hubert born the 28th of this month, of the legitimate marriage of Amable Petit and of Emelie Aubichon, his wife, the godfather Alexis Aubichon, the godmother Marianne Walès his wife, all of this parish.

L. A. LeBas,
priest, miss, apost.

S-17
Luce
Chalifoux

The 31 December, 1849, we priest undersigned have buried in this Church the body of Luce Chalifoux deceased day before yesterday at the house of her father at the age of about 11 years, in presence of André St. Martin and of Louis Pichet who have not known how to sign.

J. B. Z. Bolduc, priest
1850

S-1
Zoé
Garant

The 8 January, 1850, we priest undersigned have buried in the cemetery of this mission the body of Zoé Garant deceased yesterday at the age of 6 weeks, in presence of Andrée St. Martin and of Charles Petit who have not known how to sign.

J. B. Z. Bolduc, priest

p. 25
S-2
F. Xavier
Lavigueur

The 8 January, 1850, we priest undersigned have buried in the cemetery of this mission the body of Francois Xavier Lavigueur deceased day before yesterday; in presence of Cuthbert Lambert and of André St. Martin who have not known how to sign.

J. B. Z. Bolduc, priest

S-3
Marie
Guilbeau

The 9 February, 1850, we priest undersigned have buried in the cemetery of this mission the body of Marie Guilbeau deceased yesterday, at the age of about 9 years; in presence of Amable Petit and of André Hophop who have not known how to sign.

J. B. Z. Bolduc, priest

B-1
Moise
Bargevin

The 10 February, 1850, we priest undersigned have baptized Moise born this morning of the legitimate marriage of Louis Bargevin and of Magdelaine Servant. The godfather has been Augustin Rochon and the godmother Celeste Jeaudoin who alone has known how to sign.

Celeste Jeaudoin
J. B. Z. Bolduc, priest

B-2
Augustin
Sepiho

The 15 February, 1850, we priest undersigned have baptized Augustin born today of the legitimate marriage of Pierre Sepiho and of Catherine. The godfather has been Augustin Garant and the godmother Lucie his wife who have not known how to sign.

J. B. Z. Bolduc, priest

B-3
Clarisse
Bernier

The 25 February, 1850, we priest undersigned have baptized Clarisse born day before yesterday of the legitimate marriage of Francois Bernier and of Pelagie Lussier. Godfather Pierre Lacourse (Senior); godmother Marguerite wife of Etienne Lussier, who have not known how to sign.

J. B. Z. Bolduc, priest

B-4
Cécile
Salopan

The 26 February, 1850, we priest undersigned have baptized Cécile Salopan, Indian *[girl]* born the 12th of this month, the godfather Amable Arquott the father *[Senior]*, the godmother Marianne wife of Amable Arquot the son *[Junior]*, who have not known how to sign.

L. A. LeBas,
priest, miss. apost.

p. 26
S-4
Céleste
Jeaudoin

The 3 March, 1850, we priest undersigned have buried in the cemetery of this mission the body of Céleste deceased yesterday at the age of about 6 months, in presence of Augustin Rochon and of Amable Petit who have not known how to sign.

J. B. Z. Bolduc, priest

S-5
Marie
Indian

The 30 March, 1850, we priest undersigned have buried in the cemetery of this mission the body of Marie deceased yesterday at the house of Jean Baptiste Deguire, at the age of about 1 year, Present Amable Petit and Charles Petit who alone has signed with us.

Charles Petit
J. B. Z. Bolduc, priest

B-5
Joseph
Sotshohoanni

The 1st of April, 1850, we priest undersigned have *["buried" crossed out]* privately baptized Joseph legitimate child of Jean Baptiste Sotshohoanni and of Angelique of the tribe of Pand'Oreille, at the house of the father.

J. B. Z. Bolduc, priest

S-6
Marie
Pichet

The 8 April, 1850, we priest undersigned have buried in the cemetery of this mission the body of Marie privately baptized in danger of death at the house of her father by Catherine Russie, in presence of Amable Petit and of André Hophop who have not known how to sign.

J. B. Z. Bolduc, priest

S-7
Augustin
Sepiho

The 10 April, 1850, we priest undersigned have buried in the cemetery of this mission the body of Augustin deceased yesterday at the age of 1 month and 23 days, in presence of Amable Petit and of Charles Petit who alone has signed with us.

[no signature]
J. B. Z. Bolduc, priest

B-6
André
Ménard

The 21 April, 1850, we priest undersigned have baptized André born since 4 days of the legitimate marriage of Pierre Ménard and of Josephte Youtta. Godfather André St. Martin. Godmother Genevieve St. Martin who have not known how to sign.

J. B. Z. Bolduc, priest

S-8
Joseph
Sotshohoanni

The 22 April, 1850, we priest undersigned have buried in the cemetery of this mission the body of Joseph deceased yesterday, in presence of Amable Petit and of Charles Petit who alone has signed with us.

[no signature]
J. B. Z. Bolduc, priest

p. 26 a
B-9
G. William
Asrow

The 21 April, 1850, we priest undersigned have baptized George William born since 10 days of infidel parents of the tribe of Tchinouk. Godfather Louis Lussier; godmother Maria McKay who have not known how to sign.

J. B. Z. Bolduc, priest

S-9
Louise
Boisvert

The 2 May, 1850, we priest undersigned have buried in the Church of this mission on the right hand side of the altar towards the middle, the body of Louise deceased day before yesterday, in presence of André Chalifoux and of Augustin Rochon who have not known how to sign.

J. B. Z. Bolduc, priest

S-10

The 23 May, 1850, we priest undersigned have buried in the cemetery of

Nancy Dobin	this mission the body of Nancy deceased day before yesterday, in the presence of Pierre Papin dit Lachance and of Amable Petit who could not sign. J. B. Z. Bolduc, priest
B-10 Josephte Gauthier	The 26 May, 1850, we priest undersigned have baptized conditionally Josephte born the 28th of March in California of the legitimate marriage of Pierre Gauthier and of Esther Dalcourt. Godfather Elie Gigaire, godmother Catherine Dalcourt who could not sign. J. B. Z. Bolduc, priest
B-10 Marie Indian	The 27 May, 1850, we priest undersigned have baptized a little Indian girl aged about 7 years at the place of Henry Maxwell, who [she] was in danger of death. The undersigned has been himself the godfather, no godmother at all. We have given her the name of Marie. J. B. Z. Bolduc, priest
S-11 Moyse Bargevin	The 27 May, 1850, we priest undersigned have buried in the cemetery of this mission the body of Moyse deceased yesterday at the age of 3 months and 17 days, in the presence of Jacques Servant and of Augustin Raymond who could not sign. J. B. Z. Bolduc, priest
S-12 Marie Indian	The 11 June, 1850, we priest undersigned have buried in the cemetery of this mission the body of Marie deceased the 9th at the house of Henry Maxwell in the presence of Amable Petit and of Augustin Rochon who could not sign. J. B. Z. Bolduc, priest

p. 26b

B-11 Rose Gendron	The 30 June, 1850, we priest undersigned have baptized Rose aged 3 months, legitimate daughter of Joseph Gendron and of Pauly of the nation of the Dalles - The godfather has been Amable Arcouet and the godmother Marguerite Chinouck who could not sign. J. B. Z. Bolduc, priest
B-12 Susanne Deschouquet	The 30 June, 1850, we priest undersigned have baptized Susanne born the 28th of the legitimate marriage of Francois Deschouquet and of Marie Okinagan. Godfather Andre Lonetain, godmother Nancy his wife who could not sign. J. B. Z. Bolduc, priest
B-13 Taddée H. Dupuis	The 30 June, 1850, we priest undersigned have baptized Taddée Henry born the 24 August of the last year of the legitimate marriage of Edouard Dupuis and of Marguerite Anne Dickerson. Godfather Augustin Rochon, godmother Celeste Jeaudoin who alone has signed. Celeste Jeaudoin J. B. Z. Bolduc, priest
M-2 Pierre Pariso & Marie DonPierre	The 8 July, 1850, considering the publication of three banns between Pierre Pariso, of-age son of Baptiste Pariso and of Francoise Alaric of St. Pierre diocese of Montreal on the one part and Marie DonPierre minor daughter of the late David DonPierre and of Marguerite Deshulieres on the other part; nor was any impediment discovered, we undersigned, have received their mutual consent and have given them the nuptial benediction in the presence of Andre Chalifoux and of Louis Vendal witnesses, who could not sign. J. B. Z. Bolduc, priest
M-3 Laurent Sauve & Francoise Coyouse	The 9 April, 1850, considering the publication of two banns and the dispensation of the third granted by us between Laurent Sauve, widower of Josephte Tlalam on the one part, and Francoise widow of the late Paul Guilbeau on the other part; nor any impediment having been discovered, we have received their mutual consent and have given them the nuptial benediction in the presence of Louis LaBonte (Senior) and Andre St. Martin who could not sign. J. B. Z. Bolduc, priest

p. 27

S-13	The 12 July, 1850, we priest undersigned have buried in the cemetery of

Christine Jeaudoin	this mission the body of Christine deceased yesterday at the age of 3 years and some months. Were present Amable Petit and Augustin Rochon who could not sign. J. B. Z. Bolduc, priest
B-14 Antoine Indian	The 14 July, 1850, we priest undersigned have baptized a man of about 25 years born of infidel parents and already known under the name of Antoine, name which we have kept for him. Godfather Antoine Gregoire godmother Sophie Gregoire who could not sign. J. B. Z. Bolduc, priest
M-4 Pierre Lacourse & widow McMullen widow of Jos. McLoughlin	The 18 July, 1850, in view of the dispensation of three banns granted by Monsigneur the Archbishop of Oregon City between Pierre Lacourse of-age son of Pierre Lacourse and of Archange woman of the Tchinouck tribe, on the one part; and Victoire McMullen widow of the late Joseph McLoughlin on the other part; nor any impediment to marriage being discovered, we have received the mutual consent and have given them the nuptial benediction in the presence of John Picard and of Charles Petit who alone has signed with us. Charles Petit J. B. Z. Bolduc, priest
M-5 Joseph Jacques & Elisabeth Bourgeau	The 23 July, 1850, in view of the publication of one bann and the dispensation of two others granted by us between Joseph Jacques originally of Sorel in Canada on the one part and Elisabeth Bourgeau minor daughter of Sylvain Bourgeau and of Josephte Indian woman on the other part; nor any impediment having been discovered, we have received the mutual consent and have given them the nuptial benediction in the presence of Louis Haussant and of Ferdinand Labri who could not sign. J. B. Z. Bolduc, priest
M-6 Joseph Matte & Henriette Biscornet	The 29 July, 1850, in view of the publication of one bann and the dispensation of two others granted by us between Joseph Matte farmer of St. Louis, widower of Josephte Serpent, on the one part; and Henriette Biscornet minor daughter of Pascal Biscornet and of Louise of the tribe of Tlalam on the other part, nor any impediment having been discovered, we have received their mutual consent and have given them the nuptial benediction in the presence of Gedeon Snecal and of Francois Xavier Mathieu who alone has signed with us. [no signature] J. B. Z. Bolduc, priest
p. 28 B-15 Angelle Mongrain	The 2 August, 1850, we priest undersigned have baptized Angelle born yesterday of the legitimate marriage of David Mongrain and of Catherine Lafantaisie. Godfather Theodore Gervais; godmother Angelle Lafantaisie who could not sign. J. B. Z. Bolduc, priest
B-16 Louis LaBonte	The 6 August, 1850, we priest undersigned have baptized Louis born yesterday of the legitimate marriage of Louis LaBonte and of Caroline Montour. Godfather Francois Poirier; godmother Marie Sinclair who could not sign. J. B. Z. Bolduc, priest
B-17 Moyse Servant	The 13 August, 1850, we priest undersigned have baptized Moyse born yesterday of the legitimate marriage of Jacques Servant and Josephte Okinagan. Godfather Augustin Raymond, godmother Marie Servant who could not sign. J. B. Z. Bolduc, priest
B-18 Louis Bourgeau	The 13 August, 1850, we priest undersigned have baptized Louis born today of the legitimate marriage of Sylvain Bourgeau and of Josephte. Godfather Louis Haussant, godmother Marie his wife who could not sign. J. B. Z. Bolduc, priest
B-18 Marie Indian	The 14 August, 1850, we priest have baptized a little girl of the nation of Chinouk aged about 7 years. Godmother Victoire McMullen, no godfather at all. J. B. Z. Bolduc, priest

S-14 Marie Indian	The 19 August, 1850, we priest undersigned have buried in the cemetery of this mission the body of Marie deceased yesterday; were present Amable Petit and Pierre Lacourse who could not sign. J. B. Z. Bolduc, priest
B-19 Joseph Rivet	The 24 August, 1850, we priest undersigned have baptized Joseph born the 20th of the legitimate marriage of Joseph Rivet and of Marie Anne Despard. The godfather has been Antoine Rivet and the godmother Emelie his wife, who could not sign. J. B. Z. Bolduc, priest
B-20 Emelie Caroline Raymond	The 26 August, 1850, we priest undersigned have baptized Emelie Caroline born yesterday of the legitimate marriage of Augustin Raymond and of Marie Servant. Godfather Ferdinand La Bri; godmother Anne Cosgrove who alone has signed with us. *[no signature]* J. B. Z. Bolduc, priest

p. 29

S-15 Joseph Nipissingue	The 14 September, 1850, we priest undersigned have buried in the cemetery of this mission the body of Joseph deceased yesterday at the age of 7 years; were present Laurent Quintal and Amable Petit who could not sign. J. B. Z. Bolduc, priest
M-7 Theodore Gervais & Angelle Lafantaisie	The 24 September, 1850, in view of the publication of one bann and the dispensation of two others between Theodore Gervais on the one part and Angelle Lafantaisie widow of Joseph Bourgeau on the other part; nor any impediment having been discovered, we have given them the nuptial benediction in the presence of David Mongrain and of Ferdinand Labri who could not sign. J. B. Z. Bolduc, priest
B-21 Charles Lafrete	The 26 September, 1850, we priest undersigned have baptized Charles aged 5 days, legitimate child of Michel Lafrete and of Rose Kaous. Godfather Charles Petit; godmother Catherine Sauve, who have signed with us. *[no signatures]* J. B. Z. Bolduc, priest
S-16 Rosalie Indian	The 27 September, 1850, we priest undersigned have buried in the cemetery of this mission the body of Rosalie deceased yesterday at the age of 6 years. Present Amable Petit and Joseph Pin who could not sign. J. B. Z. Bolduc, priest
B-22 Flavie LeBrun	The 30 September, 1850, we priest undersigned have baptized Flavie born today of the legitimate marriage of Hercule LeBrun and of Louise Ouvré. The godfather has been Jean Baptiste Zacharie Bolduc and the godmother Catherine Russie. J. B. Z. Bolduc, priest

p. 30

B-23 Edouard Rivet	The 2 October, 1850, we priest undersigned have baptized Edouard born the 29th of September of the legitimate marriage of Antoine Rivet and of Emilie Pend'Oreille. Godfather Joseph Rivet, godmother Sophie Gregoire who could not sign. J. B. Z. Bolduc, priest
B-24 Francois Petit	The 4 October, 1850, we priest undersigned have baptized Francois born today of the legitimate marriage of Amable Petit and of Susanne Tawakon. Godfather Francois Roland, godmother Francoise Sauve who could not sign. J. B. Z. Bolduc, priest
S-27 Jean Bapt Saste Indian	The 21 October, 1850, we priest undersigned have buried in the cemetery of this mission the body of Jean Baptiste, deceased yesterday at the age of 3 years. Present Amable Petit, who could not sign. A. Goetz, S.J.
S-28 Joseph Laframboise	The 24 October, 1850, we priest undersigned have buried in the cemetery of this parish the body of Joseph, deceased yesterday at the age of 3 years. Present Amable Petit, who could not sign. A. Goetz, S.J.

S-29
Emilie
Quesnel

The 5 November, 1850, we priest undersigned have buried in the cemetery of this parish the body of Emelie Quesnel, deceased yesterday, aged 12 years. Present Amable Petit, who could not sign.

Cenas, priest

M-8
Joseph
Champagne
&
Catherine
Sauve

The 19 November, 1850, in view of the dispensation of two banns of marriage, and the publication of the third made at the sermon of the parish Mass, between Joseph Champagne, farmer, of-age son of Joseph Champagne and of Marguerite Sauguinette of the parish of Sorel (Canada), on the one part; and Catherine Sauve, minor daughter of Laurent Sauve, farmer of this parish, and of the late Josette of the river of Frasers on the other part. Nor was any impediment discovered, and the parents having declared consent to the said marriage; we priest undersigned have received their mutual consent and have given them the nuptial benediction in the presence of Laurent Sauve, father of the bride and of Andre Longtain, as well as many other friends. The groom, the bride and one of the witnesses have signed.

Joseph Champagne
Catherine Sauve
Gedeon Berthelet
Cenas, priest

p.31
M-9
Casimir
Gardepy
&
Genevieve
Bellique

The 25 November, 1850, in view of the dispensation of two banns of marriage and the publication of the third made at the sermon of the parish Mass, between Casimir Gardepy of this parish, on the one part; and Genevieve widow Belleque, also of this parish, on the other part - nor any impediment revealing itself, and the relatives having declared consent to the said marriage, we priest undersigned have received their mutual consent and have given them the nuptial benediction, in the presence of Etienne Lussier, Jean Baptiste Jodoin, relatives of the bride, as well as many other Witnesses and friends, of whom only one has signed. The groom and the bride could not sign.

Joseph Champagne
Cenas, priest

B-25
Jean
Baptiste
(Indian)

This 7 December, 1850, we priest undersigned have baptized Jean Baptiste, aged 15 years. Godfather Jean Baptiste Delcour, who has not known how to sign.

Cenas, priest

S-30
Jean
Baptiste
Saste

The 9 December, 1850, we priest undersigned have buried in the cemetery of this parish the body of Jean Baptiste Saste, deceased yesterday aged 15 years. Present Joseph Champagne undersigned.

Joseph Champagne
Cenas, priest

[There are a number of pages inset between pp. 31-32, not numbered in any way, for the years 1854-1860, written by Father Croke on missionary tours to Southern Oregon. As these entries are not of St. Paul, they are included in the Jacksonville Register, where they properly belong.]

1850 - 1851

p 32
M-10
George
Chiffman
Aplin
and
Marie
Wagnor

The 26 December, 1850, in view of the dispensation of one ban of marriage and the publication of two others made at the sermon of the parish Masses, between George Chiffman Aplin, farmer of this parish, on the one part; and Marie Wagnor, minor daughter and legitimate of Pierre Wagnor, and of Louise, also of this parish, on the other part; nor was discovered any impediment, and the parents having declared consent to the said marriage, we Archbishop undersigned have received their mutual consent and have given them the nuptial benediction in the presence of Pierre Wagnor, father of the bride, of Joseph Champagne, of Laurent Sauve, and of many other witnesses and friends of the groom. The groom and one of the witnesses

alone have signed.
Wagner [?]
Joseph Champagne   George Chiffman Aplin
                                     F. N. Blanchet, Archbishop of
                                     Oregon City

B-25
Narcisse
Portier

The 29 December, 1850, we priest undersigned have baptized Narcisse born two days ago of the legitimate marriage of Nicolas Portier and of Marguerite Laroque [above the line] of Red River. Godfather Narcisse Morin; godmother Therese Delcour, who could not sign. Present Nicolas Portier, father of the child, and Amable Petit. See word between lines, good.

Cenas, priest

1851

B-1
Marguerite
Liard

The 3 January, 1851, we priest undersigned have baptized Marguerite, born today of the legitimate marriage of Tanis [Stanislaus] Liard, farmer of this parish, and of Celeste Rochbrune. Godfather David Mongrain; godmother Catherine Lafantaisie, who could not sign; present Tanis Liard, who could not sign.

Cenas, priest

p 33
S-1
Laurent
Irroquois

The 8 January, 1851, we priest undersigned have buried in the cemetery of this parish the body of Laurent, Irroquois, deceased yesterday, in the presence of Amable Petit, Jean Baptiste Jodoin, who could not sign.

Cenas, priest

S-2
Marie
Flathead

The 8 January, 1851, we priest undersigned have buried in the cemetery of this parish the body of Marie, wife of Francois Gervais, deceased yesterday. Present Amable Petit, Joseph Servant, who could not sign.

Cenas, priest

S-3
Flavie
Lebrun

The 19 January, 1851, we priest undersigned have buried in the cemetery of this parish the body of Flavie, deceased yesterday at the age of 3 months and a half, present Joseph Champagne and Amable Petit, who could not sign.

Cenas, priest

S-4
Susanne

The 25 January, 1851, we priest undersigned have buried in the cemetery of this parish the body of Susanne deceased 2 days ago at the age of 4 years and 9 months. Present Amable Petit and Francois Serdon [?] dit Charlot, who could not sign.

Cenas, priest

S-5
Isabelle
wife of
Peletier

The 9 February, 1851, we priest undersigned have buried in the cemetery of this parish the body of Isabelle, wife of Salomon Peletier, deceased 2 days ago. Present Amable Petit, Louis Pichet, who could not sign. Two words between the lines good. [referring to S-4, where "dit Charlot" were interlined]

Cenas, priest

B-2
Joseph
Theodore
Tellier

The 17 February, 1851, we priest undersigned have baptized Joseph Theodore, born the 20 December, 1850, of the legitimate marriage of Louis Tellier and of Angelique Pend'Oreille of this mission. Godfather Theodore Gervais; godmother Angele Lafantaisie, who could not sign.

Cenas, priest

p. 34
M-1
Theodore
Poujade
and
Marguerite
Cosgrove

The 24 February, 1851, after the publication of one ban of marriage between Theodore Poujade, of-age son of Jean-Pierre Poujade, physician, and the late Marie Noble, of the mission of St. Louis, on the one part; and Marguerite Cosgrove, minor daughter of Hugh Cosgrove, merchant, and of Marie Roster, of this mission, on the other part. Like publication having been made at St. Louis as is apparent by the certification of Mr. Delorme, officiating at the said mission of St. Louis; the parties having obtained of Monsigneur the Archbishop of Oregon City dispensation of two bans, we undersigned priest officiating at the mission of St. Louis, with the approbation of the parents of the bethrothed, have received their mutual consent to marriage and have given them the nuptial benediction in the presence of the undersigned

Witnesses   Hugh Cosgrove   Theodore C Poujade
Elizabeth Cosgrove   Margaret Cosgrove
Sophie Belleque

B. Delorme, priest, missionary

B-3
Sophie
Chalifoux

The 24 February, 1851, by us priest undersigned has been baptized Sophie, born yesterday of the legitimate marriage of Andre Chalifoux and of Catherine Russe, godfather Louis Pichet, who has not undersigned; godmother Sophie Belleque undersigned.

Sophie Belleque
Cenas, priest

B-4
William
Lacourse

The 26 February, 1851, by us priest undersigned has been baptized William, born 2 days ago of the legitimate marriage of Pierre Lacourse and of Victoire McLoughlin. Godfather Narcisse Vivet godmother Julienne Labonte, who have not undersigned.

Cenas, priest

M-2
Francois
Bolduc
&
Angele

The 3 March, 1851, after the publication of one bann of marriage between Francois Bolduc, of-age son and legitimate of Pierre Bolduc and of Josette Gagnon, of Quebec in Canada, on the one part; and Angele, metisse Tchinouck, on the other part. The parties having obtained of Monsigneuer the Archbishop of Oregon City dispensation of two banns, we undersigned priest, with the approbation of the relatives of the bethrothed have received their mutual consent to marriage and have given them the nuptial benediction in the presence of the undersigned and many others.

J. B DeGuire   (X) Francois Bolduc
J B Jeaudoin   (X) Angele
Cénas, priest

p. 35
B-5
Jean
Baptiste
(Indian)

The 4 March, 1851, by us priest undersigned has been baptized Jean Baptiste, born the day before of the legitimate marriage of Nicolas (Indian) and of Marie (Indian). Godfather Jean Baptiste Nordouest; godmother Marie, who have not undersigned.

Cénas, priest

B-6
Marie
Emaline
Cosgrove

The 5 March, 1851, by us priest undersigned has been baptized Marie Emaline, born the day before, of the legitimate marriage of Hugh Cosgrove and of Marie Roster. Godfather Amable Petit; godmother Elisabeth Cosgrove, who have not undersigned.

Cénas, priest

S-6
Joseph
PendOreille

The 6 March, 1851, by us priest undersigned has been buried in the cemetery the body of Joseph, deceased the day before, aged 1 year and a half. Present Amable Petit and Francois Rivet, who have not undersigned.

Cénas, priest

B-7
Charles
Jean
Bapt.
Jeaudoin

The 11 March, 1851, by us priest undersigned has been baptized Charles Jean Baptiste born today of the legitimate marriage of Jean Baptiste Jeaudoin and of Elizabeth Joachim. Godfather Jean Francois Guerin; godmother Isabelle McKay, who have not undersigned. The father has signed.

Jean Bapt. Jeaudoin
Cénas, priest

S-7
Jean Bapt.
(Indian)

The 15 March, 1851, by us priest undersigned has been buried in the cemetery the body of Jean Baptiste, Indian, deceased the day before, aged 10 days. Present Amable and Charles Petit, who have not undersigned.

Cénas, priest

B-8
Marie
Ignace

The 23 March, 1851, by us priest undersigned has been baptized Marie, born 7 days ago of the legitimate marriage of Baptiste Ignace and of Angelique. Godfather Louis Bargevin; godmother Magdeleine, wife of Bargevin, who have not undersigned.

Cénas, priest

S-8

The 26 March, 1851, by us priest undersigned has been [three words crossed

Magdeleine (Indian)	*out]* buried in the cemetery the body of Magdeleine, Indian, deceased the day before, aged 11 years. Present Bernier and Petit. Three words erased nul.

Cénas, priest

p. 36

B-9
Marie — The 27 March, 1851, by us priest undersigned has been baptized Marie born 5 days ago of the legitimate marriage of Francois Belenzo, Spaniard, and of Louise. Godfather Cuthbert Robillard; godmother Marie who have not undersigned.

Cenas, priest

B-10
William
Edouard
Gay — The 6 April, 1851, by us priest undersigned has been baptized William Edouard, born 5 months and a half ago of the legitimate marriage of George Gay and of Louise. Godfather Casimir Gardepy; godmother Genevieve, who have not undersigned.

Cenas, priest

S-9
Marguerite
Wagner — The 13 April, 1851, by us priest undersigned has been buried in the church, under the chapel of the right wing, the body of Marguerite, deceased 2 days ago, aged 8 years. Present Pierre Wagner, George Chiffman Aplin, who have not undersigned.

Cenas, priest

S-10
Catherine
Laurent — The 19 April, 1851, by us priest undersigned has been buried in the cemetery the body of Catherine deceased the day before aged 8 years and a half. Present Amable and Charles Petit, who have not undersigned.

Cenas, priest

S-11
Marie
wife *[of]*
Despart — The 29 April, 1851, by us priest undersigned has been buried in the cemetery the body of Marie, deceased 2 days ago, aged 43 years. Present Amable and Charles Petit who have not undersigned.

Cenas, priest

B-11
Henriette
Nausie *[?]* — The 29 April, 1851, by us priest undersigned has been baptized Henriette Nansie *[?]* metisse woman in danger of death, aged 23 years. Godfather Jean Baptiste Nordouest, godmother Henriette, who have not undersigned.

Cenas, priest

B-12
Jean
Baptiste — The 29 April, 1851, by us priest undersigned has been baptized Jean Baptiste (Indian) born of infidel parents, aged 22 years. Godfather Francois Bolduc,; godmother Angele his wife, who have not undersigned.

Cenas, priest

B-13
Marie
Papin
[Pepin] — The 30 April, 1851, by us priest undersigned has been baptized Marie, born the day before of the legitimate marriage of Pierre Papin and of Susanne Godriche *[Goodrich]*. Godfather Denis *[Tanis, Stanislaus]* Liard; godmother Celeste Laroque *[should read Rochbrune]*, who have not undersigned.

Cenas, priest

p 37

B-14
Marienne
Nipis-
singue — The 4 May, 1851, by us priest undersigned has been baptized Marianne born 1 month and 11 days ago of the legitimate marriage of Louis Nipissingue and of Lisette. Godfather Adolphe Chamberland; godmother Louise, who have not undersigned.

Cenas, priest

B-15
Genevieve
[Plouf crossed out]
Sylvestre — The 24 May, 1851, by us priest undersigned has been baptized Genevieve, born 2 days ago *[of the legitimate marriage of the late Plouf - crossed out]* *[written above the line]* natural child of Jos Sylvestre and of Rosalie *[written above the line]* widow Plouf *[his wife - crossed out]*. Godfather Etienne Gregoire, godmother Sophie, who have not undersigned. 9 words erased nul; 7 between the lines good.

Cenas, priest

B-16
Marguerite — The 25 April, 1851, by us priest undersigned has been baptized Marguerite, born 6 days ago of the legitimate marriage of Louis Pichet and of Mar-

Pichet	guerite. Godfather Francois Bernier; godmother Sophie, who have not undersigned.
	Cenas, priest
B-12 Joseph Beauchemin	The 1 June, 1851, by us priest undersigned has been baptized Joseph, born the 11 September, 1850, of the legitimate marriage of Charles Beauchemin and of Julie. Godfather Louis Bargevin; godmother Magdeleine, who have not undersigned.
	Cenas, priest
S-12 Susane Pieriche	The 3 June, 1851, by us priest undersigned has been buried in the cemetery the body of Susane deceased yesterday aged 1 year and a half. Present Paul Piedriche [sic] and Amable Petit, who have not undersigned.
	Cenas, priest
B-13 Marianne widow King	The 16 June, 1851, by us priest undersigned has been baptized Marianne, Indian woman widow of the late King, aged 22 years. Godfather John Howard, godmother Catherine, who have not undersigned.
	Cenas, priest
M-3 Basile Corville & Marianne King	The 16 June, 1851, after the publication of two banns of marriage between Basile Corville, of the parish of St. Louis, and Marianne widow King, of the parish of St. Paul, the parties having obtained from Monsigneur the Archbishop of Oregon City dispensation of one bann, we undersigned priest officiating at the mission of St. Paul, have received the mutual consent of the betrothed and have given them the nuptial benediction in the presence of Andre Lonetain and John Howard witnesses of the marriage, and of many other persons, who have not undersigned.
	Cenas, priest.
p. 38 S-13 Genevieve Sylvestre	The 19 June, 1851, by us priest undersigned has been buried in the cemetery the body of Genevieve deceased yesterday aged 1 month. Present Amable and Charles Petit, who have not undersigned.
	Cenas, priest
S-14 Antoine Tayekuarihi dit Nordouest	The 20 June, 1851, by us priest undersigned has been buried in the cemetery the body of Antoine deceased yesterday aged 7 years. Present Baptiste Tayekuarihi, called Nord-ouest and Charles Petit who have not undersigned.
	Cénas, priest
B-14 Antoine Joseph Gagnon	The 27 June, 1851, by us priest undersigned has been baptized Antoine Joseph, aged 11 years, son of Louis Gagnon and Marie. Godfather Reverend Monsieur Francis Rock, priest; godmother Sophie Beleque undersigned.
	F. Rock, pr.
	Sophie Bellique
	Cenas, priest
B-15 Calixte Chamberland	The 29 June, 1851, by us priest undersigned has been baptized Calixte, born 8 days ago of the legitimate marriage of Adolphe Chamberland and of Louise. Godfather Pierre Pepin, godmother Suzanne who have not undersigned.
	Cenas, priest
B-16 Theodore Gervais	The 4 July, 1851, by us priest undersigned has been baptized Theodore born the same day of the legitimate marriage of Theodore Gervais and of Angele Lafantaisie. Godfather Baptiste Gervais, godmother Catherine, who have not undersigned.
	Cenas, priest
P. 39 S-15 Calixte Chamberland	The 6 July, 1851, by us priest undersigned has been buried in the cemetery the body of Calixte deceased yesterday aged 15 days. Present Amable and Charles Petit, who have not undersigned.
	Cenas, priest
M-4 Thomas Tayakuarihi	The 19 July, 1851, we priest undersigned officiating have given the nuptial benediction to Thomas Tayakuarihi, and Marie, illegitimately united since 3 months, not having recourse to a priest. The witnesses have been Amable

[Norwest] & Marie B-17 Magdeleine Gendron	Petit, Charlot [Tse-tse] and Baptiste Tayakuarihi, dit Nord-ouest, who have not undersigned. *[no priest signature, Cenas handwriting]* This 20 July, 1851, by us priest undersigned has been baptized Magdeleine, born 4 months ago of the legitimate marriage of Francois Gendron and of Marguerite. Godfather Joseph Pin; godmother Catherine Plassie *[Laferte]*, who have not undersigned.
	Cenas, priest
B-18 Charles Bargevin	The 27 July, 1851, by us undersigned has been baptized Charles, born the same day of the legitimate marriage of Louis Bargevin and of Magdeleine Servant. Godfather Jacques Servant; godmother Catherine, who have not undersigned.
	Cenas, priest
S-16 Archange Plouf	The 29 July, 1851, by us priest undersigned has been buried in the cemetery the body of Archange deceased 2 days ago, aged 8 years. Present Amable and Charles Petit, who have not undersigned.
	Cenas, priest
S-17 Caroline Montour	The 3 August, 1851, by us priest undersigned has been buried in the cemetery the body of Caroline wife of Louis Labonte, deceased the 1 August, aged 26 years. Present Hugh Cosgrove, Culbert *[Cuthbert]* Lambert, Amable Petit, who have not undersigned.
	Cenas, priest
B-19 Marie [Lussier crossed out] Russi p 40	The 3 August, 1851, by us priest undersigned has been baptized Marie Angele, born the 25 July of the legitimate marriage of Augustin *[Lussier crossed out]* Russi, and of Anne *[Norwest]*. Godfather Gedeon Berthelet; godmother Cecile Tayekuarihi *[Norwest]*, who have not undersigned. Cenas, priest
B-20 Edouard Gardepy	The 8 August, 1851, by us priest undersigned has been baptized Edouard born the same day of the legitimate marriage of Casimir Gardely and of Genevieve. Godfather Edouard Hubard *[Thomas Hubbard]*; godmother Marie, his wife, who have not undersigned.
	Cenas, priest
S-18 Catherine Monique	The 12 August, 1851, by us priest undersigned has been baptized *[crossed out]* buried in the cemetery the body of Catherine, deceased the day before, aged 9 years. Present Amable and Charles Petit, who have not undersigned. Word erased nul.
	Cenas, priest
S-19 Marguerite wife [of] Pin	The 17 August, 1851, by us priest undersigned has been buried in the cemetery the body of Marguerite, deceased 2 days ago, aged 48 years. Present John Howard; Amable Petit who have not undersigned.
	Cenas, priest
B-21 Jean Joseph Geferes [Jeffers]	The 18 August, 1851, by us priest undersigned has been baptized Jean Joseph, born 2 days *[ago]* of the legitimate marriage of Edouard Geferss and of Josette. Godfather John Howard; godmother Catherine *[Longtain]* who have not undersigned. Cenas, priest
B-22 Esther Quintal	The 18 August, 1851, we priest undersigned have baptized conditionally Esther, born the 13 August last of the legitimate marriage of Laurent Quintal and of Marianne, privately baptized in the house of the parents, godfather Louis Pichet; godmother Marguerite who have not undersigned.
	Cenas, priest
S-20 Joseph Lecuyer	The 20 September, 1851, by us priest undersigned has been buried in the cemetery the body of a child privately baptized the day before at home and born the 14 September of the legitimate marriage of Francois Lecuyer and of Marie. Present Amable and Charles Petit, who have not undersigned.
	Cenas, priest
S-21	The 21 September, 1851, by us priest undersigned has been buried in the

Jean Bapt.
Sylvestre

cemetery the body of Jean Baptiste Sylvestre, deceased the day before aged 40 years. Present Louis Pichet, Amable Petit, who have not undersigned.

Cenas, priest

p. 41
B-23
Mary
McKay

The 21 September, 1851, by us priest undersigned has been baptized Marie born the same day of the legitimate marriage of James McKay, and of Cecilia Lauson. Godfather Etienne McDonald; godmother Anne Cosgrove who have not undersigned.

Cenas, priest

S-22
Pelage
wife [of]
Plante

The 23 September, 1851, by us priest undersigned has been buried in the cemetery the body of Pelage wife of Plante deceased yesterday aged 60 years. Present Charles Plante and Francois Rolland who have not undersigned.

Cenas, priest

S-23
Josette
wife [of]
Menard

The 24 September, 1851, by us priest undersigned has been buried in the cemetery the body of Josette, wife of Menard, deceased the day before aged 50 years. Present Francois Rolland and Amable Petit, who have not undersigned.

Cenas, priest

S-24
André
Chalifoux

The 26 September, 1851, by us priest undersigned has been buried in the cemetery the body of Andre deceased 2 days ago aged 62 years, present Louis Pichet, Hubert Robillard, who have not undersigned.

Cénas, priest

B-24
John
Western
[Weston]

The 27 September, 1851, by us priest undersigned has been baptized Jean, born the 12 September last of an illegitimate intercourse between one named John and Mary. [Added above the line] Legitimatized afterwards by David Western see 27 January 1852. Godfather Narcisse Vivet, godmother Julienne Labonte, who have not undersigned.

Cenas, priest

M-5
Narcisse
Cornoyer
&
Sophie
Bellique

The 29 September, 1851, after the publication of one bann of marriage between Narcisse Cornoyer, of-age son and legitimate of the late [both] Narcisse Cornoyer and Marie Anne Bercier, on the one part; and Sophie Bellique, minor daughter and legitimate of the late Pierre Bellique and of Genevieve [St.] Martin, on the other part, nor any impediment having been discovered, and the oath of two trustworthy men having been given, the one before the mayor of Oregon City, the other before us priest under-signed, to attest that the Sieur Narcisse Cornoyer, coming from the county of St. Clair, State of Illinois, has not there contracted any matrimonial engagement, we undersigned priest, with the approbation of the relatives of the betrothed, have received their mutual consent to marriage and have given them the nuptial benediction in the presence of the undersigned. The parties have obtained the dispensation of two banns.

Pierre Lacourse   Narcisse A. Cornoyer
Etienne Gregoire   Sophie Bellique
Thomas J. Hubbard
Robert Deer
Francois Bernier

Cenas, priest

p. 42
S-25
Marie
Ignace

The 3 October, 1851, by us priest undersigned has been buried in the ceme-tery the body of Marie deceased the day before aged 8 months. Present Amable and Charles Petit who have not undersigned.

Cenas, priest

Act
concerning
the
confirmation
of 37
persons

The 5 October, 1851, by Monsigneur F. N. Blanchet, Archbishop of Oregon City have been confirmed the following persons:

George Chiffman Aplin   Susanne (Indian)
Jacques (Indian)   Genevieve [St.] Martin
John Handson   Sophie Dubreuil
Michel Rivet   Esther Belleque

Michel Dubreuil
Jean Baptiste Dubreuil
Joseph Lonetain
Antoine Servant
Jean Baptiste Ouvre
Jean Baptiste Bourgeau
Roch Pichet
Charles Petit
Charles Dupre
Francois Rivet
Louis Quintal
Paul Hypolite
Charles Rivet
Eubert Lacourse

Catherine Sauve
Marguerite Despart
Josette Lavigueur
Rosalie Plouf
Victoire Masta
Esther Pichet
Catherine Aubichon
Philomene Aubichon
Zoe Chamberland
Marie Petit
Marie Wagner
Adelaide Rivet
Marguerite Lacourse
Genevieve Lonetain
Marguerite Pin
Louise

Cenas, priest

p. 43

S-26
Rose
wife of
Michel
Saste

The 6 October, 1851, by us priest undersigned has been buried in the cemetery the body of Rose, wife of Michel, Saste Indian, aged 33 years. Present Amable and Charles Petit, who have not undersigned.

Cenas, priest

B-25
Angelique
Laframboise

The 18 October, 1851, by us priest undersigned has been baptized Angelique, born the 5 October of the same month *[sic]* of the legitimate marriage of Michel Laframboise and of Emelie Picard. Godfather Joseph Sylvestre; godmother Angelique Laframboise, who have not undersigned.

Cenas, priest

S-27
Joseph
Jacques

The 31 October, 1851, by us priest undersigned has been buried in the cemetery the body of Joseph, deceased the day before aged 26 years. Present Louis Pichet and Gedeon Berthelot, who have not undersigned.

Cenas, priest

B-26
Marie
Louise
Philomene
Lebrun

The 4 November, 1851, by us priest undersigned has been baptized Marie Louise Philomene, born yesterday of the legitimate marriage of Hercule Lebrun and of Louise Ouvré. Godfather Firmin Lebrun; godmother Sophie widow Portus, who have not undersigned.

Cenas, priest

S-28
Francois
Gillebeau

The 8 November, 1851, by us priest undersigned has been buried in the cemetery the body of Francois, deceased 2 days ago aged 4 years. Present Hugh Cosgrove, James McKay, Amable Petit, who have not undersigned.

Cenas, priest

B-27
Thomas
Deguire

The 16 November, 1851, by us priest undersigned has been baptized Thomas, born 6 days ago of the legitimate marriage of Jean Baptiste Deguire and of Marie Anne. Godfather Narcisse Cornoyer; godmother Marie, who have not undersigned.

Cenas, priest

M-6
Firmin
Lebrun
&
Sophie,
Portus
[Porteus]

The 18 November, 1851, after the publication of one bann of marriage between Firmin Lebrun, of-age son and legitimate of Pierre Lebrun and of Josette Grinier, both dead, on the one part; and Sophie, widow of William Portus on the other part. The parties having obtained of Monsigneur the Archbishop of Oregon City dispensation of two banns, nor any impediment having been discovered, and the oath of Jean Olivier having been given before us and the witnesses undersigned to attest that the Sieur Firmin Lebrun, of the District of Three Rivers (Canada), has not there contracted any matrimonial engagement, we undersigned priest officiating at the Mission of St. Paul - Wallamete, with the approbation of the relatives of the betrothed, have received their mutual consent to marriage and have given them the nuptial benediction in the presence of the undersigned and many others.

Narcisse A Cornoyer	Firmin LeBrune
J. O. Chevrefils	Sophie widow Portus

Cenas, priest

p. 44
B-28
Marcelline
Bertrand

The 22 November, 1851, by us priest undersigned has been baptized Marcelline born 4 days ago of the legitimate marriage of Cirille Bertrand and of Angele. Godfather Pierre Papin; godmother Susanne Gaudriche, who have not undersigned.

Cenas, priest

M-7
Edward
Eldridge
&
Anne
Cosgrove

The 27th of November, 1851, after the publication of one bann of marriage, the dispensation of the two others being obtained, the dispensation of disparity of worship being moreover obtained from Most Reverend Blanchet Archbishop of Oregon City, I have received the mutual consent of marriage of Freeman Edward Eldridge, son of Gardener Eldridge and Pamelia Mecham both living in Knox county State of Illinois, and Anne Cosgrove, daughter of Hugh Cosgrove and Mary Rositer of the parish of St. Paul in the presence of the said Hugh Cosgrove, Thomas Fitzgerald, William Goulder, Theodore Poujade, Mary Cosgrove who have signed with us as well as the spouses.

B. Delorme [crossed out]

Freeman Edward Eldridge	Anne Cosgrove
Hugh Cosgrove	Thomas Fitzgerald
Theodore C. Poujade	Wm A. Goulder
Mary Cosgrove	M Dougherty

B Delorme

p. 45
B-29
Celestin
Gravel

The 7 December, 1851, by us priest undersigned has been baptized Celestin [male] born a month and 4 days ago of the legitimate marriage of Gedeon Gravel and of Anne Pin. Godfather Pierre Papin; godmother Susanne Gaudriche, who have not undersigned.

Cenas, priest

M-8
Charles
Plante
&
Marguerite
widow
Dubreuil

The 17 December, 1851, Charles Plante and Marguerite, widow Dubreuil, having obtained of Monsigneur the Archbishop of Oregon City the double dispensation of prohibited time and that of three banns of marriage we undersigned priest officiating at the mission of St. Paul [their - crossed out] have received their mutual consent to marriage and have given them the nuptial benediction in the presence of Louis Lucier and of Joseph Despart, who have not undersigned. One word erased nul.

Cenas, priest

B-30
Francois
Bernier

The 25 December, 1851, by us priest undersigned has been baptized Francois born since the 5 of this month of the legitimate marriage of Francois Bernier and of Pelagie Lucier. Godfather Narcisse Cornoyer; godmother Sophie Belleque, who have not undersigned.

Pretot, priest

S-29
Laurent
Sedé

The 26 December, 1851, by us priest undersigned has been buried in the cemetery the body of Laurent deceased since the day before aged 4 years. Present Charlot, and Amable Petit, who have not undersigned.

Cenas, priest

S-30
Charles
Sasté

The 31 December, 1851, by us priest undersigned has been buried in the cemetery the body of Charles deceased the day before aged 25 months. Present Charles Petit and Michel Saste, who have not undersigned.

Cenas, priest
1852

B-1
Auguste
Tayekuarihi

The 4 January, 1852, by us priest undersigned has been baptized Auguste, born 5 days ago of the legitimate marriage of Thomas Tayekuarihi and of Marie. Godfather Francois Guillebeau; godmother Marie Anne, who have not undersigned.

Cénas, priest

p 46

S-1
Eusebe
Tayekua-
rihi
[Norwest]

The 4 January, 1852, by us priest undersigned has been buried in the ceme-
tery the body of Eusebe, deceased the day before aged 6 years and 7 months.
Present Michel Saste and Baptiste Tayekuarihi who have not undersigned.
Cenas, priest

M-1
Louis
Loucier
[and]
Celestine
Gervais

The 7 January, 1852, after the publication of three bans of marriage between Louis Loucier, of-age son and legitimate of Etienne Loucier and of
Marguerite, on the one part; and Celestine Gervais minor daughter and
legitimate of Jean Baptiste Gervais and of Marie Lucie(r), on the other part.
Nor any impediment having been discovered, we undersigned priest officia-
tion at the mission of St. Paul - Wallamette, with the approbation of the
parents of the betrothed, have received their mu- to consent to marriage and
have given them the nuptial benediction in the presence of witnesses undersigned and of many others.
Louis Loucier

Joseph Gervais
Culbert Lambert
Cenas, priest

S-2
Joachim
Fennelly
[Finlay]

The 13 January, 1852, by us priest undersigned has been buried in the ceme-
tery the body of Joachim deceased the day before aged 15 years. Present
Eubert Lacourse and Charles Petit, who have not undersigned.
Cenas, priest

M-2
Michel
Laferte
[and]
Angelique
Sibonne
[Assiniboine]

The 20 January, 1852, after the publication of three bans of marriage between Michel Laferte and Angelique Sibonne, nor having been discovered
any impediment, we undersigned priest officiating at the mission of St. Paul
- Wallamete, with the approbation of the relatives of the betrothed, have
received their mutual consent to marriage and have given them the nuptial
benediction in the presence of Joseph Despart, and of Thomas Tayekuarihi
[Norwest], who have not undersigned.
Cenas, priest

p 46 a
M-3
David
Western
[and]
Marie
Saintclair

The 27 January, 1852, after the publication of one ban of marriage between
David Western on the one part; and Marie Saintclair, on the other part. The
parties having obtained from Monsigneur the Archbishop of Oregon City
dispensation of two bans, nor any impediment being discovered; and the
solemn declaration of Baptiste Deguire having been given before us and the
witnesses undersigned to attest that David Western, known to him since 10
years, has not to his knowledge contracted any matrimonial engagement.
The said David Western having on this occasion consented to make legitimate in his name and to regard as his own child John, natural child of Marie
Saintclair, We undersigned priest have received their mutual consent to
marriage, in presence of the undersigned and of several others.

J.B.DGuire
Louis Labonte
John Moll

David (X) Western
Mary Saintclair

Cenas, priest

S-3
Xavier
Menard

The 14 February, 1852, by us priest undersigned, has been buried in the
cemetery the body of Xavier, deceased the day before aged 4 years. Present
Charles Petit who has not undersigned.
F. Veyret, priest

S-4
Henriette
wife of
Nordouest

The 23 February, 1852, by us priest undersigned has been buried in the
cemetery the body of Henriette deceased the day before, aged 38 years.
Present Bapt. Nordouest and Charles Petit, who have not undersigned.
F. Veyret, priest

p 46 b
M-6
Louis
Boisvert

The 24 February, 1852, Louis Boisvert and Elisabeth having obtained of
Monsigneur the Archbishop of Oregon City dispensation of three proclamations of bans of marriage, We priest undersigned have received their mutual
consent of marriage and have given them the benediction nuptial in the

and
Elisabeth
[Snowden]

presence of Reverend Monsieur Delorme, priest, and of Charles Sete [Tse-te]. The first has signed.

B Delorme, pr.
Cenas, priest

S-5
Joseph
Rivet

The 16 March, 1852, by us priest undersigned has been buried in the cemetery the body of Joseph Rivet deceased the 11th [?] at Oregon City, aged 40 years - present Garant, and Champagne.

Gr. Mengarini, S.J.

S-6
Joseph
Menard

The 17 March, 1852, by us priest undersigned has been buried in the cemetery the body of Joseph Menard deceased the day before aged 15 years. Present Garant.

Gr. Mengarini S.J.

S-7
Stanislas
Leard
[Liard]

The 18 March, 1852, by us priest undersigned has been buried in the cemetery the body of Stanislas Leard deceased the day before, aged 35 years in the presence of Garant.

Gr. Mengarini S.J.

S-8
Marie
Russi

The 2 April, 1852, by us priest undersigned has been buried the body of Marie deceased the day before aged 8 months. Present Augustin Russi and Dalcourt, who have not undersigned.

Cenas, priest

S-9
Julie
Beauchemin

The 9 May, 1852, by us priest undersigned has been buried in the cemetery the body of Julie deceased the day before aged 30 years. Present Delcourt, Bourgeau, Gervais, who have not undersigned.

Cénas, priest

S-10
Catherine
Sauve
wife [of]
Champagne

The 17 May, 1852, by us priest undersigned has been buried in the cemetery the body of Catherine deceased the day before aged 13 years [sic]. Present Joseph Champagne, Laurent Sauve and Louis Pichet, who have not under-signed.

Cenas, priest

p. 47
M-5
Louis
Labonte
&
Euphrasie
Gervais

The 18 May, 1852, after the publication of three banns of marriage between Louis Labonte, son of Louis Labonte and of Marguerite, on the one part; and Euphrasie Gervais, daughter of Jean Baptiste Gervais and of the late Marie Lucie, on the other part. Nor any impediment having been discovered, we undersigned priest have received their mutual consent to marriage in the presence of Pierre Lacourse and of Eubert Lambert, witnesses, and have given them the benediction nuptial. The spouses nor the witnesses, have not signed.

Cenas, priest

B-2
Pierre
Bourgignon

The 17 June, 1852, by us priest undersigned has been baptized Pierre born since the 16 March, 1851,. of the legitimate marriage of Pierre Bourgignon and of Marguerite. Godfather Amable Petit; godmother Suzanne who have not undersigned.

Cenas, priest

B-3
Rosalie
Bourgignon

The 17 June, 1852, by us priest undersigned has been baptized Rosalie, born since 3 years and 2 months of the legitimate marriage of Pierre Bourgignon and of Marguerite. Godfather Augustin Garant; godmother Lucie, who have not undersigned.

Cenas, priest

B-4
Augustin
Reymond

The 18 June, 1852, by us priest undersigned has been baptized Augustin born 3 days ago of the legitimate marriage of Augustin Reymond and of Marie Servant. Godfather Charles Beauchemin; godmother Celeste, widow Liard who have not undersigned.

Cenas, priest

M-6
Pierre
Menard
[&]
Marie

The 21 June, 1852, [some words crossed out] after the publication of one ban of marriage between Pierre Menard on the one part, and Marie Blackfoot on the other part. The parties having obtained of Monsigneur the Archbishop of Oregon City, dispensation of two proclamations of banns, nor was presented any impediment, we priest undersigned have received their

Blackfoot mutual consent to marriage and have given them the nuptial benediction in the presence of Amable Petit, of Ambroise Jean and of one other witness, who have not undersigned.

Cenas, priest

p. 48
B-5 The 28 June, 1852, by us priest undersigned has been baptized Marie, Indian woman in danger of death.

Cenas, priest

S-11
Marie
Indian The 29 June, 1852, by us priest undersigned has been buried in the cemetery the body of Marie Indian woman aged 79 years. Present Narcisse Cornoyer and Louis Pichet, who have not undersigned.

Cenas, priest

S-12
Acadie
Bernier The 5 July, 1852, by us priest undersigned has been buried in the cemetery the body of Adacie aged 5 years. Present Francois Bernier and Louis Pichet, who have not undersigned.

Cenas, priest

S-13
Marie
Attalon The 24 July, 1852, by us priest undersigned has been buried in the cemetery the body of Marie, aged 25 years. Present Amable Petit, Masta, Gingras, who have not undersigned.

Cenas, priest

B-6
Robert
Hartgran [?]
Allen The 25 July, 1852, by us priest undersigned has been baptized Robert born 3 months ago of the legitimate marriage of Thomas Hartgran [?] and Edwin Allen [sic]. Godfather Antoine Lussier; godmother Julie Aubichon who have not undersigned.

Cenas, priest

B-7
Marguerite
wife [of]
Bourgignon The 25 July, 1852, by us priest undersigned has been baptized Marguerite, wife of Prospere Bourgignon.

Cenas, priest

p. 49
M-7
Prospere
Bourgignon
&
Marguerite
Indian The 25 July, 1852, Prospere Bourgignon and Marguerite Indian wife, having obtained dispensation of all banns, in view of the state of cohabitation in which they have found themselves by reason of a natural marriage which they have contracted since several years in the Indian regions, we priest undersigned have received their mutual consent to marriage and have given them the nuptial benediction, in the presence of Amable Petit and of Antoine Masta, who have not undersigned. The spouses have consented before the above said witnesses, to regard as legitimate the 4 children following, born before their ecclesiastic marriage, namely: Louis, Julie, Rosalie and Pierre.

Cenas, priest

B-8
Genevieve
Indian The 8 August, 1852, by us priest undersigned has been baptized Genevieve born 3 months ago of the legitimate marriage of Pierre and of Catherine both Indians. Godfather Louis Bergevin; godmother Genevieve wife of Gardepy, who have not undersigned.

Cenas, priest

B-9
Jean
Gingras The 19 August, 1852, by us priest undersigned has been baptized Jean, born the day before of the legitimate marriage of Jean Gingras and of Bethzee. Godfather Jean Gingras; godmother Olive, who have not undersigned.

Cenas, priest

B-10
Fabien
Chamberland The 27 August, 1852, by us priest undersigned has been baptized Fabien born 4 days ago of the legitimate marriage of Adolphe Chamberland and of Louise. Godfather Fabien Malois [Malouin]; godmother Octavie Laderoute who have not undersigned.

Cenas, priest

B-11
Charles
[Boisvert] The 29 August, 1852, by us priest undersigned has been baptized Charles born 3 days ago of the legitimate marriage of Louis Boisvert and of Bethzee [Betsy?]. Godfather Casimir Gardepy; godmother Catherine, widow Chali-

foux, who have not undersigned.

Cenas, priest

[Inset between pp. 49-50]

S-14   The 1 October, 1852, by us priest undersigned has been buried in the cemetery the body of Marie Florence, wife of Charles Prevost, deceased the day before aged 43 years. Present Moll, Prevost and Mesplié, who have not undersigned.

Cenas, priest

p. 50

B-12
Joseph
Barnabe

The 5 September, 1852, by us priest undersigned has been baptized Joseph, aged 16 years, son of Joseph Barnabe and of Marie, now dead. Godfather Jacques Servant; godmother Isabele Bouche, who have not undersigned.

P. Mangarini

B-13
Marie
Cornouyer

The 5 September, 1852, by us priest undersigned has been baptized Marie born the day before of the legitimate marriage of Narcisse Cornouyer and of Sophie Belleque. Godfather Francois Bernier; godmother Genevieve, who have not undersigned.

Cenas, priest

B-14
Louis
Lacourse

The 11 September, 1852, by us priest undersigned has been baptized Louis, born the day before of the legitimate marriage of Pierre Lacourse and of Victoire Mullen *[McMillan]*. Godfather Louis Labonté; godmother Marie, who have not undersigned.

Cenas, priest

B-15
Joseph
Jodoin

The 23 September, 1852, by us priest undersigned has been baptized Joseph born the day before of the legitimate marriage of Baptiste Jodoin and of Elisabeth Joachim. Godfather Joseph Barnabe; godmother Claudine who have not undersigned.

Cenas, priest

S-14
John
Western

The 27 September, 1852, by us priest undersigned has been buried in the cemetery the body of John deceased the day before aged 1 year. Present Joseph Champagne and David Western, who have not undersigned.

Cenas, priest

S-15
Francois
Rivet

The 27 September, 1852, by us priest undersigned has been buried in the cemetery the body of Francois deceased 2 days ago aged 95 years. Present Antoine Rivet and Narcisse Cornouyer, who have not undersigned.

Cenas, priest

S-16
Catherine

The 7 October, 1852, by us priest undersigned has been buried in the cemetery the body of Catherine deceased the day before aged 32 years. Present Bertrand and Petit who have not undersigned.

Cenas, priest

p. 51

B-16
Joseph
Poujade

The 7 October, 1852, by us priest undersigned has been baptized Joseph Hugh, born the day before of the legitimate marriage of Theodore Poujade and of Marguerite Cosgrove. Godfather Louis Poujade; godmother Marie Cosgrove, undersigned.

Louis Poujade

Mary Cosgrove

Cenas, priest

S-17
Therese
wife *[of]*
Rivet

The 13 October, 1852, by us priest undersigned has been buried in the cemetery the body of Therese deceased the day before aged 97 years. Present Francois Bernier, Antoine Rivet, who have not undersigned.

Cenas, priest

S-18
Jean
Gingras

The 15 October, 1852, by us priest undersigned has been buried in the cemetery the body of Jean deceased the day before aged 2 months. Present Jean Gingras and Amable Petit, who have not undersigned.

Cenas, priest

B-17
George
Anderson

The 31 October, 1852, by us priest undersigned has been baptized George born 8 days ago of the legitimate marriage of Peter Anderson, and of Angelique Carpentier. Godfather Michel Laferté; godmother Marie Anne,

who have not undersigned.
Cenas, priest

S-19
Marie
Costello

The 19 November, 1851 *[sic, probably 1852 intended]* by us priest undersigned has been buried in the cemetery the body of Marie Anne deceased 2 days ago aged 10 years. Present Messieurs Guerin, Costello and Russis, who have not undersigned.
Cenas, priest

S-20
Olivier
Laferte

The 23 November, 1852, by us priest undersigned has been buried in the cemetery the body of Olivier deceased the day before aged 23 years. Present Michel Laferté, and Adolphe Chamberland, who have not undersigned.
Cenas, priest

p. 52
S-21
Celestine
Gervais

The 25 November, 1852, by us priest undersigned has been buried in the cemetery the body of Celestine deceased the day before aged 20 years. Present Louis Loucier and Firmin Lebrun, who have not undersigned.
Cenas, priest
1853

S-1
James
Sheil

The 4 January, 1853, by us priest undersigned has buried in the cemetery the body of James, deceased the day before aged 35 years. Present Messieurs Murphy, Cosgrove, McKay, who have not undersigned.
Cenas, priest

S-2
Charles
Indian

The 10 January, 1853, by us priest undersigned has been buried in the cemetery the body of Charles deceased the day before aged 35 years. Present Pierre Parisot and Amable Petit, who have not undersigned.
Cenas, priest

B-1
Marguerite
Russi

The 16 January, 1853, by us priest undersigned has been baptized Marguerite born the day before of the legitimate marriage of Augustin Russi and of Anne. Godfather Francois Bernier; godmother Marguerite Lacourse, who have not undersigned.
Cenas, priest

B-2
Julienne
Bergevin

The 16 January, 1853, by us priest undersigned has been baptized Julienne born the day before of the legitimate marriage of Louis Bergevin and of Magdeleine. Godparents, Augustin Reymont and Genevieve, who have not undersigned.
Cenas, priest

B-3
Louise
Petit

The 14 January, 1853, by us priest undersigned has been baptized Louise born the day before of the legitimate marriage of Amable Petit and of Suzanne. Godfather Louis Pichet; godmother Marie Petit, who have not undersigned.
Cenas, priest

p. 53
S-3
Jean
Indian

The 27 January, 1853, by us priest undersigned has been buried in the cemetery the body of Jean deceased the day before aged 15 years. Present Amable Petit and Joseph Champagne, who have not undersigned.
Cenas, priest

B-4
Joseph
Papin

The 27 January, 1853, by us priest undersigned has been baptized Joseph, born the day before of the legitimate marriage of Pierre Papin, and of Suzanne Gaudriche. Godfather Cirille Bertrand, godmother Angèle, who have not undersigned.
Cenas, priest

B-5
Emilie
Goin

The 30 January, 1853, by us priest undersigned has been baptized Emilie born 2 days ago of the legitimate marriage of Pierre Goin and of Felicite Kany[?]. Godfather Maurice Brouillet; godmother Catherine, widow Chalifoux, who have not undersigned.
Cenas, priest

M-1
Honore
Picard
&

The 1 February, 1853, after the publication of two banns of marriage between Honoré Picard, on the one part and Celeste Larocque, widow Liard, on the other part. The parties having obtained dispensation of one bann nor any impediment having been discovered, we priest undersigned

Celeste
Larocque
[Rochbrune]

have received their mutual consent to marriage and have given them the nuptial benediction in the presence of witnesses undersigned, and of many other persons.

Hercule Lebrun
Francois Bernier
Cénas, priest

S-4
Child *[of]*
Gervais

The 6 February, 1853, by us priest undersigned has been buried in the cemetery the body of a child privately baptized and deceased the day of birth.
Cénas, priest

p. 54
B-6
Jerome
Rivet

The 7 February, 1853, by us priest undersigned has been baptized Jerome born 3 days ago of the legitimate marriage of Antoine Rivet and of Marie. Godfather Adolphe Chambrelant; godmother Louise, who have not undersigned.
Cénas, priest

B-7
Marie
Pichet

The 7 February, 1853, by us priest undersigned has been baptized Marie born the day before of the legitimate marriage of Louis Pichet and of Marguerite. Godfather Louis Pichet; godmother Catherine, widow Chalifoux, who have not undersigned.
Cenas, priest

B-8
Narcisse
Bertrand

The 8 February, 1853, by us priest undersigned has been baptized Narcisse born 2 days ago of the legitimate marriage of Cirille Bertrand and of Angele. Godfather Narcisse Gingras; godmother Therese Delcourt, who have not undersigned.
Cenas, priest

B-9
Daniel
Mongrain

The 10 February, 1853, by us Archbishop undersigned has been baptized Daniel born the same day of the legitimate marriage of David Mongrain and of Catherine Lafantaisie. Godfather Louis Pichet, godmother Suzan Okenagan who have not undersigned.
+ F. N. Archbishop of Oregon City

B-10
Francois
Indian

The 19 February, 1853, by us priest undersigned has been baptized Francois born the day before of the legitimate marriage of Michel and of Catherine, both Indians. Godfather Joseph Lucier; godmother Genevieve Belleque, who have not undersigned.
M. Accolti

B-11
Genevieve
Aplin

The 22 February, 1853, we priest undersigned have supplied the ceremonies of Baptism to Genevieve born the 11 of this month of the legitimate marriage of George Chiffman Aplin and of Marie Wagner.
Cenas, priest.

p. 55
S-5
Etienne
Loussier

The 9 March, 1853, by us priest undersigned has been buried in the cemetery the body of Etienne deceased the day before aged 60 years. Present Bernier, Pichet, Champagne, who have not undersigned.
Cenas, priest

[of Pierre]

S-6
Pierre
Bourgignon

The 24 March, 1853, by us priest undersigned has been buried in the cemetery the body deceased the day before aged 3 years. Present Amable Petit and Prospere Bourgignon, who have not undersigned.
Cenas, priest

S-7
Marguerite
wife of
Bourguignon

The 25 March, 1853, by us priest undersigned has been buried in the cemetery the body of Marguerite deceased the day before aged 30 years. Present Prospere Bourguignon and Amable Petit who have not undersigned.
Cenas, priest

B-12
Pierrette
Arquoit

The 3 April, 1853, by us priest undersigned has been baptized Pierrette born 8 days ago of the legitimate marriage of Amable Arquoit and of Pierrette. Godfather Michel Arquoit; godmother Genevieve Beleque, who have not undersigned.
Cenas, priest

B-13 Catherine Westron	The 17 April, 1853, we priest undersigned have baptized Catherine, born the 28 March last, of the legitimate marriage of David Westron, and of Mary Sinclair of this parish. Godfather William Gladman, who has signed with us, godmother Genevieve Longtain who could not sign. William Gladman B Delorme, priest
S-8 Agathe Delcour	The 4 May, 1853, we undersigned have buried Agathe, Indian wife of Baptiste Delcour, inhabitants of the parish of St. Paul, deceased the day before yesterday aged about 40 years. Witnesses Louis Aussan, Felix Bergevin, Cuthbert Lambert. B Delorme
S-9 Ant Rivet	The 4 May, 1853, we undersigned priest of St. Paul have buried Antoine son of Antoine Rivet and Emelie his wife, deceased the day before aged about 5 years. Witnesses Louis Aussan, Felix Bergevin. B Delorme

p. 56

1853

B-14 Luce Gardepi	The 31 May, 1853, we Archbishop of Oregon City have baptized Luce born yesterday of the legitimate marriage of Casimire Gariessi, farmer of this place and of Genevieve St. Martin. Godfather Louis Bergevin, godmother Madeleine Servant who as well as the father could not sign. + F. N. Archbishop of Oregon City
B-15 Michel Laferte	The 12 June, 1853, we undersigned priest of St. Paul have baptized Michel born the day before yesterday of the legitimate marriage of Michel Laferte and of Angelique Assiniboine, inhabitants of this parish. Godfather Joseph Laferté, godmother Sophie Aubichon who could not sign. B Delorme, priest
B-15 [sic] Florence Gagnon	The 26 June, 1853, we undersigned Parish priest of St. Paul have baptized Florence aged about 2 years born outside of marriage, of Francois Gagnon of the parish of St. Louis and of Marie Monique of the parish of St. Paul. Godfather Eluy Ducharme godmother Esther Belleque who could not sign. B Delorme, priest
M-2 Julien Marie Bihan & Emilie Pelletier	The 4 July, 1853, we undersigned parish priest of St. Paul, after the publication of three banns of marriage made at the sermons of our parish Masses, of St. Louis and of St. Paul between Julien Marie Bihan of-age son of Jacques Marie Bihan resident of Cruisie Department of the Lower Loire, France, and of Lealie [?] Francoise Navette, deceased, of the same place, on the one part; and Emilie Pelletier of-age daughter of Jean Baptiste Pelletier and of Rosalie Blanchet, both deceased of St. Francois district of Quebec, Canada, on the other part; Messieurs Francois Menes and Jean Francois Guerin having certified before us that the said Julien Bihan was free of all matrimonial engagements, and not having encountered, moreover any impediment, we have received their mutual consent to marriage and have given them the nuptial benediction in the presence of M. Guilliam Leclaire, priest, Jean Francois Guerin, Cuthbert Lambert, and of Charles Prevost. The two first have signed with us as well as the groom. Julien Marie Bihan. G. Leclaire, priest Jean Francois Guerin B Delorme, priest

p. 57

B-16 Louis Leclaire	The 25 July, 1853, we undersigned parish priest of St. Paul have baptized Louis born the day before of the legitimate marriage of Francois Xavier Leclaire, and of Rachel Halsey of this parish. Godfather Louis Forcier, godmother Sophie Dubreuil who could not sign. B Delorme, priest
B-17 Edouard Bellanger	The 1 August, 1853, we undersigned parish priest of St. Louis and of St. Paul have baptized Edouard born the 24 of July last of the legitimate marriage of Edouard Bellanger, and of Angelique Marcellai of this parish. God-

father Louis Gagnon, godmother Ursule Gagnon who could not sign.

B Delorme, priest

S-10
Rosalie
Perrault

The 29 August, 1853, we undersigned parish priest of St. Paul have buried in the cemetery of this parish Angele *[sic]* brought up by Baptiste Perrault, deceased at the house of Baptiste Deguire 2 days ago, aged about 16 years. Witnesses Joseph Champagne, Charles Prévot.

B Delorme,

M-3
James
Costello
[&]
Mary
Cosgrove

On the 27 October, 1853, after the publication of one bann of marriage which has been performed at the sermon of our parish Masses of St. Louis and St. Paul between James Costello of the parish of St. Paul, son, of-age, of John Costello, deceased, in Fortwain *[Fort Wayne]* Indiana North America, and of Ellen Burns of the same parish on the one side and Mary Cosgrove, daughter, of-age, of Hugh Cosgrove of Mary Rosida of the same parish of St. Paul on the other side; whereas a dispensation of two banns has been granted by Mons. Rev. F.N. Blanchet, Archbishop of Oregon City; whereas moreover no legal impediment has appeared to exist; we the undersigned parish priest of the parishes of St. Paul and St. Louis have received their mutual consent of marriage and have given them the nuptial benediction in the presence of Hugh Cosgrove, father of the bride, John D. Crawford, Ellen Mary Costello and some other friends of the parties who have signed with us as well as the new married couple.

James Costello	Mary Cosgrove
Hugh Cosgrove	John D Crawford
Ellen Mary Costello	F.E. Eldridge
John Costello	Robert Newell
Anne Eldridge	Virginia F. Burns

B Delorme, c.p.

p. 58
S-11
Jerome
Rivet

The 4 November, 1853, we undersigned have buried in the cemetery of this mission the body of Jerome legitimate son of Antoine Rivet farmer of this place and Emelie Moyse, deceased day before yesterday aged 10 months. Present Antoine Rivet and Charles Prevost, who could not sign.

+ F. N. Archbishop of Oregon City

M-4
Manuel
Felix
&
Sophie
Dubreuil

The 21 November, 1853, after the publication of three banns of marriage made at the sermons of the parish Masses of this mission as well as that of St. Louis as it appears by the certificate of the missionary, between Manuel Felix, domiciled at St. Louis, of-age son of Antoine Felix, farmer and of the late Marguerite des Chaudieres, of the same place, on the one part; and Sophie Dubreuil, domiciled at St. Paul, minor daughter of the late Jean Baptiste Dubreuil, during his lifetime farmer, and of Marguerite Tchinouk, of the same place, on the other part, nor having been discovered any impediment to the said marriage and with the consent of the mother of the bride, and the relatives of the groom, we undersigned have received their mutual consent to marriage and have given them the nuptial benediction in the presence of Antoine Felix Palaquin, father, David Mongrain friend of the groom, and of Charles Plante step-father, of Francois Xavier Plante step brother of the bride who as well as the spouses could not sign.

+ F. N. Archbishop of Oregon City

p. 59
S-12
Thomas
Deguire

The 7 December, 1853, by us undersigned has been buried in the cemetery of this mission the body of Thomas legitimate son of Jean Baptiste Deguire husbandman, and of Marie Anne Perault, deceased the day before yester-day, aged 2 years, in the presence of Jean Bte Deguire and of Louis Guilbeau who have not undersigned.

+ F. N. Archbishop of Oregon City

B-18
Adele
Picard

The 21 December, 1853, we undersigned have baptized Adele born today of the legitimate marriage of Henri Picard farmer and of Celeste Rochbrun, of this mission. Godfather Jacques Servant; godmother Catherine Russie

who as well as the father could not sign.
+ F. N. Archbishop of Oregon City

B-19
Alexandre
illegitimate

The 31 May, 1853, we undersigned have baptized Alexandre born illegitimate the 24 April last, in this parish. Godfather we undersigned for want of another.
Fr. Mengarini S.J.

B-20
Mary Ann
Helene
Durett

The 25 September, 1853, we undersigned have baptized Mary Ann Helene born the 14 May last of the legitimate marriage of Benedict G. Durett, merchant and of Louisa J Waddille of this parish. Godfather James Costello, godmother Helenn [sic] Costello undersigned as well as the father.
B. G. Durrett
[no other signatures]
Gr. Mengarini, S.J.

p. 60

1854

B-1
Julie
Gravel

The 5 January, 1854, we undersigned have baptized Julie born the 10 of last month of the legitimate marriage of Gedeon Gravel farmer of this place, and of Nancy Pin. Godfather Charles Prevost Sr. godmother Marguerite Pin who could not sign, nor could the father.
+ F. N. Archbishop of Oregon City

B-2
Euphemie
Chamberland

The 6 January, 1854, we undersigned have baptized Euphemie born today of the legitimate marriage of Adolphe Chamberland farmer of this place and of Louise Emperville. Godfather Pierre Gautier, godmother Esther Dalcourt who could not sign. The father undersigned.
Adolphus Chamberlain
+ F. N. Archbishop of Oregon City

S-1
Joseph
Jacques

The 13 January, 1854, we undersigned have buried in the cemetery of this mission Joseph son of the late Joseph Jacques, in his lifetime farmer, and of Betsy Bourgeau, of this place, deceased day before yesterday aged 2 years and a half. Present Joseph Barnabe, and David Mongrain who could not sign.
+ F. N. Archbishop of Oregon City

S-2
Cuthbert
Lacourse

The 21 January, 1854, we undersigned have buried in the cemetery of this mission the body of Cuthbert legitimate son of Pierre Lacourse and of Archange of the tribe of Nesqualy, deceased day before yesterday, aged 16 years. Present Pierre Lacourse father and Francois Bernier who could not sign.
+ F. N. Archbishop of Oregon City

B-3
Bibianne
Lafantaisie

The 30 January, 1854, we priest undersigned have baptized Bibiane born the 26 of this month, of the legitimate marriage of Charles Lafantaisie farmer of this place and of Genevieve Rondeau. Godfather Jean Francois Guerin, undersigned, godmother Isabelle McKay who as well as the father could not sign.
J.F. Guerin
+ F. N. Archbishop of Oregon City

B-4
M. Melanie
Lebrun

The 4 February, 1854, we undersigned have baptized Marie Melanie born yesterday of the legitimate marriage [of] Hercule Lebrun farmer of this place and Louise Ouvre. Godfather Antoine Gregoire, godmother Therese Ouvre, who has signed also the father, the godfather could not sign.
Hercule Lebrun   Therese Ouvre
+ F. N. Archbishop of Oregon City

p. 61
B-6
Jean
Laframboise

The 5 February, 1854, we undersigned have baptized Jean born 21 days ago of the legitimate marriage [of] Michel Laframboise farmer, and of Emelie Picard; of this mission. Godfather Cuthbert Lambert, godmother Marie Okinagan who could not sign. The father absent.
+ F. N. Archbishop of Oregon City

M-1
Hyacinthe

The 13 February, 1854, in view of the dispensation of two banns granted by us undersigned and the publication of the third at the sermon of the parish

Comartin & Catherine Russie	Mass between Hyacinthe Comartin, domiciled in this place, of-age son of Antoine Comartin, husbandman and of Felicite Sylvestre, of St. Barthelemi, District of Montreal in Canada, on the one part; and Catherine Russie, domiciled in this place, widow, of-age, of the late Andre Chalifou, in his lifetime farmer, in this mission, on the other part; nor was discovered any impediment, and the future groom having brought two witnesses who have declared under oath that he was free for the three or four *[years]* that they had seen and known him in the United States, We Archbishop of Oregon City, undersigned, have received their mutual consent to marriage and have given them the nuptial benediction in the presence of Louis Pichet, relative of the bride, of Casimire Gariessy and of Francois Bernier friends of the groom who could not sign nor could the spouses.

+ F. N. Archbishop of Oregon City

B-7 Francois Raimond	The 15 February, 1854, we undersigned have baptized Francois born yesterday of the legitimate marriage of Augustin Raimond, husbandman, and of Marie Servant, of this mission. Godfather Francois Bernier, godmother Josephte Okinagan who as well as the father could not sign.

+ F. N. Archbishop of Oregon City

B-8 Genevieve Bernier	The 22 February, 1854, we undersigned have supplied the ceremonies of baptism upon Genevieve born yesterday of the legitimate marriage of Francois Bernier, husbandman and of Pelagie Lucie *[sic]* of this mission; Godfather David Mongrain, godmother Catherine Lafantaisie. The said Genevieve having been privately baptized the same day of her birth in danger of death by Michel Laframboise.

Gr. Mengarini S.J.

Inset above pp 61-62
[see M-1 above]
Affidavit of Michel Pellicier in favor of Hy Comartin
Before us Archbishop of Oregon City has appeared Michel Pelicier formerly of the parish of St Michel of Yamaska, district of Three Rivers, which he left 6 years ago, who declares under the fidelity of the oath that he has known the said Hyacinthe Comartin formerly of St. Barthelimi, during 4 years at St. Paul, at the River of the Swan, at the little falls, that he had worked 7 months with him, that he had encountered him many a time during the year and that he had not ever heard said, nor learned not knew that he was married neither there nor anywhere.
Done at St Paul the 10 February, 1854, in the presence of Louis Pichet and of Cazimire Gariepy who have signed by a cross as well as the one sworn.

Louis (X) Pichette   Michel (X) Pelicier
Casimire (X) Gariessy

+ F. N. Archbishop of Oregon City

Before us Archbishop of Oregon City has appeared the said Michel Bonneau formerly of Chateauguay district of Montreal, Canada, who declares under the fidelity of the oath that he has known the said Hyacinthe Comartin formerly of St. Barthelimi, Canada, at the Fort Guiner *[?]* for the first time, that he has seen him afterwards during three years at different times, that he has worked himself with him, that he had come with him into the country and that he had never heard said, nor learned, nor known that he was ever married there or anywhere - done the 10 February, 1854, in the presence of witnesses undersigned by the means of a cross as well as the one sworn.

Louis (X) Pichet   Michel (X) Bonneau
Cazimire (X) Gariessy

+ F. N. Archbishop of Oregon City

[Cenas signed at the bottom edge of the page]

p. 62

B-9 Rodolphe Auguste Desrivieres	The 23 February, 1854, we undersigned have supplied the ceremonies of baptism upon Rodolphe Auguste Maximilien born the 17 of this month of the legitimate marriage of Isidore Adelard De*[s]*rivieres, Doctor, and Elisabeth Bourgeau. Godfather Silvain Bourgeau, godmother Angele Lafantaisie, who could not sign. The father absent.

Gr. Mengarini S.J.

S-3	The 3 March, 1854, we undersigned have buried in the cemetery of this mis-

Marguerite Kalapouia	sion the body of Marguerite legitimate daughter of Antoine Kalapouya and of Marguerite Kalapouia, deceased yesterday, aged 2 years. Present Charles Petit and Narcisse Vivet who could not sign. + F. N. Archbishop of Oregon City
S-4 Louis Lacourse	The 11 March, 1854, we undersigned have buried in the cemetery of this mission the body of Louis legitimate son of Pierre Lacourse farmer and of Victoire McMullen, of this mission, deceased yesterday in the morning aged 1 and a half [years] Present Louis Labonte and Pierre Lacourse who could not sign. + F. N. Archbishop of Oregon City
B-10 Marie Quintal	The 28 March, 1854, we undersigned have baptized Marie born about 2 months ago of the legitimate marriage of Laurent Quintal farmer and of Marie Anne Tchinook, of this mission. Godfather Augustin Russie, godmother Anne Nordouest who could not sign. + F. N. Archbishop of Oregon City
S-5 Edouard Rivet	The 6 April, 1854, we undersigned have buried in the cemetery of this mission the body of Edouard son of Antoine Rivet, farmer, and of Emelie Moyse, of this place, deceased yesterday aged 2 years. Present Antoine Rivet and Francois Rivet who could not sign. + F. N. Archbishop of Oregon City
B-11 Catherine Gingras	The 9 April, 1854, we undersigned have baptized Catherine born the 31 March last of the legitimate marriage of Joseph Gingras farmer and of Marie Anne Bastien of this mission. Godmother Catherine Laferte who as well as the father could not sign. + F. N. Archbishop of Oregon City
p. 63 S-6 Charles Prevost by explosion of the Gazelle	The 11 April, 1854, we undersigned have buried in the cemetery of this mission the body of Charles son of Charles Prevost farmer, and of the late Marie Florence Peltier, of the same place deceased Saturday evening about 6 hours, the 8th of the month, at Oregon City in consequence of the explosion of the steamboat Gazelle at Canemeh about 7 hours in the morning of the same day, after having been administered [the Sacraments]. Present Charles Prevost, father, Louis Prevost, brother of the deceased and a great number of friends. + F. N. Archbishop of Oregon City
B-12 Esther Matte	The 28 May, 1853 [sic], by us undersigned Archbishop of Oregon City has been baptized Esther born today of the legitimate marriage of Louis Matte blacksmith and of Therese Piedgane of this mission. Godfather Rock Pichet, godmother Esther Pichet who as well as the father could not sign. + F. N. Archbishop of Oregon City
S-7 Jacques Servant	The 4 June, 1854, by us Archbishop undersigned has been buried in the cemetery of this mission Jacques Servant in his lifetime farmer and [husband] of Josephte Okinagan, of this place, deceased day before yesterday aged . . . Present Louis Bergevin and Augus Raimond who could not sign. + F. N. Archbishop of Oregon City
B-13 Philomene Indian	The 4 June, 1854, by us priest Archbishop undersigned has been baptized Philomene born 8 months ago of the natural marriage of Baptiste Clamath and a Saste woman. Godfather Amable Arquoite, godmother Marguerite Clackmas who could not sign. F. N. Archbishop of Oregon City
B-14 Calliste Gingras	The 6 June, 1854, we priest undersigned have baptized Calliste born yesterday of the legitimate marriage of Jean Gingras and of Olive Forcier of this parish. Godfather Pierre Pepin (alias LaChance) and godmother Susanne Bash [Lachance?] who as well as the father could not sign. Gr. Mengarini S.J.
B-15 Pascal Oawhy	The 10 June, 1854, we Archbishop undersigned have baptized Pascal born 2 years ago of the natural marriage of Charles Oawhy and of Melie woman of the country. Godfather Pascal Biscornet, godmother Louise Kawitchin who could not sign. F. N. Archbishop of Oregon City

P 64
S-8
Nameless
of
Pichet

The 19 June, 1854, by us undersigned Archbishop has been buried in the cemetery of this mission the body of an un-named boy child legitimate of Louis Pichet, father, farmer, and of Marguerite Bercier, of this place, deceased shortly after having been privately baptized at home, day before yesterday. Present Louis Pichet, jr., and Rock Pichet who could not sign.

F. N. Archbishop of Oregon City

B-16
Christine
Deschamps

The day 10 July, 1854, we priest undersigned have baptized Christine born the 2 July, 1854, of the legitimate marriage of Pierre Deschamps and Marie Louis Monique of this parish. Godfather Louis Loucie [Lucier]; godmother Marguerite Frederique [Despard] who as well as the father could not sign.

Gr. Mengarini S.J.

B-17
Louis
Cantal
[Quintal]

The 17 July, 1854, we priest undersigned have baptized Louis born 2 months ago of the marriage of Louis Cantal and of Cecile Laderisse [Norwest] of this parish. Godfather Auguste Russie; godmother Anne Laderisse [Norwest] who could not sign.

m. OReilly, priest

M-2
Regis
Picard
&
Marie
Petit

The 24 July, 1854, after the publication of one bann of marriage between Regis Picard, minor son of the late Andre Picard and of Marie Okinagan on the one part, and Marie Petit, minor daughter of Amable Petit and Suzanne Indian, both with the consent of their parents. The parties having obtained dispensation of 2 banns, and not having discovered any impediment, we undersigned priest have received their mutual consent to marriage and have given them the nuptial benediction in the presence of Cuthbert Lambert, of Amable Petit, Casimir Gardepi, and of Etienne Gregoire who could not sign.

M. OReilly, c.p.

p. 65
S-9
Louise
Petit

The 8 August, 1854, we undersigned Archbishop have buried in the cemetery of this mission Louise legitimate daughter of Amable Petit, verger, and Susanne Thomas, of this mission, deceased yesterday in the morning aged 1 year and a half. Present Amable Petit and Cuthbert Lambert who could not sign.

+ F. N. Archbishop of Oregon City

M-3
J Bte
Goye
&
Louise
Tawatawakon

The 16 August, 1854, in view of the dispensation of one bann of marriage granted by us undersigned and the publication of two others between Jean Baptiste Goyé domiciled in this place, of-age son of Augustin Goyé and of Lisette Roy, of St. Laurent Island of Montreal, Canada, on the one part; and Louise Tawatawakon, domiciled in this place, minor daughter of the late Thomas Tawatawakon and of Francaise Cayouse, of this mission, on the other part; nor having been discovered any impediment and with the consent of the mother of the bride, we Archbishop of Oregon City have received their mutual consent to marriage and have given them the nuptial benediction in the presence of Laurent Sauve, stepfather of the girl, of Cuthbert Lambert of Gratien Leblanc and of Joseph Rigail, the two last undersigned, the others as well as the spouses could not sign.

Joseph Rigail   Gratien leblanc
+ F. N. Archbishop of Oregon City

B-18
Marie
Gervais

The 29 August, 1854, by us Archbishop undersigned has been baptized Marie born yesterday of the legitimate marriage of Theodore Gervais farmer and of Angelique Lafantaisie, of this mission. Godfather Jean Baptiste Dalcourt, godmother Susanne Okinagan who as well as the father present could not sign.

+ F. N. Blanchet

S-10
William
Canon

The 30 August, 1854, by us Archbishop undersigned has been buried in the cemetery of this mission the body of William Canon, widower of a Chinouk woman, deceased supplied with the Sacraments of the Church yesterday aged 97 years. Present Cuthbert Lambert and Casimire Gardipy who could not sign.

+ F. N. Archbishop of Oregon City

p. 66

B-19
Mary Ann
Costello

On the 10th of September 1854, we undersigned Archbishop have baptized Mary Ann born on the 11th of August last, from the lawful marriage of James Costello, merchant of Champoeg and of Mary Cosgrove, of this mission. Godfather Myles McDonald, godmother Helenn Mary Costello signed with us and the father and mother.

Ellen Ma Costello
Miles McDonnald

Mary Costello
James Costello

+ F. N. Archbishop of Oregon City

B-20
Euphreme
Jeaudoin

The 22 September, 1854, we undersigned have baptized Euphreme born yesterday of the legitimate marriage of Jean Baptiste Jeaudoin farmer, and of Elisabeth Joachim, of this mission. Godfather Francois Lefevre, godmother Therese Dalcourt who could not sign. The father has signed with us.

Jean Bapt Jeaudoin
+ F. N. Archbishop of Oregon City

Abj. 1
James
Robinson

The 24 September, 1854, we undersigned archbishop of Oregon City, have received the abjuration of protestantism of James Robinson, formerly soldier at the barracks of the Dalles, and his profession of the faith Catholic, Apostolic and Roman, in the presence of Myles McDonald and D.M. Murphy signed with the new member of the church.

Miles McDonnell
D MC Murphy

James Robinson

+ F. N. Archbishop of Oregon City

B-21
James
Robinson

The 24 September, 1854, we undersigned Archbishop of Oregon City have baptized conditionally James Robinson aged 40 years, heretofore a soldier at the Dall, husband of Mary Ann Engrem [Ingrahm?] Godfather Myles McDonald, godmother Cecilia Lawson undersigned as well as the baptized.

Cecilie Lawson
Miles McDonnell

James Robinson

+ F. N. Archbishop of Oregon City

Bapt 22
Moise
Rivet

The 15 October, 1854, we undersigned priest have baptized Moise born the 25 September, 1854, of the legitimate marriage of Antoine Rivet and of Amelia Noitpi [?] of this mission. Godfather Narcisse Cornoyer and godmother Marie Sophie Belleque who have signed.

Gr. Mengarini S.J.
Narcisse A Cornoyer   Marie Sophie Belleque

p. 67

B-23
Celestine
Pepin

The 18 October, 1854, we undersigned priest have baptized Celestine born yesterday of the legitimate marriage of Pierre Pepin (dit LaChance) and of Susanne Godridge farmers. Godfather Elois DuCheneau. Godmother Zoë Chamberlain who could not sign.

Gr. Mengarini S.J.

S-11
Felecite
Gervais

The 22 October, 1854, we undersigned have buried in the cemetery of this mission the body of Felecite Gervais, wife of Louis Labonte farmer of this place, deceased day before yesterday in the evening, aged 16 years and a half. Present Louis Labonte and Francois Bernier who could not sign.

+ F. N. Blanchet Archbishop of Oregon City

B-24
Soulanges
Bergevin

The 2 November, 1854, we undersigned have baptized Souslanges born yesterday of the legitimate marriage of Louis Bergevin farmer and of Magdeleine Servant of this mission. Godfather Theodore Gervais, godmother, Marie Servant who as well as the father could not sign.

+ F. N. Archbishop of Oregon City

S-12
Archange
Lacourse

The 3 November, 1854, we undersigned Archbishop have buried in the cemetery of this mission the body of Archange of the tribe of . . . , wife of Pierre Lacourse senior, deceased the 1 of the month aged about 50 years. Present Cuthbert Lambert and Francois Bernier who could not sign.

+ F. N. Archbishop of Oregon City

B-25
B-25
Joseph
Clovis
Cornoyer

The 25 November, 1854, we undersigned have baptized Joseph Clovis born yesterday of the legitimate marriage of Narcisse Cornoyer farmer and of Sophie Beleque of this mission. Godfather Casimire Gardepie godmother Marie St. Martin Huburd who could not sign. The father absent.

+ F. N. Archbishop of Oregon City

p. 68
B-26
Francois
Laderoute

The 26 November, 1854, we undersigned have baptized Francois born the 18th of this month, of the legitimate marriage of Xavier Laderoute farmer, and of Marie Anne Ouvre, of this mission. Godfather Louis Labonte, godmother Genevieve Lonetain who no more than the father, could not sign.

+ F. N. Archbishop of Oregon City

S-13
Eloi
Ducheneau

The 4 December, 1854, we undersigned have buried in the cemetery of this mission the body of Eloi Ducheneau son of the late . . . Ducheneau and of . . . Ducheneau, deceased day before yesterday aged about 26 years. Present Cuthbert Lambert and . . . Bertrand who could not sign.

+ F. N. Archbishop of Oregon City

B-14, 15
Claude
&
Sara
Lacourse

The 7 December, 1854, we undersigned have baptized Claude and Sara, twins, born yesterday of the legitimate marriage of Pierre Lacourse, farmer, and Victoire McNolen [McMillan], of this mission. Godfathers and godmothers of Claude, Louis Labonte jr., and Marie St. Martin; of Sara, Francois Poirier and Julienne Labonte, who no more than the father could not sign.

+ F. N. Archbishop of Oregon City

B-16
George
Edouard
Applin

The 10 December, 1854, we undersigned have baptized George Edouard born the 5 of this month of the legitimate marriage of George Applin farmer, and Marie Waguener, of this mission. Godfather Jean Baptiste Mesplié and [godmother] Elizabeth Waguener, who has not signed. The father and the godfather undersigned.

George Chiffman Aplin
Jean Mesplié
+ F. N. Archbishop of Oregon City

S-14
Catherine
Weston

The 11 December, 1854, we undersigned have buried in the cemetery of this mission the body of Catherine legitimate daughter of David Weston, blacksmith, and of Mary Sinclair, deceased yesterday in the morning, aged about 20 months. Present Louis Labonte who could not sign. David Weston undersigned.

[no signature]
+ F. N. Archbishop of Oregon City

p. 69
B-17
Felicite
Comartin

The 15 December, 1854, we undersigned have baptized Felicite born day before yesterday of the legitimate marriage [of] Hyacinthe Comartin, farmer, and of Catherine Russie, of this mission. Godfather Francois Bernier, godmother Pelagie Lussier who as well as the father present could not sign.

+ F. N. Archbishop of Oregon City

S-15
Frs
Pascal
Biscornet
dit
Caillé

The 23 December, 1854, we undersigned have buried in the cemetery of this mission the body of Francois Pascal Biscornet, farmer, husband of Louise, of the Fraser River, deceased yesterday aged about 63 years. Present Jos. Matte and Cazimire Gardipie who could not sign.

+ F. N. Archbishop of Oregon City

Baptisms 17
Sepultures 15
Marriages 3

1855

B-1
Honore
Desire
Bertrand

The 1 January, 1855, we undersigned have baptized Honore Desire born this morning of the legitimate marriage of Cyril Bertrand farmer and of Angele Gingras, of this mission. Godfather Honore Picard, godmother Celeste Rocquebrune who could not sign.

+ F. N. Archbishop of Oregon City

M-1 Joseph Rocbrune & Mgte Souliere	The 8 January, 1855, after the publication of three banns of marriage between Joseph Rocbrune, farmer, widower of Lisette Wallawalla, formerly of the mission of St. Louis, on the one part; and Marguerite Souliere, of this mission, widow of the late David Dompierre, in his lifetime farmer, on the other part, nor any impediment having been discovered, we undersigned have received their mutual consent to marriage and have given them the nuptial benediction in the presence of Sylvain Bourgeau and of Jean Pierre Sanders witnesses who as well as the spouses could not sign. + F. N. Archbishop of Oregon City
B-2 Pierre Garant	The 13 January, 1855, we undersigned have supplied the ceremonies of baptism to Pierre born the 6 March, 1853 of the legitimate marriage of Augustin Garant, and Lucie of Cowlitz, of this mission, privately baptized at home during the while by the Rev. Mr. Cenas, at that time officiating priest *[of the parish]*. + F. N. Archbishop of Oregon City
p. 70 B-3 Thomas Garant	The 13 January, 1855, we undersigned have baptized Thomas born the 9 of the present *[month]* of the legitimate marriage of Augustin Garant, farmer, and of Lucie of Cowlitz, of this mission. Godfather Pierre Bonin, godmother Rosalie Waguener undersigned. The father and the godfather could not do *[sign]*. Rose Wagner + F. N. Archbishop of Oregon City
S-1 Euphreme Jeaudoin	The 16 January, 1855, we undersigned have buried in the cemetery of this mission the body of Euphreme legitimate son of Jean Baptiste Jeaudoin farmer and of Elisabeth Joachim, of this place, deceased the day before yesterday, aged 4 months. Present Jean Bte Jeaudoin and Amable Petit who have not signed. + F. N. Archbishop of Oregon City
M-2 Pre Bonin & Rose Waguener	The 29 January, 1855, in view of the dispensation of the publication of one bann of marriage, granted by us, and the publication of two others in this mission as well as in that of St. Louis as it appears by the certificate between Pierre Bonin, farmer, domiciled at the mission of St. Louis, of-age widower of the late Louise Rondeau, on the one part; and Rose Waguener, domiciled in this mission, minor daughter of Pierre Waguener, farmer and of Marie of the Island of Vancouver, also of St. Paul, on the other part; not any impediment having been discovered and with the consent of the father of the bride, we undersigned Archbishop have received their mutual consent to marriage and have given them the nuptial benediction in the presence of Augustin Lambert and Cubert Lambert, witnesses, of Pierre Waguener and of Pierre Lacourse who as well as the groom could not sign. The bride has signed with us. Rose Wagner + F. N. Archbishop of Oregon City
S-2 Moyse Rivet	The 31 January, 1855, we undersigned have buried in the cemetery of this mission the body of Moise legitimate son of Antoine Rive farmer and Amelie Calispell, deceased yesterday, aged 4 months. Present Narcisse Cornoyer and Antoine Rive. Gr. Mengarini S.J.
p. 70a B-4 Louisa Philomena Petit	The 7th day of February, 1855, we the undersigned missionary priest, now at St. Paul, Oregon Territory, have baptized Louisa Philomena, born the 6th instant the legitimate daughter of Amable Petit and Susanna Wacko - (Sponsors) Charles Prevost and Maria Lambert. Patrick Mackin C.P.
S-3 John	The 8th day of February, 1855, we the undersigned missionary priest, now at St. Paul, Oregon Territory, have given Christian burial to John an Indian, about 23 years old, and resided with Peter Lacours *[Pierre Lacourse]*. Patrick Mackin C. Pr.

S-4 **Joseph** **Laframboise**	The 15th day of February, 1855. We the undersigned missionary priest now at St. Paul, Oregon Territory, have given Christian burial to Joseph 13 years old and the legitimate son of Michel Laframboise and Emelie Picard. Patrick Mackin C. Pr.
B-5 **Marie** **La Forte** *[Laferte]*	The 4 March, 1855, we undersigned have baptized Marie born yesterday of the legitimate marriage of Michel la Forte and Angelique de Rivieres, of this mission. Godfather Peter Pepin, godmother Catherine La Fort who could not sign. M. OReilly, priest
B-6 **Baptiste** **La Phantasie**	The 12 March, 1855, we undersigned have supplied the ceremonies of baptism to Baptiste born the 6 March of the legitimate marriage of Charles La Phantasie and Genevieve Rondeau, of this mission, privately baptized at home in danger of death by us undersigned. Godfather Justin de L'or *[Augustin Delard]* godmother Nancie Empreville *[Humpherville]* who could not sign. M. OReilly, priest
S-4 *[sic]* **Michel** **La Ferte**	The 15 March, 1855, we undersigned have buried in the cemetery of this mission the body of Michel, legitimate son of Michel La Ferte and of Angelique de Rivieres, of this place, deceased day before yesterday, aged 18 months. Present Thomas Norruss Michel La Ferte, and Amable Petit, who could not sign. M. OReilly, priest
p. 70b **B-7** **Catherine** **illegitimate**	The 18 March, 1855, we undersigned have baptized Catherine, born the 14th of the present *[month]* illegitimate daughter of Catherine Lonetain of this mission. Godfather Francois Toupain, godmother Genevieve Lonetain, who could not sign. M. OReilly, priest
B-8 **John** **Neal** **McKay**	On the 19th day of March, 1855, we the undersigned have baptized John Neal, born March 7th *[?]* of the lawful marriage of James McKay and Cecilia Lauson of this mission. Sponsors Myles McDonald and Elisabeth Cosgrove. M. OReilly, priest
B-9 **Clarissa** **Mongrain**	The 21 March, 1855, we undersigned have baptized Clarissa, born yesterday of the legitimate marriage of David Mongrain and Catherine La Phantasie, of this mission. Godfather Francois Bernier, godmother Marguerite Bertier, who could not sign. M. OReilly, priest
S-5 **Therese** **Dalcourt**	The 23 March, 1855, we undersigned have buried in the cemetery of this mission the body of Therese, legitimate daughter of Baptiste Dalcourt and of Agate Indian, deceased yesterday, aged 18 years. Present Baptiste Dalcourt, Francois Bernier, Baptiste Jervais, who could not sign. M. OReilly, priest
S-6 **Augustin** **Russie**	The 6 April, 1855, we undersigned have buried in the cemetery of this mission the body of Austin *[sic]* Russie, son of Augustin Russie and Rose Chinook, deceased yesterday, aged 30 years. Present Catherine Russie, Pierre Lacourse, who could not sign. M. OReilly, priest
B-10 **Eulalie** **Deguire**	The 8 April, 1855, we undersigned have supplied the ceremonies of baptism to Eulalie born the 2 January last of the legitimate marriage of Baptiste Deguire and Marie Anne Perault, of this mission, privately baptized by Mgr. F.N. Blanchet. Godfather Jean Mesplié, godmother Marie Hubbard. M. OReilly, priest
S-7 **James** **Robinson**	On the 17th day of April, 1855, we the undersigned have interred in the cemetery of this mission the body of James Robinson, deceased the 15th inst. aged 41 years, in presence of Dr. W. Shiels, Patrick Quinnen, Charles Prevost. M. OReilly, priest

p. 71

B-11 Hyacinthe Russie	The 23 April, 1855, we undersigned have baptized Hyacinthe born of the legitimate marriage of Augustin Russie, now dead, and of Agnes . . . Godfather Hyacinthe Comartin, godmother Genevieve Gardipie, who could not sign. M. OReilly, priest
S-8 Baptiste Norouest	The 25 April, 1855, we undersigned have buried in the cemetery of this mission the body of Baptiste Norouest, of this place, deceased day before yesterday, aged 60 years, Present Thomas Baptiste Norouest, Charles Prevost and Amable Petit, who could not sign. M. OReilly, priest
B-12 Robert James Fitzmaurice	On the 22nd day of May, 1855, we the undersigned have baptized Robert James, born on the 14th of April last, of the lawful marriage of Michael Fitzmaurice and Anne Garven of Polk County, Sponsor Nelson Johnson. M. OReilly, priest
B-13 Caroline Gardepie	The 25 May, 1855, we undersigned have baptized Caroline, born this morning of the legitimate marriage of Casimir Gardepie and Genevieve St. Martin. Godfather Narcisse Cornoyer, godmother Marie Sophie Cornoyer. Narcisse A Cornoyer M. OReilly, priest
B-14 Francois N. Harcouet [Arquoet]	The 3 June, 1855, we undersigned have baptized Francois Napoleon, born the 15 May of the legitimate marriage of Amable Harcouet, and Marie Anne Norwest, of Butteville. Godfather Baptiste Goyet, godmother Louise Goyet. M. OReilly, priest
B-15 Harriett M Dunlap	On the 10th day of June, 1855, we the undersigned have baptized conditionally Harriett Mary Dunlap aged 8 years, daughter of Smith Dunlap and Harriett . . . in presence of Julia M. Sheils and Mrs. McKay. M. OReilly, priest

p. 72

S-9 Sarah Lacourse	The 11 June, 1855, we undersigned have buried in the cemetery of this mission the body of Sarah, legitimate daughter of Pierre Lacourse and Victoire Borrisson [Macmillan?], died the 8th of this month, aged 6 months. Present Pierre Lacourse, Cuthbert Lambert. M. OReilly, priest
S-10 Anders Norouest	The 23 June, 1855, we undersigned have buried in the cemetery of this mission the body of Anders, legitimate son of Thomas Norouest, and of Louise Pierre of this mission, died yesterday, aged 3 years. Present Thomas Norouest and Amable Petit who could not sign. M. OReilly, priest
M-3 Leon Morel & Marguerite Despar	The 3 July, 1855, in view of the dispensation of two publications of banns granted by power conceded by Archbishop F.N. Blanchet, and considering also the dispensation of the impediment of public propriety by reason of the betrothal contracted with the sister of the wife and after the publication of one bann of marriage between Leon Morel son of Louis Morel and of Josette Chaudiere of Canada, of Vancouver's Island, on the one part, and Marguerite Despar, daughter of Joseph Despar and Lisette Chinouk, of this mission, nor having discovered any impediment, and with the consent of the father of the bride, we priest undersigned have received their mutual consent to marriage, and have given them the nuptial benediction in the presence of Joseph Despar and of Adolphe Chamberland, Casimire Gardipie. Adolphus Chamberlain M. O'Reilly, priest
B-16 Thomas John Anderson	The 8 July, 1855, we undersigned have baptized Thomas John, born the 14 May of the marriage of John Anderson and of Isabel of Pudding River. Godfather John Hord [Howard]. Godmother Mary Westron. M. O'Reilly, priest

p. 73

B-17
Anne
Yamhill

The 26 July, 1855, we undersigned have baptized conditionally Anne Yam-hill, Indian, in danger of death.

M. O'Reilly, priest

B-18
Clothilde
Deguire

The 29 July, 1855, we undersigned have baptized Clothilde, born the 17th of August of last year, of the legitimate marriage of Francois Deguire and Leonore St. James. Godfather Baptiste Deguire godmother Marie Anne Deguire.

J.B. Deguire
M. O'Reilly, priest

B-19
Baptiste
Goyet

The 20 August, 1855, we undersigned have baptized Baptiste, born yester-day of the legitimate marriage of Baptiste Goyet and of Louise Thomas *[Norwest]*. Godfather Xavier Roy, Godmother Celeste Petit.

Xavier Roy
M. O'Reilly, priest

B-20
Elizabeth
Brummer

The 23 day of August, 1855, we the undersigned have baptized Elizabeth born on the 18th day of June last of the lawful marriage of Henry Brummer and Agnes Yunker, of Yamhill. Sponsors, Myles McDonald and Fanny Coleman.

M. O'Reilly,

Transfer
of the
body
of Sister
Renilde

The 20 September, 1855, we undersigned have transferred the body of Sister Renilde of Notre Dame, which had been interred in the cemetery of the Sisters, to the parish Church, where it rests buried in the corner of the chapel of Sainte Vierge, Present Monsigneur Blanchet Archbishop of Oregon City, Charles Prevost, Baptiste Goyet.

+ F. N. Archbishop of Oregon City
M. OReilly, priest

Abj. 1
B-21
Clarissa
Isom

The 28 September, 1855, we undersigned have baptized conditionally Clarissa, wife of James Jefferson Isom, aged 33 years, after having received her abjuration of Protestantism and her profession of the Catholic Faith in the presence of Madame Catherine Murphy.

M. OReilly, priest

p. 74
Abj. 2
B-22
Louisa
Durett

The 4 October, 1855, we undersigned have baptized conditionally Louisa, wife of Benedict G. Durett, of Champoeg after having received her abjura-tion of Protestantism and her profession of the Catholic Faith in the presence of B. G. Durett and of Catherine Lonetain witnesses.

M. OReilly, priest

S-11
Clarissa
Isom

The 7 October, 1855, we undersigned have buried in the cemetery of this parish the body of Clarissa, wife of James Jefferson Isom, aged 33 years, in the presence of Hugh Cosgrove, Amable Petit and of others.

M. OReilly

B-23
Esther
Lebrun

The 7 October, 1855, we undersigned have baptized Esther, born yesterday of the legitimate marriage of Hercule Lebrun and Louise Ouvre of this parish. Godfather Dominique Pichet Godmother Angelique Dupre, who could not sign.

M. OReilly, priest

B-24
John
William
Isom

The 14 October, 1855, we undersigned have baptized John William son of James Jefferson Isom and of Clarissa Wenn, aged more than one year, God-father Eugene Leblanc, Godmother Pauline Leblanc, who could not sign.

M. OReilly, priest

M-4
Miles
McDonnell
&
Maria
Galloway

On the 15th day of October, 1855, we the undersigned, having granted a dispensation from the three banns of marriage between Miles McDonnell, son of Owen McDonnell and Mary McKeon, of Armagh, Ireland, on the one side, and Maria Galloway, daughter of Charles Galloway and Mary Henny of Polk County, Oregon, and nor having discovered any impediment, have received their mutual consent of marriage in presence of George Crosson, James Coleman and James Coyle.

M. OReilly, pastor

S-12 Lisette Indian	The 28 October, 1855, we undersigned have buried in the cemetery of the parish the body of Lisette Indian, died yesterday, aged about 60 years, living at the house of Michel La Ferte, in the presence of Michel La Ferte, M. Peltire [Peltier] Amable Petit. M. OReilly, priest miss.
B-25 Mary Weston	The 28 October, 1855, we undersigned have baptized Mary, born the 24 of this month of the legitimate marriage of David Weston and Mary Sinclair of Champoeg. Godfather Narcisse Vivet, Godmother Josephte La Framboise, who could not sign. M. OReilly, priest

p. 75

S-13 Jacques Poirier	The 29 October, 1855, we undersigned have buried in the cemetery of the parish the body of Jacques son of Alexander Poirier and Julienne LaBonté, deceased day before yesterday, aged 2 years and a half, in the presence of Alexander Poirier and Amable Petit, who could not sign. M. OReilly, priest
B-26 Marie Menard	The 2 December, 1855, we undersigned have baptized Marie Blackfoot, wife of Pierre Menard, of this place, aged about 30 years. Godfather Baptiste Goyet. Godmother Louise Goyet, who could not sign. M. OReilly
B-27 Gedeon Gravel	The 14 December, 1855, we undersigned have baptized Gedeon, born the 10 November last of the legitimate marriage of Gedeon Gravel and Nancy Pain of Yamhill County. Godfather Baptiste Pain, Godmother Josephte Laframboise who could not sign. Gedeon Gravel M. OReilly
B-28 Eleanore Picard	The 16 December, 1855, we undersigned have baptized Eleanore, born the 12th of the month, of the legitimate marriage of Henri Picard and Celeste Brun of this place. Godfather Damien Ledoux, godmother Josette Laframboise. Damien Ledoux M. OReilly
B-29 Barthelemy Chamberlain	The 17 December, 1855, we undersigned have baptized Barthelemy, born the 14th of this month of the legitimate marriage of Adolphe Chamberlain and Louise Hompherville of this place. Godfather Louis B. Vandal. Godmother Nancy Hompherville, who could not sign. Adolphus Chamberlain M. OReilly

Baptisms	29
Burials	13
Marriages	4

p 76

1856

M-1 Edouard Daignon [Degneau] and Marguerite Lussier	The 5 January, 1856, seeing the dispensation of three bans of marriage granted by us between Edouard Daignon son of Boisch Daignon and of Marguerite Mitlette of the District of Montreal, Lower Canada, on the one part, and Marguerite widow of the late Etienne Lussier of this place on the other part, and not having discovered any impediment, we undersigned have received their mutual consent to marriage and have given them the nuptial benediction in the presence of Casimir Gardipie, George Applin and of Peter Wagner, witnesses. George Aplin. M. OReilly
B-1 Jean Octave Rivet	The 10 January, 1856, we undersigned have baptized Jean Octave, born the 7th of this month of the legitimate marriage of Antoine Rivet and Emelie Spokan of this place. Godfather Firmin Lebrun, godmother Sophie Lebrun. Firmin Lebrun M. OReilly
B-2	The 13 January, 1856, we undersigned have baptized Medard born the . . .

Medard
Jeaudoin

of this month of the legitimate marriage of Baptiste Jeaudoin and Elizabeth Joachim of this place. Godfather Firmin Duteau Godmother Josette Lavigueur

M. OReilly, priest

B-3
Christine
Jeaudoin

The 13 January, 1856, we undersigned have baptized Christine born the . . . of this month of the legitimate marriage of Baptiste Jeaudoin and Elizabeth Joachim of this place. Godfather Louis Bergevin. Godmother Madeleine Bergevin.

M. OReilly, priest

S-1
Marie
OKanagan

The 20 January, 1856, we undersigned have buried in the cemetery the body of Marie daughter of Balanso and of Aloyse OKanagan, deceased the 17, aged about 4 years, in the presence of Cuthbert Lambert, Casimir Gadepie.

M. OReilly, priest

B-4
Marie
Klikitat

The 21 January, 1856, we undersigned have baptized Marie, aged about 11 months, born of the legitimate marriage of Joseph Klikitat and Isabelle Klikitat. Godfather Amable Petit.

M. OReilly

p. 77
S-2
Francois

The 3 February, 1856, we undersigned have buried in the cemetery the body of Francois Indian deceased day before yesterday, aged 4 years, in the presence of Casimir Gardipie and Amable Petit and others.

M. OReilly

B-5
Catherine
Indian

The 3 February, 1856, we undersigned have baptized Catherine Indian, aged about 30 years, in danger of death. Godmother Mary Weston.

M. OReilly

M-2
Matthew
Murphy
&
Ellen
Costello

On the 4th day of February, 1856, after one proclamation of the banns of marriage (a dispensation having been granted for the other two) between Matthew Murphy, son of Daniel Murphy and Catherine Dillon of this parish, on the one side, and Ellen Costello daughter of John Costello deceased and Ellen Burns, wife of John Gearin of this parish, no impediment being discovered, we the undersigned have received their mutual consent of marriage and have given them the nuptial benediction in presence of Andrew Murphy. Rebecca Shiel, and the parents and friends of the parties

Elizabeth Cosgrove	. . . Murphy
Mary E. White	
Catherine Murphy	Andrew Murphy
Mrs. Eldridge	Rebecca Shiel
Mary Costello	Maria Shiel

M. OReilly, priest

B-6
Louis
Depot

The 8 February, 1856, we undersigned have baptized Louis, born yesterday of the legitimate marriage of Pierre Depot and Marie Dijerle [Desjarlais] of this place. Godfather Louis Forcier. Godmother Olive Gingras, who could not sign.

M. OReilly

S-3
Luce
Gardipie

The 20 February, 1856, we undersigned have buried in the cemetery of this parish the body of Luce, daughter of Casimir Gardepie and Genevieve St. Martin, deceased yesterday in the morning, aged 2 years 8 months and a half, present Casimir Gardepie, Narcisse Cornoyer and others.

M. OReilly, priest

p. 78
S-4
Clarisse
Montour

The 27 February, 1856, we undersigned have buried in the cemetery of this parish the body of Clarisse, daughter of Marguerite Montour and of an unknown father, deceased yesterday, aged 1 year and a half. Present George Groom, and Francis Newel, witnesses.

M. OReilly, pastor

S-5
William
Gladman

The 7 March, 1856, we undersigned have buried in the cemetery of this parish the body of William Gladman, deceased yesterday at the house of Andre Lonetain, aged about 24 years. Present Joseph Lonetain, Thomas Hubbard, Mark Stevens and others.

M. OReilly, priest

S-6 Elizabeth Jeaudoin	The . . . March, 1856, we undersigned have buried in the cemetery of the parish the body of Elizabeth, wife of Baptiste Jeaudoin, deceased day before yesterday, aged . . . years. Present Baptiste Jeaudoin, Amable Petit and others. M. OReilly
B-7 Cecile Pichet	The 6 April, 1856, we undersigned have baptized Cecile born the 30 March of the legitimate marriage of Louis Pichet and Marguerite Bercier of this place. Godfather Pierre Bellique. Godmother Esther Pichet. M. OReilly
B-8 Julienne Picard	The 6 April, 1856, we undersigned have baptized Julienne, born day before yesterday of the legitimate marriage of Regis Picard and Marie Petit, of this place. Godfather Henri Picard. Godmother Julienne Labonté. M. OReilly, priest
B-9 Henry Jefferson	The 12 April, 1856, we undersigned have baptized Henry, born the 29 March of the marriage of Edward Jefferson and Josette Cornoyer, of this parish. Godfather Thomas Hubbard, Godmother Geneviève Lonetain. Thomas Hubbard M. OReilly, priest
B-10 David Bernier	The 13 April, 1856, we undersigned have baptized David, born the 31 March last, of the legitimate marriage of Francois Bernier and Pelagie Lucier of this place. Godfather Hyacinth Comartin, Godmother Catherine Comartin. M. OReilly
p. 79 M-3 Louis Labonté & Josette Laframboise	The 14 April, 1856, after the publication of 1 bann of marriage, dispensation being accorded for the two others, between Louis Labonte, widower, son of Louis Labonte and Marguerite Clatsop of Yamhill County, on the one part, and Josette Laframboise, minor daughter of Michel Laframboise and of Emelie Picard, by the consent of whom she has proceeded, on the other part, we undersigned have received their mutual consent to marriage and have given them the nuptial benediction, in the presence of Cuthbert Lambert and of Charles Laprette, witnesses. M. OReilly, priest
B-11 Emelie Norouest [Norwest]	The 20 April, 1856, we undersigned have baptized Emelie born yesterday of the legitimate marriage of Thomas Baptiste Norouest and of Louise Seguin, of this place. Godfather Hyacinthe Comartin, Godmother Catherine Comartin. M. OReilly
S-7 Maxime Moise Pend'oreille	The 24 April, 1856, we undersigned have buried in the cemetery of the parish the body of Maxime legitimate son of Maxime Moise and Anne Paulin, of the country of the Pend'Oreille, deceased yesterday, aged 4 years, in the presence of Francois Rivet and Amable Petit, witnesses. M. OReilly
S-8 Rose Baptiste Indian	The 3 May, 1856, we undersigned have buried in the cemetery of the parish the body of Rose Baptiste, Indian of the Falls living at the house of Amable Arquoit of the Butte, deceased day before yesterday, aged about 11 years. Witnesses Cuthbert Lambert and Jean Arquoit. M. OReilly
B-12 Eliza Jane Coleman	The 9 May, 1856, we undersigned have baptized Eliza Jane, legitimate daughter of James Coleman and Fanny Murray of Yamhill, aged about 5 months. Godfather Michael Horan, Godmother Catherine Horan. M. OReilly
B-13 Matilda Raleigh	The 10 May, 1856, we undersigned have baptized Matilda Maria, legitimate daughter of Patrick Raleigh and Mary Kane of Yamhill, aged about 3 months. Godfather Myles McDonald. Godmother Maria McDonald. M. OReilly, priest
p. 80 S-9 Pierre	The 7 June, 1856, we undersigned have buried in the cemetery of the parish the body of Pierre, son of Thomas Baptiste and of Louise Peter of this place,

Baptiste	aged 2 years and a half, died yesterday. Witnesses Jules Siuste, Charles Prevost and others. Jules Siuste M. OReilly, priest
S-10 Pelagie Bernier	The 10 June, 1856, we undersigned have buried in the cemetery of this parish the body of Pelagie Lussier, wife of Francois Bernier, of this place, deceased day before yesterday, aged . . . , in the presence of Rev. M. Le-Bas, Firmin Lebrun, Andre Lachapelle, witnesses. L. A. LeBas, priest, miss., apost. M. OReilly, priest
M-4 Francois Moray & Catherine Laferté	The 8 July, 1856, after the publication of 1 bann of marriage, dispensation being granted for the two others, between Francois Moray, widower of Sophie Finlay, son of Francois Moray and Marie Laroque of the parish of St. Louis, Wilamette, on the one part, and Catherine Laferte, of-age daughter of Michel Laferte and Josette Pend'Oreille of this place, and not having discovered any impediment, we undersigned have received their mutual consent to marriage and have given them the nuptial benediction in the presence of Antoine Moray and of Marguerite Gagnon, Michel Laferté and others. M. OReilly, priest
S-11 Baptiste Dalcourt	The 8 July, 1856, we undersigned have buried in the cemetery of the parish the body of Baptiste Dalcourt dit Champagne, drowned yesterday in the morning, aged about 55 years, tennant-farmer of this place, in the presence of Pierre Gautier, Cuthbert Lambert, Augustin Raymond and other witnesses. M. OReilly, priest
B-14 Francois Comartin	The 22 July, 1856, we undersigned have baptized Francois, born this morning, of the legitimate marriage of Hyacinth Comartin and Catherine Russie, of this place. Godfather Dominique Pichet. Godmother Louise Martineau. M. OReilly, priest
p. 81 B-15 Clementine Pepin	The 27 July, 1856, we undersigned have baptized Clementine, born the 22 of this month of the legitimate marriage of Pierre Pepin and of Susanne Gaudrich, of this place. Godfather Amable Arquoit Godmother Marguerite Harquoit. M. OReilly, priest
M-5 Pierre Lacourse & Josette Servant	The 4 August, 1856, after one publication of banns of marriage (dispensation being granted for the others) between Pierre Lacourse, widower, of this place, on the one part, and Josette Servant, widow of Jacques Servant, of this place also, and not having discovered any impediment, we undersigned have received their mutual consent to marriage in the presence of Cuthbert Lambert and Louis Bergevin, witnesses. M. OReilly
B-16 Charles Gingras	The 24 August, 1856, we undersigned have baptized Charles born the 21 of this month, of the legitimate marriage of Jean Gingras and Olive Forcier, of this place. Godfather Damien Ledoux. Godmother Louise Gingras. Damien Ledoux M. OReilly, priest
B-17 Helena Bertrand	The 19 September, 1856, we undersigned have baptized Helena, born the 16 of this month of the legitimate marriage of Cyrille Bertrand and Angele Gingras, of this place. Godfather Cuthbert Lambert, Godmother Marie Lambert, who could not sign. M. OReilly
M-6 Dominique Pichet & Marguerite	The 22 September, 1856, after the publication of 3 banns of marriage between Dominique Pichet minor son of Louis Pichet and Marguerite Bercier, of this place, on the one part, and Marguerite Lacourse minor daughter of Pierre Lacourse and Archange, Indian, of this place, on the other part, both with the consent of their parents, and not having discovered any impedi-

Lacourse

ment, we undersigned have received their mutual consent to marriage and have given them the nuptial benediction in the presence of Rocque Pichet and Esther Bellique, Louis Pichet and Pierre Lacourse, Augustin Raymond, Theodore Gervais and others.

M. OReilly, priest

p. 82
S-12
Jean
Gingras

The 7 October, 1856, we undersigned have buried in the cemetery of this parish, the body of Jean Gingras of this place, deceased the 5 of this month aged . . . years, in the presence of Francois Bernier and of Amable Petit.

L. A. LeBas,
priest, miss., apost.

S-13
Madeleine
Pend'Oreille

The 11 October, 1856, we undersigned have buried in the cemetery of this parish, the body of Madeleine, daughter of Maxime PendOreille and Pauline Spokan, aged 2 years, in the presence of Amable Petit.

M. OReilly, priest

B-18
Jean
Baptiste
Bergevin

The 19 October, 1856, we undersigned have baptized Jean Baptiste, born yesterday of the legitimate marriage of Louis Bergevin and Madeleine Servant, of this place. Godmother Esther Pichet. Godfather Pierre Belique.

T. Mesplié, priest, m.

B-19
Louisa
Gay

The 19 October, 1856, we undersigned have baptized Louisa, born the 27 July of the marriage of George Gay and Louisa Henry. Godfather Francois Poirier. Godmother Mary Weston.

T. Mesplie, priest, m.

S-14
Francois
Rivet

The 31 October, 1856, we undersigned have buried in the cemetery of this parish, the body of Francois legitimate son of Antoine Rivet and Emelie Pend'Oreille of this place, deceased yesterday, aged 17 years, in the presence of Francois Bernier, and Magloire Alard and others.

M. OReilly, priest

M-7 Andrew
Daniel
Murphy
&
Elizabeth
Cosgrove

The 24th day of November, 1856, after one publication of the banns (dispensation granted for the other two) between Daniel Murphy, son of Michael Murphy and Catherine Murphy, both deceased, of Illinois, on the one side, and Elizabeth Cosgrove, daughter of Hugh Cosgrove and Mary Rositer of this parish, and no impediment being discovered, we the undersigned have received their mutual consent of marriage and have given them the nuptial benediction in presence of Daniel H. Murphy, Susan Cosgrove, Hugh Cosgrove, H. Elridge and others.

Andrew Murphy	Daniel H. Murphy
Elizabeth Cosgrove	Susannah Cosgrove
Mary Costello	Hugh Cosgrove

[no priest's signature]

p. 83
B-20
Bridget
McDonald

On the 9th day of November, 1856, we the undersigned have baptized Bridget, one month old, born of the lawful marriage of Miles McDonald and Maria Galloway, of Yamhill. Sponsors James Coyle and Mary Raliegh.

Jas. Croke R.C.P.

B-21
James
Murphy

On the 14th day of December, 1856, we the undersigned have baptized James born on the . . . of the lawful marriage of Matthew Murphy and Ellen Costello, of this parish. Sponsors Peter Murphy and Susan Cosgrove.

M. OReilly, pastor

B-22
Charles N.
Laderoute

The 27 December, 1856, we undersigned have baptized Charles Noel, born the 25 of this month, of the legitimate marriage of Xavier Laderoute and Marianne Ouvré, of this place. Godfather Charles Prevost. Godmother Marie Picard.

M. OReilly, priest

M-8
Theodore
Lacourse
&
Helene

The 29 December, 1856, after the publication of 1 bann of marriage between Theodore Lacourse, son of Charles Lacourse, deceased, and Marianne Fanché, of Canada, on the one part; and Helene Bourgeau, daughter of Sylvain Bourgeau and Josette Chinook of this place, on the other part; nor having discovered any impediment, we undersigned have received their

Bourgeau	mutual consent to marriage in the presence of Theodore Gervais and Baptiste Bourgeau, who could not sign.
	M. OReilly, priest
B-23 Abraham Laframboise	The 31 December, 1856, we undersigned have baptized Abraham, born the 25 of this month, of the legitimate marriage of Michel Laframboise and Emelie Picard, of this place. Godfather Regis Picard. Godmother Marie Picard.
	M. OReilly, priest

Baptisms 23
Burials 14
Marriages 8
p. 84

1857

S-1 Marie Menard	The 8 January, 1857, we undersigned have buried in the cemetery of this parish the body of Marie Blackfoot, wife of Pierre Menard, of this place, deceased day before yesterday, aged about 30 years. Witnesses Pierre Wagner and Amable Petit, Pierre Menard.
	M. OReilly, priest
S-2 Caroline Gardepie	The 2 February, 1857, we undersigned have buried in the cemetery of this parish the body of Caroline, aged near 2 years legitimate daughter of Casimir Gardepie and Genevieve St. Martin, deceased yesterday. Witnesses Casimir Gardepie, Baptiste Goyet and others.
	M. OReilly, priest
B-1 Alexandre Raymond	The 5 February, 1857, we undersigned have baptized Alexandre, born the 2 of this month, of the legitimate marriage of Augustin Raymond and Marie Servant, of this place. Godfather Francois Etu and Marianne Angelique Dupres.
	M. OReilly
B-2 William Deguire	The 8 February, 1857, we undersigned have baptized William, born the 30 January last, of the legitimate marriage of Baptiste Deguire and Marianne Perrault, of this place. Godfather Pierre Belleque. Godmother Rosalie Gervais.
	M. OReilly, priest
B-3 Louis Labonte	The 22 February, 1857, we undersigned have baptized Louis, born the 30 January past, of the legitimate marriage of Louis Labonte jr. and Josette Laframboise, of this place. Godfather Michel Dubreuil. Godmother Julienne Labonte.
	M. OReilly, priest
B-4 Catherine McKay	The 25th day of February, 1857, we the undersigned have baptized Catherine, born on the 21st inst. of the lawful marriage of James McKay and Cecilia Lawson of this parish. Sponsors Hugh Cosgrove Mrs. Costello.
	Hugh Cosgrove
	Mary Costello
	M. OReilly, priest
B-5 Ellen Larisson	The 1 March, 1857, we undersigned have baptized Ellen, born the 28 December, 1856, of the marriage of John Larisson and Ellen Perault, of the Butte. Godfather J. Baptiste Deguire. Godmother Genevieve Bellique.
	M. OReilly, priest
B-6 Larose Goyet	The 11 March, 1857, we undersigned have baptized Larose, born yesterday of the legitimate marriage of Baptiste Goyet and Louise Thomas, of this place. Godfather Charles Prevost. Godmother, Catherine Comartin.
	M. OReilly, priest
p. 85 B-7 Antoine Laferte	The 29 March, 1857, we undersigned have baptized Antoine, born the 25 of the month, of the legitimate marriage of Michel Laferte and Angelique Peter, of this place. Godfather Pierre Belleque. Godmother Marie Ducharme.
	M. OReilly, priest
B-8	The 12 April, 1857, we undersigned have baptized Lucius, aged 4 years, son

Lucius Delerma	of Lucius S. [?] Delerma and . . . Godfather, Hugh Cosgrove. Godmother Cecilia McKay. M. OReilly, priest
M-1 Felix Gregoire & Genevieve Belleque	The 20 April, 1857, after the publication of one bann of marriage between Felix Gregoire, of-age son of Etienne Gregoire and Marguerite Chouchonave [*Souchonabe, Shuswap*] of the parish of St. Louis of the Willamette, on the one part, and Genevieve Belleque, of-age daughter of Pierre Belleque, deceased, and Genevieve St. Martin, of this parish on the other part, nor having discovered any impediment, we undersigned have received their mutual consent to marriage and have given them the nuptial benediction in the presence of Louis Bergevin and Pierre Lacourse, the parents of the married and others. M. OReilly, priest
B-9 Patrick Fitzmaurice	The 23 April, 1857, we undersigned have baptized Patrick Francis, born the 12 January last, of the legitimate marriage of Michael Fitzmaurice and Anne Garvy, of Polk County, Oregon Territory. Godmother Marguerite Berg. M. OReilly, priest
B-10 Virginie Lebrun	The 3 May, 1857, we priest undersigned have baptized Virginie, born the 27 April last of the marriage of Hercule Lebrun and of Louise Ouvray; the godfather David Mongrin, the godmother Catherine Russy, all of this parish. L. A. LeBas, priest, miss., apost.
B-11 John George Raley	The 3 May, 1857, we undersigned have baptized John George born the 2 June 1853, of the marriage of John G. Raley and of Marguerite Dwyer, the father is a soldier of the United States. Godfather John Smith. Godmother Anne Smith. M. OReilly, priest
p. 86 B-12 Louis E. Raley	The 3 May, 1857, we undersigned have baptized conditionally Louis Edward, born the 13 March 1855 of the marriage of John G. Raley, soldier of the United States, and of Marguerite Dwyer. The godmother has been Mary Pickett. M. OReilly, priest
B-13 Sarah Jane Burns	The 3 May, 1857, we undersigned have baptized Sarah Jane, born the 29 November last of the marriage of Patrick Burns, soldier of the United States, and of Marguerite Connelly. Godfather Thomas Monaghan. Godmother Marguerite Ryan. M. OReilly, priest
S-3 Josette Bourgeau	The 10 May, 1857, we undersigned have buried in the cemetery of this parish the body of Josette, wife of Sylvain Bourgeau, of this place, deceased day before yesterday. Witnesses Amable Petit. M. OReilly, priest
M-2 Joseph Lucier & Louise Martineau	The 11 May, 1857, after the publication of banns of marriage between Joseph Lucier, minor son of the late Etienne Lucier and Josette, Indian, and residing at the house of Francois Bernier his guardian, by the consent of whom he proceeded, on the one part, and Louise Martineau, of the parish of St. Louis, minor daughter of Pierre Martineau and Lisette Humpherville, both deceased in Oregon, and residing at the house of Pierre Humpherville, her guardian, by the consent of whom she proceeds, on the other part, and not having discovered any impediment, we undersigned have received their mutual consent to marriage and have given them the nuptial benediction in the presence of Firmin Lebrun and Augustin Lambert, witnesses. Firmin LeBrun M. OReilly, priest
B-14 Agnes	The 17 May, 1857, we undersigned have baptized Agnes, born day before yesterday of the legitimate marriage of Pierre Lacourse jr. and of Victoire

Lacourse	McMullen, of this place. Godfather Cuthbert Lambert. Godmother Julienne Labonte. M. OReilly, priest
p. 87 B-15 Genevieve Aplin	The 17 May, 1857, we undersigned have baptized Genevieve, born the 20 April last, of the legitimate marriage of George Aplin and of Marie Wagner, of this place. Godfather, Victorin Mesplie. Godmother Genevieve Lonetain. M. OReilly, priest
B-16 Flavie Petit	The 18 May, 1857, we undersigned have baptized Flavie, born today of the legitimate marriage of Amable Petit, and of Susanne Thomas of this place. Godfather Augustin Raymond. Godmother Marie Raymond. M. OReilly, priest
B-17 Julienne Pichet	The 21 June, 1857, we undersigned have baptized Julienne, born the 18 of this month of the legitimate marriage of Louis Pichet and of Marguerite Bercier, of this place. Godfather Dominique Pichet. Godmother Marguerite Pichet. M. OReilly, priest
B-18 Amable Arquoit	The 27 July, 1857, we undersigned have baptized Amable, born the 18 of the month, of the legitimate marriage of Amable Arquoit, jr. and of Marianne Norouest of the Butte. Godfather Charles Petit. Godmother Anne Russie. M. OReilly, priest
B-19 Joseph Brummer	The 2 September, 1857, we undersigned have baptized Joseph, born the 1st of August last of the legitimate marriage of Henry Brummer and Agnes Yunker, of Yamhill. Godfather James Coleman: Godmother Catherine Horan. M. OReilly, priest
M-3 Joseph Laderoute & Rosalie Gervais	The 22 September, 1857, after the publication of 3 banns of marriage between Joseph Laderoute, of-age son of Xavier Laderoute and Julie Gervais deceased, of St. Paul, on the one part, and Rosalie Gervais of-age daughter of Joseph Gervais and Marie Indian of St. Paul, on the other part, and not having discovered any impediment, we undersigned have received the mutual consent to marriage and have given them the nuptial benediction in the presence of Baptiste Deguire and William Tison, witnesses: J. B. Deguire M. OReilly, priest
p. 88 S-4 Elizabeth Boisverd	The 23 September, 1857, we undersigned have buried in the cemetery of the parish the body of Elizabeth Snowden, wife of Louis Boisverd of this place, deceased day before yesterday. Witnesses, Firmin Lebrun, Jean Mesplie, Louis Boisverd and others. Firmin LeBrun M. OReilly, priest
Sep. 5 Josephte Servant	The 24 September, 1857, we undersigned have buried in the cemetery of the parish the body of Josette, deceased day before yesterday, aged 12 years, daughter of Jacques Servant and Josephte . . . , in the presence of Firmin Lebrun, Jean Mesplie, Amable Petit and others. M. OReilly, priest
B-20 Louis Nepesine [Nipissing]	The 25 September, 1857, we undersigned have baptized Louis, aged about 3 months, born of the legitimate marriage of Louis Nepesine and Lisette Klikattat, both living at the Reservation of Grande Ronde, Yamhill Co. Godfather Amable Petit, Godmother Madame Petit. M. OReilly, priest
B-21 Julie Tete-Plate [Flathead] Confirmation of	The 10 October, 1857, we undersigned have baptized Julie Tete-Plate, aged about 50 years, living at the house of her daughter Madame McKindlay of Champoeg. Godfather David Mongrain. Godmother Catherine Lafantasie. M. OReilly, priest The 11 October, 1857, have been confirmed at the Church of St. Louis of the Willamette by Msgr. A. M. Blanchet, Bishop of Nesqualy, the persons

30 persons	here named, of the parish of St. Paul.	

Michael Costello	Leandre leMaloin	Celeste Petit
Peter Murphy	Pierre Servant	Marie Robillard
Joseph Paulding	Pierre Laferte	Josephte Pierre
Edwin Paulding	Andre Chalifoux	Rosalie Laderoute
Joseph Lacourse	Francois Norouest	Marie Ducharme
Louis Lacourse	Charles Norouest	Therese Rivet
Norbert Bernier	Lazare Norouest	Luce Lonetain
Charles Pichet	Anasie Guilbeau	Louise Gingras
Joseph Bourgeau	Julie TetePlate	Angelique Dupre
Isidore Laderoute	Emilie Pichet	Caroline Cosgrove

M. OReilly, priest

p. 89
B-22
Mary
Cecilia
Murphy

On the 25th day of October, 1857, I, the undersigned, have baptized Mary Cecilia, born on the 17th inst. of the lawful marriage of Andrew Murphy and Elizabeth Cosgrove of this parish. Sponsors, Joseph Paulding and Caroline Cosgrove.

M. OReilly, pastor

M-4
Peter
Kitson
&
Angelique
Dupre

The 26 October, 1857, after the publication of one bann of marriage (dispensation being granted for the others) between Peter Kitson, of-age son of William Kitson, deceased, and Marie Walla Walla on the one part, and Angelique Dupre, daughter of Nazaire Dupre, deceased, and Catherine Lafantasie, on the other part, both of this parish, and not having discovered any impediment, we undersigned have received their mutual consent to marriage and have given them the nuptial benediction in the presence of David Mongrain and Henri Hogue.

Henri Hogue
M. OReilly, priest

B-23
Ellen
Eliza
Realeigh

On the 23rd day of November, 1857, we the undersigned have baptized Ellen Eliza, born on the 5th inst. of the lawful marriage of Patrick Raleigh and Mary Kain, of Yamhill Co. Sponsors Michael Horan and Catherine Horan.

M. OReilly, priest

B-24
Stephen
Henry
Coleman

On the 24th day of November, 1857, we the undersigned have baptized Stephen Henry, born on the 19th inst. of the lawful marriage of James Coleman and Fanny Murray, of Yamhill Co. Sponsors James McPhillips and Mrs. McDonald.

M. OReilly, priest

B-25
Narcisse

The 28 November, 1857, we undersigned have baptized Narcisse, born the 23 of this month of Louise . . . and of an unknown father. Godfather Charles Petit. Godmother Marie Robillard.

M. OReilly, priest

B-26
Marianne
Jeff[ries]

The 29 November, 1857, we undersigned have baptized Marianne, born the 13 of June last, of the marriage of Edward Jeff and Josephte Quesnel, of this place. Godfather Joseph Lonetain. Godmother Genevieve Lonetain.

M. OReilly

p. 90
B-27
Moise
Lacourse

The 30 November, 1857, we undersigned have baptized Moise, born yesterday of the legitimate marriage of Theodore Lacourse and Helen Bourgeau, of this place. Godfather Louis Bergevin. Godmother Magdeleine Bergevin.

M. OReilly, priest

B-28
Benjamin
Ducharme

The 18 December, 1857, we undersigned have baptized Benjamin, born yesterday of the legitimate marriage of Baptiste Ducharme and Catherine Paul of this place. Godfather Andre Lonetain. Godmother Julie Tete Plate [Flathead].

M. OReilly, priest

B-29
Baptiste

The 25 December, 1857, we undersigned have baptized Baptiste, born the 21 of the month of the legitimate marriage of Thomas Norouest and Louise

Norouest	Pierre, of this place. Godfather Lazare Norouest. Godmother Josephte Pierre.
	M. OReilly, priest
M-5 Sylvain Bourgeau & Angele Perault	The 28 December, 1857, after the publication of 2 banns of marriage (the other having been dispensed) between Sylvain Bourgeau, widower, son of Joseph Bourgeau and of Angelique Henri of Canada, on the one part, and Angele Perault, widow of Baptiste Perault, on the other part, nor having discovered any impediment, we undersigned have received their mutual consent to marriage and have given them the nuptial benediction in the presence of Baptiste Ducharme and Amable Petit, witnesses.
	M. OReilly, priest

Baptisms   29
Burials   5
Marriages   5

1858

S-1 Virginie Lebrun	The 2 January, 1858, we undersigned have buried in the cemetery of the parish the body of Virginie, aged 9 months deceased . . . daughter of Hercule Lebrun and Louise Ouvre, in the presence of Firmin Lebrun and Amable Petit and others.
	M. OReilly, priest
S-2 Celeste Petit	The 2 January, 1858, we undersigned have buried in the cemetery of this parish the body of Celeste deceased day before yesterday, aged about 14 years, daughter of Amable Petit and of Susanne Thomas. Witness, Amable Petit.
	M. OReilly, priest
p. 91 M-1 Francois Catheu & Zoe Chamberlaine	The 18 January, 1858, after the publication of 1 bann of marriage between Francois Catheu of-age son of Joseph Catheu and of Angelique DeRosier, deceased, of Canada, on the one part, and Zoe Chamberlaine, of-age daughter of Adolphe Chamberlaine and of Juliane Wateyes [Watice], deceased, of this place, on the other part, and not having discovered any impediment, we undersigned have received their mutual consent to marriage and have given them the nuptial benediction in the presence of Pierre Pepin and Augustin Raymond, witnesses.
	M. OReilly, priest
S-3 Catherine Lonetain	The 19 January, 1858, we undersigned have buried in the cemetery of this parish, the body of Catherine Lonetain, wife of John Hord [Howard], deceased day before yesterday, aged about 30 years, in the presence of Andre Lonetain, Charles Prevost, Cuthbert Lambert, and others.
	M. OReilly
S-4 Charles Norouest	The 24 January, 1858, we undersigned have buried in the cemetery of this parish, the body of Charles son of Antoine Norouest and Louise Indian of this place, in the presence of Amable Petit.
	M. OReilly
M-2 Antoine Servant & Louise Gingras	The 1st of February, 1858, after the publication of 1 bann of marriage (dispensation being granted for the 2 others) between Antoine Servant, son of Pierre Servant and of Josephte Okinagan, of this parish, on the one part, and Louise Gingras, daughter of Jean Gingras and of Charlotte Okinagan, both deceased, on the other part, and not having discovered any impediment, we undersigned have received their mutual consent to marriage and have given them the nuptial benediction, in the presence of Francois Bernier and Cuthbert Lambert, witnesses.
	M. OReilly, priest
M-3 Narcisse Vivet & Julienne Labonte	The 9 February, 1858, after the publication of 1 bann of marriage (dispensation being granted for the others) between Narcisse Vivet, of-age son of Louis Vivet and of Josephte Tchinook, both deceased, on the one part, and Julienne Labonte, of-age daughter of Louis Labonte and Marguerite Clatsop, of Yamhill on the other part, nor having discovered any impediment, we undersigned have received their mutual consent to marriage and have

given them the nuptial benediction in the presence of Henri Hogue and Francois Quesnel, witnesses.

Henri Hogue

M. OReilly, priest

p. 92
S-5
Philomene
Lebrun

The 28 February, 1858, we undersigned have buried in the cemetery of the parish the body of Philomene aged 10 years, daughter of Hercule Lebrun and of Louise Ouvre, of this place. Witnesses, Firmin Lebrun and Amable Petit.

M. OReilly, priest

B-1
Selime
Picard

The 28 February, 1858, we undersigned have baptized Selime, born the 12 of this month of the legitimate marriage of Henri Picard and Celeste Rockbrun of this place. Godfather Augustin Raymond. Godmother Marie Raymond.

M. OReilly, priest

S-6
Charles
Gingras

The 1st of March, 1858, we undersigned have buried in the cemetery of the parish, the body of Charles, aged about 18 months, legitimate son of Jean Gingras, deceased, and of Olive Forcier, of this place. Witnesses, Narcisse Gingras, and Pierre Petit.

M. OReilly, priest

S-7
Esther
Lebrun

The 8 March, 1858, we undersigned have buried in the cemetery of the parish the body of Esther, died yesterday, aged 2 years, daughter of Hercule Lebrun and of Louise Ouvre, of this place. Witnesses, Charles Prevost and Amable Petit.

M. OReilly, priest

B-2
Francois
Labonte

The 14 March, 1858, we undersigned have baptized Francois, born the 3 of this month, of the legitimate marriage of Louis Labonte and of Josephte Laframboise, of Yamhill Co. Godfather Joseph Lonetain. Godmother Genevieve Lonetain.

M. OReilly, priest

p. 93
B-3
Lucy
Indian

The 22 March, 1858, we undersigned have baptized conditionally, Lucy, Indian, in danger of death, at the house of Peter Wagner, of this place, and aged about 15 years. Godfather, Peter Wagner.

M. OReilly, priest

S-8
Lucy
Indian

The 24 March, 1858, we undersigned have buried in the cemetery of the parish the body of Lucy, Indian, died day before yesterday, at the house of of Peter Wagner, and aged about 15 years. Witnesses, Peter Wagner and Amable Petit.

M. OReilly, priest

B-4
Charles
Indian

The 11 April, 1858, we undersigned have baptized Charles, son of Charles, Indian and Therese Calapooia, of the Grand Ronde [Reservation] in Yamhill. Godfather Charles Petit. Godmother Louise, Indian of Oregon City.

M. OReilly, priest

S-9
Child of
Joseph
Laderoute

The 18 April, 1858, we undersigned have buried in the cemetery the body of a child [male] of Joseph Laderoute and Rosalie Gervais, of this place, died after having been privately baptized, in the presence of Amable Petit, and Pierre Petit.

M. OReilly

B-5
Louis
James
Deguire

The 25 April, 1858, we undersigned have baptized Louis James, born the 2 August, 1856, of the legitimate marriage of Francois Deguire and of Ellen St. James, of this place. Godfather Louis Bergevin. Godmother Ellen Murphy.

M. OReilly, priest

B-6
Josephte
Picard

The 25 April, 1858, we undersigned have baptized Josephte, born the 20 of this month, of the legitimate marriage of Regis Picard and of Marie Petit, of this place. Godfather, Charles Petit. Godmother Josephte Labonte.

M. OReilly, priest

B-7

On the 9th day of May, 1858, I, the undersigned have baptized, Ellen, born

Ellen
Coffey

on the 29th ult. of the lawful marriage of Edward Coffey and of Mary
Ronan, of this parish. Sponsors, Robert Keating and Anne O'Brien.

M. OReilly, priest

p. 94
M-4
Adolphe
l'Oiseau
&
Louise
Lebrun

The 10 May, 1858, after the publication of one bann of marriage (dispensation having been granted for the others) between Adolphe l'Oiseau, of-age
son of Adolph l'Oiseau and of Catherine Given [Gwen?], of Canada, on the
one part, and Louise Lebrun, widow of Hercule Lebrun, on the other part,
nor having discovered any impediment, we undersigned have received their
mutual consent to marriage and have given them the nuptial benediction in
the presence of Baptiste Goyet and Amable Petit, witnesses.

M. OReilly, priest

M-5
Louis
Bernier
and
Josephte
Lavigueur

The 17 May, 1858, after the publication of three bans of marriage between
Louis Bernier, of-age son of Charles Bernier and of Marianne Morin (?) of
the parish of St. Joseph in Canada on the one part, and Josephte Lavigueur
daughter of Hyacinthe Lavigueur and of Marguerite Spokan, both deceased, on the other part, and not having discovered any impediment, we
undersigned have received their mutual consent to marriage and have given
them the nuptial benediction in the presence of Louis Bergevin, Narcisse
Cornoyer, Joseph Lavigueur, Esther Pichet and others.

Narcisse A. Cornoyer

M. OReilly, priest

M-6
Francois
Bernier
and
Marie
Despar

The 22 May, 1858, dispensation having been granted for the 3 bans of marriage between Francois Bernier, son of Francois Bernier and of Genevieve
Ayotte on the one part, and Marie Despard, of-age daughter of Joseph
Despard and Lizette Chinook on the other part, we undersigned have received their mutual consent to marriage and have given them the nuptial
benediction, in the presence of Amable Petit and of William Tison, witnesses.

M. OReilly, priest

p 95
B-8
Theresa
Gubser

The 23 May, 1858, we undersigned have baptized Theresa, born the . . . of
the legitimate marriage of . . . Gubser and of . . . of Chehalim. Godfather
John Dowd, godmother Catherine Coffey.

M. OReilly, priest

B-9
John W. B.
Durett

The 30 May, 1858, we the undersigned have baptized John William Bene-
dict, born on the 17th of March last of the lawful marriage of Benedict G.
Durett and Louisa J. Waddile of Fairfield, Marion County. Sponsor John B.
P. Piette.

John B. P. Piette

M. OReilly, priest

B-10
Jacques
Pichet

The 13 June, 1858, has been baptized by us undersigned priest, Jacques
born the 22nd of July, 1857, son of Roch Pichet and of Victoire Despard, the
godfather Pierre Lacourse, the godmother Marie St. Martin.

L. A. LeBas, Pt.

B-11
David
Weston

The same day [13 June, 1858 in B-10] has been baptized by us priest under-
signed, David, born the 15 January, 1858 of David Weston and of Marie
Saintclair, the godfather Narcisse Vivet and the godmother Marie St.
Martin.

L. A. LeBas,

B-12
Ellen
McDonald

On the 16th day of June, 1858, we the undersigned have baptized Ellen,
born on the 23rd of May last, of the lawful marriage of Miles McDonald
and Maria Galloway of Yamhill. Sponsors, James Coleman and Fanny
Coleman.

M. OReilly, priest

p. 96
M-7
Baptiste
Bourgeau

The 19 June, 1858, after the publication of two banns of marriage (dispensation granted for the 3rd) between Baptiste Bourgeau, of-age son of Sylvain
Bourgeau, of this place, and of Josephte Chinook, deceased, on the one

&
Genevieve
Martineau

part; and Genevieve Martineau, of-age daughter of Michel Martineau *[Pierre]* and of Lisette Spokan, both deceased, on the other part, and not having found any impediment, we undersigned have received their mutual consent to marriage, and have given them the nuptial benediction in the presence of Baptiste Goyet and A. Hartz, witnesses.

M. OReilly, priest

B-13
Adolphine
Pepin

The 20 June, 1858, we undersigned have baptized Adolphine, born the 14 of this month of the legitimate marriage of Pierre Pepin and Susan Gaudritch, of this place. Godfather Louis Vandal. Godmother Marianne Vandal. *[Delard]*

M. OReilly, priest

B-14
Jeremie
Clement
Chamberlain

The 27 June, 1858, we undersigned have baptized Jeremie Clement, born the 13 of this month, of the legitimate marriage of Adolphus Chamberlain and Louise Humpherville, of this place. Godfather Narcisse Cornoyer. Godmother Mary Cornoyer.

Narcisse A Cornoyer
Marie S. Cornoyer
M. OReilly, priest

M-8
Francois
Lefevre
&
Adelaide
Rivet

The 19 July, 1858, after the publication of three banns of marriage between Francois Lefevre, of-age son of Francois Lafevre and Marianne Bastien of the parish of Soulanges, Canada, on the one part, and Adelaide Rivet, daughter of Joe *[sic]* Rivet and of Rose Lacourse, both deceased, on the other part, and not having found any impediment, we undersigned have received their mutual consent to marriage and have given them the nuptial benediction in the presence of Gedeon Senechal, Joseph Hybert, witnesses.

Joseph Hebert
M. OReilly, priest

p. 97
M-9
Roque
Pichet
&
Victoire
Despar[d]

The 21 July, 1858, after the publication of one bann of marriage (dispensation being granted for the others) between Roque Pichet, son of Louis Pichet and of Marguerite Bercier, of this place, on the one part, and Victoire Despar, minor daughter of Joseph Despard, of this place, and of Lisette Chinook, deceased, on the other part, we undersigned have received their mutual consent to marriage and have given them the nuptial benediction in the presence of Charles Prevost and of Francois Poirier, witnesses.

M. OReilly, priest

S-10
Laurent
Sauve

The 3 August, 1858, we undersigned have buried in the cemetery of the parish, the body of Laurent Sauve, of this place, aged about . . . years, deceased yesterday. Present Baptiste Goyet, Peter Wagner and others.

M. OReilly, priest

B-15
Catherine
Murphy

On the 15th day of August, 1858, we the undersigned have baptized Catherine, born on the 6th inst, of the lawful marriage of Matthew Murphy jr. and Ellen Costello, of this parish. Sponsors Daniel Murphy and Mary Connor.

Mary Connor
Daniel H Murphy
M. OReilly, pastor

S-11
Michel
Laferte

The 22 August, 1858, we undersigned have buried in the cemetery of the parish, the body of Michel Lafertê, of this place, deceased yesterday, and aged . . . years, in the presence of Pierre Pepin Etienne Peltier, and others.

M. OReilly, priest

B-16
George

The 29 August, 1858, we undersigned have baptized George born the 6 of this month of the marriage of . . . and of Marianne . . . the godfather Culbert Lambert dit Robillart, the godmother Marie Weston.

L. A. LeBas,
priest, miss., apost.

p. 98
B-17
Louis

The 5 September, 1858, we undersigned have baptized Louis, born day before yesterday of the legitimate marriage of Louis Bergevin and Madeleine

Bergevin

Servant, of this place. Godfather Louis Bernier; Godmother Josephte Bernier.

M. OReilly, priest

B-18
Nazaire P.
Kitson

The 5 September, 1858, we undersigned have baptized Nazaire Peter, born the 29 of August last, of the legitimate marriage of Peter Kitson and of Angelique Dupres, of this place. Godfather, Charles Dupres. Godmother, Marie Ducharme.

M. OReilly, priest

B-19
Josephine L.
Delaunais

The 10 October, 1858, we undersigned have baptized Josephine Lina, born the 28 October, A.D. 1856, of the legitimate marriage of Louis Delaunais and of Isabelle Montour, of Umpqua. Godfather John B.P. Piette. Godmother Margaret OBrien.

M. OReilly, priest

B-20
Pierre
Vivet

The 10 October, 1858, we undersigned have baptized Pierre, born the 25 September past of the legitimate marriage of Narcisse Vivet and of Julienne Labonte, of Yamhill. Godfather, Pierre Lacourse. Godmother, Victoire McMullan.

M. OReilly, priest

B-21
Esthere
Catheu

The 7 November, 1858, we undersigned have baptized Esthere, born the 31 of last month, of the legitimate marriage of Francois Catheu, and of Zoe Chamberlain, of this place. Godfather, Louis Pichet. Godmother, Marguerite Pichet.

M. OReilly, priest

B-22
Marie
Clotilde
Jette

The 14 November, 1858, we undersigned have baptized Marie Clotilde legitimate daughter of Adolphe Jette and of Julie Indian, born the 9 of this month, the godfather Georges C. Aplin, the godmother Marie Wagner. The father and the godfather have signed with us.

Adolphe Jette
George C. Aplin
L. A. LeBas,
priest, miss., apost.

p 99
M-10
William
Tison
and
Agnes
Russie

The 22 November, 1858, after the publication of 2 bans of marriage between William Tison, of-age son of Francois Tison, deceased, and of Hyacinthe bruly of St. Louis on the one part, and Agnes Iroquois, widow of the late Augustin Russie on the other part, and not having discovered any impediment, we undersigned have received their mutual consent to marriage in the presence of Firmin Lebrun and David Mongrain, witnesses.

Firmin Lebrun
M. OReilly, priest

M-11
Thomas
Hubbard
[Herbert]
and
Genevieve
Lonetain

The 2 December, 1858, dispensation having been granted of three bans of marriage between Thomas Hubbard [Herbert] of Yamhill Co., of-age son of Thomas Hubbard [Herbert] and of Catherine Hart of the County Kildare, Ireland, on the one part, and Genevieve Lonetain, of-age daughter of Andre Lonetain and of Nancy Okanagan of Champoeg on the other part, nor having found any impediment, we undersigned have received their mutual consent to marriage in the presence of Margaret McKinlay and of Charles Matthieu, witnesses.

M. OReilly, priest

M-12
Joseph
Osborne
and
Luce
Lonetain

The 2 December, 1858, after 2 publications of bans of marriage between Joseph Osborne of Champoeg, of-age son of Joseph Osborne, deceased, and of Margaret Hammond of Baltimore, Maryland, on the one part, and Luce Lonetain, minor daughter of Andre Lonetain and of Nancy Okanagan of Champoeg, she having the consent of her parents, on the other part, and after dispensation of the impediment of mixed faith, we undersigned have received their mutual consent to marriage in the presence of J.J. Murphy and of Esthere Bellique, witnesses.

M. OReilly, priest

S-12 Francois Dupre	The 13 December, 1858, we undersigned have buried in the cemetery of this parish the body of Francois Dupre, died day before yesterday, aged about 90 years. Witnesses Peter Kitson, Charles Prevost. M. OReilly, priest
p. 100 B-23 Rosalie Raymond	The 19 December, 1858, we undersigned have baptized Rosalie, born the . . . of this month of the legitimate marriage of Augustin Raymond and of Marie Servant. Godfather Francois Xavier Matthieu. Godmother Rose Matthieu. M. OReilly, priest
B-24 Marguerite Lozeau [l'Oiseau]	The 27 December, 1858, we undersigned have baptized Marguerite, born the 18 of this month of the legitimate marriage of Adolphe Lozeau [l'Oiseau] and of Louise Ouvré, of this place. Godfather Magloire Allard. Godmother Esthere Pichet. M. Allard M. OReilly, priest
S-13 Kennedy	The 31 December, 1858, has been buried in the cemetery of this parish the body of . . . Kennedy, deceased . . . Witnesses Hugh Cosgrove and James McKay. [no priest's signature] 1859
S-1 Catherine Petit	The 3 January, 1859, we undersigned have buried in the cemetery of this parish the body of Catherine, deceased yesterday, aged 11 years, daughter of Amable Petit and of Susanne Thomas. Witnesses, Amable Petit, Charles Prevost, Baptiste Goyet. M. OReilly, priest
B-1 Josette Iroquois	The 3 January, 1859, we undersigned have baptized Josette, aged 3 months, born of the marriage of Michel Iroquois and of Marie Calapooia, of the Grand Ronde [Reservation]. Godfather, Charles Petit. Godmother Josette Labonte. M. OReilly, priest
S-2 Child Aplin	The 23 January, 1859, we undersigned have buried in the cemetery of this parish, the body of a child [male], died day before yesterday, legitimate son of George Aplin and of Marie Wagner, of this place, who formerly had been privately baptized in danger of death. Witnesses Amable Petit, Edward Coffey, and others. M. OReilly, priest
B-2 Edouard Pelissier	The 6 February, 1859, we undersigned have baptized Edouard, born the 20 of January last, of the legitimate marriage of Michel Pelissier and of Catherine Aubichon, of this place. Godfather Louis Vandal, godmother, Marianne Vandal [Delard]. M. OReilly, priest
p 101 S-3 Hyacinthe Russie	The 15 March, 1859, we undersigned have buried in the cemetery of the parish the body of Hyacinthe, aged 6 years, died yesterday, son of Augustin Russie, deceased, and of Agnes Norouest. Witnesses William Tison and Charles Petit. M. OReilly, priest
S-4 [Marie Emy Blanche Franconi]	The 8 April, 1859, we undersigned have buried in the cemetery of the parish the body of Marie Emy Blanche, aged 6 years and 4 months, daughter of Louis Franconi [?] and of Clementine Frick, deceased the 6 of April. Witnesses J. B. Piet [Piette] and G. Davidson. P. Congioto
S-5 Joseph Longtain	The 2 September, 1859, we undersigned parish priest of St. Louis have buried Joseph Longtain legitimate son of Andre Longtain and of Nancy Okinagan of the parish of St. Paul, deceased the day before, aged about 21 years. Present Gedeon Senecal and Louis Bargevin, who could not sign. B. Delorme, Vg
S-6	The 19 October, 1859, we undersigned parish priest of St. Louis have buried

Antoine Laferte	in the cemetery of the parish of St. Paul Antoine legitimate son of Michel Laferte and Angelique Desrivieres, of this place, deceased the day before aged about 2 years and a half. Present Pierre Laferte and Andre Chalifoux. B Delorme V.g
B-3 Clement illegit- imate	The 11 December, 1859, we parish priest undersigned have baptized Clement illegitimate, born ["nee" is used, feminine gender] the 23 November of the same year. Godfather Amable Petit, Godmother Dame Robillard dit Lambert. J. F. Malo, parish priest

[Inset between pp 100-101 is a small paper containing two Acts of Faith]:

B-6	The 3rd day of April I undersigned baptized a child born the 30th of March, 1859, daughter of Charles Petit and Olive Forcier: and given the name Felicite. Godfather was Regis Picard, Godmother was Marie Pierre. P. Congioto S.J.
B-7	The 17th April I undersigned baptized a child born the 14th of April, 1859, legal daughter of Baptiste Goyet and Louise Thomas; and given the name Francisca. Godfather was the Indian Jacob, commonly called Jacque, godmother was Philomene Thomas. P. Congioto S.J.

p 102 B-4 Marie Pariseau	The 28 December, 1859, we parish priest have baptized Marie, born the 12 of the same month of the legitimate marriage of Pierre Pariseau, farmer of this parish and of Genevieve Dompierre. Godfather, Joseph Rochbrune, Godmother Catherine Lafantaisie who, as well as the father, could not sign. J. F. Malo, parish priest
B-5 Marguerite Pariseau	The 28 December, 1859, we parish priest undersigned have baptized Marguerite born the 12 of the same month, of the legitimate marriage of Pierre Pariseau, farmer of this parish, and of Genevieve Dompierre. Godfather David Mongrain. Godmother Marguerite Souliere, who, as well as the father, could not sign. J. F. Malo, parish priest
S-7 Marguerite Pariseau	The 29 December, 1859, we priest undersigned have buried in the cemetery of this place Marguerite legitimate daughter of Pierre Pariseau, farmer, and of Genevieve Dompierre of this parish. Present Pierre Pariseau and Joseph Rochbrune who could not sign. A. J. Croquet 1860

Year 1860 B-1 Andrew Allen Osborn	The 8 January, 1860 [fifty crossed out], we parish priest undersigned have baptized Andrew Allen, born the 8 of December preceeding of the legitimate marriage of Joseph Alexander "husband" [in English, the rest of the entry in French], carpenter, and of Luce Lonetain, of this parish. Godfather Thomas Hubbard, Godmother Genevieve Lonetain, who could not sign. The godfather and the father have signed with us. One word erased nul. Thos. Hubbard Joseph A. Osborn J. F. Malo, priest
B-2 Honore Picard	The 15 January, 1860, we parish priest undersigned have baptized Honore born the 3 of the same month of the legitimate marriage of Honore Picard, farmer, and of Celeste Rochbrune, of this parish. Godfather, Louis Bergevin, Godmother Madeleine Servant, who as well as the father, could not sign. J. F. Malo, priest
p. 103 B-3 Andre Labonte	The 15 January, 1860, we parish priest undersigned have baptized ["Honore" crossed out] Andre aged 1 month, born of the legitimate marriage of Louis Labonte farmer and of Josephte Laframboise of this parish. Godfather, Andre Chalifou, Godmother [Josephte] Petre who could not sign. The father absent. One word erased nul. J. F. Malo, priest

B-4 **Elie** **Marie** **Vivet**	The 29 January, 1860, we parish priest undersigned have baptized Elie Marie, aged 1 month, born of the legitimate marriage of Narcisse Vivet and of Julienne Labonte of this parish. Godfather J Bte P. Piette, Godmother, Marie St. Martin who as well as the father could not sign. The godfather has signed with us.

John B. P. Piette
J. F. Malo, priest

B-5 **Adolphe** **Chamberlain**	The 18 February, 1860, we parish priest undersigned have baptized Adolphe, born the 29 January of the same year, of the legitimate marriage of Adolphe Chamberlain and of Louise of this parish. Godfather Arthure Grenier, Celeste Picard *[godmother]* who could not sign, the father and the godfather have signed with us.

Adolphus Chamberlain
Arthur Grenier
J. F. Malo, priest

B-5 **Michel** **Indian**	The 19 February, 1860, we parish priest undersigned have baptized Michel Indian aged about 45 years. Godfather George Applin, godmother Marie Applin who have signed with us.

G. Aplin
Mary Aplin
J. F. Malo, priest

[Inset between pp 102-103]

The 6 February 1860

M-1 **John B. P.** **Piette** **and** **Francis M.** **Million**	The 6 February, 1860, we parish priest undersigned have received the consent of marriage of John B. P. Piette with Francis M. Million, both of this parish. The Catholic party, John B. P. Piette, having obtained a dispensation "ex infidelitate" of Msgr. the Archbishop of Oregon City, under date of 15th November, 1859, the non-Catholic party having agreed to let the children raised in the Catholic religion. All done and passed in the presence of the witnesses undersigned. The two parties have signed with us.

John B. P. Piette   Francis M. Million

Witnesses   J. B. A. Brouillet
Louis Bergevin
Augustin Raymond
Charles Prevost
J. F. Malo, priest of St. Paul

p 104

M-2 **James** **Cosgrove** **and** **Mary** **Cavanaugh**	The 20 February, 1860, after one publication of bans of marriage between James Cosgrove, minor son of Hugh Cosgrove and of Mary Cosgrove of this parish, who has the consent of his parents, on the one part, and Mary Cavanaugh, of-age daughter of the late Peter Cavenough and Allen *[Ellen]* Cavanough of the parish of St. Louis on the other part, we parish priest undersigned have received their mutual consent to marriage and have given them the nuptial benediction in the presence of:

Hugh Cosgrove
Walter D. Paulding
Patrick McCan
Andrew Murphy
James Cosgrove
Mary A. Cavanough
J. F. Malo, priest

S-1 **Margaret** **Fraley**	The 16 February, 1860, we parish priest undersigned have buried in the cemetery of this place the body of Margaret, legitimate daughter of James P. Fraley and of Elizabeth Fraley, deceased 2 days ago, aged 2 days. Present James and Hugh Cosgrove who could not sign.

J. F. Malo, priest

S-2 **Child of**	The 23 February, 1860, we parish priest undersigned have buried in the cemetery of this place the child *[son]* privately baptized of Thomas Nord-

Thomas
Nordwest

west, aged 4 days, deceased 2 days ago. Present Michel and Pierre Placie who could not sign.

J. F. Malo, priest

B-7
Isadore
Picard

The 25 February, 1860, we parish priest undersigned have baptized Isadore born the 19th of the same month of the legitimate marriage of Regis Picard and of Marie Petit, of this parish. Godfather Culbert Lambert [godmother] Marie Okinagan, who could not sign. The father absent.

J. F. Malo, priest

p 105
B-8
Amable
Bergevin

The 3 March, 1860, we parish priest undersigned have baptized Amable born 2 days ago of the legitimate marriage of Louis Bergevin and of Madeleine Servant of this parish. Godfather, Amable St. Germain, godmother Catherine Chalifou, who could not sign.

J. F. Malo, priest

B-9
Jhon
[sic]
Gingras

The 3 March, 1860, we parish priest undersigned have baptized Jhon born the 13 February of the same year, of the marriage "non encore legitimate" of Narcisse Gingras and of Louise Indian (Okinagan) of this parish. Godfather, J Bte Goyer. Godmother Louise Thomas who could not sign. His mother present.

J. F. Malo, priest

S-3
Agnes
Lacourse

The 10 March, 1860, we parish priest undersigned have buried in the cemetery of this place the body of Agnes, aged 3 years, legitimate daughter of Pierre Lacourse and of Victoire Lacourse of this parish. Present, Pierre Lacourse, Narcisse Vivet, who could not sign.

J. F. Malo, priest

M-3
Charles
Brady
&
Anne
widow
Paulding

The 17 March, 1860, we parish priest undersigned have received the mutual consent of marriage of M. Charles Brady living at Water Bay, with Anne, widow Paulding living in this parish. Witnesses, Amable Petit, and others.

Charles Brady   Ann A Brady

J. F. Malo, priest

B-10
Artibule
Isaac
Lacourse

The 11 March, 1860, we parish priest undersigned have baptized Artibule Isaac born the day before of the legitimate marriage of Pierre Lacourse (Junior) and of Victoire McMallen, of this parish. Godfather, Jacques Coutoir, Godmother Therese Rivet who as well as the father could not sign.

J. F. Malo, priest

p. 106
B-11
Esther
Pichet

The 18 March, 1860, we parish priest undersigned have baptized Esther, born this day of the legitimate marriage of Roch Pichet and of Victoire Despart, of this parish. Godfather Dominique Pichet. Godmother Marguerite Lacourse who as well as the father could not sign.

J. F. Malo, priest

S-4
Amable
Arcouette

The 27 March, 1860, we parish priest undersigned have buried in the cemetery of this place the body of Amable, deceased 2 days ago, aged 2 years, son [of the] legitimate marriage of Amable Arcouette (Jr.) and of Marianne Arcouette, of this parish. Witnesses Amable Arcouette, father of the child and Francois Caillé who could not sign.

J. F. Malo, priest

B-12
Daniel
Murphy

The 6 May, 1860, we parish priest undersigned have baptized Daniel, legitimate son of Matthieu OC Murphy and of Helene OC Murphy, born the 16 of April preceeding, of this parish. Godfather Walter Paulding, Godmother Marthe Jeanne O'Conor who have signed with us as well as the father and the mother.

Matthew O'C Murphy
Ellen M. Murphy
Walter D. Paulding
J. F. Malo, priest

B-13

The 6 May, 1860, we parish priest undersigned have baptized Jean, son born

Jean Rochbrune	the . . . April preceding, legitimate son of Joseph Rochbrune and of Marguerite Soulliere of this parish. Godfather, Joseph Rochbrune, Jr., godmother Veronique Rochbrune, who, as well as the father, could not sign. J. F. Malo, priest
B-14, 15, 16 Michel Jacques Marie, Indians	The 29 April, 1860, we parish priest undersigned have baptized three Indians, Michel, aged about 26 years, Jacques and his wife Marie, aged about 33 years *[both]*. George Applin, godfather of the first, Amable Petit, godfather of the second, the mother Wagner, godmother of the last. J. F. Malo, priest
p 107 S-5 Rosalie Bourguignon	The 4 May, 1860, we parish priest undersigned have buried the body of Rosalie Bourguignon, aged 12 years, deceased 2 days ago; she was an orphan, having been raised at the house of George Applin. Witnesses, Mary and George Applin. J. F. Malo, priest
B-17 Josephine Weston	The 27 May, 1860, we parish priest undersigned have baptized Josephine, born in December last, of the legitimate marriage of David Weston and of Marie Weston of this parish. Godfather Thomas Hubert *[Hubbard]*, godmother Madame Hubert who could not sign. The father absent. J. F. Malo, priest
B-18 Hellen Johnson	The 27 May, 1860, we parish priest undersigned have baptized Helen, born the 14th of April preceding of the legitimate marriage of John Johnson and of Mary Johnson of the parish of Louis *[St. Louis]*. Godfather James Cosgrove and godmother Suzane Cosgrove. J. F. Malo, priest
B-19 Jacques Hug. McKay	The 24 June, 1860, we priest undersigned have baptized Jacques Hugues, born the 18th of June of the legitimate marriage of Jacques McKay and of Cecile Looson. Godfather Hugues Kosgrove and godmother Caroline Kosgrove. A. J. Croquet, priest
B-20 Delmer Jeanne Pepin	The 24 June, 1860, we priest undersigned have baptized Delmer Jeanne, born yesterday of the legitimate marriage of Pierre Pepin and Susanne Gaudrich. Godfather, Pierre Gauthier, godmother Lester *[Esther]* Delcour. A. J. Croquet, priest
S-6 Catherine Comartin	The 13 July, 1860, we parish priest undersigned have buried in the cemetery of this place the body of Catherine Comartin, deceased 2 days ago, aged about 40 years. Witnesses, Frs. Bernier, and Louis Pichet who could not sign. J. F. Malo, priest
p 108 B-21 Elie Pellan	The 15 July, 1860, we parish priest undersigned have baptized Elie, born the 8 of the same month, of the legitimate marriage of Elie Pellan and of Elizabeth Pellan, of this parish. Godfather, Georges Aplin, Godmother Dame Georges Aplin. J. F. Malo, priest
B-22 Marie Jaquet	The 15 July, 1860, we parish priest undersigned have baptized Marie, born the day before of the legitimate marriage of Amadee Jaquet and of Marie Jaquet of this parish. Godfather Frs. Bernier and godmother Marie Bernier. J. F. Malo, priest
B-23 Pierre Kitson	The 22 July, 1860, we parish priest undersigned have baptized Pierre born the day before, of the legitimate marriage of Peter Kitson and of Angelique Kitson of this parish, Godfather, David Mongrain, godmother Catherine Mongrain, who as well as the father, could not sign. J. F. Malo, priest
B-24 Domitille Lacourse	The 22 July, 1860, we parish priest undersigned have baptized Domitille born the 11, of the legitimate marriage of Theodore Lacourse and of Helene Lacourse, of this parish. Godfather, J Bte Bourgeault, godmother Genevieve Bourgeault, who as well as the father, could not sign. J. F. Malo, priest

B-25
Celeste
(Indian)

The 27 July, 1860, we parish priest undersigned have baptized Celeste, born the day before, of the legitimate marriage of Benjamin (Indian) and of Marianne (ditto) of this parish. Godfather Pierre Pepin (Jr.) godmother Julie Pepin who as well as the father could not sign.

J. F. Malo, priest

p 109
M-4
Charles
Petit
and
Sophie
Gendron

The 25 July, 1860, we parish priest undersigned have received the mutual consent of marriage Charles Petit on the one part and of Sophie Gendron on the other part, who had contracted marriage six months previously, before a Protestant minister. Witnesses, Amable Petit, father of the groom, and myself, priest undersigned.

J. F. Malo, priest

B-26
Narcisse
Pichet

The 29 July, 1860, we parish priest undersigned have baptized Narcisse, born the 19th, of the legitimate marriage of Louis Pichet and Marguerite Pichet of this parish. Godfather Narcisse Arpin [Herpin], godmother Olive Arpin, who could not sign.

J. F. Malo, priest

M-5
John J.
Cook
and
Mary
[Bridget]
Lee

The 11 September, 1860, we parish priest undersigned have received the mutual consent to marriage of John J. Cook, of-age son of Patrick Cook, deceased, of Illinois, and of Luanna Calahen, on the one part, and of Bridgit Lee, of-age daughter of Patrick Lee and of Mary Burns living in Ireland on the other part, the parties having obtained dispensation of bans. The parties have signed with us, as well as the witnesses.

John J. Cook
Bridget Lee
John Gearin
J. F. Malo, priest

M-6
John Cook
and
Bridgit Lee
[the above
crossed out]
Louis
Simon and
Anne
Langrez

The 17 September, 1860, we parish priest undersigned have received the mutual consent to marriage of Louis Simon, of-age son of Jean Louis Simon and of Victoire Lamet living formerly in the department of Ille et Vilaine in France, on the one part, and of Anne Augustine Langrez, of-age daughter of Olivier Langrez and of Helene Fanchard of the same place in France. The spouses and the witnesses have signed with us.

Louis Simon   Anne Langrez
Fran. Menes   Chs. (X) Prevost
J. F. Malo, priest

p 110
M-7
Nicolas
Dupuis
and
Lareine
Gagnon

The 17 September, 1860, we parish priest [vicar crossed out] undersigned have received the mutual consent to marriage of Nicolas Dupuis of-age son of Nicolas and of Julienne Demers living at Vancouver, on the one part, and of La Reine Gagnon minor daughter of the late Frs Gagnon and of Angelique Marcellais of this parish on the other part. The spouses and the witnesses have signed with us.

Nicolas Dupuis
La Reine Gagnon
Charles Derome
Joseph Laferte
J. F. Malo, priest

M-8
Georges
Hawkens
and
Margueret
Kearnan

The 5 October, 1860, we parish priest undersigned have received the mutual consent to marriage of Georges Hawkens of-age son of William Hawkens and of James [sic] Hawkens on the one part, and of Marguerite Kearnan, widow [of] William Kearnan, on the other part, both coming from foreign places. The spouses and the witnesses have signed with us.

Go Hawkens
Margueret (X) Hawkens
John B.P. Piette
Thomas Ryan
J. F. Malo, priest

S-7
"Pere"
[father,
the elder]
Louis
Labonte
p 111

The 13 September, 1860, we parish priest undersigned have buried the father Louis Labonte deceased 2 days ago, aged about 80 years, in the presence of all the parish; of his children and grandchildren who could not sign.
J. F. Malo, priest

B-27
Marie
Josephine
Applin

The 7 October, 1860, we parish priest undersigned have baptized Marie Josephine born the 15 September, of the legitimate marriage of Georges Applin and of Marie Applin of this parish. Godfather Helie Pellan, godmother Josephine Bernier, who could not sign.
J. F. Malo, priest

B-28
Salomee
Raymond

The 7 October, 1860, we parish priest undersigned have baptized Salomee, born the 27 September of the legitimate marriage of Augustin Raymond and of Marie Raymond of this parish. Godfather Israel Langlois, Godmother Adelaide Lefebvre who could not sign.
J. F. Malo, priest

M-9
Matthew
Murphy
&
Sarah
Ellen
Grim

The 19 October, 1860, we parish priest undersigned, have received the mutual consent to marriage [of] Matthew Murphy of-age son of John Murphy and Mary Murphy, living in Ireland, on the one part; and of Sarah Ellen Grim, minor daughter of Jacob Grim. The groom having obtained dispensation of banns and of disparity of cult the same day. The spouses have signed with us. The bride consenting to let the children be raised in the Catholic religion.

Matthew Murphy
Louis (X) Forcier, witness
Sarah Ellen Grim
J. F. Malo

38 Confirm.
21 Oct 1860

The 21 October, 1860, in the parish of St. Paul, Mgr. Frs. Norbert Blanchet, Archbishop of Oregon City, has administered the sacrament of confirmation to the following persons:

p. 112

Alfred Pepin	Marie Anne Gagnon
Paul Menard	Marie Bernier
Pierre Menard	Marguerite Rochbrune
Francois Dubreuil	Marie Bourgeau
Thomas Longtain	Marie Agnes Bourguignon
Paul Roussie	Marie, Indian
Joseph Rochbrune	Gertrude Cosgrove
Francois Rochbrune	Genevieve Murphy
Pierre Pepin	Isabelle Bourgeau
Isaac Arcouette	Anastasie Laframboise
Gedeon Forcier	Elize Pichet
Alexie Forcier	Soulange Pichet
Louis Gingras	Marie Anne Rochbrune
Vital Pichet	Veronique Rochbrune
Andree Thomas	Marie Lacourse
Jacques Indian	Marie Thomas
Michel Indian	Isabelle Quintal
Julien Laderoute	Marguerite Arcouette
Marie Pellan	Elizabeth Chamberlan
Total 38	Marie Coyle

J. F. Malo, parish priest
[there are actually 39]

M-10
Cyrile
Richter
and
Veronique

The 29 October, 1860, after the publication of one ban of marriage, we parish priest undersigned have received the mutual consent to marriage between Cyrile Richter, of-age son of Joseph Richter and of Marie Labelle, living in Canada, on the one part, and Veronique Rochbrune, minor daughter of Joseph Rochbrune and of Lizette Walla Walla of this parish on the

Rochbrune

other part; nor having discovered any impediment, and the girl having the consent of her parents, we have received their mutual consent to marriage in the presence of Charles Prevost, friend, and Joseph Rochbrune, father of the bride. The spouses and witnesses could not sign.

J. F. Malo, priest

p 113
S-8
Adele
Rowland

The 7 November, 1860, we parish priest undersigned have buried in the cemetery of this place the body of Adele Rowland, wife of JBte Jodoin, deceased 2 days ago aged 10 years *[sic]*. Witnesses, Pierre Pariseau, Joseph Delard, who could not sign.

J. F. Malo, priest

B-29
Adele
Jodoin
S-10

The 7 November, 1860, we parish priest undersigned have baptized Adele, born 2 days ago of the legitimate marriage of JBte Jodoin and of Adele Rowland of this parish. Godfather Pierre Pariseau, godmother Marianne Vandal, who could not sign. Which child died and was buried 15 days later.

J. F. Malo, priest

S-9
Esther
Lavigueur

The 8 November, 1860, we parish priest have buried in the cemetery of this place the body of Esther Pichet, wife of Joseph Lavigueur, deceased 2 days ago, aged 21 years. Witnesses, Louis Pichet, father, Firmin Lebrun, Joseph Lavigueur, husband.

J. F. Malo, priest

S-11
Marie
Vivet

The 19 December, 1860, we parish priest undersigned have buried in the cemetery of this place the body of Marie, child of Narcisse Vivet and of Julienne Labonte, deceased 2 days ago, aged 11 months. Witnesses, the father and the mother of the child, who could not sign.

J. F. Malo, priest

S-12
Louis
Lacourse

The 24 December, 1860, we parish priest have buried in the cemetery of this place the body of Louis, legitimate child of Pierre Lacourse (Senior) and of Archange, Indian, deceased 2 days ago, aged 14 years. Witnesses Louis Pichet, and Pierre Lacourse, father, who could not sign.

J. F. Malo, priest

p. 114
S-13
Joseph
Jerome
Jackson

. . . November, 1860, we parish priest, undersigned, have buried in the cemetery of this place the body of Joseph Jerome Jackson, deceased 2 days ago, aged 4 days, legitimate child of Jerome Jackson and of Mary Jackson, of this parish. Witnesses Hugh and James Cosgrove.

J. F. Malo, priest

B-30
Josephine
Mongrain

. . . November, 1860, we parish priest undersigned have baptized Josephine, born 8 days before, of the legitimate marriage of David Mongrain, and of Angelique *[Catherine]* Mongrain. Godfather Georges Rondeau Godmother, Madame Rondeau.

J. F. Malo, priest

B-31
Ellen
Anna
Petty

The 30 December, 1860, we parish priest undersigned, have baptized Ellen Anna, aged 3 weeks, born of the legitimate marriage of Joseph Petty, butcher at Champoeg, and of Mary Petty. Godfather Michel Coyle, Godmother Mary Ellen Coyle who could not sign.

J. F. Malo, priest

1861

M *[no #]*
DieuDon
Maneigre
&
Emelie
Pichet
dit
Dupres

The 8 January, 1861, after the publication of one bann of marriage, we parish priest undersigned, have received the mutual consent to marriage between Dieudonne Maneigre, of-age son of the late Pierre Maneigre and of Judith Chevrette, on the one part; and Emelie Pichet dit Dupres, minor daughter of Louis Pichet dit Dupres and of Marguerite Bercier on the other part; in the presence of Louis Pichet dit Dupres, of Frs. Bernier, Magloire Allard, who have signed with us, as well as the spouses.

Louis (X) Pichet dit Duprés
Francois (X) Bernier
Magloire Allard
DieuDonne (X) Maneigre
Emelie (X) Pichet dit Duprés
J. F. Malo, priest

p. 115

1-B
Francis
Eugenie
Piette

The 12 January, 1861, we parish priest undersigned have baptized Francis Eugenie Piette, wife of Jean Baptiste P. Piette of this parish. Godfather Francois Xavier Matthieu, Godmother Rose Matthieu his wife, the godfather has signed with us.

Francois Xavier Matthieu
J. F. Malo, priest

B-2
Henri
Clovis
Matthieu

The 12 January, 1861, we parish priest, undersigned, have baptized Henri Clovis, born the 9 November preceeding, of the legitimate marriage of Francois X. Matthieu and of Rose Matthieu, of this parish. Godfather Jean Baptiste P. Piette, Godmother Francis Eugene Piette who have signed with us.

John B. P. Piette
Frances E. Piette
J. F. Malo, priest

B-3
Gedeon
Brouillard

The 9 February, 1861, we parish priest undersigned have baptized Gedeon, born the day before, of the marriage, that by the way lawful, of Francois Brouillard and of Olive Forcier, of this mission. Godfather Gédéon Forcier, Godmother Louise, Indian who could not sign.

J. F. Malo, priest

S-1
Michel
Laframboise

The 28 January, 1861, we parish priest undersigned, have buried the body of Michel Laframboise, deceased the 25th aged about 75, of this parish. Witnesses Culbert Lambert, Pierre Lacourse, etc. and etc. who could not sign.

J. F. Malo, priest

B-4
Daniel
Lucier

The 3 February, 1861, we parish priest undersigned have baptized Daniel, aged 15 days, born of the legitimate marriage of Joseph Lucier and of Louise Martineau, of this parish. Godfather J.Bte Bourgeau Godmother Marie Bourgeau who could not sign.

J. F. Malo, priest

p. 116

M-2
Etienne
Pelletier
&
Catherine

The 12 February, 1861, we parish priest undersigned have received the mutual consent to marriage between Etienne Pelletier of this parish on the one part, and Catherine Saste, also of this parish, on the other part, the parties having obtained dispensation of the banns. Witnesses Charles Prevost, friend of the groom, Michel father of the bride, who could not sign, the groom has signed with us.

Etienne Peltier
Catherine (X)
Charles (X) Prevost
Michel (X) Saste
J. F. Malo, priest

B-5
Thomas
Nordouest

The 17 February, 1861, we parish priest undersigned have baptized Thomas born the 8 before, of the legitimate marriage of Thomas Nordouest and of Luise [sic] Nordouest of this parish. Godfather Amable Arcouette, [Godmother] Marie Arcouette who could not sign.

J. F. Malo, priest

B-6
&
S-2
Thomas
Smith

The 17 February, 1861, we parish priest undersigned have buried the body of Thomas, baptized 3 days before, child of John Smith and of Dame Smith of Champoeg, in this parish. Witnesses, Charles Prevost, the elder ["pere"] Forcier.

J. F. Malo, priest

M-3
Luger
Camiran
&
Marie
Ducharme

The 19 February, 1861, we parish priest undersigned have received the mutual consent to marriage of Luger Camiran, of-age son of the late Joseph Camiran and of Luce Lord of St. Monique of the Diocese of Three Rivers, in Canada, on the one part; and of Marie Ducharme, widow Longtain, of this parish, on the other part, the parties having obtained dispensation of banns and of "Prohibited Times" from the Vicar General, under date of the same day. Witnesses, Frs. Lefebvre, Pierre Carpentier, who could not sign.

J. F. Malo, priest

p. 117

B-7
Clementine
Servant

The 25 February, 1861, we parish priest undersigned have baptized Clementine, born the 15 of the same month, of the legitimate marriage of Antoine Servant and of Louise Servant *[Gingras]* of this parish. Godfather Registe Picard, Godmother Marie Picard who could not sign.

J. F. Malo, priest

B-8
Charles
Henry
Petit

The 17 March, 1861, we parish priest undersigned have baptized Charles Henry born the 16 February preceeding, of the legitimate marriage of Amable Petit and of Emelie Petit *[Aubichon]* of this parish. Godfather Pierre Gauthier, Godmother Esther Gauthier who could not sign.

J. F. Malo, priest

S-3
Hilaire
Gariessy
[Gardipie]

The 19 March, 1861, we parish priest undersigned have buried in the cemetery of this place the body of Hilaire, deceased 2 days ago, aged about 1 year, legitimate son of Casimir Gariessy and of Genevieve Gariessy *[St. Martin, Belique]*, of this parish. Witnesses the father and the mother and a great number of relatives; Pierre belique, and etc., who could not sign.

J. F. Malo, priest

M-4
Frs.
Dubreuil
and
Marie
Bourgeau

The 2 April, 1861, we parish priest undersigned have received without any solemn ceremony (because of previous proceedings taken before a justice of the peace) the consent to marriage of Francois Dubreuil, minor son of the late JBte Dubreuil and Marguerite, on the one part; and of Marie Bourgeau, minor daughter of Sylvain Bourgeau and of . . . *[Josephte Sok, Chinook]* of this parish on the other part. Witness Louis Forcier who could not sign.

J. F. Malo, priest

B-9
Isabelle
Bourgeau

The 7 April, 1861, we parish priest undersigned have baptized Isabelle, born the 1st of April, legitimate child of JBte Bourgeau and M. Martineau. Godfather, Joseph Lucier. godmother his wife.

J. F. Malo, priest

p 118

S-4
Pierre
Lacourse

The 18 April, 1861, we parish priest undersigned have buried in the cemetery of this place the body of Pierre Lacourse (Jr.), deceased 2 days ago, aged 33 years. Witnesses, Louis Pichet, Aug, Raymond, and etc.

J. F. Malo, priest

S-5
Joseph
Lacourse

The 26 April, 1861, we parish priest undersigned have buried the body of Joseph Lacourse, deceased 2 days ago, aged 18 years, of-age son of Pierre Lacourse (Sr.) of this parish. Witnesses Louis Bergevin, Narcisse Cornoyer, and stc.

J. F. Malo, priest

B-10
Jean
Baptiste
Labonte

The 12 May, 1861, we parish priest undersigned have baptized Jean Baptiste born the 19 April preceding, of the legitimate marriage of Louis Labonte and Josephte Laframboise of this parish. Godfather, J. F. Malo, parish priest, godmother Marie Petit, who could not sign.

J. F. J. Malo, priest

B-11
Georges W.
Brouillet

The 2 June, 1861, we parish priest have baptized George Washington, born 14 December, 1860, of the legitimate marriage of Maxime Brouillet and of Adelaide Br. of this parish. Godfather, Frs. Xavier Matthieu, godmother Rose Matthieu, who could not sign.

J. F. Malo, priest

B-12
Andrew
James
Murphy

On the 23 of June, 1861, we the undersigned priest of Oregon City, have baptized Andrew James, born on the . . . son of the lawful marriage of Andrew Murphy and Elizabeth Murphy of this parish. The godfather was James Cosgrove and the godmother Emeline Cosgrove, also both of this parish.

J. F. Fierens, miss. priest

B-13
Floride
Jeanne
Laferte

The 23 June, 1861, we priest of Oregon City, undersigned, have baptized Floride Jeanne born the 12 of the same month, daughter of the legitimate marriage of Michel Laferte and of Angelic De Riviere. Godfather Thomas . . . and godmother . . . all of the parish of St. Paul.

J. F. Fierens, priest miss.

p. 119

B-14
Joseph
Laderoute

The 23 of the month of June 1861, we priest of Oregon City, undersigned have baptized Joseph born the 16 of this month, son of Joseph Laderoute and of Rosalie Gervais born the 16 June. Godfather Charles Prevost Godmother Sophie Gregoire who could not sign.

J. F. Fierens
miss. priest

B-15
Catherine
Osburn

The 14 July, 1861, we parish priest undersigned have baptized Catherine, born the 1st of July, of the legitimate marriage of Joseph Osburn and of Luce Lonetain of this parish. Godfather Andree Lonetain, and Godmother Nancy Okinagan who could not sign.

J. F. Malo, priest

S-6
Joseph
Gervais

The 15 July, 1861, we parish priest undersigned have buried in the cemetery of this place the body of Joseph Gervais, the elder ["*pere*"], deceased 2 days ago, aged 84 years, in the presence of Louis Pichet, David Mongrain and etc. and etc. who could not sign.

J. F. Malo, priest

16 B
Francois
Roby
[*Raby*]

The 11 August, 1861, we parish priest undersigned have baptized Francois, born the 5, of the legitimate marriage of Abraham Roby and of Julienne [*Lirdi ?*] of this parish. Godfather, Frs. Chartier, Godmother Marguerite Arcouette who could not sign.

J. F. Malo, priest

B-17
Joseph
Leon
Lefebvre

The 11 August, 1861, we parish priest undersigned have baptized Joseph Leon born the 5 of the legitimate marriage of Francois Lefebvre and of Adelaide Rivet of this parish. Godfather Israel Langlois, Godmother Therese Rivet who could not sign.

J. F. Malo, priest

p. 120

B-18
Marie
Aurelie
Simon

The 18 August, 1861, we parish priest undersigned have baptized Marie Aurelie born the 17th of the legitimate marriage of Louis Simon and of Anne Langrez of this parish. Godfather Eugene Langrez, Godmother Amelie Peltier who have signed with us.

Amelie (X) Peltier

L Simon Langrez

J. F. Malo, priest

B-19
Nicolas
Cooke

On the 25th day of August, 1861, we the undersigned priest of Oregon City have baptized Nicolas, born on the 31 of July, son of the lawful marriage of John Joseph Cooke and Brigity Lee of this parish. The godfather James Lee and the godmother Hellen Mary Costello, also both of this parish.

J. F. Fierens, miss. priest

B-20
Julie
Indian
[*Jette*]

The 19 August, 1861, we parish priest undersigned have baptized Julie Indian wife of Adolphe Jette aged about 23 years, myself being the godfather, godmother Henriette Plamondon who could not sign.

J. F. Malo, priest

M-5
Pierre
Menard
and
Therese
Sastee

The 6 September, 1861, we parish priest undersigned have received the mutual consent to marriage between Pierre Menard, widower and old citizen ["*ancien citoyen*"] of this parish, on the one part, and Therese Sastee (Indian) resident in this parish since three months; having granted them dispensation of bans and of "disparity of cult", which had been allowed to me by Mgr. the Archbishop of Oregon City, the month of December preceeding. Witnesses, Amable Petit, Frs. X. Laderoute who could not sign.

J. F. Malo, priest

B-21
Joseph
Bernier

The 7 September, 1861, we parish priest undersigned have baptized Joseph, born the 5 of the legitimate marriage of Frs. Bernier and Marie Despart, of this parish. Godfather Amable Petit, godmother Victoire Despart, who could not sign.

J. F. Malo, priest

p 121

M-6

The 10 September, 1861, we parish priest undersigned have received the

Eusebe M.
Plamondon
and
Elizabeth
Illidge

mutual consent to marriage between Eusebe Michel Plamondon, domiciled at Salem, on the one part; and Elizabeth Illidge, of-age daughter of George Alfred Illedge and of Elizabeth Illedge on the other part; having granted them dispensation of bans and of mixed faiths which we have been allowed by Mgr. the Archbishop of Oregon City in December preceeding. The spouses have signed with us.

Witnesses
Amable Petit   Eusebe Plamondon
Jean Campagnas   Elizabeth Illidge
J. F. Malo, priest

22 B
Agnes
Armenie
Jette

The 15 September, 1861, we parish priest undersigned have supplied the ceremonies and prayers of baptism to Agnes Armenie, born and baptized the 2 of this month, child of the legitimate marriage of Adolphe Jette, and of Julie Roque (Indian) of this parish. Godfather, Honore Picard, Godmother Celeste Picard who could not sign.
J. F. Malo, priest

23 B
Edouard
Vivet

The 6 October, 1861, we parish priest undersigned have baptized Edouard, born the 13 September of the current year, of the legitimate marriage of Narcis Vivet and of Julienne Labonte of this parish. Godfather A Jette, Godmother, Marguerite Labonte, who could not sign.
J. F. Malo, priest

B-24
Mary
Anne
Johnson

The 13 October, 1861, we parish priest undersigned have baptized Mary Anne born the 16 September preceeding of the legitimate marriage of John Johnson and of Mary Johnson of this parish. Godfather Machael Horen, Godmother Catherine Horen who could not sign.
J. F. Malo, priest

p. 122
B-25
David
Laderoute

The 20 October, 1861, we priest undersigned have baptized David born the 9 of the current month of the legitimate marriage of Frs. X. Laderoute and of Suzanne Indian of this parish. Godfather Adolphe Jette, Godmother Marie Weston who could not sign.
J. F. Malo, priest

B-26
Louis
Desire
Maneigre

The 24 October, 1861, we parish priest undersigned have baptized Louis Desire, born of the legitimate marriage of Dieudonne Maneigre and of Emelie Pichet of this parish. Godfather Louis Pichet, Godmother Marguerite Pichet who could not sign.
J. F. Malo, priest

M-7
Adolphe
Jette
&
Julie
Indian

The 21 of December, 1861, we parish priest undersigned have received the mutual consent to marriage of Adolphe Jette, of the parish of Repentigny in Canada, district of Montreal in Canada, on the one part, and Julie (Indian) on the other part, the parties having contracted marriage . . . 8 years previously, afterwards acknowledged before a justice of the peace, three or four [years] after; then finally before the Catholic Church on this day, both recognizing as their own children, Matilde aged 6 years the 4 of May last, Clotilde aged 3 years the 9 November last, Armenie Agnes aged 3 months the 2 of the present month, in the presence of Charles Prevost, and A. Petit. who could not sign. The groom has signed with us.
Adolphe Jette
Chls (X) Prevost
Amable Petit
J. F. Malo, priest

B-27
Narcisse
Chamberlan

The 3 December, 1861, we parish priest undersigned have baptized Narcisse, born the 24th of November of the same year, legitimate son of Adolphe Chamberlan and of Louise Wacan [Humphreville] of this parish. Godfather, Narcisse Arpin [Herpin], Olive Arpin, who could not sign.
J. F. Malo, priest

p 123
B-28
Mary

The 25 December, 1861, we priest undersigned have baptized Marie Helene, born the 1st of this month, of the legitimate marriage of Matthieu

Helen Murphy B-29 Clementine Dubreuil	Murphy and of Helene Costelo of this parish. Godfather John Fitzgiben, godmother Catherine Coffey who could not sign. J. F. Malo, priest The 25 December, 1861, we parish priest undersigned have baptized Clementine, born the 23rd of this month of the legitimate marriage of Francois Dubreuil and of Madeleine Bourgeault. Godfather, JBte Bourgeault, godmother Sophie Manuel *[Felix]* who could not sign. J. F. Malo, priest

1862

Erection of the Stations of the Cross in the Chapel of the Sisters

The 1st day of January, 1862, we priest undersigned in this authorization by Monsigneur F. N. Blanchet, Archbishop of Oregon City (as it appears by the letter herewith, dated the 2nd of December, 1861, addressed to the Mother Superior of the Sisters of Jesus and Mary, the Reverend Mother Alphonse, complying to her request made in writing the 2nd of December, 1861) have raised the Stations of the Cross in the Chapel of Ste. Victoire adjoining the Convent by us for the said Sisters of the Sacred Hearts of Jesus and Mary in the parish of St. Paul, in the presence of Reverend Father Malo, parish priest of this place, and of the Sisters at that time in charge of the convent, and others who have signed with us.

Sister Marie Febronie	Ellen Coyle
Sister Marie Perpetue	Caroline Raymond
Mary McKormick	Mary McKay

A. Z. Poulin, priest miss.

J. F. Malo, priest

[Inset between pp. 122-123 is the "letter herewith" mentioned in the preceeding entry.]

p. 124

1 B Georges Picard	The 12 January, 1862, we parish priest undersigned have baptized Georges born the 31 December preceeding of the legitimate marriage of Regist Picard and of Marie Petit of this parish. Godfather James Coutoir, Godmother Anasthasie Laframboise, who could not sign. J. F. Malo, priest
1 S Joseph Deguire	The 17 January, 1862, we parish priest undersigned have buried Joseph deceased 2 days ago, aged 2 years, son of JBte Deguire and of M. Deguire of this parish. Witnesses A. Petit P. Lachance who could not sign. J. F. Malo, priest
B-2 Euphrosine Kitson	The 19 January, 1862, we parish priest undersigned have baptized Marie Euphrosine born the 5 of this month of the legitimate marriage of Petre Kitson and Angelique Kitson of this parish. Godfather Fir. Lebrun, godmother Sophie Gregoire, who could not sign. J. F. Malo, priest
B-3 Pierre Pellan	The 26 January, 1862, we parish priest undersigned have baptized Pierre born the 18, of the legitimate marriage of Hele Pellan and of Elise Wagner of this parish. Godfather Louis Prevost, godmother Marie Elizabeth Chamberlan who could not sign. The father was present. J. F. Malo, priest
S-2 Joseph Longtain	The 31 January, 1862, we parish priest undersigned have buried in the cemetery of this place the body of Joseph, aged 2 years, deceased 2 days ago, legitimate son of Joseph Lonetain and of Marie Ducharme, of this parish. Witnesses, Ludger Camiran, M. Senecal and Andree Lonetain, who could not sign. J. F. Malo, priest

p 125

B-4 Martin James Higly	The 4 February, 1862, we parish priest undersigned have baptized Martin Jacques, born the 23 July, 1857, of the legitimate marriage of Harvy Higly (a protestant) and of Amanda Higly of this parish. Godfather, I undersigned, godmother Adele Petit who could not sign. J. F. Malo, priest

B-5
Anne
Higly

The 4 February, 1862, we parish priest undersigned have baptized Anne, born the 22 July, 1855, of the legitimate marriage of Harvy Higly and of Amanda Higly of this parish. Godfather, I undersigned, godmother Marguerite Pichet, who could not sign.

J. F. Malo, priest

B-6
Joseph
Ogdon

The 16 February, 1862, we parish priest undersigned have baptized Joseph, born the 12, illegitimate child of Irrita *[Euretta]* Ogdon of Champoeg. Godfather David Mongrain, godmother Catherine Lafantaisie who could not sign.

J. F. Malo, priest

S-3
Henri
Clovis
Matthieu

The 21 February, 1862, we parish priest undersigned have buried in the cemetery of this place the body of Henri Clovis, deceased 2 days ago, aged 15 months, legitimate son of F. X. Matthieu and Rose Oscent of this parish. Witnesses, Charles and Frs. X. Matthieu, etc.

J. F. Malo, priest

B-7
Eugene
Jean
Bapt.
Blanchet

The 24 February, 1862, we priest undersigned have baptized Eugene Jean Baptiste, born the 20 of this month at 2 hours 10 minutes of the morning, of the legitimate marriage of Oliver Blanchet and of Marie Anne Laurent. Godfather Francois Banget, Godmother Adelaide Lescarbeault who could not sign.

A. Z. Poulin, priest

p. 126
M-1
Joseph
E.
Bertrands
and
Isabelle
Aubichon

The 3 March, 1862, we parish priest undersigned after the publication of one bann of marriage between Joseph E. Bertrands, of-age son of Louis Bertrands, deceased in the Province of Alsace in France, and of Elizabeth Wolf, on the one part, and Isabette Aubichon, of-age daughter of Alexie Aubichon and of Marianne of this parish, on the other part, nor any impediment being declared, have received their mutual consent to marriage and have given them the nuptial benediction in the presence of Joseph Laferte, taking the place *["tenant lieu"]* of the father, of Amable Petit, brother-in-law, and Frs. Banget friend of the bride who have signed with us.

Joseph (X) Laferte   J. E. Bertrands
Francois Banget   Isabelle (X) Aubichon
Amable Petit

J. F. Malo, priest

M-2
Simon
Gregoire
&
Victoire
McMollen

The 12 March, 1862, we parish priest, undersigned, have received the mutual consent to marriage between Simon Gregoire of-age son of Etienne Gregoire and of Marguerite (Indian) of the parish of St. Louis, on the one part; and Victoire McMollen widow of Pierre Lacourse, of this parish, the parties having obtained dispensation of "Times Prohibited" and the same for the banns from the Vicar General of the diocese under date of 11 of this same month. Witnesses, Felix Gregoire, brother, and Jean Baptiste Jodoin who as well as the spouses have signed.

Felix (X) Gregoire
Simon Gregoire   Jean Bapt. Jeaudoin
Victoire (X) McMollen

J. F. Malo, priest

p. 127
B-8
Catherine
Elisabeth
Hickey

The 2 May, 1862, we, priest undersigned, have baptized Catherine Elisabeth, born the 9 May, 1861 of the legitimate marriage of Andre Hickey and of Marie Haten, of this parish. Godfather Nicolas Carlin, godmother Catherine Smith.

A. J. Croquet, priest

B-9
Marcelline
Gingras

The 4 May, 1862, we priest undersigned have baptized Marcelline, born the 17 February last of the legitimate marriage of Narcisse Gingras and of Louise, of this parish. Godfather Honore Picart, godmother Julienne Labonte.

A. J. Croquet, priest

B-10

The 23 March, 1862, we parish priest undersigned have baptized Virginie

Sophie Virginie Picard	born the 11 of this month of the legitimate marriage of Honore Picard and of Celeste Rochbrune of this parish. Godfather Firmin Lebrun, Godmother Sophie Gregoire who could not sign. J. F. Malo, priest
B-11 Rose [Mary] Amanda Higly	The 19 April, 1862, we parish priest undersigned have baptized Mary Amanda, born the ["13 July" crossed out] 31 Dec. 1850, of the legitimate marriage of Harvey Higly and of Amanda Higly of this parish. Godfather I undersigned, Godmother Mary McKay J. F. Malo, priest
B-12 Mary Elizabeth Higly	The 19 April, 1862, we parish priest undersigned have baptized Mary Elizabeth born the 15 June, 1853, of the legitimate marriage of Harvey Higly and of Amanda Higly of this parish. Godfather I undersigned, Godmother Caroline Raymond J. F. Malo, priest
B-13 Christine Petit	. . . May, 1862, we parish priest undersigned have baptized Christine born the same day of the legitimate marriage of Charles Petit and of Sophie Jandron [Gendron] of this parish. Godfather Charles Prevost, Godmother Marie Picard. J. F. Malo, priest
p. 128 B-14 Dalbert Senecal	The 25 May, 1862, we parish priest undersigned have baptized Dalbert born the 4 of this month of the legitimate marriage of Gedeon Senecal and of Lucie Ducharme of this parish. Godfather Louis Bergevin, Godmother Madeleine Sarvant [Servant] who could not sign. J. F. Malo, priest
B-15 Cecilia McKay	The 25 May, 1862, we priest have baptized Cecilia born the 9 of this month of the legitimate marriage of James McKay and of Cecilia McKay of this parish. Godfather James Coleman, Godmother Anny [or Fanny] Coleman. J. F. Malo, priest
B-16 Honore Camiran	The 1 June, 1862, we parish priest undersigned have baptized Honore born the 4 May of the legitimate marriage of Ludger Camirand and of Marie Ducharme of this parish. Godfather Aug. Raymond, Godmother Lucie Senecal [Ducharme] who could not sign. J. F. Malo, priest
B-17 Sarah Louisa Matthieu	The 1 June, 1862, we parish priest undersigned have baptized Sarah Louisa born the 1 November, 1850, of the civil marriage of Charles Matthieu, and of Marguret McKinly, of this parish. Godfather, Charles Matthieu, uncle, Godmother Philomene Matthieu who has signed with us. [no signature] J. F. Malo, priest
B-18 Ellen Flora Matthieu	The 1 June, 1862, we parish priest undersigned have baptized Ellen Flora born the 23 November, 1861, of the civil marriage of Charles Matthieu and of Margueret McKinly of this parish. Godfather Charles Matthieu, uncle, Godmother Clarissa Matthieu who could not sign. J. F. Malo, priest
B-19 Frances Em Colman	The 8 June, 1860 [1862] we priest undersigned have baptized Francis Emely, born the 30th of May of the legitimate marriage of James Colman and of Francis Murry of this parish. Godfather Ed. Coffey, godmother Mary Coffey. J. F. Malo, priest
p 129 B-20 Ellen E. V. Laroque	The 18 June, 1862, we parish priest undersigned have baptized Ellen Eunice Virginie, born the 2nd of October, 1855, of the civil marriage of Georges M. Laroque and of Arcinoue Matilde Clark of this parish. Godfather J. Francois Benger [Banget], godmother Adelaide Benger, who could not sign. J. F. Malo, priest
B-21 George C.	The 18 June, 1862, we parish priest undersigned have baptized Georges Clark, born the 21st of July, 1857, of the civil marriage of Georges M.

Laroque	Laroque and of Arcinoue Matilde Clark of this parish. Godfather, J. Francois Benger *[Banget]*, godmother Adelaide Benger, who could not sign. J. F. Malo, priest
B-22 *[George crossed out]* Albion Alphonse Laroque	The 18 June, 1862, we parish priest undersigned have baptized Albion Alphonse, born the 20th of December, 1858, of the civil marriage of Georges M. Laroque and of Arcinoue Matilde Clark of this parish. Godfather J. Francois Benger *[Banget]*, Adelaide Benger, who could not sign. J. F. Malo, priest
B-23 Mary H. Laroque	The 18 June, 1862, we parish priest undersigned have baptized Mary Henriat, born the 5th of February, 1861, of the civil marriage of Georges M. Laroque and of Arcinoue Matilde Clark of this parish. Godfather, J. Frs. Benger *[Banget]*, godmother Adelaide Benger who could not sign. J. F. Malo, priest
B-24 Marie Mad. Bergevin	The 19 June, 1862, we parish priest undersigned have baptized Marie Madeleine, born the 17th, of the legitimate marriage of Louis Bergevin and of Madeleine Servant of this parish. Godfather, Louis Prevost, godmother Apoline Prevost who could not sign. J. F. Malo, priest
p. 130 S-4 Helene Laroque	The 25 June, 1862, we parish priest undersigned have buried at the Butte the body of Helene Laroque deceased the day before, aged 6 years, legitimate daughter of Georges Laroque and of Arcinoue M. Clark of this parish. Witnesses, F. X. Matthieu, J. J. B. Piette and others. J. F. Malo, priest *[This is probably "Ellen E. V." of B-20, p. 129]*
B-25 Mary Kennedy	The 26 June, 1862, we parish priest undersigned have baptized Mary Arah, born the 20 February, 1856, of the legitimate marriage of Bernard Kennedy, and M. Kennedy (infidel) of this parish. Baptized privately and without the ceremonies. J. F. Malo, priest
B-26 Sarah Kennedy	The 26 June, 1862, we parish priest undersigned have baptized Sarah born the 13 June, 1858, of the legitimate marriage of Bernard Kennedy and M. Kennedy (infidel) of this parish. Baptized privately and without the ceremonies. J. F. Malo, priest
B-27 Rose Brouillard	The 6 July, 1862, we parish priest undersigned have baptized Rose, born the day before of the civil marriage of Frank Brouillard and of Olive Forcier of this parish. Godfather Alocie *[sic]* Forcier, Godmother Helene Laroque who could not sign. J. F. Malo, priest
B-28 Sarah Ellen Murphy	The 6 July, 1862, we parish priest undersigned have baptized Sarah Ellen born the 23 *["1861" in figures crossed out]* May, 1861, *["we parish priest undersigned" crossed out]* of the civil marriage of Daniel Murphy (junior) and of Susan Delia Harrison of Eugene City. Godfather Daniel Murphy (senior), Godmother Mary Ellen Murphy. J. F. Malo, priest
S-5 Gedeon Brouillard	The 13 July, 1862, we priest have buried in the cemetery of this place the body of Gedeon Brouillard deceased 2 days ago, aged 18 months legitimate son of Francois Brouillard and of Olive Forcier, of this parish. Witnesses Louis Bergevin, Amable Petit, who could not sign. J. F. Malo, priest
p 131 S-6 Marie Mad. Bergevin	The 13 July, 1862, we parish priest undersigned have buried in the cemetery of this place the body of Marie Madeleine, deceased 2 days ago, aged 1 month, legitimate daughter of Louis Bergevin and of Madeleine Servant, of this parish. Witnesses Frs. Brouillard and Amable Petit who could not sign. J. F. Malo, priest
S-7	The 16 July, 1862, we parish priest undersigned have buried in the cemetery

James McKay	of this place the body of Jacques Hughes, deceased the day before, aged 2 years, legitimate son of Jacques McKay and Cecile Loosson *[Lawson]* of this parish. Witnesses, John Gearin, Michael Horan. J. F. Malo, priest
B-29 Marie Jane Pichette	The 20 July, 1862, we parish priest undersigned have baptized Marie Jeanne born the 15 of the legitimate marriage of Roch Pichette and of Victoire Despart of this parish. Godfather Frs. Bernier, godmother Marie Despart who could not sign. J. F. Malo, priest
S-8 Cyrille Richter	The 21 July, 1862, we parish priest undersigned have buried in the cemetery of this place the body of Cyrille Honore, deceased the day before aged 3 weeks, legitimate son of Cyrile Richter and Veronique Laroque *[should be Rochbrune?]* of this parish. Witnesses, Honore Picard, Amable Petit. J. F. Malo, priest
B-30 Cyrille H. Richter	The 30 June, 1862, we parish priest undersigned have baptized Cyrile Honore born the same day of the legitimate marriage of Cyrile Richter and Veronique Roquebrune of this parish. Godfather, Honore Picard, godmother Marguerite Liard who could not sign. J. F. Malo, priest
p 132 B-31 Henry Gay	The 22 July, 1862, we parish priest undersigned have baptized Henri St. Clair born the 15 January, 1861, of the legitimate marriage of Georges Gay and of Louisa Gay of this parish. Godfather Jos. Roquebrune, godmother Marie St. Clair, who could not sign. J. F. Malo, priest
B-32 Elisa Montour	The 9 August, 1862, we parish priest undersigned have baptized Elisa, aged 4 weeks, illegitimate child of Julie Montour. Godfather Amable Petit, Godmother Marguerite Labonte who could not sign. J. F. Malo, priest
[A space left blank, then the record goes on with:] B-34 Pierre Chalifoux	The 27 November, 1862, we parish priest undersigned have baptized Pierre born the 21 of the same month of the legitimate marriage of Andre Chalifoux and of Josephte Petre of this parish. Godfather Louis Chalifoux, Godmother, Marguerite Gervais who could not sign. J. F. Malo, priest
B-35 Louis E Matthieu	The 29 November, 1862, we parish priest undersigned have baptized Louis Etienne, born the 14 of the legitimate marriage of F. X. Matthieu, and of Rose Matthieu of this parish. Godfather Charles Matthieu (junior) Godmother Rosy Mat *[page torn, the rest of the name gone, but probably Matthieu]*. J. F. Malo, priest
B-36 John Albert Applin	The 15 December, 1862, we parish priest undersigned have baptized John Albert born the 19 November *["one thousand eight" crossed out]* last, of the legitimate marriage of George Applin and of Marie Applin of this parish. Godfather John B.P. Piette, Godmother Francis Piette. J. F. Malo, priest

p 133

(1863)

M-1 Jos. *[Jude]* Vertefeuille & Catherine Gauthier	The 12 January, 1863, we parish priest undersigned have received the mutual consent to marriage of Jude Vertefeuille, of-age son of Joseph Vertefeuille in Canada, and of Adelaide Sevignie, on the one part; and of Catherine Gauthier minor daughter of Pierre Gauthier and of Esther d'allcourt of this parish on the other part, the parties having obtained dispensation of banns. The witnesses were: Pierre (X) Gauthier, Gedeon (X) Senecal

Amable Petit
The spouses: Juda (X) Vertefeuille
Catherine (X) Gauthier
J. F. Malo, priest

M-2
Jacques
Coutoir
&
Soulange
Pichet

The 20 January, 1863, we parish priest undersigned have received the mutual consent to marriage between Jacques Coutoir, of-age son of Pierre Coutoir and of Angele d'Alcourt in Canada, on the one part; and Soulange Pichet dit Dupres, minor daughter of Louis Pichet dit Dupres and of Marguerite Bercier of this parish on the other part; the parties having obtained dispensation of 2 banns. Witnesses Louis (X) Pichet dit Dupres,
Frs. (X) Bernier
Joseph Angelos Bonacina
The spouses: Jacques (X) Coutoir
Soulange (X) Pichet dit Dupres
J. F. Malo, priest

B-37
Daniel
[Perrault]

The 25 December, 1863 [the "3" written over "2"] we priest undersigned have baptized Daniel, born the 19 October, 1862, of Helen Perrault ("metis") [mixed-blood, but the wrong form of the word for a woman] of this parish. Godfather Louis Bergevin, Godmother Catherine Lafantaisie who could not sign.
J. F. Malo, priest

B-1
Louis
J. H.
Prevost

The 6 January, 1863, we priest undersigned have baptized Louis Joseph Hector born the 19 December (in 1862) of the marriage of Louis Prevost and of Apoline Lefort [Lefaure] of this parish. Godfather Charles Prevost, Godmother Renee Souchue who could not sign.
J. F. Malo, priest

p 134
S-1
David
Boucher

The 4 February, 1863, we priest undersigned have buried in the cemetery of this place the body of David Boucher deceased the 1st of this month, aged about 33 years. His family was of Berthier, District of Montreal, Canada. Witnesses F. X. Matthieu, Jean B. P. Piette and so on.
J. F. Malo, priest

S-2
James
Cosgrove

The 4 February, 1863, we priest undersigned have buried in the cemetery of this place the body of James Cosgrove deceased 2 days ago, aged 26 years. Witnesses, Hugh Cosgrove, Jerome Jackson and others.
J. F. Malo, priest

B-2
Marguerite
Lucier

The 1 March, 1863, we priest undersigned have baptized Marguerite, born the 23 February last, of the legitimate marriage of Joseph Lucier and of Louise Martineau, of this parish. Godfather, Wacan, Godmother Jeanne Humperville.
J. F. Malo, priest

B-3
Louis
Marie
Simon

The 5 April, 1863, we priest undersigned have baptized Louis Marie born the 29 March last of the legitimate marriage of Louis Simon and of Nancie Langrez, of this parish. Godfather Julien Bihan, Godmother Sophie Lebrun who could not sign.
J. F. Malo, priest

B-4
M.
Madeleine
Raymond

The 5 April, 1863, we priest undersigned have baptized Marie Madeleine born the 1st, of the legitimate marriage of Augustin Raymond and of Marie Servant of this parish. Godfather Marcel Raymond, Godmother Caroline Raymond.
J. F. Malo, priest

p. 135
S-6
Elizabeth
Wagner

The 21 May, 1863, we priest undersigned have buried in the cemetery of this place the body of Elizabeth Wagner wife of Heli Pellan, deceased 2 days ago, aged 23 years. Witnesses father Wagner ["Pere Wagner"] Heli Pellan and others.
J. F. Malo, priest

M-3
Norbert
Bernier
&
Therese
Rivet

The 25 May, 1863, after the publication of three banns between Norbert Bernier, minor son of Frs. Bernier and of the late Pelagie Lucier, on the one part, and Therese Rivet, of-age daughter of the late Joseph Rivet, and of the late Rose Lacourse, on the other part, both of this parish, nor any impediment being discovered, we have received their mutual consent to marriage in the presence of the witnesses following: Frs. (X) Bernier, the father, and

Louis (X) Pichette, friend of the groom, and of Pierre Lacourse (X) grandfather, and Pierre (X) Bonin friend of the bride who could not sign, nor could the spouses.

J. F. Malo, priest

B-5
Severe
Manaigre

The 25 May, 1863, we priest undersigned have baptized Severe born the 22 of the legitimate marriage of Dieudonne Manaigre and of Emelie Pichette of this parish. Godfather Narcisse Herpin, Godmother Olive Herpin who could not sign.

J. F. Malo, priest

M-4
Elie
Pellan
&
Marguerite
Lacourse

The 16 June, 1863, we priest officiating at the mission of St. Paul have received the mutual consent to marriage between Elie Pellan (widower) on the one part, and Marguerite Lacourse, widow of Dominique Pichette, on the other part; the parties having obtained dispensation of banns from the Vicar General. Witness Pierre (X) Lacourse and Francois (X) Brouillard who could not sign.

Elie (X) Pellan   Marguerite (X) Lacourse

J. F. Malo, priest

p. 136
S-6
Mary
Howard

The 6 July, 1863, we parish priest undersigned have buried in the cemetery of this place the body of Mary Howard, deceased 2 days ago, aged 12 years, child of John Howard, of this parish. Witnesses, Andree Lonetain, grandfather, and Thos. Hubbert [Herbert], [Beau-frere, brother-in-law crossed out], uncle of the departed, who could not sign.

J. F. Malo, priest

B-6
Catherine
Emma
Murphy

The 18 June [sic], 1863, we parish priest undersigned have baptized Catherine Emma, born the 23 May last of the legitimate marriage of Andrew Murphy and of Elizabeth Cosgrove of this parish. Godfather, Daniel Murphy, Godmother Ellen Coyle.

J. F. Malo, priest

B-7
Hellen
C
Feller
[Fellaire]

The 12 July, 1863, we parish priest undersigned have baptized Hellen Clarissa, born the 18 June last of the legitimate marriage of Peter Feller and of Anna Feller of this parish. Godfather, John Feller, Godmother Clarissa Matthieu.

J. F. Malo, priest

B-8
Catherine
Placie

The 9 August, 1863, we parish priest undersigned have baptized Catherine born the 16 July last of the legitimate marriage of Michel Placie and of Angelique Placie of this parish. Godfather, Gedeon Forcier, Godmother Marie Othawa.

J. F. Malo, priest

B-9
William
Ed.
Murphy

The 16 August, 1863, we parish priest undersigned have baptized William Edouard born the 25 July last, of the legitimate marriage of Matthew Murphy and of Hellen Costello of this parish. Godfather, Andrew Murphy, Godmother Elizabeth Murphy.

J. F. Malo, priest

B-10
Adolphe
Gilbert
Jette

The 16 August, 1863, we parish priest undersigned have baptized Adolphe Gilbert born the 4 of the month of the legitimate marriage of Adolphe Jette and of Julia Jette of this parish. Godfather Firmin Lebrun, Godmother Sophie Lebrun.

J. F. Malo, priest

p. 137
B-11
Dolphisse
Lacourse

The 7 June, 1863, we, parish priest undersigned have baptized Dolphisse born [male] the 15 May last of the legitimate marriage of Theodore Lacourse and of Helene Bourgeau of this parish. Godfather Pierre Menard, Godmother, Madeleine Bourgeau.

J. F. Malo, priest

B-12
Clementine
Bourgeau

The 7 June, 1863, we parish priest undersigned have baptized Clementine, born the 1st of this month of the legitimate marriage of JBte Bourgeau and of Genevieve Bourgeau of this parish. Godfather Louis Belhomme, Godmother Anne Humperville.

J. F. Malo, priest

B-13 Nettie Alice Osborn	The 22 August, 1863, we parish priest undersigned have baptized Nettie Alice born the 17 of this month of the legitimate marriage of Joseph Osborn and of Luce Lonetain of this parish. Godfather I undersigned, Godmother Angelique Lonetain. J. F. Malo, priest
S-7 Nettie Alice Osborn	The 26 August, 1863, we priest, undersigned, have buried in the cemetery of St. Paul, the body of Nettie Alice, aged 10 days, child of Joseph Osborn and of Luce Lonetain, deceased the day before. Witnesses, Thomas Osborn and Thomas Lonetain, uncles of the child who could not sign. F. X. Blanchet, priest
B-14 F. Xavier Gingras	The ["20" crossed out] 30 August, 1863, we, priest undersigned, have baptized Francois Xavier, born the 9 of this month, of the legitimate marriage of Narcisse Gingras and of La Louise (Indian) of this parish. Godfather, Narcisse Vivette, godmother Julienne Vivette, who could not sign. F. X. Blanchet, priest
p. 138 B-15 Nazaire J. Labonte	The 7 September, 1863, we, priest, undersigned, have baptized Nazaire Jeremie, born 2 days ago, of the legitimate marriage of Louis Labonte and of Josephte Laframboise of this parish. Godfather, Joseph Laderoute, godmother Rosalie Laderoute, who could not sign. F. X. Blanchet, priest
S-8 Charles ["Jacquet"? crossed out] Choquette	The 14 September, 1863, we, priest, undersigned, have buried in the cemetery of St. Paul, the body of Charles, deceased the day before; child of Amadee ["Jacquet?" crossed out] Choquette and of Marie Bernier, aged about 18 months. Present Francois Bernier and Jean Baptiste Laderoute who could not sign. F. X. Blanchet, priest
B-16 Alexis M. Bertrand	The 22 September, 1863, we, priest, undersigned, have baptized Alexis Magnus, born 3 days ago, of the legitimate marriage of Joseph Emile Bertrand and of Elizabeth Aubichon, of this parish. Godfather, Jos. Lafferty [Laferte], godmother Sophie Aubichon, who could not sign. F. X. Blanchet, priest
B-17 Firmin Bergevin	The 1 October, 1863, we, priest, undersigned, have baptized Firmin Edouard, born 3 days ago, of the legitimate marriage of Louis Bergevin, farmer, and of Magdeleine Bergevin of this parish. Godfather Firmin Le-Brun, godmother Sophie LeBrun. The godfather has signed with us. Firmin LeBrun F. X. Blanchet, priest
B-18 G. Francois Fernando	The 3 October, 1863, we, priest, undersigned, have baptized Guillaume Francois, aged 4 years and 4 months, born of Hosie [Jose] Fernando and of an unknown mother of Chinookville. Godfather, Francois Banget, godmother Adelaide Banget who could not sign. F. X. Blanchet, priest
B-19 Thomas R. Johnson	The 3 October, 1863, we, priest undersigned, have baptized Thomas Richardson, aged about 3 months, born of the marriage of Thomas Jefferson Johnson and of Mary Johnson of this parish. Godfather, James McKy [McKay], godmother Mary McKy, who could not sign. F. X. Blanchet, priest
p. 139 S-9 Mad[eleine] Servant wife of L. Bergevin	The ["4" crossed out] 5 October, 1863, we priest undersigned have buried in the cemetery of St. Paul the body of ["Marie Anne" crossed out] Madeleine Servant, wife of Louis Bergevin, deceased 2 days ago, aged about 40 years. Present J. Bte. Piette, H. Picard and F. LeBrun who would [sic] not sign. F. X. Blanchet, priest
B-20 Pierre Bernier	The 11 October, 1863, we parish priest undersigned have baptized Pierre born the 5 October current of the legitimate marriage of Frs. Bernier and of Marie Despart of this parish. Godfather, Fir. Lebrun, Godmother Therese Rivest. J. F. Malo, priest

B-21 **Isabelle** **Almina** **Pelicier**	The 11 October, 1863, we parish priest undersigned have baptized Isabelle Almina born the 27 September last of the legitimate marriage of Michel Pelicier and of Catherine Augichon of this parish. Godfather Jos. Bertrands, Godmother Isabelle Aubichon. J. F. Malo, priest
S-10 **Narcisse** **Pichet**	The 19 October, 1863, we parish priest undersigned have buried in the cemetery of this place the body of Narcisse, deceased 2 days ago, aged 3 years, son of Louis Pichette of this parish. Witnesses D. Manaigre, Louis Pichette. J. F. Malo, priest
B-22 **Esther** **Vertefeuille**	The 1 November, 1863, we parish priest undersigned have baptized Esther born the 19 October last of the legitimate marriage of Judes Vertefeuille and Catherine Gauthier of this parish. Godfather Pierre Gauthier, Godmother Esther Gauthier who could not sign. J. F. Malo, priest
B-23 **Nazar** **Dubreuil**	The 6 November, 1863, we parish priest undersigned have baptized Nazar born the 29 October last of the marriage [of] Frs. Dubreuil and of Madeleine Bourgeau. Godfather, Pierre Menard, godmother Julie Lachance. J. F. Malo, priest

p 140

S-12 **Matilde** **Jette**	The 6 November, 1863, we parish priest undersigned have buried in the cemetery of this place the body of Matilde Jette deceased 2 days ago aged 8 years. Witnesses A. Petit, C. Gariessy. J. F. Malo, priest
B-24 **F.** **Cecelia** **Matthieu**	The 8 November, 1863, we parish priest undersigned have baptized Frances Cecelia, born the 21 September last of the civil marriage of S [?] Chs. Matthieu and of Marguerite M'Canley of this parish. Godfather F. X. Matthieu, godmother Rose ditto. J. F. Malo, priest
S-13 **Olive** **Forcier**	The 30 November, 1863, we priest undersigned have buried in the cemetery of this place the body of Olive Forcier, wife of Frank Brouillard, deceased 2 days ago, aged 34 years about. Witnesses, Ls. Bergevin, Narcisse Gingras and others. J. F. Malo, priest
B-25 **and** **B-26**	The 25 December, 1863, we parish priest undersigned have baptized John (Pit River Indian California) aged about 24 years, and Catherine, his wife, (further away than the Saste) aged about 19 years. Godparents Pierre Pariseau and his wife. J. F. Malo, priest
B-27 **Joseph** **Pariseau**	The 25 December, 1863, we parish priest undersigned have baptized Joseph, aged one year, child of Pierre Pariseau and of Marie his legitimate wife. Godfather John, godmother Catherine, In. J. F. Malo, priest
B-28 **Marie** **Laderoute**	The 27 December, 1863, we parish priest undersigned have baptized Marie born this day of the legitimate [marriage of] F. X. Laderoute and of Marianne. Godparents JBte Brentano and his wife. J. F. Malo, priest **1864**

p 141

M-1 **Frs.** **Wassneff** **and** **Ellen** **Coyle**	The 13 January, 1863 [sic] we parish priest undersigned after the 3 publications of marriage have received the mutual consent to marriage with the consent of the parents, of Frs. Wassenoff and of Mary Ellen Coyle of this parish, no impediment being presented. James Coyle Francis Bosquet Annie Coleman James Coleman John B. P. Piette Mathias Goulet J. F. Malo, priest

M-2
Philomene
[Matthieu]
and
D Geer

The 27 March, 1863, we priest undersigned have received the consent to marriage of Philomene Mathieu, of-age daughter of F. X. Matthieu and of Rose Osent; and of Dwight Geer (infidel), having obtained myself the necessary dispensation, nine months previously, time at which the parties had contracted a civil marriage only at the scorn of our Sacred Religion by the Catholic party. Signed,

Philimine Geer
Theodore Dwight Geer
Witnesses, Charles Matthieu, brother
Rose (X) Matthieu, mother of the spouse
[no priest's signature]

B-1
Marie
Florence
Bernier

The 24 February, 1864, we parish priest undersigned have baptized Marie Florence born the 14 of the month of the legitimate marriage of Norbert Bernier and of Therese Rivet of this parish. Godfather Frs. Bernier, godmother Marie Bernier.

J. F. Malo, priest

p 142
M-3
Frs.
Davidson
and
Anne
Coleman

The 24 May, 1864, we parish priest undersigned have been present at the marriage of William F. Davidson (infidel) and C. Anna Coleman, minor daughter of James Coleman and W. Murray of this parish, the dispensation of disparity of cult having been obtained of the Vicar General Rev. B. Delorme, under date of 22 May, 1864.

J. F. Malo, priest

Witnesses
The spouses and so on
W. F. Davidson
A. C. Davidson
G. C. Davidson
James Coleman
John B. P. Piette
G. B. Davidson
Cornelius Murray
Mary Coleman

M-4
Sam.
Karr
and
Catherine
Coffey

The 14 June, 1864, we parish priest undersigned have received the mutual consent to marriage of Samuel Car (infidel) and of Catherine Coffey, of-age daughter of Edouard Coffey and of Mary Ronan of this parish, the dispensation of disparity of cult having been obtained of the Vicar General, B. Delorme, under date of 11 of the month.

J. F. Malo, priest

Witnesses
Edward Coffey
Catherine Kerr
James Coleman
Samuel P. Kerr

Hereby I, Samuel P. Kerr, engage myself to allow my lawful wife, Catherine Coffey, to practise freely her religion and to raise and educate my and her children, if God gives us any, in her religion, that is, the roman catholic faith.

signed
Samuel P. Kerr
Witnesses
Edward Coffey
James Coleman

p 143
B-2
Thomas
Richter

The 7 February, 1864, we parish priest undersigned have baptized Thomas born the 19 July, 1863, of the legitimate marriage of Cyrille Ritchert and of Veronique Rochbrune of this parish. Godfather H. Picard, godmother Celeste Picard who could not sign.

J. F. Malo, priest

B-3
Mary
illegitimate

The 27 March, 1864, we parish priest undersigned have baptized Mary, illegitimate, child of Mary (M. Manson's servant girl) which child born the 15 December, 1863. Godfather A. Petit, Godmother Julienne Labonte.

J. F. Malo, priest

B-4 **Therese** **Choquette**	The 11 April, 1864, we parish priest undersigned have baptized Therese Celina Virginie born the 9, of the legitimate marriage of Amadee Choquette and of Marie Bernier of this parish. Godfather Norber Bernier, Godmother Therese Rivet. J. F. Malo, priest
B-5 **Julienne** **Vivet**	The 10 June, 1864, we parish priest undersigned have baptized Julienne E. born yesterday *[one word written above, illegible]* of the legitimate marriage of Narcisse Vivet and of Julienne Labonte of this parish. Godfather Ls. Labonte. Godmother Josephte Labonte. J. F. Malo, priest
S-5 **Rosalie** **Gervais**	The 21 June, 1864, we parish priest undersigned have buried in the cemetery of this place the body of Rosalie Gervais, wife of Joseph Laderoute, deceased 2 days ago, aged 23 years. Witnesses, Jos. Laderoute and F. X. Laderoute who could not sign. J. F. Malo, priest

p. 144

B-6 **Marie** **Jakson** *[Jackson]*	The 26 June, 1864, we parish priest undersigned have baptized Agnes Marie born the 23 May of the legitimate marriage of Jerome B. Jackson and Marie Jackson of this parish. Godparents Jacques McKay and Cecile McKay who are unable to sign. J. F. Malo, priest
B-7 **Francois** **Xavier** **Mongrain**	The 26 June, 1864, we parish priest undersigned have baptized Francois Xavier born the 22 June the same year, of the legitimate marriage of David Mongrain and Catherine Mongrain of this parish. Godparents Pierre Bonin and Genevieve LaFramboise who are unable to sign. J. F. Malo, priest
B-8 **Adeline** **Christine** **Kitson**	The 29 June, 1864, we parish priest undersigned have baptized Adeline Christine born the 1 May of the legitimate marriage of Pierre Kitson and Angelique Kitson of this parish. Godparents, Marcel Raymond and Merence Mongrain who are unable to sign. J. F. Malo, priest

27 Confirmations 30 June *["27 persons" crossed out]*

List of children confirmed by His Grace the Archbishop of Oregon City, F. N. Blanchet, the 30 June, day of the Commemoration of St. Paul, 1864.

Louis Charles Allard	Andrew Menard
Louis Bourgeau	Catherine Perpetue Hunt
Charles Bergevin	Helene Larison
Antoine LeBrun	Marie Catherine Mathieu
Pierre Pariseau	Francoise Marie Piette
Jacque Coleman	Marie Elisabeth Quintal
Auguste Raymond	Marie Joannes . . .
Julien LaChance	Julie Jette
Jean Brentano	Aurelie Bonin
David Mongrain	Marie Sophie Petit
Moise Servant	Sophie Petit
Marie Elisabeth Applin	Marie Magdelaine Laframboise
Adelaide Petit	Elisab. Marie Anne Higly
	Marie Julie Brentano

Total 27

J. F. Malo, priest

p. 145

B-9 *[Elizabeth Petit]*	The 17 July, 1864, we parish priest undersigned have baptized Elisabeth legitimate child of Charles Petit and Sophie Gendron, born the 26 July. Godparents, Amable Petit and Susanne Tamasawokon *[?]* not knowing how to sign. S. Goens, priest
S-6 **Marianne** **Perrault**	The 19 August, 1864, we priest undersigned have buried in the cemetery of this place the body of Marianne Perrault, wife of Jean Baptiste Degheer *[Deguire]*, deceased 2 days ago, aged 30 years. Witnesses, Jean Baptiste DeGeer, Laurent, Piette and others. A. J. Croquet, priest

S-7 Nazaire Dubreuil	The 20 August, 1864, we priest undersigned have buried in the cemetery of this place the body of Nazaire Dubreuil, son of Francois Dubreuil and of Madeleine Bourgeau, deceased 2 days ago at the age of 10 months. Witnesses Amable Petit, Francois Dubreuil and others. <div align="right">A. J. Croquet, priest</div>
B-10 Robert Cooke	The 10 July, 1864, we parish priest undersigned have baptized Robert, born the 17 May of the legitimate marriage of J. Jos. Cooke and of Brigit Lee of this parish. Godfather John Gearin, Godmother Mary McKay. <div align="right">J. F. Malo, priest</div>
B-11 Ls Arthur Bernier	The 28 August, 1864, we parish priest undersigned have baptized Louis Arthur born 2 days ago of the legitimate marriage of Louis Bernier and of Josephte Lavigueur of this parish. Godfather Fir. Lebrun, godmother Sophie Lebrun. <div align="right">J. F. Malo, priest</div>
B-12 Frederic Ernest Geer	The 28 August, 1864, we parish priest undersigned have baptized Frederic Ernest, born the 12 July, of the legitimate marriage of Dwight Geer and of Philomene Geer of this parish. Godfather F. X. Matthieu, godmother Rose Matthieu, who could not sign. <div align="right">J. F. Malo, priest</div>
S-8 Jeanne Laferte	The 6 October, 1864, we undersigned have buried Jeanne, legitimate daughter of Michel Laferte and of Angelique Desrivieres of this place, deceased the 3rd, aged about 5 years and 3 months. Present Louis Chalifoux and Amable Petit. <div align="right">B. Delorme, V.G.</div>
p 146 **B-13** Francois Chamberlan	The 16 October, 1864, we priest undersigned have baptized Francois, born 4 days ago of the legitimate marriage of Adolphe Chamberlan and Louise Wacan of this parish. Godfather Francois Brouillart, godmother Genevieve. <div align="right">A. J. Croquet, priest</div>
B-14 James Pichet	The 16 October, 1864, we priest undersigned have baptized James (conditionally); he having been privately baptized by a lay person), born the 10 of the same month of the legitimate marriage of Roch Pichet and Victoire Frederic [Despard]. Godfather, James Comtois, godmother Soulanges Pichette. <div align="right">A. J. Croquet, priest</div>
S-8 Pierre Lacourse	The 17 October, 1864, we priest undersigned have buried Pierre Lacourse, husband of Josette, deceased the 15, aged 70 years. Present Amable Petit, Firmin Lebrun and others. <div align="right">A. J. Croquet, priest</div>
B-15 Adolphe Picard	The 10 December, 1864, we priest undersigned have baptized Adolphe born the 5 of June last of the legitimate marriage of Honore Picard and of Celeste Picard. Godfather, Adolphe Jette, godmother Helene Roquebrune. <div align="right">A. J. Croquet, priest</div>
B-16 Anne Norwest	The 18 December, 1864, we priest undersigned have baptized Anne born the 10 of the same month of the legitimate marriage of Thomas Norwest and of Louise Saint-Andre of this parish. Godfather Andre Chalifoux, godmother Josette Saint-Andre. <div align="right">A. J. Croquet, priest</div>
S-9 Xavier Laderoute	The 19 December, 1864, we priest undersigned have buried in the cemetery of this place the body of Xavier Laderoute, husband of Marianne Auvry [Ouvre], deceased 2 days ago, at the age of about 50 years. Witnesses Firmin Lebrun, Jean Brentano and others. <div align="right">A. J. Croquet, priest</div>
p. 147 **B-17** Hyacinthe Jeremie Laderoute	The 19 December, 1864, we priest undersigned have baptized Hyacinthe Jeremie born the 14 of the same month of the legitimate marriage of Xavier Laderoute and of Marianne Auvry of this parish. Godfather Joseph Laderoute, godmother Julie Lachance. <div align="right">A. J. Croquet, priest</div>

S-10
Catherine
Murphy

The 24 December, 1864, we priest undersigned have buried in the cemetery of this parish the body of Catherine Murphy, wife of Daniel Murphy, deceased 2 days ago at the age of about 50 years. Witnesses Alphonse Defois, Jean Brentano and others.

A. J. Croquet, priest

B-18
Alfred
Applin

The 25 December, 1864, we priest undersigned have baptized Alfred born the 9 of the same month of the legitimate marriage of Georges Applin and Marie Wagener of this parish. Godfather the undersigned, godmother Elisabeth Applin.

A. J. Croquet, priest
End of Vol. II
St. Paul Parish

INDEX
ST. PAUL PARISH II
1847-1864

INDEX (abbreviations used)

Page numbers listed in this index are those of the original ledger. See note regarding page numbering at top of first page of translations.

adj - abjuration
aff - affidavit
B - baptism
fa - father
G - guardian
H - "chez" (house of, place of)
L - legitimatized
M - married
mo - mother
PS - priest's signature (or mention of)
S - burial
S-fa - step-father
sig - person's own signature
V - widow or widower
W - witness or godparent

Place names are listed alphabetically with the exception of towns in Canada, which are under "Canada".

Index 1

B-16, p 128
Cameron, Joseph (in Canada, "late")
  fa, M-3, p 116
Cameron, Luger
  M-3, p 116 (to Marie Ducharme, widow
    of Joseph Longtain)
  W, S-2, p 124
  fa, B-16, p 128
Cannon, William
  (V of a Chinook woman)
  S-10, p 65 (97 yrs)
Carlin, Nicholas
  W, B-8, p 127
Carpentier, Angelica
  (& Peter Anderson)
  mo, B-17, p 51
Carpentier, Pierre
  W, M-3, p 116
Catherine, . . .
  S-16, p 50 (32 yrs)
Catherine, . . .
  W, B-18, p 39
Catherine, Indian
  (& Michel, Indian)
  mo, B-10, p 54
  B-5, p 77 (30 yrs, prob)
Catherine, Indian
  (& Pierre)
  mo, B-8, p 49
Catherine, Pit River Indian
  (& John, Pit River Indian)
  B-26, p 140
  W, B-27, p 140
Catheu, Esther
  B-21, p 98
Catheu, Francois
  M-1, p 91 (to Zoe Chamberland)
  fa, B-21, p 98
Catheu, Joseph (in Canada)
  fa, M-1, p 91
Cavenaugh, Ellen
  mo, M-2, p 104
Cavenaugh, Mary
  M-2, p 104 (to James Costello)
Cavenaugh, Peter
  fa, M-2, p 104 ("late")
Cayuse, Agathe
  (wife of J. B. Dalcour)
  S-8, p 55 (40 yrs)
  mo, S-5, p 70b ("late")
Cayuse, Francoise
  (widow of Paul Guilbeau)
  M-3, p 26b (to Laurent Sauve)
  W, B-24, p 30
Cayuse, Rose
  (& Michel Saste)
  mo, B-32, p 10
  S-26, p 43
Cayuse, Rose

(& Michel Lafrete—Laferte?)
  mo, B-21, p 29
Celeste, Indian
  B-25, p 108
Chalifou, Andre I
  (& Catherine Russie)
  fa, B-16, p 5
  W, M-3, p 9
  W, M-7, p 11
  W, B-5, p 17
  W, B-6, p 18
  W, S-11, p 21; M-4, p 21
  W, S-15, p 23
  fa, S-17, p 24
  W, S-9, p 26a
  W, M-2, p 26b
  fa, B-3, p 34
  S-24, p 41 (62 yrs)
Chalifou, Andre II
  conf, p 88
  W, S-6, p 101
  W, B-3, p 103
  fa, B-34, p 132
  W, B-16, p 146
Chalifou, Louis
  W, B-34, p 132
  W, S-8, p 145
Chalifou, Luce
  S-17, p 24
Chalifou, Marie Philomene
  B-16, p 5
Chalifoux, Pierre
  B-34, p 132
Chalifou, Sophie
  B-3, p 34
Chalifoux - see Chalifou
Chamberlain - see Chamberland
Chamberland, Adolphe I
  (& Louise Humpherville)
  fa, B-8, p 2 (mo Julienne Watiece)
  W, M-10, p 13
  W, B-14, p 37
  fa, B-15, p 38
  fa, B-10, p 49
  W, S-20, p 51
  W, B-6, p 54
  fa, B-2, p 60
  W, M-3, p 72
  fa, B-29, p 75
  fa, M-1, p 91
  fa, B-14, p 96
  fa, B-5, p 103
  fa, B-27, p 122
  fa, B-13, p 146
Chamberland, Adolphe II
  B-5, p 103
Chamberland, Barthelmy
  B-29, p 75
Chamberland, Calixte

W, B-4, p 2
W, M-7, p 11
W, M-1, p 46
W, S-9, p 46b (prob)
fa, M-3, p 87
S-6, p 119 (84 yrs)
Gervais, Marguerite
W, B-34, p 132
Gervais, Marie
B-18, p 65
Gervais, Rosalie
W, B-2, p 84
M-3, p 87 (to Joseph Laderoute)
mo, S-9, p 93
mo, B-14, p 119
W, B-15, p 138
S-5, p 143 (23 yrs)
Gervais, Theodore I
W, B-15, p 28
M-7, p 29 (to Angelle Lafantasie)
W, B-2, p 33
fa, B-16, p 38
fa, B-18, p 65
W, B-24, p 67
W, M-6, p 81
W, M-8, p 83
Gervais, Theodore II
B-16, p 38
Giguere, Elie (Helie)
W, B-10, p 26a
Gingras, Angele
(widow of Hypolite Brouillet, now wife
of Cyrille Bertrand)
mo, B-28, p 44
W, B-4, p 53
mo, B-8, p 54
mo, B-1, p 69
mo, B-17, p 81
Gingras, Calixte
B-14, p 63
Gingras, Catherine
B-11, p 62
Gingras, Charles
B-16, p 81
S-6, p 92
Gingras, Francois Xavier
B-14, p 137
Gingras, Jean I
(widower of Charlotte (Louise)
Okanogan, now married to Olive
Forcier)
W, S-13, p 48
W, B-9, p 49
fa, B-14, p 63
fa, B-16, p 81
S-12, p 82
fa, M-2, p 91 (late)
fa, S-6, p 92 (late)
Gingras, Jean II

(& Bethzee (Elizabeth) Finlay)
fa, B-9, p 49
fa, S-18, p 51
Gingras, Jean III
B-9, p 49
S-18, p 51
Gingras, John
B-9, p 105
Gingras, Joseph
(& Marie Anne Bastien)
fa, B-11, p 62
Gingras, Louis
conf, p 112
Gingras, Louise
W, B-16, p 81
conf, p 88
M-2, p 91 (to Antoine Servant)
mo, B-7, p 117
Gingras, Marcelline
B-9, p 127
Gingras, Narcisse
(& Louise Okanogan)
W, B-8, p 54
W, S-6, p 92
fa, B-9, p 105
fa, B-9, p 127
fa, B-14, p 137
W, S-13, p 140
Giroux, Marie (in Canada)
mo, M-9, p 13
Given (?), Catherine (in Canada)
mo, M-4, p 94
Gladman, William
W, B-13, p 55
S-5, p 78 (24 yrs)
Goemare, Melanie (Sister Renilde)
S-7, p 19
Transfer of body, p 73
Goin (?), Emile
B-5, p 53
Goin (?), Pierre
(& Felicite Kany?)
fa, B-5, p 53
Goodrich, Susanne
(& Pierre Pepin I)
mo, B-42, p 14
W, B-15, p 20
mo, B-13, p 36
W, B-15, p 38
W, B-29, p 45
W, B-14, p 63 (prob)
mo, B-23, p 67
mo, B-15, p 81
mo, B-13, p 96
mo, B-20, p 107
Goulder, William A. (Golder)
W, M-7, p 44
Goulet, Mathias
W, M-1, p 141

CATHOLIC CHURCH RECORDS

of the

PACIFIC NORTHWEST

St. Paul, Oregon

Vol. III

1st & 2nd pgs

Vol. III St. Paul Parish (1865 -
[Set in before the 1st page]
On April 25th, 1844, we have baptized Catherine born on the 13th instant of the legitimate marriage of André Chalifoux farmer and Catherine Russil *[Russie]* of this parish. Sponsors: Laurent Quintal & Marianne *[prob Nipissing, wife of Laurent Quintal]* who could not sign.
Ant. Langlois, priest

By George C. Chabot, Rector
St. Paul, Oregon
August 16, 1919

Page 1
III Volume of the Register of the parish of St. Paul.

This Register containing 288 pages has been bought and prepared to serve for the recording of Baptisms, Marriages, Burials, abjurations, confirmations which will take place in the parish of St. Paul, County of Marion, State of Oregon, from the beginning of the year 1865 and following.
Portland, Oregon, January 1, 1865.

F. N. Blanchet
Archbishop of Oregon City

B-1 Hélenè Louise Coleman	The 8 January, 1865, Monsigneur the Archbishop has baptized Hellen Louisa, born the 15 December last of the legitimate marriage of Jacques *[James]* Coleman and of Françoise Murray of this parish. Godfather Franck Wesley, godmother Marie Hélenè Coyle. A. J. Croquet, priest
B-2 Mathieu Murphey	The 15 January, 1865, we priest undersigned have baptized Mathieu, born the 26 December last of the legitimate marriage of Mathieu Murphey and of Hélenè Murphey of this parish. Godfather Jacques Coffey, godmother Marie Coleman. A. J. Croquet, priest
S-1 Anne Norwest	The 16 January, 1865, we priest undersigned have buried in the cemetery of this place, Anne, daughter of Thomas Norwest and Louise St. André, died 2 days ago at the age of 5 weeks. Witnesses Jean Brentano and Reginerius Brentano. A. J. Croquet, priest
B-3 Jean Joseph Flavien Mathieu	The 22 January, 1865, we priest undersigned have baptized Jean Joseph Flavien born the 30 October last of the legitimate marriage of François Xavier Mathieu and of Rose Mathieu *[Aucent]* of this parish. Godfather Charles Olivier Pellan, and godmother Clarissa Mathieu. A. J. Croquet, priest
Page 2 M-1 John Dowd and Julie Papin	The 13 February, 1865, in view of the dispensation of 2 bans and the publication of the third between John Dowd, of age son of Patrick Dowd and Hélenè Dowd (of Ireland) on the one part; and Julie Papin, minor daughter of Pierre Papin and of Susanne Gaudriche on the other part, both of this parish; nor having discovered any impediment, we priest undersigned have received their mutual consent of marriage and have given them the nuptial benediction in presence of Peter Cleary, Thomas O'Conor, Pierre Papin, John O'Conor. A. J. Croquet, priest
B-4 André Longtin	The 19 February, 1865, we priest undersigned have baptized André born the 22 January last of the legitimate marriage of Thomas Longtin and of Julienne Montour of this parish. Godfather Joseph Lucier, godmother Louise Martineau. A. J. Croquet, priest
S-2 Julie Jetté	The 25 February, 1865, we priest undersigned have buried in the cemetery of this place Julie (Indian) wife of Adolphe Jetté of this parish, deceased 2 days ago, aged about 25 years. Were present François Brouillard, John Brentano and etc. A. J. Croquet, priest

B-5 Alfred Raymond	The 26 February, 1865, we, priest undersigned, have baptized Alfred born the 3 February last of the legitimate marriage of Augustin Reymond and of Marie Servant of this parish. Godfather François Reymond, godmother Clarissa Mathieu. A. J. Croquet, priest
B-6 Esther Comtois	The 26 February, 1865, we priest undersigned, have baptized Esther born the 20 of the same month of the legitimate marriage of James Comtois and of Louise Soulanges of this parish. Godfather Louis Pichette, godmother Marguerite Bercier. A. J. Croquet, priest
Page 3 **B-7** Joseph Francois Bertrands	The 11 March, 1865, we, priest undersigned, have baptized Joseph François, born the 6 of this month of the legitimate marriage of Joseph Bertrands and of Isabelle Aubichon of this parish. Godfather François Bangé, godmother Adélaïde Banjé [Banget]. A. J. Croquet, priest
S-3 Marie Bastien	The 18 March, 1865, we, priest undersigned, have buried in the cemetery of this place Marie (Indian) wife of Isaac Bastien, of this parish, deceased 2 days ago, at the age of about 20 years. Were present Francois Brouillard, Alphonse Defois and etc. A. J. Croquet, priest
S-4 Joseph François Bertrands	The 18 March, 1865, we, priest undersigned, have buried in the cemetery of this place Joseph François, son of Joseph Bertrands and of Isabelle Aubichon, of this parish, deceased 2 days ago, at the age of 12 days. Were present François Brouillard, John Brentano, and others. A. J. Croquet, priest
S-5 Marie Waguener	The 26 March, 1865, we, priest undersigned, have buried in the cemetery of this place Marie (Indian), wife [of] . . . Waguener, of this parish, deceased 2 days ago, aged about 60 years. Were present Alphonse Defois, John Brentano and others. A. J. Croquet, priest
B-8 Marie Elisabeth Davidson	The 30 April, 1865, we, priest undersigned, have baptized Marie Elisabeth, born the 9 March last of the legitimate marriage of Frank Davidson and of Anne Colman, living actually near the Mission of St. Patrick, Yamhill Co., Godfather Jean Baptiste Piette, godmother Francess [sic] Mary Piette. A. J. Croquet, priest
B-9 Pierre Louis Chalifoux	The 30 April, 1865, we, priest undersigned, have baptized Pierre Louis, born the 15 April last of the legitimate marriage of André Chalifoux and of Josette St. André of this parish. Godfather Pierre Bonnet, godmother Elisabeth Chalifoux. A. J. Croquet, priest
Page 4 **B-10** Archange Marcellin Dupres	The 14 May, 1865, we, priest undersigned, have baptized Archange Marcellin [son] born the 7 of this month of the legitimate marriage of Charles Dupres and of Elisabeth Chalifoux of this parish. Godfather André Chalifoux, godmother, Josette St. André. [See S-7, p 148] A. J. Croquet, priest
B-11 Agnès Lacourse	The 14 May, 1865, we, priest undersigned, have baptized Agnès aged 1 month, born of Marguerite Lacourse of this parish. Godfather François Lefevre, godmother Adélaïde Rivet. A. J. Croquet, priest
B-12 Ls. Joseph Lucier	The 28 May, 1865, we priest undersigned, have baptized Louis Joseph born the 19 of this month of the legitimate marriage of Joseph Lucier and of Louise Martineau of this parish. Godfather Etienne Lucier Godmother Mérance Mongrain. J. F. Malo, priest
B-13 Ephrem Lefebvre	The 4 June, 1865, we priest undersigned have baptized Ephrem born the 25 May of the legitimate marriage of Frs. Lefebvre and of Adélaïde Rivet of this parish. Godfather Etienne Peltier, Godmother Aurélie Bonin. J. F. Malo, priest

B-14 Isabella Anderson	The 11 June, 1865, we priest undersigned have baptized Isabella born the 10 Jan. 1864, of the legitimate marriage of John Anderson and of Isabelle Lambert of this parish. Godfather Patrick McIntee [McGinty?], Godmother Geneviêvre [sic] Bourgeau. J. F. Malo, priest
B-15 Ed. Théodore Murphy	The 9 July, 1865, we priest undersigned, have baptized Edward Théodore born the 4 June of the legitimate marriage of Andrew Murphy and of Elizabeth Cosgrove of this parish. Godfather Hugh Cosgrove, Godmother Mary McKay. ["J.F. Ma" crossed out] Chls. Ls. Tierny
S-6 . . . Wagner	The 16 June, 1865, we priest undersigned have buried the body of . . . Wagner husband of Marie (Indian) deceased 2 days ago aged about 75 years, of this parish. Witnesses Geo. Applin, Pierre Bonin. J. F. Malo, priest
Page 5 1 M Pierre Bonin & Salomee Raymond	The 25 July, 1865, we priest undersigned have received the mutual consent of marriage between Pierre Bonin on the one part, and Salomée Raymond on the other part, the parties having obtained the dispensation of bans of the Vicar General under date of 23 July. Witnesses Augustin (X) Raymond Frs. (X) Bernier Pierre (X) Bonin Salomée (X) Raymond J. F. Malo, priest
S-7 Catherine Lafantaisie	The 7 August, 1865, we priest undersigned have buried in the cemetery of this place the body of Catherine Lafantaisie wife of David Mongrain, deceased 2 days ago, aged about 40 years, of this parish. Witnesses Georges Rondeau, Petre [sic] Kitson and etc. J. F. Malo, priest
B-16 Robert C. Johnson	The 1st of October, 1865, we priest undersigned have baptized Robert Amaty, born the 24 July of the legitimate marriage of John Johnson and of Mary Kennedy of this parish. Godfather James Coyle, godmother Mary Anna Goulet who have not known how to sign. J. F. Malo, priest
B-17 Mary Jane Bourgeau	The 1st of October, 1865, we priest undersigned have baptized Mary Jane born the 22 August of the legitimate marriage of J Bte Bourgeault and of Geneviève Martineau of this parish. Godfather Georges Aplin, godmother Mary Elizabeth Aplin. J. F. Malo, priest
B-18 Henri Petit	The 1st of October, 1865, we priest undersigned have baptized Henri born the 7 August of the legitimate marriage of Pierre Petit and Marianne Gendron of this parish. Godfather Amable Petit, Sr., Godmother Susanne Petit who have not known how to sign. J. F. Malo, priest
B-19 & 20 Daniel & Mary Frances McPoland	The 10 October, 1865, we priest undersigned have baptized Daniel (born July 8, 1862) and Mary Frances (born July 17, 1865), children of Pr. McPoland of this parish. Sponsors of the 1st, JBte Piette and wife, and of the 2nd, J. F. Malo and A. Higley. J. F. Malo, priest
Page 6 M-3 John Staats & Mary Toupin	The 9 November, 1865, we priest undersigned have received the mutual consent of marriage between Marie Toupin, minor daughter of the late Francois Toupin and . . . Lonetain on the one part, and John Staats, of-age son of . . . , both of this parish. The Catholic party having previously obtained of the Archbishop dispensation for disparity of worship. Further: Hereby I, the undersigned bind myself to allow my lawful wife, Mary Toupin, to practise freely her own religion, & to raise & educate my and her children, if God gives any to us, in the Roman Catholic Faith. Witnesses:

Andre Longtain   John G. Staats
F. X. Matthieu   Mary Topar
B. F. Newman
Sarah F. Jones   J. F. Malo, priest

M-4
Frs.
Brouillard
&
Aurelie
Bonin
The 7 December, 1865, we priest undersigned have received the mutual consent of marriage between Francois Brouillard, widower of Olive Forcier, on the one part; and Aurelie Bonin minor daughter of Pierre Bonin farmer of this parish, who has given his open consent to this marriage; the parties having obtained dispensation of the bans under date of the same day of the Very Rev. B. DeLorme, V.G. Witnesses Pierre Bonin, father, and Cuthbert Lambert, friend of the bride, who have not known how to sign.

J. F. Malo, priest

B-21
Paul
Pariseau
The 17 December, 1865, we priest undersigned have baptized Paul born the 13 of the legitimate marriage of Pierre Pariseau and Marie Dompierre, of this parish. Godfather James Contois, godmother Soulange Pichette.

J. F. Malo, priest

Page 7
B-22
Marie Ovide
illegitimate
The 11 November, 1865, we priest undersigned have baptized Marie Ovide child of Aurelie Bonin, born the 5. Godfather Pierre Bonin, Godmother Salomee Bonin.

J. F. Malo, priest
1866

S-1
Daniel
Murphy
The 23 January, 1866, we priest undersigned have buried in the cemetery of this place the body of Daniel Murphy deceased 2 days ago aged about 66 years. Witnesses Andrew Murphy, John Gearin, JBte Piette.

J. F. Malo, priest

M-1
Augustin
Calmels
&
Philomène
Piette
The 19 February, 1866, we priest undersigned have received the mutual consent of marriage between Augustin Calmels of-age son of Paschal Calmels and of Rose de Raymond of the Department of Tarn, in France, on the one part; and Philomène Piette, of-age daughter of Pierre Piette and of Emélie Bourré of St. Norbert County in Canada. The parties having obtained the dispensation of bans of Marriage of the Vicar General B. Delorme under date of 18 of this month. Witnesses and the bridegroom have signed with us.

J. F. Malo, priest

A. Calmels & Philomene (X) Piette
John B. F. Piette
Mary Coleman   Culbert (X) Lambert
Frances M. Piette

B-1
Marie
Virginie
Bernier
The 12 February, 1866, we priest undersigned have baptized Marie Virginie born the 1st of this month of the legitimate marriage of Norbert Bernier and of Thérèse Rivet of this parish. Godfather Amedé Choquette, Godmother Marie Bernier.

J. F. Malo, priest

Page 8
B-2
Eulalie
Foisy
The 16 June, 1866, we priest undersigned have baptized Eulalie, born the 7 April, of the legitimate marriage of Médard Foisy and of Marianne Delard, of this parish. Godfather Pierre Gauthier, Godmother Esther Champagne.

J. F. Malo, priest

B-3
Etienne
Raphaël
Bernier
The 15 July, 1866, we priest undersigned have baptized Etienne Raphaël, born the 13 of the month of the legitimate marriage of Louis Bernier and of Josephte Lavigueur of this parish. Godfather Etienne Peltier, Godmother Marguerite Liard.

J. F. Malo, priest

B-4
Antoine
Marcel
(Humpherville)
The 28 July, 1866, we priest undersigned have baptized Antoine Marcel born 25 May, illegitimate child of Jane Wakan.

J. F. Malo, priest

B-5
The 15 May *[sic]*, 1866, we priest undersigned have baptized Louis born the

Louis Picard	10 of this month, of the legitimate marriage of Régis Picard and of Marie Petit of this parish. Godfather Ls. Bernier, Godmother Joste [Josephte] Lavigueur. J. F. Malo, priest
B-6 Leo Pius Rihart	The 10 June, 1866, we priest undersigned have baptized Leo Pius, born the 5 May, of the legitimate marriage of Jos. Riart and of Elizabeth Rihart of this parish. Godfather Louis Prévost, Godmother Pauline Lefort. J. F. Malo, priest
B-7 John Cassy [Casey?]	The 29 July, 1866, we priest undersigned have baptized John born the 11 of this month of the legitimate marriage of Michael Cassy and of Marguerite Lody of this parish. Godfather JBte Piette, Godmother Mary Coleman. J. F. Malo, priest

Page 9

B-8 Anna Osburn	The 26 August, 1866, we priest undersigned have baptized Anna born the 7 March of the legitimate marriage of Jos. Osburn and of Luce Lonetain of this parish. Godfather, Marcel Raymond. Godmother Caroline Raymond. J. F. Malo, priest
B-9 Ernest Theodore Matthieu	The 20 August, 1866, we priest undersigned have baptized Ernest Theodore born 2 August of the legitimate marriage of F. X. Matthieu and of Rose Ossent of this parish. Godfather, Matt. Goulet, Godmother Mary Ann Goulet. J. F. Malo, priest
B-10 Francis Mary Pichette	The 2 September, 1866, we priest undersigned have baptized Francis Mary, born the day before, of the legitimate marriage of Rock Pichette and of Victoire Despard, of this parish. Godfather Dieudonné Manaigre, Godmother Emelie Pichette. J. F. Malo, priest
B-11 Pauline Chamberlain	The 7 October, 1866, we priest undersigned have baptized Pauline born the 20 of last month, of the legitimate marriage of Adolphe Chamberlain and of Louise Waccan of this parish. Godfather ["Jos Paulding, Godmother. . ." crossed out] Ls. Prévost and wife. J. F. Malo, priest.
B-12 Albert Siday [sic] Murphy	The 16 December, 1866, we priest undersigned have baptized Albert Sidnay, born the 22 November, of the legitimate marriage of Matt. Murphy & Ellen Costello, of this parish. Godfather Jos. Paulding, Godmother Anna Costello. J. F. Malo, priest
M-4 Jacob Bernard & Eliza Collins	The 19 December, 1866, we priest undersigned have received the mutual consent of marriage of Jacob Bernard and of Eliza Collins of Salem, the jurisdiction for this marriage having been [given?] to me the same day by Rev. Father S. Goens, Pastor of Salem. Witnesses: Andrew Murphy, Amable Petit. The spouses have signed with us. Eliza Collins, Wife Eliza Collins, Wife Jacob Bernarde Jacob Bernarde J. F. Malo, priest.

Page 10

M-3 William Duke & Helene Rochbrune	The 13 August, 1866, we priest undersigned have received the mutual consent of marriage between Helene Rochbrune, of-age daughter of Joseph Rochbrune and of the late Lisette (Indian) of this parish on the one part; and W. K. Duke (American non-Catholic) on the other part born in St. Louis Missouri. Witnesses Joseph Rochbrune, father, Honore Picard, brother-in-law of the bride. Francois Bernier friend of the groom. By the presents Mr. W. K. Duke binds hims[elf] [this part written in English, the rest in French, Father Malo's familiar tongue] to let his wife have the ful [sic] liberty of practising her religion, and moreover to raise her children, if God give them any, in the same Catholic faith. Signed & witnessed. Helene (X) Rochbrune W. K. (X) Duke J. F. Malo, priest

**2 M [sic]
Geo. Ridders
&
Bertha
Brentano**

The 1st of December, 1866, we priest undersigned have received the mutual consent of marriage between George Ridders, of the Kingdom of Hanover, Germany, and Bertha Brentano, adoptive daughter of Doctor Frs. J. Brentano, and Elizabeth Muller of this parish; after the publication of 1 ban of marriage, the parties having obtained dispensation of the two other bans. The spouses have signed with us.

Witnesses J. F. T. Brentano
Joseph Bissonet
George Ridders
Spouses
Bertha Brentano
J. F. Malo, priest

**M-5
F. X.
Martineau
&
Sophie
Chalifoux**

The 1st of November, 1866, we priest undersigned have received the mutual consent of marriage of Frs. X. Martineau & Sophie Chalifoux, minor daughter of the late Andree Chalifoux and of Catherine Roussie of this parish. Witnesses, Jos. Lucier, Amable Petit.
J. F. Malo, priest

**Page 11
B-13
[John]
Francis
Smith**

The 9 December, 1866, we priest undersigned have baptized John Francis born the 18 November of the legitimate marriage of Francis Smith and of Ellen Dolin of this parish. Godfather Michael Horan, Godmother Emeline Cosgrove.
J. F. Malo, priest

**B-14
Anna
Kitson**

The 10 July, 1866, we priest undersigned have baptized Anne, born 15 days ago, of the legitimate marriage of Peter Kitson & of Angelique Dupre of this parish. Godfather J. F. Malo, Godmother Isabelle Chalifoux.
J. F. Malo, priest

**Names of young
people confirmed
by the Archbishop
of Oregon, Fr.
Norb. Blanchet.**

A.D. 1866, 25th December, were given the Sacrament of Confirmation by the Reverend and Illustrious Archbishop Francis Norbert Blanchet, the following:

Thomas Coleman
Calixte Gingras
John Larison
Alexandre Labonti
Fabien Chamberlain
Francois Raymond
Victor Richart
Charles Richart
Thomas Garant
Francois Bernier
Philippe McPoland

Euphémie Chamberlain
Clara Mongrain
Cécile Pichette
Philomène Petit
Hélenè McPoland
Catherine Bourgeault
Marie Pichette
Adèle Picard
Francis Harriet Anderson
Soulange Bergevin
Julienne Bergevin
Marianne Costello
Alice Dunn
Anna Roy
J. F. Malo, priest
1867

**B-1
Camille
Theodore
Raymond**

The 20 January, 1867, we priest undersigned have baptized Théodore Camille born the 12 of this month of the legitimate marriage of Augustin Raymond & of Marie Servant of this parish. Godfather Edouard Gervais & Godmother Odile Raymond.
Odille Raymond
J. F. Malo, priest

**Page 12
B-2
Hilaire
Saint Martin**

The 8 February (1867), 1867, we priest undersigned have baptized Hilaire born the 4 December last, of the legitimate marriage of Isidore Saint-Martin and of Marguerite Arcouette of this parish. Godfather - Augustin Roussi; Godmother Cécile Arcouette.
Gust. Thibau

B-3 Catherine Félicite Martineau	The 6 January, 1867, we, priest undersigned, have baptized Catherine Félicite, born the 28 December, 1866, of the legitimate marriage of F. X. Martineau and of Sophie Chalifou of this parish. Godfather: J. Bte. Ménard; godmother Louise Lucier. J. F. Malo, priest
B-4 Hélenè Sharp	The 20 January, 1867, we, priest undersigned, have baptized in this parish Hélenè Sharp, aged about 12 years, of the legitimate marriage of . . . Sharp and of . . . Godfather . . . Hurtubise; godmother Rose Matthieu. Gust. Thibau
B-5 James Stephen Aplin	The 3 February, 1867, we, priest undersigned, have baptized James Stephen, born the 23 December, 1866, of the legitimate marriage of Geo. Aplin and of Marie Wagner of this parish. Godfather: James Coleman; godmother Fanny Murry. J. F. Malo, priest
B-6 Laura Elisabeth Ladd	The 17 February, 1867, we priest undersigned, have baptized Laura Elisabeth born the . . . of the legitimate marriage of John Ladd and of Mary Cavanough of this parish. Godfather: Andrew Murphy; godmother: Mary Cecilia Murphy. J. F. Malo, priest
B-7 Antoine Damas Labounty	The 22 March, 1867, we, priest undersigned, have baptized Antoine Damas born the 21 [of this month, probably], 1867, of the legitimate marriage of Louis Labounty [Labonté] and of Joséphte Laframboise. Godfather: Narcisse Vivet; godmother: Julienne Vivet. Gust. Thibau
B-8 Hélenè Dowd	The 24 March, 1867, we, priest undersigned, have baptized Hélenè Dowd born the 22 March of the legitimate marriage of John Dowd and of Julie Lachance of this parish. Godfather: Pierre Lachance; godmother: Marie Lachance. J. F. Malo, priest
B-9 Herbert John Higly	The 21 April, 1867, we, priest undersigned, have baptized in this parish Herbert John, born the 15 October, 1848, in Iowa of the legitimate marriage of Harvy Higly and of Amanda Smith. Godfather: Rev. Father Malo; godmother: Mary Elizabeth Higly. G. Thibau
Page 13 B-10 David Guay	The 21 April, 1867, we, priest undersigned, have baptized David, born the 17 March last, of the legitimate marriage of Joseph and of Philomène Bercier of this parish. Godfather: Louis Pichette; godmother: Marguerite Pichette. J. F. Malo, priest
B-11 John	The 21 April, 1867, we, priest undersigned, have baptized John, born the 20 April, 1866, of the legitimate marriage of John . . . and of Bethsée. Godfather: Narcisse Vivet; godmother: Julienne Vivet. J. F. Malo, priest
B-12 Lachance	The 10 April, 1867, we, priest undersigned have baptized at his house, one of the twin children, who was in danger of death, of Pierre Lachance, and of . . . born the 9 May [sic] of the legitimate marriage of the spouses above-mentioned, baptized the 10 May and died the same day. No godfather or godmother. G. Thibau
B-13 Thomas Lachance	The 11 May, 1867, we priest undersigned, have baptized Thomas, born the 9 May, of the legitimate marriage of ["Joseph" erased] . . . Lachance and of . . . of this parish. Godfather: Patrick Dowd; godmother Julie Lachance. G. Thibau
B-14 Alexander Hirsch	The 12 May, 1867, we, priest undersigned, have baptized Alexandre, born the 7 April last of the legitimate marriage of F. Hirsh and of M. Bork [or Rork] of this parish. Godfather and Godmother: Mr. and Mrs. Smith. G. Thibau
B-15 Michel	The 12 May, 1867, we, priest undersigned, have baptized Michel born the 29 April last, of the legitimate marriage of . . . and of . . . of this parish.

Laferté	Godfather: Pierre Lachance; Godmother: Adelaïde Bethsé.
	G. Thibau
B-16	The 12 May, 1867, we, priest undersigned, have baptized John born the 1st
John	of April last, of the legitimate marriage of Johnson and of M. Kennedy of
Johnson	this parish. Godfather: Andrew Murphy; godmother: Madame Jackson.
	G. Thibau
B-17	The 17 February, 1866 [sic] by us priest undersigned has been [baptized]
Geneviève	Geneviève born the 22 January of the legitimate marriage of Thomas Nord-
NordWest	west and of Marie of this parish. Godfather François Servant; Godmother
	Cecile Arcouette.
	J. F. Malo, priest
Page 14	
M-1	The 19 December, 1866 [sic], we priest undersigned have received the
Jacob	mutual consent of marriage of Jacob Bernard and of Widow Eliza Collins,
Bernard	both of Salem Ogn. Witnesses M. Hurtubise and Andrew Murphy.
&	J. F. Malo, priest
Eliza	
Collins	
see page 9	
M-2	The 4 July, 1867, we priest undersigned have received the mutual consent
Narcisse	of marriage of Narcisse Gingras and of Julie Montour of this parish. Wit-
Gingras	nesses Culbert Lambert and Jos. Lucier who have not known how to sign.
&	J. F. Malo, priest
Julie	
Montour	
S-2	The 27 April, 1867, we priest undersigned have buried in the cemetery of
Pierre	this place the body of Pierre Gauthier, deceased 2 days ago, aged 58 years,
Gauthier	husband of Esther Champagne. Witnesses Jerome Jackson & A Vertefeuille.
	J. F. Malo, priest
S-3	The 4 [? overwritten] May, 1867, we priest undersigned have buried in the
François	cemetery of this place the body of François Banger [Banget], deceased 2
Banger	days ago, aged 58 years, husband of Adelaïde L'Escarbeault. Witnesses
	Louis Simon, F. X. Matthieu.
	J. F. Malo, priest
S-4	The 12 June, 1867, we priest undersigned have buried in the cemetery of
Félicite	this place the body of Félicite Lucier wife of M. Manson, deceased 2 days
Lucier	ago, aged 53 years. Witnesses. Stephen Manson, Francois Bernier and etc.
	J. F. Malo, priest
S-5	The 18 July, 1867, we priest undersigned have buried in the cemetery of
Amable	this place the body of Amable Petit, verger, deceased 2 days ago, aged about
Petit	70 years, husband of Suzane Towacon. Witnesses, Regis Picard, Pierre
Verger	Charles Petit.
[Beadle]	J. F. Malo, priest
Page 15	
M-3	On the 8 day of August, 1867, we, undersigned Missionary married after
Israel	one publication of bans, a dispensation having been granted by Very Rev.
Langlois	B. Delorm [sic] V.G. from two publications, Israel Langlois, son of Jean
and	Langlois and Margaret Bissonnet of the one part; and Maria Papin daughter
Maria	of Pierre Papin and Susan Goodrich of the other part, of this parish. Wit-
Papin	nesses, Peter Papin and Odile Raymond.
	Cornelius Delahunty, Priest
["B" crossed out]	
S-6	On the 21st day of August, 1867, We, undersigned Missionary gave Chris-
Charles	tian burial to the body of Charles Norwest, son of Thomas Thomas [sic]
Norwest	Norwest and Mary, died on the 19th day of this month. Age 2 months and
	11 days.
	Cornelius Delahunty, Priest
B-18	The 13 September, 1867, we priest undersigned have baptized Jean Bap-
Jean Baptiste	tiste, born the 3 August of the legitimate marriage of John Anderson and of

Anderson	Isabella. The godfather has been Jean Baptiste Piette, the godmother Francase Piette.
	F. P. Cazeau, priest
S-7	The 13 September, 1867, we Priest undersigned have buried in the cemetery
Adolphe	of this parish the body of Adolphe, son of Liza Manson and of an unknown
Manson	father. Witnesses J. Brentano and Manson.
	F. P. Cazeau, priest
B-19	The 15 September, 1867, we Priest undersigned have baptized ["Pierre"
Elie	crossed out] Elie born [son] the 10 of the legitimate marriage of Adolphe
Chamberland	Chamberland and of Louise Chamberland of this parish. Godfather Joseph Chamberland, godmother Euphemie Chamberland.
	F. P. Cazeau, Priest
B-20	The 15 September, 1867, we priest undersigned have baptized Pierre, born
Pierre	the 11th of the legitimate marriage of Francois Brouillard and of Aurelie
Brouillard	Bonnet [Bonin]. Godfather Pierre Bonnet, godmother Salome Bonnet.
	F. P. Cazeau, Priest
Page 16	
B-21	The 18 September, 1867, we Priest undersigned have baptized Charles
Charles	Duncan born the 24th of January, 1864, of the legitimate marriage of
Duncan	Charles Mathieu and of Marguerite Mathieu. The godfather was Francosy
Mathieu	Xavier Mathieu, godmother Marie Anne Goulet.
	F. P. Cazeau, Priest
B-22	The 18 September, 1867, we Priest undersigned have baptized Jacques
Jacques	Archibald born the 8th of May of the legitimate marriage of Charles
Archibald	Mathieu and of Marguerite Mathieu. Godfather Philippe Goulet, god-
Mathieu	mother Rose Mathieu.
	F. P. Cazeau, Priest
S-8	The 23 September, 1867, we priest undersigned have buried in the cemetery
Michael	of this place the body of Michael Coyle deceased 2 days ago aged about 60
Coyle	years. Witnesses: James Coyle, brother, and Francois Wasnuff, nephew of the deceased.
	J. F. Malo, Priest
S-9	The 30 September, 1867, we Priest undersigned have buried in the cemetery
Alexis	of this place the body of Alexis Aubichon deceased the day before, aged
Aubichon	about 80 years. Witnesses: Jos. Laferte, step-son [sic], and Charles Mathieu, friend of the deceased.
	J. F. Malo, Priest
B-23	The 5 May, 1867, we Priest undersigned have baptized Stell [sic] Mary born
Stella M.	March 14th of the legitimate marriage of Theodore Dight Geer and Philo-
Geer	mene Mathieu of Butteville. Godfather Charles (junior) Matthieu, god- mother Rosa Matthieu.
	J. F. Malo, Priest
B-24	The 22 September, 1867, we Priest undersigned have baptized Rose Pelagie,
Rose	born the 4th June of the legitimate marriage of Norbert Bernier and of
Pelagie	Therese Rivet of this parish. Godfather Francois Bernier, godmother
Bernier	Clarisse Bernier.
	J. F. Malo, Priest
Page 17	
B-25	The 22 September, 1867, we Priest undersigned have baptized Esther born
Esther	the 12th of the legitimate marriage of JBte Bourgeault and of Genevievre
Bourgeault	of this parish. Godfather Francois Dubreuil, godmother Josephte Chilifou.
	J. F. Malo, Priest
B-26	The 12 October, 1867, we Priest undersigned have baptized James born the
James	25 June of the marriage of Frank Feller and Rohema Witney of Butteville.
Feller	Godfather Peter Feller, godmother Anna Feller.
	J. F. Malo, Priest
B-27	The 14 October, 1867, we Priest undersigned have baptized Norbert born
Norbert	the 4 October of the legitimate marriage of Andree Chalifou and Josephte
Chalifou	of this parish. Godfather Pierre Petit, godmother Marie Ottawa.
	J. F. Malo. Priest

B-28
Adolphe
illegitimate

The 12 June, 1867, we Priest undersigned have baptized Adolphe born the 13 March of Liza Manson. Godfather Joseph Lucier, godmother Louise.
[See S-7, p 15]   J. F. Malo, priest

B-29
Iser
Freeman
Gould

The 26 May, 1867, we Priest undersigned have baptized Iser Freeman born the 12 of the legitimate marriage of John Gould & Lucie Perrault of this parish. Godfather Firmin Lebrun and Sophie Gregoire his wife.
                    J. F. Malo, Priest

B-30
Soulange
Emelie
Manaigre

The 26 May, 1867, we Priest undersigned have baptized Soulange Emelie born the 23, of the legitimate marriage of Dieudonne Manaigre and Emelie Pichette of this parish. Godfather James Comtoir, Godmother Soulange Pichette his wife.
                    J. F. Malo, Priest

B-31
Charles
Nordouest

The 22 June, 1867, we Priest undersigned have baptized Charles born to 10 of the legitimate marriage of Thomas Nordouest and Marie of this parish. Godfather, Aug. Russie, Godmother Christine Laderoute.
[See S-6, p 15]   J. F. Malo, Priest

Page 18
M-4
Julien
Provost
&
Caroline
Raymond

The 21 October, 1867, after the publication of 1 ban of marriage, the parties having obtained the dispensation of the two other bans, We Priest undersigned have received the mutual consent of marriage of Julien Provost, of-age son of Benjamin Provost of the parish of St. Philippe in Canada; and of Caroline Raymond, minor daughter of Augustin Raymond and Marie Servant of this parish.
                    J. F. Malo, Priest

Witnesses

Aug. (X) Raymond	The spouses	Julien Provost
Olivier Thibodeau		Caroline Raymond
Brother, Marcell J. Raymond		
Clara Matthieu		
Odille Raymond		
Rosa Matthieu		
Margaret Matthieu		

B-32
Eliza
Jane
Davidson

The 3 November, 1867, we Priest undersigned have baptized Eliza Jane born the 28 September of the legitimate marriage of Franklin Davidson & of Anna Coleman of this parish. Godfather James Coleman (junior). Godmother Eliza Coleman.
                    J. F. Malo, Priest

B-33
Georges
Comtoir
[Comtois]

The 11 May, 1867, we Priest undersigned have baptized Georges born 19 April, of the legitimate marriage of Jacques Comtoir and of Soulange Pichette of this parish. Godfather Vital Pichette, Godmother Marguerite Pichette.
                    J. F. Malo, Priest

B-34
Archange
Kitson

The 30 June, 1867, we priest undersigned have baptized Archange born the 20 June of the legitimate marriage of Peter Kitson and of Angelique of this parish. Godfather And. Chalifou, Godmother Josephte.
                    J. F. Malo, Priest

Page 19
B-35
John
Kerr

The 1st of November, 1867, we Priest undersigned have baptized John born the 26 October of the legitimate marriage of Samuel Kerr & of Catherine Coffey of this parish. Godfather Mic. Horan, Godmother Catherine Horan.
                    J. F. Malo, Priest

B-36
Josephine
["Horner"
written faintly]

The 3 November, 1867, we Priest undersigned have baptized Josephine born the 7 of June, child of Marguerite Lacourse and of . . . of the County of YamHill. Godfather Norbert Bernier, Godmother Thérèse Rivest [Rivet] his wife.
                    J. F. Malo, Priest

B-37
Hugh
McPoland

The 24 November, 1867, we priest undersigned have baptized Hugh born the 16 September, of the legitimate marriage of Roger McPoland & of M. McPoland of this parish. Godfather Dr. J. F. J. Brentano & Elizabeth

W. M. Brentano.

J. F. Malo, Priest

B-38 Frs. Xavier Ridders — The 12 December, 1867, we priest undersigned have baptized Francois X. Marie Ridders, born the 21 November, of the legitimate marriage of Georges Ridders & of Elizabeth W. F. Ridders of Corvallis, Ogn. Godfather Dr. J. F. J. Brentano, Godmother Elizabeth W. M. Brentano.

J. F. Malo, Priest

B-39 Mary Francis Marshall — The 25 December, at Midnight Mass, 1867, we Priest undersigned have baptized Mary Francis, born the 22 April, 1855, of the legitimate marriage of G. T. [?] Marshall and of H. [? or K] Million of Portland, Oregon. Godfather J. B. P. Piette; Godmother Francis Piette.

J. F. Malo, Priest

B-40 Marguerite Isabella Marshall — The 25 December, at Midnight Mass, 1867, we Priest have baptized Marguerite Isabella born the . . . , 1860, of the legitimate marriage of G. T. [?] Marshall and of H [or K?] Million of Portland, Oregon. Godfather J. F. Malo, Priest; Godmother Mary E. Coleman.

J. F. Malo, Priest

Page 20

B-41 [Mary May Davidson] — The 25 December, at Midnight Mass, 1867, we Priest undersigned have baptized Mary May born the 8 May, 1860, of the legitimate marriage of Green C. Davidson and of Nancy Million of this parish, Fairfield; Godfather James Coyle; Godmother Elizabeth Coyle.

J. F. Malo, Priest

["The 19th of January" started and crossed out. The remainder of p. 20 is blank]

Page 21

Year 1868

Bapt 1 Adolphe Amédée Choquet — The 19 January, 1868, by us priest has been baptized Adolphe Amédée aged 47 days, born of the legitimate marriage of Amédée Choquet and of Marie Barnier of the Mission of St. Paul Marion County, Oregon; the godfather and godmother have been Adolphe Jetté and Clarisse Barnier, who have not been able to sign.

T. Mesplié, Priest
Miss.

Sept. 1 Julie Gingras — The 3 February, 1868, by us priest undersigned, has been buried in the cemetery of this Mission the body of Julie Gingras deceased 2 days ago aged 23 years; witnesses Xavier Martineau and Pierre Petit.

T. Mesplié, Priest

B-2 Emilia Susanna Rihart — The 9 February, 1868, by us priest undersigned has been baptized Emilia Susanna born since the 27 January of this year, of the legitimate marriage of Joseph Rihart and of Elizabeth Rye of this Mission; the godfather and godmother have been Felix Hirsh and Marianne Hirsh, who have not been able to sign.

T. Mesplié, Priest

S-2 Hirsh — The 11 February, 1868, by us priest undersigned, has been buried in the cemetery of this mission the body of a young son of Felix Hirsh - deceased 2 days ago aged 3 years and 6 months. Witnesses Doctor Brantano and the parents of the child.

T. Mesplié, Priest

B-3 Emma Agnes Pichette — The 6 April, 1868, we priest undersigned have baptized Emma Agnes, born the day before, of the legitimate marriage of Rock Pichette and Victoire Despard of this parish. Godfather Adolphe Jette, Godmother Marguerite Pichette.

J. F. Malo, Priest

B-4 Jane Osburn — The 8 March, 1868, we priest undersigned have baptized Jane born a month ago of the legitimate marriage of Jos. Osburn and Luce Longtain of this parish. Godfather J. F. Malo, priest; Godmother angelique Longtain.

J. F. Malo, Priest

Page 22

B-5 — The 8 March, 1868, we priest undersigned have baptized Mary Alice born

Mary Alice	since 4 months, illegitimate child of Mathilde Rivest. Godfather Marcel Raymond.

J. F. Malo, Priest

B-6 Mary Agnes Murphy	The 26 April, 1868, we Priest undersigned, have baptized Mary Agnes born the 4 of this month of the legitimate marriage of Matt. Murphy and Helen Costello of this parish. Godfather John Costello, Godmother Mary McKay.

J. F. Malo, Priest

B-7 Semeon Bernier	The 3 May, 1868, we Priest undersigned have baptized Semeon born the 7 April of the legitimate marriage of Frs. Bernier and Marie Desparts of this parish. Godfather Ambroise Sauvage, Godmother Marie Sauvage.

J. F. Malo, Priest

B-8 John Franklin Coleman	The 31 May, 1868, we Priest undersigned have baptized John Franklin born the 3 of this month of the legitimate marriage of James Coleman and Fanie Murry of this parish. Godfather J. B. P. Piette, Godmother Francis . . .

J. F. Malo, Priest

B-9 Mary Dowd	The 31 May, 1868, we priest undersigned have baptized Mary born the 16 of this month of the legitimate marriage of John Dowd and Julie Papin of this parish. Godfather Ed. Coffey, Godmother Ellen Gearin.

J. F. Malo, Priest

B-10 Francis Lester Matthieu	The 24 May, 1868, we Priest undersigned have baptized Francois Lester born the 25 February of the legitimate marriage of F. X. Matthieu and Rose Ossant of this parish. Godfather F. X. Matthieu, Grandfather, Godmother Adelaide Banget.

J. F. Malo, Priest

B-11 Emeline Francis Flynn	The 11 June, 1868, we Priest undersigned have baptized Emeline Francis born the 9 of this month of the legitimate marriage of John Flynn & of Mary Flynn, of this parish. Godfather Wm. John Smith, Godmother Suzan Smith.

J. F. Malo, Priest

Page 23

B-12 Mary Helen Hillery	The 14 June, 1868, we Priest undersigned have baptized Mary Helen born the 31 July of the preceeding year, of the civil marriage of Geo. Hillery and of Angelique Laframboise of this parish. Godfather J. F. Malo, Godmother Josephte Labonté.

J. F. Malo, Priest

B-13 Wm James Trevor Convert	The 14 June, 1868, we Priest undersigned have baptized William James Trevor born the 17 March, 1829, of this parish. Godfather Toussaints Mesplié, Priest, Godmother Mary Conkannon.

F. N. Blanchet, Archbishop of O.C.

B-14 William Franklin Davidson Convert	The 14 June, 1868, we Archbishop of O.C. undersigned have baptized William Franklin Davidson [born] the 28 March, 1843, of this parish. Godfather John Coleman.

+ F. N. Blanchet, Archbishop of O.C.

B-15 Samuel Js. Kerr Convert	The 14 June, 1868, we Archbishop of O.C., have baptized Samuel James Kerr born the 30 December, 1839 in Ireland. Godfather John Coffey.

+ F. N. Blanchet, Archbishop of O.C.

[The handwriting in the body of the above 3 entries is that of Father Malo. The signature that of Archbishop Blanchet.]

Sep. 3 Simeon Barnier	The 18 June, 1868, by us priest undersigned, has been buried in the cemetery of this Mission the body of Simeon Barnier deceased the day before aged 2 months and 8 days. Witnesses François Barnier and John Brantano.

T. Mesplié, Priest

B-16 Dorothea Charlotte Vanwassenhov	On the 13th day of September, 1868, I, the undersigned Priest baptized Dorothea Charlotte daughter of of [sic] Frank Vanwassenhov and Ellen Mary Coyle born on the 21st day of August last. Sp. [Sponsors] John B. P. Piette and Mary Ellen McPoland.

Cornelius Delahunty

Page 24

M-1
Thomas
Lonetain
&
Matilde
Rivest

The 3 August, 1868, we priest undersigned have received the mutual consent of marriage between Thomas Lonetain of-age son of Andrée Lonetain of this parish, and Matilde Rivest of-age daughter of the late Joseph Rivest and of Marianne Desparts, the parties having obtained dispensation of ban[s] of the Archbishop the preceeding day, and the wife recognized to be free of a civil marriage on information and testimony of Rev. Father Croquet. Further, the parties recognize & make legitimate before the priest undersigned and the witnesses, as theirs, a child aged 9 months by the name of Mary Alice.

Signed   Thomas (X) Lonetain
                 Matilde (X) Rivest

Witnesses
    Dr. J. F. J. Brentano
    Jno F. Brentano
                     J. F. Malo, Priest

S-8
Catherine
Horan

The . . . September, 1868, we Priest undersigned, have buried in the cemetery of this place the body of Catherine Horan, wife of Mic. Horan aged 58 years, of this parish. Witnesses Ls. McKay & Ls. Coleman and etc.
                     J. F. Malo, Priest

B-17
Mary Hellen
Hillery
see B-12
pag. 23

The 15 July, 1868, we Priest undersigned have baptized Mary Hellen born the 31 July, 1867, of the legitimate marriage of G. Hillery & of Angélique Laframboise of Martin's Ferry. Godfather J. F. Malo, Priest, Godmother Josephte Labonté.
                     J. F. Malo, Priest

B-18
Frs. Julien
Picard

The 16 August, 1868, we Priest undersigned have baptized Frs. Julien born of the [sic] 24 July of the legitimate marriage of Honore Picard and of Céleste Rochbrune of this parish. Godfather, Julien Provost, Godmother Emelie Provost.
                     J. F. Malo, Priest

Page 25

B-19
Frs. Albert
Brouillard

The 3 October, 1868, we Priest undersigned have baptized Frs. Albert born the 10 September of the legitimate marriage of Frs. Brouillard & of Aurelie Bonin of this parish. Godfather Narcisse Gingras, Godmother Mary E. Aplin.
                     J. F. Malo, Priest

B-20
Walter Rich.
Murphy

The 18 October, 1868, we Priest undersigned have baptized Walter Richard born the 4 January, of the legitimate marriage of Andrew Murphy & of Elizabeth Cosgrove, of this parish. Godfather, James C. Murphy, Godmother Kate McKay.
                     J. F. Malo, Priest

B-21
Eléonore
Papin

The 18 October, 1868, we Priest undersigned have baptized Eléonore born the 9 of this month of the legitimate marriage of Pierre Papin & of Suzane Goudrich, of this parish. Godfather Petrus Papin & Godmother Julienne Labonté.
                     J. F. Malo, Priest

B-22
Mary L.
Cooke

The 22 November, 1868, we Priest undersigned have baptized ["Brigitt" crossed out] Mary Louise born the 28 May, 1866, of the legitimate marriage of Jn. J. Cooke & of Brigitt Lee, of this parish. Godfather, Nicolas Cooke, Godmother Mary Coleman.
                     J. F. Malo, Priest

B-23
Elizabeth
H. Smith

The 28 November, 1868, we Priest undersigned have baptized Elizabeth Hannah born the 3 November of the legitimate marriage of Jn. W. Smith & Suzan Mcdermott of this parish. Godfather J. F. Malo, Godmother Hannah McDermott.
                     J. F. Malo, Priest

B-24
Joseph
Bernier

The 6 December, 1868, we Priest undersigned have baptized Joseph born the 18 Nov. ["28" crossed out] of the legitimate marriage of Louis Bernier & of Josephte Lavigueur of this parish. Godfather Louis Prévost, Godmother Appoline Prévost.

J. F. Malo, Priest

B-25
James
Onésime
Comtoir

The 6 December, 1868, we Priest undersigned have baptized James Onésime born the 11 November of the legitimate marriage of James Comtoir & of Soulange Pichette of this parish. Godfather Rock Pichet. Godmother Victoire desparts.

J. F. Malo, Priest

Page 26
B-26
Jean Baptiste
Langlois

The 6 December, 1868, we Priest undersigned have baptized Jean-Baptiste born the . . . October, of the legitimate marriage of Isreal Langlois, and of Marie Papin of this parish. Godfather Pierre Lachance, Godmother Suzane Goudrich his wife. [Also grandparents of this child]

J. F. Malo, Priest

B-27
Mary Eve
Gay

The 3 January, 1869, we Priest undersigned have baptized Mary Eveline born the 12 November preceeding (1868), of the legitimate marriage of Joseph W. Gay & of Philomène Bercier, of this parish. Godfather Petrus Papin, Godmother Clarissa Matthieu.

J. F. Malo, Priest

B-28
Marguerite
Ritcher

The 3 January, 1869, we Priest undersigned have baptized Marguerite born the 12 November preceeding, of the legitimate marriage of Cyrile Ritcher & of Véronique Rochbrune of this parish. Godfather Frs. Brouillard, Godmother Aurélie Bonin.

J. F. Malo, Priest

S-9
Theodore
C.
Raymond

The 29 December, 1868, we priest undersigned have buried in the cemetery of this place the body of Theodore Raymond, aged 2 years, son of August Raymond and of Marie Servant of this parish. Witnesses, Aug. Raymond, father, and Julien Prevost, brother *[sic]* of the deceased.

J. F. Malo, Priest

There were during the year 5 burials of Metis or Indian children whose names were not given.

Page 27   **Year   1869   of Our Lord**
B-1
Joseph
W. Gay
Convert

The 3 January, 1869, we undersigned Priest have baptized Joseph Whiteum Gay, aged 27 years, son of George Gay and of Louisa of this parish. Godfather Julien Papin, godmother Rosa Matthieu.

J. F. Malo, Priest

B-2
Mary S.
Duke

The 24 February, 1869, we Priest undersigned have baptized Mary Surrettes born the 2nd September, 1857, of the legitimate marriage of Wm. C. Duke (protestant) and Ellene Roquebrune of this parish. Godfather, J. F. Malo, Priest, godmother Francis Piette.

J. F. Malo, Priest

[The 2 May, 18 crossed out.]
B-3
Emelie
Jane
Staats

The 2 May, 1869, we Priest undersigned have baptized Emelie Jane born the 19th of March of the legitimate marriage of John Staats (protestant) and of Marie Toupin of this parish. Godfather Ls. Bergevin, godmother Clara Matthieu.

J. F. Malo, Priest

B-4
Alfred
Jerome
Chamberlain

The 9 May, 1869, we Priest undersigned have baptized Alfred Jerome born the 31st March of the legitimate marriage of Adolphe Chamberlain and of Louise of this parish. Godfather Aug. Raymond, godmother Marie Servant.

J. F. Malo, Priest

B-5
Theresa
Zolner

The 11 May, 1869, we Priest undersigned have baptized Theresa born the 3rd March of the legitimate marriage of Robert Zolner and of Catherine Zolner of the parish of St. Louis. Godfather Francis Nibler, godmother Marguerite Nibler.

J. F. Malo, Priest

B-6
Theresa
Juliana
Schultheis

The 21 February, 1869, we Priest undersigned have baptized Theresa Juliana born the 17th of this month of the legitimate marriage of Michael Schultheis and of Theresa Schultheis of this parish. Godfather Michael Nibler, godmother Theresa Nibler.

J. F. Malo, Priest

B-7
Jos.
Patrick
[Smith]

The 14 March, 1869, we Priest undersigned have baptized Joseph Patrick born the 10th February of the legitimate marriage of Francis Smith and of Ellen Nolin of this parish. Godfather J. F. Malo, Priest.

J. F. Malo, Priest

Page 28

B-8
James
Kerr

The 26 March, 1869, we Priest undersigned have baptized James born the 18th February of the legitimate marriage of Samuel Kerr and of Catherine Coffey of this parish. Godfather John Coffey, godmother Mary McKay.

J. F. Malo, Priest

B-9
John
Geo.
Nibler

The 28 March, 1869, we Priest undersigned have baptized John Georges born the 12th February of the legitimate marriage of John Nibler and of Mary Nibler of this parish. Godfather Georges Nibler, godmother Margy Flashman.

J. F. Malo, Priest

B-10
Marie
Louise
Lucier

The 14 March, 1869, we Priest undersigned have baptized Marie Louise born the 19th February of the legitimate marriage of Jos. Lucier and of [Marie crossed out] Louise of this parish. Godfather Louis Chalifoux, godmother Euphemie Chamberlain.

J. F. Malo, Priest

B-11
Marie
Adelaide
Vertefeuille

The 4 April, 1869, we Priest undersigned have baptized Marie Adelaide born the 6th January of the legitimate marriage of Jude Vertefeuille and of Catherine Gauthier of this parish. Godfather Aug. Raymond, godmother Adelaide Banget.

J. F. Malo, Priest

B-12
Ellen
Virginia
Ladd

The 30 May, 1869, we Priest undersigned have baptized Ellen Virginia born the 22nd December, 1868, of the civil marriage of John Ladd and of Marg. Cavenough of Portland. Godfather Hugh Cosgrove (junior), godmother Emmy Cosgrove.

J. F. Malo, Priest

B-13
Celeste
Mary R. E.
Plamondon

The 30 May, 1869, we Priest undersigned have baptized Celeste Mary Rose Edeste born the 29th April last of the legitimate marriage of Frs. F. Plamondon and Matilde Dubois of Butteville. Godfather J. F. Malo, Priest, godmother, Clara Matthieu.

J. F. Malo, Priest

Page 29

B-14
Angelique
Lonetain

The 30 May, 1869, we Priest undersigned have baptized Angelique born the 16th of this month of the legitimate marriage of Thomas Lonetain and of Matilde Rivest of Champoeg in this parish. Godfather Adolphe Jette, godmother Angelique Lonetain.

J. F. Malo, Priest

B-15
Prosper
Picard

The 18 July, 1869, we Priest undersigned have baptized Prosper born the 12th of this month of the legitimate marriage of Regis Picard and of Marie Petit of this parish. Godfather Abraham Guilbeault, godmother Julienne Bergevin.

J. F. Malo, Priest

B-16
Maria
Theresa
Nibler

The 25 July, 1869, we Priest undersigned have baptized Maria Theresa born the 16th of this month of the legitimate marriage of Nibler and of Theresa Nibler of this parish. Godfather Michael Sholdice, godmother Theresa Kolar.

J. F. Malo, Priest

S-4
Angelique
Lonetain

The 4 August, 1869, we Priest undersigned have buried in the cemetery of this place the body of Angelique deceased 2 days ago aged 3 months, child of Thomas Lonetain and of Matilde Rivest of this parish. Present, Pierre Pariseau, JBte Gobin.

J. F. Malo, Priest

B-17
Charles
Wm.
Kittson

The 8 August, 1869, We Priest undersigned have baptized Charles William born the 27th of July last of the legitimate marriage of Peter Kittson and of Angelique Dupres of this parish. Godfather Frs. Dompierre, godmother Marguerite Liard.

J. F. Malo, Priest

B-18
Jerome B.
Jackson,
a convert

The 15 August, 1869, we Priest undersigned have baptized Jerome B. Jackson, adult aged about 45 years, husband of Mary Cosgrove. Godfather J. F. Malo, Priest, godmother Elizab. Elredge.

J. F. Malo, Priest

B-19
Mary
Ellen
Jackson

The 15 August, 1869, we Priest undersigned have baptized Mary Ellen born the 7th of August, 1858, of the legitimate marriage of Jerome B. Jackson and of Mary Cosgrove of this parish. Godfather J. F. Malo, Priest, and [godmother] Anny Costello.

J. F. Malo, Priest

Page 30
B-20
Theodore
Aplin

The 15 August, 1869, we Priest undersigned have baptized Theodore born the 8th of July of the legitimate marriage of Georges Aplin and Marie Wagner of this parish. Godfather Fir. Lebrun, godmother Sophie Lebrun.

J. F. Malo, Priest

B-21
John
Michael
Cooke

The 12 September, 1869, we the undersigned parish priest of St. Paul have baptized John Michael, born the 16th of May of this year of the lawful marriage of J. J. Cooke and Bridget Lee of this parish. Sponsors: William J. Trevor, Bridget Trevor.

J. F. Malo, Priest

S-5
Josette
Chalifou

The 24 August [1869] has been buried in the cemetery of St. Paul the body of Josette wife of Andre Chalifou deceased the day before, aged about 23 years. Witnesses: Doctor Brentana, Pierre Kittson.

J. F. Malo, Priest

[Entries in English until January, 1881, rarely in French.]

B-22
Robert
Wilfred Lee
Matthew

The 12 September, 1869, we the undersigned parish priest of St. Paul have baptized Robert Wilfred born [12th del.] the 5th of August of this year of the lawful marriage of F. X. Matthew and Rosa Ossent of Butteville. Sponsors: Louis H. Ouimette, Priscilla Cloth. Matthew.

J. F. Malo, Priest

S-6
Theodore
Aplin

The 16th of September, 1869, we the undersigned parish priest of St. Louis have buried in the graveyard of St. Paul the corpse of Theodore, son of George Aplin and Mary Wagner of this parish, deceased the 15th inst., aged 2 months. Witnesses, Brentano, Parizeau.

G. C. Thibau, pr.

B-23
Antoine

The 17th of October, 1869, we the undersigned parish priest of St. Louis have baptized in St. Paul's church Antoine, born the 26th of September of this year, of the lawful marriage of Thomas . . . and Mary . . . of this parish. Sponsors: Mr. Francis and Mrs. Adelaide Lefevre.

G. C. Thibau, pr.

B-24
Christine
Dubreuil

The 17th of October, 1869, we undersigned parish priest of St. Louis have baptized Christine in St. Paul's church, born the 3rd of October inst. of the lawful marriage of Francois Dubreuil and Magdelen Bourgeau of this parish. Sponsors: Joseph Lucier and Louise Martineau.

G. C. Thibau, pr.

S-7
[Ottawa
deleted]
Noress

On the 26th of October, 1869, we the undersigned parish priest have buried in the grave yard the corpse of [Ottawa dele.] a son of . . . of this parish deceased on the 25th inst, aged 9 days. Witnesses: Pariso and some members of his family.

A. J. Glorieux, P.P.

Page 31
B-25
Peter
Fitzgerald

On the 30th of October, 1869, we the undersigned parish Priest have baptized at domicile in danger of death Peter Fitzgerald. No sponsors.

A. J. Glorieux, P.P.

S-8
Peter
Fitzgerald

On the 31st of October, 1869, we the undersigned Parish Priest have buried the corpse of Peter Fitzgerald, who died immediately after his baptism. Witnesses, Fitzgerald, Pariso and N. Vivet.

A. J. Glorieux, P.P.

Sep. 9
Anne

On the 5th of November, 1869, we the undersigned Parish Priest, have buried in the grave yard the corpse of Anne Murray, aged 34 years, wife of

Murray,
wife of
Chs. J.
Fitzgerald

Chs. Jn. Fitzgerald. Witnesses: Dr. Brentano, Parizeau, Lambert and some others.

A. J. Glorieux, P.P.

B-26
Francois
Cyan
[Wilquet]

On the 14th of November, 1869, we the undersigned Parish Priest have baptized Francois Cyan, aged 1 month, a son of [Francois Servan dele.] Charles and Silla Wallquet. Godfather Francois Servant, godmother Mary Laferte.

A. J. Glorieux, P.M.

Sep. 10
Theresia
Schultheis

On the 18th of November, 1869, we the undersigned Parish Priest have buried in the grave yard the corpse of Theresia Schultheis, born on the 17th of March last, a daughter of Michael Schultheis. Witnesses Dr. Brentano, Pariso and etc.

A. J. Glorieux, P.M.

B-27
Francois
Xavier
Matthieu

On the 25th of November, 1869, we the undersigned Parish Priest have baptized at domicile in Butteville, Francois Xavier, born on the 24th last of the lawful marriage of Stanislaus Pierre Charles Matthieu and Marguerite Matthieu. Sponsors: Mr. and Mrs. Plamondon.

A. J. Glorieux, P.M.

Page 32

S-11
Adelaide
Lambert

On the 28 of November, 1869, we the undersigned Parish Priest have buried in the grave yard of St. Paul the corpse of Adelaide Lambert aged about 10 years, a daughter of Auguste Lambert. Witnesses: P Pariso, Jn. Brentano, and her family, and a great many members of the Congregation.

A. J. Glorieux, PM

M-1
Narcisse
Lafontaine
and
Marguerite
Pichette
[In French]

The 30 November, 1869, after the publication of one ban of marriage, the parties having obtained dispensation of two others, we undersigned Priest have received the mutual consent of marriage of Narcisse Lafontaine, of-age son of Belinier Lafontaine and Nannette Boisvert of the parish of Berthier, and Marguerite Pichette, of-age daughter of Louis and Marguerite Bercier of this parish.
Witnesses: Adolphe Jette
Francois Bernier
The spouses   Narcisse (X) Lafontaine
Margaret (X) Pichette
A. J. Glorieux, priest
1869

Baptisms   27
Burials   11
Abjuration   1
Marriage   1
Page 33

1870

S-1
Sister
Marie
Olive

On the 9th of February, 1870, we the undersigned Chaplain of the Sisters of the Holy Names of J. and M. have buried in the little chapel on the Sisters' ground the corpse of Sister Marie Olive, of the Community of the Sisters of the Holy Names of Jesus and Mary. Witnesses: Father Glorieux, Sister Mary, Sister Perpetue, Sister Peter, Sister Orsinius, also signed with me.

L. Piette, C.P.

A. J. Glorieux, P.P.
Sister Mary   Sister Mary Orsinius
Sister Mary Perpetue   Sister Mary Peter

M-1
Adolphe
Jette
and
Mary
Liard
[in French]

The 1st of February, 1870, after the publication of one ban of marriage, the parties having obtained dispensation of two others, We, Priest undersigned have received the mutual consent of marriage of Adolphe Jette, widower in his first marriage of Julienne, deceased the 25 February, '65, and Marguerite Liard, daughter of Louis . . . and Celeste Rochbrune, all of the parish of St. Paul.

A. J. Glorieux, priest

The spouses, Adolphe Jette
Margaret Liard
Witnesses, F. X. Mathieu, Sen.
Joseph Rochburn [sic]

B-1
Caroline
Pichette

On the 20th of February, 1870, we the undersigned have baptized Caroline Pichette, born on the 16th instant, of the lawful marriage of Rock Pichette and Victoire Frederic [Despard]. Sponsors, Narcisse Lafontaine and Mrs. J. B. Piette.

A. J. Glorieux, PM

Page 34
S-2
Eleanore
Pepin
[Lachance]

On the 2nd of March, 1870, we the undersigned Parish Priest of St. Paul have buried in the graveyard of St. Paul the corpse of Eleonore Pepin who died in the 1st instant, a daughter of Peter Lachance Pepin and Suzanne Goodrich. Witnesses Peter Pariseau, Peter Lachance and many members of the same family.

A. J. Glorieux, PM

B-2
Josephine
Labonte

On the 6th of March, 1870, we the undersigned Parish Priest have baptized Josephine Labonte, born on the 20th of February, a daughter of Louis Labonte and Josette Laframboise. Sponsors: Etienne Gregoire and Victoire McMullen.

A. J. Glorieux, PM

S-3
Narcisse
Vivet

On the 7th of March, 1870, we the undersigned Parish Priest of St. Paul, have buried in the grave yard of St. Paul, Narcisse Vivet, born in 1831, died on the 5th instant. Witnesses: Pariseau, L. Bergevin.

A. J. Glorieux, PM

B-3
Matthias Elr.
Wasenhove

On the 3rd of April, 1870, we the undersigned Parish Priest, have baptized Mathias E. Wasenhove, born on the 28th February last, a son of Frank and Ellen Coyle. Godfather Francis Beuscher. Godmother Nancy Goulet.

A. J. Glorieux, PM.

B-4
Isidore
St. Martin

On the 11th of April, 1870, we the undersigned Parish Priest have baptized in Butteville, Isidore St. Martin, a son of Isidore St. Martin and Marguerite Arquette. He was born on the 19 of March. Godfather Amable Arquet Godmother Augustine [?] Arquet.

A. J. Glorieux, P.M.

Page 35
B-5
François
August
St. Martin

On the 11th of April, 1870, we the undersigned Parish Priest of St. Paul, have supplied the Ceremonies of Baptism on François August St. Martin found validly baptized in case of danger of death by Amable Arquette. He was a son of Isidore St. Martin and Marguerite Arquette, and born on the 16 October, 1868.

A. J. Glorieux, P.M.

S-4
François
St. Martin

On the 14th of April, 1870, we the undersigned Parish Priest, have buried in the grave yard the corpse of François St. Martin, a son of Isidore and Marg. Arquette, aged 1 year and a half. Witnesses: Isidore St. Martin, Amable Arquette.

A. J. Glorieux, PM

B-6
Elias
Eberhard
(Convert)

On the 17th of April, 1870, we the undersigned Parish Priest have baptized Elias Eberhard, born on the 24th of September, 1851. Godfather Hugh Gearin. Godmother Mary Coleman.

Elias Eberhard
A. J. Glorieux PM

[B-no#]
Bridget
Catherine
Dowd

Catherine Bridget Dowd was baptized by F. Croquet, April 21, 1870: born March 21, 1870. Sponsors H. Callinan & Honore McManara.

B-7
Norbert
Lucifique
Choquette

On the 1st of May, 1870, we the undersigned Parish Priest have baptized in St. Paul's Church Norbert Lucifique Choquette born on the 24th April last, a son of Amédée and Marie Bernier. Sponsors: Julien Provost and Caroline Raymond.

A. J. Glorieux, PM

B-8
Mary
Louisa
Provost

On the 8th of May, 1870, we the undersigned Parish Priest of St. Paul have baptized in St. Paul's Church Mary Louisa Provost born the 19th of April last, a daughter of Louis Provost and Pauling Lallefol [Lafaure] Sponsors: Joseph Remi Provost (by proxy from Chs. Provost) and Louisa Ossan (by proxy from Ellen Sharp).

A. J. Glorieux, PM

Page 36
B-9
Marguerite
Niebler

On the 22nd of May, 1870, we the undersigned Parish Priest have baptized Marguerite Niebler, born on the 17 instant of the lawful marriage of Joseph and Mary Niebler. Sponsors: Frank Niebler, Marguerite Niebler.

A. J. Glorieux, PM

M-2
Louis
Ouimette
and
Clara
Matthieu
[In French]

The 26th May, 1870, we Priest undersigned, have received the mutual consent of marriage of Louis Ouimette, son of Louis and Marguerite Ouimette, and Clara Matthieu, daughter of F. X. and Rosa Matthieu of the parish of St. Paul. The parties have obtained dispensation of two bans.

The spouses: L. H. Ouimette

Clare Ouimette

Witnesses: Chas. Matthieu, Jr.

Telesphore Diegnan

A. J. Glorieux, Priest

S-5
Robert
Daly

On the 27th of May, 1870, we the undersigned Priest have buried in the grave yard of St. Paul the corpse of Robert Daly, aged about 40 years, who died on the 24 instant. Witnesses: James McKay, Dr. Brentano, Mr. Horan, Js. Coyle and many others.

A. J. Glorieux, P.M.

B-10
James
Francis
McPoland

On the 29th of May, 1870, we the undersigned Parish Priest have baptized James Francis McPoland born on the 18th of April last of the lawful marriage of Roger McPoland and Anne McPoland. Sponsors: Frank Vanwasenhove and Ellen Mary Coyle.

A. J. Glorieux, PM

Page 37
B-11
Joseph
Picard

On the 10th of June, 1870, we the undersigned Parish Priest have baptized Joseph Picard, born on the 8 May last, a son of Henri Picard and Celeste Rochbrune. Sponsors: Joseph Rochbrune and Adele Picard.

A. J. Glorieux, PM

S-6
Cecelia
Lauson
[Lawson]

On the 15th of June, 1870, we the undersigned Parish Priest have buried in the grave yard of St. Paul the corpse of Cecelia Lauson, wife of James McKay. She was about 50 years of age. Witnesses, Rev. Father Thibau, Mich. Horan and etc.

A. J. Glorieux, P.M.

B-12
William
Bailey
(Convert)

On the 17th of June, 1870, we the undersigned have baptized William Bailey, aged 64 years. Sponsors: Mr. Matthew Murphy and Mrs. Matthew Murphy.

F. X. Weninger, Missionary

B-13
Joseph E.
Davidson
(Convert)

On the 21st of June, 1870, we the undersigned have baptized in St. Paul's Church Joseph E. Davidson, born on the 4th of May, 1826, a son of James Davidson and Mary Davidson. Sponsor: J. B. P. Piette.

F. X. Weninger, M.

Benediction
of the
little
Chapel

We the undersigned Parish Priest certify that Very Rev. Father Fierens, V.G., has solemnly blessed the little chapel on the Sisters' ground in presence of Rev. Father Piette, Mother Veronica, Sup.

A. J. Glorieux, PM

B-14
Joseph
Ausber
[Osborne]

On the 17th of July, 1870, we the undersigned have baptized in St. Paul's Church Joseph Ausber, born on the 17th of June last, a son of Joseph and Louise Ausber. Godfather F. X. Moison, Godmother, Angelique Moison.

A. J. Glorieux, PM

Page 38
B-15
Marie

On the 23rd of July, 1870, we the undersigned Parish Priest have baptized Mary Ellen McHoran, born on the 22nd instant, a daughter of Michael and

Ellen McHoran	Catherine Horan of the Parish of St. Paul. Sponsors: Patrick and Catherine Flynn. A. J. Glorieux, P.M.
B-16 Theodore Lonetain	On the 24th of July, 1870, we the undersigned Parish Priest have baptized in St. Paul's Church theodore Lonetain, born on the 27th of June last, of the lawful marriage of Thomas and Mathilda Longtain of this Parish. Sponsors: Fabien Rivet and Elizabeth Aplin. A. J. Glorieux, P.M.
B-17 James Aug. Kennedy	On the 16th of October, 1870, we the undersigned Parish Priest have baptized in St. Paul's Church James Augustin Kennedy, born on the 22nd of September last of the lawful marriage of John and Brigette Kennedy. Sponsors: James McKay and M. Coleman. A. J. Glorieux, PM
B-18 Alfred Vertfeuille	On the 20 November, 1870, we the undersigned Parish Priest have baptized in St. Paul's Church Alfred Vertfeuille, born on the 1st instant of the lawful marriage of Judei and Catherine Gauthier of this parish. Sponsors: Charles Bergevin and Olive Gauthier. A. J. Glorieux, P m
B-19 Margaret Kerr	On 31 July, 1870, we the undersigned have baptized in St. Paul's Church Margaret Kerr born on the 28 instant of the lawful marriage of Samuel J. and Catherine Coffey. Sponsors: James J. Coyle, M. Coffey. L. A. LeBas, M [?]
Page 39 B-20 Louise Celine Brouillard	On the 11 September, 1870, we the undersigned have baptized in St. Paul's Church Louise Celine, born on the 5th instant of the lawful marriage of Frank Brouillard and Aurelie Bonin of this parish. Sponsors: Charles Bergevin and Anastasie Bonin. L. A. LeBas, M.
B-21 Louise Horn[er]	On the 11 September, 1870, we the undersigned have baptized Louise Horn [Lacourse crossed out] on in [sic] September, 1869, of the marriage of Sam Horn and Marguerite Lacourse. Sponsors Augn. Raymond and Marie Servan. L. A. LeBas, M.
B-22 Henri Comtoir	On the 9 October, 1870, we the undersigned have baptized in St. Paul's Church Henri Comtoir, born on the 22 of Sept. last, of the lawful marriage of Eugene Comtois and Soulange Pichette of this parish. Sponsors; Henri Heter [?] and Marie Pichette. L. A. LeBas, M.
Sep. 7 Marguerite Waponte	On the 5 October, 1870, we the undersigned have buried in St. Paul's grave yard, Marguerite Waponte, wife of Amable Arquitte, aged seventy two years, deceased on the 3d instant. Witnesses: Michel Laferte and Moyse Sanders. L. A. LeBas, M.
B-23 Joseph Goyet	On the 18 September, 1870, we the undersigned have baptized in St. Paul's Church, Joseph Goyet, aged four years, son of Goyet and Louise Wacan [Tawakon]. Sponsors: Edward Gervais and Marie Picard. G. C. Thibau, pr.
B-24 Page 40 Pierre Bourgeault	On the 18 September, 1870, we the undersigned have baptized Pierre Bourgeault, born on the 3d instant, of the lawful marriage of J. Baptiste and Genevieve Bourgeault [Martineau], of this parish. Sponsors: Louis Amperville [Humpherville] and Mrs. Andrew Lachapelle [Adrienne Lucier]. G. C. Thibau, pr. 1870
B-25 Ellen Elizabeth Murphy	On the 18 September, 1870, we the undersigned have baptized under condition Ellen Elizabeth Murphy, born on the 13th of May of the lawful marriage of Andrew Murphy and Elizabeth Cosgrove of this parish. Sponsors Matthew Murphy and Elizabeth Cosgrove. G. C. Thibau, pr.
B-26	On the 22nd of September, 1870, we the undersigned [Parish crossed out]

Charles Pierre Pariseau	priest have baptized Charles Pariseau, born on the 12th of Sept. instant, of the lawful marriage of Pierre Pariseau and Marie Rochbrune *[Dompier]* of this parish. Sponsors, Mr. Th. Gervais and Marie Gervais. G. C. Thibau. pr.
B-27 Catherine Anson *[Anderson]*	On the 7 August, 1870, we the undersigned have baptized Catherine Anson *[Anderson]*, born on the 27 of June last of the lawful marriage of John Anson *[Anderson]* and Isabelle Lambese *[Lambert, Lumbers]*. Sponsors: Philippe J. McPoland and Clarisse Mongrain. G. C. Thibau, pr.
Sep. 8 Euphrosine Kitson	On the 18 August, 1870, we the undersigned P. Priest of St. Louis have buried in the St. Paul's grave yard Euphrosine Kitson, born on the 19 January, 1862, who died on the 16th instant. G. C. Thibau, pr.
Sep. 9 John Niebler	On the 22 of September, 1870, we the undersigned Parish Priest have buried in St. Paul's grave yard John George Niebler, a son of John Niebler and Mary Niebler, born on the 28 of March, 1869. Witness, Parizeau. G. C. Thibau, pr.
Page 41 Sep. 10 Mary Ellen Horan	On the 22 of September, 1870, we the undersigned Parish Priest, Mary Ellen M. Horan, a daughter of Mich. Horan and of Catherine Flynn, baptized on the 23 of July and deceased on the 21st instant. Witnesses, James Coyle, Parizeau. G. C. Thibau, pr.
Sep. 11 Margaret Kerr	On the 12 October, 1870, we the undersigned Parish Priest of St. Louis have buried in St. Paul's grave yard the corpse of Margaret Kerr, daughter of Sam Kerr and Cath. Coffey, baptized on the 31 of July last, deceased on the 10th instant. Witnesses: Parizeau and Dr. Brentano. G. C. Thibau, pr.
Sep. 12 Sister Mary Francis	On the 11 of December, 1870, we the undersigned Chaplain of the Sisters have buried in the graveyard of the Sisters the corpse of Sr. Mary Francis, of the Community of the Sisters of the Holy Names of Jesus and Mary. She died on the 9th instant. Witnesses: A. J. Glorieux, pr. L. A. LeBas, M., Sr. Veronica of the Crucifix, Sr. Marie Febronie. L. Piette, Chaplain

First Communions 11	Mary Kennedy Elizabeth " Anna " Manda "	Louisa Paunell Ellen Coffey Mary Kirschner Emma Patterson	Lena Patterson Albina Graton Louiza Bonin A. J. Glorieux, P.P.

1871

Page 42	Baptisms 27 Burials 12 Marriages 2
B-1 Philomine Zelia *[?]* Raymond	On the 1st of January, 1871, we the undersigned, have baptized on condition Philomine Zelia Raymond, born on the 10 December, 1869, of the lawful marriage of Augn. Raymond and Marie Servain, of this parish. Godfather: Isaac Boutan, Godmother: Philomine Langlois. A. J. Glorieux, P.P.
S-1 Sister Mary Florence	On the 5th of January, 1871, we the undersigned, Chaplain of the Sisters, have buried in the Sisters grave yard the corpse of Sr. Mary Florence, of the Community of the Sisters of the Holy Names of Jesus and Mary, who died on the 3d instant. Witnesses: A. J. Glorieux, P.P. L. Piette, Chaplain L. A. LeBas, pr. Miss. Apost.
B-2 Joseph Victor Laferte	On the 8 January, 1871, we the undersigned Parish Priest have baptized in St. Paul's Church, Joseph Victor Laferte, born on the 18th of December last of the lawful marriage of Michel Laferte and Angelique Desrivieres. Godfather: Firmin Lebrun. God Mother: Mrs. Firmin Lebrun *[Sophie Gregoire]*. A. J. Glorieux, Pr.

B-3
Theresa
Mary
Schultheis

On January 8, 1871, we the undersigned Parish Priest have baptized in St. Paul's Church Theresa Mary Schultheis, born on the 7th instant of the lawful marriage of Michael and Theresa Schultheis. Sponsors; Michael Niebler and Mrs. Michael Niebler.

A. J. Glorieux, Pr.

Page 43
B-4
Mary
Dupret
[Dupre]

On the 8 January, 1871, we the undersigned Parish Priest have baptized in St. Paul's Church Mary Dupret, born on the 2nd of December last, of the lawful marriage of Charles Dupret and Catherine Chalifou. Sponsors, Frank Lambert and Mrs. Vivet.

A. J. Glorieux, Pr.

Sep. 2
Sister
Mary
Simone

On the 9th of January, 1871, we the undersigned Chaplain of the Sisters, have buried in the Sisters graveyard in St. Paul's Parish, the corpse of Sr. Mary Simone of the Community of the Sisters of the Holy Names of Jesus and Mary, who died on the 7th instant.
Witnesses:
A. J. Glorieux, P.P.
L. A. LeBas, M.　　　　　L. Piette, Chaplain
pr. miss. apost.

Sep. 3
Margaret
Kirk

On January 16, 1871, we the undersigned Parish Priest have buried in the graveyard of St. Paul's, the corpse of Margaret Kirk, daughter of Peter Kirk, aged 6½ years; who died on the 15th instant. Witnesses Peter Kirk, Dr. Brentano, A. Murphy, and many members of the Congregation.
Feb 15, 1875. Removed to the New graveyard. : B.D.

A. J. Glorieux, Pr.

M-1
Andre
Chalifou
&
Emerance
Mongrain

On January 16, 1871, we the undersigned Parish Priest, have received, after one publication, the mutual consent of marriage of Andre Chalifou, son of Andre and Catherine Russie, widow[er] of Josette St. Andre, on one side and Emerance Mongrain, daughter of David and Catherine Lafantaisie, on the other side, they are both of this Parish.
Married persons
Andre X Chalifou
his mark
Emerance Mongrain
her mark　　　　　A. J. Glorieux
Witnesses
Augn, X Lambert
his mark
David X Mongrain
his mark

Page 44
Sep. 4
Margaret
Fleishman

On the 25th of January, 1871, we the undersigned Parish Priest have buried in St. Paul's graveyard Margaret Fleishman, wife of Peter Fleishman; she was born in 1800 and died on the 23d instant. Witnesses: P. Parizeau, Frank Vanwassnuf, etc.

A. J. Glorieux, Pr.

Sep. 5
Philomine
Raymond

On the 29th January, 1871, we the undersigned Parish Priest have buried in St. Paul's graveyard, Philomine Raymond, born on the 10th December last. Witnesses: Augn. Raymond, Gervais etc.

A. J. Glorieux, Pr.

B-5
Marcelline
Chalifou

On the 27th February, 1861, we the undersigned Parish Priest have baptized Marcelline Chalifou, a daughter of Andy and Emerance Chalifou, born on the 25 February last. Godfather: David Mongrain, Godmother Clarisse Mongrain.

A. J. Glorieux, Pr.

B-6
Francis
A.
Davidson

On the 19 March, 1871, we the undersigned Parish Priest have baptized in St. Paul's church, Francis Arcilla Davidson, a daughter of Frank and Anna Davidson, born on the 15 February last. Sponsors: Chs. Coakley and Mrs. Coyle.

A. J. Glorieux, Pr.

B-7
Francoise
Norwes

On the 26 March, 1871, we the undersigned Parish Priest have baptized in St. Paul's Church, Francoise Norwes, born on the 8th of February last of the lawful marriage of Thomas Norwes and Marie Desrivieres. Sponsors: Francois Dubreuil, Magdelein Bourgeault.
A. J. Glorieux, Pr.

Page 45
B-8
Charles
W. A.
Jette

On the 9th of April, 1871, we the undersigned Parish Priest have baptized in St. Paul's Church, Charles Wilfred Adolphe Jette, born on the 10th of February, of the lawful marriage of Adolphe Jette and of Margaret Liard of this parish. Sponsors, Chs. Mathieu, Jr, and Rosa Mathieu.
A. J. Glorieux, Pr.

B-9
James E.
Smith

On the 9th of April, 1871, we the undersigned Parish Priest have baptized in St. Paul's Church, James E. Smith, a son of Francis and Ellen Smith, born on the 12th of March last. Sponsors Mr. J. Coyle, Mary Ann Coffey.
A. J. Glorieux, Pr.

B-10
Mary A.
Manaigre

On the 9th of April, 1871, we the undersigned Parish Priest have baptized in St. Paul's Church, Mary Agnes Manaigre, a daughter of Pierre [crossed out] Dieudonne Manaigre and Emilie Pichette, born on the 28th of February last. Sponsors, Amadee Choquette, Marie Bernier.
A. J. Glorieux, Pr.

B-11
Henry M.
Geffrey

On the 9th of April, 1871, we the undersigned Parish Priest have baptized in St. Paul's Church Henry Martin Geffrey, a son of Edward Geffrey and Josephine Gauthier, born on the 23d of March last. Sponsors, Jude Vertefuelle, Josephine Gauthier.
A. J. Glorieux, Pr.

B-12
Norbert
Bernier

On the 9th of April, 1871, we the undersigned Parish Priest have baptized in St. Paul's Church, Norbert Bernier, born on the 22nd of February last, of the lawful marriage of Norbert, Theresa Bernier. Sponsors, David, Genevieve Bernier.
A. J. Glorieux, Pr.

Page 46
B-13
Susanna
Murphy

On the 23rd of April, 1871, we the undersigned Parish Priest have baptized in St. Paul's Church, Susanna Murphy, daughter of Matthew O. C. Murphy and Ellen Murphy, born on the 3rd of April last. Sponsors, Patrick Flynn and Catherine Flynn.
A. J. Glorieux, Pr.

B-14
Lucy
Murphy

On the 23rd of April, 1871, we the undersigned Parish Priest have supplied the ceremonies of baptism on Lucy Murphy, baptized in 1869 by Father Malo; she is the daughter of M. O. C. and Ellen Murphy, born on the 15th of July, 1869. Sponsors, Patrick Flynn and Annie Murphy.
A. J. Glorieux, Pr.

Sep. 6
Veronique
Rochbrune
wife of
Cyrille
Richter

On the 5th of May, 1871, we the undersigned Parish Priest have [baptized crossed out] buried in the graveyard the corpse of Veronique Rochbrune, wife of Cyrille Richter, who died on the 3rd instant. Witnesses: J. McKay, H. Cosgrove, P. Kirk, and J. P. Cook, etc.
A. J. Glorieux, Pr.

B-15
Joseph
Prosper
Pichette

On the 7th of May, 1871, we the undersigned Parish Priest have baptized in St. Paul's Church Joseph Prosper Pichette, born on the 3d of May, of the lawful marriage of Rock and Victoire Pichette. Sponsors, Firmin Lebrun, Marianne Dupati.
A. J. Glorieux, Pr.

B-16
Francis
Niebler

On the 18th of May, 1871, we the undersigned Parish Priest have baptized in St. Paul's Church Francis Xavier Niebler, born of the lawful marriage of Francis and Margaret Niebler on the 16th last. Godfather, George Niebler, Godmother Mrs. J. Niebler.
A. J. Glorieux, Pr.

Page 47
B-17

On the 18th day of May, 1871, we the undersigned Parish Priest have bap-

William
Ed.
Smythe

tized (privately) at home, William Edward Smythe, a son of John W. and Susan Smythe, born on the on the 17th instant. Ceremonies supplied 19 June. Sponsors, Diloyer *[?]*, Katie Murphy.

A. J. Glorieux, Pr.

B-18
Gilbert
Joseph
Aplin

On the 28th of May, 1871, we the undersigned Parish Priest have baptized in St. Paul's Church Gilbert Joseph Aplin, a son of George and Marie Aplin, born on the 10th instant. Sponsors, Mr. and Mrs. F. Lebrun.

A. J. Glorieux, Pr.

Sep. 7
Sylvain
Bourgeault

On the 13th of June, 1871, we the undersigned Parish Priest have buried in the graveyard the corpse of Sylvain Bourgeault, aged about 70 years, who died yesterday. Witnesses, Peter Parizeau, Peter Kirk, Bernier, etc.

A. J. Glorieux, Pr.

B-19
Mary
Agnes
Kirk

On the 18th of June, 1871, we the undersigned have baptized in St. Paul's Church Mary Agnes Kirk, a daughter of Peter and Margaret Kirk, born on the 6th instant. Sponsors: James Coyle and Mrs. Piette.

A. J. Glorieux, Pr.

Confirmation
28

The 25th of June, A.D. 1871, the Most Reverend F. N. Blanchet, Archbishop of Oregon City, administered the Sacrament of Confirmation to the following:

William Baily	David Bernier
Elias Eberhard	David Pichette
Samuel Kerr	Eleanore Picard
Charles E. Flynn	Ellen Coffey
Andrew Flynn	Mary Kennedy
Thomas Kirk	Elizabeth Kennedy
John Kirk	Salome Raymond
Charles Coleman	Albina Graton

Page 48

Rosa Raymond	Margaret Niebler
Elizabeth Kirk	Catherine Parizeau
Leonie Patterson	William Baily
Amanda Kennedy	Priscilla Matthieu
Anna Kennedy	Arsino Matthieu
Emma Patterson	Mary Kirschner

Attested by:

A. J. Glorieux, Pastor

Erection
of the
Way of
the Cross

[Here are included three short letters between Father Glorieux and Archbishop Blanchet regarding the formalities of establishing the Way of the Cross at St. Paul.]

Page 49
First
Communion
19

On the ninth of April, 1871, the following have made their first Communion:

Casimir Brentano	David Pichette
Michael Murphy	Julien Pichette
Daniel Murphy	David Bernier
Charles Coleman	Antoine Lambert
Stephen Coleman	Alexandre Raymond
Edward Flynn	J. Bte. Bergevin
William Baily	Rosa Raymond
Pierre Vivet	Salome Raymond
Margaret Niebler	Catherine Parizeau
Charles Flynn	

A. J. Glorieux, Pr.

Sep. 8
Mary R.
Coffey

On the 28th of July, 1871, we the undersigned Parish Priest have buried in St. Paul's grave yard the corpse of Mary Ronan Coffey, wife of Edward Coffey. She was born the 2d of February, 1817, and died the 27th ultimo. Witnesses: James Coyle, Catherine Murphy, M. Horan and many members of the Congregation.

A. J. Glorieux, Pr.

Sep. 9 Mary Jane Pichette	On the 6th of July, 1871, we the undersigned priest have buried in St. Paul's grave yard the corpse of Mary Jane Pichet, daughter of Roch Pichet. Born on the 15th of July, 1862. Witnesses, Dr. Brentano, Parizeau and many members of the Congregation. G. Heinrich, Pr.
B-20 Page 50 Catherine Kitson	On the 20th of August, 1871, we the undersigned Parish Priest have baptized in St. Paul's Church Catherine Kitson, a daughter of Peter Kitson and Angelique Dupres, born on the 8th instant. Sponsors: Theodore Gervais, Launda Gagnon. A. J. Glorieux, Pr.
Sep. 10 [Sister] Mary Norbert	On the 24 August, 1871, we the undersigned chaplain, have buried in the Sisters' graveyard the corpse of Sister Mary Norbert of the community of the sisters of the Holy Names of Jesus and Mary, who died on 22d instant. Witnesses, T. Heinrich Sr. Mary Perpetua S. Piette, pr.
B-21 John Statts [Staats]	On the 29 September, 1871, we the undersigned have baptized John Walter, son of John Statts and Mary Toupin, born on the 21 January last. Sponsors John Toupin and Mary Weston. S. Piette, pr.
Sep. 11 Margaret Nibler	On the 12 September, 1871, the undersigned priest has buried in St. Paul's grave yard the corpse of Margaret Nibler, aged 81 years, who died on the 10th instant, wife of [blank] Witnesses: Michael and Franc Nibler etc.
B-22 Mary Louise Matthieu	On the 17 September, 1871, we the undersigned priest have baptized in St. Paul's church Mary Louise, daughter of Francis Xavier and Rosa Matthieu, born on the 25 July of this year. Sponsors: Charles Olivier Pelland and Arsino Matthieu. G. C. Thibau, pr.
B-23 Regina Nibler	On the 17 September, 1871, we the undersigned priest have baptized Regina, daughter of John and Mary , born on the 7th instant. Sponsors: George and Margaret Nibler. G. C. Thibau, pr.
Page 51 Sep. 12 Mary Flynn	On the 23 September, 1871, we the undersigned priest have buried in the grave yard of St. Paul's parish the corpse of Mary Flynn, wife of Peter Flynn, aged 71, who died the 23d instant. Witnesses: Mr. Brentano and Michael Horan etc. G. C. Thibau, pr.
Bap. 24 Francoise Marie Langlois	On the 24 September, 1871, the undersigned priest has baptized Francoise Marie, daughter of Israel Langlois and Mary Papin of Polk County, born on the 10 December, 1870. Sponsors, Isaac Bastien and Philomene Langlois, L. A. LeBas, pr. miss. apost.
B-25 Joseph Daught [crossed out] Dowd	On the 8 October, 1871 we the undersigned priest have baptized Joseph, son of John and Julia Daught [Dowd] born on 25 September of this year. Sponsors: Dr. Brentano and his wife. L. A. LeBas, pr. miss. apost.
B-26 William Francis Feller	On the 21 October, 1871, we the undersigned, pastor of the parish of St. Paul, have baptized William Francis, born on the 19 day of May, 1870, of the lawful marriage of Francis Xavier Feller and Rheuamah Feller of Buteville. Sponsors J. B. Jackson and Mary Cosgrove, his wife. J. B. Jackson Mary Jackson B. Delorme, V.G.
Sep. 13 Francis Xavier Nibbler	On the 28 October, 1871, we the undersigned pastor of this parish have buried Frank Xavier lawful son of Francis Xavier Nibbler and Margaret Koller of this place, who died on the day before at the age of about five months. Witnesses Fr. Xavier, father of the child, and Michael Nibler, uncle to the same. B. Delorme, V.G.

B-27
Edward
John
Bernier

On 1 November, 1871, we the undersigned have baptized Edward John, born the 12 October last, of the lawful marriage of Louis Bernier and Josette Lavigueur of this Parish. Sponsors, Mr. and Mrs. Bayley [Bailey] who have signed with us.

W. H. Bailey   Julia M. Bailey
B. Delorme, V.G.

Sep. 14
Infant
of Mr.
Chamberlan

On the 10 December, A.D. 1871, we the undersigned, pastor of this parish, have buried a boy, lawful son of Adolphe Chamberlan and Louise Humpherville, privately baptized at his birth, who died yesterday about one month old. Present, Fabien Chamberlan, brother of the deceased, and Frank Brouillard of this place.

B. Delorme, V.G.

Page 52
B-28
Alexandre
Prevot

On the 30 December, 1871, we the undersigned pastor of this parish, have baptized Alexandre, born on the 19th day of the present month, of the lawful marriage of Louis Prevot and Pauline Lafort, of this place. Sponsors Louis Bernier and Josette Lavigueur, his wife, who were unable to sign.

B. Delorme, V.G.

Baptisms in the year 1871	28	
Burials " " "	14	
Confirmations	28	
First Communions	19	Marriages 1

1872

B-1
Marcelline
Pepin

On January 6, 1872, we, the undersigned, have baptized conditionally Marcelline, born 22 December last, of the lawful marriage of Pierre Pepin and Susanne Goodridge of this parish. Godfather Jules Pepin, Godmother Clementine Pepin.

B. Delorme, V.G.

M-1
Louis
Chalifoux
and
Julienne
Picard

On the 8 January, 1872, after the publication of three bans of marriage between Louis Chalifoux of this parish, son of age of the late Andre Chalifoux and Catherine Russy, of the first part; and Julienne Picard, daughter under age of Regis Picard and of Mary Petit of the same place, of the consent of whom it proceeds, of the second part; no impediment being found, we, the undersigned, pastor of the parish of St. Paul, have received their mutual consent of marriage and have given them the nuptial benediction in the presence of Regis Picard, father of the bride; Augustin Lambert, henri Picard and Julien Prevot.

Julien Porvost.
B. Delorme, Vic. Gen.

Mar. 2
John B.
Dompierre
and
Angelique
M.
Bonenfant

On 22 January, A.D., 1872, the dispensation of three bans being by us grantes on account of the parties having been married civilly six years before in California, we the undersigned pastor of the parish of St. Paul, have received the mutual consent of marriage of John Baptiste Dompier, son of age of the late David Dompierre and of Margaret Soulier, now living in this place, on the one part; and of Angelique Margaret Bonenfant, daughter of age of Antoine Bonenfant and of Francoise Departy on the other part, and have given them the nuptial benediction in the presence of Pierre Parizeau and Louis Parizeau.

B. Delorme, Vic. Gen.

B-2
Josephine
Dompierre

On the 22 January, 1872, we the undersigned, pastor of the parish of St. Paul, have baptized Josephine, born on the 13 October, 1870, of John Bapt. Dompierre and Angelique Bonenfant. Sponsors Joseph Rochbrune and Margaret Soulier.

B. Delorme, V.G.

Page 53
B-3
Joseph
Bernard
Kennedy

On the 10 March, 1872, we the undersigned parish priest of St. Paul have baptized Joseph Bernard, born on the 1 February last of the lawful marriage of John Kennedy and of Julia Scollard of this place. Sponsors, Michael Horan and Catherine Flynn, who have signed with us.

Michael Horan   Catherine Horan
B. Delorme, V.G.

B-4
Salome
Blandine
Lucier

On the 10 March, 1872, we the undersigned, pastor of the parish of St. Paul, have baptized Salome Blandine, born on the 10 February last, of the lawful marriage of Joseph Lucier and Louise Martineau of this place. Sponsors, Xavier Martineau and Sophie Chalifoux.

B. Delorme, V.G.

B-5
John
Alexander
Whitman

On the 21 April, 1872, we the undersigned pastor of the parish of St. Paul have baptized John Alexander, born on the 17th of this month of the lawful marriage of John Peter Whitman and Catherine Smith of this place. Sponsors John Coleman and Mary Elizabeth Coleman.

John Coleman   Mary E. Coleman
B. Delorme, V.G.

B-6
Joseph
Richard
Cooke

On the 5 May, 1872, we the undersigned, pastor of the parish of St. Paul, have baptized Joseph Richard, born on the 11th day of March last, of the lawful marriage of Joseph Cooke and Bridget Lee of this place. Sponsors, Michael Egan and Anna Costello.

Michael Egan   Anna Costello.
B. Delorme, V.G.

Sepult 1
Marcelline
Pepin

On the 5 May, 1872, we the undersigned pastor of the parish of St. Paul, have buried Marcelline, lawful daughter of Pierre Pepin and Susanne Goodridge, deceased on the 3d day of the same month at the age of four months and a half. Witnesses, John Paterson and Casimir Brentano.

B. Delorme, V.G.

B-7
Mary
Amanda
E.
Raymond

On the 12 May, 1872, we the undersigned, pastor of the parish of St. Paul, have baptized Mary Amanda Elsie, born on the 10th of the same month of Marcel Raymond and Odile Raymond of this parish. Sponsors, Peter Bonnin and Marie Raymond.

B. Delorme, V.G.

B-8
A. Louise
Geffries

On 2 June, 1872, we the undersigned pastor of the parish of St. Paul, have baptized Adine Louise born on the 17th day of April of John Edward Geffries and Josephine Gauthier of this place. Sponsors, Dolphie Gauthier and Olive Gauthier, who were not able to sign their names.

B. Delorme, V.G.

Page 54
B-9, 10
Walter
Theodore
Geer and
Charles
Geer

On the 2 June, 1872, we the undersigned pastor of the parish of St. Paul have baptized Walter Theodore, and Charles Banks, born, the first on the 17th of December, 1869, and the second on the 11th of December last, of the lawful marriage of DeWight Geer and Philomene Matthieu, of this place. Sponsors of Walter Theodore, Oliver Arel and Clarissa Matthieu, and of Charles, Elias Eberhard and Priscilla Matthieu.

Oliver Arel   Clarissa Matthieu
Elias Eberhard   Priscilla Matthieu
B. Delorme, V.G.

B-11
Esther
Elizabeth
Duchamp

On the 9 June, 1872, we the undersigned pastor of the parish of St. Paul have baptized Esther Elizabeth, born on the 11th of April last, of the lawful marriage of Francois Duchamp and Esther Dalcour of this place. Sponsors, Theodore Gervais and Olive Gauthier.

B. Delorme

B-12
John
Seifert

On the 21 June, A.D. 1872, we the undersigned pastor of the parish of St. Paul have administered the ceremonies of Baptism to John, born on the 7th of April last of the lawful marriage of John Seifert and Mary Brummel of the parish of St. Patrick, Yamhill County, and baptized privately by Rev. Father Croquet on the next day. Sponsors, Henry Brummel, grandfather of the child and Elizabeth Brummel, aunt of the same.

Henry Brummel   Elizabeth Brummel
B. Delorme, V.G.

B-13
William
Robert

On June 24, 1872, we the undersigned pastor of the parish of St. Paul have baptized William Robert born on the 13th of January last, of the lawful marriage of John P. Ladd and Mary Cavanaugh of Portland. Sponsors,

Ladd

Michael Hugh Murphy and Caroline V. Vantine through Mrs. Elizabeth Murphy.

Michael H. Murphy   Elizabeth Cosgrove

B. Delorme, V.G.

Marriage 3
Louis
Parizeau
&
Ellen
Larrison

On 24 June, 1872, after the publication of two bans of marriage of the parish of St. Paul, lawful son of Peter Parizeau and Mary Dompierre of the first part, and Ellen Larrison, lawful daughter under age of the late John Larrison and Reinette Perrault of the same parish, of the second part; the dispensation of the third ban being by us granted and no impediment being found, we the undersigned, pastor of this place, have received their mutual consent of marriage, and given them the nuptial benediction in the presence of the parents of the parties and of J. B. Deguire, Frank Lambert, and several other witnesses.

B. Delorme, V.G.

Page 55
B-14
John B. P.
Patterson

On 30 June, 1872, we the undersigned have baptized conditionally John Baptiste Peter, born on the 22d of December, 1859, of the lawful marriage of James Patterson and Sara O'Kelly, then living in Eugene City. Sponsors Mr. J. B. Piette and his wife.   John Patterson

John B. P. Piette   Frances M. Piette

B. Delorme, V.G.

B-15 & 16
Joseph
Leo
Patterson
&
Arra
Blandine
Patterson

On 30 June, 1872, we the undersigned pastor of the parish of St. Paul, have baptized conditionally Joseph Leo and Arra Blandine, born the first on the 18 August, 1862, and the second on the 8 June, 1865, of the lawful marriage of James Patterson and Sara O'Kelly, then living near Eugene City. Sponsors of Joseph Leo, James Coyle and Elizabeth Coyle. Sponsors of Arra Blandine, Hugh Cosgrove and Mrs. J. Bailey, represented by Mrs. Bridgit Kennedy.

James Coyle   Hugh Cosgrove

Elizabeth Coyle.

B. Delorme, V.G.

B-17
Charles
Roch
Pichette

On the 30 June, 1872, we the undersigned have baptized Charles Roch, born on the day before yesterday, of the lawful marriage of Roch Pichette, Victoire Despard. Sponsors, Charles Bergevin and Mary Pichette.

Charles Bergevin

B. Delorme, V.G.

First
Communion

On June 30, 1872, we the undersigned, pastor of the parish of St. Paul, have admitted to the first communion the following:

Henry Herren	Annie Nibler
Francis Martin	Alice Bequette
Robert E. Kirk	Victoria Graton
Alphonso Nibler	Esther Pichette
John B. Peter Patterson	Catherine McPaulin
Augustin Bonnin	Caroline Anderson
Nazaire Kitson	Christina Anderson
Isadore Picard	Cecile Lucier
Jeremiah Chamberlan	Clementine Mongrain
John Baptiste Parizeau	Josette Picard
Louis Bergevin	Josephine Mongrain
Francis Bourgeau	Rose Chalifoux
Eugene Blanchet	Salome Picard
Margaret Marshal	Louise Lemery
Theresa Nibler	Rosa Allard

B. Delorme, V.G.

Page 56
S-2
Peter
Fleishman

On the 8 July, 1872, we the undersigned, pastor of the parish of St. Paul, have buried the body of Peter Fleishman, deceased on the day before yesterday, at the age of 73 years. Present, Nicholas Fleishman and Nicolas Michaels.

B. Delorme, V.G.

| B-18 Charles Picard | On the 21 July, 1872, we the undersigned, pastor of the parish of St. Paul, have baptized Charles, born on the 18th instant of the lawful marriage of Regis Picard and Mary Petit of this place. Sponsors, Paul Guilbeau and Flavie Petit. |

Paul Guilbou   Philomena Petit
                    B. Delorme, V.G.

| B-19 Mary Bosquet | On the 11 August, 1872, we the undersigned have baptized Mary born on the 8th of May last, of the lawful marriage of Francis Bosquet and Elizabeth Bower of this parish. Sponsors, Alexander Coyle and Mary Ellen Goulet. |

Alexander Coyle   Mary Ellen Goulet
                    B. Delorme, V.G.

| B-20 Francis Leon Choquette | On the 11 August, 1872, we the undersigned pastor of the parish of St. Paul have baptized Francis Leo, born on the 3d of this month of the lawful marriage of Amadee Choquette and Mary Bernier of this place, Sponsors, Francis Bernier and Genevieve Bernier, uncle and aunt of the child. |

                    B. Delorme, V.G.

| S-3 & 4 Peter Bourgeau & Ch. Roch Pichette | On the 17 August, 1872, we the undersigned pastor of the parish of St. Paul, have buried Peter Bourgeau, lawful son of Baptiste Bourgeau and Genevieve Martineau, who died on the 15th at the age of 2 years, and Charles Roch Pichette, lawful son of Roch Pichette and Victoire Despard, who died yesterday one month and a half old. Witnesses, Baptiste Bourgeau and Roch Pichette, parents of the deceased. |

                    B. Delorme, V.G.

| B-21 Eleonore Theresa Longtain | On 18 August, 1872, we the undersigned pastor of St. Paul have baptized Eleonora Theresa, born on March 7 of the lawful marriage of Thomas Longtain and Mathilda Rivet of this place. We have stood for godfather of the child and Eleonore Theresa Ady has been the other sponsor. |

                    L. T. Ady
                    B. Delorme, V.G.

Page 57

| B-22 Elie Brouillard | On August 25, A.D. 1872, we the undersigned, pastor of the parish of St. Paul, have baptized Elie, born on the 17th of this month, of the lawful marriage of Francois Brouillard and Aurelie Bonnin of this place. Sponsors Alonzo Bonnin and Mary Lambert, who has signed with us. |

                    Mary Lambert
                    B. Delorme, V.G.

| B-23 Jerome Richard Jackson | On September 1, 1872, we the undersigned, pastor of the parish of St. Paul, have baptized Jerome Richard born on July 23 last, of the lawful marriage of Jerome Jackson and Mary Cosgrove of this place. We have been the Godfather of the child, and Annie Cosgrove has been the other sponsor. |

                    Annie Eldridge
                    B. Delorme, V.G.

| B-24 William Comtois | On September 1, 1872, we the undersigned, pastor of the parish of St. Paul, have baptized William, born on August 7 last, of the lawful marriage of James Comtois and Soulange Pichette of this place. Sponsors Francis Bernier and Cecile Pichette. |

                    B. Delorme, V.G.

| B-25 Charles Lafontaine | On September 8, 1872, we the undersigned, pastor of St. Paul, have baptized Charles, born on the 6th of this month of the lawful marriage of Narcisse Lafontaine and Margaret Pichette of this place. Sponsors Louis Pichette and Margaret Bercier his wife, grandfather and grandmother of the child. |

                    B. Delorme, V.G.

| M-4 Samuel Brothers & Adolphine Papin | On September 9, 1872, we the undersigned, pastor of the parish of St. Paul, after having granted the dispensation of the impediment commonly called *Vetitum Ecclesie*, and received from the bridegroom the solemn promise that he will leave his wife entirely free to practise the duties of her religion and to raise their children, if they have any, in the Catholic faith, no other impediment being found, have received the mutual consent of marriage of |

Samuel T. Brothers, of Yamhill County, son of age of William Brothers and Annie O'Brien of the one part, and Adolphine Papin otherwise called Lachance of this parish of St. Paul, daughter of Peter Papin and Suzan Goodrich, of the consent of whom it proceeds of the other part, and united them in the holy bonds of matrimony in the presence of Peter Papin and Peter Parizeau.

Samuel T. Brothers   Adolphine Papin Lachance
                                      B. Delorme, V.G.

Page 58
S-5
Elizabeth
Flynn

On September 14, 1872, we the undersigned pastor of the parish of St. Paul have buried Elizabeth, daughter of Bernard Flynn and Catherine Bennet, of this place, deceased on the 12th instant at the age of two years and nine months. Witnesses Patrick Flynn and Peter Parizeau.
                                      B. Delorme, V.G.

B-26
John
Arcouet

On October 19, 1872, we the undersigned, pastor of the parish of St. Paul, have baptized John, born on December 25 last, of the lawful marriage of John Arcouet and Christina Sanders of this parish. Sponsors, Michel Arcouet and Elizabeth Sanders.
                                      B. Delorme, V.G.

B-27
John
Winfield
Harner

On October 20, 1872, we the undersigned pastor of St. Paul have baptized John Winfield born on November 10, 1871, of Samuel Harner and Margaret Lacourse, of this place. Sponsors James Coleman and Fanny Coleman.
                                      James Coleman
                                      B. Delorme, V.G.

B-28
James
Henry
Kirk

On November 17, 1872, we the undersigned have baptized James Henry, born on the 7th of this month, of the legitimate marriage of Peter Kirk and Margaret Lyons of this parish of St. Paul. Sponsors, John McGrath and Mrs. Bridget Kennedy.
                                      John McGrath
                                      B. Delorme, V.G.

B-29
James
Frederic
Davidson

On November 17, 1872, we the undersigned, pastor of the parish of St. Paul, have baptized James Frederic, born on the 23d day of October last, of the lawful marriage of Frank Davidson and Anna Coleman of this place. Sponsors, James Coleman, grandfather of the child, and Emma Coleman.
James Coleman   Emma Coleman
                                      B. Delorme, V.G.

B-30
Louis
Chalifoux

On December 22, 1872, we the undersigned have baptized Louis, born on the 14th instant of the lawful marriage of Louis Chalifoux and Julienne Picard. Sponsors, Frank Martin and Frank Petit.
                                      B. Delorme, V.G.

Page 59
31, 32 B
Martha
Elizabeth
Duke
&
Thomas
Duke

On December 25, 1872, we the undersigned have baptized Martha Elizabeth and Thomas born, the first on March 26, 1867, and the second on February 20, 1871, of the lawful marriage of William Duke, now deceased, and Helene Rochbrune of Westport, Oregon. Sponsors of Martha Elizabeth, Henri Picard and Celeste Rochbrune his wife; sponsors of Thomas, Cyrille Richter and Eleanore Picard
                                      B. Delorme, V.G.

Summing up of the year 1872
Baptisms--------------------32
Burials   5
Marriages   4
First Communion   31

1873

M-1
Charles
Olivier
Pelham
[Pelland]

On January 1, 1873, after the publication of one ban of marriage at our parochial mass, between Charles Olivier Pelham of this parish of St. Paul, son of age and legitimate of Eusebe Pelham and Angele Herrard of the parish of St. Norbert, District of Montreal, Canada, on the first part; and Mary Coleman of the same parish of St. Paul, daughter of age and legiti-

&
Mary
Coleman

mate of James Coleman and Fanny Murray, on the second part; the dispensation of the two other bans and that of the Prohibited Times being granted by us, the undersigned, and moreover no other impediment having been found, we, pastor of the said parish of St. Paul, have received their mutual consent of marriage and given them the nuptial benediction in the presence of James Coleman, father of the bride, J. Baptiste Piette, James Coyle and James Coleman, groomsmen, Mary McKay and Annie Costello, who have signed with us.

Chs. O. Pelland
Mary E. Coleman
James Coleman
John B. P. Piette
James Joseph Coyle
Mary McKay
Anna Costello

B. Delorme, V.G.

M-2
Marcel
Raymond
&
Odile
Raymond

On January 6, A.D. 1873, the dispensation of three bans of marriage being granted by us the undersigned, and moreover those of their consanguinity of the second degree being also dispensed by the Most Rev. Archbishop of this

Page 60

diocese in virtue of faculties received from the Holy See with the date of July 12, 1863, no other impediment being found, We the undersigned pastor of the parish of St. Paul have have [sic] received the mutual consent of marriage of Marcel Raymond, son of age and legitimate of Augustin Raymond and Marie Servant, of the parish of St. Paul on the one part; and Odile Raymond, daughter of age and legitimate of Francis Raymond and Mary Langlois of the same parish of St. Paul on the second part, and have given them nuptial benediction in the presence of James Coleman, Augustin Lambert, L. R. Brentano. Moreover, we have declared the children of said parties, Mary Agnes and Mary Amanda Elsie, to be legitimated in the eyes of God and of the Church by the Christian marriage of their parents.

Regnier L. M. Brentano   M. J. Raymond
                                Odile Raymond
B. Delorme, V.G.

B-1
Charles
Kerr

On January 19, A.D. 1873, we the undersigned, pastor of St Paul, have baptized Charles, born on the 8th day of this month of the lawful marriage of Samuel James Kerr and Catherine Coffey of this parish. Sponsors, Patrick Flynn and Catherine Flynn, his wife.

B. Delorme, V.G.

B-2
Joseph
Bourgeau

On January 19, 1873, we the undersigned, pastor of St. Paul, have baptized Joseph born on the 31st day of December last of the lawful marriage of J. Baptiste Bourgeau and Genevieve Martineau, of this parish. Sponsors Joseph Lucier and Cecile Lucier.

Joseph Lucier
B. Delorme, V.G.

B-3
Olivier
Placy
dit
Laferte

On January 25, 1873, we the undersigned have baptized Olivier, born on the 16th day of the month of the lawful Marriage of Michel Laferte, otherwise Placy, and Angelique Desrivieres of this place. Sponsors, Frank Comartin and Rose Chalifoux.

B. Delorme, V.G.

M-3
Felix
Delisle
&
Mary
Pichette

On February 9, A.D. 1873, after the publication of one ban of marriage between Felix Delisle, of this parish of St. Paul, son of age and lawful of Joseph Delisle and Mary Lamotte, both deceased at Cap Sante, district of Quebec, Canada, of the first part, and Mary Pichette, daughter of age and lawful of Louis Pichette and Margaret

Page 61

Bercier of the said parish of St. Paul, of the second part, the dispensation of the two other bans having been granted by us and no impediment being found, we, the undersigned, pastor of the parish of St. Paul, have received

their mutual consent of marriage and have given them the nuptial benediction in the presence of Louis Pichette, father of the bride, Francis
Bernier, Vital Pichette and Eleonore Oicard.

B. Delorme, V.G.

B-4
Elizabeth
McPaulin

On February 16, 1873, we the undersigned have baptized Elizabeth, born
on the 11th day of January last, of the lawful marriage of Roger McPaulin
and Mary Haner of this place; sponsors, John P. Wittman and Elizabeth
Aplin.

Elizabeth Aplin
B. Delorme, V.G.

B-5
John
Murphy

On February 23, A.D. 1873, we, the undersigned, have baptized John born
on the 8th instant of the lawful marriage of Matthew O'C, Murphy and
Helen M. Costello of this parish of St. Paul. Sponsors John F. B. Brentano
and Mary Cecelia Murphy who have signed with us.

Jno. F. Theo. B. Brentano   Mary Cecelia Murphy
B. Delorme, V.G.

S-1
Celina
Brouillard

On March 17, 1873, we the undersigned have buried Celina, lawful daughter of Francis Brouillard and Aurelie Bonnin of this place, deceased the day
before yesterday at the age of two years and a half. Witnesses Narcisse
Gingras and Peter Bonnin.

B. Delorme, V.G.

B-6
Catherine
Dupre

On April 20, 1873, we the undersigned have baptized Catherine, born the
fifth of this month, of the lawful marriage of Charles Dupre and Catherine
Chalifoux, of this place. Sponsors, Louis Chalifoux and Sophie Chalifoux.

B. Delorme, V.G.

B-7
Peter
Clement
Smythe

On May 11, 1873, we the undersigned have baptized Peter Clement, born
on the 22d day of April last, of the lawful marriage of Francis Smythe and
Ellen Nolan. , of this place. Sponsors, Patrick Mullen and Bridget Trevor.

Patrick Mulen   Bridgit
B. Delorme, V.G.

B-8
Joseph
Parizeau

On May 11, A.D., 1873, we the undersigned have baptized Joseph born on
the 6th day of the month of the lawful marriage of Louis Parizeau and
Ellen Larrison of this place. Sponsors, Peter Parizeau and Philomene Petit.

Philomena Petit
B. Delorme, V.G.

Page 62
M-4
Cyprien
Bellique
&
Julienne
Bergevin

On May 13th, A.D. 1873, the dispensation of three bans of marriage having
been dispensed by us, and no impediment being found, we the undersigned
have received the mutual consent of marriage of Cyprien Bellique of the
parish of St. Louis, son of age of Pierre Bellique and Genevieve St. Martin,
deceased, of the first part; and of Julienne Bergevin of this parish of St. Paul,
daughter of age of Louis Bergevin now living and of Magdeleine Servant,
deceased, of the second part; and have given them the nuptial benediction in
the presence of Louis Parizeau and Moyse Servant.

Julienne Bergevin
B. Delorme, V.G.

S-2
Eulalia
Deguire

On May 17, 1873, we the undersigned, pastor of the parish of St. Paul,
have buried Eulalie Deguire, lawful daughter of Baptiste Deguire, and
Mary Ann Perrault, deceased on the day before yesterday, she being eighteen years old. Witnesses, Louis Parizeau and John Wittman.

B. Delorme, V.G.

B-9
Violette
Adelaide
Mathieu

On May 18, 1873, we the undersigned, pastor of the parish of St. Paul,
have baptized Violette Adelaide, born on the 21st day of August last, of the
lawful marriage of Francois Xavier Mathieu and Rosa Aussan, of this place.
Sponsors, William Trevor and Bridget Trevor.

William Trevor   B. Delorme, V.G.
Bridget Trevor

B-10
Clara

On May 18th, A.D. 1873, we, the undersigned pastor of the parish of St.
Paul, have baptized Clara Adelaide, born April 21 last, of the lawful mar-

Adelaide Ouimette	riage of Louis Ouimette Clarissa Mathieu of this place. Sponsors, Francis Bernier and Rosa Aussan.
	B. Delorme, V.G.
B-11 Louis Andrew Vertfeuille	On May 18, A.D. 1873, we the undersigned pastor of the parish of St. Paul have baptized Louis Andrew, born on the 29th of November last, of the lawful marriage of Jude Vertfeuille and Catherine Gauthier, of this place. Witnesses, Charles O. Pelland and Mary Coleman, his wife.
	Chs. O. Pelland Mary E. Pelland
	B. Delorme, V.G.
Page 63 B-12 Marie Louise [Vertfeuille]	On May 18, A.D. 1873, we the undersigned, pastor of the parish of St. Paul, have baptized Marie Louise, born on the 28 day of November last, of the lawful marriage of Jude Vertfeuille and Catherine Gauthier of this parish. Sponsors, Dolphis Gauthier and Mary Weston.
	B. Delorme, V.G.
B-13 Rose Maneigre	On May 18, A.D. 1873, we the undersigned, pastor of the parish of St. Paul, have baptized Rose, born on the 9th day of April last of the lawful marriage of Dieudonne Maneigre and Emily Pichette of this place. Sponsors, Francis Bernier junior and Roch Pichette.
	B. Delorme, V.G.
S-3 Peter Flynn	On May 20, A.D. 1873, we the undersigned, pastor of the parish of St. Paul, have buried Peter Flynn of this place, deceased on the 18th of the same month, he being then 87 years old. Witnesses John Brentano, James Coleman, Math Murphy and many others.
	B. Delorme, V.G.
M-5 Francis Dompierre & Soulange Bergevin	On May 25, A.D. 1873, we the undersigned, pastor of the parish of St. Paul, have received the renewed consent of marriage of Francis Dompierre of this parish, son of age of the late David Dompierre and Margueret Soulier, now living, for the first part; and Soulange Bergevin of the same parish, daughter of age of Louis Bergevin and of the late Mary Ann Magdelen Servant, for the second part; and we have given them the nuptial benediction in the presence of Augustin Raymond and Peter Parizeau.
	Soulange Bergevin
	B. Delorme, V.G.
B-14 Walter Louis Gay	On the 27 May, 1873, we the undersigned, pastor of the parish of St. Paul, have baptized Walter Louis, born on the 26th of February last, of the marriage of Joseph Gay and Philomene Bercier of this parish. Sponsors, Charles Mathieu and Arsinoe Mathieu.
	Chas. Mathieu Arsinoe Mathieu
	B. Delorme, V.g.
B-15 Rose Rochbrune	On June 1, 1873, we the undersigned have baptized Rose, born April 29 of the lawful marriage of Joseph Rochbrune and Victoire Charlebois of this place. Sponsors, Joseph Rochbrune and F. Soulange Dompierre.
	B. Delorme, V.G.
Page 64 M-6 Michael O'Loughlin & Elizabeth Aplin	On June 3d, 1873, we the undersigned, pastor of the parish of St. Paul, have received the mutual consent of marriage of this parish, son of age of the late John O'Loughlin and of Catherine Ryan still living, for the first part; and of Elizabeth Aplin also of this parish, daughter of age of George Aplin and Mary Wagner, for the second part, and have given them the nuptial benediction in the presence of William Trevor and John Wittman. Michael O'Loughlin Mrs. Michael O'Loughlin William Trevor
	B. Delorme, V.G.
S-4 Mary Petit R. Picard's wife	On June 15, 1873, we the undersigned, pastor of the parish of St. Paul, have buried Mary Petit, wife of Regis Picard of this place, deceased on the day before yesterday, being then about thirty five years of age. Witnesses, Jean Brentano and Narcisse Gingras.
	B. Delorme, V.G.
M-7	On June 19, 1873, we the undersigned, pastor of the parish of St. Paul,

Patrick Geelan & Elizabeth Goodrich	after having granted the dispensation of the impediment called *Vetitum Ecclesia*, and received from the non-Catholic bride the solemn promise to raise her children, if she has any by this marriage, in the belief and practise of the Catholic religion, and besides no other impediment being found, have received the mutual consent of marriage of Patrick Geelan of this parish, son of age of the late James Geelan and Jane O'Connor residing in Ireland, for the first part; and of Elizabeth Goodrich, widow of John Goodrich, of the same place, for the second part, and we have joined them in the holy bonds of matrimony in the presence of Patrick Mullen and Caledonia Orton.

Patrick Mullen   Patrick Geelan
Caledonia Orton   Elizabeth Goodrich
B. Delorme, V.G.

S-5 Charles Petit	On June 21, 1873, we the undersigned, pastor of the parish of St. Paul, have buried Charles Petit, son of the late Amable Petit and of Susan Thomas, deceased on the day before, at the age of 39 years. Witnesses, Narcisse Gingras and Regis Picard.

B. Delorme, V.G.

S-6 Clementine Dubreuille	On June 21, 1873, we the undersigned, pastor of the parish of St. Paul, have buried Clementine Dubreuille, daughter of Francois Dubreuille and Magdeleine Bourgeau, deceased on the day before at the age of 12 years. Present, John Wittman and Baptiste Bourgeau.

B. Delorme, V.G.

Page 65 B-16 & 17 Emma Julia Ogden & Sara May Ogden	On June 27, 1873, we the undersigned, pastor of the parish of St. Paul, have baptized conditionally Emma Julia, born on the second day of November, 1864 of the lawful marriage of Isaac Ogden and Anna Manson, and Sara May, born on the tenth of May, 1866 of the same parents. We stood godfather for both children, and Miss Katie Murphy was the godmother for Emma Julia, and Miss Emma Patterson was the godmother for Sara May. The sponsors have signed with us along with the mother of the children.

Annie Ogden   Katie Murphy   Emma Patterson
B. Delorme, V.G.

S-7 Sister Mary of the Visitation	On July 1, 1873, we the undersigned, pastor of the parish of St. Paul, have buried, in the Sisters' mortuary chapel, Sister Mary of the Visitation, of the Congregation of the Holy Names of Jesus and Mary, deceased on the 29th of June last, at the age of fourty *[sic]* years. Witnesses, Mother LeMary Stanislas, Superior of the said Congregation, Sister Mary Perpetua and Sister Mary Febronia.

B. Delorme, V.G.

First Communion	On June 29, 1873, we the undersigned have admitted to the first communion the following persons.

Andrew Murphy	Zenaide Gregoire
Leo Joseph Patterson	Josephine Aplin
Nicholas Cook	Suzan Deshotel
Philippe Raymond	Caroline Kennedy
Francis Raymond	Fr. Emily Coleman
Narcisse Gingras	Josephine E. Jackson
Louis Manaigre	Mary Simon
Charles Bernier	Bridget Connor
Henry Picard	Catherine Flynn
Amable Bergevin	Esther Sanders
James Cook	

B. Delorme, V.G.

S-8 Mary Jane Bourgeau	On June 11, 1873, we the undersigned, pastor of the Parish of St. Paul, have buried Mary Jane, daughter of J. Baptiste Bourgeau and Genevieve Martineau of this place, deceased on the day before at the age of seven years. Witnesses, Xavier Martineau and Charles Dupre.

B. Delorme, V.G.

B-15
Patrick
Bartholomew
Aplin

On July 13, 1873, we the undersigned, pastor of the parish of St. Paul, have baptized Patrick Bartholomew, born on the 17th of June last, of the lawful marriage of George Aplin and Mary Wagner of this place. Witnesses Dr. W. Bailey and Mrs. Bailey, who have signed with us.

W. J. Bailey   Julia N. Bailey
B. Delorme, V.G.

Page 66
S-9
Margaret
Labonte
[Kilakotah]

On July 20, 1873, we the undersigned have buried Margaret, wife of the late Louis Labonte of this parish of St. Paul, deceased on the day before yesterday at the age of 80 years. Witnesses, Peter Kitson and Firmin Lebrun.
B. Delorme, V.G.

B-19
J. Baptiste
Chamberlan

On July 20, 1873, we the undersigned, pastor of the parish of St. Paul, have baptized John Baptiste, born on the 23rd of June last, of the lawful marriage of Adolphe Chamberlan and Louise Humpherville of this place. Sponsors, J. B. Piette and wife.

Frances M. Piette   John B. P. Piette
B. Delorme, V.G.

B-20
Mary Jane
Roch
Pichette

On July 20, 1873, we the undersigned, pastor of the parish of St. Paul, have baptized Mary Jane, born on the 6th instant, of the lawful marriage of Roch Pichette and Victoire Despard of this place. Sponsors, Charles Dupre and Soulange Contois.

Charles Dupre
B. Delorme, V.G.

B-21
David
Louis
[Labonte]

On August 3, 1873, we the undersigned, pastor of the parish of St. Paul, have baptized David Louis, born on the 26th of July last of Julienne Labonte, Widow Vivet, and of an unknown father. Sponsors, Augustin Lambert and Mary Weston.
B. Delorme, V.G.

B-22
Eulalia
Jette

On August 17, 1873, we the undersigned, pastor of the parish of St. Paul, have baptized Eulalia, born on the 13th of July last of the lawful marriage of Adolphe Jette and Margaret Liard of this place. Sponsors, Amadee Choquette and Mary Bernier his wife.

Amadee Choquette
B. Delorme, V.G.

B-23
Andre
Chalifoux

On August 23, A.D. 1873, we the undersigned pastor of the parish of St. Paul, have baptized Andrew, born on the 4th instant, of the lawful marriage of Andrew Chalifoux and Emerance Mongrain of this place. Sponsors, Charles Dupre and Catherine Chalifoux.
B. Delorme, V.G.

Page 67
S-10
Margaret
Kirk
[Lyons]

On September 2, 1873, we the undersigned pastor of the parish of St. Paul, have buried Margaret Lyons, wife of Peter Kirk of this place, deceased the day before yesterday at the age of fourty-two *[sic]* years. Witnesses, Rev. Fathers Croquet and Goens and Dr. Brentano, who have signed with us.

A. J. Croquet   S. Goens, Pr.   T. F. J. Brentano
B. Delorme, V.G.
Feb. 15, 1875. Removed to new graveyard.

B-24
Narcisse
Pepin

On September 7, 1873, we the undersigned pastor of the parish of St. Paul have baptized Narcisse, born on the third instant of the lawful marriage of Pierre Pepin and Suzan Goodrich of this place. Sponsors, Dr. Brentano and Mrs. Brentano.

T. F. J. Brentano   E. W. J. M. Brentano
B. Delorme, V.G.

B-25
Rose
Justine
Kitson

On Sept 14, 1873, we the undersigned, pastor of St. Paul, have baptized Rose Justine born on the second day of this month of the lawful marriage of Peter Kitson and Angelique Dupre of this place. We have stood godfather to the child and Mary Lambert was the other sponsor.
B. Delorme, V.G.

S-11

On September 15, 1873, we the undersigned, pastor of the parish of St.

Rev. Father Julian DeCraene	Paul, have buried in the right wing of the church of said parish, near the west side wall, Reverend Father Julian DeCraene pastor of Salem, deceased at the last mentioned town on the 12th instant, aged 30 years and 7 months. Witnesses, Very Rev. J. F. Fierens, Rev. P. Gibney, Rev. P. McCormick, Rev. F. Sebastian Goens, Rev. Fr. Hylebos.

P. F. Gibney   P. F. Hylebos
S. Goens, Pr.   J. F. Fierens
B. Delorme, V.G.

S-12 Mary Jane Pichette	On September 15, 1873, we the undersigned, pastor of the parish of St. Paul, have buried Mary Jane, daughter of Roch Pichette and Victoire Despard, of this place, deceased on yesterday, she being then about two months old. Witnesses: Roch Pichette, father of the child, and J. Patterson. B. Delorme, V.G.
Page 68 S-13 Mary Rositer wife of H. Cosgrove	On September 17, 1873, we the undersigned, pastor of the parish of St. Paul, have buried Mary Rositer, wife of Hugh Cosgrove of this place, deceased on the day before yesterday at the age of 65 years. Witnesses, Rev. F. Thibau, Jerome Jackson, Michael Dougherty and many others. Mrs. Cosgrove was born in the county of Wexford, Ireland. G. C. Thibau, pr. B. Delorme, V.G.
B-26 Francis Bernier	On September 21, 1873, we the undersigned, pastor of the parish of St. Paul, have baptized Francis [born] on the 27th of August, of the lawful marriage of Norbert Bernier and Therese Rivet of this place. Sponsors, Amedee Seguin and Eleanore Picard. Amedee Seguin B. Delorme, V.G.
M-8 Callyxte Gingras & Josette Picard	On October 14, 1873, after the publication of one ban of marriage between Callyxte Gingras, son of the late John Gingras & Olive Forcier, for the first part; and Josette Picard of the same parish, daughter underage of Regis Picard, of the consent of whom it proceeds, and of the late Mary Petit, for the second part; the dispensation of the other two bans having been by us granted and no impediment being found, we the undersigned, pastor of the parish of St. Paul, have received their mutual consent of marriage and given them the nuptial benediction in the presence of Regis Picard, father of the bride, Louis Chalifoux, Vincent Guilbeau, Philomene Petit. Colice [Callyxte] B. Delorme, V.G.
S-14 Augustine Raymond	On October 14, 1873, we the undersigned, pastor of the parish of St. Paul, have buried Augustine Raymond, deceased on the day before yesterday at the age of _____ Witnesses, Firmin Lebrun, A. Chamberland, Joseph Matte and many others. B. Delorme, V.G.
B-27 Henry Joseph Langlois	On October 20, 1873, we the undersigned, pastor of the parish of St. Paul, have baptized Henry Joseph born on the 15th day of December last of the lawful marriage of Israel Langlois and Mary Pepin of this place. The sponsors were John Dowed and Julia Pepin his wife. B. Delorme, V.G.
Page 69 B-28, 29, 30 Adeline Dompierre Marie Louise Dompierre Edouard Dompierre	On October 26, 1873, we the undersigned, have baptized Adeline, Marie Louise and Edouard born of the lawful marriage of John Baptiste Dompierre and Angelique Bonenfant, Adeline on the 11th of December, 1867, Mary Louise on the 15th of April, 1869, and Edouard on the 23d day of March of the present year. The sponsors were: for Adeline, Louis Parizeau and Ellen Larrison, for Mary Louise Peter Parizeau and Julienne Bergevin, and for Edouard Francois Dompierre and Soulange Bergevin.

Ellen Larrison   Julienne Bergevin
Soulange Bergevin
B. Delorme, V.G.

B-31
Charles
Gregory

On November first, 1873, we the undersigned pastor of the parish of St. Paul have baptized Charles, born on the 21st of May of the lawful marriage of Charles Gregory and Mary Jane Bird of this place. Sponsors, Simon Connor & Lizzy Kirk.

Simon Connor   Lizzie Kirk
                B. Delorme, V.G.

S-15
Sister
Mary
Praxede

On November 4, 1873, we the undersigned pastor of the parish of St. Paul, have buried, in the Sisters' mortuary Chapel, the body of S. Mary Praxede, of the Congregation of the Holy Names of Jesus and Mary, deceased on the first day of the present month, at the age of 33 years. Witnesses, Rev. Sister Praxede of the Congregation of Providence, and Rev. Sister Assistant of Portland, along with Sister Mary Perpetua, S. Mary Pierre, Mary Leocadia, Mary Edward, ets.

                B. Delorme, V.G.

S-16
Josette
Servant
widow of
Lacourse

On the November 4, 1873, we the undersigned pastor of the parish of St. Paul, have buried Josette Servant, widow of Peter Lacourse, Sr., deceased the day before yesterday at the age of 76 years. Witnesses, Peter Bonnin, Aug. Lambert, Peter Kirk.

                B. Delorme, V.G.

B-32
Suzanna
Smyth

On November 15, 1873, we the undersigned pastor of the parish of St. Paul, have baptized Suzanna born on the 13th instant of the lawful marriage of John William Smyth and Suzan McDermott of this place. Sponsors, Thomas Coakley and Anna McDermot who have signed with us.

Thomas Cockley   Hannah McDermot
                B. Delorme, V.G.

Page 70
B-33
John
Prosper
Brothers

On November 23, 1873, we the undersigned pastor of the parish of St. Paul have baptized John Prosper, born on the third instant of the lawful marriage of Sam Brothers & Delphine Lachance of this parish. Sponsors, Pierre Lachance and Suzan Goodrich his wife.

                B. Delorme, V.G.

B-34
Mary
Emma
Wittman

On November 23, 1873, we the undersigned pastor of the parish of St. Paul, have baptized Mary Emma, born on the 20th instant, of the lawful marriage of John P. Wittman & Catherine Smith of this place. Sponsors, John Brentano & Emma Patterson.

John Brentano   Emma Patterson
                B. Delorme, V.G.

M-9
Peter H.
Flynn
&
Mary Ann
Coffey

On November 26, 1873, after the publication of one ban of marriage between Peter Harvey Flynn of the parish of St. Paul, son of age of John Flynn and Mary Harvey of the first part; and Mary Ann Coffey daughter underage of Edward Coffey of the same parish, of the consent of whom it proceeds, and of the late Mary Ronan, of the second part, the dispensation of the two other bans having been granted by us, and no impediment being found, we the undersigned, pastor of the said parish of St. Paul, have received their mutual consent of marriage and given them the nuptial benediction in the presence of Patrick A. Flynn, the bridegroom man, Eliza Coleman the bridemaid, John Coffey, brother of the bride.   P. H. Flynn

        P A. Flynn   E. J. Coleman   M. A. Coffey
        John Coffey
                B. Delorme, V.G.

B-35
Josephine
Mathilda
["Crete"
written
faintly]

On December 11, 1873, we the undersigned have baptized Josephine Mathilda, natural child of Rosalie Raymond of this parish, born on the 26th day of November last. Sponsors, Francis Dompierre and Soulange Bergevin.
                B. Delorme, V.G.

B-36
James
Picard

On December 25, 1873, we the undersigned pastor of the parish of St. Paul, have baptized James, born on the 22d of November last of the lawful marriage of Honore Picard and Celeste Rochbrune of this place. Sponsors,

Page 71

Francis Bernier and Leonore Picard, sister of the child.
B. Delorme, V.G.

Recapitulation for the year 1873

Baptisms	36
Burials	16
Marriages	7
First Communions	21

1874

B-1
Joseph
Delille

On January 4, 1874, we the undersigned pastor of the parish of St. Paul, have baptized Joseph born on the 30th day of December last of the lawful marriage of Felix Delille and Mary Pichette of this place. Sponsors, Louis Pichette and Margaret Bercier, his wife, grandparents of the child.
B. Delorme, V.G.

B-2
Louis
Bernier

On January 18, 1874, we the undersigned, pastor of St. Paul, have baptized Louis Alfred, born on the 13th instant of the lawful marriage of Louis Bernier and Josette Lavigneur of this place. Sponsors, Julien Provost and Caroline Raymond, his wife.
Julien Provost   Caroline Raymond
B. Delorme, V.G.

S-1
J. B.
Chamberland

On February 6, 1874, we the undersigned have buried Jean Baptiste Chamberlan, lawful son of Adolphus Chamberland and Louise Humpherville of this parish of St. Paul, deceased on the 4th instant, at the age of about six months. Witnesses, Francis Bergevin and Louis Bergevin.
B. Delorme, V.G.

B-3
Charles
Albert
Pelland

On February 22, 1874, we the undersigned pastor of the parish of St. Paul have baptized Charles Albert, born on the 11th instant, of the lawful marriage of Charles Olivier Pelland and Mary E. Coleman of this parish. Sponsors, James Coleman, grandfather of the child, and Annie Davidson.
James Coleman
Chs. O. Pelland   Annie C. Davidson
B. Delorme, V.G.

B-4
Josephine
Barons

On February 22, 1874, we the undersigned have baptized Josephine, born on the 13th instant, of the lawful marriage [of] Dominick Baron now deceased and Josephine Raymond of this parish. Sponsors, Isreal Raymond and Eleonore Picard.
B. Delorme, V.G.

Page 72
B-5 & 6
Alfred
Lucier
&
Josphine
C. Lucier

On February 26, 1874, we the undersigned, pastor of the parish of St. Paul, have baptized Alfred and Josephine Clarisse born on the 24th instant of the lawful marriage of Joseph Lucier & Louise Martineau. Sponsors of Alfred, Amadee Choquette and Marie Bernier his wife. Sponsors of Josephine, the same Amadee Choquette and Clarisse Bernier.
Amedee Choquette
B. Delorme, V.G.

S-2
Louis
Bernier

On March 7, 1874, we the undersigned have buried Louis Bernier, lawful son of Louis Bernier and Josette Lavigneur of this place, deceased yesterday at the age of two months. Witnesses. Peter Bonnin and Ben Lambert.
B. Delorme, V.G.

B-7
Cecile
Dubreuil

On March 22, 1874, we the undersigned, pastor of the parish of St. Paul, have baptized Cecile, born on the 28th of February last of the lawful marriage of Francis Dubreuil and Magdeleine Bourgeau of this place. Sponsors, Francis Bernier, Junior, and Cecile Lucier.
B. Delorme, V.G.

M-1
Isaias
Crete
&
Rosa

On March 24, 1874, We, the undersigned, pastor of the parish of St. Paul, after having granted the dispensation of three bans and that of the impediment of prohibited time, no other impediment being found, have received the mutual consent of marriage of Isaias Crete, of the parish of St. Pouis, widower of Isabelle Gobin, and son of the late Oliver Crete & Margaret

Raymond

Toupin of the first part; and Rosa Raymond, of this parish of St. Paul, daughter under age of the late Augustin Raymond and of Mary Servant, of the consent of whom it proceeds, and have given them the nuptial benediction in the presence of the said Mary Servant, mother of the bride, Augustin Lambert and Francis Raymond.

Isaia Crete
Rosy Raymond
B. Delorme, V.G.

S-3
James
Picard

On March 26, 1874, we the undersigned, pastor of the parish of St. Paul, have buried James Picard lawful son of Henry Picard and Celeste Rochbrune of this place, deceased yesterday at the age of four months. Present, James Patterson and A. Lucier.
B. Delorme, V.G.

Page 73
S-4
Alfred
Lucier

On April 8, 1874, We, the undersigned, pastor of the parish of St. Paul, have buried Alfred Lucier, lawful son of Joseph Lucier and Louise Martineau, of this place, deceased yesterday, he being then about 7 weeks old. Present, James Patterson and Baptiste Dubreuil.
B. Delorme, V.G.

S-5
Thomas
Hubbard
[Herbert]

On April 22, 1874, we the undersigned have buried Thomas Hubbard [Herbert] of this parish of St. Paul, husband of Genevieve Longtain and deceased the day before yesterday at the age of . . . Present, Dr. Bayley, Dr. Brentano, J. B. Piette, etc.
B. Delorme, V.G.

B-8
Emilia
Philomena
Longtain

On April 22, 1874, we the undersigned pastor of the parish of St. Paul, have baptized Emilia Philomena, born on the 14th day of March last, of the lawful marriage of Thomas Longtain and Mathilda Rivet of this place. The sponsors were Xavier Moisan and Philomene Moisan.
Philomene Moisan
F. X. Moisan
B. Delorme, V.G.

B-9
Jane
Geelan

On April 26, 1874, we the undersigned pastor of the parish of St. Paul have baptized Jane, born on the 3d instant of the lawful marriage of Patrick Geelan and Elizabeth Ady, of this parish. Sponsors, Patrick MCantee and Mrs. Elizabeth Coyle.
P. MCantee   Elizabeth Coyle
B. Delorme, V.G.

B-10
Annie
Suzan
Dowd

On May 14, 1874, we the undersigned, pastor of the parish of St. Paul, have baptized Annie Suzan born on the 25th of April last, of the lawful marriage of John Dowd and Julia Pepin of this place. Sponsors, Peter Cleary and Miss Mary Murphy, represented by her mother Mrs. A. Murphy.
Peter Clery
Minnie C. Murphy
B. Delorme, V.G.

B-11
Louis
Clement
Raymond

On May 31, 1874, we the undersigned, pastor of the parish of St. Paul, have baptized Louis Clement, born on the 18th instant of the lawful marriage of Marcel Raymond and Odile Raymond of this place. Sponsors, Charles Bergevin and Caroline Provost.
Charles Bergevin   Caroline Provost
B. Delorme, V.G.

Page 74
B-12
Marie
Mary
[Margaret]
Comtois

On May 31, 1874, we the undersigned, pastor of the parish of St. Paul, have baptized Mary Margaret, born on the 7th of the lawful marriage of James Comtois and Soulange Pichette of this place. Sponsors, Louis Prevot and Pauline his wife.   Louis Prevot   Poline Prevost
B. Delorme, V.G.

B-13
Mary
Malvina

On June 4, 1874, we, the undersigned, pastor of the parish of St. Paul, have baptized Mary Malvina, born of the lawful marriage of Cyprien Bellique and Julienne Bergevin of this place, on the 1st instant. Sponsors, Charles

Bellique	Bergevin and Soulange Bergevin.

Charles Bergevin Soulange Bergevin
B. Delorme, V.G.

B-14
Ann
Etu
On June 7, 1874, we the undersigned, pastor of the parish of St. Paul, have baptized Ann, born of the marriage of Henry Etu and Archange Deshotel of Fort Vancouver, on the 18th of December last. Sponsors, George Connor & Salome Picard.

George Connor
B. Delorme, V.G.

S-6
Henry
Joseph
Langlois
On June 9, 1874, Henry Joseph, lawful son of Israel Langlois and Mary Pepin of Yamhill County, deceased on the 6th instant, was buried in the grave yard of this parish of St. Paul. Present, James Patterson & Ben Lambert.

B. Delorme, V.G.

B-15
Agnes
Bosquet
On the 14th day of June, 1874, we, the undersigned pastor of the parish of St. Paul, have baptized Agnes, born on the 7th of April last of the lawful marriage of Francis Bosquet and Elizabeth Bowers [Bauer] of this place. Sponsors, George Goulet and Kathy Murphy.

George Goulet Katie Murphy
B. Delorme, V.G.

Page 75
S-7
Andrew
Chalifoux
On June 20, 1874, we the undersigned, pastor of the parish of St. Paul, have buried Andrew, lawful son of Andrew Chalifoux and Emerance Mongrain, of this place, deceased the day before yesterday, at the age of ten months. Present, James Patterson and Roch Pichette.

B. Delorme, V.G.

B-17 [sic]
John
O'Loughlin
On June 24, 1874, we the undersigned, pastor of the parish, have baptized John, born on the 8th instant, of the lawful marriage of Michael O'Loughlin and Elizabeth Aplin of this place. Sponsors, Etienne Simon Gregoire and Josephine Aplin.

Etienne Simon Gregoire Josephine Aplin
B. Delorme, V.G.

B-18
Louis
Brouillard
On June 28, 1874, we the undersigned, pastor of the parish of St. Paul, have baptized Louis, born on the 18th instant, of the lawful marriage of Francis Brouillard and Aurelie Bonnin of this place. Sponsors, Baptist AYotte and Josephine Raymond.

B. Delorme, V.G.

1st
Communions
This is to certify that, on June 28, 1874, the following persons have made their first communion in the Church of St. Paul, Most Rev. F. N. Blanchet officiating:

Peter David Chalifoux	Mary Ann Saxe
John Baptist Gauthier	Elizabeth Cecelia Connor
Olivier Louis Rochbrune	Mary Cecelia McKay
Joseph Bernier	Anna Blandine Johnson
Theodore Philippe Boutin	Mary Ellen Johnson
Charles Andrew Smith	Mary Jane Connor
Joseph Louis Prevot	Ellen Agnes Flynn
Thomas Francis McGrath	Mary Agnes Jette
Patrick Henry Connor	Angelique Rose Dupre
Frank John Arhens	Isabelle Mary Bourgeau
	John Julien Rochbrune

In all 21 first communions

B. Delorme, V.G.

Confirm-
ations
66
This is to certify that on June 28, 1874, the Sacrament of Confirmation has been administered by Most Rev. F. N. Blanchet, Archbishop of Oregon City, to the following persons:
James Cyprian Patterson
John Peter Patterson
Leo Joseph Patterson

Andrew Henry Murphy
Nicholas D. Cook
James Joseph Cook
Matthew Henry Connor
Thomas Joseph Connor
Robert Joseph Kirk
Richard Joseph Kirk
Eugene Joseph Blanchet
Stephen Alfred Fitzgerald

Page 76

Peter David Chalifoux	Cecile Julie Lucier
John Baptist Gauthier	Clementine Virginia Mongrain
Olivier Louis Rochbrune	Josephine Esther Mongrain
John Julien Rochbrune	Salome Mary Picard
Joseph Bernier	Rose Christine Chalifoux
Theodore Philippe Boutin	Esther Euphrosine Pichette
Ch. Andrew Smyth	Mary Ann Connor
Joseph Louis Prevot	Alice Blandine Bequette
Thomas Francis McGrath	Zenaide Helen Gregoire
Patrick Henry Connor	Josephine Agnes Aplin
Francis John Arhens	Bridget Veronica Connor
Nazaire David Kitson	Mary Ann Veronica McGrath
Augustin Joseph Bonnin	Martha Agnes Connor
Jeremie Chamberlan	Alice Bridget Connor
Francis Bourgeau	Catherine Agnes McGrath
Louis Mongrain	Catherine Esther Connor
Charles Francis Bernier	Mary Emily Coleman
Peter Vivet	Esther Jos. June Jackson
Louis Bergevin	Catherine Marietta Flynn
Jules Francis Raymond	Mary Amelia Helen Simon
Amable Joseph Bergevin	Suzan Deshotel
Philippe Nazaire Raymond	Mary Ann Saxe
Henry Picard	Elizabeth Cecelia Connor
	Mary Cecelia McKay
	Anna Blandina Johnson
	Mary Helena Johnson
	Mary June Connor
	Ellen Agnes Flynn
	Mary Agnes Jette
	Angelique Rose Dupre
	Isabel Mary Bourgeau

In all 66 confirmations

B. Delorme, V.G.

S-8 Adelaide Lambert

On July 11, 1874, we the undersigned, pastor of the parish of St. Paul, have buried Adelaide, daughter of Augustin Lambert and Margaret Sanders of this place, deceased the day before yesterday, at the age of six years. Present, James Patterson and Hugh Cosgrove.

B. Delorme, V.G.

B-19 Louis Narcisse Lafontaine

On August 30, 1874, we the undersigned pastor of St. Paul, have baptized Louis Narcisse, born the 21st instant of Narcisse Lafontaine and Margaret Pichette of this place. Sponsors, James Comtoir & Angelique Pichette.

B. Delorme, V.G.

B-20 Joseph Pichette

On August 30, 1874, we the undersigned pastor of St. Paul, have baptized Joseph, born on the 25th instant, of the lawful marriage of Roch Pichette and Victoire Despard of this place. Sponsors, Amedee Choquette and Mary Bernier.

A. Choquette
B. Delorme, V.G.

Page 77

B-21
Eva
Adilia
Gear

On September 13, 1874, we the undersigned pastor of St. Paul have baptized Eva Adilia born on the 7th of March last of the lawful marriage of T. D. Gear and Philomene Mathieu of this place. Sponsors, Charles Bergevin and Arsinoe Mathieu.

Charles Bergevin   Arsinoe Matthieu
                              B. Delorme, V.G.

B-22
James
Nicholas
Patterson

On September 13, 1874, we the undersigned pastor of St. Paul have baptized James Nicholas, born on the 11th instant of the lawful marriage of James Patterson and Sara O'Kelly of this place. Sponsors, Nicholas Flashman and Margaret Flashman.

Nichlas Flishman
                              B. Delorme, V.G.

S-9
Victoire
Charlebois

On September 22, 1874, Rev. Father B. Mackin buried in the cemetery of St. Paul, Victoire Charlebois, wife of Joseph Rochbrune, junior, of this place, deceased on the 20th instant at the age of about 30 years. Present, James Patterson and Joseph Rochbrune.

B-23
Josephine
Pepin

On September 27, we the undersigned pastor of St. Paul have baptized Josephine, born on the 31st of December last, of the civil marriage of Peter Pepin or Lachance and Amanda Grim of this place. Sponsors, Alonzo Bonnin and Mary Wagner.
                              B. Delorme, V.G.

B-24
Francis
Paul
Ernst

On September 27, 1874, we the undersigned pastor of St. Paul, have baptized Francis Paul, born on the 25th instant of the lawful marriage of Francis Henry Ernst and Magdelen Vesper of this place. Sponsors, Paul Beaudry and Marie Raymond.
                              B. Delorme, V.G.

S-10
N.C. 1
Helen
Lyons

On September 29, 1874, We, the undersigned pastor of the parish of St. Paul, have buried in the new grave yard of said parish, Helen Lyons, mother of the late Mrs. Kirk, deceased yesterday at the age of 75 years. Witnesses, John Brentano, Math. Murphy, James Patterson, etc.

[Marginal note] Henceforth N.C. means New Cemetery, & O.C. means Old Cemetery.

Page 78

B-25
Caroline
Labonte

On October 5, 1874, we the undersigned pastor of St. Paul, have baptized Caroline, born on the 6th of August last, of the civil marriage of Alexandre Labonte and Clementine Pepin otherwise Lachance of this place. Sponsors, Julien Pepin and Sara Charlebois.
                              B. Delorme, V.G.

S-11 O.C.
Louis
Clement
Raymond

On October 9, 1874, we the undersigned pastor of St. Paul, have buried in the old grave yard Louis Clement, lawful son of Marcel Raymond and Odile Raymond of this place, deceased the 8th instant, at the age of 7 months. Witnesses, Peter Kirk & James Patterson.
                              B. Delorme, V.G.

B-26
Margaret
Catherine
Manaigre

On October 17, 1874, we the undersigned, pastor of St. Paul, have baptized Margaret Catherine, born on the 2nd instant of the lawful marriage of Dieudonne Manaigre and Emilie Pichette of this parish. Felix Delille, godfather; Godmother, Marie Pichette.
                              B. Delorme, V.G.

S-12 O.C.
Priscilla
Mathieu

On November 9, 1874, we the undersigned, pastor of the St. Paul parish, have buried in the old grave yard Priscilla Mathieu, lawful daughter of Fr. Xavier Mathieu & Rose Aussant of this place, deceased on the 7th instant at the age of 20 years. Witnesses, John Brentano, James Patterson, Firmin Lebrun, etc, etc.
                              B. Delorme, V.G.

S-13 O.C.
Francois
Dubreuil

On December 1, 1874, We the undersigned pastor of St. Paul, have buried in the old grave yard Francis, lawful son of Francis Dubreuil & Magdelen Bourgeau, deceased on the 29th of November last, at the age of 3 years and 8 months. Present, Joseph Lucier and Xavier Martineau.
                              B. Delorme, V.G.

S-14 N.C.
Rose
Rochbrune

On December 5, 1874, we the undersigned pastor of St. Paul have buried in the new grave yard Rose Rochbrune, lawful daughter of Joseph Rochbrune and Victoire Charlebois, deceased yesterday at the age of 17 months. Present, James Patterson and John Dowd.

B. Delorme, V.G.

Page 79
B-27
Eleonore
Pelage
Choquette

On December 6, 1874, we the undersigned, pastor of the parish of St. Paul, have baptized Eleonore Pelage, born on the 30th of November last, of the lawful marriage of Amadee Choquette and Mary Bernier of this place. Sponsors, David Bernier & Salome Picard.

B. Delorme, V.G.

B-28
John
Franklin
Davidson

On December 8th, 1874, we the undersigned pastor of St. Paul, have baptized John Franklin, born on the 16th of November of the lawful marriage of Frank Davidson and Annie Coleman. Sponsors, John Coleman & Louise Coleman.

B. Delorme, V.G.

S-15 O.C.
Josephine
Bourgeau

On December 23, 1874, we the undersigned pastor of St. Paul have buried Josephine, lawful daughter of J. Bpt. Bourgeau and Genevieve Martineau, deceased, after being privately baptized, at the age of 14 days. Present, James Patterson & Louis Humpherville.

B. Delorme, V.G.

B-29
Eliza
Ann
Wassenhove

On December 25, 1874, we the undersigned pastor of St. Paul have baptized Eliza Ann, born on the 29th of November last, of the lawful marriage of Frank Wassenhove and Ellen Coyle of this place. Sponsors, Patrick Karrigan & Eliza Coleman.

Patrick Kerrigan   Eliza Coleman
B. Delorme, V.G.

B-30
Alfred
Prevot

On December 27, 1874, we the undersigned, pastor of St. Paul, have baptized Alfred, born on the 8th instant of the lawful marriage of Louis Prevot & Pauline T. Lefot of this place. Sponsors, James Comtois & Soulange Pichette.

B. Delorme, V.G.

S-16 N.C.
Thomas
Kirk

On December 31, 1874, we the undersigned pastor of St. Paul, have buried in the new cemetery Thomas Kirk, deceased on the 29th instant, at the age of about 87 years. Present, J. Brentano, M. Murphy, John Coffey, etc.

B. Delorme, V.G.

Recapitulation for the year 1874

Baptisms	30	First Communions	31
Burials	16	Confirmations	66
Marriages	1		

1875

Page 80
M-1
Frederic
Fortin
&
Mary
Servant

On January 7, 1875, after the publication of two bans of marriage between Frederic Fortin of this parish of St Paul, lawful son and of age of Christophe Fortin & Elizabeth Paulin, now residing at St. Valentine, District of Montreal Canada, of the first part; and Mary Servant, widow of Augustine Raymond, of the second part; the dispensation of the other ban being by us granted; and no impediment whatever being found; we the undersigned, pastor of the said parish of St. Paul, have received their mutual consent of marriage and have given them the nuptial benediction in the presence of Peter Bonnin, Francis Bernier and Augustine Lambert.

Frederic Fortain   Mary Servant
B. Delorme, V.G.

M-2
J. B.
Ayote
&
Josephine
Baron

On January 25, 1875, after the publication of one ban of marriage made at our parochial mass, between John Baptiste Ayote, of the parish of St. Paul, son of age and lawful of Peter Ayote and Margaret Biron, deceased at Maskinonge Canada for the first part; and Josephine Raymond, of the same parish of St. Paul, widow of Dominic Baron, of the second part; the dispensation of the two other bans being granted by us, Vicar General, and no impediment whatever being discovered, We, the undersigned, pastor of the said parish of St. Paul, have received their mutual consent of marriage, and bestowed on them the nuptial benediction in the presence of Francis Raymond, father of the bride, Peter Bonnin, Israel Raymond and Leonore Picard.

B. Delorme, V.G.

B-1 Marie Philomene Chalifoux

On January 30, 1875, we the undersigned have baptized Mary Philomene, born on the 11th instant of the lawful marriage of Louis Chalifoux and Julienne Picard of the parish of St. Paul. Sponsors, Francis Bernier and Rose Chalifoux.

B. Delorme, V.G.

Page 81 S-1 O.C. Pascal Parizeau

On March 12, 1875, we the undersigned have buried Pascal Parizeau, son of Peter Parizeau and Mary Dompierre of Lane County, deceased at the age of 8 years. Witnesses, Peter Kirk and P. Connor.

B. Delorme, V.G.

S-2 N.C. Mathew Connor

On March 24, 1875, we the undersigned, pastor of the parish of St. Paul, have buried in the new grave yard Mathew Connor of this place, deceased on the 22nd at the age of 51 years. Witnesses, Mathew Murphy, Patrick Connor, Peter Kirk, and many others.

B. Delorme, V.G.

B-2 Samuel Kerr

On April 4, 1875, we the undersigned pastor of St. Paul have baptized Samuel, born on the 1st instant of the lawful marriage of Samuel James Kerr and Catherine Coffey of this place. Sponsors, Peter H. Flynn and Mary Coffey.

P. H. Flynn　　　　　　　Mary Ann Flynn

B. Delorme, V.G.

B-3 Mary Agnes Goodrich

On the 4 April, 1875, we the undersigned pastor of St. Paul have baptized Mary Agnes, daughter by a civil marriage of John Goodrich, now deceased, and of Elizabeth Ady of this place, the child being born July 12, 1868. Sponsors, Charles Pelland and his wife, Mary Coleman.

Mary Coleman　　　Chs. O. Pelland　　　Mary E. Pelland

B. Delorme, V.G.

S-3 N.C. Patrick Connor

On April 14, 1875, we the undersigned pastor of St. Paul have buried in the new graveyard, Patrick Connor, of this place, deceased on the 12th instant at the age of 69 years. Witnesses: Dr. Brentano, James Coyle, Andrew Hughes, John McGrath, etc.

B. Delorme, V.G.

M-3 Charles Bergevin & Rosa Mathieu Page 82

On April 15, 1875, we the undersigned pastor of the parish of St. Paul, after the publication of one ban of marriage at our parochial mass, between Charles Bergevin, of the same parish, son of age and lawful, of Louis Bergevin and Mary Ann Servant, of the first part; and Rosa Mathieu of the same parish of St. Paul, daughter of age and lawful of Francis Xavier Mathieu & Rose Aussant for the second part; the dispensation of the two other bans being granted by us, the undersigned, and no impediment whatever being found, Have received their mutual consent of marriage and given them the nuptial benediction in the presence of Louis Bergevin, father of the bridegroom, Francis X. Mathieu, father of the bride, James Coleman and Charles Mathieu, bridegroom's men, & Arsinoe Mathieu & Catherine Barclay, bridemaids, who have signed along with the parties.

Louis Bergevin　　　　　　Charles Bergevin
F. X. Matthieu　　　　　　Rosa Matthieu
James R. Coleman　　　　　Arsinoe Matthieu
Charles Matthieu　　　　　Catherine Barclay

B. Delorme, V.G.

B-4 Virginia Rose Vertfeuille

On April 15, 1875, we the undersigned, pastor of St. Paul, have baptized Virginia Rose, born on the 27th of January last, of the lawful marriage of Jude Vertfeuille and Catherine Gauthier, from Buteville. Sponsors, Charles Bergevin and Rosa Mathieu.

B. Delorme, V.G.

B-5 Felicite Lucier	On April 18, 1875, we the undersigned pastor of St. Paul, have baptized Felicite, born on the 5th instant, of the lawful marriage of Joseph Lucier & Louise Martineau of this place. Sponsors, Fabien Chamberland & Isabelle Bourgeau. B. Delorme, V.G.
S-4 N.C. Sister Mary Lazare	On April 23, 1875, we the undersigned pastor of St. Paul parish, have buried in the little chapel of the Sisters, Sister Mary Lazare, of the Holy Names of Jesus and Mary, deceased on the 21st instant at the age of 40 years & 8 months. Present, Rev. Sister Superior from Portland, Sr. Mary Peter, Peter Kirk, John McGrath, etc. B. Delorme, V.G. Transferred to chapel of N.C.
Page 83 Ab. 1 B.C. First Com. 1	On April 25, 1875, we the undersigned, pastor of St. Paul's parish, having received the profession of faith of Elizabeth Ady, born on September 3, 1852, wife of Patrick Geelan of the said parish of St. Paul, and the required absolution being imparted, have solemnly admitted her into the bosom of the Holy Roman Catholic Church, in the presence of the whole congregation, and we have baptized her conditionally, her sponsors being James Coleman and Mary McKay; and moreover we have admitted her for the first time, to Holy communion. Elizabeth A. Geelan James Coleman Mary McKay B. Delorme, V.G.
B-7 Emerance Catherine Chalifoux	On April 25, 1875, we the undersigned, pastor of St. Paul's parish, have baptized Emerance Catherine, born on the 15th instant, of the lawful marriage of Andrew Chalifoux and Emerence Mongrain of this place. Sponsors, Dieudonne Manaigre and Emily Pichette. B. Delorme, V.G.
S-5 O.C. Adeline Josephine Bellique	On April 30, 1875, we, the undersigned, pastor of St. Paul's parish, have buried Adeline Josephine, daughter of J. B. Bellique and Victoire Vassal, of this place, deceased on the 28th instant, at the age of about ten months. Present, Firmin Lebrun and Peter Kitson. B. Delorme, V.G.
S-6 N.C. Louis Humpherville	On May 1, 1875, we the undersigned, pastor of St. Paul's church, have buried in the new graveyard, Louis Humpherville of this place, deceased on the 29th of April last at the age of about 40 years. Present, J. B. Bourgeau, Xavier Martineau, etc. B. Delorme, V.G.
S-7 O.C. Joseph Frederic Despard	On May 11, 1875, we the undersigned pastor of St. Paul have buried Joseph F. Despard of this place, deceased on the 9th instant, at the age of 87 years. Present, Roch Pichette and David Mongrain. B. Delorme, V.G.
B-8 Joseph Abraham Jackson	On May 16, 1875, we the undersigned, pastor of St. Paul's church, have baptized Joseph Abraham, born on the 13th of March last, of the lawful marriage of Jerome B. Jackson and Mary Cosgrove, of this place. Sponsors, Esther Jackson and ourselves. B. Delorme, V.G.
Page 84 B-9 Rosa McGrath	On May 16, 1875, we the undersigned, pastor of St. Paul, have baptized Rosa, born on the 14th instant of the lawful marriage of John McGrath and Mary Hughes of this place. Sponsors, Mathew Connor and Bridget Connor. Mathew Connor Bridget Connor John McGrath B. Delorme, V.G.
B-10 Mary Olive Gingras	On May 23, 1875, we the undersigned, pastor of St. Paul have baptized Mary Olive, born on the 6th of December last of the lawful marriage of Calixte Gingras & Josette Picard of this place. Sponsors, Francis Bernier, jun, and Flavie Petit. Frank Bernier Flavie Petit B. Delorme, V.G.

B-11
Marie
Celeste
Picard

On May 23, 1875, we the undersigned pastor of St. Paul have baptized Mary Celeste, born on the 4th instant of the lawful marriage of Henry Picard and Celeste Rochbrune of this place. Sponsors, Calixte Lebeau and Dorilda Gagnon.

Calixte Lebeau   Dorilda Gagnon
B. Delorme, V.G.

B-12
John
Albert
Jette

On June 6, 1875, we the undersigned, pastor of St. Paul's parish, have baptized John Albert born on the 14th of May last of the lawful marriage of Adolph Jette and Margaret Liard of this place. Sponsors, J. Baptiste Piette and Frances Million his wife.

John B. P. Piette   A. Jette
Frances M. Million
B. Delorme, V.G.

B-13
Frances
Rosa
Lavigueur

On June 25, 1875, we the undersigned have baptized Frances Rosa, born on the 14th instant of Josette Lavigueur and of an unknown father. Sponsors, J. B. Piette and Frances M. Million his wife.

John B. P. Piette
Frances M. Million
B. Delorme, V.G.

B-14
Mary
Josephine
Gould

On July 4, 1875, we the undersigned have baptized Mary Josephine Gould, born on the 4th of June last of the lawful marriage of John Gould and Lucy Perrault of this place. Sponsors, Adolph Jette and Mary Weston.

Adolphe Jette
B. Delorme, V.G.

Page 85
B-15
Charles
Nazaire
Dupre

On the 4 July, 1875, we the undersigned have baptized Charles Nazaire, born on the 17th of June last, of the lawful marriage of Charles Dupre and Catherine Chalifoux of this place. Sponsors, Bartholomew Chamberland and Angelica Dupre.

B. Delorme, V.G.

B-16
Thomas
Alexan-
der
McLaugh-
lin

On July 6, 1875, we the undersigned, pastor of St. Paul's parish, have baptized conditionally Thomas Alexander, born on the 26th of May last, of Catherine McLaughlin and of an unknown father. Sponsor, Matilde Rivet.

B. Delorme, V.G.

B-17
William
Hugh
Brothers

On July 11, 1875, we the undersigned, pastor of St. Paul's church, have baptized William Hugh, born on the last day of April of the same year, of the lawful marriage of Sam T. Brothers and Adolphine Pepin of this place. Sponsors, Hugh Cosgrove & John Dowd.

H. Cosgrove
B. Delorme, V.G.

B-18
Francis
Leo
Smyth

On July 25, 1875, we the undersigned, pastor of St. Paul, have baptized Francis Leo, born on the 9th instant of the lawful marriage of Frank Smyth and Ellen Nolan of this parish. Sponsors, Charles Smyth and Alicia Nolan.

Alicia Nolan
B. Delorme, V.G.

First
Commu-
nion

This is to certify that on the 27th day of June, 1875, the following persons have made their first communion at St. Paul.

William Murphy   Edmont Bergevin
Mathew Murphy   Francis Mongrain
Philip Flashman
John Gately   Louisa Coleman
Daniel Larrison   Agnes Jackson
Adolph Chamberland   Magdelen Raymond
Narcisse Chamberland   Martha Connor
Etienne Lucier   Jane Erskin
Daniel Lucier   Clementine Bourgeau
George Picard

Page 86

M-4
John
Charles
McDowell
&
Margaret
Connor

On August 11, 1875, after having granted the dispensation of the publication of three bans and also of the prohibition known as prohibition of the Church or Vetitum Ecclesia, no other impediment being found, and the bridegroom, the non-Catholic part, having solemnly promised beforehand to let his wife entirely free in her religious belief and in the practise of her Christian duties, and moreover to have their children, if God give them any, raised according to the Roman Catholic faith; We the undersigned Vicar General of the Diocese of Oregoncity and pastor of the parish of St. Paul, have received the mutual consent of marriage of John Charles McDowell of the County of Solano in California, son of age of the late Thomas McDowell and Ellen Donahoe of the first part; and of Margaret Connor of the parish of St. Paul in the County of Marion, State of Oregon, daughter of age of the late Patrick Connor and Elizabeth Dunn; and have joined them in the holy bonds of matrimony in the presence of Mary Connor, Patrick Gately, Bridget Connor, Lizzy Connor, and Jane Gately.

Patrick Gately	J. C. McDowell
Jane Gately	Margaret McDowell
Mary Connor	Bridget Connor
	B. Delorme, V.G.

M-5
Anton
Deniople
or
Adamapple
&
Philomene
Petit

On August 27, 1875, after having granted the dispensation of three bans and no impediment being found, we, the undersigned, pastor of the parish of St. Paul and Vicar general have received the mutual consent of marriage of Anton A. Deniople or Adamapple of the County of Clapsop in Oregon, son of age of the late George Deniople or Adamapple and Helen Constantin still living of the first part; and Philomene Petit of the parish of St. Paul, daughter of the late Amable Petit and Suzan Petit, yet living, of the second part; and having bestowed on them the nuptial benediction in the presence of Leon Deloney, Suzan Petit and Flavie Petit.

Leon Delauney	Anton X. Deniople
Flavie Petit	Philomene Petit
	B. Delorme, V.G.

P 87

B-19
Frederic
Joseph
Murphy

On the 29th of August, 1875, we the undersigned pastor of St. Paul have baptized Frederic Joseph born on the 25th of July last of the lawful marriage of Andrew Murphy and Elizabeth Cosgrove of this place. Sponsors, William Murphy and Cecelia McKay.

William Murphy	Andrew Murphy
Cecelia McKay	Elizabeth Murphy
	B. Delorme, V.G.

B-20
Joseph
Albin
Sharp

On August 29, 1875, we the undersigned pastor of St. Paul's Parish have baptized Joseph Albin born on the 25th inst. from Helen Sharp of this place and from an unknown father. Sponsor, Caroline Raymond.
B. Delorme, V.G.

B-21
Agnes
Kitson

On the 12th of September, 1875, we the undersigned pastor of St. Paul's church have baptized Agnes, born on the 20th day of August last of the lawful marriage of Peter Kitson and Angelie Dupre of this place. Sponsors, Baptiste Gagnon and Cloris Mongrain.
B. Delorme, V.G.

S-8 O.C.
Frances
Rosa
Lavigueur
Benediction
of the
Mortuary
Chapel and
Vault at the
New Graveyard

On September 17, 1875, we the undersigned pastor of St. Paul have buried Frances Rosa Lavigueur, daughter of Josette Lavigueur of this place, deceased at the age of three months. Witnesses J. B. Piette and H. Ernst.
B Delorme, V.G.

On September 18, 1875, we the undersigned Vicar General of the Diocese of Oregoncity and pastor of St. Paul have solemnly blessed the mortuary chapel at the new cemetery under the invocation of St. Joseph, patron of a happy death, along with the vault underneath, the same to be used as a burying place for the Sisters of the Holy Names of Jesus and Mary in the state of Oregon; and we have moreover transferred and buried therein the

and transfer of the remains of remains of the following Rev. Sisters:

Sister Renilde, deceased April 1, 1849
Sister Mary Olive, deceased January 7, 1870
Sister Mary Florence, deceased January 3, 1871
Sister Mary Simone, deceased January 7, 1871
Sister Mary Francis, deceased December 9, 1870
Sister Mary Norbert, deceased August 22, 1871
Sister Mary of the Visitation, deceased June 29, 1873
Sister Mary Praxede, deceased November 1, 1873
Sister Mary Lazare, deceased April 21, 1875, in the presence of Very Rev. T. Fierens, Rev. T. Thibau, Rev. J. Croquet, and of the Rev. Sisters: Mary of the

Page 88

Seven Dolors, Superior of the Community in Oregon; Mary of the Sacred Heart, Superior of the House in Salem, Mary Perpetua, Superior of the house at Grand Round, Mary Peter, Sup. of the House at St. Paul and seventeen others of the same community, along with Sr. Blandine and Sr. Peter Claver of the Order of Providence, and moreover a large congregation of people.

Sister Mary of the Seven Dolors, Sup.
Sister Mary of the Sacred Heart
Sister Mary Perpetua
Sister Mary Peter
G. C. Thibau
A. J. Croquet, pr.
F. Fierens, V.G.
B. Delorme, V.G.

B-22 Marguerite De Lima Delille

On September 19, 1875, we the undersigned pastor of St. Paul's church have baptized Margaret Delima, born on the 9th of this month of the lawful marriage of Felix Delille and Mary Pichette of this place. Sponsors, Roch Pichette and Soulange Pichette.
B. Delorme, V.G.

S-9 O.C. Thomas Alexander McLaughlin

On September 29, 1875, we the undersigned pastor of St. Paul have buried Thomas Alexander McLaughlin, son of Catherine McLaughlin of this parish, deceased yesterday about four months old. Witnesses, Henry Ernst and Fabien Rivet.
B. Delorme, V.G.

B-23, 24 Louis Parizeau & Rachel F. Parizeau

On October 10, 1875, we have baptized Louis born on the 20th of August last of the lawful marriage of Louis Parizeau and Ellen Larrisson, and Rachel Florence, born on the 21st of June last, of the lawful marriage of Peter Parizeau and Mary Dompierre, all of Lane Co., Oregon. Sponsors of Louis, Louis Dompierre and Euphemie Chamberland. Sponsors of Rachel, John B. Dompierre and Angelie Bonenfant.
B. Delorme, V.G.

B-25 Eliza Eugenia Wittman

On October 17, 1875, we the undersigned pastor of St. Paul have baptized Eliza Eugenia, born on the 14th instant of the lawful marriage of John Wittman and Catherine Smith of this place. Sponsors, James Coyle, Jun., and Eliza Coleman.
B. Delorme, V.G.

Page 89
S-10 Lucy Goule

On October 20, 1875, we the undersigned, pastor of St. Paul, have buried in the new Graveyard Lucy Perrault, wife of John Goule of this place, deceased on the 18th instant at the age of 35 years. Witnesses, John Brentano and Cas. Brentano.
B. Delorme, V.G.

B-26 Mary Ann

On October 23, 1875, we the undersigned pastor of St. Paul have baptized Mary Ann, born on the 20th instant, of the lawful marriage of Andrew Hughes and Rosa Connor Of this place. Sponsors, Simon Connor and

Hughes

Catherine McGrath.
Simon Connor   Catherine McGrath
                                B. Delorme, V.G.

B-27
Joseph
Longtain

On October 24, 1875, we the undersigned, pastor of St. Paul, have baptized Joseph, born on the 26th day of September last of the lawful marriage of Thomas Longtain and Matilda Rivet of this place. Sponsors, Adolph Jette and Genevieve Herbert.
                               Adolphe Jette
                                B. Delorme, V.G.

Erection
of the
Way of
the Cross
at the
Convent

On October 29, 1875, we the undersigned, Vicar General of the Diocese of Oregoncity, being duly authorized therefore by the General of the Brothers Minors, in view of a power granted to us May 13, A.D. 1870, have erected the Stations of the Cross in the Chapel of the Convent of St. Paul, in the presence of Rev. S. White, Rev. Sr. Mary Peter, along with the Sisters and Pupils of the Community.
                                B Delorme, V.G.

B-28
Elizabeth
Orton

On October 31, 1875, we the undersigned, pastor of St. Paul, have baptized Elizabeth, born on the 15th of January, 1855, of the marriage of Ira Orton and Martha Burton of Yam Hill Co. Oregon. Sponsors, Frank Davidson and Eliza Coleman.
                                           W. F. Davidson
                   E. J. Coleman   Elizabeth Orton
                                B. Delorme, V.G.

Page 90
M-6
W.
Thomas
Coleman
&
Caledonia
Elizabeth
Orton

On November 4, 1875, after the publication of two bans of marriage between William Thomas Coleman of this parish of St. Paul, son of age and lawful of James Coleman and Fanny Murray, of the first part, and Caledonia Elizabeth of the same parish, daughter of age of Alfred Orton and Martha Burton, of the second part, the dispensation of the other ban having been granted by us, Vicar General of the Diocese of Oregoncity, and no impediment whatsoever being found, we the undersigned, pastor of the said parish of St. Paul, have received their mutual consent of marriage and bestowed on them the nuptial benediction in the presence of James Coleman, father of the bridegroom, Oliver Abernathey, brother-in-law of the bride, James Coleman, junior, and James Coyle, bridegroomsmen, Eliza Jane Coleman and Martha Abernethy, bridemen [sic], and Frank W. Davidson, who have signed with us along with the newly married couple.
          James R. Coleman, Jr.   William Thomas Coleman
          James Joseph Coyle   Caledonia Elizabeth Orton
          Eliza J. Coleman   James Coleman
          Martha Abernethy   Oliver Abernethy
          W. F. Davidson
                                B. Delorme, V.G.

Erection
of the
Stations
of the
Cross
at the
Mortuary
Chapel
of the
Sisters

On November 2, 1875, we the undersigned, Vicar General of the Diocese of Oregoncity, being duly authorized therefore by the General of the Brothers Minors through a power granted to us May 13, A.D. 1870, have erected the stations or Way of the Cross in the Mortuary Chapel of the Sisters of the Holy Names of Jesus and Mary, in the presence of Rev. S. White, Rev. Sr. Mary Peter, Superior of the Convent of St. Paul, Sr. Mary John, etc, etc.
                                B. Delorme, V.G.

B-29
Harriet
Rosina
Ouimette

On November 7, 1875, we the undersigned, pastor of St. Paul, have baptized Harriet Rosa, born on the 11th of October of the lawful marriage of Louis Hercules Ouimette and Clara Mathieu of this place. Sponsors, Charles Bergevin and Rosa Mathieu.
          Chas. L. Bergevin   Rose Bergevin
                                B. Delorme, V.G.

Page 91

M-7
Jake
Bellanger
&
Cloris
[Clarisse]
Bernier

On November 8, 1875, after the publication of one ban of marriage at our parochial mass, between Jake Bellanger of this parish of St. Paul, son of age of Frank Bellanger and the late Margaret Kingston, of the one part; and Clhoris Bernier of the same parish, daughter of age and lawful of Francis Bernier and of the late Pelage Lucier, of the second part; the dispensation of the two other bans having been granted by V.G. and no impediment whatever being found, we, the undersigned, pastor of the said parish of St. Paul, have received their mutual consent of marriage and bestowed on them the nuptial benediction in the presence of Francis Bernier, father of the bride, Antoine Seguin, Cleophas Seguin, and Mary Choquette.

Cleophas X Seguin	Jake X Bellanger
Mary Choquette	Clarice Bernier
Antoine Seguin	Francis Bernier

B. Delorme, V.G.

S-11 N.C.
Chloris
Lucier

On November 18, 1875, we the undersigned, pastor of St. Paul, have buried in the new Graveyard Chloris Lucier, lawful daughter of Joseph Lucier and Louise Martineau, deceased on the 16th instant at the age of 19 months. Present, Baptiste Bourgeau and Henry Ernst.

B. Delorme, V.G.

B-30
J.
Baptiste
Dompierre

On September 5, 1875, we the undersigned pastor of St. Paul, have baptized John Baptiste, born on the 17th of October last, of the lawful marriage of John Baptiste Dompierre and Angelie Bonenfant of this place. Sponsors, Louis Dompierre and Mary Lambert.

Mary Lambert
B. Delorme, V.G.

Recapitulation for the year 1875

Baptisms	30
Burials	11
Marriages	7
Abjuration	1

Translation of nine deceased Sisters of the Holy Names
Blessing of the Mortuary Chapel
Erection of the Ways of Cross

1876

Page 92

M-1
Frank
Lambert
&
Clementine
Mongrain

On January 1, 1876, we the undersigned pastor of St. Paul's parish, after having published twice at our parochial masses the bans of marriage of Frank Lambert of this parish, son of age and lawful of Augustin Lambert and Catherine Piche of the first part; and of Clementine Mongrain of the same parish, daughter of age and lawful of David Mongrain and Catherine Lafantaisie, of the second part; the dispensation of the third ban and of the impediment known as the Vetitum Ecclesia having been granted by us, Vicar General, have received their mutual consent of marriage and given them the nuptial benediction in the presence of Augustin Lambert, father of the bridegroom, David Mongrain, father of the bride, David Mongrain, junior, and Mary Lambert.

Mary Lambert
B. Delorme, V.G.

B-1
Joseph
Murphy

On January 2, 1876, we the undersigned pastor of St. Paul, have baptized Joseph, born on the 15th of August last, of the lawful marriage of Mathew Murphy and Helen Costello of this parish. Sponsors, Hugh Gearin and Lizzy Coleman.

Hugh B. Gearin
Eliza Coleman
B. Delorme, V.G.

B-2
Maxime
Lafontaine

On January 2, 1876, we the undersigned, pastor of St. Paul, have baptized Maxime, born on the 13th of November last, of the lawful marriage of Narcisse Lafontaine and Margaret Pichette of this parish. Sponsors, Felix

Delille and Mary Pichette.

B. Delorme, V.G.

B-3 & Ab. 1

On January 9, 1876, we the undersigned pastor of St. Paul have baptized conditionally John McLaughlin, born on the 23rd of May, 1851, of the marriage of John McLaughlin and Mary Bayley; and we have at the same time received his abjuration and profession of faith. Sponsors, Peter Kirk and Mary Connor.

John Jobe McLaughlin
Peter Kirk
Mary Connor

B. Delorme, V.G.

Page 93
B-4 Eliza Henrietta Ray

On January 9, 1876, we the undersigned, pastor of the parish of St. Paul, have baptized Eliza Henrietta, born on the 6th day of March, 1855, of the marriage of Charles Ray and Emily Eyre. Sponsors, Charles Pelland and Kathe McKay.

Eliza Henrietta Ray
Charles O. Pelland
Katie McKay

B. Delorme, V.G.

B-5 Allie Mary Ray

On the 9 January, 1876, we the undersigned, pastor of the parish of St. Paul, have baptized Allie Mary, born on the 25th of November, 1858, of the marriage of Charles Ray and Emily Eyre. Sponsors, Anthyme Charbonneau and Mary McKay.

Awntime Charbonneau   Allie Mary Ray
Mary McKay

B. Delorme, V.G.

S-1 O.C. Charles Gaston Dueuron

On January 13, 1876, we the undersigned, pastor of St. Paul, have buried in the new cemetery Charles Gaston Dueuron, deceased yesterday, at the age of 24 years. Present, Leon Delony and Prosper T Lachance.

B Delorme, V.G.

S-2 O.C. Joseph Pichette

On January 14, 1876, we the undersigned have buried in the old grave-yard Joseph Pichette, son of Roch Pichette and Victoire Despard of this parish. Present, John Patterson and Amedee Choquette.

B. Delorme, V.G.

S-3 & 4 N. C. Magdelen Dubreuil & her child

On January 22, 1876, we the undersigned pastor of St. Paul have buried Magdelen Bourgeau, wife of Frank Dubreuil of this parish, deceased Thursday last at the age of 30 years and her daughter, deceased after receiving private baptism. Witnesses, Joseph Lucier and John McGrath.

B. Delorme, V.G.

B-6 Marcel Isadore Raymond

On February 6, 1876, we the undersigned pastor of St. Paul' parish have baptized Marcel Isadore, born on the first instant, of the lawful marriage of Marcel Raymond and Odile Raymond of the said parish. Sponsors, Israel Raymond and Salome Raymond.

Salome Raymond

B. Delorme, V.G.

Page 94
S-5 N.C. William Bayley

On February 17, 1876, we the undersigned, pastor of the St. Paul's parish, have buried in the New Cemetery thereof Dr. William Bayley, deceased on the 5th instant at the age of 70 years. Present: Mrs. Jul. Bayley, his wife, Sister Mary of the Seven Dolors, Sr. Mary Peter, Dr. Brentano, Charles Pelland, and a large congregation.

B. Delorme, V.G.

B-7 Josephine Clothilda Bellique

On the 21st of February, 1876, we the undersigned, pastor of St. Paul's parish, have baptized Josephine Clothilda, born the 13th instant of the lawful marriage of Cyprien Bellique and Julienne Bergevin of this place. Sponsors, Edward Gardipie and Salome Raymond.

Edward Garipy   Salome Raymond

B. Delorme, V.G.

B-8 & S-6
Daughter
of M.
O'Loughlin

On February 23, 1876, we the undersigned pastor of St. Paul's parish have buried a daughter of Michael O'Loughlin and Elizabeth Aplin, deceased yesterday after being privately baptized and she being 22 days old. Witnesses, W. Trevor and George Aplin.

B. Delorme, V.G.

S-7 N.C.
Francis
Lefebvre

We the undersigned pastor of St. Paul's parish have buried Francis Lefebvre deceased on the 25th instant at the age of 65 years, said burial done on the 28th of February, 1876. Present, Peter Bonnin and Louis Simon.

B. Delorme, V.G.

S-8 N.C.
Magdelen
Wittman

On March 10, 1876, we the undersigned pastor of St. Paul's parish, have buried in the New Cemetery thereof Magdelen Gossman, widow of Stephen Wittman, deceased on the 8th instant at the age of 109 years old. Witnesses, Andrew Hughes and John McGrath.

B. Delorme, V.G.

S-9 N.C.
Nancy
Longtain

On March 17, 1876, we the undersigned pastor of St. Paul's parish, have buried Nancy Longtain, wife of Andrew Longtain of this place, deceased on the 15th instant at the age of 80 years. Present, Xavier Moisan and John Brentano.

B. Delorme, V.G.

B-9
Elizabeth
Dowed

On March 19, 1876, we the undersigned pastor of St. Paul's parish, have baptized Elizabeth, born on the 10th of February last, of the lawful marriage of John Dowed and Julia Pepin of this place. Sponsors, James Murphy and Elizabeth Geelan.

James C. Murphy   Elizabeth Geelan
B. Delorme, V.G.

Page 95
B-10
Florence
Gertrude
Pelland

On March 19, 1876, we the undersigned pastor of St. Paul's parish, have baptized Florence Gertrude, born on the first of February last, of the lawful marriage of Charles Pelland and Mary Coleman of Champoeg. Sponsors, James Coleman and Fanny Coleman, his mother.

James Coleman, Jr.   Fanny Coleman.
B. Delorme, V.G.

B-11
Mary
Julia
Etu

On April 2, 1876, we the undersigned pastor of the parish of St. Paul have baptized Mary Julia, born on the 27th of January of the civil marriage of Henry Etu and Archange Deshotel. Sponsors, Etienne Deshotel and Mary Magdelen Ernst.

Marie Madeshrine [?] Ernst
B. Delorme, V.G.

B-12
Margaret
Mary
Kirk

On April 3, 1876, we the undersigned pastor of St. Paul have baptized Margaret Mary, born on March 31st last, of the lawful marriage of Peter Kirk and Margaret Gogan of this place. Sponsors, Simon Connor and Lizzy Kirk.

Simon Connor   Lizzy Kirk
B. Delorme, V.G.

B-13
Valerie
Lia
Boutin

On April 9, 1876, we the undersigned pastor of St. Paul, have baptized Valerie Lian, born on the 3rd of March last of the lawful marriage of Isaac Boutin and Philomene Langlois of this place. Sponsors, Marcel Raymond and Odile Raymond.

M. J. Raymond   Odille Raymond
B. Delorme, V.G.

S-10 O.C.
Louise
Chamberland

On April 17, 1876, we the undersigned pastor of St. Paul, have buried Louise Humpherville, wife of A. Chamberland, deceased on the 15th instant, at the age of about 50 years. Witnesses, Peter Bonnin and Fr. Broulliard.

B. Delorme

B-14
Page 96
Arsinoe
Mary

On April 23, 1876, we the undersigned, pastor of St. Paul, have baptized Arsinoe Mary, born on the 30th of March last, of the lawful marriage of Roch Pichette and Victoire Despard of this place. Sponsors, Amedee

Pichette	Choquette and Mary Bernier of the same place. A. Choquette B. Delorme, V.G.
S-11 N.C. Myles McDonald	On May 1, 1876, we the undersigned, pastor of St. Paul's parish, have buried Myles McDonald of this place, deceased on the 29th of April last at the age of 70 years. Witnesses, And. Hughes, Peter Kirk, John McGrath, etc. B. Delorme, V.G.
M-2 William Hanigan & Ellen Coffey	On May 2, 1876, after having published one ban of marriage between William Hanigan, son of age of the late William and Magdelen Hanigan of the first part; and Ellen Coffey, daughter of age of Edward Coffey and the late Mary Ronan, both being of the parish of St. Paul, in the County of Marion, State of Oregon; after having moreover granted the dispensation of the two other bans and also the impediment known as the prohibition of the Church, or Vetitium Ecclesiae, no other impediment being found, and the bridegroom, the non-Catholic part, having solemnly promised beforehand to let his wife entirely free in her religious belief and practise of Christian duties, and also to have their children, if God give them any, raised in the Catholic faith; We, the undersigned Vicar General of Oregoncity and pastor of the said parish of St. Paul, have received their mutual consent of marriage and joined them in the holy bonds of matrimony in the presence of Sam Kerr, John Coffey, Mary Ann Flynn and Hannah Deloney. William Hannegan S. J. Kerr Ellen Coffey John Coffey Mrs. Mary A. Flynn B. Delorme, V.G.
B-15 J. Bapt. Bourgeau	On May 7, 1876, we the undersigned, pastor of St. Paul, have baptized John Baptist, born on the 30th day of April last, of the lawful marriage of Baptist Bourgeau and Genevieve Martineau of this place. Sponsors, Anthony Lambert and Emerance Chalifoux. B. Delorme, V.G.
Page 97 S-12 N.C. Felicite Lucier	On May 12, 1876, we the undersigned, pastor of St. Paul, have buried Felicite, lawful daughter of Joseph Lucier and Louise Martineau, deceased on the 6th instant at the age of three months. Witnesses, Xavier Martineau and Fabien Chamberlan. B. Delorme, V.G.
B-16 Marg. Aglae Ayotte	On May 14, 1876, we the undersigned pastor of St. Paul, have baptized Margaret Aglae, born on the 15th of March last, of the lawful marriage of Baptiste Ayotte and Josephine Raymond of this place. Sponsors, Francis Raymond and Odile Raymond. Frank Raymond B. Delorme, V.G.
M-3 Daniel McCann & Genevieve Herbert	On May 16, 1876, after having granted the dispensation of three bans of Marriage between Daniel McCann of this parish of St. Paul, son of age of John McCann and Annie McCormick residing in Antrim Co, Ireland, of the first part; and Genevieve Longtain, widow of Thomas Herbert, of the same parish, for the second part; no impediment whatever being found, we, the undersigned, pastor of the said parish of St. Paul, and Vicar General of the Diocese of Oregoncity, have received their mutual consent of marriage, and given them the nuptial benediction in the presence of Adolphe Jette, Thomas Longtain, Mrs. Bayley, Mrs. Toupin, Mrs. Osborn, and Mrs. Jette. Daniel McCann Adolphe Jette Genevieve Herbert Julia M. Bailey B. Delorme, V.G.
M-4 Calyxte Lebeau &	On May 22, 1876, after the publication of one ban of marriage at our parochial mass, between Calyxte Lebeau of the parish of St. Paul, son of age and lawful of Joseph Lebeau and Delphine Rinfrow residing at Maskinonge, Dominion of Canada, of one part; and Clhoris Mongrain of the same place,

Clhoris
Mongrain

daughter of age and lawful of David Mongrain and the late Catherine Lafantaisie of the other part; the dispensation of two other bans having been granted by us, and no impediment whatever being found, We, the undersigned pastor of the said parish of St. Paul, have received their mutual consent to marriage and given them the nuptial benediction in the presence of David Mongrain, father of the bride, J. B. Ayotte, David Mongrain, jun., and Mary Lambert.

Calixte Lebeau   Mary Lambert
Clhoris Mongrain
                    B. Delorme, V.G.

Page 98
B-17
Mary
Agnes
Comtois

On May 25, 1876, we undersigned have baptized Mary Agnes, born on the 26th of April last, of the lawful marriage of James Comtois and Soulange Pichette of this parish. Sponsors, Frederic Fortin and Mary Servant.
                    Frederic Fortain
                    B. Delorme, V.G.

B-18
Ignatius
McDonald
[Peter]

On May 28, 1876, we the undersigned, pastor of St. Paul, have baptized Ignatius, born on the 8th of March last of the lawful marriage of Myles McDonald and Anna Maria Galloway of this place. Sponsors, James McDonald *[sic]* & Mary McGrath.
James Coleman   Mary McGrath
                    B. Delorme, V.G.

B-19
Francis
Ed.
Smith

On June 12, 1876, we the undersigned, pastor of St. Paul, have baptized Francis Edward, born on the 9th day of January, 1875, of the lawful marriage of Francis M. Smyth and Josephine Durett of this parish. Sponsors, F. Richard Durett and Leonie Patterson.
Francis R. Durett   Mary Leona Patterson
                    B. Delorme, V.G.

S-13 O.C.
Soulange
Dompierre

On June 13, 1876, we the undersigned pastor of St. Paul have buried in the old graveyard Soulange, wife of Fr. Dompierre, deceased at St. Louis, she being about 20 years old. Witnesses, J. B. Piette and Peter Kitson.
                    B. Delorme, V.G.

S-14 N.C.
Rev. Sr.
Mary Emer-
entienne

On June 17, 1876, we the undersigned, pastor of St. Paul, have buried, in the mortuary chapel of the Srs, of the Holy Names, Sr. Mary Emerentianne, deceased at Portland on the 14th instant, she being then 36 years old, after 18 years of religious life in the said Congregation of the Holy Names of Jesus and Mary. Witnesses, Sr. Mary Mary of the seven Dolors, Sup. and Sr. Mary Peter, etc.
Sr. Mary of the Seven Dolors   Sr. M. Peter
                    B. Delorme, V.G.

Page 99
B-20
Alfred
Eugene
Feller

On June 18, 1876, we the undersigned, pastor of St. Paul, have baptized Alfred Eugene, born on the 18th of October, 1873, of the lawful marriage of Francis Feller and Rheuamah Wittney of this parish. Sponsor, Elizabeth Miller.
                    Francis Feller
                    Rheuama Feller, Witnes.
                    B. Delorme, V.G.

B-21
John
Henry
Miller

On June 18, 1876, we the undersigned, pastor of St. Paul, have baptized John Henry, born on the 11th day of November, 1875, of the lawful marriage of Jacob Miller and Elizabeth Feller. Sponsor, Francis Feller.
                    Elizabeth Miller
                    Jacob Miller, Witn.
                    B. Delorme, V.G.

B-22
Mary
Rosa
Elizabeth
Hincks

On June 23, 1876, we the undersigned, pastor of St. Paul have baptized Mary Rosa Elizabeth Hincks, daughter of Isaac Hincks and Jane Kell, she being then about 15 years old. We have stood sponsor for her, and Mrs. Adeline Manning was her godmother.
                    B. Delorme, V.G.

B-23 Wilfred Aplin	On June 25, 1876, we the undersigned, pastor of St. Paul, have baptized Wilfred, born on the 29th day of May last of the lawful marriage of George Aplin and Mary Wagner of this place. Sponsors, Simon Gregoire and Eleonore Picard. E. S. Gregoire B. Delorme, V.G.
Transla- tion 2	On June 27, 1876, we the undersigned pastor of St. Paul have solemnly transferred from the old graveyard to the new one the remains of Dr. James Shiel, deceased Jan. 3, 1853, and of Thomas Herbert, deceased on the 19th of April, 1874. Present, And. Hughes, John Brentano, Hugh Cosgrove, Dan McKay, etc. B. Delorme, V.G.
S-15 N.C. Louis Bergevin	On June 29, 1876, we the undersigned, pastor of St. Paul, have buried Louis Bergevin, deceased on the 27th day of June at the age of 68 years. Witnesses, J. B. Piette, F. X. Mathieu, James Coyle, Edward Coffey, and a large congregation.
Page 100	John B. P. Piette B. Delorme, V.G.
B-24 Inis Weston	On July 23, 1876, we the undersigned pastor of St. Paul, have baptized Inis Agnes, born on the 6th day of June last of the marriage of the late David Weston and Mary Sinclair of this place. Sponsor Mary Weston: M. J. Weston B. Delorme, V.G.
B-25 Mary Octavia Murphy	On August 28, 1876 we the undersigned have baptized Mary Octavia, born on the 21st instant of the Lawful marriage of Mathew Murphy and Ellen Costello of this place. Sponsors, James Murphy and Kathe Murphy. James Murphy Katie Murphy B. Delorme, V.G.
B-26 Elizabeth Virginia Brouillard	On September 24, 1876, we the undersigned, pastor of St. Paul, have baptized Elizabeth Virginia, born on the 19th of August last, of the lawful marriage of Frank Brouillard and Aurelie Bonnin of this place. Sponsors, Augustin Bonnin and Anastasie Bonnin. Augustine Bonin A. Bonin B. Delorme, V.G.
B-27 Rosa Zimmerman	On October 8, 1876, we the undersigned pastor of St. Paul's parish have baptized Rosa, born on the 6th of June last of the lawful marriage of Peter Zimmerman and Christina Seelig of this place. Sponsor, Minnie Seelig who signed with us. Minnie Seelig Peter Zimmerman B. Delorme
M-5 Francis Bernier & Mary Lambert	On October 10, 1876, after the publication of one ban of marriage in the parochial churches of St. Paul and St. Louis, between Francis Bernier of the parish of St. Louis, son of age and lawful of Francis Bernier, domiciled in the parish of St. Paul, and of the late Pelagie Lucier, for the first part; and Mary Lambert, of the parish of St. Paul, daughter of age and lawful of Augustin Lambert and Catherine Piche, of the same place, for the second part; the dispensation of the two other bans having been granted by us, Vic. Gen. of the Diocese of Oregoncity, and as no impediment whatever being discovered, we the undersigned pastor of the said parish of St. Paul have received their mutual consent of marriage and have imparted to them the nuptial benediction in the presence of Augustin Lambert, father of the bride, Amedee Choquette, Guilbert Lambert and Genevieve Bernier. A. Choquette Frank Bernier Jane Bernier Mary Lambert B. Delorme, V.G.
Page 101 B-25 Arthur Bergevin	On October 15, 1876, we the undersigned pastor of St. Paul's Church have baptized Arthur Leslie, born on the 1st instant of the lawful marriage of Charles Bergevin and Rosa Mathieu of this place. Sponsors, Anthyme

Charbonneau and Rosa Aussan, grandmother of the child.

A. Charbonneau

B. Delorme, V.G.

S-16 N.C.
Louis
Pichette

On October 30, 1876, we the undersigned have buried Louis Pichette of this parish of St. Paul, deceased on the 28th Inst. at the age of 79 years. Witnesses, Felix Delille and Dieudonne Manaigre.

B. Delorme, V.G.

S-17 N.C.
Child of P.
Geelan

On November 7, 1876, we the undersigned, pastor of St. Paul, have buried a little girl, lawful daughter of Patrick Geelan and Elizabeth Ady of this parish, deceased a few hours after being born, she having received private baptism. Present, John Dowd and Leo Patterson.

B. Delorme, V.G.

M-6
Napoleon
Lafontaine
&
Ellen
Sharp

On November 11, 1876, after having granted the dispensation of three bans of marriage and no impediment being discovered, we the undersigned, pastor of the parish of St. Paul, have received the mutual consent of marriage of Napoleon Lafontaine, widower of Bibiane Lafantaisie, for the first part, of the same parish; and Helen Sharp, daughter of age of Mr. Sharp for the second part; and have given them the nuptial benediction in the presence of Hugh Cosgrove and John Wittman.

H. Cosgrove   Napoleon Lafontaine

J. P. Wittman   Ellen Sharp

[no priest's signature]

B-29
Ed.
William
Hanigan

On December 10, 1876, we the undersigned, pastor of the parish of St. Paul, have baptized Edward William, born on the second instant of the lawful marriage of William Hanigan and Ellen Coffey of this place. Sponsors, John Coffey and Catherine Kerr.

John Coffey   Catherine Kerr

B. Delorme, V.G.

Page 102
B-30
Mary
Susan
Labonte

On November 15, 1876, we the undersigned, pastor of the parish of St. Paul, have baptized Mary Susan, born on the 9th of August last of the marriage of Alexander Labonte and Clementine Lachance Pepin, of this place. Sponsors, Pierre Vivet and Flavie Petit.

Flavie Petit   Peter Vivette

B. Delorme, V.G.

N.C.
S-18, 19
Celecte
Picard
and her
little
girl

On December 26, 1876, we the undersigned, pastor of St. Paul, have buried Celeste Rochbrune, wife of Henry Picard of this place, deceased on the 24th instant at the age of 42 years, and we also have buried her child, deceased after being baptized. Witnesses, Adolphe Jette and Amedee Seguin.

Amedee Seguin   Adolphe Jette

B. Delorme, V.G.

Total for the year 1876

Baptisms	30
Marriages	6
Burials	17
Abjurations	1

1877

B-1 & 2
Emma
Hileary
Charles
Hileary

On January 7, 1877, we the undersigned, pastor of St. Paul's parish, have baptized Emma, born June 30, 1873, and Charles, born August 22, 1875, of the civil marriage of George Hileary and Angelie Laframboise, Nez Perce Co., Wash. Ter. Sponsors of Emma, Peter Bonnin and Mary Fortain; Sponsors of Charles, Augustin Raymond and Salome Raymond.

Augustin Raymond   Salome Raymond

B. Delorme, V.G.

S-1 O.C.
Francis
Bernier

On January 12, 1877, we the undersigned, pastor of St. Paul's parish, have buried Francis Bernier, deceased on the 10th instant, at the age of 70 years. Witnesses, Dieudonne Manaigre and Felix Delille.

B. Delorme, V.G.

Page 103

M-1
Henry
Cameron
&
Eleonore
Picard

On January 22, 1877, after the publication of one ban of marriage having been made at our parochial mass, between Henry Cameron of this parish of St. Paul, son of age and lawful of Thomas Cameron and Mary Ramsay, residing at Leeds, District of Quebec, Dominion of Canada, for the first part; and Eleonore Picard of the same parish of St. Paul, daughter of age and lawful of Honore Picard and of the late Celeste Rochbrune, for the second part; the dispensations of the two other bans having been granted by us, Vicar General of the Diocese of Oregoncity, and no impediment whatever being discovered, We, the undersigned pastor of the said parish of St. Paul, have received their mutual consent of marriage and given them the nuptial benediction in the presence of Hugh Cosgrove and James Patterson, who have signed with us and the bridegroom.

H. Cosgrove　　　　　　　Harry Cameron
J. C. Patterson　　　　　　Eleonore Picard
　　　　　　B. Delorme, V.G.

S-2 N.C.
Sister
Mary
Cecelia

On January 23, 1877, we the undersigned have buried in the mortuary chapel of the Sisters of the Holy Names of Jesus and Mary, Sister Mary Cecelia, deceased on the 20th instant at the age of 21 years, in the presence of Rev. Father Vermesh, Rev. Sr. of the Seven Dolors, Rev. Sr. Mary Peter, and of a large attendance.

Rev. P. A. Vermeersch, P.
Sister Mary, Sup.　　　　　　Sr. Mary Peter
　　　　　　B. Delorme, V.G.

B-3
Eugene
Clarence
Davidson

On January 28, 1877, we the undersigned, pastor of St. Paul's parish, have baptized Eugene Clarence, born on the 29th of December last of the lawful marriage of Frank Davidson and Annie Coleman of this place. Sponsors, William Kaiser and Elizabeth Coleman.

W. M. Kaiser　　　　　　Elizabeth Coleman
　　　　　　B. Delorme, V.G.

S-3 N.C.
Joseph
Longtain

On February 5, 1877, we the undersigned, pastor of the parish of St. Paul, have buried Joseph Longtain, deceased on the 3rd instant, aged 15 months, son of Thomas Longtain and Matilde Rivet of this parish. Witnesses, Dan McCann and Joseph Howard.

　　　　　　B. Delorme, V.G.

Page 104

S-4 N.C.
J. B.
Bourgeau

On February 21, 1877, we the undersigned, pastor of St. Paul's parish, have buried John Baptist Bourgeau, son of B. Bourgeau and Genevieve Martineau of this place, deceased yesterday, aged about 11 months. Present, Xavier Martineau and Frank Dubreuil.

　　　　　　B. Delorme, V.G.

B-4
Mary
Frances
Delia
Choquette

On February 25, 1877, we the undersigned pastor of St. Paul's parish, have baptized Mary Frances Delia, born on the 18th instant of the lawful marriage of Amedee Choquette and Mary Bernier. Sponsors, Jake Bellanger and Mary Lambert.

Mary Bernier
　　　　　　B. Delorme, V.G.

S-5 N.C.
Esther
Pichette

On March 3, 1877, we the undersigned pastor of St. Paul's parish have buried Esther Pichette, lawful daughter of Roch Pichette and Victoire Frederic of this place, deceased yesterday morning at the age of 17 years. Present, Amedee Choquette and Dieudonne Manaigre.

　　　　　　B. Delorme, pastor of St. Paul

B-5
Mary
Lucile
Delille

On March 15, 1877, we the undersigned have baptized Mary Lucile, born on the 7th instant of the lawful marriage of Felix Delille and Mary Pichette of this parish. Sponsors, Narcisse Lafontaine and Margaret Pichette.

　　　　　　B. Delorme, V.G.

S-6 N.C.
Michael
O'Loughlin

On March 23, 1877, we the undersigned have buried Michael O'Loughlin, deceased on the 21st instant, at the age of 50 years. Witnesses, John McGrath and John Dowd.

　　　　　　B. Delorme, V.G.

B-6
Alvina
Mary
Jette

On April 1, 1877, we the undersigned, pastor of St. Paul's parish have baptized Mary Alvina, born on the 2nd of March last of the lawful marriage of Adolphe Jette and Margaret Liard of this place. Sponsors, Henry Cameron and Eleonore Picard his wife.
Harry Cameron
B. Delorme, V.G.

S-7 O.C.
Mary
Genevieve
Bellanger
Page 105

On March 10, 1877, we the undersigned, pastor of the parish of St. Paul, have buried Mary Genevieve, daughter of Jake Bellanger and Chloris Bernier, deceased on the 8th instant at the age of 8 months. Witnesses, Amedee Choquette and Roch Pichette.

B-7
Mary
Patricia
Malvina
Lavigneur

On April 13, 1877, we the undersigned pastor of St. Paul's have baptized Mary Patricia Malvina, illegitimate daughter of Josette Lavigneur, born about 3 months ago. Sponsors, Cuthbert Lambert and Frances Piette.
B. Delorme, V.G.

B-8
Frank
Chalifoux

On May 6, 1877, we the undersigned pastor of St. Paul have baptized Frank, born on the 23rd of April last of the lawful marriage of Andre Chalifoux and Emerance Mongrain of this place. Sponsors, Amable Bergevin and Josephine Mongrain.
B. Delorme, V.G.

B-9
Virginia
Lebeau

On May 6, 1877, we the undersigned pastor of St. Paul have baptized Virginia, born on the 17th of March last of the lawful marriage of Callyxte Lebeau and Clhoris Mongrain of Chehalem Valley. Sponsors, Frank Lambert and Clementine Mongrain.
B. Delorme, V.G.

B-10
J. B.
Dupre

On May 19, 1877, we the undersigned pastor of St. Paul have baptized Jean Baptiste, born on the 15th instant of the lawful marriage of Charles Dupre and Catherine Chalifoux. Sponsors, J. B. Bourgeau and Genevieve Martineau.
B. Delorme, V.G.

B-11
Joseph
Aug.
Lucier

On May 22, 1877, we the undersigned pastor of St. Paul's parish have baptized Joseph Aug., born on the 29th of April last of the lawful marriage of Joseph Lucier and of Louise Martineau of this place. Sponsors, Charles Lebrun and Dorilda Gagnon.
Charles Lebrun   Dorilda Gagnon
B. Delorme, V.G.

B-12
Mary
Virginia
O'Loughlin

On May 31, 1877, we the undersigned pastor of St. Paul have baptized Mary Virginia, born on the 14th day of April last of the lawful marriage of Michael O'Loughlin, now deceased, and Elizabeth Aplin of this place. Sponsors, George Aplin and Mary Wagner.
G. C. Aplin
B. Delorme, V.G.

B-13
Andrew
Horner

On June 3, 1877, we the undersigned pastor of St. Paul have baptized Andrew Horner, born on the 31st of March, 1874, of the civil marriage of Simon Horner and Margaret Lacourse of Yam Hill County. Sponsors, Clara Lacourse and Zenaide Gregoire.
Zenaide Gregoire
B. Delorme, V.G.

Page 106
B-14
Aloysius
Anthyme
Ernst

On June 10, 1877, we the undersigned pastor of St. Paul have baptized Aloysius Anthyme, born on the 29th of May last, of the lawful marriage of Henry Ernst and Magdelen Vesper of this place. Sponsors, Anthyme Charbonneau and Lizzy Kirk . . . Charbonneau.
Lizzie Kirk
B. Delorme, V.G.

B-15 & Abj.
William
Hunter

On June 23, 1877, we the undersigned have baptized conditionally William Hunter, lawful son of Robert Hunter and Elizabeth Train, born on the 3rd of August, 1857, and moreover having made his abjuration of heresy and profession of faith, we have received into the bosom of the Catholic Faith. Sponsors, Charles Bergevin and Rosa Mathieu his wife.

Charles Bergevin   William Hunter
Rosa Bergevin
B. Delorme, V.G.

B-16
Philomene
Dompierre

On June 24, 1877, we, the undersigned pastor of St. Paul, have baptized Philomene, born on the 10th day of June last of the lawful marriage of J. Baptiste Dompierre and Angelique Bonenfant of this place. Sponsors, J. B. Piette and Rose Aussant.

John B. P. Piette
B. Delorme, V.G.

1st Commun-
ion   22

This is to certify that on June 24, 1877, the following persons have received their first communion in the Church of St. Paul.

Joseph McGrath	Cassie Murphy
Peter Fitzgerald	Lizzy Kennedy
Edward Mathieu	Florence Bernier
William Hunter	Mary Amanda Seguin
Jacob Walker	Blandine Manning
Alfred Aplin	Mary J. Davidson
Bernard Smyth	Theresa Dodson
George Connor	Elizabeth Sax
Severe Manaigre	Thecla McDonald
Augustin Lambert	Pauline Picard
Thomas Richie	Archange Dupre

B. Delorme, V.G.

Page 107
57
Confirmation

This is to certify that on June 24, 1877, the following persons were confirmed by the Most Rev. F. Norbert Blanchet, in the church of St. Paul.

Ferdinand Edward Wirfs	Elizabeth Mary Geelan
Edward Mathieu	Mary Josephine Wirfs
William Mathew Hunter	Agnes Margaret Jackson
William Stephen Murphy	Eleonore Eliz. Wall
Mathew Philippe Murphy	Caroline Victoria Kennedy
Bernard Smyth	Mary Magd. Choquette
Jacob Walker	Magdelen Blandina Raymond
Peter Joseph Fitzgerald	Cassie Murphy
Alfred Aplin	Elizabeth Cecelia Kennedy
Joseph McGrath	Mary Davidson
George Connor	Mary Amanda Fel. Seguin
Robert Daniel Cook	Blandine Carole Manning
Thomas Joseph Kerr	Elizabeth Blandina Sax
Albert Murphy	Thecla Blandina McDonald
Francis Ridder	Florence Theresa Bernier
John Job Jonas McLoughlin	Pauline Mary Picard
Jacob Aplin	Ellen Cecelia Dowd
Edward Bergevin	Lucy Elizabeth Connor
George Picard	Theresa Cecelia Manning
Etienne Lucier	Mary Cook
Daniel Lucier	Mary Magd. Ernst
Alphonse Boutin	Mary Frances Dowd
Alfred Lambert	Archange Fel. Dupre
Francis Mongrain	Rosa Picard
Adolphe Bapt. Chamberlan	Clementina Bourgeau
Jeremias John Labonte	Theresa Mary Dodson
Narcisse Chamberlan	
Augustin Lambert	
Severe Manaigre	
John Adolphe Picard	
Thomas Richi	

B. Delorme, V.G.

Benediction of the New Graveyard

On June 24, 1877, we the undersigned, Archbishop of the Diocese of Oregoncity, have solemnly blessed the new cemetery of the parish of St. Paul, in the presence of V. Gen. B. Delorme, Vic. Gen. Rev. Father Jos. Sam. White and of a very large congregation.

B. Delorme, V.G.
J. S. White, Pt.
F. N. Blanchet
Archbp. of O.C.

B-17 Margaret Prevost

On July 1, 1877, we the undersigned, pastor of St. Paul, have baptized Margaret, born on the 2nd of June last of the lawful marriage of Louis Prevot and Pauline Lefort of this place. Sponsors, Alphonse Seguin and Rose Seguin.

Rosa Seguin
B. Delorme, V.G.

Page 108 B-18 Sara Julia Bernier

On June 1, 1877, we the undersigned, pastor of St. Paul's, have baptized Sara Julia, born on the 25th of May last, of the lawful marriage of Norbert Bernier and Theresa Rivet of this place. Sponsors, Charles Pelland and Mary Choquette.

Chs. O. Pelland   Mary Choquette
B. Delorme, V.G.

B-19 Ellen Eberhard

On the 17th day of July, 1877, we the undersigned, have baptized Ellen Eberhard, lawful daughter of Bernard Eberhard and Elizabeth Stalie, born on the 14th of September, 1854. Sponsors, James Coyle and Mary McKay.

J. J. Coyle   Mary McKay
[No priest's signature]

M-2 Alexander Coyle & Ellen Eberhard

On July 17, 1877, after the publication of one ban of Marriage between Alexander Coyle, son of age of James Coyle and of the late Charlotte Scot, of the parish of St. Paul, for the first part; and Ellen Eberhard of the same place, daughter of age of Bernard Eberhard and Elizabeth Stalie for the second part, the dispensation of the two other bans having been granted by us, Vic. Gen. of the Diocese of Oregoncity, and no impediment whatever being found, we the undersigned, pastor of the said parish of St. Paul, have received their mutual consent of marriage and have given them the nuptial benediction in the presence of James Coyle the bridegroom man and Mary McKay the bridemaid and of many others.

James J. Coyle   Alexander Coyle
Mary McKay   Ellen Eberhard
B. Delorme, V.G.

S-8 N.C. Cecile Dubreuil

On July 20, 1877, we the undersigned have buried Cecile daughter of Fr. Dubreuil and Magdelen Bourgeau, deceased yesterday age 3 years and 5 months. Present, Jo Lucier and Dan Lucier.

B. Delorme, V.G.

Page 109 B-20 Remy Lambert

On August 26, 1877, we the undersigned, pastor of St. Paul's parish have baptized Remy, born on the 22nd instant of the lawful marriage of Frank Lambert and Clementine Mongrain of this place. Sponsors, David Mongrain and Catherine Piche.

B. Delorme, V.G.

S-9 R. Pichette's child

On August 21, 1877, we have buried a son of Roch Pichette and Victoire Frederic his wife, deceased the day before, after being privately baptized, at the age of 8 days. Witness, Henry Ernst.

V. Delorme, V.G.

M-3 John Scollard & Alice Kelly

On September 4, 1877, after the publication of one ban of marriage between John Scollard of this parish of St. Paul, son of age and lawful of Maurice Scollard and Margaret Connor for the first part; and Alice Kelly of the same parish, daughter of age and lawful of Patrick Kelly, deceased, and of Rose Kennedy, residing at Castleray, County of Donegal, Ireland, for the second part; the dispensation of the two other bans having been granted by us, V.G. of the Diocese of Oregoncity, and no impediment whatever being found, we the undersigned, pastor of the said parish of St. Paul, have received their mutual consent of marriage and given them the nuptial benediction in the presence of William McKay, John McCormick, Sarah Kennedy and Mary Schollard, who have signed with us along with the newly married couple.

W. R. McKay   John Scollard
J. H. McCormick   Alice Kelly
Sarah Kennedy
Mary Scollard

B. Delorme, V.G.

B-21 William Nicholas Wittman

On September 9, 1877, we the undersigned, pastor of St. Paul's parish, have baptized William Nicholas born on the 7th instant of the lawful marriage of John P. Wittmann and Catherine Smyth of this place. Sponsors, Nicholas Wittmann and Magdelen Vesper.

Nicholas Wittmann   M. Vesper

B. Delorme, V.G.

Page 110
B-22 Louis Wilfred Lafontaine

On September 17, 1877, we the undersigned, pastor of St. Paul have baptized Louis Wilfred born on the 7th instant of the lawful marriage of Napoleon Lafontaine and Helen Sharp of this place. Sponsors, Charles Prevot and Pauline Prevot.

B. Delorme, V.G.

S-10 Sedec Raymond

On September 23, 1877, we the undersigned pastor of St. Louis have buried Sedec Raymond, son of Marcel Raymond and Odile Raymond of this parish, deceased on the 21st instant, aged 18 months. Witnesses, Augustus Raymond and Cuthbert Lambert.

B. Delorme, V.G.

O.C. S-11 & 12 Archange & Catherine Kittson

On October 28, 1877, we the undersigned have buried Archange and Catherine, lawful daughters of Peter Kitson and Angelie Dupre, deceased on the 26th instant aged 10 and 6 years respectively. Witnesses, David Mongrain and Andre Chalifoux.

B. Delorme, V.G.

S-13 O.C. Rose Justine Kitson

On October 29, 1877, we the undersigned, pastor of St. Paul, have buried Rose Justine, lawful daughter of Peter Kitson and Angelie Dupre of this place, deceased yesterday, aged 4 years. Witnesses, And. Chalifoux and David Mongrain.

B. Delorme, V.G.

M-4 Charles Wilson & Elizabeth O'Loughlin

On November 9, 1877, we the undersigned, pastor of St. Paul and Vicar General of Oregoncity, after granting the dispensation of three bans of marriage and also that of the impediment known as *Vetitium Ecclesiae* or prohibition of the Church, have received the mutual consent of matrimony of Charles Wilson of this parish; son of age of Charles Wilson and Hannah Sublem, residing in Stockholm, Sweden, for the first part; and of Elizabeth Aplin, widow of the late Michael O'Loughlin of the said parish of St. Paul for the second part; and joined them in the bonds of lawful wedlock in the presence of George Aplin and Mary Aplin parents of the bride; and moreover the said Charles Wilson, the non-Catholic part has solemnly promised beforehand that he would let his wife entirely free in the practise of her religion and have the children, if he has any, raised according to the faith and duties of the Catholic Church.

Carsius   G. C. Aplin
Mrs. C. Wilson   Mary Aplin

B. Delorme, V.G.

Page 111
B-23 Felix B. Lafontaine

On November 11, 1877, we the undersigned pastor of St. Paul have baptized Felix Bellani, born on the 2nd instant of the lawful marriage of Narcisse Lafontaine and Margaret Pichette of this place. Sponsors, Dieudonne Manaigre and Emilie Pichette.

B. Delorme, V.G.

S-14 N.C.
Charles
Dupre

On November 11, 1977, we the undersigned, pastor of St. Paul, have buried Charles Dupre, son of Charles Dupre and Catherine Chalifoux of this place, deceased on the 9th instant, aged 2 years and 5 months. Witnesses, Frank Lambert and Thomas McGrath.

B. Delorme, V.G.

S-15 O.C.
Child of
Denoipl

On November 17, 1877, we, the undersigned, have buried a lawful child of Anton Denoipl and Philomene Petit, deceased on the 15th instant, after being privately baptized by us. Witnesses, Louis Labonte and Henry Ernst.

B. Delorme, V.G.

B-24
Helen
Denoipl

On November 25, 1877, we the undersigned, pastor of St. Paul, have baptized Helen, born on the 23rd instant of the lawful marriage of Anton Denoipl and Philomene Petit of this place. Sponsors, George Picard and Flavie Petit.

Flavie Petit

B. Delorme, V.G.

B-25
Martha
Jane
Hughes

On December 9, 1877, we the undersigned pastor of St. Paul have baptized Martha Jane born this morning of the lawful marriage of Andrew Hughes and Rosy Connor, of this place. Sponsors, Matthew Connor and Martha Connor.

Matthew Connor   Martha Connor

B. Delorme, V.G.

S-16 N.C.
Child of
F. Delille

On December 10, 1877, we have buried a child of Felix Delille and Mary Pichette his wife, born and deceased yesterday after being privately baptized. Witnesses, D. Manaigre and Henry Ernst.

B. Delorme, V.G.

Page 112
B-26
Edward
Kitson

On December 13, 1877, we the undersigned, pastor of St. Paul's parish, have baptized Edward, born on the 4th of November last, of the lawful marriage of Peter Kitson and Angelique Dupre of this place. Sponsors, Dr. Brentano and Josephine Mongrain.

J. P. J. Brentano   Josephine Mongrain

B. Delorme, V.G.

S-17 O.C.
Edward
Kitson

On December 14, 1877, we the undersigned have buried Edward Kitson, son of Peter Kitson and Angelique Dupre, his wife, deceased yesterday at the age of 5 weeks. Witnesses, David Mongrain and Charles Dupre.

B. Delorme, V.G.

S-18 N.C.
Sr. Mary
Raphael

On December 18, 1877, we the undersigned, pastor of the parish of St. Paul, have buried in the mortuary chapel of the Sisters of the Holy Names of Jesus and Mary, Sister Mary Raphael, deceased on the 15th instant, aged years, in the presence of Rev. Father Thibau, Rev. Sr. Mary Margaret, Rev. Sr. Mary of Alcantara, John D. Kennedy, and Bridget Kennedy, parents of the deceased, and of a large attendance.

G. C. Thibau, pr.

B. Delorme, V.G.

S-19 N.C.
Margaret
Marshal

On December 15, 1877, we the undersigned pastor of St. Paul have buried Margaret Marshal, a niece of J. B. Piette and Frances Piette, deceased on the 13th at the age of 18 years. Witnesses, Peter Kirk and Peter Bonnin.

B. Delorme, V.G.

Total for the year 1877

Baptisms	26
Abjuration	1
Marriages	4
Burials or Sepultures	19
First Communions	25
Confirmations	57
Easter Communions	320
Communions at Christmas 1875	175

Names to be found
in another book

1878

Page 113
S-1 N.C.

On January 9, 1878, we the undersigned, pastor of St. Paul, have buried

Mary Mullen	Mary Mullen, widow of N. Keating and Thomas Mullen, deceased on the 7th instant, aged 74 years. Witnesses, Peter Kirk and John McGrath. <div align="center">B. Delorme, V.G.</div>
B-1 James Joseph Hanigan	On January 13, 1878, we the undersigned pastor of St. Paul, have baptized James Joseph, born on the 4th instant of the lawful marriage of William Hanigan and Ellen Coffey of this place. Sponsors, John D. Kennedy and Bridget Kennedy. <div align="center">B. Delorme, V.G.</div>
B-2 Mary Melicia Chalifoux	On January 13, 1878, we the undersigned, pastor of St. Paul, have baptized Mary Melicia, born on the 17th of December last, of the lawful marriage of Louis Chalifoux and Julienne Picard, of this parish. Sponsors, Peter Chalifoux and Flavie Petit. <div align="center">B. Delorme, V.G.</div>
M-1 Alexander Labonte & Clementine Lachance	On January 28, 1878, we have received the mutual consent of marriage of Alexandre Labonte, he being on the point of death, and of Clementine Lachance, of Yam Hill County, and given them nuptial benediction in the presence of Julianna Vivet. <div align="center">B. Delorme, V.G.</div>
B-3 Francis J. McGrath	On January 30, 1878, we the undersigned, pastor of the parish of St. Paul, have baptized Francis James, born yesterday of the lawful marriage of John McGrath and Mary Hughes of this place. Sponsors, James Coyle and Elizabeth Leonard his wife. James Coyle Elizabeth Coyle <div align="center">B. Delorme, V.G.</div>
B-4 Charles Ruben Bergevin	On February 17, 1878, we the undersigned pastor of St. Paul have baptized Charles Ruben, born on the 5th of this month of the lawful marriage of Charles Bergevin and Rosa Mathieu of this place. Sponsors, J. B. Bergevin and Clara Ouimette. J. B. Bergevin Clara Ouimette <div align="center">B. Delorme</div>
B-5 Mary E. D. Bellanger	On February 23, 1878, we the undersigned, pastor of St. Paul, have baptized Mary Euphrasia D., born on the 13th instant of the lawful marriage of Jacob Bellanger and Chloris Bernier, of this place. Sponsors, Amedee Choquette and Mary Choquette. Amedee Choquette Mary Choquette <div align="center">B. Delorme, V.G.</div>
Page 114 B-6 Louis Zetique Comtois	On February 24, 1878, we the undersigned, pastor of St. Paul, have baptized Louis Zetique, born on the 4th instant of the lawful marriage of James Comtois and Soulange Pichette of this place. Sponsors, Amedee Choquette and Mary Bernier. <div align="center">A Choquette B. Delorme, V.G.</div>
B-7 Mary Rosa Veronica Dowd	On February 25, 1878, we the undersigned, pastor of St. Paul, have baptized Mary Rosa Veronica, born yesterday, of the lawful marriage of John Dowd and Julia Lachance, otherwise Pepin, of this place. Sponsors, Emmet R. Kirk and Lizzy Kirk. Robert Kirk Lizzie Kirk <div align="center">B. Delorme, V.G.</div>
B-8 Mary Louise Bourgeau	On March 10, 1878, we the undersigned, pastor of St. Paul, have baptized Mary Louise, born on the 23rd of February last, of the lawful marriage of B. Bourgeau and Genevieve Martineau of this place. Sponsors, Alonzo Bonnin and Angelique Dupre. <div align="center">B. Delorme, V.G.</div>
B-9 Mary Eliza Cameron	On March 17, 1878, we the undersigned, pastor of St. Paul, have baptized Mary Eliza, born on the 26th of January last, of the lawful marriage of Henry Cameron and Eleonore Picard of this place. Sponsors, Adolphe Jette and Margaret Liard, his wife. Adolphe Jette Margaret Liard <div align="center">B. Delorme, V.G.</div>

S-2 N.C.
Moses
Lacourse

On March 23, 1878, we the undersigned, pastor of St. Paul, have buried Moses Lacourse, son of the late Theodore Lacourse and Ellen Bourgeau, deceased at Champoeg on the day before, aged about 20 years. Witnesses, J. B. Piette and Henry Ernst.

B. Delorme, V.G.

S-2 O.C.
Narcisse
Chamberland

On March 31, 1878, we the undersigned, pastor of St. Paul, have buried Narcisse Chamberlan, son of A. Chamberlan and Louise Humpherville, deceased on the 29th instant, aged about 17 years. Witnesses, Anthyme Charbonneau and Jack Bellanger.

B. Delorme, V.G.

B-10
Sara
Jane
Longtain

On March 7, 1878, we the undersigned have baptized Sara Jane, born on the first day of October last of the lawful marriage of Thomas Longtain and Mathilda Rivet of this parish. Sponsors, Michael McPartland and Minnie Jette.

Minnie Jette

Page 115

B. Delorme, V.G.

B-11
James
Patrick
Geelan

On April 21, 1878, we the undersigned have baptized James Patrick, born on the 19th day of March last of the lawful marriage of Patrick Geelan and Elizabeth Ady of this parish, St. Paul. Sponsors, Edward Geelan, and Mary Agnes Goodrich.

Edward Geelan

B. Delorme, V.G.

B-12
Louis
Gustave
Bellique

On April 21, 1878, we the undersigned, pastor of St. Paul's parish, have baptized Louis Gustave, born on the 9th instant of the lawful marriage of Cyprian Bellique and Julienne Bergevin of this place. Sponsors, J. B. Bergevin and Josephine Mongrain.

J. B. Bergevin   Josephine Mongrain

B. Delorme, V.G.

B-13
William
Linus
Smyth

On April 28, 1878, we the undersigned pastor of the parish of St. Paul have baptized William Linus, born on the 13th instant of the lawful marriage of Francis Smyth and Ellen Nolan of this place. Sponsors, William J. Trevor and Kathe Connor.

William Trevor   Katie Connor

B. Delorme, V.G.

B-14
Julia
Ayot

On May 26, 1878, we the undersigned pastor of St. Paul have baptized Julia, born on the 11th instant, of the lawful marriage of Baptist Ayot and Josephine Raymond of this place. Sponsors, Augustine Raymond and Salome Raymond.

Augustin Raymond   Salome Raymond.

B. Delorme, V.G.

B-15
Mary
Parisot

On June 9, 1878, we the undersigned pastor of St. Paul have baptized mary, born on the 20th of August last, of the lawful marriage of Louis Parisot and Ellen Larrison of Lynn County, Oregon. Sponsors, John Hubbard Larrison and Cecile Lucier.

John Hubard Larison

B. Delorme, V.G.

First
Communion

On the 30th day of June, 1878, the following have made their first communion:

Alfred Mathew	Esther Comtois
Robert Cook	Maggie Lucier
Alfred Patterson	Mary Fr. Pichette
Herman Hecker	Mary Hecker
Albert Murphy	Mary Cook
Edward Kennedy	Mrs. Ellen Coyle
Thomas Kerr	Rosa Picard
Peter Bernier	Sara Osborn
John Picard	Mary Ernst
Alphonse Boutin	Mary Wassenhove
James R. Pichette	Josephine Wassenhove

Page
116

B-16
 Charles
 H.
 Scollard
	On July 23, 1878, we the undersigned have baptized Charles Henry, born on the 5th instant of the lawful marriage of John Scollard and Alice Kelly of this parish. Sponsors, Nicholas Schollard and Annie Johnson.
	     Nicholas Schollard Annie Johnson
	               B. Delorme, V.G.

B-16
Charles
H.
Scollard

On July 23, 1878, we the undersigned have baptized Charles Henry, born on the 5th instant of the lawful marriage of John Scollard and Alice Kelly of this parish. Sponsors, Nicholas Schollard and Annie Johnson.
Nicholas Schollard   Annie Johnson
        B. Delorme, V.G.

S-4
Mary
Lucier

On August 10, 1878, we the undersigned have buried Mary Lucier, daughter of Joseph Lucier and Louise Martineau, deceased on the 8th instant, aged about 11 years. Witnesses, Louis Chalifoux and Henry Ernst.
        B. Delorme, V.G.

B-17, 18,
19, 20
Otto H.
Hohbach
Ernest L.
Hohbach
Henry J.
Hohbach
Jerome
Hohbach

On August 11, 1878, we the undersigned pastor of St. Paul have baptized Otto Henry, born March 11th, 1870, Ernest Louis, born on July 3rd, 1872, Henry Joseph, born on June 27, 1874, and Jerome, born on the 27th of November, 1876, of the lawful marriage of Herman Hohbach and Magdelen Weigle, of Butteville. Sponsors, Henry Ernst for Otto, Anthyme Charbonneau for Ernest, Agnes Jackson for Henry, and Mrs. Mary Jackson for Jerome.
  Henry Ernst   Agnes Jackson
  A. Charbonneau   Mary Jackson
  H. Hohbach   [sig. in German]
        B. Delorme, V.G.

B-21
Mary
Salome
Hockin

On September 1, 1878, we the undersigned pastor of St. Paul have baptized Mary Salome, born on October 11th, 1877, of the civil marriage of Jabes Hockin, now residing in San Francisco, and Alice Bequette, now residing at this place. Sponsors, Anthyme Charbonneau and Salome Raymond.
  Antime Charbonneau   Salome Raymond
        B. Delorme, V.G.

B-21 *[sic]*
Page 117
John
Henry
[Woods]

On September 22, 1878, we the undersigned, pastor of St. Paul's parish, have baptized John Henry, born on May 6th last, of the lawful marriage of George W Woods and Helen Rochbrune of this place. Sponsors, Joseph Rochbrune and Angelica Dupre.
  Joseph Rochbrune   Joshua Woods
        B. Delorme, V.G.

S-5 O.C.
Flavie
Petit

On September 25, 1878, we the undersigned, pastor of St. Paul, have buried Flavie Petit, deceased the day before yesterday, aged about 25 years. Witnesses, Louis Chalifoux and Henry Ernst.
        B. Delorme, V.G.

B-22
Josephine
Ady

On October 6, 1878, we the undersigned have baptized Josephine Ady of this parish, daughter of Robert Ady and Mary Ann Michel, born September 11, 1861. Sponsors, Patrick Geelan and Elizabeth Ady.
  Robert Geelan   Elizabeth Geelan   Josephine Ady
        B. Delorme, V.G.

B-23
Annie
Edna
Davidson

On October 6, 1878, we the undersigned pastor of St. Paul have baptized Annie Edna, born on the 4th of September last, of the lawful marriage of Frank Davidson and Annie Coleman of this place. James Murphy and Bridget McDonald have been sponsors.
  James c. Murphy   Bridget McDonald
        B. Delorme, V.G.

B-24
Ferdinand
Giacoma
Gothard
Rotto

On November 3, 1878, we the undersigned, pastor of St. Paul, have baptized Ferdinand Giacomo Gothard, born on the 8th of March of the lawful marriage of Joseph Rotto and Felicita Arriotta, of this parish. Sponsors, Gothard Quaglia and Amelia Rotto.   Gothard Quaglia,   Amelia Rotto,
  Rotto, Guiseppi   Ariotti, Felicita   Rotto, Pietro
        B. Delorme, V.G.

B-25
Mary
Catherine
Genevieve
Bernier

On November 10, 1878, we the undersigned have baptized Mary Catherine Genevieve, born on the second instant, of the lawful marriage of Francis Bernier and Mary Lambert of this place. Sponsors, Augustin Lambert and Catherine Piche.
        B. Delorme, V.G.

B-26
Alphonse
Remy
Aplin

On November 24, 1878, we the undersigned pastor of St. Paul, have baptized Alphonse Remy, born on the 10th of October last, of the lawful marriage of George Aplin and Mary Wagner of this place. Sponsors, Henry Ernst and Magdelen Vesper his wife.

H. Ernst   Maderlaine Vesper
                    B. Delorme, V.G.

Page 118
B-27
Isaac
Wilson

On November 25, 1878, we the undersigned pastor of St. Paul have baptized Isaac, born on the 8th instant, of the lawful marriage of Charles Wilson and Elizabeth Aplin of this place. Sponsor, Catherine Chalifoux.
                    B. Delorme, V.G.

S-6
O.C.
Susan
Petit

On November 26, 1878, we the undersigned, pastor of St. Paul, have buried Susan, widow of the late Amable Petit, deceased on the 22nd instant. Witnesses, J. B. Piette and Henry Ernst.
                    B. Delorme, V.G.

S-7
Isaac
Wilson

On November 27, 1878, we the undersigned, pastor of St. Paul, have buried Isaac Wilson, lawful son of Charles Wilson and Elizabeth Aplin, deceased the day before a few days old. Witnesses, George Aplin and Henry Ernst.
                    B. Delorme, V.G.

B-28
Fred
Louis
Pichette

On December 1, 1878, we the undersigned have baptized Frederic Louis Pichette, born on the 22nd day of the last month of the lawful marriage of Roch Pichette and Victoire Despard of this place. Sponsors, Augustin Raymond and Cecile Pichet.
                    Augustin Raymond
                    B. Delorme, V.G.

B-28
Charles
Ferdinand
Wilson

On December 29, 1878, we the undersigned have baptized Charles Frederic, born on the 8th of November last of the lawful marriage of Charles Wilson and Elizabeth Aplin of this place. Sponsors, Timothy Joseph Concannon and Josephine Aplin.

Josephine Aplin   Timothy Joseph Concannon
                    B. Delorme, V.G.

Recapitulation for the year 1878

Baptisms	28
Burials	7
Marriages	1
First Communions	23

1879

Page 119
S-1 N.C.
Mary
Delille

On January 13, 1879, we the undersigned, pastor of St. Paul, have buried Mary Pichette, wife of Felix Delille, deceased on the 10th instant, aged 25 years. Present, Amedee Choquette and Dieudonne Manaigre, with a large congregation.
                    B. Delorme, V.G.

S-2 O.C.
Josette
Labonte

On January 15, 1879, we the undersigned, have buried Josette Laframboise, wife of Louis Labonte, of this parish, deceased on the 13th instant at the age of 40 years. Present, Thomas McGrath and Joseph McGrath.
                    B. Delorme, V.G.

S-3 N.C.
Fred.
Louis
Pichette

On the 25 January, 1879, we have buried Frederic Louis, son of Roch Pichette and Victoire Despard of this place, deceased yesterday at the age of 2 months. Witnesses, Felix Delille and Peter Cleary.
                    B. Delorme, V.G.

S. Leon Deloney was buried by us on February 5, A.D. 1879. Died on February 3; age 49 years and 7 months. B. Delorme, V.G.

B-1
Louis
B. Diel-
schnider

On February 16, 1879, we the undersigned, pastor of St. Louis, have baptized Louis, born on the 9th of August last of the lawful marriage of Louis B. Dielschnider and Julia Bancasser of this place. Sponsors, Anthony Ahrens and Mrs. Fanny Coleman.

L. Dielschnieder   Anthony Ahrens
Julia Dielschneider   Fanny Coleman
                    B. Delorme, V.G.

S-4 N.C. Andrew Longtain	On February 23, 1879, we the undersigned, pastor of St. Paul, have buried Andrew Longtain, lately of the parish deceased at Salem on the 21st instant, aged about 97 years. Present, Xavier Moisan and Dan McCan. B. Delorme, V.G.
Marriage 1 Augustin Raymond & Josephine Mongrain	On February 24, 1879, after having published at our parochial mass one ban of marriage between Augustin Raymond of this parish of St. Paul, son of age of the late Augustin Raymond and of Mary Servant, for the first part; and Josephine Mongrain of the same parish, daughter of age of David Mongrain and of the late Catherine Lafantaisie for the second part; after having, moreover, granted the dispensation of the two other bans, and no impediment being found, we the undersigned pastor of the said parish of St. Paul have received their mutual consent of marriage and given them the nuptial benediction in the presence of David Mongrain, Salome Raymond, David Mongrain, Sen., and Frederic Fortain.

Augustin Raymond   Jos. Mongrain
Salome Raymond   F. Fortin
B. Delorme, V.G.

[Pages 120 and 121 are blank]

Page 122 S-5 N.G. John Cunningham	On March 1, 1879, we the undersigned have buried John Cunningham, commonly known as Dr. John, of this place. Present, Frederic Fortin and Roch Pichette. B. Delorme, V.G.
S-6 N.G. Charles Ferdinand Wilson	On March 1, 1879, we the undersigned have buried Charles Ferdinand, son of Charles Wilson and Elizabeth Aplin, Deceased yesterday at the age of 4 months. Present, George Aplin and William Trevor. B. Delorme, V.G.
S-7 N.G. Charles Pelland's child	On March 7, 1879, we the undersigned have buried a child of Ch. Pelland and of his wife Mary Coleman, deceased on the 9th instant, a few days after being born and privately baptized. Present, J. Brentano and James Coleman. B. Delorme, V.G.
B-2 Amina Marie Lambert	On March 12, 1879, we the undersigned, parish of the parish of St. Paul, have baptized Amina Marie, born on the 6th instant, of the lawful marriage of Frank Lambert and Clementine Mongrain of this place. Sponsors, Andre Chalifoux and Emerance Mongrain. B. Delorme, V.G.
B-3 Eugene Ralph Murphy	On March 17, 1879, we the undersigned, pastor of St. Paul, have baptized Eugene Ralph, born on the 23rd of January last, of the lawful marriage of Matthew Murphy and Ellen Costello of this place. Sponsors, John Kirk and Lizzy Kirk.

John Kirk   Lizzie Ann Kirk
B. Delorme, V.G.

B-4 Rosalie Judith Bellanger	On March 30, 1879, we the undersigned, pastor of this parish, have baptized Rosalie Judith, born on the 22nd instant, of the lawful marriage of Jake Bellanger and Cloris Bernier of this place. Sponsors, Norbert Bernier and Therese Rivet.

Norbert Bernier
B. Delorme, V.G.

S-8 N.G. Eugene Ralph Murphy	On April 1, 1879, we the undersigned, pastor of St. Paul, have buried Eugene Ralph, lawful son of Mathew Murphy and Ellen Costello, of this place, deceased on the 30th of March last, aged about two months. Present, Peter Kirk and John McGrath. B. Delorme, V.G.
B-5 & S-9 N.G. Joseph Kerr	On April 1, 1879, we the undersigned, pastor of St. Paul, have buried Joseph, lawful son of Sam Kerr and Catherine Coffey of this place, deceased on the 30th of March last, after being baptized by us a few days before, aged about one month. Witnesses of burial, Mathew Murphy and John Coffey. B. Delorme, V.G.

Page 123
S-10 O.G.
Moses
Servant

On April 3, 1879, we the undersigned, pastor of St. Paul have buried Moses Servant of this place, deceased on the 1st instant at the age of 29 years. Present, John Brentano and Fred. Fortain.

B. Delorme, V.G.

B-6 & S-11
N.G.
Mary
Jane
Kerr

On April 8, 1879, we the undersigned have buried Mary Jane, lawful daughter of Samuel Kerr and Catherine Coffey of this place, deceased on the 7th instant, after being baptized by us a few days before: aged about one month. Present, Samuel Kerr and John Coffey.

B. Delorme, V.G.

B-7
Frank
Alexander
Kitson

On April 11, 1879, we the undersigned have baptized Francis Alexander, born on the 9th of December last, of the lawful marriage of Peter Kitson and Angelique Dupre of this place. Sponsors, Frank Lambert and Clementine Mongrain.

B. Delorme, V.G.

S-12 N.G.
Clothilde
Jette

On April 16, 1879, we the undersigned have buried Mary Clothilde, lawful daughter of Adolphe Jette and July, deceased on the 14th instant, aged 20½ years. Present, Frank Davidson and Amedee Choquette with a large congregation.

B. Delorme, V.G.

M-2
Alphonse
Van
Hoomissen
&
Mary
Josephine
Wirfs

On April 21, 1879, publications of bans being duly made in the parochial church of Portland, and being therefor authorized by the Rev. pastors of Portland and McMinnville churches, we the undersigned, pastor of the parish of St. Paul, have received the mutual consent of marriage of Alphonse Van Hoomissen, of the parish of Portland, son of age of [sic] lawful of Philip Van Hoomissen, residing in Kansas, and Josephine Van Dosche, deceased, for the first part; and Mary Josephine Wirfs of the mission of McMinnville, daughter of age and lawful of Peter Wirfs and Mary Catherine Hoffman, for the second part, and have given them nuptial benediction in the presence of Peter Wirfs, father of the bride, Peter J. Wirfs and Paulina Hirsch who have signed with us and the married couple.

Peter Wirfs
Peter Joseph Wirfs
Pauline Maggie Hirsch

Alphonse Van Hoomissen
Mary Josephine Wirfs

B. Delorme, V.G.

B-8
Mary Jane
McCann

On April 27, 1879, we the undersigned, pastor of St. Paul, have baptized Mary Jane, born on the 23rd of March last, of the lawful marriage of Dan McCann and Genevieve Longtain of this same parish. Sponsors, Michael McFarland and Mary Staats.

M. McFarland   Mary Staats
B. Delorme, V.G.

B-9
Rosa
Emma
Choquette

On May 16, 1879, we the undersigned, pastor of the parish of St. Paul, have baptized Rosa Emma, born on the 8th instant of the lawful marriage of Amedee Choquette and Mary Bernier of this place. Sponsors, Charles Choquette and Eleonora Seguin.

Page 124
B-10
Mary
Elizabeth
Lucier

B. Delorme, V.G.

On May 18, 1879, we the undersigned, pastor of St. Paul, have baptized Mary Elizabeth, born on the 12th instant, of the lawful marriage of Joseph Lucier and Louise Martineau of this place. Sponsors, Daniel Lucier and Isabelle Bourgeau.

B. Delorme, V.G.

B-11
James
Alphonsus
Ernst

On May 22, 1879, we the undersigned, pastor of St. Paul, have baptized James Alphonsus, born on the 14th instant of the lawful marriage of Henry Ernst and Mary Magdelen Vesper. Sponsors, Henry Wolfart and Bridget Kennedy.

Henrich Wolfart   Bridget Kennedy
B. Delorme, V.G.

M-2
Antoine

On May 24, 1879, Anthony Favre, lawful son of Jean Favre and Estelle Morrisseau, and Rose Laprate, lawful daughter of Alexis Laprate and

Favre & Rose Laprate	Louise Okanagan, having been married civilly about a year ago, have renewed their consent of marriage before us, the undersigned, and we have given them the nuptial benediction in the presence of Henry Ernst and Anthyme Charbonneau.

        H. Ernst   Antoine Favre X
        Antime Charbonneau   Rose Laprate X
                          B Delorme, V.G.

B-12 Joseph Amed Jette
On May 25, 1879, we the undersigned, pastor of St. Paul, have baptized Joseph Amed, born on the 30th of March last, of the lawful marriage of Adolphe Jette and Margaret Liard of this place. Sponsors, Adolphe Jette, junior, and Adele Picard.

                     Adolphe Jette
                     B. Delorme, V.G.

S-13 N.G. Helen Patterson
On May 28, 1879, we the undersigned, pastor of St. Paul, have buried Helen Patterson, lawful daughter of James Patterson and Sara O'Kelly, deceased on the 26th instant, at the age of 20 years. Witnesses: Louis Poujade, John McGrath and a large attendance.

                     B. Delorme, V.G.

S-14 N.G. Patrick Kerrigan
On May 30, 1879, we the undersigned, pastor of St. Paul, have buried Patrick Kerrigan of this parish, deceased on the 27th instant, in the hospital of Portland, at the age of 36 years. Present, Michael McPartaland and John Coffey with a large attendance.

        Michael McPartaland   John Coffey

Page 125

                     B. Delorme, V.G.

M-3 Philip McPaulen & C. Josephine Ady
On June 10, 1879, we the undersigned, pastor of St. Paul, after publishing at our parochial mass one ban of marriage between Philip McPaulin of this parish, son of age and lawful of Roger McPaulin and Hannah Hathaway for the first part; and C. Josephine Ady of the same parish, daughter of age and lawful of Robert Ady and Mary Mitchell for the second part; the publication [sic] of the two other bans having been by us granted, and [no] impediment whatever being discovered, have received their mutual consent of marriage and given them the nuptial benediction in the presence of H. L. Eberhard and Sara Kennedy who have signed with us and the newly married couple.

        Philip McPaulan   Henry L. Eberhard
        Josephine Ady   Sarah Kennedy
                     B. Delorme, V.G.

B-13 Joseph Antoine Favre
On June 15, 1879, we the undersigned, pastor of St. Paul, have baptized Joseph Antoine, born on the 29th of May last, of the lawful marriage of Antoine Favre and Rose Laprate of this place. Sponsors, Joseph LaFlemme and Louise Laprate.

                    Joseph Laflemme
                     B. Delorme, V.G.

B-14 Simeon Dupuis
On June 17, 1879, we the undersigned pastor of St. Paul have baptized Simeon, born on the 15th instant, of the lawful marriage of Elziar Dupuis and Esther Brien of this parish. Sponsors, Edward Mathieu and Arsinoe Mathieu,

        Edward Mathieu   Arsinoe Mathieu
                     B. Delorme, V.G.

First Communion
On June 22, 1879, the following persons have made their first communion in the church of St. Paul:

Francis Coleman	Julia Calmels
John Smyth	Lucy Murphy
Eugene Flynn	Jane Davidson
James Aplin	Mary Grenier
Narcisse Manaigre	Lucy Connor
Alfred Lambert	Helen Dowd
Francis Lambert	Mary Dowd
Joseph Lucier	

Andrew Longtain
Jeremie Labonte

B. Delorme, V.G.

S-15 N.G.
F. X.
Mathieu,
Sen.

On July 12, 1879, we the undersigned, pastor of St. Paul, have buried Francis Xavier Mathieu, Sen., from Butteville, deceased on the 10th instant at the age of 85 years. Witnesses, Louis Lemery and Matt. McCormick and a large attendance.

B. Delorme, V.G.

Page 126
B-15
Xavier
George
Washing-
ton
Lachapelle

On July 13, 1879, we the undersigned, pastor of St. Paul, have baptized Xavier George Washington, born on the 4th instant of the lawful marriage of Victor Lachapelle and Christine Laderoute of this place. Sponsors, Daniel Lucier and Cecile Lucier.

B. Delorme, V.G.

B-16
James
Albert
Osborn

On July 16, 1879, we the undersigned priest have baptized James Albert, born on the 18th of October, 1878, of the lawful marriage of Joseph Osborn and Lucy Osborn of this place. Sponsors, Michael McPortland and Katy Osborn.

A. J. Croquet

M-4
Amedee
Lachapelle
&
Euphemie
Chamberlan

On July 21, 1879, we the undersigned, pastor of the parish of St. Paul, after having published three times, at our parochial mass, the bans of marriage between Amedee Lachapelle of the parish of St. Louis, son underage of Andrew Lachapelle and Adrienne Lucier, of the consent of whom it proceeds, for the first part; and Euphemie Chamberlan of this parish of St. Paul, daughter of age of Adolphe Chamberlan and of the late Louise Humpherville for the second part; the same publications being made at St. Louis, and no impediment whatever being found, have received their mutual consent of marriage and have given them the nuptial benediction in the presence [of] Andrew Lachapelle, Adolph Chamberlan, Bartholomew Chamberlan, and Mary Odile Lachapelle.

Amedy Lachapelle   Mary Lachapelle
Euphemie Chamberlain

B. Delorme, V.G.

B-17
Frederic
Adam
Manaigre

On July 27, 1879, we the undersigned pastor of St. Paul have baptized Frederic Adam, born on the 11th instant of the lawful marriage of Dieudonne Mainagre and Emelie Pichette of this place. Sponsors, Severe Manaigre and Emelie Manaigre.

Severe Manaigre
B. Delorme, V.G.

B-18
David
Lebeau

On July 27, 1879, we the undersigned pastor of St. Paul have baptized David, born on the 26th of June last of the lawful marriage of Calyxte Lebeau and Cloris Mongrain of Washington County. Sponsors, David Mongrain Senior and Marguerite Pichette.

Page 127
B-18 [sic]
Helena
Christina
Fershweiler

B. Delorme, V.G.

On August 10, 1879, we the undersigned, pastor of St. Paul, have baptized Helena Christina, born of the lawful marriage of Peter J. Fershweiler and Elizabeth Domayer of this place, on the 5th instant. Sponsors, Michael Fershweiler and Josephine Wassenhove.

M. Fershweiler   Josephine
B. Delorme, V.G.

B-19
Charles
Dupre

On August 10, 1879, we the undersigned, pastor of St. Paul, have baptized Charles, born on the 6th instant, of the lawful marriage of Charles Dupre and Catherine Chalifoux of this place. Sponsors, Frederic Fortain and Mary Servant.

Frederic Fortain
B. Delorme, V.G.

B-20
Margaret

On the 10th of August, A.D. 1879, we the undersigned, pastor of St. Paul, have supplied the ceremonies of baptism to Margaret Irene, born on the

Irene Murphy	3rd of March, 1878, of the lawful marriage of Andrew Murphy and Elizabeth Cosgrove of this place and privately baptized by us about 4 weeks after her birth. Sponsors, Michael Murphy and Laura Elizabeth Ladd. Michael Murphy Laurria E. Ladd B. Delorme, V.G.
S-16 N.G. James M. Osborn	On August 11, 1879, we the undersigned have buried James M. Osborn, son of Joseph Osborn and Lucy Longtain, deceased on the 9th instant, aged about 10 months. Witnesses, Dan McCan and Michael McPortland. B. Delorme, V.G.
B-21 Emma Constance Smith	On August 13, 1879, we the undersigned, pastor of St. Paul, have baptized Emma Constance born on the 15th of July, 1878, of the lawful marriage of Charles Thomas Smith and Leonie Mary Patterson of this place. We stood as godfather for the child and the godmother Emma Patterson being absent, was represented by Martha Connor. Martha Connor B. Delorme, V.G.
S-17 Frederic Adam Manaigre	On September 9, 1879, we the undersigned, pastor of St. Paul, have buried Frederic Adam, lawful son of Dieudonne Manaigre and Emilie Pichette, deceased yesterday aged about 2 months. Witnesses, Felix Delille and Roch Pichette. B. Delorme, V.G.
B-22 Joseph F. Raymond	On September 27, 1879, we the undersigned, pastor of St. Paul, have baptized Joseph Fabian, born on the 14th instant of the lawful marriage of Marcel Raymond and Odile Raymond, of Cowlitz, Washington Territory. Sponsors, Augustine Raymond and Josephine Mongrain. B. Delorme, V.G.
Page 128 B-23 Charles Hilaire Chalifoux	On October 5, 1879, A.D., we the undersigned, pastor of St. Paul, have baptized Charles Hilaire, born on the 26th of September last of the lawful marriage of Andre Chalifoux and Emerance Mongrain of this place. Sponsors, Cyprien Bellique and Julienne Bergevin. Julienne Bellique B. Delorme, V.G.
B-24 Marguerite Mary Alice Lafontaine	On November 2, 1879, we the undersigned pastor of the parish of St. Paul have baptized Margaret Mary Alice, born on the 26th of July last of the lawful marriage of Narcisse Lafontaine and Margaret Pichette of Washington County. Sponsors, Severe Manaigre and Cecile Pichette. Severe Manaigre B. Delorme, V.G.
S-18 N.G. Joseph Amed Jette	On November 22, 1879, we the undersigned, pastor of St. Paul, have buried Joseph Amedee Jette, lawful son of Adolph Jette and Margaret Liard deceased the *[day]* before yesterday, aged about 8 months. Present, Henry Ernst and Honore Picard. B. Delorme, V.G.
B-25 Paul Louis Chester Bergevin	On November 30, 1879, we the undersigned, pastor of St. Paul, have baptized Paul Louis Chester, born on the 16th day of the present month of the lawful marriage of Charles Louis Bergevin and Rosa Mathieu of this place. Sponsors, William Hunter and Salome Raymond. William Hunter Salome Raymond B. Delorme, V.G.
B-26 Mary Amelia Raymond	On December 7, 1879, we the undersigned, pastor of St. Paul's parish, have baptized Mary Amelia born on the 30th day of November last of the lawful marriage of Augustine Raymond and Josephine Raymond of this parish. Sponsors, Francois Dompierre and Mary Fortain. B. Delorme, V.G.
S-19 N.G. Mrs. Ellen Gearin	On December 8, A.D. 1879, we the undersigned, pastor of St. Paul's parish, have buried Mrs. Ellen Gearin, wife of John Gearin of this parish, deceased on the 6th instant, aged 70 years. Present, Mathew Murphy, John McKay, John McGrath, with a large congregation. B. Delorme, V.G.

Rec. for 1879   Baptisms, 26, Burials 19, Marriages 4, First Com. 17
1880

Page 129

S-1 O.G.
Ch.
Hilaire
Chalifoux

On February 9, 1880, we the undersigned, have buried Charles Hilaire, lawful son of Andre Chalifoux and Emerence Mongrain of this parish, of St. Paul, deceased on the 8th instant at the age of 4 months. Present, D. Mongrain and Cyprien Bellique.

B. Delorme, V.G.

M-1
James
Coyle
&
Henrietta
Ray

On the 10th day of February, 1880, after the publication of one ban of marriage between James Coyle of this parish of St. Paul, son of age of James Coyle and Charlotte Scot, for the first part, and Henrietta E. Ray, of the same parish, daughter of age of Charles Ray and Emelia Eyre, for the second part; the dispensation of the two other bans having been granted by us, Vicar General of the Diocese of Oregoncity, and no impediment whatever being discovered, we the undersigned Rector of the said parish of St. Paul have received their mutual consent of marriage and given them the nuptial benediction in the presence of Wallace Munsy, Ch. Coleman, Ally Ray and Milly Ray, Charles F. Ray, father of the bride.

James J. Coyle	Charley Coleman	Millie Ray
Ettie H. Ray	Allie Ray	
C. F. Ray	W. Munzy	

B. Delorme, V.G.

B-1
J. Peter
Dowd

On February 15, 1880, we the undersigned pastor of St. Paul have baptized John Peter, born on the 10th instant of the lawful marriage of John Dowd and Julia Papin Lachance, of this parish. Sponsors, Peter Joseph Orth and Hannah McDermott.

Peter Joseph Orth

B. Delorme, V.G.

S-2 N.G.
Cuthbert
Lambert

On March 11, 1880, we the undersigned pastor of St. Paul have buried Cuthbert Lambert, lawful son of Augustin Lambert and Catherine Piche, of this parish, deceased on the day before at the age of about 25 years. Present, J. B. Piette and John McGrath.

B. Delorme, V.G.

S-3 O.G.
Francis
Aug.
Bernier

On March 28, 1880, we the undersigned, pastor of St. Paul have buried Francis Augustin Bernier, deceased on the 26th instant, aged 2 years and 9 months. Present, Francis Bernier and Mary Lambert, parents of the child, and Amedee Choquette, with Jake Bellanger.

B. Delorme, V.G.

Page 130

S-4 O.G.
J. Jack-
son's child

On April 6, 1880, we the undersigned, pastor of St. Paul, have buried a boy, son of Jerome Jackson and Mary Cosgrove his wife, deceased on the day before, half an hour after being born and private Baptism having been administered to him. Present, Jerome Jackson and Agnes Jackson.

B. Delorme, V.G.

B-2
Elizabeth
Helen
Geelan

On April 18, A.D. 1880, we the undersigned have baptized Elizabeth Helen, born on the 22nd of March last, of the lawful marriage of Patrick Geelan and Elizabeth Ady of this place. Sponsors, Math. Connor and Bridget Pembrook.

Matthew Connor   Bridget Pembrook

B. Delorme, V.G.

B-3
James
Am.
Wilson

On April 24, A.D. 1880, we the undersigned, pastor of the parish of St. Paul, have baptized James Amior, born on the 4th instant of the lawful marriage of Charles Wilson and Elizabeth Aplin of this place. Sponsors, James Aplin and Josephine Aplin.

James Aplin   Josephine Aplin

B. Delorme, V.G.

B-4
Anna
Malvina

On April 25, A.D. 1880, we the undersigned pastor of St. Paul's parish, have baptized Anna Malvina, born on the 29th of March last of the lawful marriage of Charles Mathieu and Tina Holland of this place. Sponsors,

Bergevin [sic, Mathieu]	J. B. Piette and Mrs. Rosa Mathieu. B. Delorme, V.G.
S-5 N.G. Sr. Mary Francoise	On April 29, 1880, we the undersigned, Rector of the parish of St. Paul, have buried in the vault of the Rev. Sisters of the Holy Names of Jesus and Mary, Rev. Sr. Mary Francoise (Francoise Dubreuil) deceased on the 27th instant in the 59th year of her age and after 32 years of religious profession. Present, Rev. Fathers Dols and Capelle, Rev. Mother Superior of the Seven Dolors, Rev. Sr. Mary Peter, etc. B. Delorme, V.G.
S-6 N.G. Alice Longtain	On May 1, A.D. 1880, we the undersigned, Rector of the parish of St. Paul, have buried Alice, daughter of Thomas Longtain and Mathilda Rivet of Champoeg, deceased on the 29th of April at the age of 13 years. Present, Dan McCann and Fabien Rivet. B. Delorme, V.G.
B-5 Joseph Henry Deilschneider	On May 2, 1880, we the undersigned, Rector of St. Paul's Church, have baptized Joseph Henry, born on the 21st day of March last, of the lawful marriage of Louis Deilschneider and Julia Bangasser of this place. Sponsors, Joseph Orth and Magdelen Ernst. Peter Joseph Orth Madeleine Ernst B. Delorme, V.G.

Page 131

B-6 Francis Bertrand Bellique	On May 9, 1880, we the undersigned, pastor of St. Paul, have baptized Francis Bertrand, born on the 26th of April last, of the lawful marriage of Cyprien Bellique and Julienne Bergevin of this place. Sponsors, Felix Gregoire and Genevieve Bellique. Genevieve Gregoire B. Delorme, V.G.
S-7 N.G. Julia Baily	On May 7, 1880, we the undersigned, Rector of the parish of St. Paul, have buried Julia Bailey of this place, widow of Dr. J. Shiel and W. Bailey, deceased on the 5th instant, aged about 60 years. Present, Peter Kirk, John McGrath, James McKay, John Gearin, and a large congregation. B. Delorme, V.G.
B-7 Mary Ellen Hanigan	On May 23, 1880, we the undersigned, Rector of St. Paul, have baptized Mary Ellen, born on the 29th of June last, of the lawful marriage of William Hanigan and Ellen Coffey. Sponsors, Samuel James Kerr and Catherine Coffey. Samuel James Kerr Catherine Kerr B. Delorme, V.G.
B-8 Alexander Celest. Langlois	On May 23, 1880, we the undersigned, rector of St. Paul's Church, have baptized Alexander Celestine, born on the 3rd day of February last, of the lawful marriage of Israel Langlois and Mary Pepin of Yamhill County. Sponsors, Alexander Labonte and Clementine Papin. B. Delorme, V.G.
B-9 J. Baptiste Manaigre	On June 27, 1880, we the undersigned, pastor of St. Paul, have baptized John Baptist, born on the 14th instant, of the lawful marriage of Dieudonne Manaigre and Emilie Pichette of this parish. Sponsors, John Baptiste Piette and Francis Piette. B. Delorme, V.G.
S-8 N.G. Charles Smith	On June 28, 1880, we the undersigned have buried Charley Smith, son of Charles Smith and Leonie Patterson, deceased on the 26th instant, at the age of 6 months and 21 days. Present, Leo Patterson and Emma Patterson. B. Delorme, V.G.
S-9 O.G. Amable Arcouet	On July 8, 1880, we the undersigned, pastor of St. Paul, have buried Amable Arcouet of this parish, deceased at the age of about 81 years. Present, J. B. Piette and Henry Ernst. B. Delorme, V.G.

Page 132

S-10	On July 9, 1880, we the undersigned, pastor of St. Paul, have buried in the

Rev. L. Lajeunesse

Rev. Sisters' vault Rev. Louis Lajeunesse, deceased at Portland on the 7th instant at the age of 27 years. Present, Rev. A. Glorieux, Rev. V. Capelle, Rev. J. J. Dols, Rev. L. Schram, Rev. G. C. Thibau, Rev. White, Rev. F. Metayer, Rev. Mother Sup. of the Seven Dolors, etc.

B. Delorme, V.G.

B-10 James Albert Longtain

On July 7, 1880, we the undersigned, Rector of the parish of St. Paul, have baptized James Albert, born on the 17th of October last, of the lawful marriage of Mathilda Rivet of this place. Sponsors, Daniel Lucier, Marianne Departy.

B. Delorme, V.G.

S-11 N.G. Hermine Agnes Jette

On July 20, 1880, we the undersigned, Rector of St. Paul's parish, have buried Hermine Agnes Jette, daughter of Adolph Jette [and] Julie, his wife, deceased on the 18th instant at the age of 18 years and 10 months. Present, Joseph Orth and William Trevor.

B. Delorme, V.G.

S-12 Sara Julia Bernier

On July 23, 1880, we the undersigned, rector of St. Paul's parish, have buried Sara Julia, daughter of Norbert Bernier and Therese Rivet, deceased yesterday at the age of 3 years and 2 months. Present, Amedee Choquette and Francis Bernier.

B. Delorme, V.G.

B-11 Ralph Sylvester Davidson

On July 25, 1880, we the undersigned, pastor of St. Paul, have baptized Ralph Sylvester, born of the lawful marriage of W. Franklin Davidson and Annie Coleman on the 1st instant. Sponsors, John Kirk and Louise Coleman.

John Kirk   Louisa Coleman

B. Delorme, V.G.

B-12 John Albert McPaulin

On August 1, 1880, we the undersigned, rector of St. Paul's parish, have baptized John Albert, born on June 3 of the lawful marriage of Philip McPaulin and Josephine Ady of this place. Sponsors, Simon Connor and Kathe McKay.

Simon J. Connor   Katie McKay

B. Delorme, V.G.

B-13 Joseph Peter Hubert Lucier

On August 8, 1880, we the undersigned, rector of St. Paul's parish, have baptized Joseph Peter Hubert, born on the 25th of July last, of the lawful marriage of Peter Lucier and Thais Senecal of this place. Sponsors, Joseph Lucier and Louise Martineau.

Joseph Loucier

B. Delorme, V.G.

Page 133

S-13 N.G. Andrew Chalifoux

On August 9, 1880, we the undersigned, rector of the parish of St. Paul, have buried Andrew Chalifoux of this place, deceased on the 7th instant, at the age of 39 years. Present, Charles Dupre and Peter Kitson.

B. Delorme, V.G.

B-14 Mathew Eugene McGrath

On September 12, 1880, we the undersigned, rector of [St.] Paul, have baptized Mathew Eugene, born on the 11th instant, of the lawful marriage of John McGrath and Mary Hughes, of this place. Sponsors, Thomas McGrath and Mary Ann McGrath.

Thomas McGrath   Mary Ann Mcgrath

B. Delorme, V.G.

B-15 Francis A. Jette

On October 10, 1880, we the undersigned, rector of the parish of St. Paul, have baptized Francis Amedeus, born on the 8th of September of the lawful marriage of Adolph Jette and Margaret Liard of this place. Sponsors, Louis Prevot and Caledonia Coleman.

Louis Prevost   C. Elizabeth Coleman

B. Delorme, V.G.

S-14 N.C. Augustine Lambert

On October 10, 1880, we the undersigned, rector of the parish of St. Paul, have buried Augustine Lambert of this place, son of Augustine Lambert, Sen., and Catherine Pichet, deceased on the 8th instant at the age of 39 years. Present, J. B. Piette and John McGrath.

B. Delorme, V.G.

B-16
Rosa
Octavia
Hughes

On October 12, 1880, we the undersigned, rector of the church of St. Paul, have baptized Rosa Octavia, born on the day before of the lawful marriage of Andrew Hughes and Rosa Connor of this place. Sponsors, Joseph Mc-Grath and Bridget Connor.

Joseph McGrath   Bridget Connor
                    B. Delorme, V.G.

B-17
Peter
George
Choquette

On October 24, 1880, we the undersigned, rector of the parish of St. Paul, have baptized Peter George, born on the 15th instant of the lawful marriage of Amedee Choquette and Mary Bernier of this place. Godfather, Joseph Bernier and [godmother] Cecile Lucier.
                    B. Delorme, V.G.

S-15 N.C.
Jane
Kirby

On the 4th of November, 1880, we the undersigned, rector of St. Paul, have buried Jane Kirby, of St. Patrick's parish, in Yam Hill County, daughter of Thomas Kirby and Mary Burns, deceased on [the] 2nd instant at the age of 26 years. Present, Fath. P. Gibney and Charles Pellan.
                    B. Delorme, V.G.

Page 134
B-18
Josephine
Labonte

On November 8, 1880, we the undersigned, rector of the parish of St. Paul, have baptized Josephine, born on the 18th of October last, of the lawful marriage of Alexander Labonte and Clementine Lachance, of Yam Hill County. Sponsors, Louis Labonte and Mary Lachance.
                    B. Delorme, V.G.

M-2
Patrick
Mullen
&
Mary
Flynn

On November 10, 1880, after the publication of one ban of marriage between Patrick Mullen of the parish of St. Paul, son of age of Thomas Mullen and Mary McNaven, both deceased, for the first part; and Mary A. Flynn of the same parish, daughter of age of Bernard Flynn and Catherine Bennet, for the second part; the dispensation of the other two bans having been granted by us, Vicar Gen. of the Diocese of Oregoncity, and no impediment whatever being discovered, we the undersigned, rector of the said parish of St. Paul, have received their mutual consent of marriage and given them the nuptial benediction in the presence of Andrew Flynn and Catherine M. Flynn, who have signed with us and the new married couple.

Patrick Mulen   Mary Ann Flynn
Andrew Flynn   Catherine M. Flynn
                    B. Delorme, V.G.

B-18
John
Francis
Firshweiler

On November 21, 1880, we the undersigned, rector of the parish of St. Paul, have baptized John Francis, born on the 16th instant, of the lawful marriage of John Benjamin Firshweiler and Philomena Schramer of this parish. Sponsors, Francis Van Wassenhove and Catherina Keppinger.
                    B. Delorme, V.G.

S-16
Sr. Mary
Bernadette

On November 27, 1880, we the undersigned, rector of St. Paul parish, have buried in the vault of the Rev. Sisters of the Holy Names, Rev. Sister Mary Bernadette, deceased on the 25th instant, after 5 years of profession and at the age of [blank] years. Present, Sr. Mary Margaret and Sr. Mary Peter, etc.
                    B. Delorme, V.G.

B-19
Francis
Laurence
Bellanger

On December 19, 1880, we the undersigned, pastor of St. Paul, have baptized Francis Laurence, born on the 4th instant of the lawful marriage of Jake Bellanger and Cloris Bernier of this place. Sponsors, Amedee Seguin and Celina Choquette.

Amede Seguin   Celina Choquette
                    B. Delorme, V.G.

M-3
Edward
Bellanger
&
Rose
Chalifoux

On December 21, 1880, we the undersigned have received the renewed consent of marriage of Edward Bellanger and Rose Chalifoux of this place, who had before married civilly, and given them the nuptial benediction in the presence of Henry Ernst and Magdelen Ernst, who have signed with us and the bridegroom.

E. Bellanger   Henry Ernst   Magdelene Ernst
                    B. Delorme, V.G.

Page 135

B-20
William
Ray

On December 25, 1880, we rector of the parish of St. Paul have baptized William, born on the 25th of November last of the lawful marriage of James Coyle, jun., and Eliza Henriette Ray of this Place. Sponsors, William Richard McKay and Annie Mary Kennedy.

William R. McKay   Annie M. Kennedy
B. Delorme, V.G.

B-21
Charles
Alonzo
Aplin

On December 31, 1880, we the undersigned, rector of St. Paul, have baptized Charles Alonzo, born on the 19th of October, of the lawful marriage of George Aplin and Magdelen Raymond.

George E. Aplin   Magdelen Raymond
B. Delorme, V.G.

Recapitulation

Baptisms	21
Burials	16
Marriages	2
Easter Communions	315

1881

[Hereafter the entries are written in Latin]

M-1
John
Baptist
Bergevin
&
Salome
Picard

On January 28, 1881, after the publication of two bans of marriage, the first on the 9th and the second on the 16th of this month, and the dispensation of the third having been granted by me, Vicar General, and no impediment being found, I, rector of the parish of St. Paul, having received their mutual consent to Marriage, have joined in matrimony John Baptist Bergevin, son of Louis Bergevin and Magdelene Servant, and Salome Picard, daughter of Henri Picard and Celeste Rochbrune, both of this parish of St. Paul, in the presence of Henri *[Picard]* father of the bride, Etienne Gregoire, Henri Picard and John Picard, brothers of the bride, Salome Raymond, relative *[cousin]* of the groom, and Marie Choquette.

John B Bergevin   Salome Picard   Salome Raymond
Henry Picard   E. S. Gregoire   Mary Choquette
B. Delorme, Rector

Page 136

B.C. 1
Caroline
Lambert

On January 23, 1881, I the undersigned, Rector of the parish of St. Paul, have baptized an infant, born on the 19th instant of the lawful marriage of Francis Lambert and Clementine Mongrain of this place, to whom was given the name Caroline. Sponsors were John Brentano and Catherine Dupre.

John F. Theo. B. Brentano
B. Delorme, V.G.

B-2
J. B.
Bourgeau

On February 20, 1881, I, the undersigned, rector of the parish of St. Paul, have baptized an infant, born on the 8th instant, of the lawful marriage of J. Baptiste Bourgeau and Genevieve Martineau of this place, to whom has been given the name Jean Baptiste. Sponsors were Daniel Lucier and Marguerite Lucier, of this place.

B. Delorme, V.G.

S-1 N.G.
Augustin
Lambert

On February 15, 1881, Augustin Lambert, of St. Paul, aged 70 years, was buried in the cemetery of this mission, in the presence of Francois Bernier and Amedee Choquette, etc.

B. Delorme, V.G.

S-2 N.G.
Frances
Piette

On February 8, 1881, we the undersigned have buried Frances Million, Wife of John Baptist Piette of the parish of St. Paul, deceased the day before at the age of 50 years, having received the holy sacraments, in the presence of Charles Pelland, James Coleman, Mathew Murphy, and many others.

B. Delorme, rector

B-3
Maria
Melissa
Chalifoux

On March 13, 1881, I, the undersigned rector of the parish of St. Paul, have baptized an infant born the 12th of this month of the lawful marriage of Andre Chalifoux and Emerance Mongrain of this place, to whom is given the name Maria Melissa. Sponsors, Theophyles Lecuyer and Angelica Dupre.

T. E. Lecuyer
B. Delorme, rector

B-4
Alfred
Augustin
Crete
	On March 13, 1881, I the undersigned rector of the parish of St. Paul, have baptized an infant born the 14th of November of the preceding year of the lawful marriage of Isaac Crete and Rosa Raymond, to whom is given the name of Alfred Augustin. Sponsors, Adolphus Page and Magdelen Raymond.
	    Adolphe Page Magdalen Raymond
	            B. Delorme, rector

B-5 Rosa S. Bellanger	On March 17, 1881, I the undersigned, rector of this parish of St. Paul, have baptized an infant, born on the 19th of the month [sic] to Edward Bellanger and Rosa Chalifoux of this place, to whom is given the name Rosa Salome. Sponsors, Baptiste Gagnon and Emerance Mongrain of this place. B. Delorme, V.G.
Page 137 S-3 N.G. John Rochbrune	On April 19, 1881, John Rochbrune of this parish of St. Paul, deceased the day before, aged 22 years, was buried in the cemetery of this place in the presence of J. B. Piette and Charles Pelland. B. Delorme, rector

B-6 & 7
Stephen
Smithe
&
Mary A.
Smithe
	On May 1, 1881, I the undersigned, rector of the parish of St. Paul, I have baptized the infants born on the 14th of November last of the lawful marriage of Francis Smithe and Helena Nolan, to whom were given the names Stephen and Marie Alice. Sponsors, Andrew Murphy, Marie Cecelia Murphy, and Elizabeth Cecile Connor.
	  Andrew J. Murphy Mary C. Murphy Elizabeth C. Connor
	            B. Delorme, rector

B-8
Mary
Smith
	On May 10, 1881, I the undersigned, rector of the parish of St. Paul, have baptized an infant, born the 18th of April last of the legitimate marriage of Charles Smith and Leonie Patterson, to whom was given the name Marie. Sponsors, Leo Patterson and Elmina Patterson.
	    Leo J. Patterson Elmina Patterson
	            B. Delorme, rector

S-4 N.G. Emma Patterson	On May 12, 1881, Emma Patterson, of the parish of St. Paul, daughter of James Patterson and Sara O'Kelly, aged 26 years, deceased the day before, having duly received the sacraments of the church, was buried by me, the undersigned, in the cemetery of this place in the presence of John Brentano, Joseph Orth, Andrew Hughes, Rev. Sr. Mary Margaret, and many others. B. Delorme, Rector

B-9
Augustin
Nathan
Raymond
	On May 15, 1881, I the undersigned, rector of the parish of St. Paul, have baptized an infant, born the 1st of February last, of the lawful marriage of Marcelle Raymond and Odile Raymond of this place, to whom were given the names Augustin and Nathan. Sponsor, Salome Raymond.
	            Salome Raymond
	            B. Delorme, Rector

B-10 Marc J. Baptist [McFarland]	On May 21, 1881, I the undersigned rector of the parish of St. Paul, have baptized an infant, born the 9th of February last, of McFarland and Olive Gauthier, to whom was given the name Mark John Baptist. Sponsor, Mary Jackson. B. Delorme, Rector
B-11 & 12 Henry & Mary M. Pariseau	On May 19, 1881, I the undersigned, rector of the parish of St. Paul, have baptized two infants, Henry, born June 20th, A.D. 1879, and Marie, born the 29th of April last, of the lawful marriage of Louis Pariseau and Helene Larrison of Lane County. Sponsors of Henry, Francis Dubreuil and Angelique Dupre; of Mary, Pariseau [sic] and Salome Raymond. Salome Raymond
Page 138 S-5 N.G. James Wilson	B. Delorme, Rector On June 24, 1881, James Wilson, son of Charles Wilson and Elizabeth Aplin of this place, deceased at the age of 14 months, was buried by me in the presence of Peter Kirk and George Aplin. B. Delorme, rector

S-6 N.G.
Mary
Bellique

On June 25, 1881, Mary Bellique, daughter of John Bellique and Victoire Vassal, deceased at the age of 9 years, has been buried by me the undersigned in the presence of Peter Bellique and Edward Kennedy.

B. Delorme, rector

M-2
Henry
Picard
&
Mary
Choquette

On July 5, 1881, after the publication of one ban, made on the third of this month, and dispensation of the other two having been obtained, and no impediment being found, have received the mutual consent of marriage between Henry Picard, of St. Louis, son of Henry Picard and Celeste Rochbrune, and Mary Choquette of the parish of St. Paul, daughter of Amedee Choquette and Marie Bernier, have joined them in holy wedlock in the presence of these witnesses, namely, Henry Picard, Amedee Choquette, David Bernier, John Picard and Celina Choquette.

Amedee Choquette	H. Picard
Celina Choquette	M. Choquette

B. Delorme, rector

First
Communion

On July 3, 1881, the following received their first communion in the church of St. Paul:

Edward Murphy	Susanna Murphy
John Mathieu	Laura Davidson
William Flynn	Mary Kirk
Antoine Labonte	Marie Helen Jackson
John Kerr	Elizabeth Deilshneider
James Kerr	Bridget Dowd
Jacob Kennedy	Mary Agnes Goodrich
William Mooney	Marguerite Richi
Peter Kirk	Emilia Manaigre
Henry Ernst	Elizabeth Dupre
Joseph Richi	
Peter Martineau	In witness whereof, B. Delorme
Julius Picard	Rector
Andre Grenier	
Charles Bernier	

Page 139
M-3
John
Coleman
&
Mary
Kennedy

On July 13, 1881, after the publication of one ban, made on the 10th of July, the dispensation of the other two bans having been granted, and no impediment being found, I the undersigned, rector of the parish of St. Paul, have received the mutual consent to marriage of John Coleman, of this parish of St. Paul, son of James Coleman and Frances Murray, and Mary Kennedy of the same place of St. Paul, daughter of John Kennedy and Bridget Nagle, and have united them in matrimony in the presence of witnesses, namely: Stephen Coleman, Charles Coleman, Elizabeth Coleman and Anna Kennedy.

Stephen Coleman	John Coleman
Charles Coleman	Mary Kennedy
Eliza Coleman	
Annie Kennedy	

B. Delorme, rector

S-7 N.C.
Mary
Lambert

On the 25th of July, 1881, I, the undersigned, have buried Mary Lambert, wife of Francis Bernier, of this parish of St. Paul, aged 23 years, deceased the day before, having received the Holy Sacraments, in the presence of John Brentano and Amedee Choquette.

B. Delorme, Rector

B-13
Mary
Helen
Livingston

On July 31, 1881, I the undersigned, pastor of the parish of St. Paul, have baptized an infant born the 17th instant of the lawful marriage of Richard Livingston and M. Dugan of this place, to whom is given the name Mary Helen. Sponsors, James H. Mooney and Mary Ann Livingston.

B. Delorme, Rector

B-14
Elizabeth

On July 31, 1881, I the undersigned, rector of the parish of St. Paul, have baptized an infant born the 8th instant of the lawful marriage of Narcisse

Helene Lafontaine	Lafontaine and Mary *[Marguerite]* Pichette of this place, who has been given the name Elizabeth Helene. Sponsors, Amedee Choquette and Marie Bernier. B. Delorme, Rector
S-8 N.C. Mary Duke	On August 4, 1881, Mary Duke, daughter of William Duke and Helen Rochbrune, of the parish of St. Paul, aged 14 years, was deceased after receiving the Holy sacraments and buried by me, the undersigned, in the presence of Henry Picard and John B. Piette. B. Delorme, Rector
B-15 Michel Jeremie Lucier	On August 7, 1881, I the undersigned, pastor of the parish of St. Paul, have baptized an infant, born the 22nd of July last of the lawful marriage of Joseph Lucier and Louise Martineau of this place, to whom was given the name Michel Jeremie. Sponsors, Francis Bourgeau and Adele Picard.
Page 140	B. Delorme, Rector
S-10 N.C. Stella Eberhard	On August 30, A.D. 1881, Stella Irene Eberhard, daughter of Elias Eberhard and Sara Jane Lucey, of this parish of St. Paul, aged 8 months and 4 days, was buried by me the undersigned in the presence of J. B. Piette and Henry Ernst. B. Delorme, Rector
S-11 N.C. Thomas Longtain	On September 2, A.D. 1881, Thomas Longtain, of the parish of St. Paul aged about 36 years, deceased the day before after receiving the holy sacraments, was buried by the undersigned in the presence of Xavier Moisan and Dieudonne Manaigre and others. B. Delorme, Rector

B-16
Phillipina
Agnes
Martha
Ernst
	On September 4, A.D. 1881, I the undersigned, rector of the parish of St. Paul, have baptized an infant born the day before of the lawful marriage of Henry Ernst and Magdelen Vesper, who was given the name Philippina Agnes Martha. Sponsors were Joseph Orth and Martha Connor.
	               Peter J. Orth Martha Connor
	                                                     B. Delorme, Rector

B-17 William Wood	On September 19, A.D. 1881, I the undersigned, rector of the parish of St. Paul, have baptized an infant born the 30th of April last of the lawful marriage of Joshua Wood and Helen Rochbrune of this place, to whom was given the name William. The sponsor was Charles Prevost. B. Delorme, Rector
S-12 N.C. William Wood	On September 22, A.D. 1881, I the undersigned have buried William Wood, infant son of Joshua Wood and Helen Rochbrune of the parish of St. Paul, deceased at the age of 5 months, in the presence of Henry Picard and Henry Ernst. B. Delorme, Rector
S-13 N.C. Mary Prevot	On September 23, A.D. 1881, Mary Prevot of the parish of St. Paul, daughter of Louis Prevost and Pauline Lallefod, deceased at the age of 11 years, having received the Holy Sacraments, was buried by me, the undersigned, in the presence of J. B. Piette, Charles Pelland and others. B. Delorme, Rector

B-18
Mabel
Rosa
Bergevin
	On September 25, A.D. 1881, I the undersigned, rector of the parish of St. Paul, have baptized an infant born on the 26th of July last of the lawful marriage of Charles Bergevin and Rosa Mathieu of this parish, to whom was given the name Mabel Rosa. Sponsors, J. Baptist Piette and Salome Bergevin.
	                                      John B. P. Piette
	                                                     B. Delorme, Rector

S-14 N.C. Joseph Prevot	On September 30, A.D. 1881, Joseph Prevot of the parish of St. Paul, son of Louis Prevot and Pauline Lallefot, aged 19 years, died after receiving the Holy Sacraments and was buried by me, the undersigned, in the presence of Peter Kirk and Charles Pelland. B. Delorme, Rector
Page 141 M-4	On October 4, A.D. 1881, after the publication of one ban, made on the

John McCormick & Kathe McKay

2nd instant in the churches of Gervais and St. Paul, and the dispensation of two other bans having been granted by the Archbishop of Oregoncity, and no impediment being found, I, the undersigned, pastor of the parish of St. Paul, after receiving their mutual consent to marriage, have united in holy matrimony John McCormick, of Gervais, son of Mathew Mc-Cormick and Joanna Clancy, and Catherine McKay of the parish of St Paul, daughter of James McKay and Cecelia Lawson, in the presence of witnesses, namely, Mathew McCormick, father of the groom, James McKay, father of the bride, John McKay, John McCormick, Mary Murphy and Cecelia McKay, who have undersigned with us.

Mathew McCormick	John McCormick
James McKay	Kate McKay
Charles McCormick	John McKay
Minnie Murphy	Cecelia McKay

B. Delorme, Rector

Confirmation

On October 9, 1881, the following received the Holy Sacrament of confirmation from the Most Reverend D. Charles Seghers, Archbishop of Oregoncity, in the church of St. Paul. Sponsors were, for the boys, James Coyle, and for the girls, Mary Connor.

James Raphael Kennedy	Antoine Eugene Labonte
Peter William Kirk	Edward James Murphy
Henry Joseph Ernst	Francis Napoleon Coleman
William Joseph Mooney	Edward Joseph Kennedy
William John Flynn	Henry Joseph Ahrens
John James Cook	Narcisse Edward Manaigre
John William Mathieu	Julius Edward Picard
John Francis Kerr	Joseph Eugene Richi
Gualtierrus John Murphy	Charles John Bernier
Eugene Philip Flynn	Joseph James Lucier
James Michael Kerr	Peter Francis Martineau
Andrew Peter Grenier	Peter James Bernier
Joanna Elizabeth Davidson	Andrew Daniel Longtain
Laura Em. Blandine Davidson	Helen Louise Agnes Coleman
Mary Margaret Agnes Richi	Elizabeth Anna Deilshnider
Mary Julia Kennedy	Mary Virginia Kirk
Susanne Agnes Murphy	Lucy Virginia Murphy
Elizabeth Mary Smyth	Mary Agnes Ruth Goodrich
Josephine Cecelia Wassenhove	Helen Carol Eberhard
Mary Clara Wassenhove	Bridget Julia Dowd
Celina Rosa Choquette	Henrietta Ray
Mary Helen Edith Jackson	Mary Anna Lucier
	Emilie Anna Manaigre
	Elizabeth Mary Dupre

In witness hereof,

B. Delorme, Rector of the parish of St. Paul

B-19 Josephine Richi

On October 9, A.D. 1881, I the undersigned, rector of the parish of St. Paul, have baptized an infant born on the 9th of August last, of Cyrille Richi and Josette Lavigneur of this parish, who was given the name Josephine. Sponsors were Charles Bernier and Amanda Mary Seguin.

B. Delorme, Rector

Page 142 B-20 Sara Magdalen Raymond

On October 9, A.D. 1881, I the undersigned, rector of the parish of St. Paul, have baptized an infant born the 2nd instant, of the lawful marriage of Augustin Raymond and Josephine Mongrain of this place, to whom has been given the name Sara Magdelen. Sponsors, Francis Mongrain and Magdelen Raymond.

B. Delorme, Rector

B-21 Mathilda

On October 10, 1881, I the undersigned, rector of the parish of St. Paul, have baptized an infant born the 24th of August last, of the lawful marriage

Flora Longtain	of Thomas Longtain and Mathilda Rivet of this place, who has been given the name of Mathilda Flora. Sponsors were Joseph Rivet and Marie Bernier.
	B. Delorme, Rector
M-5 Willis D. Shaw & Ellen McDonald	On the 11th of October, 1881, the dispensation of the impediment of different faiths having been granted by the Archbishop of Oregoncity, and no other impediment found, I the undersigned, rector of the parish of St. Paul, having heard their mutual consent to marriage given, have united in marriage Willis Dean Shaw, son of Hanson Dean Shaw and Marie Gy [rest illegible] of the parish of St. Paul, and Helen, of the same place, daughter of Myles McDonald and Anne Marie Galloway, in the presence of the following witnesses: William F. Graham, James Henry Mooney, Monica McDonald and [illegible].

Willis D. Shaw
Ellen McDonald

William Findley Graham
James Henry Mooney
Monica McDonald

B. Delorme, Rector

St. Paul, Marion Co. Oregon Oct. 11, 1881 I, the undersigned, solemnly promise Ellen McDonald, whom I am going to marry, to give her full liberty in regard to her religion, and also to raise our children, if we have any, in the Roman Catholic faith, according to her wishes.

Willis D. Shaw

Attests: Peter Kirk

S-15 O.C. Sara Magdelen Raymond	On the 12 October, 1881, I the undersigned have buried Sara Magdelen Raymond, daughter of Augustin Raymond and Josephine Mongrain of this parish of St. Paul, aged 10 days, in the presence of Peter Kitson and Henry Ernst.
	B. Delorme, Rector
B-22 Philip Mullen	On October 23, 1881, I the undersigned, rector of the parish of St. Paul, have baptized an infant born the 23rd of August last of the lawful marriage of Patrick Mullen and Mary Anna Flynn of this parish, who was given the name Philip. Sponsors, Charles E. Flynn and Helen Agnes Flynn.

Charles Flynn
Ellen Agnes

B. Delorme, Rector

M-6 Hugh B. Gearin & Mary Cecelia Murphy	On October 27, 1881, after the publication of one ban, made on the 23rd of this month, in the parish of St. Paul, and the dispensation of the other two having been granted, and no impediment being found, I the undersigned, rector of the parish of St. Paul, having received their mutual consent to marriage, have united in matrimony Hugh B. Gearin of this parish, son of John Gearin and Helen Burns; and Mary Cecilia Murphy of this same place, daughter of Andrew Murphy and Elizabeth Cosgrove, in the presence of the following witnesses: John, father of the groom, Andrew Murphy, father of the bride, Daniel Murphy and Catherine Murphy.

John Gearin
Andrew Murphy
Daniel Murphy

Hugh B. Gearin
Mary Cecelia Murphy
Cassie C [?] Murphy

B. Delorme, Rector

Page 143 S-16 N.C. Mathilda Flora Longtain	On December 2, A.D. 1881, I the undersigned have buried Mathilda Flora Longtain, daughter of Thomas Longtain and Mathilda Rivet of this parish of St. Paul, deceased on the 30th of November three months after her birth. Witnesses, George Corner and Fabien Rivet.
	B. Delorme, Rector

Total for 1881

Baptisms 22   Marriages 6   Burials 16
First communions 25   Confirmations 46

1882

B-1	The second of January, 1882, I the undersigned, rector of the parish of St.

Mary **Lebeau**	Paul, have baptized an infant born the 8th of November of last year of the marriage of Calixte Lebeau and Chloris Mongrain of Washington to whom was given the name Mary. Sponsors, Augustin Raymond and Josephine Raymond.

Augustin Raymond   Josephine Mongrain

B. Delorme, Rector

M-1 **James E.** **Eldridge** **&** **Mattie** **Abernethy**	On January 11, A.D. 1882, the dispensation of the disparity of faiths having been obtained from the Archbishop of Oregoncity, the promise to educate freely the children in the Roman Catholic faith from the infidel party, namely the groom, being made, and no other impediment being found, I the undersigned, Rector of St. Paul's parish, have received the mutual consent of marriage and have joined in holy matrimony James Edward Eldridge, from the parish of St. Louis, of-age son of F. Edward Eldridge and Ann Cosgrove, and Martha Abernethy of the parish of St. Paul, of-age legitimate daughter of Oliver Abernethy and Elizabeth A. Orton, in the presence of these witnesses, namely, Oliver Abernethy, F. Edward Eldridge and Antoine Arhens.

J. E. Eldridge

F. E. Eldridge   Mattie E. Abernethy

O. Abernethy

A. Ahrens

B. Delorme, Rector

Page 144 **B-2** **John** **Hanigan**	On January 22, A.D. 1882, I the undersigned, rector of the parish of St. Paul, have baptized an infant born the 14th of December last of the lawful marriage of William Hanigan and Helene Coffey of this place, who has been given the name of John. Sponsors were James Coyle and Henrietta, his wife.

J. J. Coyle   Mrs. J. J. Coyle

B. Delorme, Rector

S-1 N.C. **Child** **McPaulen**	On January 22, A.D. 1882, I the undersigned buried the infant son of Philip McPaulen and Josephine Ady of the parish of St. Paul, deceased at the age of one day, after baptism by me, in the presence of Henry Ernst and Patrick Geelan.

B. Delorme, Rector

M-2 **James** **Murphy** **&** **Elizabeth** **A. Kirk**	On February 20, A.D. 1882, the publication of one ban having been made in the parish of St. Paul and the dispensation of the other two having been granted, and no impediment being found, I the undersigned, rector of the parish of St. Paul, having received their mutual consent to marriage, have united in holy wedlock James Murphy of this parish, son of Mathew Murphy and Helen Costello, and Elizabeth Kirk of the same place, daughter of Peter Kirk and Margaret Lyons, in the presence of the following witnesses: Mathew Murphy, Peter Kirk, John Kirk, Daniel Murphy, Cecelia McKay and Elizabeth Coleman.

James C. Murphy   Lizzie Kirk   Cecelia McKay

M. O'C. Murphy   John Kirk   E. Coleman

Peter Kirk   Daniel Murphy

B. Delorme, Rector

B-3 **Albert** **Coleman**	On March 2, 1882, an infant son of W. Thomas Coleman and Elizabeth C. Orton of the parish of St. Paul, born on the 4th of February, to whom was given the name Albert, was baptized by me, rector of the parish of St. Paul. Sponsors: Charles O. Pelland and Emma Frances Coleman.

Charles O. Pelland   Emma F. Coleman

B. Delorme, Rector

B-4 **Nazaire** **Dupre**	On March 4, A.D. 1882, I the undersigned, rector of the parish of St. Paul, baptized an infant born the 25th of February last of the lawful marriage of Charles Dupre and Catherine Chalifoux of this parish, to whom was given the name Nazaire. Sponsors were Francis Raymond and Madelen Raymond.

B. Delorme, Rector

S-2 O.C.	On April 17, A.D. 1882, Francis Labonte, son of Alexander Labonte and

Francis Labonte	Clementine Lachance of St. Paul, deceased at the age of three years and six months, was buried by me in the presence of Louis Labonte and John Dowd.

M-3 Eusebe Forcier & Salome Raymond

B. Delorme, Rector

On May 8, 1882, the publication of one ban having been made in the church of St. Paul and the dispensation of the other two having been granted, I the undersigned, rector of the parish of St. Paul, having received their mutual consent of marriage, have joined in holy wedlock Eusebe Forcier, of the parish of Portland, son of Eusebe Forcier and Marie Lachapelle, and Salome Raymond, daughter of August Raymond and Marie Servant of this place, in the presence of the following witnesses: John Baptiste Piette, Frederic Fortain, Paul Duchos and Magdelene Raymond.

John B. P. Piette	Eusebe Forcier
F. Fortain	Salome Raymond
Paul Duchos	
Magdelen Raymond	

B. Delorme, Rector

B-5 Laurina Amanda Manaigre

On May 14, A.D. 1882, an infant, daughter of Dieudonne Manaigre and Emilie Manaigre, of this parish of St. Paul, husband and wife, born the 26th of April last, was baptized by me, rector of St. Paul, and given the name Laurina Amanda; sponsors were Edmond Dupuis and Rose Seguin.

Edmond Dupuis	Rosa Dupuis

B. Delorme, Rector

B-6 Daniel McCann

On May 21, A.D. 1882, an infant, son of Daniel McCann and Genevieve Longtain of the parish of St. Paul, born the 9th of February last, was baptized by me, the undersigned rector of St. Paul, to whom was given the name Daniel. Sponsors were Elias Eberhard and Sara Osborn.

Elias Eberhard	Sarah Osborn

B. Delorme, Rector

B-7 Minnie (Mary) Emilie Miller

On May 28, A.D. 1882, an infant, daughter of Jacob Miller and Elizabeth Feller of the parish of St. Paul, born the 11th of last year, to whom was given the name Marie Emilie, was baptized by me, the undersigned rector of St. Paul. Sponsors were Francis Wassenhove and Helen Coyle.

Ellen Mary Vanwassenhove

B. Delorme, Rector

B-8 W. Benedict Pillet

On June 4, A.D. 1882, an infant, son of Joseph Pillet and Marie Elizabeth Morissette, parents, living in St. Paul, born the 9th of May last and given the name W. Benedict, was baptized by me, rector of the parish of St. Paul. Sponsors, Cleophus Seguin and Josephine Aplin.

Cleophas Seguin	Josephine Aplin

B. Delorme, Rector

B-9 Honore John Baptist Bergevin

On June 18, A.D. 1882, an infant, son of John Baptist Bergevin and Salome Picard, husband and wife of the parish of St. Paul, born the 8th instant, to whom was given the name Honore John Baptist, was baptized by me, the undersigned, rector of the parish of St. Paul. Sponsors were Honore Picard and Marie Fortain.

B. Delorme, Rector

S-3 N.C. David Mongrain

On June 26, A.D. 1882, I the undersigned [rector] of St. Paul parish, have buried David Mongrain of this place, deceased at the age of 75 years after receiving the Holy Sacraments, in the presence of John Brentano, John McGrath and others.

B. Delorme, Rector

M-4 Francis Raymond & Angelica Dupre

On July 24, A.D. 1882, the publication of one ban having been made the preceding Sunday in the church of St. Paul and the dispensation of two others having been granted, and no impediment being found, I, the undersigned, rector of the parish of St. Paul, having received their mutual consent to marriage, have united in holy matrimony Francis Raymond, son of August Raymond and Marie Servant, and Angelica Dupre, daughter of

Charles Dupre and Catherine Chalifoux, in the presence of the following witnesses: Frederic Fortain, Charles Dupre, Peter Vivet and Magdelen Raymond.

| Frederic Fortain | Frank Raymond |
| Peter Vivette | Angelica Dupre |

B. Delorme, V.G.

B-10
Blanche
Geraldine
Davidson

On July 2, A.D. 1882, an infant, daughter of Francis Davidson and Anna Coleman of this place, born June 5th last, has been baptized by me, the undersigned rector of St. Paul, and given the name Blanche Geraldine. Sponsors were Charles Pelland and Marie Coleman.

| Chas. O. Pelland | Mary Coleman |

B. Delorme, Rector

B-11
Mary
Lelia
Bellique

On July 2, A.D. 1882, I the undersigned rector of the parish of St. Paul have baptized an infant born on June 20th last of the lawful marriage of Cyprian Bellique and Julienne Bergivin of this place, to whom was given the name Marie Leila. Sponsors were Amable Bergeving and Angelique Dupre.

Amable Bergevin

B. Delorme, Rector

S-4 N.C.
Nazaire
Dupre

On July 5, A.D. 1882, I the undersigned, rector of the parish of St. Paul, have buried Nazaire, son of the legitimate marriage of Charles Dupre and Catherine Chalifoux of this place, deceased yesterday at the age of six months. Present, Peter Kitson and Francis Lambert.

B. Delorme, Rector

Page 147
B-12
Theodore
Patrick
Dowd

On July 9, A.D. 1882, I the undersigned, pastor of the parish of St. Paul, have baptised an infant, born the second instant, of the lawful marriage of John Dowd and Julia Lachance of this place, to whom was given the name Theodore Patrick. The sponsor was Marie Dowd.

Mary Dowd

B. Delorme, Rector

B-13
Ernest
Melvin
Feller

On July 9, A.D. 1882, I the undersigned, rector of the parish of St. Paul, have baptized the son of Francis Feller and Rhuamah Whitney of Butteville, born the 28th of April last, to whom was given the name Ernest. Sponsors were Ernest Mathieu and Clara Mathieu.

| Ernest Matthieu | Clara Ouimette |

B. Delorme, Rector

B-14
Mary
Magdelen
[Ayote]

On July 9, A.D. 1882, I the undersigned, rector of the parish of St. Paul, have baptized an infant born on the 20th of June last, daughter of Baptiste Ayot and Josephine Raymond of Cowlitz, to whom was given the name Marie Magdalen. Sponsor was Marie Magdalen Raymond.

Magdalen Raymond

B. Delorme, Rector

B-15
Alice
Adelaide
Geelan

On July 23, A.D. 1882, I the undersigned rector of the parish of St. Paul, have baptized an infant, born the 21st of June last, of the legitimate marriage of Patrick Geelan and Elizabeth Ady of this place, to whom was given the name Alice Adelaide. Sponsors, Joseph Orth and Anna Kennedy.

| Joseph Orth | Anna M. Kennedy |

B. Delorme, Rector

B-16
Frederic
John
Gearin

On August 27, A.D. 1882, I, the undersigned pastor of St. Paul parish, have baptized an infant, born the 23rd instant, of the legitimate marriage of Hugh Gearin and Mary Murphy of this place, to whom was given the name Frederic John. Sponsors were Edward Murphy and Catherine Murphy.

| Ed Ward | Cassie Murphy |

B. Delorme, Rector

B-17
Anna
Elizabeth

On August 29, A.D. 1882, I the undersigned, rector of the parish of St. Paul, have baptized an infant born the 17th of July last of the legitimate marriage of Charles Wilson and Elizabeth Aplin of this place, to whom was given the

Wilson — name Anna Elizabeth. Sponsors were Stephen Pelletier and Magdalen Ernst.

E. Peltier Magdeilene Ernst
B. Delorme, Rector

Page 148
S-5 N.C.
Daniel
McCann
On November 11, A.D. 1882, I the undersigned, rector of St. Paul, have buried Daniel, son of Daniel McCann and Genevieve Longtain of this place, deceased at the age of 9 months. Witnesses, Francis Wassenhove, John Dowd, etc.

B. Delorme, Rector

S-6 N.C.
Anthony
Lambert
On November 25, A.D. 1882, I the undersigned, rector of the parish of St. Paul, have buried Anthony, son of Augustin Lambert and Catherine Piche, of this place, deceased at the age of 25 years, after receiving the holy sacraments, in the presence of Francis Lambert and John B. Piette, with others.

B. Delorme, Rector

B-18
Mary
Ellen
Murphy
On November 26, A.D. 1882, I the undersigned, Rector of St. Paul parish, have baptized an infant, born the 21st instant, of the lawful marriage of James C. Murphy and Elizabeth Kirk of this place, to whom was given the name Marie Helen. Sponsors were Thomas F. Kirk and Lucy E. Murphy.

Thomas F. Kirk Lucy E. Murphy
B. Delorme, Rector

B-19
Mary
Celina
Lambert
On December 3, A.D. 1882, I the undersigned, rector of the parish of St. Paul, have baptized an infant born on the 29th of November last, of the lawful marriage of Francis Lambert and Clementine Mongrain of this place, to whom was given the name Mary Celina. Sponsors were Stephen Pelletier and M. M. Ernst.

E. Pelletier M. M. Ernst
B. Delorme, Rector

B-20
Alexander
Louis
Raymond
On December 4, A.D. 1882, I the undersigned, rector of the parish of St. Paul, have baptized an infant born on the 22nd of November last of the legitimate marriage of Marcel J. Raymond and Odile Raymond of this place, to the name Alexander Louis was given. Sponsors were Alexander Raymond and Magdalene Ernst.

B. Delorme, Rector

S-7 N.C.
Archange
Dupre
On December 9, A.D. 1882, I the undersigned, rector of St. Paul, have buried Archange Dupre, daughter of Charles Dupre and Catherine Chalifoux, who died after have received the Holy Sacraments, at the age of 17 years on the 17th instant. Witnesses, John Dowd and James Coyle.

B. Delorme,

[Recorded as son, B-10, p 4.]

Page 149
B-21
Mathilda
Coyle
On December 19, A.D. 1882, I the undersigned, rector of St. Paul's parish, have baptized an infant, daughter of James Coyle and Henrietta Ray, of this place, born November 4th last, to whom the name Mathilda is given. Sponsors were Chas. O. Pelland and Caroline Kennedy.

Chas. O. Pelland Caroline Kennedy
B. Delorme, pr.

S-8 O.G.
Alex.
Louis
Raymond
On December 23, A.D. 1882, I the undersigned, rector of the parish of St. Paul, have buried Alexander Louis, son of the lawful marriage of Marcel Raymond and Odile Raymond of this place, aged one month. Present, J. B. Piette and Andrew Hughes.

B. Delorme, Rector

B-22
Alfred
Raymond
On December 23, A.D. 1882, I the undersigned, rector of the parish of St. Paul, have baptized an infant, son of Augustin Raymond and Josephine Mongrain of this place, born on the 9th instant, to whom was given the name Alfred. Sponsors were John B. Piette and Angelique Raymond.

B. Delorme, Rector

B-23
Charles
On December 30, A.D. 1882, I the undersigned, rector of the parish of St. Paul, have baptized an infant born the 26th instant to Patrick Mullen

Mullen	and Mary Flynn of this place, to whom was given the name Charles. Sponsors were Thomas Coakley and Susan Marie Smyth.

Thomas Coekly
B. Delorme, Rector

Total in 1882

Baptisms 23   Marriages 3   Burials 8

Page 150

S-1 N.C.
John
Cook

On January 2, A.D. 1883, I the undersigned, rector of St. Paul parish, buried John Cook of this place, deceased the 30th of December last at the age of 50 and . . . years, after receiving the Holy Sacraments, in the presence of Mathew Murphy and Andrew Hughes.

B. Delorme, Rector

B-1
James
Edward
Darnielle

On January 9, 1883, I the undersigned, rector of St. Paul parish, baptized a child born the 20th of October last of James Darnielle and Margaret Kennedy of The Dalles, to whom was given the name Edward. Sponsors were James Coleman and Mary Coleman.

B. Delorme, Rector

S-2
[Francis]
Lambert

On February 6, 1883, I the undersigned, rector of St. Paul, buried Francis Lambert, aged 16, having received the Holy Sacraments, son of Augustin Lambert and Marguerite Sanders of this place, in the presence of John McGrath and James Coyle.

B. Delorme, Rector

B-2
Catherine
Theresa
Fershweiler

On February 11, 1883, I the undersigned, rector of St. Paul, baptized an infant born the 29th of January last to John Fershweiler and Philomene Schraner of this place, to whom the name Catherine Theresa was given. Sponsors were Joseph Orth and Barbara Fershweiler.

P. J. Orth
B. Delorme, Rector

S-2 [sic]
N.C.
Mary
Bourgeau

On March 3, 1883, I the undersigned, rector of St. Paul, buried Mary Bourgeau, aged 5 years, daughter of Baptist Bourgeau and Genevieve Martineau of this place, in the presence of Alphonse Bonnin and Francis Dubreuil.

B. Delorme, Rector

B-3
Rosa
Doryla
Choquette

On March 11, 1883, I the undersigned, rector of St. Paul, baptized an infant born on the 7th instant of the lawful marriage of Amedee Choquette and Marie Bernier of this place, to whom was given the name Rosa Doryle. Sponsors, Henry Picard, junior, and Mary Choquette.

Henry Picard
B. Delorme, Rector

Page 151
B-4
Mary
Glory
Lily
Bellanger

On March 18, 1883, I the undersigned, rector of St. Paul, baptized an infant born the 4th instant to Jake Bellanger and Cloris Bernier, to whom was given the name Mary Glory Lily. Sponsors were Joseph Bernier and Genevieve Bernier.

B. Delorme, Rector

B-5
Mary
Philomene
Forcier

On March 24, 1883, I the undersigned, rector of St. Paul, baptized an infant born the 22nd instant to Eusebe Forcier and Salome Raymond of this place, and gave her the name Mary A. Philomene. Sponsors were Frederic Fortain and Marie Servant.

B. Delorme, Rector

S-3
John
Baptist
Labonte

On March 30, 1883, I the undersigned, rector of St. Paul, buried John Baptist Labonte, deceased at the age of 20 years, having received the Holy Sacraments, son of Louis Labonte and Josette Laframboise of this place, in the presence of John Dowd, Peter Kitson and others.

B. Delorme, Rector

B-6
Esther
Malanie
Parisot

On April 1, 1883, I the undersigned, rector of St. Paul, baptized an infant born the 20th of March last to Louis Parisot and Helene Larrison of this place, and gave her the name Esther Melanie. Sponsor was Marie Magdalen Raymond.

Magdalen Raymond
B. Delorme, Rector

B-7
Mary
Louise
Pelland

On April 10, 1883, I the undersigned, rector of St. Paul, baptized an infant born the 4th instant to Charles Pelland and Mary Coleman of this place, and gave her the name Marie Louise. Sponsors were James Baptiste Piette and Amedile Piette.

John B. P. Piette   Amidile Piette
                    B. Delorme, Rector

B-8
Bertha
Hughes

On April 24, 1883, I the undersigned, rector of St. Paul, baptized an infant born yesterday to Andrew Hughes and Rose Connor of this place, and gave her the name Bertha. Sponsors were Thomas McGrath and Jane Connor.

Thomas McGrath   Jane Connor
                    B. Delorme, Rector

B-8 [sic]
Louis
Dupre
p 152

On May 20, 1883, I the undersigned, rector of St. Paul, baptized an infant born the 6th instant to Charles Dupre and Catherine Chalifoux of this place, and gave him the name Louis. Sponsors were
[Missing] [This page would record the death of Archbishop F. N. Blanchet on June 18, 1883.]
[A later writer condensed the original entry and that of June 23, 1884, to read as follows:]
On June 21, 1883, the Most Rev. Archbishop Francis Norbert Blanchet, first Archbishop of Oregon, was buried in the cemetery of his mission in St. Paul; Solemn Requiem Mass was celebrated by the Most Reverend Aegidus Junger, Bishop of Nesqually; Archbishop Seghers pronounced the funeral eulogy. On June 23, 1884, his body was transferred from the small chapel to a crypt provided near the central cross of the Cemetery in St. Paul.
                    B. DeLorme, Rector
Francois Raymond and Angelica Dupre.
                    B. Delorme   Rector

B-10 [sic]
August
Albert
Robert

May 27, 1883, August Albert, son of Robert Robert and Marguerite Dupre his wife of this place, born the 31st of March, was baptized by me, undersigned Rector of the Church of St. Paul. Sponsors were Elzear and [sic] Dupuis and Rosa Mathieu.
                    B. Delorme   Rector

B-11
Josephine
Mabel
Foley

June 5, 1883, Josephine Mabel, daughter of John Foley and Sara Josephine Ayer, his wife, of this place, born last night [?] was baptized by me, undersigned Rector of the Church of St. Paul. Sponsors were Edward Kennedy and Lucy Connor.

Edward Kennedy   Lucy E. Connor
                    B. Delorme   Rector

S-4
Most Rev.
F. Norbert
Blanchet

June 21, 1883, after solemn mass offered by the Illustrious and Reverend D. D. Aegidius Junger, Bishop of Nesquallie, in the city of Portland, the body of Francis Norbert Blanchet, Archbishop Amidensis i.p.i. and formerly first Archbishop of the Diocese of Oregoncity, was transported to the Church of St. Paul, and complete absolution having been given, was deposited in a crypt in the cemetery of this mission until a proper tomb should be provided, the celebrant being the Illustrious and Most Reverend D.D. Charles John Seghers, Archbishop of this diocese, assisted by the above named priest of Nesquallie as well as the presbyters whose names follow, and in the presence of a multitude of the faithful from various missions of this diocese.

Aegidius Junger, Bishop of Nesquallie

B. Delorme	J. T. Fierens	F. X. Blanchet
A. J. Glorieux	L. Dielman	P. F. Gibney
T. J. Duffy	J. Ed. Hermann	J. S. White
P. Adehelm Odermatt O.S.B.		G. B. VanLin
Louis Metayer	Jacob Rauw	P. Barnabas Held O.S.B.
Edward O'Dea		

Chas. John   Arch. Oregon

B-12
Mary

June 8, 1883, Mary Lily, daughter of Adolphe Jette and his wife Mary Liard of this place, born the 10th of June, was baptized by the undersigned,

Lily Jette	Rector of St. Paul. Sponsors were John Picard and Magdelen Raymond.
Page 153	B. Delorme Rector

M-1
Lars [Nels]
Presto
Lind
&
Veronica
McDonald

On July 25, 1883, the dispensation over the impediment of mixed religions having been granted by the Archbishop of Oregoncity, and no other impediment having been found, I, the undersigned, rector of St. Paul, having received their mutual consent to marriage, have joined in matrimony Nils Presto Lind of the city of Portland, son of Lars Lind and Anna Henson, and Veronica McDonald of St. Paul, daughter of the late Myles McDonald and Anna Mary Galloway, his wife, in the presence of the following witnesses, Udell Clarke and Monica McDonald.

Udell N. Clark   N. P. Lind
Monica McDonald   Veronica McDonald
B. Delorme, Rector

B-13
William
Kerr

On August 5, 1883, I the undersigned, rector of St. Paul, have baptized an infant, born the 30th of July last, son of Samuel Kerr and his wife Catherine Kerr of this place, to whom was given the name William. Sponsors were William McKay and Josephine Wassenhove.

William R. McKay   Josephine Van Wassenhove
B. Delorme, Rector

B-14
Mary
Celina
Salome
Lucier

On August 26, 1883, I the undersigned, rector of St. Paul, baptized an infant, daughter of Peter Lucier and Thais Senecal, his wife, of this place, to whom was given the name Marie Celina Salome, the above born on the 15th instant. Sponsors were Joseph Bernier and Celina Choquette.

Celina Choquette
[no priest's signature]

S-5 N.C.
Patrick
Murray

On September 1, 1883, I the undersigned, rector of St. Paul, buried Patrick Murray of this place, aged 62 years, deceased yesterday after receiving the Holy Sacraments. Present, Francis Davidson, Thomas Coleman and others.

B. Delorme, Rector

S-6 O.C.
Nathan
Augustin
Raymond

On September 25, 1883, I the undersigned, rector of St. Paul, buried Nathan Augustin Raymond, son of Marcel Raymond and his wife Odile Raymond, deceased yesterday at the age of six months. Present, Baptiste Piette, James Coyle and others.

B. Delorme, Rector

S-7
Zilda
Boutin

On October 4, 1883, I the undersigned, rector of St. Paul, buried Zilda Boutin, daughter of Isaac Boutin and . . . his wife, of this place, deceased yesterday at the age of 14 years. Present, James Coyle, John McGrath and others.

B. Delorme, Rector

Page 154
S-8 N.C.
Mary
Agnes
Raymond

On October 5, 1883, I the undersigned, rector of St. Paul, have buried Mary Agnes Raymond, daughter of Marcel Raymond and his wife, Odile Raymond of this place, deceased yesterday at the age of 13 years, after receiving the Holy Sacraments. Present, James Coyle, Joseph Orth and others.

B. Delorme, Rector

S-9 N.C.
Mary
Dupre

On October 20, 1883, I the undersigned, rector of St. Paul, have buried Mary Dupre, daughter of Charles Depre and Catherine Chalifoux of this place, deceased yesterday at the age of 12 years, having received the Holy Sacraments. Present, Peter Kitson and John Dowd.

B. Delorme, Rector

S-10 N.C.
Alphonse
Ernst

On October 20, 1883, I the undersigned, Rector of St. Paul, have buried Alphonse, son of Henry Ernst and Magdelen Vesper, his wife, deceased yesterday at the age of 4 years. Present, Henry Wolfhart and Lino Patterson.

B. Delorme, Rector

S-11 N.C.
Catherine

On October 22, 1883, I the undersigned, rector of St. Paul, have buried Catherine, daughter of Charles Dupre and Catherine Chalifoux, deceased

Dupre	yesterday at the age of 10 years. Present, John Dowd and Charles Prevot.
	B. Delorme, Rector
S-12 O.C.	On October 24, 1883, I the undersigned, rector of St. Paul, have buried
August	August, son of Isaac Crete and Rosa Raymond his wife, of this place, de-
Crete	ceased yesterday at the age of 4 years. Present, John Dowd and Lino
	Patterson.
	B. Delorme, Rector
S-13 N.C.	On October 26, 1883, I the undersigned, rector of St. Paul, have buried
Paul	Paul Ernst, son of Henry Ernst and his wife Magdalen of this place, de-
Ernst	ceased yesterday at the age of 9 years, after receiving the Sacrament of
	Extreme Unction. Present, John McGrath and Henry Wolfhart.
	B. Delorme, Rector
S-14 O.C.	On October 29, 1883, I the undersigned, rector of St. Paul, have buried
Virginia	Virginia Crete, daughter of Isaac Crete and his wife, Rosa Raymond, of
Crete	this place, deceased yesterday at the age of 5 years. Present, Lino Patterson
	and Henry Ernst, etc.
	B. Delorme, Rector
Page 155	
S-15 O.C.	On November 6, 1883, I the undersigned, rector of St. Paul, have buried
Charles	Charles Kitson, son of Peter Kitson and Angelica Dupre, deceased yesterday
Kitson	at the age of 13 years, after receiving the Holy Rites. Present, Lino Patterson
	and Henry Ernst.
	B. Delorme, Rector
S-16 N.C.	On November 10, 1883, I the undersigned, rector of St. Paul, have buried
Andrew	Andrew Longtain, deceased yesterday, son of Thomas Longtain and the
Longtain	late Marie Montour. Present, Lino Patterson and Henry Ernst.
	B. Delorme, Rector
S-17 N.C.	On November 22, 1883, I the undersigned, rector of St. Paul, have buried
Mary M.	Mary Melissa, daughter of the late Andre Chalifoux and Emerance Mon-
Chalifoux	grain of this place, deceased yesterday at the age of 3 years. Present, Peter
	Kitson and Henry Ernst.
	B. Delorme, Rector
S-18 N.C.	On November 24, 1883, I the undersigned, rector of St. Paul, have buried
Mary	Mary, daughter of J. Osborn and Luce Longtain, his wife, of Salem, de-
Osborn	ceased yesterday at the age of 7 years. Present, Isaac Boutin and David
	[Daniel] McCann.
	B. Delorme, Rector
B-15	On December 27, 1883, I the undersigned, rector of St. Paul, have baptized
Blandine	a daughter of Charles Smyth and Leonie Patterson of this place, born the
Elmina	25th of this month, to whom was given the name Blandine Elmina. Sponsors
Smith	were Lino Patterson and Blandina Patterson.

Linus Patterson   Blandina Patterson

B. Delorme, Rector

Total for 1883

Baptisms   15   Marriages 1   Burials   18

1884

Page 156	
B-1	On January 13, 1884, I the undersigned have baptized an infant born
Mary	the 6th instant, daughter of Henri Picard and Marie Choquette of this
Hedwidge	parish, to whom was given the name Mary Hedwidge. Sponsors were Jake
Picard	Bellanger and Clarisse Bernier.
	B. Delorme
M-1	On January 21, 1884, I the undersigned rector of this parish, one publication
John	of the bans having been made in St. Paul church and the dispensation of
Kirk	two others having been granted, and no other impediment being found,
&	have joined in holy matrimony, having received their mutual consent to
Cecelia	marriage, John Kirk, son of Peter Kirk and Margaret Lyons, and Cecelia
McKay	McKay, daughter of James McKay and Cecelia Lawson, both of this parish,
	in the presence of witnesses, namely, Thomas Kirk, Daniel Murphy, Lucy

Murphy and Caroline Murphy, with Peter Kirk, the father of the groom.

Thomas Kirk	Lucy Murphy	John Kirk
D. R. Murphy	Caroline Kennedy	Cecelia McKay
Peter Kirk		

B. Delorme, Rector

S-1 N.C. John Kennedy

On January 21, 1884, I the undersigned, rector of St. Paul, have buried John Kennedy of this place, deceased yesterday at the age of 79 years, having received the Holy Sacraments, in the presence of James Coyle and Patrick Kelly and others.

B. Delorme, Rector

M-2 Louis Bergevin & Rosa Virginia Picard

On January 30, 1884, the publication of one ban having been made in the church of St. Paul the preceding Sunday and the other two bans having been dispensed with, and no other impediment being found, I the undersigned, have united in marriage Louis Bergevin, son of Louis Bergevin and the late Magdelen Servant, and Rosa Virginia Picard, daughter of Henri Picard and the late Celeste Rochbrune, both of this place, having received their consent to marriage, in the presence of the following witnesses: Hugh Cosgrove, Stephen Gregoire, Amable Bergevin and Magdelen Raymond.

Louis Bergevin	Hugh Cosgrove
Rosa Virginia Picard	E. S. Gregoire
Amable Bergevin	
Magdeleine Raymond	

B. Delorme, Rector

Page 157

B-2 Hugh Laflemme

On January 31, 1884, I baptized an infant, born the 24th instant, to Joseph Laflemme and Josephine Cecelia Ray, his wife, of this place, to whom was given the name Hugh by me, the undersigned, Rector of St. Paul. Sponsors were Hugh Cosgrove and Mary T. Williams.

Hugh Cosgrove   Mary T. A. Williams

B. Delorme, Rector

B-3 Peter Besset

On February 3, 1884, I the undersigned, rector of St. Paul, have baptized an infant born the 31st of January last to Cyrile Besset and Mary Laflemme of Gervais, to who was given the name Peter. Sponsors were Cleophas Seguin and Josette Laflemme.

Cleophas

B. Delorme, Rector

B-4 Francis H. Raymond

On February 24, 1884, I the undersigned, rector of St. Paul, have baptized Francis Hilaire, son of Francis Raymond and Angelique Dupre his wife, of this place, born the 11th instant, to whom was given the name Francis Hilaire. Sponsors were Charles Dupre and Catherine Dupre.

B. Delorme, Rector

B-5 Mary Agnes Lacourse

The 27 of February, 1884, I the undersigned, rector of St. Paul, have baptized an infant born the 1st instant to Claude Lacourse and Marie McKay, his wife, of this place, to whom was given the name Marie Agnes. Sponsors were David Gregoire and Helen McKay.

J. D. Gregoire

B. Delorme, Rector

B-6 Francis Henry Livingstone

On March 30, 1884, I the undersigned, rector of St. Paul, baptized Francis Henry, born the 11th instant to Richard Livingston and Mary Dugan of Woodburn, to whom was given the name Francis Henry. Sponsors were Thomas Kirk and Mary Kirk.

Thomas Kirk   Mary Kirk

B. Delorme, Rector

B-7 Paul Louis McGrath

On March 31, 1884, I the undersigned, rector of St. Paul, have baptized an infant, born today, son of John McGrath and Marie Hughes, of this place, to whom was given the name Paul Louis. Sponsors were P. Joseph McGrath and Catherine Agnes McGrath.

Peter Joseph McGrath   Catherine Agnes McGrath

B. Delorme, Rector

S-2
Antony
Labonte

On April 3, 1884, I the undersigned, rector of St. Paul, have buried Anthony, son of Louis Labonte and Josette Laframboise of this place, deceased yesterday, after receiving the Holy Sacrament, at the age of 17 years. Present were John Dowd and Simon Connor.

B. Delorme, Rector

Page 158
M-3
Nehemiah
S. Jones
&
Mary
Frances
McPaulin

On April 29, 1884, the impediment of mixed religions having been removed, and no other impediment being found, I the undersigned, rector of St. Paul, having received their mutual consent to marriage, have united in matrimony Nehemiah S. Jones of Champoeg, son of S. L. Jones and Julia McAllister, and Mary Francis of this parish of St. Paul, daughter of Roger McPaulen and his wife Ann Hathaway in the presence of the following witnesses, namely: S. L. Jones and F. E. Osborn, and Emma Jones.

| Emma Jones | S. L. Jones |
| N. S. Jones | F. E. Osborn |

B. Delorme, Rector

Frances Mary X McPaulen

S-3 N.C.
Mary
Hedwige
Picard

On May 3, 1884, I the undersigned, rector of St. Paul, have buried Marie Hedwige, daughter of Henry Picard and Mary Choquette his wife, of this place, deceased yesterday at the age of 4 months, in the presence of Amedee Choquette and Henry Ernst.

B. Delorme, Rector

B-8
Mary
Adeline
Hughes

On May 5, 1884, I the undersigned, rector of St. Paul, have baptized an infant born today to Andrew Hughes and his wife Rosa Connor of this place, to whom was given the name Marie Adeline. Sponsors were Thomas Hughes and Lucy Connor.

Thomas Hughes   Lucy G. Connor

B. Delorme, Rector

M-4
John
Ventura
&
Ellen
Dowd

On May 8, 1884, I the undersigned, rector of St. Paul, the dispensation of bans having been granted and no other impediment being found, have received the consent of marriage of John Ventura of Yam Hill county, son of John Ventura and Marie Leonard, and Helen Dowd of the parish of St. Paul, daughter of John Dowd and Julie Papin, and have united them in holy matrimony in the presence of the following witnesses, namely; John Dowd and Julia Papin.

John X Ventura   Ellen Dowd
[no priest's signature]

B-9
Margaret
Hilda
Davidson

On May 16, 1884, I the undersigned, rector of St. Paul, have baptized an infant, born the 4th of April last, of Francis Davidson and Anna Coleman, his wife, of this place, to whom was given the name Margaret Hilda. Sponsors were Simon Connor and Thecla McDonald.

S. J. Connor   Thecla McDonald

B. Delorme, Rector

[Notation filed with page 158]
I the undersigned, solemnly promise Mary Frances McPaulin, whom I am going to marry, to let her have full liberty to the practice of her religion, and also to raise our children, if we have any, in the Roman Catholic Faith, according to her wishes.

N. S. Jones

Page 159
B-16
Thomas
McKay

On May 17, 1884, I the undersigned, rector of St. Paul, have baptized Thomas, born the 26th of March last, to John McKay and Sophie Biscornet his wife, of this place. Sponsor, Helen McKay.

B. Delorme, Rector

S-4
Translation
of the body
of the Most
Reverend F. N.
Blanchet

On June 23, 1884, the body of Francis Norbert Blanchet, first Archbishop of Oregon, was transferred from a cell in the cemetery of St. Paul to a crypt near the central cross, where it has been built in the same cemetery. Witnesses were Rev. Sister Mary Margaret, Andrew Hughes, John McGrath, and others.

B. Delorme, Rector

B-12
Thomas
Mullen

On July 16, 1884, I the undersigned, rector of St. Paul, have baptized an infant, born June 18 to Patrick Mullen and Mary Flynn his wife, of this place, to whom was given the name Thomas. Sponsors were George Connor and Hannah Delauney.

B. Delorme, Rector

B-13
Arthur
Benjamin
Hedges

On July 20, 1884, I the undersigned, rector of St. Paul, have baptized Arthur Benjamin, son of B. F. Hedges and Anna M. Smyth his wife, living in Portland, who was born July 20, 1880. Sponsors were Adolphe Jette and Marie Weston.

Adolphe Jette, Jr.   M. J. Weston

B. Delorme, Rector

B-14
William
Clarence
Wilson

On August 10, 1884, I the undersigned, rector of St. Paul, have baptized William Clarence, son of Charles Wilson and Elizabeth Aplin his wife, of this place, born the 23rd of July last. Sponsors were John Picard and Clara McKay.

John Picard

B. Delorme, Rector

B-15
M. Rose
Fortier

On August 24, 1884, I the undersigned, rector of St. Paul, have baptized Mathilda Rose, daughter of Eusebe Fortier and Salome Raymond his wife, of this place, born the 15th of this month. Sponsors were I. Boutin and Rosa Raymond.

B. Delorme, Rector

Page 160
S-5
F. Graton's
child

On September 6, 1884, I the undersigned, rector of St. Paul, have baptized an infant, son of Felix Graton and Sophie Ouimette his wife, of this place, born and died yesterday, after being baptized. Present, Henry Ernst and Charles Coleman.

B. Delorme, Rector

B-15
Laura E.
Bergevin

On September 14, 1884, I the undersigned, rector of St. Paul, have baptized an infant born the 24th of August last, to John Bergevin and Salome Picard his wife, of this place, to whom was given the name Laura. Sponsors were Charles Bergevin and Rosa Mathieu.

B. Delorme, Rector

S-6
Maria
Galloway

On September 16, 1884, I the undersigned, rector of St. Paul, buried Maria Heeny of this place, wife of Charles Galloway, deceased yesterday at the age of 70 years. Present, Peter Kirk, James Coyle and others.

B. Delorme, Rector

B-16
William
L. Shaw

On September 20, 1884, I the undersigned, rector of St. Paul, have baptized an infant born the 8th of July last to William D. Shaw and Helen McDonald his wife, of this place, to whom was given the name William L. Sponsor was Mary McDonald.

B. Delorme, Rector

S-7
Esther
Field

On September 22, 1884, I the undersigned, rector of St. Paul, have buried Esther Dalcour, wife of Francis Field, deceased yesterday at the age of 55 years, after receiving the sacraments. Present, Mathew McCormick and Felix Gregoire, and others.

B. Delorme, Rector

M-5
John Th.
Brentano
&
Catherine
Ahern

On October 14, 1884, I the undersigned, rector of St. Paul, after the publication of two bans and *[the dispensation]* of the third being granted, and their consent to marriage having been obtained, have united in matrimony John Theodore Brentano, of this place, son of John Frederic Brentano and Elizabeth Muller; and Catherine Ahern of the same parish, daughter of Charles Ahern and Catherine Linane, in the presence of James Coyle, Reignier Brentano and Josephine Wassenhove.

James Coyle   John F. Theo. B. Brentano
Regnier L. M. Brentano   J. Kate Ahern
Josie Vanwassenhove

B. Delorme, Rector

Page 161
B-17

On October 16, 1884, I the undersigned, rector of St. Paul, have baptized

Denys Albert Lafontaine	an infant born the 22nd of September last, son of Narcisse Lafontaine and Margaret Pichette his wife, of this parish, to whom was given the name Denys Albert. Sponsors were Charles Pelland and Marie Pelland.

Chas. O. Pelland   Mary E. Pelland

B. Delorme, Rector

M-6
John
Lynch
&
Mary
Pillet

On October 19, 1884, I the undersigned, rector of St. Paul, after the publication of one ban and the dispensation of the other two, and no impediment having been found, and having received their mutual consent to marriage, have joined in matrimony John Lynch of Holden, in the county of Johnson, Missouri, son of Michael Lynch and Mary Coffey; and Mary Pillett of St. Paul, daughter of Joseph Pillett and Elizabeth Morrissette in the presence of Joseph Pillett, Louis Prevot, Edward Pillett and Josephine Wassenhoven.

Joseph Pillett   Ed. Pillett   John Lynch
L. Prevost   Josie Vanwassenhoven   Mary Pillett
M. Pillett   C. Seguin
A. Seguin

B. Delorme, Rector

[B-18]
William
Joseph
[Grissenhoven?]

On November 13, 1884, I have baptized an infant born the 10th instant, son of John Jacob Grissenhoven and Mary Karstor his wife, of this place, to whom was given the name William Joseph. Sponsors were John Frederic Joseph Brentano and Elizabeth Wilhelmina Josephine Mary Brentano.

J. F. J. Brentano   E. W. J. M. Brentano

B. Delorme, Rector

M-7
Francis
Hammond
&
Eliza
Coleman
Page 162

On November 19, 1884, I the undersigned, rector of St. Paul, the dispensation of three bans having been granted, have united in marriage Francis Hammond of Champoeg, son of Fletcher Hammond and Mary Hunt, and Elizabeth Coleman of this parish, daughter of James Coleman and Frances Murray, having received their mutual consent to marriage, in the presence of the following witnesses, Thomas Coleman, Charles Coleman, Emily Coleman, Louisa Coleman and John Davidson.

Charles D. Coleman   Frank C. Hammond
Emma F. Coleman   Eliza Coleman
Louisa E. Coleman
Jene Davidson

B. Delorme, Rector

Total for 1884

Baptisms   17   Marriages   7   Burials   7

1885

B-1
Rosa
Justina
Bellique

On January 6, 1885, I the undersigned, rector of St. Paul, have baptized an infant born the 29th of December last to Cyprian Bellique and Julienne Bergevin his wife, of this place, to whom was given the name Rosa Justina. Sponsors were Francis Raymond and Angelique Kitson.

Frank Raymond

[no priest's signature]

B-2
Alexander
Baptiste
Chaves

On February 5, 1885, I the undersigned, rector of St. Paul, have baptized an infant born the 31st of January last to Joseph Marie Chaves and Marie Anne Pion his wife, of this place, to whom was given the name Alexander Baptiste. Sponsors were Hugh Cosgrove and Mary Theresa Williams.

Mary T. A. Williams   Hugh Cosgrove

B. Delorme, Rector

B-3
Priscilla
Raymond

On February 22, 1885, I the undersigned, rector of St. Paul, have baptized an infant born the 12th instant, daughter of Augustin Raymond and Josephine Mongrain, to whom was given the name Priscilla. Sponsors were Isaac Boutin and Angelica Kitson.

B. Delorme, Rector

B-4
Charles
Remi

On March 20, 1885, I the undersigned, rector of St. Paul, have baptized an infant born March the second, son of Charles Bernier and Nathalie Mackay his wife, of this place, to whom was given the name Charles Remi.

Bernier

Sponsors were John McKay and Sophie Biscornet.

B. Delorme, Rector

Page 163

B-5
Raphael
Daniel
Kirk

On March 25, 1885, I the undersigned, rector of St. Paul, have baptized an infant born the 21st instant, to John William Kirk and Cecelia McKay his wife, of this place, to whom the name Raphael Daniel was given. Sponsors were Daniel Murphy and Mary Agnes Kirk.

Daniel Murphy
Mary Agnes Kirk
B. Delorme, Rector

M-1
Daniel
Murphy
&
Caroline
V.
Kennedy

On April 16, 1885, I the undersigned, rector of St. Paul, after the publication of one ban and the dispensation of two others, and no impediment having been found, and having received their mutual consent to marriage have united in holy matrimony Daniel Murphy, of this place, son of Mathew Murphy and Helen Costello, and Caroline Victoria Kennedy of the same place, daughter of J. D. Kennedy and Bridget Nagle his wife, of the same place, in the presence of the following witnesses, namely: William Murphy, Elizabeth Kennedy, etc.

William Murphy	Daniel Murphy
Elizabeth Kennedy	Caroline V. Kennedy
John Costello	

B. Delorme, Rector

B-6
Priscilla
Catherine
Wolf

On April 19, 1885, I the undersigned, rector of St. Paul, have baptized an infant born the 18th of March last to Joseph Bernard Wolf and his wife Catherine Rough, of the same place, to whom was given the name Priscilla Catherine. Sponsors were John Ferschweiler and Philomene Ferschweiler.

J. B. Ferschweiler   Philomene Ferschweiler
B. Delorme, Rector

B-7
Minnie
Bergevin

On April 26, 1885, I the undersigned, rector of St. Paul, have baptized an infant born the 30th of March last, daughter of Louis Bergevin and Rosa Virginia Picard his wife, of this parish, to whom the name Marie was given. Sponsors were Alphonse Boutin and Marcelline Chalifoux.

Alphonse Boutin
B. Delorme, Rector

B-8
J. Andrew
Gearin

On May 2, 1885, I the undersigned, rector of St. Paul, have baptized an infant born the 21st of April last, to Hugh B. Gearin and Marie Cecelia Murphy, his wife, to whom the name John Andrew was given. Sponsors were Walter Murphy and Elizabeth Murphy.

Walter Murphy   Bessie Murphy

Page 164

B. Delorme, Rector

B-10
Peter
Wirf

On May 10, 1885, I the undersigned, rector of St. Paul, have baptized an infant born the 24th of April last, to Peter Joseph Wirf and his wife Susanna Schuller of this place, to whom the name Peter was given. Sponsors were Peter Wirf and Elizabeth.   Peter Wirfs   Lizzie Wirfs.

B. Delorme, Rector

B-11
Ida
Jane
Bernier

On May 30, 1885, I the undersigned, rector of St. Paul, have baptized Ida Jane, daughter of Norbert Bernier and his wife Theresa Rivet, of this place, born March 4, 1882. Sponsors were William Lacourse and Mary Bernier.

Guillelmus Lacourse   Mary Bernier
[B. Delorme's writing]

B. Delorme, Rector

M-no#
Connor
S. &
Scully, Ag.

On June 1, 1885, after the publication of one ban and the dispensation of two others having been granted, and no impediment having been found, I the undersigned, rector of St. Paul, have united in marriage Simon Connor, son of the late Mathew Connor and Mary Mary, *[sic]* Lynch, and Agnes Scully, daughter of John Scully and Mary Horan, having received their mutual consent in the presence of Mathew Connor and Emma Martin.

Simon J. Connor	Mathew Connor
Agnes Scully	Emma Martin

B. Delorme, Rector

B-12
[Joseph
Peter
Ferschweiler]

On June 11, 1885, I the undersigned, rector of St. Paul, have baptized an infant born the day before to John Ferschweiler and his wife, Philomene Schraner, of this place, to whom was given the name Joseph Peter. Sponsors were Joseph Orth and Mary Wassenhove.

P. J. Orth   Mary VanWassenhove
[no priest's signature]

B-13
Francis
George
Lambert

On July 6, 1885, I the undersigned, rector of St. Paul, have baptized an infant born the 4th instant, son of Francis Lambert and Clementine Mongrain of this place, to whom was given the name Francis George. Sponsors were Francis Bernier and Marcelline Chalifoux.

Francis Bernier   Marceline Chalifoux
B. Delorme, Rector

Page 165
S-1
Laura
Bergevin

On July 13, 1885, I the undersigned, rector of St. Paul, have buried Laura, daughter of John Bergevin and his wife Salome Picard, of this place, deceased yesterday at the age of 10 months. Witnesses, Peter Kitson and Edward Coffey.

B. Delorme, Rector

B-14
Ann
Cecelia
Geelan

On July 16, 1885, I the undersigned, rector of St. Paul, have baptized Ann Cecelia, daughter of Patrick Geelan and Elizabeth Ady, born the second instant. Sponsors were Adolphe Pillett and Antoinette Pillet.

Adolphus Pillett   A. Pillette
B. Delorme

B-15
John
Arthur
Bellanger

On August 23, 1885, I the undersigned, rector of St. Paul, have baptized an infant born the 10th instant to Jake Bellanger and his wife Cloris Bernier, of this place, to whom was given the name John Arthur. Sponsors were Henry Picard and Marie Bernier.

B. Delorme, Rec.

B-16
Albert
Alexander
Hanigan

On December *[September?]* 20, 1885, I the undersigned, rector of St. Paul, have baptized an infant born the 31st of August last, son of William Hanegan and Helen Coffey, to whom was given the name Albert Alexander. Sponsors were John McGrath and Mary McGrath.

John McGrath
B. Delorme, Rector

B-17
Peter
Francis
Choquette

On October 11, 1885, I the undersigned, rector of St. Paul, have baptized an infant, born the 6th instant, to Amedee and his wife Marie Bernier, of this place, to whom was given the name Peter Francis. Sponsors were Amedee Chaquette and Celina Choquette.

B. Delorme, Rector

B-18
Mary
Gertrude
Picard

On October 11, 1885, I the undersigned, rector of St. Paul, have baptized an infant born the 7th instant, daughter of Henry Picard and Marie Choquette, his wife, of this place, to whom was given the name Marie Gertrude. Sponsors were John Picard and Genevieve Bernier.

John Picare   jane Bernier
B. Delorme, Rector

Page 166
B-19
Augustin
Raymond

On October 18, 1885, I the undersigned, rector of St. Paul, have baptized an infant born the 10th instant to Francis Raymond and his wife Angelica Dupre, of this place, to whom was given the name Augustin. Sponsors were Eusebe Fortier and Salome Raymond.

Salome Fortier
[no priest's signature]

B-20
John Fr.
Charles
Brentano

On October 21, 1885, I the undersigned, rector of St. Paul, have baptized an infant, born yesterday, son of John Frederic Theodore Boniface Brentano and his wife Catherine Ahern, of this place, to whom was given the name John Frederic Charles. Sponsors were John Frederic Joseph *[Brentano]* and Elizabeth Wilhelmina Josephine Mary Brentano.

J. F. J. Brentano   E. W. J. M. Brentano
B. Delorme, Rector

B-21
Barbara
Antoinette
Jones

On November 1, 1885, I the undersigned, rector of St. Paul, have baptized an infant born the 25th of October last, daughter of Nehemiah Jones and Mary Francis McPaulin of this place, to whom was given the name Barbara Antoinette. Sponsors were Edward Pillett and Elizabeth Anna Smyth.

     Edward Pillett   Elizabeth Hannah Smyth
                           B. Delorme, Rector

B-22
Agnes
Hughes

On November 8, 1885, I the undersigned, rector of St. Paul, have baptized an infant born yesterday, daughter of Andrew Hughes and Rose Connor, to whom the name Agnes was given. Sponsors were Mary McGrath and William McGrath.

                    William McGrath
                         B. Delorme, Rector

S-2
Jerome
Jackson

On November 13, 1885, I the undersigned, rector of St. Paul, have buried Jerome Jackson of this place, husband of Mary Cosgrove, aged 50 years, deceased the day before after receiving the Holy Sacraments. Present, James McKay, Hugh Cosgrove, Peter Kirk and many others.

                         B. Delorme, Rector

Page 167
S-3
Martha
Connor

On December 30, 1885, I the undersigned, rector of St. Paul, have buried Martha Connor of this place, daughter of the late Mathew Connor and Mary Connor, aged 20 years, deceased day before yesterday after having received the Holy Sacraments. Present, Rev. A. Croquet, Peter Kirk, James Coyle and many others.

                         B. Delorme, Rector

Total for 1885
Baptisms   22   Marriages   1   Burials   3

1886

B-1
Louis
Alphonse
[Mongrain]

On January 28, 1886, I the undersigned, rector of St. Paul, have baptized Louis Alphonse, born today, son of Emerance Mongrain and an unknown father. Sponsor was Mary Magdelen Ernst.

                         B. Delorme, Rector

B-2
Rosa
Ann
Smyth

On February 11, 1886, I the undersigned, rector of St. Paul, have baptized an infant born the 7th of December last, daughter of Francis Smyth and his wife Eleonore Nolan, of this place, to whom the name Rosa ann was given. Sponsors were Edward Coffey and Anna Delauney.

                    E. Coffey
                         B. Delorme, Rector

B-3
James
Daniel
Stanislaus
McKay

On March 16, 1886, I the undersigned, rector of St. Paul, record that an infant born the 11th instant, son of William McKay and Ann Kavanaugh, was baptized by Rev. P. Wernher and given the name James Daniel Stanislaus. Sponsors were Thomas Coleman and his wife Caledonia.

                         B. Delorme, Rector

B-4
George
Bergevin

On March 21, 1886, I the undersigned, rector of St. Paul, have baptized an infant born the 8th instant, son of John Bergevin and Philomene Picard, to whom was given the name George. Sponsors were Cyprien Bellique and Julienne, his wife.

                         B. Delorme, Rector

B-5
Page 168
Caroline
Amelia
York

On March 25, 1886, I the undersigned, rector of St. Paul, have baptized an infant born on the 15th of this month of the protestant marriage of Henry York and Charlotte York, his wife, to whom was given the name Caroline Amelia. The sponsor was Magdelen Ernst.

                         B. Delorme, Rector

S-1
Rev. Sr.
Mary
Columba

On April 4, 1886, I the undersigned, rector of St. Paul, have buried Reverend Sister Mary Columbo (Marguerite Trees) of the Congregation of the Holy Names of Jesus and Mary, deceased the day before at the age of 21 years, in the assembled Congregation [?], and the presence of the Reverend Mother of the Seven Dolors, Peter Kirk, Joseph Orth, Reverend Father Thibau and others.

                         B. Delorme, Rector

B-6 Maria Elizabeth White	On *[April]* 24, 1886, Maria Elizabeth, daughter of William Thomas White and Elizabeth France of Columbia County, Oregon, three years of age, was baptized by me, the undersigned, rector of St. Paul. Sponsors were William Trevor and Bridget Trevor.

Mary E. S. White

William Trevor   Bridget Trevor

B. Delorme, Rector

B-7 Victor George Connor	On April 24, 1886, the infant son of Simon J. Connor and Agnes Scully, his wife, of this place, born yesterday, was baptized by me, the undersigned rector of St. Paul, and given the name Victor George. Sponsors were Thomas Connor and Lucy Connor.

Thomas Connor   Lucy Connor

B. Delorme, Rector

B-8 Joseph Ignatz *[Thomas]*	On April 25, 1886, I the undersigned, rector of St. Paul, baptized an infant son of Thomas Ignatz and Barbara Hartman, of Dayton, born the 12th of July, 1883, to whom was given the name Joseph. Sponsors were Francis Bernier and Genevieve Bernier.

Francis Bernier   Jane Bernier

B. Delorme, Rector

Page 169

B-9 Ann Venice *[Marpele]*	On May 6, 1886, I the undersigned, rector of St. Paul, have baptized an infant daughter of Richard Ezekial Marpele and Julia Ann Rizeor, his wife, of this place, born the 12th of March last. Sponsor was Mary Apple *[sic]*.

Mary Aplin
B. Delorme, Rector

B-10 W. Joseph Coyle	On June 20, 1886, I the undersigned, rector of St. Paul, have baptized the infant son of James Coyle and his wife Henrietta Elizabeth Ray, born the 21st of May last, to whom was given the name Walter Joseph. Sponsors were Francis Wassenhoven and Emma Coleman.

Emma Coleman
B. Delorme, Rector

B-11 Mary Albertina Wilson	On June 24, 1886, I the undersigned, rector of St. Paul, have baptized the infant daughter of Charles Wilson and Elizabeth Aplin, born the 8th instant, to whom was given the name Mary Albertina. Sponsors were Firmin Lebrun and Sophie Lebrun.

F. Lebrun
B. Delorme, Rector

First
Communion

On the 24th day of June, A.D. 1886, the following members of the congregation of St. Paul were admitted for the first time to Holy Communion.

James William Kirk	Caroline Magdelen Ryan
John James Murphy	Mary Margaret White
Sebastian McDonald	Gertrude Cecelia Pelland
William McGrath	Mary Ann Fahy
Thomas Mathew Hughes	Catherine Gertrude Rivey
Albert Pelland	Margaret Alice Kirk
Joseph Guilbert Aplin	Mary Ann Martha Hughes
Leo Choquette	Rosa Mary McGrath
Edward Peter Kerr	Lily Agnes Jette
William Joseph Smyth	Emma Frances White
Joseph James Dowd	Rosa Elizabeth Manaigre
Joseph Delille	Rosa Magdelen Bernier
Frederic Stephen Davidson	

B. Delorme, Rector

Page 170

B-12 Chester Aloys Davidson	On July 11, 1886, I the undersigned, rector of St. Paul, have baptized the infant son of Francis Davidson and Anna Coleman, born the 23rd of June last, to whom was given the name Chester Aloys. Sponsors were Thomas Kirk and Susanna Murphy.

Thomas Kirk   Susie Murphy

B. Delorme, Rector

B-13
George
B. Dowd

On September 15, 1886, the infant son of John Dowd and Julie Papin, his wife, of this place, born the 11th instant, was baptized by me, the undersigned, rector of St. Paul, and given the name of George Bartholomew. Sponsors were George Wolfhart and Theresa Wolfhart.

Georg Wohlfart   Teresa Wohlfart

B. Delorme, Rector

B-14
Peter
Thomas

On October 3, 1886, I the undersigned have baptized Peter, born the 25th of June last, of Ignatz Thomas and Barbara Hartman, his wife. Sponsors were Francis Bernier and Genevieve Bernier.

J. S. White, Pr.

Confir-
mation

On December 8, 1886, I testify that the Sacrament of Confirmation was received from the Most Reverend and Illustrious Archbishop of Oregon City, William H. Gross, by these faithful in the Church of St. Paul. Sponsors were, for the boys, James Coyle, and for the girls, Elizabeth Wilhelmina Mary Brentano.

Edward Joseph Gratton
Peter Joseph Manaigre
Amedee Adolphe Choquette
Charles Thomas Lafontaine
Joseph Peter Bernier
James William Choquet
Alexander James Van Wassenhove
Louis Laurence Ernst
John William McGrath
Joseph John Smith

Page 171
Confirm-
ation (continued)

Alben James Burns

James Edward Smith
Thomas Mathew Hughes
Frederic James Stephen Davidson
Charles Albert Pelland
Edward James Kerr
Leo Peter Choquet
Joseph Gilbert Aplin
Joseph Thomas Delisle
James William Kirk
Sebastien Joseph McDonald
John James Murphy
Joseph Arthur Murphy
John Frank Davidson

Frances Thecla Jones
Ellen Cecelia Coffey
Mary Gertrude Coffey
Mary Ann Driscoll
Rosa Liza Manaigre
Mary Jane Manaigre
Theresa Elizabeth Wohlfhart
Frances Aurelia Martha Davidson
Martha Prudentia Blandina Reevey
Catherine Gertrude Reevey
Susie Martha Smith
Barbara Cecelia Ferschweiler
Christina Agnes Ferschweiler
Lizzie Gertrude Ferschweiler
Antoinette Blanche Pillett
Maggie Catherine Kirk
Rosa Mary McGrath
Florence Gertrude Cecelia Pelland

Attest:

G. B. Van Lin
J. S. White, Pr.

Mary Octavia Agnes Murphy
Carrie Mary Ryan
Mary Ann Martha Hughes
Grace Frances McClinchie

Page 172
B-15
Robert
Scollard

On December 18, 1886, I the undersigned, have baptized in the church of St. Paul Robert, born the 30th of October of this year of John Scollard and Alice Kelly his wife of this parish. Sponsors were: Edward Coffey and his wife Margaret.

J. S. White, Pr.

B-16
Mary
Elizabeth
Mullen

On December 20, 1886, I the undersigned have baptized in the church of St. Paul Mary Elizabeth, born the 17th of August of this year of Patrick Mullen and Mary Ann Flynn, his wife, of this parish. Sponsors were: William Smith and Elizabeth Smith.

J. S. White, Pr.

Baptisms	16
Marriages	0
Burials	1
First Communions	25
Confirmations	47

1887

S-1
Angelique
Toupin

On January first, 1887, I the undersigned have buried in the cemetery of St. Paul the body of Angelique Longtain, wife of [Francois] Toupin, who had received the Holy Rites and died at Dufur, said to be near the Dalles, at the age of 55 years. Witnesses, Daniel McCann, Joseph Orth, and many others.

J. S. White

S-2
Thomas
Coakley

On January 12, 1887, I the undersigned have buried in the cemetery of St. Paul the body of Thomas Coakley, who received all the Holy rites and died on the 10th day of this month and year at the age of 63 years. Witnesses, Edward Coffey, John D. Kennedy, and others.

J. S. White

Page 173
B-1
Antoinette
Frances
Fick

On February 12, 1887, I the undersigned have baptized Antoinette Frances, born the 8th of this month, of George Fick and Antoinette Kuesting, his wife, of this parish. Sponsors: Charles Kuesting and Antonia Kuesting.

J. S. White, Pr.

B-2
[Augustin
Alphonse
Isaac
Boutin]

On February 18, 1887, I the undersigned have baptized Augustin Alphonse Isaac, born the 9th of this month, of the illegitimate union of Alphonse Boutin and Rosa Crete. The sponsor was Mrs. Mary Magdelen Ernst.

J. S. White, Pr.

S-3
Peter
Servant

On February 19, 1887, I the undersigned have buried in the new cemetery of St. Paul the body of Peter Servant, who received all the Holy Sacraments and was deceased on the 17th of this month at the age of 46. Witnesses, Joseph Orth, Charles Pelland and many others.

J. S. White, Pr.

B-3
Philip
Oliver
Pelland

On March 9, 1887, I the undersigned have baptized Philip Oliver, born not long ago on 24th of February of Charles Oliver Pelland and Mary E. Coleman, his wife, of this parish. Sponsors, John Coleman and his wife Mary.

John Coleman   Chas. O. Pelland
Mary Coleman
Helen Louise Coleman

J. S. White, pr.

Page 174
B-4
Freeman

On March 12, 1887, I the undersigned have baptized Aloys, born the 9th of February of this year of Eusebe Fortier and Salome Raymond, his wife,

Aloys
Fortier

B-5
Amanda
McCullough
(new con-
vert)

S-4
Margaret
Gratton

S-5
Amanda
McCullough

B-6
Jennie
Mabel
McKay

Page 175
B-7
Elizabeth
Pearl
Jones

B-8
Frank
Wirf

B-9
John
Pichette

B-10
John
Hughes

B-11
Pearl
Anne
Lily
Lafontaine

Page 176
B-12
Geraldine
Euphemia
Kirk

S-6
William
Henry
Kirby

First
Commu-
nion

of this parish. Sponsors, Julien Prevost (absent) and Magdelen Payne.
J. S. White, Pr.
On March 23, 1887, I the undersigned, in the privacy of the home of George McCullough, her husband, have baptized Amanda, born January 27, 1869 — she being in peril of death. Sponsor: Mary Aplin.
J. S. White, Pr.

On March 21, 1887, I the undersigned have buried the body of Margaret, who was born March 20, 1882, of Felix Gratton and his wife Sophie, and died the 21st of this month. Witnesses: Felix Gratton, Charles Pelland and many others.
J. S. White, Pr.
On March 30, 1887, I the undersigned have buried in the new St. Paul cemetery the body of Amanda Hogel, wife of George McCullough. She died the 28th of this month at the age of 21 years. Witnesses: George McCullough, John McGrath and many others.
J. S. White, Pr.
On April 3, 1887, I the undersigned priest have baptized Joanne Isabel, born the 27th of March last of Ambrose McKay and his wife, Clementine Bourgeau, according to Civil law. Sponsors, J. Baptiste Bourgeau and Genevieve Martineau.
J. S. White, Pr.
On April 3, 1887, I the undersigned priest have baptized Elizabeth, born the 27th of March last, of Nehemiah Jones and Frances Thecla McPoland, his wife, of this place. Sponsors were Henry Ernst, Jr., and Monica McDonald.
J. S. White, Pr.
On April 17, 1887, I the undersigned priest have baptized Francis Xavier Wirf, born the third of this month and year of Peter Wirf of this place and his wife Susanna Schuller. Sponsors: Francis Wirf and Mary Van Hoomissen (absent).
J. S. White, Pr.
On April 17, 1887, I the undersigned priest have baptized John, born the first of December, 1881, of Roch Pichette and Victoire Despard, his wife. Sponsors: Francis Bernier and Celina Choquette.
J. S. White, Pr.
On May 2, 1887, I the undersigned priest have baptized John, born yesterday of Andrew Hughes and his wife Rosa V. Connor, of this place. Sponsors: Simon Connor and his wife Agnes.   S. J. Connor   Agnes Connor
J. S. White, Pr.
On June 11, 1887, I the undersigned priest, have baptized Pearl Anne Lily, born the 5th of April last of Narcisse Lafontaine and Margaret Pichette, his wife. Sponsors, Charles Lafontaine and Rosa Lima Delisle.
J. S. White, Pr.

On June 19, 1887, I the undersigned priest have baptized Geraldine Euphemia, born yesterday of John Kirk and his wife Cecelia McKay, of this parish. Sponsors, James McKay and Ellen M. Murphy.
J. S. White, Pr.
On June 20, 1887, I the undersigned priest have buried in the cemetery of St. Paul, the body of William Henry Kirby, who was born July 24, 1859, of Thomas Peter Kirby and Mary Burns, his wife, of Yamhill, and who died the 18th instant, having received all the Holy Sacraments. Witnesses: Thomas P. Kirby and his wife, Henry Gee, Peter Kirk, Louis Hirsch, and many others.
J. S. White, Pr.
On June 24, 1887, the boys and girls whose name follow have observed the first duty of the Holy Sacrament:
Francis Ignatius McDonald   Peter Clement Smith

Joseph Arthur Murphy
Charles Kerr
John Fr. Davidson
Mary Octavia Murphy
Susanna Dowd
Lily Mary Boutin
Joanne Gleeson
Martha Joanne Hughes
Margaret Rosa Lima Delisle

Patrick Bartholomew Aplin
Francis McGrath

Grace McClinchie
Catherine Coffey
Elizabeth Ferschweiler
Elizabeth Anna Vanwassenhoven
Margaret Catherine Manaigre
Josephine Matilda Crete
J. S. White, Pr.

B-13
Charles
Regnier
Brentano

On July 3, 1887, I the undersigned priest have baptized Charles Regnier, born the 30th of June last, of John Frederic Theodore Boniface Brentano and his wife, Catherine Ahern of this place. Sponsors: Regnier L. Brentano and Hannah Delauney.

J. S. White, Pr.

Page 177
B-14
Herbert
Joseph
Wirf

On July 31, 1887, I the undersigned priest have baptized Herbert Joseph, born on the 3rd instant, of Ferdinand Wirf and his wife, Christina Kloetch, of Yamhill. Sponsors: Peter J. Wirf and Susanna Wirf.

J. S. White, Pr.

S-7
Rev. Sr.
Mary
Encratis

On August 23, 1887, I the undersigned, vicar for the Sisters of the Holy Names of Jesus and Mary in Portland, have buried in the way of the Sisters of St. Paul, the body of Sister Mary Enchratis (Annie Bow), who died the day before yesterday, after receiving all the Holy Sacraments. Present, Rev. J. S. White, Mother Superior, and a great number from the parish.

G. C. Thibau

B-15
Francis
A.
Geelan

On September 11, 1887, I have baptized in the church of St. Paul Francis Aloys born the 17th of last month, of Patrick and Elizabeth Geelan, his lawful wife, of this parish. Sponsors: John and Joanne Geelan, father and sister of the child.

Janie Geelan   Elizabeth Geelan
James P. Geelan

F. X. Blanchet, Rector

B-16
Henry L.
Raymond

On October 16, 1887, I have baptized in the church of St. Paul Henry Louis, born the 12th instant of August and Josephine Raymond, legally married, of this parish. Sponsors: Henry Ernst and Mary Magdelen Ernst.

Augustin Raymond
Henry Ernst
Mary Madeleine Ernst

F. X. Blanchet, Rector

Page 178
First
Commu-
nion

On November 20, 1887, Mary Anna Burns received the first holy communion in the chapel of the Sisters of the Most Holy Names.

F. X. Blanchet, Rector

S-8
Rev.
Julien
DeCraen

On November 22, 1887, after a solemn requiem mass, the body of Rev. Julien DeCraene, inhumed in a cell in the church of St. Paul on September 15, 1873, was reinterred in the new cemetery near the body of Archbishop F. N. Blanchet. Witnesses, Joseph Orth, John McGrath, Andrew Hughes, John Kirk, R. Emmet Kirk, and others.

F. X. Blanchet, Rector

B-17
Irene
Gearin

On December 9, 1887, I have baptized at home Irene, born the 17th of November last, daughter of Hugh and Mary Gearin, his wife, of this parish. Sponsors, Louisa and William Murphy, sister and brother.

F. X. Blanchet, Rector

B-18
Edward
Lambert

On December 26, 1887, I have baptized in the church of St. Paul Edward, born the 20th instant, son of Francis and Marie Lambert, his wife, of this parish. Godparents, Edward and Margaret Coffey.

F. X. Blanchet, Rector
[1887]

Baptisms	18
Marriages	0
Burials	8
1st Communions	20
Confirmations	0

1888

Page 179

S-1
Reinetta
Larrison

On February 14, 1888, Reinette Larrison, widow, died 2 days ago at the age of about 80 and was buried in the new cemetery of St. Paul. Witnesses, John McGrath, Joseph Orth, and many others.

F. X. Blanchet, Rector

B-1
J. B.
Silas
Labonte

On February 26, 1888, I have baptized in the church of St. Paul Silas John Baptist, born the 17th instant, of Alexander and Clementine Labonte, his wife, of this parish. Godparents, J. B. Gagnon and Mrs. Juliana Vivet.

F. X. Blanchet, Rector

B-2
Georgia
L. Anna
Belanger

On March 4, 1888, I have baptized in the church of St. Paul, Georgia Laura Anna, born the 11th last, of Jake and Clorice Belanger, his wife, of this parish. Godparents, Amedee Choquette and Rosa Manaigre.

F. X. Blanchet, Rector

S-2
F.
Adolphe
Chamberlan

On March 6, 1888, Francis Adolphe Chamberland, widower, aged about 70 years, died and was buried in the old cemetery of St. Paul. Witnesses, M. Seguin, Woodburn, Lachapelle the same, A. Choquette, John McGrath, and many others.

F. X. Blanchet, Rector

S-3
Virginia
McKay

On March 10, 1888, Virginia, aged 10 years, daughter of Moise and Josephine McKay, his wife, of Champoeg, died and was buried in the new cemetery of St. Paul. Witnesses, Bernard Flynn and Henry Ernst and others.

F. X. Blanchet, Rector

B-3
Josephine
L.
Wilson

On March 10, 1888, I have baptized in the church of St. Paul Josephine Lily, born the 31st of January last, daughter of Charles and Elizabeth Wilson (mixed marriage) of this parish. Godparents, Louis Ernst and Mary Ernst.

F. X. Blanchet, Rector

Page 180

B-4
William
Arthur
McKay

On March 24, 1888, I have baptized in the church of St. Paul William Arthur, born the 15th instant, of William R. and Annie McKay, his wife, of this parish. Godfather, John N. McKay, godmother, Sarah Kavenaugh.

Sarah Kavenaugh
John N. McKay
F. X. Blanchet, Rector

B-5
Mary
Sarah
Gaeser
First
Communion

On March 31, 1888, I have baptized in the church of St. Paul, Maria Sarah Gaeser, born July 18, 1877, to John and Emma Gaeser, his wife, of Yamhill County. Godfather, Joseph Orth, Godmother, Antoinette Pillette.

F. X. Blanchet, Rector

On April 17, 1888, Henrietta Rosa Ouimette, of Butteville, received the first Holy Communion in danger of death.

F. X. Blanchet, Rector

B-6
Catherine
Mullen

On April 21, 1888, I baptized in the church of St. Paul born the 9th instant, of Patrick Mullen and his wife Mary Mullen, of this parish. Godfather, Anthony Ahrens, godmother, Magdelen Ernst.

F. X. Blanchet, Rector

B-7
Lily
Mary
Ogle

On April 29, 1888, I baptized at home in danger of death Lily Mary Ogle, aged 21 years the 5th of November last, of this parish.

F. X. Blanchet, Rector

B-8
Joseph
C. Ogle

On May 6, 1888, I baptized in the church of St. Paul Joseph Claude, born March 30th, last year, of Lily Mary Ogle of this parish, and an unknown father. Godfather, R. E. Kirk, godmother, Mrs. Genevieve Bernier.

R. E. Kirk
F. X. Blanchet, Rector

M-1
John A.
Picard
&
Celina
Virginia
Choquette

On May 7, 1888, after the publication of one ban and the dispensation of the other two, and no impediment being found, I the rector of St. Paul, having received their mutual consent, united in marriage John A. Picard and Celina Virginia Choquette, of age, in the presence of:

  A. Amedee   A. Choquette
  Georgia Seguin

       F. X. Blanchet, Rector

Page 181
M-2
F. X.
Goyette
&
Anna
Delauney

On May 14, 1888, no proclamation having been made by reason of a dispensation by R.R.D.D. W. H. Gross, Archbishop of Oregon City, and no impediment found, I, the rector of St. Paul, having received their mutual consent, have joined in matrimony Francis Xavier Goyette and Anna Deloney, of age, witnesses: William E. Smyth and Lizzie W. Smyth.

       F. X. Blanchet, Rector

B-9
Charles
R
Picard

On May 15, 1888, I have baptized at home, in danger of death, Charles Raoul, born the 13th of January last, of Henry and Marie Picard, his wife, of this parish. Godfather, Joseph Bernier, godmother, Mrs. Celina Virginia Picard.

       F. X. Blanchet, Rector

S-4
Wilfred
Aplin

On May 21, 1888, Wilfred Aplin, aged about 12 years, [son] of George and Marie Aplin, died and was buried today in the new cemetery of St. Paul. Witnesses: Joseph Pilett, Mathew Murphy and others.

       F. X. Blanchet, Rector

B-10
Bertha
J. Wolf

On May 27, 1888, I baptized in the church of St. Paul Bertha Josephine, born the 28th of April last, to Joseph Bernard and Catherine Wolf, his wife, of Butteville. Godfather, Thomas McGrath, godmother, Elizabeth Van Wassenhove. Eliza Van Wassenhove Thomas McGrath

       F. X. Blanchet, Rector

B-11
Felix
A.
Choquette

On May 28, 1888, I have baptized in the church of St. Paul Felix Arthur, born the 20th instant, of Amedee and Marie Choquette, his wife, of this place. Godfather, Felix Gratton, Godmother, Sophie Gratton.

  Felix Gratton   Sophie Gratton
       F. X. Blanchet, Rector

B-12
Justin
Connor

On May 29, 1888, I have baptized in the church of St. Paul Justin, born yesterday, of the legitimate marriage of Simon A. and Agnes Connor, of this place. Godfather, Thomas M. Hughes, godmother, Mary Ann Hughes.

    Simon A. Connor
    Mary Ann Hughes
    Thomas M. Hughes
       F. X. Blanchet, Rector

Page 182
B-13
Marie
Eva
Pinard

On May 31, 1888, I have baptized Marie Eva, born the 23rd of April last, to Theophylus and Flora Pinard, his wife, of Butteville. Godfather, Anthony Rihard, godmother, Eva Heft.

       F. X. Blanchet, Rector

B-14
Mary A.
Aplin

On May 31, 1888, I baptized Mary Amanda, born the 26th of April last, to George E. and Amelia Aplin, his wife, of this parish. Godfather, George Aplin, Sr., godmother, Marie Aplin.

       F. X. Blanchet, Rector

B-15
Flora
Dora
Lebeau

On June 8, 1888, I have baptized in the church of St. Paul have baptized Flora Dora, born the 14th of October last, of the legitimate marriage of Calixte and Clarisse LeBeau of Washington County. Godfather, Francis Bernier, godmother, Flora Dealuney.

       F. X. Blanchet, Rector

B-16
Arthur
Fr.
Jette

On June 27, 1888, I have baptized Arthur Freeman, born the 23rd of September last, of the marriage of Adolph and Marguerite Jette of Champoeg. Godfather, Julien Prevost, godmother Caroline E. Provost.

       F. X. Blanchet, Rector

B-17

On June 17, 1888, I have baptized Francis allen, born the 24th of May

Francis
A.
Chamberland
of the marriage of Fabien and Leocadie Chamberland of Woodburn. God-parents, Francis and Genevieve Bernier.

F. X. Blanchet, Rector

B-18
William
Theodore
Gaeser
On June 23, 1888, I have baptized William Theodore, born the 27th of September, 1875, of the mixed marriage of Peter and Anna Catherine Gaeser of Yamhill County. Godfather, Alexander Wassenhove, godmother, Helen Wassenhove.

F. X. Blanchet, Rector

First
Commun-
ion
On June 24, 1888, in the church of St. Paul the first Holy Sacrament was received by the following:

Lily Cunningham
Marie Smith
Lucy Delisle
Sarah Gaeser

William Gaeser
Henry Pilett
John Driscoll
Anthyme Ernst
Maxime Lafontaine
Louis Lafontaine
Benoni Lafontaine
Francis Smith
Samuel Kerr

F. X. Blanchet, Rector

Page 183
B-19
Mary
Elizabeth
Wirf
On July 8, 1888, I have baptized Mary Elizabeth, born the 17th of June, of the marriage of Francis and Elizabeth Wirf of this parish. Godfather, P. J. Wirf, godmother, Mary Josephine Van Hoomissen.

P. J. Wirf   Mary Josephine Van Hoomissen

F. X. Blanchet, Rector

First
Commun-
ion
On July 21, 1888, Mary Lily Ogle received the first Holy Communion in her home, in danger of death.

F. X. Blanchet

S-5
Lily
Mary
Ogle
On August 20, 1888, Lily Mary Ogle, aged about 22 years, died and was buried today in the new cemetery. Witnesses, Francis Smith, Hugh Gearin, Joseph Pilett.

F. X. Blanchet, Rector

B-20
Lucy
Hughes
On August 20, 1888, I baptized Lucy, born today, of the marriage of Andrew and Rosa Hughes, of this parish. Godfather, Francis McGrath, godmother, Rosa McGrath.

Andrew Hughes

F. X. Blanchet, Rector

B-21
Matthew
Hughes
On August 20, 1888, I, rector of St. Paul, have baptized in the church matthew, born today of the marriage of Andrew and Rosa Hughes of this parish. Godfather, F. X. Blanchet, godmother, Sister Matthew.

F. X. Blanchet, Rector

B-22
Ethel
Beatrice
Payne
On September 2, 1888, I the rector of St. Paul, have baptized in the church Ethel Beatrice, born the 9th of last month, of C. T. and Marie Payne, his wife, of this parish. Godfather, Henry Ernst, godmother, Salome Fortier.

Fortier.   Salome Fortier   Herny Ernst

F. X. Blanchet, Rector

S-6
Daniel
David
On September 2, 1888, Daniel David, aged about 19 years, died yesterday and was buried today in the new cemetery. Witnesses: Joseph McGrath, Joseph Dowd and Bud Larson.

F. X. Blanchet, Rector

Page 184
B-23
Anna
Elizabeth
Wirf
On September 16, 1888, I, rector of St. Paul, have baptized in the church Anna Elizabeth, born the 14th of August last, of Ferdinand J. and Christina Wirf, husband and wife of Yamhill County. Godfather, F. C. Wirf, god-mother, Elizabeth Wirf, his wife.

F. X. Blanchet, Rector

S-7
Gertrude
On September 27, 1888, Gertrude, aged about 5 months, daughter of Mathew and Marie Murphy of Sprague, W.T., died and was buried today

Murphy	in the new cemetery of St. Paul. Witnesses, Narcisse Lafontaine, Simon Connor and others.
	<div align="right">F. X. Blanchet</div>
B-24 Catherine M. Fick	On September 30, 1888, I, rector of St. Paul, baptized in the church Catherine Marie, born the 18th of this month of the legitimate marriage of George and Antoinette Fick of this parish. Godfather, John Bearshorst, godmother M. Kuensting.
	John Bearhost Mary Kuensting
	<div align="right">F. X. Blanchet, Rector</div>
B-25 Joseph Victor Lafontaine	On October 21, 1888, I baptized in the church Joseph Victor, born the 15th of this month, to Narcisse and Marguerite Lafontaine, his wife, of this parish. Godfather, Joseph Delisle, Godmother, Lucy Delisle.
	Joseph Delisle Lucy Delisle
	<div align="right">F. X. Blanchet, Rector</div>
M-3 Chas. P. McCormick & Mary C. Wassenhove	On October 24, 1888, after the dispensation of two bans and the publication of the third, and no impediment being found, I, rector of St. Paul, having received their mutual consent, have joined in holy matrimony Charles P. McCormick of St. Gervais and Mary Clara Wassenhove of this parish, of age. Witnesses, Anna Kennedy and A. J. Wassenhove.
	A. J. Wassenhove Miss Anna Kennedy
	<div align="right">F. X. Blanchet, Rector</div>
M-4 Thomas J. Kerr & Joephine C. Wassen- hoven	On October 24, 1888, after the publication of one ban and the dispensation of the other two, I, rector of St. Paul, having found no impediment, and having received their mutual consent, have united in marriage Thomas J. Kerr and Josephine C. Wassenhoven, both of age, of this parish. Witnesses, Elizabeth Wassenhoven and F. W. Coleman.
	Miss Eliza Van Wassenhove T. W. Coleman
	<div align="right">F. X. Blanchet, Rector</div>

S-8
Rev.
Sister
Mary
Hilaria

Page 185

On November 27, 1888, I the undersigned, capellanus of the Sisters of the Holy Names of Jesus and Mary, from Portland, have buried with the Community of the Sisters in St. Paul Sister Mary Hilaria (Mary Anna Hagerty) who died the 25th of this month, having received the Holy Sacraments. Present was the Mother Superior and many others from the parish.

Jacob Rauw, Capellanus

B-26
Mary
Elizabeth
Dwyer

On December 8, 1888, I, Archbishop of Oregon *[City]* have baptized in the church of St. Paul Mary Elizabeth, born February 22, 1875, of the marriage of Franklin and Mary Ann Dwyer of Multnomah County. Godfather, William Trevor, godmother, Bridget Trevor. (First Communion in the church the next day.)

Wm. H. Gross
Archbp. Oregon

First
Commun-
ion

On December 9, 1888, the undersigned faithful have received from the Most Reverend and Illustrious Archbishop of Oregon, William H. Gross, in the church of St. Paul. Sponsors were: John Coleman for the boys and Mrs. Mary McGrath for the girls:

Bartholomew David Aplin	Samuel James Kerr
Alex. Francis Prevost	Eugene Louis Davidson
Frank James Smith	Ig. F. Peter McDonald
Peter Francis Smith	Ben. Peter Lafontaine
Louis John Lafontaine	Chas. Andrew Kerr
Wm. James Gaeser	Anthyme Ignatz Ernst
James H. Francis Pillett	Frank Philip McGrath
Maxime Peter Lafontaine	Remy John Aplin

Page 186

Mary Agnes Smith	Joan Victoria Hughes
Mary Lily Cecelia Dwyer	Edna Cecelia Davidson
Delima Agnes Delisle	Mary Matilda Wilson

Agnes Mary Burns
Eliza Margaret Wassenhove
Lucy Victoria Delisle
Lily Victoria Cunningham
Mary Teresa Reilly
Gussie Mary Miller

Sara Flavia Gaeser
Anna Victoria Gratton
Matilda Agnes Crete
Leonora Magdelen Choquette
Lily Cecelia Boutin

Wm. H. Gross
Archbp. Oregon

S-9
Mathew
Hughes

On December 18, 1888, Mathew, aged about four months, son of the legitimate marriage of Andrew and Rosa Hughes of this parish, died and was buried today in the new cemetery of St. Paul. Witnesses, Mathew Murphy, Sr., Thomas McGrath and others.

F. X. Blanchet, Rector

B-27
Charles
Herman
Coyle

On December 23, 1888, I, rector of St. Paul, have baptized in the church Charles Herman, born the 23rd of November last to James and Elizabeth Coyle, his wife, of this parish. Godfather, Thomas Kerr, godmother, Josephine C. Kerr.

F. X. Blanchet, Rector

B-28
Agnes
V.
Fortier

On December 23, 1888, I, rector of St. Paul, have baptized in the church Agnes Valma, born the 30th of last month, of the legitimate marriage of Eusebe and Salome Fortier of this parish. Godparents, Julien and Caroline Emilie Provost.

F. X. Blanchet, Rector

First
Commun-
ion

On December 25, 1888, Hugh McPaulin received the First Communion in the church of St. Paul.

Relics of
Saint
Victoria

On December 8, 1888, I testify that the relics of Saint Victoria, martyr, non virginis, was exposed for the first time for the public veneration of the faithful in the church of St. Paul by the Right Reverend Archbishop of Oregon, W. H. Gross.

F. X. Blanchet, Rector

Page 187

Recapitulation for 1888

	Baptisms	28
	Marriages	4
	Burials	9
	First Communions	25
	Confirmations	33
X	St. Victoria's Relics	X

1889

B-1
Jesse
Amadeus
Picard

On January 10, 1889, I, rector of St. Paul, have baptized in the church Jesse Amadeus, born the 4th instant of the legitimate marriage of John and Celina Picard of this parish. Godfather, Amadee Choquette, godmother, Marie Choquette.

F. X. Blanchet, Rector

B-2
Christina
C. Wirfs

On January 27, 1889, I, rector of St. Paul, have baptized in the church Christina Catherine, born the 12th instant of the legitimate marriage of Peter and Susanna Wirfs of this parish. Godfather, Alphonse Van Hoomissen, godmother, Christins Wirfs.

F. X. Blanchet, Rector

[A slip of paper included between pages 186 and 187 contains the following notation regarding Saint Victoria's relics, page 186:]

The body of Saint Victoria, martyr, was found in the cemetery of Hermetis about February 7, 1846, along with a red vessel on which the name was inscribed.

B-3
Mary
Elsie
Jordan

On February 3, 1889, I, rector of St. Paul, have baptized in the church Mary Elsie, born the 14th of October last of the lawful marriage of Henry and Anna Jordan of Champoeg. Godfather, Charles McCormick, godmother, Mary McCormick.

Mrs. Mary McCormick   Charles McCormick
F. X. Blanchet, Rector

B-4
William
Joseph
Living-
stone

On February 10, 1889, I, rector of St. Paul, have baptized in the church William Joseph, born the 11th of November last of the lawful marriage of R. H. and Mattie Livingstone of Dundee. Godfather, Richard A. Kirk, godmother, Margaret Kirk.

Richard H. Kirk   Maggie Kirk
F. X. Blanchet, Rector

Page 188
B-5
Lucy Mary
Country-
man

On February 22, 1889, I, rector of St. Paul, baptized in the church Lucy Mary Countryman, born the 13th of July, 1884, of the lawful marriage of Francis and Basilesse Countryman of this parish. Godmother, Mrs. Margaret Coffey.

F. X. Blanchet, Rector

B-6
John F.
Country-
man

On February 22, 1889, I, rector of St. Paul, baptized in the church John Franklin, born the 23rd of March, 1886, of the lawful marriage of Francis and Basilesse Countryman of this parish. Sponsor, Mr. Anton Ahrens.

F. X. Blanchet, Rector.

Via
Crucis

On March 8, 1889, I, rector of St. Paul, in the absence of the Right Reverend Archbishop of Oregon City, W. H. Gross, have blessed and erected the way of the cross in the church of St. Paul, because it had been removed, pending repairs, in the presence of the congregation.

F. X. Blanchet, Rector

S-1
Georgia
Laura
Belanger

On March 19, 1889, Georgia Laura Anna, born the July 13, 1884, to Jake and Clarice Belanger, husband and wife of this parish, died and was buried today in the cemetery of St. Paul. Witnesses, Peter Kirk, Narcisse Lafontaine and others.

F. X. Blanchet, Rector

S-2
Rev.
Sister
Mary
Cassilda

On April 23, 1889, I the undersigned, have buried in the Community of the Sisters of the Holy Names of Jesus and Mary at St. Paul, the body of Sister Mary Cassilda (Mary Dunn), who died the 9th of this month, having received the Holy Sacraments. Witnesses, Mother Justina, Sister Marguerite and many others from the parish.

James Rebmann, S.J.

B-7
Charles
Edwin
Feller

On April 28, 1889, I, rector of St. Paul, have baptized in the church Charles Edwin, born the 28th of August, 1886, to Francis and Rhuamah Feller, lawfully married (of which the mother is non-catholic) of Butteville. Godfather, William Trevor.

F. X. Blanchet, Rector

B-8
Anna May
Feller

On April 28, 1889, I, rector of St. Paul, have baptized in the church Anna May, born the 17th of March, 1888, to Francis and Rheuamah Feller, lawfully married, the mother an a-catholic, of Butteville. Godmother, Mary Elizabeth Dwyer.

F. X. Blanchet, Rector.

Page 189
B-9
Charles
Albert
Jones

On April 28, 1889, I, rector of St. Paul, have baptized in the church Charles Albert, born the 25th of November last of the lawful marriage of Noemi and Francis Jones of Champoeg, the marriage being non-catholic. Godfather, Joseph Orth.

F. X. Blanchet, Rector

B-10
Francis
Ottawa
Durant

On May 2, 1889, I, rector of St. Paul, baptized in the church Francis Ottawa, born the 26th of June last, to Francis and Monica Durant, legally married, of Yamhill County. Godfather, Robert Emmett Kirk.

R. E. Kirk
F. X. Blanchet, Rector

B-11
Wilfred
Leo
McKay
First
Communion

On May 26, 1889, I the undersigned have baptized in the church of St. Paul Wilfred Leo, born the 4th of March last, to Moise and Josephine McKay of Champoeg, husband and wife. Sponsors, Henry and Magdelen Ernst.

Geo. Vermeersch, Presbyter

On June 16, 1889, Basilesse Countryman, wife of Francis Countryman, received the first communion in the church of St. Paul.

F. X. Blanchet, Rector

B-12
Elizabeth
C.
Brentano

On June 19, 1889, I testify that Elizabeth Catherine, born the day before of the legitimate marriage of John F. T. and Catherine Brentano of this parish, was baptized at home by the Reverend Father Lynch of Corvallis. Godparents, Casimer F. Brentano and Elizabeth Wirfs.

F. X. Blanchet, Rector

B-13
Charles
F.
Lembke

On June 30, 1889, I, rector of St. Paul, have baptized in the church Charles Frederic, born the 22nd of April last, of the lawful marriage of Charles and Mary Lembke of Butteville. Godmother, Elizabeth Miller.

F. X. Blanchet, Rector

B-14
Agnes
Martha
Langtry

On July 7, 1889, I, rector of St. Paul, have given private baptism at home in extremity to Agnes Martha, aged about one year *[written above the line, 14th of April, 1888]* daughter of Moise and Emma Langtry, non-catholic husband and wife of this parish. Godmother, Mrs. Mary Coleman. *[added]* The omission was supplied September 15, following.

F. X. Blanchet, Rector

Page 190
M-1
Casimer
Brentano
&
Dora V.
Thoma

On July 18, 1889, after the publication of one ban and the dispensation of the other two, and no impediment being found, I, rector of St. Paul, having received their mutual consent, have joined in marriage Casimer F. Brentano of Oregon and Dora V. Thoma of Yamhill, both of age. Witnesses: Regnier L. M. Brentano and Mary M. Ernst.

Regnier L. M. Brentano   Mary M. Ernst

F. X. Blanchet, Rector

S-3
Albert
Sidnay
Murphy

On July 21, 1889, Albert Sidney, aged about 23 years, died and was buried today in the cemetery of St. Paul, the son of the lawful marriage of Mathew and Helen Murphy. Witnesses, Daniel Murphy, William Foley and many others.

F. X. Blanchet, Rector

B-15
John W.
Geelan

On July 21, 1889, I, rector of St. Paul, have baptized in the church John William, born the 5th instant, of the lawful marriage of Patrick and Elizabeth Geelan of this parish. Godparents, Peter J. Wirfs and his wife.

F. X. Blanchet, Rector

B-16
James
Urban
Kirk

On August 17, 1889, I, the rector of St. Paul, baptized in the church James Urban, born the 13th of this month, of the lawful marriage of John W. and Cecelia Kirk of this parish. Godfather, William R. McKay, godmother, Anna McKay.

Annie McKay   W. R. McKay

F. X. Blanchet, Rector

B-17
Helen L.
Pelland

On September 1, 1889, I, rector of St. Paul, have baptized in the church Helen Loretta, born the 25th last, of the lawful marriage of Charles and Marie Pelland of this parish. Godfather, Nicholas Cooke, godmother Laura Davidson.

F. X. Blanchet, Rector

B-18
Bertha
Langtry

On September 15, 1889, I, rector of St. Paul, baptized in the church Bertha, born January 30, 1883, of the lawful marriage of Moses and Emma Langtry, non-catholic of this parish. Godfather, Julien Provost, godmother Mrs. Margaret Coffey.

Julien Provost

Page 191
S-4
Felix
Gratton

F. X. Blanchet, Rector

On September 19, 1889, Felix Gratton, aged about 50 years, married man, died and was buried in the cemetery of St. Paul. Witnesses, F. Davidson, Hugh Cosgrove, John Gearin and many others.

F. X. Blanchet, Rector

B-19
Joseph
Scollard

On September 28, 1889, I, rector of St. Paul, baptized in the church Joseph, born the 10th of this month, to John and Alice Scollard of Champoeg. Godfather, Joseph B. Kennedy, godmother, Margaret Kennedy.

Joseph Kennedy   F. X. Blanchet, Rector
Maggie Kennedy

B-20

On October 28, 1889, I, rector of St. Paul, baptized in the church Charles,

Charles
Kerr

born yesterday of the lawful marriage of Thomas and Josephine Kerr of this parish. Godfather, Francis Wassenhove, godmother, Mrs. Catherine Kerr.

F. X. Blanchet, Rector

B-21
Amelia
Edna
Aplin

On October 12, 1889, I, rector of St. Paul, baptized in the church Amelia Edna, born the 7th instant, of the lawful marriage of George and Amelia Aplin, of this place. Godfather, Dieudonne Peter Manaigre, godmother, Amelia Manaigre.

F. X. Blanchet, Rector

M-2
H. G.
Kirkpatrick
&
Mary E.
Davidson

On October 30, 1889, the dispensation of disparity of religion having been obtained from the Archbishop of Oregon City and no impediment being found, I, the undersigned, rector of St. Paul, having received their mutual consent to marriage, have united in holy matrimony H. G. Kirkpatrick of the state of Washington and Mary E. Davidson of St. Paul, in the presence of witnesses, namely, Mrs. Emma Coleman and Charles O. Pelland.

F. X. Blanchet, Rector

I, the undersigned, solemnly promise Mary E. Davidson, whom I am going to marry, to give her full liberty in regard to her religion, and also to raise our children, if we have any, in the Roman Catholic Faith, according to her wishes.

H. G. Kirkpatrick

B-22
Patrick
Joseph
Mullen

On November 16, 1889, I, rector of St. Paul, have baptized in the church Patrick Joseph, born the 24th of October last, of the lawful marriage of Patrick and Mary Ann Mullen of this parish. Godfather, F. X. Blanchet, Godmother, Mrs. Catherine McGrath.

Page 192

F. X. Blanchet, Rector

S-5
George
C.
Aplin

On December 20, 1889, George C. Aplin, married man, aged 65 years, died and was buried in the cemetery of St. Paul. Present, Firmin Lebrun, John Gearin, D. Gagnon and others.

F. X. Blanchet, Rector

First
Communion

On December 25, 1889, Mrs. Dora Thoma Brentano and Eleonora Choquette received the first Holy Communion in the church of St. Paul.

B-23
Cecelia
Estelle
McKay

On December 29, 1889, I, rector of St. Paul, have baptized in the church Cecelia Estelle, born the 19th of this month, of the lawful marriage of William R. and Anna McKay of this parish. Godfather, John McCormick, godmother, Catherine McCormick.

John MCormick   Katie MCormick

F. X. Blanchet, Rector

Recapitulation for 1889

Baptisms	23
Marriages	2
Burials	5
First Communions	3
Confirmations	0

1890

B-1
Francis H.
Lafontaine

On January 11, 1890, I, rector of St. Paul, baptized in the church Francis Hormis [?], born today, of the lawful marriage of Narcisse Lafontaine and Marguerite of this place. Godfather, Hormis [?] Fortin, godmother, Mrs. Magdelen Ernst.

F. X. Blanchet, Rector

M-1
Victor
A.
Demacon
&
Marie C.
Bellique

On January 13, 1890, I, rector of St. Paul, after the publication of three bans, and no impediment being found, have received their mutual consent to marriage and have united in holy matrimony Victor August Demacon and Marie Clementine Bellique, of age, of the parish of St. Louis. Witnesses, Theodule Martin, Mary Bellique.

F. X. Blanchet, Rector

Page 193
M-2

On January 14, 1890, the dispensation for the disparity of religion having

A. J.
Crosby
&
Rosa
Manaigre

been obtained from the Archbishop of Oregon City, and no other impediment being found, I, rector of St. Paul, having received their mutual consent, have united in marriage A. J. Crosby and Rosa Manaigre, underage, of this parish in the presence of witnesses: L. M. Fortier and Mrs. Mary Manaigre.

F. X. Blanchet, Rector
ST Paul, Marion Co. Or. Jany 14, 1890

I, the undersigned, solemnly promise Rose Manaigre, whom I am going to marry, to give her full liberty in regard to her religion, and also to raise our children, if we have any, in the Roman Catholic Faith, according to her wishes.

A. J. Crosby

Attest: L. H. Fortin

S-1
Marguerite
Pichette

On February 1, 1890, Marguerite Pichette, widow, aged 76 years, died and was buried in the cemetery of St. Paul. Witnesses, Peter Manaigre, Narcisse Lafontaine, and others.

F. X. Blanchet, Rector

B-2
Charles
D.
Lambert

On February 2, 1890, I, rector of St. Paul, baptized in the church Charles David, born the 27th last, of the lawful marriage of Francis and Clementine Lambert of this place. Godfather, R. L. M. Brentano, godmother, Mary Ernst.

M. M. Ernst   R. L. M. Brentano
F. X. Blanchet, Rector

B-3
Ambrose
Connor

On February 9, 1890, I, rector of St. Paul, baptized in the church Ambrose, born yesterday of the lawful marriage of Simon and Agnes Connor of this parish. Godfather, Mathew Connor, godmother, Elizabeth Connor.

Mathew Connor   Lizzie Connor
F. X. Blanchet, Rector

S-2
Francis H.
Lafontaine

On February 10, 1890, Francis D., aged about one month, legitimate son of Narcisse and Marguerite Lafontaine, died and was buried in the cemetery of St. Paul. Witnesses, Emmet R. Kirk, Felix Delisle and others.

F. X. Blanchet, Rector

B-4
Infant
Hughes

On February 11, 1890, the infant of Hughes received private baptism in danger of death.

F. X. Blanchet, Rector

S-3
Infant
Hughes
Page 194

On February 12, 1890, the infant of Hughes died yesterday and was privately buried in the St. Paul cemetery.

F. X. Blanchet, Rector

S-4
Mary A.
Aplin

On February 24, 1890, Mary A., aged about 10 months, of the lawful marriage of George E. and Amelie Aplin, died yesterday and was buried today in St. Paul Cemetery. Witnesses, Dr. Peltier, Peter Manaigre, and others.

F. X. Blanchet, Rector

B-5
Mary M.
Belanger

On March 9, 1890, I, rector of St. Paul, have baptized in the church Mary Margaret, born the 2nd of this month, of the lawful marriage of Jake and Clarice Belanger of this parish. Godfather, Anthony Ahrens, godmother, Magdalena Ernst.

F. X. Blanchet, Rector

B-6
Lucy
Virginia
Raymond

On April 6, 1890, I, rector of St. Paul, have baptized in the church Lucy Virginia, born the 19th of last month, of the lawful marriage of August and Josephine Raymond of this parish. Godfather, Severe Manaigre, godmother, Matilda Crete.

Matilda Crete   Sevare Managre
F. X. Blanchet, Rector

B-7
F. G. F.
Wirfs

On April 20, 1890, I, missionary of Mt. Angel, have baptized in the church Francis William Ferdinand, born the 1st of this month, of the lawful marriage of Francis and Elizabeth Wirfs of St. Paul parish. Godfather, Ferdinand Wirfs, Godmother, Elizabeth Geelan.

P. Adelhelm, O.S.B.

B-8	On April 30, 1890, I, rector of St. Paul, have baptized in the church Peter
Peter	Joseph, born the 27th of this month of the lawful marriage of Adolph and
Joseph	Christina Pfeifer of this parish. Godfather, Joseph Orth, godmother,
Pfeifer	Teresa Wolfhart.

Teresa Wohlfart   P. Joseph Orth

F. X. Blanchet, Rector

B-9	On May 25, 1890, I, rector of St. Paul, have supplied an omission in the
Charles	church, for Charles Arthur, born the 12th of last month and baptized at
Arthur	once, in danger of death, son of William and Helen Hannigan, legitimately
Hannigan	married (this marriage was non-catholic) of this parish. Godfather, Peter
	Kirk, godmother, Mrs. Peter Wirfs.

Peter Kirk

F. X. Blanchet, Rector

Page 195
First Com-
munion
21

On June 5, 1890, twenty-one children received in the Church of St. Paul their First Communion, namely:

James Geelan	Helen Geelan
Benjamin Lambert	Mary Reilly
Elizabeth Merten	Mary Belanger
Marganta Pitt	Mary Oberdoester
Genevieve Bernier	Anna E. Davidson
Agnes Burns	Gertrude Miller
Regina M. Fitzpatrick	Emma Lambert
Eugenia Lebeau	Eulalia Malone
Eugene Davidson	Mary Lemery
Ramy Aplin	Rosa Hughes

F. X. Blanchet

Rector

Confir-
mations
25

On June 5, 1890, the underwritten faithful received confirmation by R.R.D.D. Archbishop W. H. Gross in the church of St. Paul: Sponsors were, for the boys, Math. Connor, and for the girls, Mrs. Mary McKay.

Louis Joseph Vivet	Joseph John Gooding
Frederic John Prevost	Henry Joseph Rehemaun
Eugene Joseph McGrath	Adolph Charles Oberdoester
James Peter Geelan	William Joseph Hannigan
Francis Paul Crete	Benjamin Joseph Lambert
Margaret Pauline Prevost	Mary Flavia Lemery
Rosa Mary Hughes	Margaret Victoria Manaigre
Mary Anna Josephine Bellarts	Helen Victoria Geelan
Eulalia Leocadie Malone	Margaret Cecelia Pitt
Genevieve Magdelen Bernier	Mary Clara Belanger
Emma Elizabeth Lambert	Elizabeth Victoria Merten
Eugenia Victoria Lebeau	Mary Regina Fitzpatrick
Mary Helen Oberdoester	

F. X. Blanchet, Rector

B-10	On June 15, 1890, I, rector of St. Paul, have baptized in the church John
John	Frederic Joseph, born today of the lawful marriage of Casimer F. and
Fred. J.	Dora Victoria [?] Brentano of this parish. Godfather, J. F. J. Brentano,
Brentano	godmother, E. W. J. Muller.

J. Fr. J. Brentano   E. W. J. M. Muller

Page 196
S-5
Jake
Belanger

F. X. Blanchet, Rector

On June 18, 1890, Jake Belanger, married man, of this parish, deceased at the age of about 40 years, was buried today in the cemetery of St. Paul. Witnesses, Amedee Choquette, Mr. Lebrun, Pat. Mullen.

F. X. Blanchet, Rector

S-6
Indian
Michel

On July 23, 1890, Indian Michel, unmarried, of this parish, deceased yesterday at the age of about 70 years, was buried today in the cemetery of St. Paul. Witnesses, William Trevor, John McGrath and others.

F. X. Blanchet, Rector.

B-11
Joseph
Labonte

On July 27, 1890, I, rector of St. Paul, have baptized in the church Joseph, born the 27th of April last of the lawful marriage of Alexander and Clementine Labonte of this parish. Godfather, Stephen Merten, godmother, Theresa Merten.

F. X. Blanchet, Rector

M-3
Laurence
H. Fortin
&
Mary Agnes
Manaigre

On July 29, 1890, after the publication of one ban and the dispensation of two others by R.R.D.D. Archbishop of Oregon City, and no impediment being found, I, rector of St. Paul, having received their mutual consent to marriage, have united in holy matrimony Laurence H. Fortin and Mary A. Manaigre, of age, of this parish. Witnesses, Miss Maggie Manaigre, Mr. Leo Choquette.

F. X. Blanchet, Rector

S-7
Cecelia
Krechter

On August 13, 1890, Cecelia, daughter of August and Anna Krechter of this parish, deceased yesterday at the age of about 12 months, was buried today in the cemetery of St. Paul. Witnesses, Peter Kirk, Joseph Bramberger.

F. X. Blanchet, Rector

M-4
Robert
E. Kirk
&
Agatha
McDonald

On September 2, 1890, after the publication of one ban and the dispensation of two others by R.R.D.D. archbishop of Oregon City, and no legitimate impediment being found, I, rector of St. Paul, having received their mutual consent to marriage, have joined in holy wedlock Robert E. Kirk and Agatha McDonald, of age, of this parish, Witnesses, C. D. Coleman and J. Orth.

F. X. Blanchet, Rector

Page 197
B-12
Basil
Hugh
Gearin

On September 14, 1890, I, rector of St. Paul, have baptized at home Basil Hugh, born the 9th of this month, of the lawful marriage of Hugh and Mary Cecelia Gearin of this parish. Godfather, Edward Pillett, godmother, Matilda Pillett.

F. X. Blanchet, Rector

B-13
Elmer
Thomas
Picard

On September 21, 1890, I, rector of St. Paul, baptized in the church Elmer Thomas, born the 17th of July last, of the lawful marriage of Henry and Marie Picard of this parish. The following are godmother and godfather:
Adolphe Jette   Marguerite Jette

F. X. Blanchet, Rector

B-14
Edna
Matilda
Jette

On September 28, 1890, I, rector of St. Paul, have baptized in the church Edna Matilda, born the 23rd of August last, of Adolphe and Marguerite Jette of Champoeg. Godfather and godmother were the following:
Matilda Pillett   E. Pillett

F. X. Blanchet, Rector

B-15
John
A. F.
Choquette

On October 20, 1890, I, rector of St. Paul, have baptized in the church John Alvord Freeman, born the 24th of this month, of the lawful marriage of Amedee and Marie Choquette of this parish. Sponsors were: John Picard and Eleonore Choquette.

F. X. Blanchet, Rector
                                              at home

B-16
Mary Ida
Swain

On October 30, 1890, I, rector of St. Paul, have baptized at once, in danger of death, Mary Ida, born in the month of September, 1882, of James and Anna Swain of Washington.

F. X. Blanchet, Rector

B-17
George
Stephen
Fick

On November 2, 1890, I, rector of St. Paul, have baptized in the church George Stephen, born the 22nd last, of the lawful marriage of George and Antoinette Fick of this parish. Godparents were:
Steven Merten   Elizabeth Buskay

F. X. Blanchet, Rector

B-18
Infant
Crosby

On November 9, 1890, I testify that Mrs. Ernst gave immediate baptism to an infant born to A. J. and Rose Crosby, husband and wife of this parish; the child later died.

F. X. Blanchet, Rector

Page 198

S-8
Infant
Crosby

On November 10, 1890, the infant of A. J. Crosby and Rose Crosby of St. Paul was buried in the St. Paul cemetery. Witnesses, N. Lafontaine and Peter Manaigre.

F. X. Blanchet, Rector

M-5
P. J. Orth
&
M. A.
Krechter

On November 28, 1890, after the publication of one ban and the dispensation of the other two by the R.R.D.D. Archbishop of Oregon City, and no impediment being found, I, rector of St. Paul, having received their mutual consent to marriage, have joined in Holy Matrimony Peter Joseph Orth and Mary Anna Krechter, of age, of this parish. Witnesses, Francis Schmidt and Dora Krechter.

Frank Schmitz   Dora Krechter.

F. X. Blanchet. Rector

M-6
W.
Murphy
&
Emma
Coleman

On November 25, 1890, after the publication of one ban and the dispensation of the other two by the R.R.D.D. Archbishop of Oregon City, and no legal impediment being found, I, rector of St. Paul, having received their mutual consent to marriage, have joined in holy wedlock William Murphy and Emma Coleman, of age, of this parish. Witnesses:

Helen Louise Coleman
Stephen Henry Coleman

F. X. Blanchet, Rector

B-19
Laurence
T. E.
Bernard

On December 20, 1890, I, rector of St. Paul, have baptized in the church Laurence Thomas Edward, born the 13th of November last, illegitimate, of Edward and Marguerite Bernard, of this parish. Godfather, Charles Prevost, godmother, Magdelena Ernst.

F. X. Blanchet, Rector

Recapitulation for 1890

Baptisms	19
Marriages	6
Burials	8
First Communions	21
Confirmations	25

1891

Page 199

B-1
Mary
Elsie
Virginia
Picard

On January 11, 1891, I, rector of St. Paul, have baptized in the church Mary Elsie Virginia, born the 17th of December, of the lawful marriage of John and Celina Picard of this parish. Godfather, Joseph Bernier, godmother, Clara Belanger.

F. X. Blanchet, Rector

M-1
Regnier
L. M.
Brentano
&
Mary A.
Ernst

On January 14, 1891, after the publication of one ban and the dispensation of the other two by the R.R.D.D. Archbishop of Oregon City, and no impediment being found, I, rector of St. Paul, having received their mutual consent to marriage, have joined in holy matrimony Regnier L. M. Brentano and Mary Ann Ernst, of age, of this parish.

Witnesses, Antoinette Pillett   Henry C. Ernst

F. X. Blanchet, Rector

M-2
Thomas J.
Connor
&
Catherine
A.
McGrath

On January 25, 1891, after the publication of one ban and the dispensation of two others by the R.R.D.D. Archbishop of Oregon City, and no impediment being discovered, I, rector of St. Paul, having received their mutual consent, have joined in marriage Thomas Joseph Connor and Catherine Agnes McGrath, of age, of this parish.

Witnesses: Lucy Connor   Thomas McGrath

F. X. Blanchet, Rector

S-1
Anna
Edna
Davidson

On January 30, 1891, Anna Edna, daughter of Francis and and Anna Davidson, deceased at the age of 12 years and 4 months, was today buried in the cemetery of St. Paul. Witnesses, Amedee Choquette, James Coleman and many others.

F. X. Blanchet, Rector

M-3

On February 2, 1891, after the publication of one ban and the dispensation

Alphonse
Buyserie
&
Mary
Berhorst

of two others by the R.R.D.D. Archbishop of Oregon City, and no impediment being found, I, rector of St. Paul, having received their mutual consent to marriage, have joined in matrimony Alphonse Buyserie and Mary Berhorst, of age, of this parish.
Witnesses: Dora Krechter   Isidore Buyserie
                                    F. X. Blanchet, Rector

Page 200
B-2
John
Nalweissa
[?]

On February 1, 1891, I, rector of St. Paul, baptized in the church John, born the 26th last, of the lawful marriage of Thomas and Hedwige Nalweissa of this parish. Sponsors, Mrs. Christina Pfeifer   Fred Hoerner
                                    F. X. Blanchet, Rector

S-2
Thomas
Mullen

On February 3, 1891, Thomas, son of the lawful marriage of Thomas and Mary Mullen of this parish, deceased at the age of 6 years and 7 months, was buried today in the cemetery of St. Paul. Witnesses, John McGrath, John Kirk, and others.
                                    F. X. Blanchet, Rector

B-3
George
Firmin
Lafontaine

On March 1, 1891, I, rector of St. Paul, have baptized in the church George Firmin, born the 21st of February last, of the lawful marriage of Narcisse and Marguerite Lafontaine of this parish. Godfather and godmother,
        F. LeBrun   Sophie LeBrun
                                    F. X. Blanchet, Rector

Confirma-
tions   3

On March 1, 1891, the following received confirmation from the Illustrious D.D. Archbishop of Oregon City in the church of St. Paul; Joanna *Victoria* Kirk, Cerida [?] *Cecelia* Kelly, and *Catherine.*
                                    F. X. Blanchet, Rector

B-4
Mary
Louise
Bernard

On March 12, 1891, I, rector of St. Paul, have baptized at home Mary Louise, born the 10th of January, 1887, of the lawful marriage of Margaret and Edward Bernard of this parish. Godmother, Mary Magdelen Ernst.
                                    F. X. Blanchet, Rector

B-5
Mary A.
Bernard

On March 12, 1891, I, rector of St. Paul, baptized at home Mary Angelica, born the 15th of April, 1888, of the lawful marriage of Edward and Margaret Bernard of this parish. Godfather, Charles Prevost.
                                    F. X. Blanchet, Rector

B-6
George
A.
Aplin

On March 14, 1891, I, rector of St. Paul, have baptized in the church George Albert, born the 26th of January last of the lawful marriage of George and Amelia Aplin of this parish. Godfather and godmother were: Peter and Emilie Manaigre.
                                    F. X. Blanchet, Rector

Page 201
B-7
Rosa
Anna
Fortin

On March 27, 1891, I, rector of St. Paul, have baptized in the church Rose Anna, born today of the lawful marriage of Laurence and Mary Agnes Fortin of this parish. Godfather, Peter Manaigre, godmother, Emelie Manaigre.
        L. H. Fortin   Peter Manaigre   Emelie Manaigre
                                    F. X. Blanchet, Rector

First
Commu-
nion

On March 29, 1891, Robert Henry and John McKinney, brothers, received their First Communion in the church of St. Paul.
                                    F. X. Blanchet, Rector

S-3
Stephen
Pelletier

On April 18, 1891, Stephen Pelletier, unmarried, aged 65 years, died three days ago and was buried today in the cemetery at St. Paul. Witnesses, John Brentano and William Trevor.
                                    L. A. Brousseau, Presbyter

S-4
James
Henry
Kirk

On April 27, 1891, James Henry Kirk, aged about 19 years, was buried today in the cemetery at St. Paul. Witnesses, James Coleman, A. Choquette, James Cooke and many others.
                                    F. X. Blanchet, Rector

B-8
Peter
Alexander

On May 5, 1891, I, rector of St. Paul, baptized in the church Peter Alexander, born the first day of this month of the lawful marriage of Henry and Elizabeth Bellarts of this parish. Godfather, Peter Bellarts, godmother

Bellarts   Catherine Bellarts.

         Peter Bellarts   Katrina Bellarts
                                 F. X. Blanchet, Rector

B-9
Ferdinand
William
Wirfs

On May 10, 1891, I, rector of St. Paul, baptized in the church Ferdinand William, born the 23rd last, of the lawful marriage of Peter J. and Susanna Wirfs of this parish. Godfather, Ferdinand Wirfs per Regnier Brentano, Godmother Elizabeth Geelan per Mrs. Mary Brentano.

         R. L. M. Brentano   M. M. Brentano
                       F. X. Blanchet, Rector

Page 202
S-5
Mary
Elsie
Virginia
Picard

On May 17, 1891, Mary Elsie Virginia, aged six months, legitimate daughter of John and Celina Picard, of this parish, was today buried in the St. Paul cemetery. Witnesses, C. A. Robert, Peter Manaigre, W. F. Davidson and many others.

                       F. X. Blanchet, Rector

B-10
Albert
Goodell

On May 17, 1891, I, rector of St. Paul, am informed that Mrs. Adolph Jette of Champoeg has given private baptism to Albert, in danger of death, aged about 3 years, lawful son of Henry and Mary Goodell, on the first of this month.

                       F. X. Blanchet, Rector

First
Communion
19

On May 28, 1891, nineteen young people received their first communion in the church of St. Paul, as follows:

Sophia G. Elliot	William L. Gooding
Delia A. Choquette	William J. Hannigan
Elizabeth L. Elliott	Eugene McGrath
Maria L. Lafontaine	Charles Scollard
Rosa J. Belanger	Joseph A. Krechter
Mary H. Hannigan	William L. Smith
Eugenia Steiner	James J. Hannigan
Catherine Fitzpatrick	Frederic Pelland
Justina Calmels	Laurence Belanger
Mary Raymond	

                       F. X. Blanchet, Rector

Confirm-
ations
18

On May 28, 1891, the undersigned faithful received the sacrament of confirmation from R.R.D.D. Archbishop W. H. Gross in the church at St. Paul. Sponsor for the boys was Marhew Connor, for the girls, Mrs. Mary McKay.

	William Peter L. Gooding
Sophia Cecelia G. Elliott	William Joseph Smith
Delia Victoria A. Choquette	Charles William Scollard
Elizabeth Agnes L. Elliott	Joseph John A. Krechter
Mary Rosa Lafontaine	James Thomas J. Hannegan
Rosalie Mary Judith Belanger	Joseph Pelland
Mary Elizabeth H. Hannigan	Laurence Joseph Belanger
Eugenia Jennie Steiner	
Catherine Christine Fitzpatrick	
Justina Cecelia Calmels	
Mary Agnes Raymond	
Dora Victoria Barbara Brentano	

                       F. X. Blanchet, Rector

Page 203
S-6
Mrs.
Hirsch,
Mary

On July 9, 1891, Mrs. Hirsch, daughter of Thomas Kirby, married, aged 30 years, of Yamhill, was buried today in the cemetery at St. Paul. Witnesses, Thomas Kirby, Narcisse Lafontaine, Peter Kirk.

                       F. X. Blanchet, Rector

S-7
Josephine
McKay

On June 23, 1891, Josephine, born on the 12th, of the lawful marriage of Moses and Josephine McKay of Champoeg, was given private baptism by Sophie McKay, was deceased yesterday and buried in the St. Paul cemetery today. Witnesses, Moses McKay, N. Lafontaine and others.

                       F. X. Blanchet, Rector

B-11
Clarence
Ruben
Coyle

On June 28, 1891, I, rector of St. Paul, have baptized in the church Clarence Ruben, born the 7th instant, of the lawful marriage of James and Henrietta Coyle of this parish. Godfather, Alexander Wassenhove, godmother, Elizabeth Wassenhove.

Eliza Van Wassenhove   Aleck Van Wassenhove

F. X. Blanchet, Rector

B-12
Agnes
Bernardine
Wolf

On July 26, 1891, I, rector of St. Paul, have baptized Agnes Bernardine, born the 19th of last month, of the lawful marriage of Joseph B. and Catherine Wolf of Butteville. Godfather, George Fick, godmother, Mrs. Antoinette Fick.

F. X. Blanchet, Rector

B-13
Joseph
James
Grant

On August 12, 1891, I, rector of St. Paul, have baptized in the church Joseph James, born yesterday, of the lawful marriage of William and Bridget Grant of this parish. Godfather, Thomas Hughes, godmother, Mrs. Rosa Hughes.

Thomas M. Hughes   Rose V. Hughes

F. X. Blanchet, Rector

S-8
Peter
Alexander
Bellarts

On August 28, 1891, Peter Alexander, aged four months, of the lawful marriage of Henry and Elizabeth Bellarts of this parish, died yesterday and was buried in the St. Paul Cemetery. Witnesses, L. H. Fortin, Sebastien Wachter and others.

F. X. Blanchet, Rector

B-14
Ruben
Raymond
Fortier

On August 30, 1891, I, rector of St. Paul, have baptized in the church Ruben Raymond, born the 8th of this month of the lawful marriage of Eusebe and Salome Fortier of this parish. Godfather, August Raymond, godmother, Mrs. Josephine Raymond.

F. X. Blanchet, Rector

Page 204
B-15
Charles
Eugene
Geelan

On September 6, 1891, I, rector of St. Paul, have baptized in the church Charles Eugene, born the 17th of last August, of the lawful marriage of Patrick and Elizabeth Geelan of this parish. Godfather, James Geelan, godmother, Catherine Connor.

James Geelan   Mrs. Thomas Connor

F. X. Blanchet, Rector

B-16
Bernard
Thomas
Mullen

On September 13, 1891, I, rector of St. Paul, have baptized in the church Bernard Thomas, born the 3rd of last August, of the lawful marriage of Patrick and Mary Mullen of this parish. Godfather, Mathew Connor, godmother, Mary Kirk.

Mary Kirk   Mathew Connor

F. X. Blanchet, Rector

B-17
Paul
Laurence
Kronenburg

On September 25, 1891, I, rector of St. Paul, have baptized in the church Paul Laurence, born the 3rd of this month of the lawful marriage of Francis and Josephine Kronenburg of this parish. Godfather, Thomas Fuchs, godmother, Elizabeth Fuchs.

Thomas Fuchs   Elizabeth Fuchs

F. X. Blanchet, Rector

B-18
Nunia
Catherine
Lemcke

On September 27, 1891, I, rector of St. Paul, have baptized in the church Nunia Catherine, born the 29th of last June, of the lawful marriage of Charles and Mary Lemcke of Butteville. Godfather, John Miller, godmother, Carrie Miller.   Mr. John Miller   Miss Carrie Miller

F. X. Blanchet, Rector

B-19
Oliver
Abernethy
neo Cath-
olic

On October 8, 1891, I, rector of St. Paul, testify that Mrs. James Eldridge gave private baptism to Oliver Abernethy, aged 59 years, her father, in danger of death, after repeated requests.[?]

F. X. Blanchet, V.G., Rector

S-9
Oliver
Abernethy

On October 10, 1891, Oliver Abernethy, aged 59 years, married, of Yamhill County, died and was buried in the cemetery at Champoeg. Witnesses, James Eldridge, Mr. Cohn, Francis Wassenhove, John Gearin, Mr. Hofer,

F. Davidson, W. R. McKay, Peter Kirk and many others.

F. X. Blanchet, V.G., Rector

Page 205
B-20
Frederic
H.
Brentano

On October 25, 1891, I, rector of St. Paul, have baptized in the church Frederic Henry, born yesterday, of the lawful marriage of Regnier and Mary Brentano of this parish. Godfather, Henry Ernst, godmother, Magdelen Ernst.

F. X. Blanchet, V.G., Rector

B-21
Arthur
Edward
Crosby
neo-
Catholic

On November 3, 1891, I, rector of St. Paul, have baptized conditionally in the church Arthur Edward, born Sept. 9, 1863, lawful husband of Rose Manaigre (Crosby). Godfather, Peter Manaigre, godmother, Mary Manaigre.

Peter Manaigre　　　　　　Emeley Managre

F. X. Blanchet, V.G., Rector

B-22
John A.
Bunning

On November 8, 1891, I, rector of St. Paul, have baptized in the church John Adolph, born the 5th of this month, of the lawful marriage of Christian Bunning and Mary Teresa Weekamp of this parish. Godfather, Adolph Pfeifer, godmother, Mrs. Anna Krechter.

F. X. Blanchet, V.G., Rector

B-23
Mary
G.
Connor

On November 9, 1891, I, rector of St. Paul, have baptized in the church Mary Gertrude, born today, of the lawful marriage of Thomas Connor and Catherine McGrath of this parish. Godfather, Eugene McGrath, godmother, Rosa McGrath.

Rose McGrath　　　　　　Eugene McGrath

F. X. Blanchet, V.G., Rector

S-10
Sister
Mary
Octavia

On November 17, 1891, I the undersigned, have given burial in the vault of the Sisters of the Holy Names of Jesus and Mary in St. Paul to the body of Sister Mary Octavia (Mary L. Ladue) who died the 25th of this month, having received the Holy Sacraments. Witnesses, Sister Francis Xavier, Sister Mathew and many others from this parish.

James Rauw, priest

B-24
Albert
F. Kerr

On November 22, 1891, I, rector of St. Paul, have baptized in the church Albert Francis, born the 16th of this month of the lawful marriage of Thomas Kerr and Josephine Wassenhove of this parish. Godfather, Samuel Kerr, godmother, Helen Coyle.

F. X. Blanchet, V.G., Rector

Page 206
M-4
John J.
Casey
&
Helen L.
Coleman

On November 23, 1891, after the publication of one ban, the other two being dispensed, and no impediment being found, I, rector of St. Paul, having received their mutual consent, have joined in matrimony John J. Casey and Helen Louise Coleman, of age, from East Portland and from this parish. Witnesses,

Stephen H. Coleman　　　　Jennie E. Davidson

F. X. Blanchet, V.G., Rector

B-25
Julien
Charles
Provost

On November 12, 1891, I, rector of St. Paul, testify that Mrs. Mary Magdelen Vesper (Ernst) gave private baptism in danger of death to Julien Charles, born the day before, of the lawful marriage of Julien Provost and Caroline Philomene Raymond of this parish.

F. X. Blanchet, V.G., Rector

S-11
Julien
C. Provost
[O.C.]

On November 12, 1891, I, rector of St. Paul, buried in the Old Cemetery Julien Charles, born the day before, to Julien Provost and Philomene Caroline Raymond of this Parish.

F. X. Blanchet, V.G., Rector

B-26
Mary
Loretta
Kirk

On November 26, 1891, I, rector of St. Paul, have baptized in the church Mary Loretta, born today, of the lawful marriage of John Kirk and Cecelia McKay of this parish. Godfather, Peter Kirk, godmother M.K.

Margaret M. Kirk　　　　　Peter P. Kirk

F. X. Blanchet, V.G., Rector

S-12

On December 9, 1891, I, rector of St. Paul, buried in the mortuary of the

Sister Mary Achille 36a.5m. & 14 d.	Sisters of the Holy Names of Jesus and Mary at St. Paul the body of Sister Mary Achille (Delia Rousseau) who died the 7th of the month, having received the Holy Sacraments. Witnesses, R. D. Rauw, priest, Mother Provincial Margaret Sister Assenium, Sister Joseph and many others. F. X. Blanchet, V.G., Rector
B-27 Wilhelm- ina M. Brentano	On December 27, 1891, I, rector of St. Paul, have baptized in the church Wilhelmina Mary, born the 25th of this month of the lawful marriage of Casimir Brentano and Dora M. Thoma of this parish. Godfather, Regnier M. Brentano, godmother, Mrs. Mary Ernst.

Regnier L. M. Brentano   Mary Brentano
F. X. Blanchet, V.G., Rector

Page 207 B-28 Sophia Victoria Buyserie	On December 30, 1891, I, rector of St. Paul, have baptized in the church Sophia Victoria, born the 24th of this month of the lawful marriage of Alphonse Buyserie and Mary Bearhorst of this parish. Godfather, William McKay, godmother, Anna Kavanaugh.

W. R. McKay   Anna McKay
F. X. Blanchet, V.G., Rector

Recapitulation in 1891

Baptisms of infants	26	
" " Adults	2	= 28
Marriages	4	
Burials	12	
First Communions	19	
Confirmations	18	

1892

B-1 William Reiland	On January 11, 1892, I, rector of St. Paul, have baptized in the church William, born today, of the lawful marriage of Christian Reiland and Mary Kirchbum of this parish. Godfather, Joseph Bramberger, godmother, Mrs. Mary Magdelen Ernst.

Joseph Bramberger   Mary Ernst
F. X. Blanchet, V.G., Rector

S-1 Cornelius Murray	On February 5, 1892, Cornelius Murray, unmarried, aged 78 years, was buried today in the cemetery of St. Paul. Witnesses, P. Mullen, Peter Kirk, James Cooke, J. McGrath and many others. F. X. Blanchet, V.G., Rector
B-2 Robert E. Pfeifer	On February 13, 1892, I, rector of St. Paul, have baptized in the church Robert Emmett, born three days ago of the lawful marriage of Adolph Pfeifer and Christina Oberdoester of this parish. Godfather, Robert Emmett Kirk, godmother, Mrs. Agatha McDonald.

Robert E. Kirk   Mrs. Agatha Kirk
F. X. Blanchet, V.G., Rector

Page 208 M-1 Edward Pillett & Dora K. Krechter	On February 22, 1892, after the publication of one ban and the dispensation of the other two, and no impediment being found, I, rector of St. Paul, having received their mutual consent, have united in marriage Edward Pillett and Dora K. Krecter, of age, of this parish. Witnesses,

Joseph Smith   Matilda Pillett
F. X. Blanchet, V.G., Rector

B-3 Cecelia Victoria Hughes	On March 11, 1892, I, rector of St. Paul, have baptized in the church Cecile Victoria, born today of the lawful marriage of Andrew Hughes and Rose Connor of this parish. Godfather, Eugene McGrath, godmother, Mary Ann Hughes.

Xavier Goyette   Hannah Goyette
F. X. Blanchet, V.G., Rector

B-4 Martha A. Hughes	On March 11, 1892, I, rector of St. Paul, have baptized in the church Martha Angela, born today, of the lawful marriage of Andrew Hughes and Rose Connor of this parish. Godfather, Xavier Goyette, godmother, Hannah Deloney.

Eugene McGrath   Mary Ann Hughes
F. X. Blanchet, V.G., Rector

B-5
Dieudonne
Augustin
Lambert

On March, 1892, I, rector of St. Paul, have baptized in the church Dieudonne Augustin, born the 20th of this month, of the legitimate marriage of Francis Lambert and Clementine Mongrain of this parish. Godfather, Dieudonne Manaigre, Godmother Emilia Pichette.

F. X. Blanchet, V.G., Rector

B-6
Leo
Justin
McKay

On March 30, 1892, I, rector of St. Paul, have baptized in the church Leo Justin, born the 22nd of this month, of the lawful marriage of William R. McKay and Anna Kavanaugh of this parish. Godfather, John Kirk, godmother, Cecelia McKay.

John Kirk   Cecelia Kirk

F. X. Blanchet, V.G., Rector

S-2
Agnes
Bernard-
ina Wolf

On April 11, 1892, Agnes Bernardine, born the 9th of this month, of the lawful marriage of Joseph and Catherine Wolf of Butteville, was buried today in the cemetery at St. Paul. Witnesses, Narcisse Lafontaine and John McKay.

F. X. Blanchet, V.G., Rector

Page 209
First
Communion

On April 17, 1892, Francis Murphy received the Holy Sacrament for the first time in the church of St. Paul.

F. X. Blanchet, V.G., Rector

B-7
Helen
J. W.
Jones

On April 17, 1892, I, rector of St. Paul, have baptized in the church Helen Joanna Wanita, born the 22nd of August last, of [Nehemiah] Jones and Francis McPaulin (mixed marriage) of Champoeg. Godfather, Hugh McPaulin, godmother, Matilda Pillett.

F. X. Blanchet, V.G., Rector

B-8
Bartholomew
Labonte

On April 17, 1892, I, rector of St. Paul, have baptized in the church Bartholomew, born the 11 of March last, of the lawful marriage of Alexander Labonte and Clementine Lachance of Champoeg.

F. X. Blanchet, V.G., Rector

M-2
J. E.
Kennedy
&
Lucy E.
Connor

On April 20, 1892, after the publication of one ban and the dispensation of two others, and no impediment being found, I, rector of St. Paul, having received their mutual consent, have united in marriage J. Edward Kennedy and Lucy E. Connor, of age, of this parish. Witnesses,

John Coleman   Mary A. Hughes

F. X. Blanchet, V.G., Rector

B-9
John
J.
Brentano

On May 1, 1892, I have baptized in the church of St. Paul John Joseph, born the 27th of April last of the lawful marriage of J. F. T. B. Brentano and Catherine Ahern of this parish. Godfather, Joseph Pillett, godmother, Elizabeth Pillett.

Leo Huebscher, O.S.B.

B-10
William
Chamberlain

On May 1, 1892, I baptized at home William Chamberlain, protestant, non-married, aged 25 years, of this parish. Godfather, Patrick Geelan, Godmother, Elizabeth Goodrich Geelan.

Leo Huebscher, O.S.B.

Page 210
S-3
Henry
Picard

On May 19, 1892, Henry Picard, widower, aged 65 years, who died three days before in Walla Walla, was today buried in the cemetery at St. Paul. Witnesses, A. Choquette, Fr. Van Wassenhove and many others.

F. X. Blanchet, V.G., Rector

B-11
Josephine
A. Raymond

On May 26, 1892, I, rector of St. Paul, have baptized in the church Amanda Josephine, born the 15th of this month of the lawful marriage of August Raymond and Josephine Raymond of this parish.

Godfather, Euseb Fortier   Godmother, Salome Fortier

F. X. Blanchet, V.G., Rector

13
First
Commu-
nion

On June 16, 1892, the following young people received their First Communion in the church of St. Paul:

George M. Pillett   Mary M. Merten
Mary T. Wilson   Rose Scollard
Mary S. Lebrun   Domitilla G. Lebrun

Evelina V. Pearson   Cecelia M. Pearson
Inez R. Weston   Eva B. Morissey
Mary A. Smith   Helen E. Lafontaine
Mary Rose Robert

F. X. Blanchet, V.G., Rector

S-4 Mary Bernier called Choquette
On June 18, 1892, Mary Bernier, wife of Amedee Choquette, aged 45 years, 1 month and 15 days, was buried today in the cemetery at St. Paul. Witnesses, Francis Wassenhove, Charles Pelland, F. W. Davidson and many others.

F. X. Blanchet, V.G., Rector

S-5 Martha Agnes Langtry
On June 24, 1892, Martha Agnes, aged 4 years and 2 months, lawful daughter of Moses and Emma Langtry, was buried today in the cemetery at St. Paul. Witnesses, Julien Provost, Hugh Cosgrove, Peter Kirk and others.

F. X. Blanchet, V.G., Rector

Page 211

B-12 Clarissa S. Lebeau
On July 3, 1892, I, rector of St. Paul, have baptized in the church Clarissa Stella, born the 29th of September last, of the lawful marriage of Calixte Lebeau and Clarisse Mongrain of Milton, Washington County. Godfather, N. Lafontaine, godmother, Margaret Pichet (Lafontaine).

F. X. Blanchet, V.G., Rector

S-6 Sister Mary Rosalind Aged 19 years
On August 11, 1892, I, rector of St. Paul, have buried in the mortuary of the Sisters of the Holy Names of Jesus and Mary at St. Paul the body of Sister Mary Rosalind, born Matilda Guilbeault, who died the 10th of this month, having received the Holy Sacraments. Witnesses, Rev. Mother Margarita, Sister Joseph, and others from this parish.

F. X. Blanchet, V.G., Rector
H. J. Baert, priest

M-3 Norbert Zetique Choquette & Elma Morel
On September 22, 1892, after the publication of one ban and the dispensation of two others, no impediment being found, I, rector of St. Paul, having received their mutual consent, have united in marriage Norbert Zetique Choquette and Elma Morel, of age, of this parish. Witnesses:
Mrs. Leo Choquette   Miss Augusta Seguin

F. X. Blanchet. V.G. Rector

S-7 John C. Maneely
On September 23, 1892, John Charles, born the 9th of this month, of the lawful marriage of C. O. Maneely and Elizabeth M. Smith of Portland, died three days ago and was buried today in the cemetery at St. Paul. Witnesses, Peter Kirk, Julien Provost, Peter Manaigre.

F. X. Blanchet, V.G., Rector

S-8 Cecelia Victoria Hughes
On September 25, 1892, Cecelia Victoria, aged six months, lawful daughter of Andrew Hughes and Rose Connor, died yesterday and was buried today in the cemetery at St. Paul. Witnesses: John Kirk, Matt. Connor and many others.

F. X. Blanchet, V.G., Rector

Page 212

B-14 Charles S. F. Fick
On November 1, 1892, I, rector of St. Paul, have baptized in the church Charles San Francisco, born the 25th of October last, of the lawful marriage of the late George Fick and Antoinette Kuesting of this parish. Godfather, Francis Kuesting per Charles Kuesting and Antoinette Kuesting.

F. X. Blanchet, V.G., Rector

B-15 Mary Alta Crosby
On November 5, 1892, I, rector of St. Paul, have baptized in the church Mary Alta, born the 9th of October last, of the lawful marriage of Arthur Crosby and Rose Manaigre of Woodburn. Godfather, Peter Manaigre, godmother, Emilie Pichette.

F. X. Blanchet, V.G., Rector

B-16 Francis R. Coleman
On December 11, 1892, I, rector of St. Paul, have baptized in the church Francis Rosswell, born the 29th of November of the lawful marriage of F. N. Coleman and Mary Helen Jackson of this parish. Godparents were:
Stephen H. Coleman   Agnes M. Jackson

F. X. Blanchet, V.G., Rector

Total in 1892

Baptisms of Infants	15	
" " Adults	1	= 16
Marriages	3	
Burials	8	
First Communions	13	
Confirmations	0	

1893

B-1 Mary Lucy Lafontaine

On January 8, 1893, I, rector of St. Paul, have baptized in the church Mary Lucy, born yesterday, of the lawful marriage of Narcisse Lafontaine and Margaret Pichet of this parish. Godfather, Maxime Lafontaine, godmother, Mary Lafontaine.

F. X. Blanchet, V.G., Rector

B-2 Mary H. Lafontaine

On January 8, 1893, I, rector of St. Paul, have baptized in the church Mary Henrietta Albina, born today (twin daughters) of the lawful marriage of Narcisse Lafontaine and Margaret Pichette of this parish. Godfather, John Picard, godmother, Celina Choquette.

F. X. Blanchet, V.G., Rector

Page 213 B-3 Francis Orlando Coolidge

On January 13, 1893, I, rector of St. Paul, have baptized in the church Francis Orlando Coolidge, born the 27th of October, 1868, non married, of Champoeg.

F. O. Coolidge

F. X. Blanchet, V.G., Rector

First Communion

On January 14, 1893, I testify that Francis Orlando Coolidge received for the first time the Holy Sacrament in the church of St. Paul.

F. X. Blanchet, V.G., Rector

B-4 Mathew Connor

On January 15, 1893, I, the rector of St. Paul, baptized in the church Mathew, born today of the lawful marriage of Thomas Connor and Catherine McGrath of this parish. Godfather, Simon Connor, godmother, Mary Connor.

F. X. Blanchet, V.G., Rector

B-5 Francis Provost

On January 18, 1893, I, rector of St. Paul, testify that Mrs. Mary Magdelen Vesper (Ernst) gave private baptism in danger of death to Francis, born today, of the legitimate marriage of Julien Provost and Caroline Philomene Raymond of this parish.

F. X. Blanchet, V.G., Rector

S-1 John Gearin

On January 23, 1893, John Gearin, widower, aged 81 years, of this parish, died day before yesterday and was buried today in the cemetery of St. Paul. Witnesses, D. Bosquet, Matt Murphy, Fr. Pilette, F. Wassenhove and many others.

F. X. Blanchet, V.G., Rector

M-1 Julius Picard & Eleonora P. D. Choquette

On January 24, 1893, after the publication of one ban and the dispensation of two others, and no impediment being found, I, rector of St. Paul, having received their mutual consent, have united in marriage Julius Picard and Eleonore Pelagie Dolly Choquette, of age of this parish. Witnesses: [one illegible. dim]   Delia Choquette
A. A. Choquette

F. X. Blanchet, V.G., Rector

B-6 Elizabeth H. Brentano

On January 28, 1893, I, rector of St. Paul, have baptized in the church Elizabeth Henrietta, born day before yesterday of the lawful marriage of Regnier Brentano and Mary Ernst. Godparents, Doctor Brentano and his wife.

F. X. Blanchet. V.G., Rector

Page 214 B-7 Octavia Ouida Fortier

On January 29, 1893, I, rector of St. Paul, have baptized in the church Octavia Ouida, born the 15th of this month of the lawful marriage of Eusebe Fortier and Salome Raymond of this parish. Godfather, Henry Ernst, godmother, his wife.

F. X. Blanchet. V.G.. Rector

M-2
Joseph
Proulx
&
Margaret
C.
Manaigre

On February 13, 1893, after the publication of one ban and the dispensation of the other two, and no impediment being found, I, rector of St. Paul, having received their mutual consent, have united in marriage Joseph Proulx and Margaret Catherine Manaigre, of age, of this parish. Witnesses:

Lillie Jette   Sevare Managre

F. X. Blanchet, V.G., Rector

B-8
William
Henry
Winkleman

On February 27, 1893, I, rector of St. Paul, baptized in the church William Henry Winkleman, born the 31st of March, 1868, unmarried, of Mount Angel. Sponsor, Henry Bellarts.

F. X. Blanchet, V.G., Rector

M-3
William
H.
Winkleman
&
Elizabeth
Fessler

On February 28, 1893, [inserted, "ex tempore ultito"?] three bans having been dispensed and no impediment found, I, rector of St. Paul, having received their mutual consent, have united in marriage William Henry Winkleman and Elizabeth Fessler, of age, of this parish. Witnesses:

Mary Kirk   Thomas Kirk

F. X. Blanchet, V.G., Rector

B-9
Rachel
Eliz.
Pillett

On March 4, 1893, I, rector of St. Paul, have baptized in the church Rachel Elizabeth born the 1st of this month of the lawful marriage of Edward Pillett and Dora Krechter of this parish. Sponsors:

Aug. Krechter   Elizabeth Pillett

F. X. Blanchet, V.G., Rector

B-10
Catherine
Van

On March 4, 1893, I, rector of St. Paul, have baptized in the church Catherine Van, born the 24th of May, 1879, of this parish. Sponsors, Walter and Elizabeth Murphy.

F. X. Blanchet, V.G., Rector

B-11
N.
George
Joseph
Merten

On March 17, 1893, I, rector of St. Paul, have baptized in the church N. George Joseph, born the day before yesterday, of the lawful marriage of Stephen Merten and Teresa Gooding of this parish. Sponsors, Nicholas Gooding and Mary (overwritten), his wife.

F. X. Blanchet, V.G., Rector

Page 215
M-4
John F.
Kerr
&
Eliz. A.
Van Was-
enhove

On April 3, 1893, after the publication of one [ban] and the dispensation of two others, and no impediment being found, I, rector of St. Paul, having received their mutual consent, have united in holy matrimony John F. Kerr and Elizabeth A. Van Wassenhove, of age, of this parish. Witnesses:

Miss Elizabeth Murphy   Aleck Van Wassenhove

F. X. Blanchet, V.G., Rector

B-12
Caroline
Elizabeth
McCormick

On April 7, 1893, I, rector of St. Paul, baptized in the church Caroline Elizabeth, born the 3rd of this month, of the lawful marriage of Charles McCormick and Mary Van Wassenhove of this parish. Godfather, Alex. Van Wassenhove, godmother, Agnes Bosquet.

F. X. Blanchet, V.G., Rector

B-13
Marzella
Elizabeth
Gearin

On April 16, 1893, I, missionary, have baptized at home Marzella Elizabeth, born the 8th of this month, of the lawful marriage of Hugh B. Gearin and Minnie Murphy of the parish of St. Paul. Godfather, Frederic Murphy, godmother, Margaret Murphy.

P. William Kramer, O.S.B.

B-14
Mary
Lucy
Kennedy

On April 23, 1893, I, missionary, baptized in the church Mary Lucy, born today, of the lawful marriage of Edward J. Kennedy and Lucy E. Connor of the parish of St. Paul. Godfather, John Coleman, godmother, Mary Kennedy his wife.

P. William Kramer, O.S.B.

B-15
Genevieve
Mabel
Picard

On May 9, 1893, I, rector of St. Paul, have baptized in the church Genevieve Mabel, born the 6th of this month of the lawful marriage of John Picard and Celina Choquette of this parish. Godfather, A. Choquette, godmother, Genevieve Bernier.

F. X. Blanchet, V.G., Rector

B-16
Warren
Francis
Smith
11
First
Commu-
nions

On May 22, 1893, I, rector of St. Paul, testify that Peter kirk gave private baptism yesterday to Warren Francis Smith, in danger of death, aged 72 years the 10th of last April.

F. X. Blanchet, V.G., Rector

On June 1, 1893, the following children received their First Communion in the church of St. Paul:

Stephen James Smith   Lena Ida Krechter
Philippina Martha Ernst   Amanda Manaigre
Caroline Lambert   Mary Pelland
Theresa Philomena Merten   Elizabeth Pitt
Mary Gloria Lily Bellanger   Mary Joanne McCann
Bertha Hughes

F. X. Blanchet, V.G., Rector

Page 216
21
Confir-
mations

On June 1, 1893, the following faithful received the Sacrament of Confirmation from R.R.D.D. Archbishop of Oregon City W. H. Gross in the church of St. Paul. Sponsors were Thomas Connor and Mrs. Mary McKay.

Justina H. Victoria Davidson
Amanda Helen Manaigre
Teresa Philomene Barbara Merten
Elizabeth Mary Lafontaine
Mary Cecelia Smith
Mary Angela Pelland
Domatilla Helen Lebrun
Lena Ida Cecelia Krechter
Philippina Teresa Ernst
Arthur Edward Crosby
Milton John Pillett
Rosa Margaret Pelland
Mary Joanne Cecelia McCann
Inez R. Margaret Weston
Elizabeth Victoria Pitt
Mary Agnes Lebrun
Mary Gloria Lily Victoria Bellanger
Caroline Victoria Lambert
Bertha Mildred Hughes
Stephen Louis Smith

William
Archbishop of Oregon City
F. X. Blanchet, V.G., Rector

B-17
Winifred
Lucy
Woolf

On June 4, 1893, I, rector of St. Paul, have baptized in the church Winifred Lucy, born the 19th of last March of the lawful marriage of J. F. Woolf and Catherine Rorsch of this parish. Godfather, Joseph Singer, godmother, Anna Schneider, his wife.

F. X. Blanchet, V.G., Rector

B-18
Henry
Bunning

On June 9, 1893, I, rector of St. Paul, have baptized in the church Henry Francis, born the 5th of this month of the lawful marriage of Christian Bunning and Mary Theresa Weekamp of this parish. Godfather, Henry Ernst, Godmother, Magdelen Vesper, his wife.

F. X. Blanchet, V.G., Rector

B-19
Norbert
Stephen
Pfeifer

On June 11, 1893, I, rector of St. Paul, have baptized in the church Norbert Stephan, born the 6th of this month of the lawful marriage of Adolph Pfeifer and Christine Oberdoester of this parish. Godfather, Stephen Merten, godmother Anna Krupp.

F. X. Blanchet, V.G., Rector

S-2
Sister
Mary Juliana
nee Rosa

On July 12, 1893, rector of St. Paul, have buried in the mortuary of the Sisters of the Holy Names of Jesus and Mary the body of Sister Mary Juliana (Rosa Manning) aged about 33 years, who died the day before yesterday, after having received the Holy Sacraments. Witnesses, Mother Rosinante [?]

Manning	Margaret, Sisters Infant Jesus, Arsenius, Rosa, Barnabas and many others.
	F. X. Blanchet, V.G., Rector

B-20
Julia
Helen
Hughes

On June 17, 1893, I, rector of St. Paul, have baptized in the church Julia Helen, born the 14th of this month, of the lawful marriage of Andrew Hughes and Rosa Connor of this parish. Godfather, Joseph Bramberger, godmother, Isabella Effinger, his wife.

F. X. Blanchet, V.G., Rector

B-21
Mary
Frances
Pearl
Picard

On July 2, 1893, I, rector of St. Paul, have baptized in the church Mary Frances Pearl, born the 3rd of December last, of the lawful marriage of Henry Picard and Marie Chpquette of this parish. Godfather, Julius Picard, godmother Eleonore Choquette, his wife.

F. X. Blanchet, V.G., Rector

B-22
Mary
Trenholm
Dixon

On July 11, 1893, I, rector of St. Paul, have baptized conditionally in the church Mary Trenholm (Dixon), married, born the 8th of February, 1833, in England, educated in the Episcopal church, now of this parish.

F. X. Blanchet, V.G., Rector

B-23
Mary
Matilda
Boles

On July 11, 1893, I, rector of St. Paul, have baptized conditionally (she had been baptized earlier by Sister Mary Victor, in danger of death), Mary Matilda, born the 11th of January, 1885, of unknown parents. Mrs. Goyette was godmother.

F. X. Blanchet, V.G., Adm.

B-24
Georgiana
Boles

On July 11, 1893, I, rector of St. Paul, have baptized in the church Georgiana Amelia, born Feb. 15, 1886, of unknown parents. Godmother, Matilda Dixon, their guardian [?].

F. X. Blanchet, V.G., Adm.

B-25
Agatha
Lorita
Lind

On July 25, 1893, I, rector of St. Paul, have baptized in the church Agatha Lorita, born the 16th of November last, of the lawful marriage of Nelson P. Lind (non-catholic) and Veronica McDonald, of East Portland. Sponsors:

Agatha Kirk   R. E. Kirk

B-26
Laurence
D.
Desjardins

On August 1, 1893, I, rector of St. Paul, have baptized in the church Laurence Damase, born yesterday, of the lawful marriage of Fabien Desjardins and Anne Remillard of this parish. Godfather, L. M. Fortin, Godmother, Agnes M. Manaigre, his wife.

L. H. Fortin   Agnes M. Manaigre
F. X. Blanchet, V.G., Rector

B-27
Mary
Catherine
Bellarts

On September 11, 1893, I, rector of St. Paul, baptized in the church Mary Catherine, born today, of the lawful marriage of Henry Bellarts and Elizabeth Zolner of this parish. Godfather, Francis Zollner per R. E. Kirk, and godmother, Mrs. Catherine Bellarts.

R. E. Kirk   Mrs. K. Ballert
F. X. Blanchet, V.G., Rector

B-28
M. Celina
Georgiana
Choquette

On September 24, 1893, I, rector of St. Paul, baptized in the church Mary Celina Georgiana, born the 17th of this month of the lawful marriage of Norbert Zetique Choquette and Elma Morel of this parish. Godfather, Amedee Choquette, godmother Celina Choquette (Picard).

F. X. Blanchet, V.G., Rector

B-29
Reina
Helen
Combest

On October 1, 1893, I, rector of St. Paul, have baptized in the church Reina Helen, born the 26th of November, 1886, to Thomas Combest and Loysa Helen Bennett (Combest), non-catholic, of this parish. Godfather, Peter Kirk, Godmother, Josephine Wassenhove (Kerr).

F. X. Blanchet, V.G., Rector

B-30
Grace
Amy
Combest

On October 1, 1893, I, rector of St. Paul, have baptized in the church Grace Amy, born the 19th of May, 1889, to Thomas Combest and Helen Bennett (Combest), non-catholic, of this parish. Godfather, L. Simon, godmother, Mary Simon.

F. X. Blanchet, V.G., Rector

B-31 Francis Loyd Combest	On October 1, 1893, I, rector of St. Paul, have baptized in the church Francis Loyd, born the 25th of May *[1893 added later in margin]* to Thomas Combest and Helen Loysa Bennett (Combest), non-catholic, of this parish. Godfather, James Coyle, godmother, Elizabeth Ray (Coyle). F. X. Blanchet, V.G., Rector
B-32 Teresa McLoughlin	On October 14, 1893, I, rector of St. Paul, have baptized in the church Teresa, born the 7th of September last, to William McLoughlin and Clementine Lambert, non-catholic, husband and wife of Newberg. Godmother, Emma Lambert. Wm. McLoughlin Emma Lambert F. X. Blanchet, V.G., Rector
Page 219 S-3 Julia Helen Hughes	On October 23, 1893, Julia Helen, aged 4 months, lawful daughter of Andrew Hughes and Rose Connor of this parish, died yesterday and was today buried in the cemetery at St. Paul. Witnesses: John McGrath, Thomas Connor and others. F. X. Blanchet, V.G., Rector
S-4 Margaret Kirk	On November 10, 1893, Margaret Lyons *[Lynes]*, wife of Peter Kirk, aged 50 years, of this parish, died day before yesterday and was today buried in the cemetery at St. Paul. Witnesses: Matth. Murphy, F. Van Wassenhove, J. McKay, J. Coleman and many others. F. X. Blanchet, V.G., Rector
B-33 Charles I. Francis Brentano	On November 9, 1893, I, rector of St. Paul, have baptized in the church Charles Ignatius Francis, born today, of the lawful marriage of Casimer Brentano and Victoria Dora Thoma of this parish. Godfather, Anthony Ahrens, godmother, Margaret Coffey. F. X. Blanchet, V.G., Rector
B-34 Virginia Jette	On November 10, 1893, I, rector of St. Paul, baptized at home Virginia, aged about 5 months, (first baptism) of the lawful marriage of Adolphe and Margaret Jette of Champoeg. F. X. Blanchet, V.G., Rector
B-35 Margaret T. Geelan	On November 12, 1893, I, rector of St. Paul, have baptized in the church Margaret Teresa, born the 9th of October last, of the lawful marriage of Patrick Geelan and Elizabeth Goodrich (Geelan) of this parish. Godfather, Hugh B. Gearin, godmother, Mary Agnes Bearhorst (Buyserie). F. X. Blanchet, V.G., Rector
S-5 Marguerite Dubreuil	On November 14, 1893, Marguerite Dubreuil, aged 90 years, widow, died the day before yesterday and was today buried in the cemetery at St. Paul. Witnesses: Francis Lambert, Chas. Lafontaine and a few others. F. X. Blanchet, V.G., Rector
B-36 Thomas Combest	On November 26, 1893, I, rector of St. Paul, have baptized in the church Thomas Combest, born the 18th of September, 1844, husband of Loysa Helen Bennett (Combest) of this parish. Godfather, Patrick Mullen. F. X. Blanchet, V.G., Rector
Page 220 B-37 Loysa H. Bennett Combest	On November 26, 1893, I, rector of St. Paul, have baptized in the church Loysa Helen Bennett (Combest), born the 17th of January, 1858, wife of Thomas Combest of this parish. Godmother, Elizabeth Coyle. F. X. Blanchet, V.G., Rector
B-38 William Combest	On November 26, 1893, I, rector of St. Paul, have baptized in the church William, born the 9th of April, 1875, of the lawful marriage of Thomas Combest and Loysa Helen Bennett (Combest) of this parish. Godfather, William Trevor. F. X. Blanchet, V.G., Rector
B-39 Arthur J. Combest	On November 26, 1893, I, rector of St. Paul, have baptized in the church Arthur James, born the 14th of April, 1877, of the lawful marriage of Thomas Combest and Loysa Helen Bennett (Combest) of this parish. Godmother, Teresa Merten. F. X. Blanchet, V.G., Rector

B-40
John S.
Combest

On November 26, 1893, I, rector of St. Paul, have baptized in the church
John Sidney, born August 20th, 1879, of the lawful marriage of Thomas
Combest and Loysa Helen Bennett (Combest) of this parish. Godfather,
Stephen Merten.

F. X. Blanchet, V.G., Rector

B-41
Thomas
E.
Combest

On November 26, 1893, I, rector of St. Paul, have baptized in the church
Thomas Everett, born the 27th of December, 1881, of the lawful marriage
of Thomas Combest and Loysa Helen Bennett (Combest) of this parish.
Godfather, R. E. Kirk, godmother, Agatha McDonald (Kirk).

F. X. Blanchet, V.G., Rector

First
Commu-
nion
Page 221

On November 27, 1893, Emma Julia Ogden, aged about 30 years, received
her first communion at home in Champoeg.

F. X. Blanchet, V.G., Rector

B-42
Mary
Emilie
Proulx

On December 6, 1893, I, rector of St. Paul, have baptized in the church
Mary Emlile Victoria, born two days ago, of the lawful marriage of Joseph
Proulx and Margaret Manaigre (Proulx) of this parish. Godfather, Peter
Manaigre, godmother, Emilie Pichette (Manaigre).

F. X. Blanchet, V.G., Rector

First
Commu-
nion

On December 8, 1893, Margaret Irene Murphy and Emilie Thoma received
the First Holy Sacrament in the church of St. Paul.

F. X. Blanchet, V.G., Rector

First
Commu-
nion

On December 25, 1893, Thomas Combest, Ellen Bennett (Combest),
William Combest, Arthur Combest, and Mary Thoma received their first
Holy Communion in the church of St. Paul.

F. X. Blanchet, V.G., Rector

Summary	1893	
Baptisms of Infants	35	
" " Adults	7	= 42
Marriages	4	
First Communions	20	
Confirmations	21	
Easter Duty	307	
Burials	5	

1894

S-1
Mary
Loretta
Kirk

On January 4, 1894, Mary Loretta, aged two years and two months, daughter of John Kirk and Cecelia McKay, died the day before yesterday and
today was buried in the cemetery at St. Paul. Witnesses, W. R. McKay,
Peter Manaigre and others.

F. X. Blanchet, V.G., Rector

S-2
Charles
David
Lambert

On January 16, 1894, Charles David, aged about 4 years, son of Francis
and Clementine Lambert, died the day before yesterday and was buried
today in the cemetery at St. Paul. Witnesses, Julius Picard, Peter Manaigre
and many others.

F. X. Blanchet, V.G., Rector

Page 222
B-1
Julius
F.
Picard

On January 28, 1894, I, rector of St. Paul, have baptized in the church
Julius Francis, born the 22nd of this month of the lawful marriage of
Julius Picard and Eleonore Choquette of this parish. Godfather, Amedee
Choquette, godmother, Delia Choquette.

F. X. Blanchet, V.G., Rector

M-1
Joseph
Ridders
&
Emilie
Thoma

On January 29, 1894, after the publication of one ban and no impediment
being found, I, rector of St. Paul, having received their mutual consent,
have united in marriage Joseph Ridders of Corvallis and Emilie Thoma
of McMinnville, of age, in the presence of:

Louis Ernst   Miss Mary Thomas

F. X. Blanchet, V.G., Rector

B-2
Joseph

On February 27, 1894, I, rector of St. Paul, have baptized in the church
Joseph Henry, born yesterday, of the lawful marriage of Joseph Haas and

222nd, 223rd, & 224th pgs

H. Haas	Mary Prager (Haas) of this parish. Godfather, Joseph Bramberger, god-mother, Isabelle Bramberger.
	Joseph Bramberger Isabelle Bramberger
	[signatures written in German]
	F. X. Blanchet, V.G., Rector
B-3	On March 21, 1894, I, rector of St. Paul, have baptized in the church Mary
Mary	Adeline, born the 17th of this month of the lawful marriage of Alphonse
Adeline	Buyserie and Mary Bearhorst of this parish. Godfather and godmother:
Buyserie	Mary McKay Isadore Buyserie
	F. X. Blanchet, V.G., Rector
B-4	On March 22, 1894, I, rector of St. Paul, baptized in the church Elizabeth,
Elizabeth	born the 26th of January last of the lawful marriage of James Coyle and
Coyle	Henrietta Ray of this parish. Godfather and godmother:
	F. X. Blanchet Eliz. Coyle
	F. X. Blanchet, V.G., Rector
First Commu-nion	On March 29, 1894, I, rector of St. Paul, testify that Mary Trenholm Dixon received her First Communion.
	F. X. Blanchet, Rector

Page 223

B-5	On March 31, 1894, I, rector of St. Paul, have baptized in the church
Eliza	Elizabeth Victoria, born the 4th of this month of the lawful marriage
Victoria	of Eusebe Fortier and Salome Raymond of this parish. Godfather and
Fortier	godmother:
	Matilda Crete Hector Beaudry
	F. X. Blanchet, V.G., Rector
B-6	On April 8, 1894, I, rector of St. Paul, have baptized in the church Irene
Irene	Alice, born the 28th of February last of the lawful marriage of Patrick
Alice	Mullen and Mary Flynn of this parish. Godfather and godmother:
Mullen	Emma Murphy W. M. Murphy
	F. X. Blanchet, V.G., Rector
S-3	On April 29, 1894, I the undersigned have buried in the cemetery of St.
Helen	Paul Helen Lebeau, aged 2 years and 7 months, daughter of Calixte Lebeau
Lebeau	and Clara Lebeau.
	In the absence of the rector,
	fr. Dominic Wadenschwiler, O.S.B.
B-7	On May 6, 1894, I the undersigned have baptized in the church of St. Paul
Rosa	Rosa Octavia, born February 12, 1894, to George Aplin, father, and Emilie
Octavia	Aplin, his wife, of the parish of St. Paul. Godparents were: Rosa Crosby
Aplin	and Other *[Arthur]* Crosby, both of St. Paul parish.
	Rosy Crosby Arthur Crosby
	fr. Dominic Wadenschwiler
	in the absence of the rector
B-8	On May 27, 1894, I the undersigned have baptized in the church of St. Paul
John	John Edward, born the 23rd of October, 1893, of Edward Lempeke and
Edward	Mary Miller of Butteville. Godparents were: Edward Miller and Elizabeth
Lempeke	Miller, both of Butteville.
	Elizabeth Miller
	Fr. Dominic
	in the absence of the rector

Page 224

B-9	On . . . *[May or June?]*, 1894, I completed the ceremony of baptism of
Mary	Mary Louisa Jones (the infant had been privately baptized at home),
Louisa	daughter of Nehemiah S. Jones and Frances McPaulin of Champoeg.
Jones	Witnesses were:
	Joseph Pillett Elizabeth Pillett
	fr. Dominic,
	in the absence of the rector.
B-10	On July 10, 1894, I, rector of St. Paul, Baptised conditionally in the church

John W. Dixon	William Dixon, born Dec. 25, 1838, in Hartford, England. Peter Kirk, sponsor. <div align="right">F. X. Blanchet, V.G., Rector per Fr. Dominic, O.S.B.</div>
S-4 Alphonse Remi Aplin	On August 2, 1894, Alphonse Remi Aplin, aged about 16, died the day before yesterday and was buried today in the cemetery at St. Paul. Witnesses, C. O. Pelland, Julien Provost and many others. <div align="right">F. X. Blanchet,.V.G., Rector</div>
B-11 James Edwin Scollard	On August 2, 1894, I, rector of St. Paul, have baptized in the church James Edwin, Born the 29th of June last, of John Scollard and Alice Kelly, husband and wife of Champoeg. Sponsor, Charles Scollard, godmother, Anna Kennedy. Annie S. Kennedy Charles Scollard <div align="right">F. X. Blanchet, V.G., Rector</div>
B-12 Rosa Eunice Connor	On August 10, 1894, I, rector of St. Paul, have baptized in the church Rosa Eunice, born today of the lawful marriage of Thomas Connor and Catherine McGrath of this parish. Godfather, Joseph McGrath, godmother, Rosa Hughes (Connor). Rose V. Hughes P. J. McGrath <div align="right">F. X. Blanchet, V.G., Rector</div>
Page 225 B-13 Frederic William Garnett	On August 15, 1894, I, rector of St. Paul, have baptized in the church Frederic William Garnett, born the 21st of June, 1826. Mr. Garnett received conditional baptism because of his former Lutheran belief. Hugh B. Gearin William Garnett <div align="right">F. X. Blanchet, V.G., Rector</div>
S-5 Rachel Elizabeth Pilette	On August 16, 1894, Rachel Elizabeth, aged 18 months, lawful child of Edward Pilett and Dora Krechter (Pilett) of St. Gervais and Protaise died the day before yesterday and was buried today in the cemetery at St. Paul. Witnesses: August Krechter, Joseph Pilette and many others. <div align="right">F. X. Blanchet, V.G., Rector</div>
B-14 Catherine Raymond	On August 19, 1894, I, rector of St. Paul, baptized in the church Catherine, born the first of this month of the lawful marriage of August Raymond and Josephine Mongrain (Raymond) of this parish. Godfather, Joseph Goyette, godmother, Hannah McDermott (Goyette). <div align="right">F. X. Blanchet, V.G., Rector</div>
B-15 Dyonisius M. Winkleman	On August 26, 1894, I, rector of St. Paul, have baptized in the church Dyonisius Martin, born the 24th of this month, of the lawful marriage of Julius Winkleman and Elizabeth Fessler (Winkleman) of Hubbard. Godfather, Martin Fessler, godmother, Mary Winkleman. Mary Winkleman Martin Fessler <div align="right">F. X. Blanchet, V.G., Rector</div>
B-16 Edward M. Peter Shaw	On August 30, 1894, I, rector of St. Paul, have baptized in the church Edward Marion Peter, born the 18th of April last, of the lawful marriage of William M. Shaw (non-catholic) and Helen McDonald of this parish. Godfather, Peter Kirk, godmother Mary McDonald. <div align="right">F. X. Blanchet, V.G., Rector</div>
First Commun- ion	On September 2, 1894, Frederic William Garnet received for the first time the Holy Eucharist in the church of St. Paul. <div align="right">F. X. Blanchet, V.G., Rector</div>
Page 226 B-17 Mary Ethel Cosgrove	On September 13, 1894, I baptized privately at home Mary Ethel, lawful daughter of Hugh Francis Cosgrove and Emma Stanley (Cosgrove) of this parish, born August 6th last. (Mother non-catholic) Godmother, Margaret Murphy. The ceremonies withheld to be completed later. <div align="right">F. X. Blanchet, V.G., Rector</div>
S-6 Elizabeth Coyle	On October 1, 1894, Elizabeth Coyle, wife of James Coyle, aged about 62 years, died two days ago and was buried today in the cemetery at St. Paul. Witnesses, James Coleman, John Kirk and many others. <div align="right">F. X. Blanchet, V.G., Rector</div>

B-18
Infant
Brentano

On October 2, 1894, I, rector of St. Paul, testify that Dr. Brentano baptized an infant *[born]* of the lawful marriage of Regnier Brentano and Mary Ernst (Brentano) of this parish.
F. X. Blanchet, V.G., Rector

S-8
Eliza
Victoria
Fortier

On October 9, 1894, Elizabeth Victoria, born the 7th of this month of the lawful marriage of Eusebe Fortier and Salome Raymond of this parish died yesterday at the age of 7 months and was buried today in the cemetery at St. Paul. Witnesses, John Kirk and Peter Manaigre and others.
F. X. Blanchet, V.G., Rector

S-9
Emma
Ogden

On October 31, 1894, Emma Ogden, aged 25 years, unmarried, died the day before yesterday and was buried today in the Champoeg cemetery. Witnesses, A. Jette, Marguerite Jette, Mrs. Scollard and others.
F. X. Blanchet, V.G., Rector

S-10
Winifred
Lucy
Wolf

November 11, 1894, Winifred Lucy, aged 20 months, born of the legitimate marriage of J. B. Wolf and Catherine Rorsch (Wolf) Of Butteville, died yesterday and was today buried in the cemetery at St. Paul. Witnesses: Stephen Merten, W. F. Davidson, and others.
F. X. Blanchet, V.G., Rector

Page 227
M-2
J. F.
Miller
&
M. U.
Pilette

On December 26, 1894, the dispensation for disparity of religion having been granted and no other impediment being found, after the publication of one ban, I, rector of St. Paul, having received their mutual consent, have united in marriage James F. Miller and Matilda Ursula Pilette, of age, of this parish. Witnesses, Antoinette Pilette and Adolph Pilette.
F. X. Blanchet, V.G., Rector
1895

B-1
George
Frederic
Pfeifer

On January 20, 1895, I, rector of St. Paul, have baptized in the church George Frederic born yesterday of the lawful marriage of Adolph Pfeifer and Christina Oberdoester of this parish. Godfather, Frederic Hoerner, godmother, Mary Bunning.
Fred Hoerner   M. T. Bunning
F. X. Blanchet, V.G., Rector

B-2
Anna
Kennedy

On February 26, 1895, I, rector of St. Paul, have baptized in the church Anna, born yesterday, of the lawful marriage of Edward Kennedy and Lucy Connor of this parish. Godfather, Andrew Hughes, godmother, Mary Anna Hughes.
Mary A. Hughes   Andrew Hughes
F. X. Blanchet, V.G., Rector

[Inserted beside pp. 227 and 228 is a paper of declaration, as follows:]
St. Paul, Marion Co. Or. Dec. 26, 1894
I, the undersigned, solemnly promise Matilda Ursula Pilette, whom I am going to marry, to give her full liberty in regard to her religion, and also to raise our children, if we have any, in the Roman Catholic Faith, according to her wishes.
J. F. Miller
Attest: Patrick Geelan

B-3
Amanda
Jane
Crosby

April 21, 1895, I baptized conditionally Amanda Jane, born the 29th of March last, to Arthur Crosby, Woodburn, and Rose Manaigre of this parish, parents. Godparents were: Joseph Prue and Margaret Prue *[Proulx]*.
D. Faber, Rector

B-4
Joseph
Bernard
Wolf

April 23, 1895, I baptized Joseph Bernard, born the 20th of March last, to Joseph Bernard Wolf, of Sech *[?]*, Tyrol, and Catherine Rauch, of Iowa, husband and wife. Godparents were Joseph Singer and Helen McKay.
D. Faber, Rector

Page 228
B-5
Angela
Teresa
Wolf

April 23, 1895, I baptized Angela Teresa, born the 20th of March last, to Joseph Bernard Wolf, Sech, Tyrol, and Catherine Rauch, of Iowa, parents. Godparents were: Joseph Singer and Mary Anna Singer.
D. Faber, Rector

B-6
Mary
Flavia
Caroline
Miller

May 12, 1895, I baptized Mary Flavia Caroline, born Dec. 16, 1878, in California, to Leander Miller, of Maine, and Fannie M. Banks, of Australia. Godparents were: Stephen Merten and Teresa Merten.

D. Faber, Rector

S-1
Charles
Prevost

June 1, 1895, I buried in the cemetery of St. Paul Charles Prevost, aged 84, who died May 30 in this same parish.

D. Faber, Rector

B-7
Cora
Augusta
Picard

June 1, 1895, I baptized Cora Augusta, born the 25th of May last to John Picard and Celina Choquette, both of this place. Godparents were: Julius Picard and Leonarda Picard.

D. Faber, Rector

B-8
James
Howard
Coleman
Murphy

June 2, 1895, I baptized James Howard Coleman, born the 18th of May last, to William Murphy and Emma Coleman, both of this place. Godparents were William Thomas Coleman and Caledonia Elizabeth Coleman.

D. Faber, Rector

B-9
Joseph
Boniface
Bunning

June 7, 1895, I baptized Joseph Boniface, born June 5th of this year, to Christopher Bunning, of Germany, and Mary Teresa Weekamp, from Illinois. Godparents were: Joseph Hoerner [?] and Christina Pfeifer.

D. Faber, Rector

Page 229

B-10
Joseph
Edward
Faber

August 1, 1895, I baptized Joseph Edward, born the 30th of July last to George Faber, of Bavaria, and Mary Haas, from Ohio. Godparents were Joseph Haas and Rose Hughes.

D. Faber, Rector

B-11
Mary
Elizabeth
Bellarts

August 15, 1895, I baptized Mary Elizabeth, born today to Henry Bellarts, of Prussia, and Elizabeth Zollner, of Mount Angel. Godparents were: Stephen Merten and Teresa Merten.

D. Faber, Rector

B-12
Simon
Andrew
Connor

August 18, 1895, I baptized Simon Andrew, born today to Simon James Connor, of Illinois, and Agnes Scully, of Pennsylvania. Godparents were: Andrew Hughes and Agnes Burns.

D. Faber, Rector

[A slip of paper is inserted here, recording an act B that was apparently omitted in writing the page.]

B
Charles
Leonard
D.
Picard

August 26, 1895, I baptized Charles Leonard D. Picard, born the 18th of April last, to Henry Picard and Mary Choquette, both of St. Paul. Godparents were: Dieudonne Manaigre and Mary Bellanger.

D. Faber, Rector

M-1
Joseph
Delisle
&
Mary
Frances
Delia
Choquette

August 29, 1895, the publication of all bans having been dispensed with [?], I have joined in holy matrimony Joseph Delisle, son of Felix Delisle and Mary Delisle, and Mary Frances Delia Choquette, daughter of Amedee Choquette and Mary Choquette. Witnesses were: Francis Bernier and Rosa Delisle.

D. Faber, Rector

B-13
Francis
Conrad
Berhorst

September 1, 1895, I baptized Francis Conrad, born the 27th of August last to John Berhorst, of Missouri, and Barbara Seger, of Baden, Europe. Godparents were: Alphonse Joseph Marie Buyserie and Mary Buyserie.

D. Faber, Rector

Page 230

B-14
Elsie
Virginia
Jette

October 7, 1895, I baptized Elsie Virginia, born the 19th of June, 1893, to Adolphe Jette, of Canada, and Marguerite Liard, of this place. Godparents were: Edward Krechter and Eulalie Jette.

D. Faber, Rector

Sum [?]

B-15

October 12, 1895, I baptized Felix Xavier, born the 17th of September

Felix Xavier Delisle	last, to Joseph Delisle and Mary Frances Delia Choquette, both of this place. Godparents were: Amedee Choquette and Eleonore Choquette. <div align="center">D. Faber, Rector</div>
B-16 Louise Brule	October 13, 1895, I baptized Louise, born October 10th of this year, to Ange Brule, of Canada, and Helen Connor, also of Canada. Godparents were: Xavier Goyette and Anne Goyette. <div align="center">D. Faber, Rector</div>
M-2 James Frederic Davidson & Mary Anna Gooding	October 23, 1895, I have joined in marriage James Frederic Davidson, son of Francis and Anna Davidson, and Mary Anna Gooding, daughter of Nicholas and Mary Gooding, the dispensation of two and the publica- tion of the third ban having been made. Witnesses were: John Davidson and Elizabeth Merten. <div align="center">D. Faber, Rector</div>
B-17 Josephine Elizabeth Adeline Bruce	December 8, 1895, I baptized Josephine Elizabeth Adeline Bruce, born June 4, 1880, of James N. Bruce and Elizabeth Riddle, Godparents were: John Berhorst and Mary McKay. <div align="center">D. Faber, Rector</div>
Page 231	
B-18 Elmer Romey Baptiste Manaigre	December 22, 1895, I have baptized Elmer Romey Baptiste born November 8th last, to Sevare Manaigre of St. Paul and Mary Alice Vandale of St. Louis, Oregon. Godparents were Jean Baptiste Vandale and Clementine Vandale. <div align="center">D. Faber, Rector</div>
B-19 Thomas Roland Connor	December 22, 1895, I baptized Thomas Roland, born the 21st of this month and year to Thomas Joseph Connor of Minnesota and Catherine Agnes McGrath, also of Minnesota. Godparents were: Mathew Connor and Mary McGrath. <div align="center">D. Faber, Rector</div>
S-2 Sister Mary Bertilia	December 23, 1895, I gave burial in the mortuary of the Sisters of the Holy Names of Jesus and Mary at St. Paul to the body of Sister Mary Bertilia (Jane Margaret Larkin) who died the 21st in Portland of pulmonary congestion (quick consumption), aged 34 years, 1 month and 27 days. <div align="center">D. Faber, Rector</div>
S-3 Genevieve Bernier	December 24, 1895, i buried in the cemetery of St. Paul Genevieve Bernier, deceased the 22nd of this month in Woodburn of pulmonary congestion, aged 41 years. <div align="center">D. Faber, Rector</div>
B-20 Elsie Agnes Lebeau	December 28, 1895, I baptized Elsie Agnes, born May 2nd of this year to Calixte Lebeau, of Canada, and Clarisse Mongrain of St. Paul, Oregon. Godparents were: Ange Brule and Helene Brule. <div align="center">D. Faber, Rector</div>
Page 232	
	<div align="center">1896</div>
B-1 Herman Polycarp Pillett	January 1, 1896, I baptized Herman Polycarp, born the 26th of December last, to Edward Pillett of Illinois and Dorothy Catherine Krechter of Indiana. Godparents were: Henry James Pillett and Magdelen A. Krechter. <div align="center">D. Faber, Rector</div>
B-2 Irene Lucretia Merten	January 8, 1896, I baptized Irene Lucretia Merten, born the 7th of this month, to Stephen Merten, of Morbach [?] Germany, and Teresa Gooding, of Indiana. Godparents were: James Frederic Davidson and Anna Mary Davidson. <div align="center">D. Faber, Rector</div>
S-1 Felix Xavier Delisle	January 8, 1896, I have buried Felix Xavier Delisle, deceased yesterday of pulmonary congestion at the age of 3 months and 10 days, son of Joseph Delisle and Mary Frances Delia Choquette. <div align="center">D. Faber, Rector</div>
B-3	January 17, 1896, I baptized Alphonse Casimer, born the 14th of this month

Alphonse
Casimer
Brentano

and year, of Regnier Lambert Marie Brentano, of Holland, and Mary Magdelen Ernst, of Paris, France. Godparents were: Casimer Frederic Brentano and Victoria Brentano.

D. Faber, Rector

B-4
Rudolph
Regnier
Brentano

January 17, 1896, I baptized conditionally Rudolph Regnier, born the 14th of this month and year, to Regnier Lambert Marie Brentano, of Holland, and Mary Magdelen Ernst, of Paris, France. Godparents were: Henry Charles Ernst and Philippina Agnes Ernst (by proxy).

D. Faber, Rector

Page 233
B-5
Francis
Xavier
Miller

January 22, 1896, I baptized Francis Xavier, born the 8th of this month and year, to James Francis Miller, of Ohio, and Matilda Ursula Pillett, of Illinois. Godparents were: Joseph Pillett and Elizabeth Pillett.

D. Faber, Rector

B-6
Anna
Delia
Choquette

January 29, 1896, I baptized Anna Delia, born the 9th of this month and year, to Norbert Lucifugue Choquette, St. Paul, and Mary Elma Morrell, Prineville, Oregon. Godparents were Joseph Morrell and Marie Anne Morrell.

D. Faber, Rector

S-2
Mary
Kirk

February 7, 1896, I buried Mary Kirk, aged 61 years and 11 months, who died the 5th of this month of the illness commonly called dropsy.

D. Faber, Rector

S-3
John
O'Loughlin

February 18, 1896, I buried John O'Loughlin, deceased the 16th of this month of the illness commonly called pleurisy, at the age of 21 years, 8 months and 12 days.

D. Faber, Rector

B-7
Helen
Isabelle
Brentano

March 13, 1896, I baptized Isabelle Helen, born today to Casimer Frederic Brentano, of Kansas, and Victoria Thoma, of St. Peter's, Minnesota. Godparents were: Joseph Bramberger and Isabelle Bramberger.

D. Faber, Rector

B-8
Gertrude
Frances
Iva
Picard

March 18, 1896, I baptized Gertrude Frances Iva, born the 6th of this month and year to Julius Picard and Genevieve Nora Choquette, both of this place. Godparents were: Adolphe Picard and Celina Picard.

D. Faber, Rector

Page 234
B-9
Philip
Eugene
Wolf

April 20, 1896, I baptized Philip Eugene, born the 24th of March last, to Joseph Bernard Wolf, of Tyrol, and Catherine Rauch, of Davis Co., Iowa. Godparents were: Henry Wolfhart and Mary Ferschweiler.

D. Faber, Rector

S-4
Sister
Mary
Sebastien

April 11, 1896, I gave burial in the mortuary of the Sisters of the Holy Names of Jesus and Mary at St. Paul to the body of Sister Mary Sebastien (Rose de Lima Roy), deceased in Portland the 9th of this month at the age of 49. Cause of death was cancer.

D. Faber, Rector

S-5
Frederic
Fortin

April 22, 1896, I buried Frederic Fortin, who died the 20th of this month of heart dropsy at the age of 55 years.

D. Faber, Rector

S-6
Francis
Coleman

April 28, 1896, I buried Francis Coleman, who died the 26th of this month of apoplexy and advanced age; his age was 71 years, 1 month, 12 days.

D. Faber, Rector

B-10
Mary
Helen
Gearin

May 15, 1896, I baptized Mary Helen, born the 28th of March to Hugh Burns Gearin, of Indiana, and Mary Cecelia Murphy of this place. Godparents were: Joseph Pillett and Elizabeth Pillett.

D. Faber, Rector

Page 235
S-7
Andrew
Murphy

May 30, 1896, Andrew Murphy died and on the 2nd of June was buried in the cemetery of St. Paul. Andrew Murphy died of asthma and dropsy at the age of 71.

D. Faber, Rector

B-11
Theo
Aglae
Margaret
Matthieu

June 4, 1896, I baptized Theo Aglae Margaret, born the 26th of February last to Theodore Matthieu, of Butteville, and Josephine Mary Neibert, of Wisconsin. Godparents were: Lester A. Matthieu and Aglae Clara O. Matthieu.

D. Faber, Rector

B-12
Joseph
William
Kirk

June 17, 1896, I baptized Joseph William, born the 16th of this month to Peter Kirk, of Ireland, and Matilda M. Dixon, of England. Godparents were: Peter Pius Kirk and Mary Agnes Kirk.

D. Faber, Rector

M-1
Jerome
Richard
Jackson
&
Laura
Amelia
Davidson

June 22, 1896, I joined in marriage Jerome Richard Jackson, son of Jerome B. and Mary Jackson, and Laura Amelia Davidson, daughter of Francis and Anna Davidson. Witnesses were: Joseph G. Jackson and Florence G. Pelland. Two bans had been published.

D. Faber, Rector

M-2
Alfred
Lambert
&
Mathilda
Crete

June 28, 1896, the publication of two bans having been excused [?], I united in marriage Alfred Lambert, son of August and Catherine Lambert, and Mathilda Crete, daughter of Isaac and Rosalie Crete. Witnesses were: Remy Lambert and Mary Raymond.

D. Faber, Rector

B-13
Francis
Joseph
Opitz

August 17, 1896, I baptized Francis Joseph, born the 4th of this August, to August Opitz, of Hungary, and Elizabeth Goelde [?] of Hungary. Godparents were: Francis Tinschut and Mary Magdelen Brentano.

D. Faber, Rector

Page 236

B-14
James
Erwin
Kennedy

September 20, 1896, I baptized James Erwin, born the 18th of this month to Edward John Kennedy, of Harrisburg, and Lucy Connor, of Wasica, Minnesota. Godparents were: James Arthur Kennedy and Martha Jane Hughes.

D. Faber, Rector

B-15
Bertha
Mary
Lambert

October 4, 1896, I baptized Bertha Mary, born the 29th of September last, to Francis Lambert and Clementine Mongrain, both of St. Paul. Godparents were Peter Manaigre and Mary Lambert.

D. Faber, Rector

S-18
August
Krechter

October 4, 1896, August Krechter died and on the 6th was buried; from Prussia, Europe, aged 63 years, 4 months, and 15 days, of pulmonary and heart failure.

D. Faber, Rector

B-16
Amabel
Viola
Gravel

October 10, 1896, I baptized Amabel Viola, born the 30th of August last year, to Augustin Joseph Gravel, of Canada, and Julie Juineaux, of Canada. Godparents were: L'Ange Brule and Helen Brule.

D. Faber, Rector

B-17
Joseph
Combest

October 17, 1896, I baptized Joseph, born the 10th of this month, to Thomas Combest, of Kentucky, and Louisa Ellen Bennett, of Iowa. Godparents were: Joseph Xavier Goyette and Hannah Goyette.

D. Faber, Rector

S-9
Angela
Teresa
Wolf

October 31, 1896, Angela Teresa died and on November 2 was buried, aged one year, seven months and seven days.

D. Faber, Rector

Page 237

M-3
Joseph
Bierward
&
Margaret

November 3, 1896, I joined in matrimony Joseph Bierward, son of Anthony Bierward and Rosa Vouer, and Margaret De Lima Delisle, daughter of Felix Delisle and Mary Pichet. Godparents were: John Bierward and Rosa Delisle.

D. Faber, Rector.

de Lima
Delisle
S-10
Albert
Murphy

December 9, 1896, I buried Albert, son of Andrew James and Myrtle Luella Murphy, born the 17th of this month in Portland, deceased of acute infant sickness at the age of 3 months and 17 days.

D. Faber, Rector

[1897]

M-1
Charles
Wilfred
Adolph
Jette
&
Mary
Elizabeth
Thibodeau

January 2, 1897, after the publication of three bans, I have united in marriage Charles Wilfred Adolphe Jette, son of Adolphe Jette and Marguerite Liard, and Mary Elizabeth Thibodeau, daughter of Napoleon Thibodeau and Mary Elizabeth Sannasee. Witnesses were: Louis Thibodeau and Nellie Duke.

D. Faber, Rector

M-2
Frank
Bernier
&
Mary
Lucile
Delisle

January 7, 1897, I have joined in matrimony *[several words illegible, but seem to refer to a dispensation of the impediment of consanguinity]* Francis Bernier, son of Julian Bernier and Celeste Girving *[?]*, and Mary Lucile Delisle, daughter of Felix Delisle and Margaret Pichette. Witnesses were: Peter Manaigre and Mary Philomene Fortier.

D. Faber, Rector

B-1
Peter
Laurence
Bellarts

January 21, 1897, I baptized Peter Laurence, born the 20th of this month to Henry John Bellarts, of Prussia, and Elizabeth Zollner, of Mount Angel, Oregon. Godparents were: Peter Laurence Gooding and Anna Mickle.

D. Faber, Rector

M-3
James
Edward
Smith
&
Elizabeth
Jane
Davidson

February 22, 1897, I have united in marriage *[several words illegible]* James Edward Smith, son of Francis S. and Ellen Smith, and Elizabeth Jane Davidson, daughter of William Franklin Davidson and Anna C. Davidson. Witnesses were: F. S. Smith and Eliza Davidson.

D. Faber, Rector

Page 238
B-2
John
Christian
Pfeifer

February 28, 1897, I baptized John Christian Pfeifer, born yesterday, to Adolphe Pfeifer, of Germany, and Christina Oberdoester, of Ohio. Godparents were: Christian Bunning and Mary Brentano.

D. Faber, Rector

B-3
Joseph
Felix
Delisle

March 21, 1897, I baptized Joseph Felix, born the 17th of this month, to Joseph Delisle and Mary Francis Delia Choquette, both of this place. Godparents were: Felix Delisle and Cecelia Pichette.

D. Faber, Rector

B-4
Albert
Joseph
McKay

April 4, 1897, I baptized Albert Joseph, born the 27th of March last, to William Richard McKay and Anna Kavanaugh, of St. Pouis, Oregon. Godparents were: Alphonse Joseph Buyserie and Catherine Kavanaugh.

D. Faber, Rector

B-5
Margaret
Elvina
Picard

April 5, 1897, I baptized Margaret Elvina, born the 18th of March last, to John Adolphe Picard and Celina Choquette, both of this place. Godparents were: Adolphe Jette and Marguerite Jette.

D. Faber, Rector

B-6
William
Herman
Bunning

April 6, 1897, I baptized William Herman, born the 4th of this month, to Christopher Bunning, of Germany, and Mary Teresa Weekamp, of Illinois. Godparents were: William Grant and Bridget Grant.

D. Faber, Rector

S-1
Peter
Kirk

April 6, 1897, on the third of this month, Peter Kirk died at the age of 66 years, 4 months and 9 days, of apoplexy, and was buried in this cemetery.

D. Faber, Rector

Page 239

S-2
James
Coyle
April 10, 1897, I buried in this cemetery James Coyle, who died the 8th of this month of advanced age, that being 80 years, 2 months and three days.
D. Faber, Rector

S-3
Edward
Coffey
April 13, 1897, I buried in this cemetery Edward Coffey, who died the 10th of this month of advanced age, that being 80 years, nine months and seventeen days.
D. Faber, Rector

B-7
Teresa
Laura
Haas
May 19, 1897, I baptized Teresa Laura, born today to Joseph Haas, of Cincinnati, Ohio, and Mary Prager, of Wisconsin. Godparents were: Stephen Merten and Teresa Merten.
D. Faber, Rector

B-8
Gerald
Patrick
Connor
May 21, 1897, I baptized Gerald Patrick, born the 20th of Simon James Connor, of Illinois, and Agnes Elizabeth Scully, of Pennsylvania. Godparents were: Robert Emmett Kirk and Mary Magdelen Burns.
D. Faber, Rector

B-9
Joseph
Oliver
Proulx
May 21, 1897, I baptized Joseph Oliver, born the 20th of April last, of Joseph Proulx, of . . . , and Margaret Manaigre, of this place. Godparents were: Laurence Amedee Fortin and Mary Agnes Fortin.
D. Faber, Rector

B-10
Freda
Loraine
Lambert
May 30, 1897, I baptized conditionally Freda Loraine, born the 13th of this April to Alfred Lambert and Matilda Crete, both of this place. Godparents were: Francis Crete and Mary Philomena Fortier.
D. Faber, Rector

Page 240

S-4
Sister
Mary
Crescentia
June 2, 1897, I buried in the mortuary of the Sisters of the Holy Names of Jesus and Mary at St. Paul, Sister Mary Crescentia (Rosa Becket). She died the 31st of May last in Portland at the age of 25 years, 2 months and 24 days, of consumption.
D. Faber, Rector

B-11
Amelia
Julia
Anna
Labonte
June 13, 1897, I baptized Amelia Julia Anna, born the 29th of April last, to Louis Labonte, of this place, and Josephine Bellique, of St. Louis, Oregon. Godparents were: Francis N. Coleman and Mary Helen Coleman.
D. Faber, Rector

B-12
Minnie
Stella
McKay
June 30, 1897, I baptized Minnie Stella, born the 17th of January last, to Moses McKay of St. Louis, Oregon, Josephine Aplin of this place. Godparents were: John McKay (by proxy) and Sophia McKay.
D. Faber, Rector

B-13
Jerome
Raphael
Jackson
July 3, 1897, I baptized Jerome Raphael, born June 8th of this year, to Jerome Richard Jackson and Laura Emily Davidson, both of this place. Godparents were: William Franklin Davidson and Anna Catherine Davidson.
D. Faber, Rector

B-14
Rosa
Raymond
July 3, 1897, I baptized Rosa Raymond, born the 6th of June last, of August Raymond and Josephine Mongrain, both of this place. Godparents were: John F. T. B. Brentano and Catherine Brentano.
D. Faber, Rector

S-5
Alexander
Gauthier
July 6, 1897, I buried in the new cemetery the body of Alexander Gauthier, who died the 4th of this month of dropsy at the age of 72 years, 3 months.
D. Faber, Rector

Page 241

B-15
Aloysius
Buyserie
July 11, 1897, I baptized Aloysius, born yesterday, to Alphonse Joseph Buysery, of Flanders, Belgium, and Mary Cunigunda [?] Berhorst, of Missouri. Godparents were: John Berhorst and Barbara Berhorst.

B-16
Anna
Elizabeth
Kuensting
July 18, 1897, I baptized Anna Elizabeth born the 11th of this month [?] to Charles Kuensting, of Missouri, and Mary Kenin [?] of Missouri. Godparents were: Stephen Merten and Elizabeth Anna Buskey.
D. Faber, Rector

B-17
Mary
Beatrix
Kirk

July 28, 1897, I baptized Mary Beatrix, born the 22nd of this month to John William Kirk, of Minnesota, and Cecile McKay, of this place. Godparents were: Thomas Francis Kirk and Agnes Kirk.

D. Faber, Rector

S-6
Patrick
Joseph
McGrath

August 2, 1897, I buried in the new cemetery Patrick Joseph McGrath, who was drowned in the Willamette River on July 31, aged 33 years, 7 months and 11 days.

D. Faber, Rector

S-7
Thomas
Riley
Combest

August 21, 1897, I buried Thomas Riley Combest, who died of exhaustion the 26th of this month, aged 52 years, 11 months and 1 day.

D. Faber, Rector

S-8
Andre
Labonte

August 30, 1897, I buried Andre Labonte, who died yesterday of a fractured skull, at the age of 37 years, 8 months and 13 days.

D. Faber, Rector

S-9
Antoinette
Blanche
Pillett

September 1, 1897, I buried in the cemetery, new, Antoinette Blanche Pillett, who died the 30th of August of consumption at the age of 29 years, 3 months and 29 days.

D. Faber, Rector

M-4
Jesse
Allen
Wallace
&
Amanda
Laura
Manaigre

September 7, 1897, after the dispensation of disparity of religion [word illegible], I have united in marriage Jesse Allen Wallace, of Ohio, now living in Cowlitz, Washington, and Amanda Lucy Manaigre, of this place. Witnesses were: Louis Manaigre and Emilie Manaigre.

D. Faber, Rector

Page 242
B-18
Mary
Anna Rosa
Bierward

September 12, 1897, I baptized Mary Anna Rosa, born the 8th of this month, to Joseph Bierward, of Wisconsin, and Margaret De Lima Delisle, of this place. Godparents were: Anthony Bierward and Cecelia Pichette.

D. Faber, Rector

B-19
Hermina
Camilla
Fortier

October 31, 1897, I baptized Hermina Camilla, born the 14th of September last, to Eusebe Fortier, of Canada, and Salome Raymond, of this place. Godparents were: Robert Emmett Kirk and Agatha Kirk.

D. Faber, Rector

B-20
Edward
Frederic
Davidson

November 21, 1897, I baptized Edward Frederic, born the 20th of this month, to James Frederic Davidson, of this place, and Mary Anna Gooding, . . . Prussia. Godparents were: Nicholas Gooding and Mary Gooding.

D. Faber, Rector

B-21
Cecelia
Mullen

December 18, 1897, I baptized Cecelia, born the 26th of November last, to Patrick Mullen, of C . . . Co, Ireland, and Mary Anna Flynn, of Albany, N.Y., his wife. Godparents were: Peter Pius Kirk and Margaret Mary Kirk.

D. Faber, Rector

1898

B-1
William
McKinley
Smith

January 9, 1898, I baptized William McKinley, born the 30th of December last, to James Edward Smith and Elizabeth Jane Davidson, both of this place. Godparents were: Joseph Patrick Smith and Frances Ursula Davidson.

D. Faber, Rector

Page 243
B-2
Joseph
Francis
Connor

January 11, 1898, I baptized Joseph Francis, born today to Thomas Joseph Connor, of Minnesota, and Catherine McGrath, his wife, also of Minnesota. Godparents were: Joseph Bramberger and Isabelle Bramberger.

D. Faber, Rector

B-3
Grace
Gloriunda
Wolf

February 2, 1898, I baptized Grace Gloriunda, born the 5th of January of this year, to Joseph Bernard Wolf, of Vorailberg, Austria, and Catherine Rauch, of Iowa, his wife. Godparents were: Peter George Wolfhart and Olga Joanna Wolf.

D. Faber, Rector

S-1 Sister Mary Lucretia	February 21, 1898, I buried in the vault of the Sisters of the Holy Names of Jesus and Mary at St. Paul, Sister Mary Lucretia (Mary Dugan), who died at Portland the 18th of this month of the illness commonly called consumption, at the age of 36 years, 4 months and 14 days. D. Faber, Rector
B-4 Edward George Pillett	February 27, 1898, I baptized Edward George, born the 5th of this month, to Edward Xavier Pillett, of Illinois, and Dorothea Krechter, of Indiana, his wife. Godparents were: George Milton Pillett, (by proxy) Matilda Eunice [?] Miers. D. Faber, Rector
S-2 Infant 6 years Brentano	March 4, 1898, I buried in this cemetery a boy, baptized today, by J. T. Brentano, and deceased shortly after, of whom the father was R. L. M. Brentano and the mother M. M. Ernst. D. Faber, Rector
B-5 Clement Emery Picard	March 6, 1898, I baptized Clement Emery, born the 24th of January last, to Julius Picard and Eleonore Choquette his wife, both of this place. Godparents were: Adolphe Jette and Marguerite Jette. D. Faber, Rector
Page 244 B-6 Edward Francis Manaigre	May 1, 1898, I baptized Edward Francis, born the 20th of April last to Sevare Manaigre, of this place, and Alice Vandale of St. Louis. Godparents were: Dieudonne Manaigre and Emilie Manaigre. D. Faber, Rector
B-7 Grace Winnie Wallace	May 3, 1898, I baptized conditionally Grace Winnie, born the 29th of April last, to Jesse Allen Wallace, of Ohio, and Amanda Laura Manaigre, his wife, of this place. Godparents were: Dieudonne Manaigre and Emilie Manaigre. D. Faber, Rector
S-3 Grace Winnie Wallace	May 14, 1898, I buried in the cemetery Grace Winnie Wallace, who died yesterday, at the age of 14 days. D. Faber, Rector
S-4 Helen Mary Van Wassenhove.	June 23, 1898, I buried Helen Mary Van Wassenhove, who died the 21st of June of paralysis at the age of 52 years 9 months and 14 days. D. Faber, Rector
B-8 Mary Lucretia Faber	June 23, 1898, I baptized Mary Lucretia, born today to George Faber, of Bavaria, and Mary Haas, his wife, of Ohio. Godparents were George Hiller and Mary Marguerite Albers. D. Faber, Rector
B-9 Frances Louise Murphy	July 25, 1898, I baptized Frances Louise, born the 20th of June last, to William Murphy and Frances Emma Coleman, his wife, both of this place. Godparents were: Stephen Henry Coleman and Blanche Geraldine Davidson. D. Faber, Rector
B-10 Cornelius Dewey Gearin	August 15, 1898, I baptized Cornelius Dewey, born the 1st of July last, of Hugh Burns Gearin, of Indiana, and Mary Cecelia Murphy, his wife, of this place. Godparents were: John Andrew Gearin and Catherine Delila Vann. D. Faber, Rector
Page 245 B-11 Elizabeth Hazel Murphy	August 15, 1898, I baptized Elizabeth Hazel, born the 21st of October of last year, to Edward Theodore Murphy, of this place, and Cora Sanfield, of Indiana, his wife. Godparents were: Frederic John Gearin (by proxy [?]) and Catherine Delisle Vann. D. Faber, Rector
S-5 James	August 31, 1898, I buried James McKay, of County Down, Ireland, who died the 29th at the age of 80 years, 4 months and 14 days, of the illness

McKay	commonly called kidney disease.
	D. Faber, Rector
S-6 Sister Mary Genevieve	September 6, 1898, I buried in the mortuary of the Sisters of the Holy Names of Jesus and Mary at St. Paul the body of Sister Mary Genevieve, of Canada, (Elizabeth Leblanc), aged 68 years, 1 month and 8 days, at Portland the 4th of this month of heart failure.
	D. Faber, Rector
B-12 Teresa Margaret Opitz	October 23, 1898, I baptized Teresa Margaret, born the 15th of this month to Christian Opitz, of Hungary, and Elizabeth Goeldl, his wife, also of Hungary. Godparents were: George Peter Wohlfart and Mary Catherine Goeldl.
	D. Faber, Rector
Page 246 B-13 Herb. Wilfred Adolphe Jette	November 6, 1898, I baptized Herb. Wilfred Adolphe, born the 27th of September last, to Charles Wilfred Adolphe Jette, of Champoeg, and Mary Elizabeth Thibodeau, of . . . his wife. Godparents were: Adolphe Jette and Marguerite Jette.
	D. Faber, Rector
B-14 William Alfred Lambert	November 23, 1898, I baptized William Alfred, born the 12th of this month, to Alfred Lambert and Matilda Crete, both of this place, husband and wife. Godparents were: William Trevor and Bridget Trevor.
	D. Faber, Rector
S-8 John William Smith	December 9, 1898, I buried John William Smith, deceased the 6th of this month, of . . . *[unfinished, no signature]*
B-15 James Lorin Kirk	December 22, 1898, I baptized James Lorin, born the 28th of November last, of Robert Emmett Kirk, of Minnesota, and Agatha McDonald, his wife, of Yamhill Co. Godparents were: Ignatius Peter McDonald and Veronica Lind.
	D. Faber, Rector
S-9 Sister Mary Misera- cordia	December 28, 1898, I buried in the mortuary of the Sisters of the Holy Names of Jesus and Mary, Sister Mary Miseracordia (Mary of Mercy), born Adelaide Rainault, who died the 26th of this month at the age of 67 years, 9 months and 28 days.
	D. Faber, Rector

Note: In Vol. III the names of witnesses and godparents are not indexed.

INDEX
ST. PAUL PARISH III
1865-1898

INDEX (abbreviations used)

Page numbers listed in this index are those of the original ledger. See note regarding page numbering at top of first page of translations.

adj - abjuration
aff - affidavit
B - baptism
fa - father
G - guardian
H - "chez" (house of, place of)
L - legitimatized
M - married
mo - mother
PS - priest's signature (or mention of)
S - burial
S-fa - step-father
sig - person's own signature
V - widow or widower
W - witness or godparent

Place names are listed alphabetically with the exception of towns in Canada, which are under "Canada".

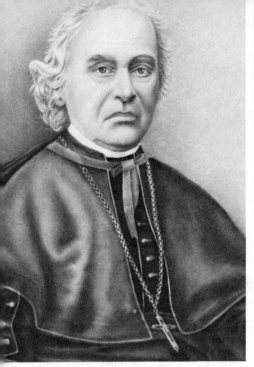

Left: Francis Norbert Blanchet, first pastor of St. Paul and first archbishop in Oregon. Right: Pierre DeSmet, S.J. (Woodcut by Father Nicolas Point).

Left: Rev. Joseph Fabian Malo, rector of St. Paul from 1859 to 1869. Right: Rev. Bartholomew Delorme, rector of St. Paul from 1853-55 and 1871-87.

Vande Steene.

Lith. de V.e Vander S.

MISSION S.t PAUL À WALLAMET. Lettres 1 et XVIII.

1. Cathédrale et maison de l'Archévêque. 4. Ancienne église. 7. Forge.
2. Couvent des Sœurs de Notre Dame. 5. Résidence S.t François Xavier. 8. Montagne Hood.
3. Collège S.t Joseph. 6. Fermes etc. 9. Montagne Molélis.

St. Paul Mission in 1847, from a Father Point woodcut. The "ancient church" (No. 4) is the original long chapel of 1836.

Part of original altar, St. Paul Church.

Festival, about 1898, at brick church, St. Paul, built in 1846.

Old altar in St. Paul Church with figure of Ste. Victoria beneath.

Left: Brick church as renovated in 1901-1902. Note wood-stove chimney. Right: Detail of column capital in church.

Left: Bell sent from Belgium as gift for new brick church. Latin inscription: "Lord, thus Thy praise goes to the ends of the earth." Right: St. Paul Church, 1979.; Note windows in wings, cross, and landscaping.

Ste. Marie du Willamette, 1861-1891. Original school was built by Sisters of Notre Dame, 1844-1853.

St. Paul Academy, 1891-1911.

Father Rauw, Sisters and pupils at St. Paul Academy, about 1904.

St. Paul Academy, 1912-1970.

Left: Sister M. Febronia, Superior at St. Paul, Oregon foundress. Right: Sister M. Misericordia, Oregon foundress.

Left: Sister M. Agatha, Oregon foundress. Right: Sister Mary Raphael, first St. Paul woman to enter the Sisterhood. (Elizabeth Kennedy, 1854-1877)

Old Cemetery, St. Paul, 1839-1890.

New Cemetery, St. Paul, about 1930.

Left: Tomb of Archbishop F.N. Blanchet, 1960. Right: Mortuary Chapel, New Cemetery.

Left: Altar from Mortuary Chapel in New Cemetery, St. Paul, 1875-1937. Right: Helen Lyons (1799-1874), first recorded burial in New Cemetery.

Wheat growing on old farm of Etienne Lucier.

River logging at Lambert's Bend on the Willamette, French Prairie.

Hugh Gearin's ferry across the Willamette River.

Main Street, St. Paul, about 1906. Front to back: Kirk store, Miles McDonald house, Old Cemetery just beyond small white house in rear.

Left: Felix Choquette with beaver traps of his great-grandfather, Etienne Lucier. Right: Louis V. Quintal (Chantell), mail carrier through the Coast Mountains.

Flour-sack stencil.

James McKay, miller.

Log cabin—Joseph Lavadour.

Board cabin—Etienne Lucier II.

Simple frame—David Weston

Elaborate frame—Hugh Cosgrove.

Left: Cyprian Belique and Madeleine Bergevin, with children Malvina and Josephine, 1876.
Right: Peter Kirk and Margaret Lyons, with children.

Left: Mary, daughter of Genevieve Longtain, and Daniel McCann, 1885. Right: (Right) Cecile Delore, daughter of Marie Poirier (left) and Joseph Delore, about 1868.

Left: Francois Xavier Dompier and Soulange Bergevin. Right: Francois Comartin and Josette Morrisette (left) and Edouard Belanger II and Rose Chalifoux (right).

Left: John B.P. Piette and Frances Million. Right: Charles F. Ray and Amelia Eyre, about 1900.

Left: Frank Lambert, 1849-1932. Right: Clementine Mongraine Lambert, 1857-1924.

Left: David Mongraine, 1806-1882. Right: Catherine Lafantaisie, 1825-1865.

Left: John J. Cooke, 1829-1882. Right: Bridgit Lee Cooke, 1831-1908.

Left: Dr. John Frederick Joseph Brentano. Right: Elizabeth Wilhelmina Josephina Marie Muller Brentano.

Left: Marie Servant Raymond, about 1830—Right: Fanny Murray Coleman, 1824-1896.

Left: Amelia Aubichon Petit, 1830-1924. Isabel Aubichon Bertrand, 1843-1933. Right: Josephine Lavigueur Moore, 1840-1932.

Left: Adolphe Jette, 1825-1917. Right: Daniel Andrew Murphy, 1826-1896.

Left: Amable Petit, 1817-1890. Right: Michel Arcouet, 1834-1915.

CATHOLIC CHURCH RECORDS

of the

PACIFIC NORTHWEST

St. Paul, Oregon

ANNOTATIONS, Vol. I, II and III

Accolti, Michael 1807-1878
Father Accolti was an Italian Jesuit who came to Oregon with a group of priests and Sisters of Notre Dame du Namur on the ship *l'Infatigable* in 1844. He helped to establish the Mission of St. Francis Xavier at St. Paul, full of hopes for the development of the Willamette Valley as an educational and religious center. His nature "had no predilection for work among the Indians", wrote one commentator. The gold rush to California ended the dream of a college at St. Paul, although Accolti remained as missionary in charge of a churchless and illdefined region to the southwest known as St. Patrick's Mission. In 1850 he was sent to California, where, with Father John Nobili, he established the College of Santa Clara. His name is found, however, on various land records in Oregon as late as 1854.

Acock, John
Acock seems to have been one of the many Hudson's Bay Company employees working on the farms outside the Fort. His wife Susanne may have been the daughter of Richard Lane, an employee from Red River who had been transferred to the West coast.

Ady, Josephine 1861-
Josephine Ady was the daughter of an American settler, Robert Ady, who had acquired the old Michel Laframboise claim on the south side of the Willamette River at Champoeg. Although a grandson says the Ady girls were educated in a Methodist school, at least two of them, Josephine (McPaulin) and Elizabeth (Geelan) married Catholics and were baptized in that faith.

Algonquin Tribe
The Algonquin linguistic group inhabited a vast area in central Canada and the United States, many tribes of different characteristics sharing the same basic language. The tribe living near the mouth of the Ottawa River was called simply Algonquin, while others bore their own distinctive names. Jean Baptiste Dupaté, appearing throughout the records in the West, was an Algonquin half-breed, for example, of the Temiskaming band. The Indian boatmen and trappers recruited in the East were chiefly Iroquois, and as the Iroquois and Algonquin tribes were traditional enemies, few of the latter are found on Company rolls.

Alipas, Benon (Benenso)
Alipas was a Spaniard of whom little is recorded. He was the son of Matheo Alipas and Isabelle Borondo, he married Louise Okanogan in 1846, and had two recorded children before he disappears from view. He may have been working for Michel Laframboise, leader of the California Brigade for many years, as the child of Alipas was privately baptized before death by Laframboise. A daughter Marie was born in 1849 and died at the age of four years.

Allen, Thomas
The garbled entry in St. Paul II, p 48, probably refers to the same Thomas Allen in St. Louis I, pp 93, 112, 126, where his wife is given as Elizabeth, Indian.

Anderson, Peter
Tracing this Anderson is an exercise in confusion. At the time of Angelique Carpentier's death in 1859, the **Oregonian** reported that she "had previously lived with a negro and a Kanaka, and had children by both". One Winslow Anderson, negro, was an early resident of Oregon, having come up from California with Ewing Young in 1834. He had a way of changing his name, sometimes to Anderson Winslow, and is thus hard to trace. It is possible that the negro and the Kanaka reported by the **Oregonian** were one and the same man, and that Peter Anderson was another of his name shifts. If not, the above Anderson is impossible to identify.

Anson, John
John Anson seems to have been an English employee of the Company, loaned to the missionaries as an interpreter. He accompanied Father DeVos on a mission to the mouth of the Columbia, on which expedition he was a witness to numerous rites. A son John was born to him and Hélène Chinook in 1836, after which the pair went separate ways, for when son John was baptized at St. Paul in 1840, Hélène was the wife of Ignace Iroquois.

Aplin, George Chiffman 1824-1889
Aplin came from Dorchester, England, and is said to have been an employee of the Hudson's Bay Company before retiring to the Prairie. His Donation Land Claim record states that he had arrived in Oregon in 1848 and "was temporarily absent 30 to 60 days in 1850, helping neighbors with harvest" in the same year in which he had settled his own claim at Champoeg. His wife was

Marie Wagner, daughter of Peter Wagner, a butcher at Fort Vancouver. Fourteen children are said to have been born to the Aplins, but few descendants bearing the name remain today. The Pioneer Memorial cabin at Champoeg Park is modelled after the Aplin house and contains one of the original box stoves that had belonged to the Mission and was later bought by Aplin. His home not far from the site of the present building was badly damaged by the great flood of 1890-91, but the stove was salvaged. The Aplin lot in the present St. Paul Cemetery is well marked.

Arcouët, Amable (I)   1802-1880
Arcouët was born in Montréal; he entered the service of the Hudson's Bay Company as a middle-man in 1823. He was one of the settlers from French Prairie who went to California for cattle in 1837 and went again for three months during the gold rush. He took a claim north of the village of Donald and became a naturalized citizen in 1851. While at work in helping blast a mill canal around the Falls in Oregon City he was permanently blinded. Eight or nine children were born to him and his Chinook wife, Marguerite. She died at St. Paul in 1870, and Amable in 1880. Both lie in the Old Cemetery there, for although the old cemetery was no longer in general use, those families whose earlier members had been buried there continued the practise, the priest noting O.C. or N.C. in the margin of the entry.

Arcouet, Amable II   1831-
Amable II was the eldest son of Amable Arcouet I and Marguerite Chinook, whose name is once given as Waponte. He married Marie Anne Norwest and was the father of five recorded children, though there were probably others. Two, John and Hyacinthe, appear in the St. Louis register. For a time Amable II seems to have lived at or near The Dalles, where he was godfather to Augustin ("Wild Gus") Delard (Delore), son of Pierre Delard, in 1862. He is not found later in Prairie records.

Arcouet, Leon (brother of Amable I)   -1843
Peter Skene Ogden, leader of the brigade on which Leon Arcouet was lost, reported to his superior, Dr. John McLoughlin, "Since I last wrote you, our Brigade has been at this place, and in going up, one of the boats, I am sorry to say, was swamped in a whirlpool, most of the property in her lost, and one of the men, named Arcouet, drowned—and another, Swanson, his setting pole slipped, he fell out of the boat into the water, and never appeared again." (Swanson's body, as well as that of Arcouet, was recovered.)

Arcouet, Leon (son of Amable I)   1842-
The name Leon or Napoleon seems to have been a family tradition. Besides Leon, son of Amable I, there was a brother Leon (above) and a Napoleon, grandson, son of Amable II, who was probably the same Napoleon who died on the Grand Ronde Reserve, aged 30, in 1883.

Arcouet, Marguerite   1846-
Marguerite married Isadore St. Martin in 1864 and helped him develop the hot springs resort known as St. Martin's Springs on Wind River, Washington. She was a most capable woman and was still living on the home place at the Springs at the age of eighty-five, greatly beloved by all who knew her.

Arcouet, Michel   1834-1915 c.
Michel was another son of Amable I. He was severely hurt by a fall from his horse during the campaign of Captain Nathan Olney's "Forty Thieves" against Chief Paulina's band, but lived to tell about his share in that great adventure. He lived out his life on a foothill farm above Colton in the mountains of Clackamas County, joined in later years by his brother John with his family of motherless children. Both he and John were known as Indians locally (which is only half true) for their hunting and tracking abilities. Michel is buried, military marker, in the nearby Bonney Cemetery.

Aubichon, Alexis (I)   1787-1867
Aubichon came from Berthier, Canada, a trapper for the Hudson's Bay Company. He was with Work to establish Fort Langley on the Fraser River, with Laframboise on various expeditions, and to California in the 1830's. On one such expedition his son Alexis was killed by the Indians. The story, as recalled by descendents, was that the infant of one of the families in the train had died, and the parents wished it to be buried at home. But a brigade moves slowly, so young Alexis volunteered to ride on ahead with the dead baby. A band of roving Indians, seeing a man with a bundle riding in haste, thought he must be a thief and shot him. Finding nothing of value on him,

they left him where he fell, to be found later by the brigade. The tale may have been distorted over the years.

Aubichon took up a claim that included La Butte, and with F. X. Matthieu platted the town of Butteville on part of the land, Aubichon's share to be called St. Alexie. Becoming interested in shipping wheat both for himself and for his neighbors, he established a landing on the river bank just below his house and for some years did a thriving business there. The place is still called "Aubichon's Landing", although it has not been used for shipping for many years.

Seven children were recorded to Aubichon and his wife Marie Anne (Elmermach) Chinook. He died in 1867 and was buried in the old cemetery at St. Paul.

Aubichon, Catherine   1837-1902
Catherine, daughter of Alexis Aubichon and Marie Anne Chinook, was twice married. To her first husband, Michel Pelissier, she bore ten children, whose records may be found in the St. Louis and St. Paul parishes. Her second husband was Nelson Tellier, whose family was well-known in the region around Walla Walla. Two children by Tellier are recorded in **Rolls of Certain Indian Tribes, House Document No. 133.**

Aubichon, Elizabeth (Isabel)   1843-1933
Elizabeth, often called Isabel, married Joseph Bertrand in 1862 and was the mother of fourteen children. Their record does not appear on the Prairie.

Aubichon, Emelie   1830-1922
Emelie Aubichon was called Amelia or Mary as well as Emelie. The name on her grave marker in the Ilwaco (Washington) Cemetery is Amelia. She married Amable Petit II in 1845 at St. Louis. Most of their married life was spent in the fishing town of Ilwaco, where many descendants remain today.

Aubichon, Jean Baptiste   1790-1879
Very little is on record about this man called "Father", aside from his two marriages to natives, first to Marie Tsalile in 1839 (see Vancouver, Vol. I) and second to Isabelle "of a tribe to the south" in 1847 at St. Louis. Three children of the latter are found in the St. Louis records: Jean Baptiste, Marie and Antoine, the last dying in 1854 at the age of eighteen months. He was followed eight weeks later by his mother Isabelle, aged 26 years. Aubichon himself died at the age of eighty-nine at Gervais, but was buried at St. Louis.

Aubichon, Julie   1833-1902
Julie Aubichon was three times married: to Antoine Lucier, to Joseph Roberts, and to one Price, having children by the first and the third. She is buried on the Ducheney lot in Fern Hill Cemetery at Skamokawa, Washington, under the name Price. Some discrepency is noted between the Church records and the dates on her stone, but nothing greatly significant.

Aubichon, Philomene   1840-
The record of Philomene is sketchy indeed. She married Francois Xavier Roi in 1855 at St. Louis. It appears that she later married one Perkins and died young, without issue.

Aubichon, Sophie   1826-1905
Sophie Aubichon married Joseph Laferte, a man somewhat older than herself, in 1845. Five children are recorded, but at least three of these died in infancy.

Aucent, Louis I *[Ossant]*   1800 c-1856
Aucent was with Samuel Black in the Rocky Mountains of Canada in 1824. Black did not trust him, claiming he was easily led by others to desert. Upon retiring, he took a land claim north of St. Louis in 1840 and later became a United States citizen in order to hold it. After the death of his wife, Catherine Kohassa, he married Mary Molalla in 1848 at St. Louis. His death occurred in 1856; his widow married Joseph Simoneau "of France" in 1858.

Aucent, Rose   1828-1901
While living in the home of Pierre Belique on French Prairie in 1842, Rose Aucent met F. X. Mathieu, a newcomer in the home of Etienne Lucier just across the fence. They were married shortly and reared a large family on their farm at Butteville. Although she is given in the records as the daughter of Catherine Kohassa *[Cayuse?]*, Mathieu on later times gave a different version of his wife's childhood. "She was born in Manitoba in 1828. Her mother died when she was a

young babe. She came to Fort Vancouver by boat when but three years old to be with her father, who was then in the employ of the Hudson's Bay Company at that place. Her earliest recollections were of journeyings on horseback with the parties of her father and of Michel Laframboise. She recalled how, on one of these jaunts, when she was a mere tot of three years, and she had for a companion a little daughter of Laframboise, they were delighted as they passed under the expansive oaks of the Sacramento Valley to hear the dry leaves rustle under their horses' hoofs." Being orphaned of a mother, Rose was brought up in the household of Belique.

Ayote, Jean Baptiste
J. B. Ayote's wife, Josephine Raymond, was the daughter of Francois Raymond and Mary Langloire (St. Louis Register). She had married Dominic Baron in 1870; two of their children died, and Baron himself was killed by a fall from his horse early in 1874. His wide Josephine married Ayote a year later.

Azur   1819-
Antoine Azur was a metis from Red River, the son of Antoine Azur, Sr., and Marguerite Assiniboine. The elder Azur had been a North West Company man at Fort George in the very early days. The first Azur entries in the Church Registers are in St. Paul, where his children Ursule and Joseph were baptized in 1841 and 1842. These are followed in the Vancouver records with his marriage to Lisette Killimaux, mother of the children. The birth and death of a son Pierre, the death of Lisette and his marriage to Marie Magdeleine, Cascades, appear also in the Vancouver records. A little son, who may have been Joseph, died in 1844. After Marie Magdeleine, Cascades, died in 1847, a daughter also named Marie Magdeleine was born to Antoine and Catherine Shoshone, whom Azur married in 1855. The name does not appear again.

Bailey (Fernandez), William Henry   1859-1925
William Fernandez was the son of a roving Spaniard and a Chinook mother. A stabbing affray on the Washington coast broke up his parents' home and the four-year-old boy was adopted by Dr. William Bailey and his wife Julia. As the child's mother was said to have lived earlier in the Willamette Valley, it is possible she was known to them. After the death of his foster parents, William Bailey, as he was now called, returned to Washington to seek his own mother. He married Lucy Ramsay and was the father of five children. For many years he worked as fireman on coastal steamers, a highly regarded citizen and general favorite. His burial was in Bay Center, Washington.

Bailey, William J.   1807-1876
William Bailey, born in Ireland, had been educated in medicine but his propensity for liquor caused his family to ship him off to America and a fresh new start, they hoped. He drifted to California and then northward to Oregon, suffering en route an Indian attack that nearly ended his life and disfigured his face permanently. He reached the Methodist Mission near Salem in dire straits; there he recovered from his wounds, reviewed his medical studies and married Margaret Smith, a teacher at the Mission. Their life on his claim southeast of Champoeg was stormy from the first, and after fourteen years of strife, ended in divorce, with bitter recriminations on each side. Margaret declared her husband was a dangerous sot, and Bailey that she was "a long tall banshee" impossible to live with. Eighteen months later Bailey made a much happier marriage with Julia Nagle, widow of another doctor, James Sheil. He built a new house near Champoeg, practiced medicine successfully and was converted to the Catholic religion of his wife. The first lot in the New Cemetery of St. Paul was sold to Dr. Bailey on the first of January, 1876, and there he was buried five weeks later. During the year his wife had the body of her first husband moved from the Old Cemetery to the same lot, and there she joined them both in 1880.

Baker, James
James Baker, probably an Indian or half-blood, was a canoeman out of Fort Vancouver in 1828. He was at Fort Walla Walla in 1829, and later the same year on a trading vessel on the Columbia, where he was loud in his demands for the same rations as the sailors, for rum and a leave in order to convey Mrs. Poirier somewhere, all of which demands were denied. By 1841 he was living on French Prairie in close association with the negro Winslow Anderson, who was working for Ewing Young at the time. Baker made various purchases from Young's store, and in the sales following Young's death, he bought various small household items and a few head of stock, including "one very old tame work horse".

Bancasser, Julia (Bangasser)
Julia's father, George Bancasser I, was born near Strassbourg, France, in 1820. He came to America as a boy of 10 years, married Barbara ------ in Buffalo, New York, in 1845, and took up a land claim in Washington County, Oregon, in 1853. He died in 1886, his wife Barbara in 1863. The birth of a daughter, Barbara Ellen, to Julia Bancasser and her husband, Louis Deilschneider, in 1875 is recorded in St. Michael's Grand Ronde, and that of a son Edward in 1877 in St. James, McMinnville.

Banget, François (Jean)   1809-1867
Banget first appears on the Prairie when he bought three lots in Butteville in 1856-57; the next year he bought an entire acre adjacent to his first purchase. This space was later occupied by a vinegar factory, which Banget may have established. He was a continental Frenchman, and in 1860 he married a Canadian Frenchwoman, Adelaïde Lescarbeau, at St. Louis. They were godparents for the little Spanish-Indian boy adopted by their Butteville neighbors, Dr. William Bailey and his wife Julia. François Banget died in 1867 at the age of fifty-eight. His widow sold their Butteville holdings within a few months and disappears from view.

Barclay, Forbes (Doctor)   1812-1873
Forbes Barclay was born in the Shetland Islands, coming at the age of twenty-seven to Fort Vancouver as chief physician for the Hudson's Bay Company at that post. He remained at Vancouver until 1850, when he moved to Oregon City. He was mayor, coroner, superintendent of schools and physician. His wife was Marie Pambrun, eldest daughter of Chief Trader Pierre Pambrun; seven children were born to them. He was a man of great heart and breadth of interest; numerous places in Oregon City bear his name today. His home on the river bank above the rock ledge where the boats anchored was always filled with orphans, relatives or visitors and was the social hub of the young town. The house has since been moved to a park on top of Singer Hill next to the McLoughlin House, which was also moved from the riverside. Barclay and many of his family are buried in Mountain View Cemetery on the crest of the ridge to the east of the city.

Barnabé, Adelaïde   1838-
Adelaïde, eldest recorded child of Joseph Barnabé and Isabelle Boucher, married Joseph Roussin in 1855 at St. Louis. Two months earlier the same register had entered the birth of a daughter Felicite, "born the 9 of this month (June) outside of marriage to George Herren (Heron) and Adeline Barnabé of the parish of St. Paul". George Heron, a cousin of sorts of Adelaïde, was generally considered unreliable and something of a scamp. What became of Felicite is not recorded, nor is the death of Adelaïde. Her later life appears to have been spent in Idaho or Montana. Some confusion results to searchers of records between the above Adelaide, daughter of Joseph Barnabé, and Adelaïde Marguerite (or Adeline), daughter of François Barnabé, who married Joseph Pin (sometimes written Parr) at Walla Walla in 1859.

Barnabé, Joseph   1812-
Joseph Barnabe of Montréal settled on a claim near Broadacres in 1850, becoming a naturalized citizen the next year. He was one of the delegates from Champoeg County in 1846 to prepare a pre-territorial memorial to Congress. Besides the children recorded in the Vancouver and St. Paul Registers, there appear Thèrése, Julienne, Christine and John in St. Louis, the last born in 1853. No more Barnabés are entered on the Prairie, which would indicate the family moved to Wasco County about this time. Later they moved on to the vicinity of Newman Lake, Washington. No dates for the death of Joseph or his wife have been found.

Baron, Dominique   -1874
The brief records of Dominique Baron are found mostly in St. Louis. There he married Josephine Raymond, daughter of François, and there his three children were born; two died as infants. Baron was killed by a fall from a horse in 1874 and was buried at St. Louis. A year later his widow married Jean Baptiste Ayote at St. Paul.

Bastien Isaac
Only scattered references to the name Bastien occur in the records. Isaac Bastien was said to have been a laborer on the Cowlitz Farm. In testimony given in the dispute over Company property still claimed years later in the United States, the following deposition was made:

> Isaac Bastien, although a former HBC man, was active in shooting the Company cattle running loose on the Washington prairies in the closing days of the regime—chiefly for

American poachers who hauled them away by boatloads (1853-54).
By 1865 Bastien was living at St. Paul, where his young wife Marie died.

Bauer, Andreas (Andrew) 1811-1884
Andrew Bauer was born in Bavaria and married there, coming to America in 1837. Ten years later, after pausing for some years in Indiana and Missouri, he crossed the plains to Oregon, arriving at Champoeg "with a wife, three children and five dollars". He was befriended by Barney Kennedy until he could buy land from the proceeds of a successful mining venture in California, and set up a blacksmith shop. Nine children were born to him and his wife Theresa, who died in 1869.

Beauchemin, Charles
Charles Beauchemin was a gold seeker in California in 1849 when he married Julie Jenota (?), the widow of another miner, Jean Baptiste Godin. Julie had two small children at the time; a son Joseph was born to her and Beauchemin in 1850 in Oregon, and Julie died in 1852. Charles Beauchemin "of Frenchtown" near Walla Walla, probably the same man, married another Julie at St. Andrew's Mission near Pendleton in 1872, with several more children recorded in the Walla Walla register.

Beauchemin, Jean Baptiste
Beauchemin is a name found sparingly in the early Northwest records, but plentifully in later times in the Walla Walla country. The earliest record is that of Antoine Beauchemin, who was one of the overland party of the Astor enterprises under Hunt, but as he is mentioned only once, he may have dropped out. He was called a Canadian voyageur at his enlistment. One item only concerning Jean Baptiste Beauchemin occurs at Vancouver, where he was a witness at the marriage of François Laframboise. Another, on a loose leaf inserted in St. Paul, Volume I, records the baptism of Beauchemin's nine year old daughter Angèle in 1845 by Father Soderini at an unspecified place, apparently eastern Washington.

Beaudoin, Césaire
Nothing more appears about Beaudoin than is contained in the entries at St. Paul. As his mother was Cécile Jobin of Montréal, and as the godfather of his son François Xavier was Sigfroid Jobin, there may have been some relationship; the Jobins also disappear from the records after a few entries.

Beaulieu, Joseph 1792-
Joseph Beaulieu, engagé of the Hudson's Bay Company, was the son of another Joseph Beaulieu and a Cree woman of Red River. He was probably the brother of Charlotte Beaulieu, wife of James Birnie. He married Betsy Tillamook in 1844; she died two years later.

Bélèque, Cyprien (Belique) 1848-1914
Cyprien was the youngest son of Pierre Bélèque I, and was an infant in arms when his father died returning from the gold fields. He married Julienne Bergevin in 1873, and became the father of ten children. He is remembered as tall and spare, a quiet, kindly man, and a good fiddler. His wife was tragically burned to death in a kitchen fire in 1901, while her small children tried vainly to tear away her burning clothing. Both husband and wife are buried on the Bergevin lot in St. Paul.

Bélèque, Esther 1840-1915
Esther was the youngest daughter of Pierre Bélèque I and Geneviève St. Martin. After Pierre's death, Geneviève married Casimer Gardipe; the family went to the Walla Walla country to live, and there Esther's life was spent. In some unrecorded place she married Joseph Hebert; he lost his mind and committed suicide at Walla Walla in 1869 at the age of thirty-nine. Two years later Esther married Moise Tessier of eastern Canada in what must have been an impressive service from the space given it by Father Brouillet in the register, with five witnesses. All, including the bride and groom, appear to have signed their own names. Esther and Moise are buried with the Cornoyers and Marie St. Martin Hubbard in the Catholic section of Mountain View Cemetery in Walla Walla under massive stones. Esther's birth date is there given as 1833.

Bélèque, Jean Baptiste 1845-1925
Jean Baptiste Bélèque came from a musical family; he himself is said to have been a violin teacher on the Grand Ronde Reserve. His record is widely scattered through the registers. He married

Victoire Vassal, widow of Edouard Gendron, at St. Louis in 1871. All her children by Gendron had died as infants, and her luck with those by Bélèque was not much better, due, the family hints darkly, to ignorance and credulity in quack remedies. A daughter Josephine born to the Bélèques at St. Louis in 1871 died at St. Andrew's Mission near Pendleton the following year; a daughter Mary Evaline, aged nine years, died at St. Paul in 1881; a daughter Josephine Adeline, born at Walla Walla in 1874, died at St. Paul at the age of ten months. The marriage was a failure and ended in divorce. A faded snapshot of Jean Baptiste shows a tall, thin old man standing by a log cabin in the timber, "My mountain home". His last years were spent with his brother Pierre at Woods, Oregon, where he is buried.

Bélèque, Joseph   1843-1847
Joseph died at the age of five. He was the only child not mentioned by his father Pierre in the will he made in preparation for his tragic trip to the gold fields.

Bélèque, Pierre (I)   1793-1849
Bélèque joined the North West Fur Company in 1818 in New Caledonia and remained in the trade until about 1830, when he took up a claim on French Prairie. This claim embraced the old Henry House trading post and surrounding Company pasture land, now marked with a State Historical Marker. He resided in the old post house with his wife, Geneviève St. Martin, where they reared seven children. Many descendants remain locally.

Bélèque and his eldest son, a lad of thirteen, went to the California gold fields and were said to have been unusually successful. Pierre died on the homeward journey and was buried at sea off the mouth of the Columbia. The gold dust was lost overboard by the boy. Bélèque was described by a contemporary as "mild and honest". He was one of the leaders in petitioning for priests to be sent to the settlement on the Prairie. His will, thoughtfully made prior to his departure to the gold fields, was the first to be recorded in Marion County, Book One, page one. His widow married Casimer Gardipe.

Bélèque, Sophie   1832-1920
In 1851 Sophie married Narcisse Cornoyer, who was captain of a volunteer army of métis against the Cayuse in 1855-56, and later Indian Agent on the Umatilla Reserve. Most of Sophie's adult life was spent in Eastern Oregon, where she reared a large family. She and her husband are buried in Mountain View Cemetery (Catholic section) in Walla Walla, along with others of her family.

Bellaire, Lizette (Louise)   -1836 c.
Lizette was the daughter of Register Bellaire, one of the earliest recorded men with the Fur Trade in the Northwest, who had been with Thompson in Montana from 1808 to 1811, and was listed as "a free man hunter in the Willamette" in 1813-14. Lizette became the first recorded wife of Charles Rondeau, another old fur company employee, to whom she bore at least three children, Angelique, George and Geneviéve.

Bellanger (Blanchey), Edouard   1826-1858
Edouard Bellanger's span of time on the Prairie was brief. Circumstances would indicate that he may have come up from California after the gold rush there, and went on to the Fraser River country when gold was discovered in 1858. On the Prairie he married Angélique Marcellais, widow of another miner who had died in California, François Gagnon. Children Edouard and Esther were born on his land claim near Brooks. Bellanger was drowned on the Fraser River by the upsetting of a canoe. His widow married Charles Derome, and Bellanger's half of the claim was lost by sheriff's sale.

Bercier, François   1821-
François Bercier was the son of Pierre Bercier I and Emélie Finlay. He married Betsy Chinook at Cowlitz in 1839. Tolmie, in charge of Fort McLoughlin in 1836, wrote, "Have sent François Bercier to Vancouver, having at this place no occasion for his services and of late I have frequently been annoyed with complaints of his bad conduct, which were generally discovered upon enquiry to be well founded."

Bercier, Marguerite   1819-1890
Marguerite Bercier married Louis Pichet in 1840 and became the mother of a large number of children, sometimes given as twenty-one; not all lived to maturity. Her entire married life seems

to have been spent on a farm near St. Paul. An early picture shows her a large, placid woman in a neat print dress, holding the hand of her husband, whose other hand grips an unmistakable bull whip. The pair are buried in the St. Paul Cemetery, their graves marked with good stones.

Bercier, Pierre (I)   -1830 c.
Numerous Berciers appear in the fur trade; Pierre was one of the earliest, being recorded as "my guide" by David Thompson of the North West Company in 1808. He was a boatman and horse keeper at Spokane House in 1813 and with Ogden in the Snake River country in 1824-26. He died about 1830 and his widow, Emélie Finlay, married Simon Plamondon the elder.

Bergevin, Julienne   1853-1901
Julienne, daughter of Louis Bergevin and Magdeleine Servant, married Cyprien Bélèque and reared a family of ten children. She was burned to death when her clothing caught fire at the kitchen stove.

Bergevin, Louis   1820-1876
Bergevin came from Canada after the Hudson's Bay Company had waned, in 1843, according to Bancroft, and took a claim south of St. Paul without much delay. He gave his birthdate as 1820; his stone in St. Paul Cemetery gives 1812. He married Magdeleine Servant, the young widow of Charles Jeaudoin, and fathered nine children. His wife died in 1863 at the birth of the ninth child. Bergevin was a prosperous man, generous with his neighbors and kindly disposed. His tombstone reads, "A good father and a true citizen. In God he trusted. May he rest in peace."

Bergevin, Soulange   1854-1876
See Dompierre, François Xavier, Sr.

Bernier, François   1806-1876
Bernier was a miller employed at McKay's grist mill on Champoeg Creek in 1844. He took a land claim near the heart of the Prairie in 1845. During the California gold rush he was absent for five months, leaving his wife, Pélagie Lucier, and their three small children on the claim. In all, eight children were born to them. Pélagie died in 1856. Two years later Bernier married Marie Despard, to whom two more children were born. He died in 1876 and was buried beside his first wife in the Old St. Paul Cemetery, unmarked.

Bernier, Louis (Charles)
The marriage of the Canadian, Louis Charles Bernier, to Josette Lavigueur did not prosper, and after some years they parted. Josette was left with several small children to support as best she could. Bernier later married Stella McKay at Gervais.

Bernier, Marcel Isidore   1819-1889
From: **Legislative Handbook and Manual of the State of Washington, circa 1889-90.**
"Marcel Bernier died at his home on Newaukum Prairie, Lewis Co., Washington, on Friday, Dec. 27th, 1889, and was buried in the Catholic cemetery on Cowlitz Prairie the Sunday following. He was born November 10, 1819, near Spokane Falls. His father was a trusted Hudson's Bay Company traveler and trapper, and came here from Canada in their employ. Marcel was sent to school at St. Boniface, Red River, Manitoba, in 1830, and in 1841 came back to Cowlitz Prairie. In 1842 he went with Father Blanchet to Puget Sound on the first missionary tour among the Indians, and directed the building of the log church on Whidby Island. In 1842 he accompanied Father Demers to Vancouver Island and Cariboo. Returning to Cowlitz Prairie in 1844, he married Celeste Bercier, and settled on his donation claim on Newaukum Prairie, where he died. His wife and several children survive him, and he leaves quite an estate. In later years Mr. Bernier has followed wagon making until rheumatism crippled him so that he could not do much at his trade. Some three weeks before his death he was somewhat injured by his horse running away and throwing him from the buggy. He was well known to the early settlers of Washington, and many of them owe much to his assistance and generosity."

Bernier was mentioned by Father Blanchet as having rescued several of the crew from a canoe wreck on the Cowlitz. He was also one of the witnesses to testify at hearings in the disputed land case at Fort Vancouver in 1887.

Bernier, Marie   1845-1892
Marie was the eldest daughter of François Bernier and Pelagie Lucier. She married Amadée Choquette in 1859 and was the mother of 15 children. A photograph taken a year or two before

her death at the age of forty-seven shows her a lovely, slender woman with large dark eyes in a thin face, looking quite like her aunt Adrienne Lucier Lachapelle; their charm may have been a family inheritance of all the Lucier women whose likenesses are not known. "Marie, beloved wife of A. Choquette" reads the stone for her and her son Pierre in the St. Paul Cemetery.

Bernier, Norbert   1844-1910 c.
Norbert Bernier, eldest son of François Bernier and Pélagie Lucier, grew up to marry Thérèse Rivet. Seven children were born to them. Thérèse died of tuberculosis while living in a tent, the prescribed treatment in such cases, at Champoeg. Her husband went to live with a son at Oregon City. On a visit to Champoeg he became ill, returned to Oregon City, and died in a few days. Both he and Thérèse are buried with other members of their family in the Champoeg Cemetery.

Bernise (Biernise, Bernaise), Etienne
Etienne Bernise was a Frenchman, but whether from France or Canada we are not told. He married Agnélique Rondeau in 1846. A son, Etienne II, was born the following year and died at the age of two months. A daughter Angelica was born at St. Louis in 1840; her mother died within a few months, aged twenty-three. Bernise then married Marie Laroc, daughter of Joseph Sebastian Laroc and Marianne Cayuse. The Etienne Burness, Third Corporal in the Walla Walla Mounted Volunteers in the Yakima Indian War in 1856 was probably the same man.

Bertrand, Cyrille
The difficult genealogy of a "jack-knife" family is typically illustrated in the case of Cyrille Bertrand, the last blade to be added. The following events took place in the space of four years:
>   Elizabeth Finlay, wife of Hypolite Brouillet died
>   Brouillet married Angèle Gingras
>   Cyrille Bertrand married Marguerite Servant
>   Marguerite died at the birth of Cyrille, Jr.
>   Brouillet died in the gold fields of California
>   Cyrille Bertrand married Angèle Gingras Brouillet
Young Cyrille Bertrand died a short while after the death of his mother. By his second wife, Angèle, Bertrand had several more children.

Bihan, Julian M.   1819-1863
Julian Bihan of France married one of the three Pelletier sisters who came from Canada to join their uncle, Bishop F. N. Blanchet, about 1850. Emélie was the youngest of these sisters. Three children were born to the Bihans, Amelia, Virginia and Louis. Bihan died in 1863 at St. Louis. His widow married one Schnable and lived out her life in Washington State where she died in 1895.

Bilodeau, François
"Mr. Bilodeau" was the new teacher of French at St. Joseph's College for Boys that was to open at St. Paul in 1843.

Blanchet, Francois Norbert   1795-1883
Three Blanchet priests labored in the Northwest, all related Canadians. François Norbert was the earliest Catholic missionary, together with Modeste Demers, to the Oregon country, arriving at the Hudson's Bay Company Fort Vancouver late in 1838. The two priests traveled widely through Oregon and Washington, establishing churches and holding missions. Blanchet worked chiefly at Fort Vancouver and in the country south of the Columbia. He was the first Archbishop in Oregon, ordered the brick church at St. Paul built in 1846, and was buried in the parish cemetery there.

Boisvert, Louis   1787-1867
Boisvert married Elizabeth (Betsy) Snowden in 1852. Whether she was the mother of the child Louise who was buried in the Church at St. Paul in 1850 is not stated. Betsy died at St. Paul in 1857; Louis died ten years later in a Salem hospital, "aged about eighty", and was buried in that town.

Bolduc, Jean Baptiste Zacharie   1818-
Two young priests, Bolduc and Langlois, left Canada for the West via Cape Horn in 1842, arriving the next year. After a mission to Puget Sound, where he is said to have "preached to upwards of a thousand", Bolduc took charge of the newly established Boys' School at St. Paul,

having in 1844, "28 boarders, all children of Canadians or Americans, except only one that is of pure native blood". During the depopulation of the Prairie during the gold rush, the school was closed, never to reopen.

Bonenfant, Antoine (I)   1794-
Antoine Bonenfant from Canada married Françoise Dupaté (Depati), daughter of Jean Baptiste Desportes (Dupaté) McKay and a Calapooya woman. He had two older sons by another wife, whose name is given in the St. Louis register as Marie Spokane, before his marriage to Françoise. The Bonenfants made their home in Douglas County, Oregon, where many descendants remain.

Bonenfant, Antoine (II)   1831-
Antoine Bonenfant II, aged 17, enlisted in Co. D of the 5th Regiment hastily formed in 1848 to subdue the Cayuses after the Whitman massacre. He paused in Oregon City long enough to be baptized, "he then passing here on his way to the Indians", wrote Father McCormick. He does not appear again.

Bonenfant, Martin   1830 c.-1858 c.
Martin was the elder of two sons of Antoine Bonenfant and "another woman", who is later called variously Marie Spokane, Marguerite Indian and Mary Ann Pend d'Oreille. His baptism, his marriage to Angélique Laroc in 1853, and the births of four children are recorded in St. Louis. At the baptism of the last, Marie Louise, in June, 1858, the priest noted that her father Martin was "probably dead". By October all doubt seems to have ended, for at that time Angélique, "widow of Martin Bonenfant" married Joseph Dépot. The gold rush to the Fraser River in 1858 might be offered as the explanation for Bonenfant's disappearance and uncertain death.

Bonin, Pierre   1816 c.-
Bonin came from Montréal in 1843 and settled on the Prairie. The **Oregon City Spectator** of May 14, 1846, carried the item:
> "Married: On the 4th inst. at 6 o'clok A.M. by Rev. Father DeVos, at the Catholic Church in Oregon City, Mr. Pierre Bonin of Champoeg to Miss Louise Rondeau of the former place."

This was the first wedding to be recorded in the new church of St. John the Evangelist, which had been dedicated in February, and was apparently an occasion of importance, attended by Dr. McLoughlin, among others. Louise died in 1851, leaving a small daughter, Aurelie. Bonin then married Rose Wagner. The baptisms of their children Alonzo, Anastasie and August and the death of Rose Wagner appear in the St. Louis register. Bonin's third wife was Salome Raymond.

Bosquet, François   1840-
François Bosquet, whose name became Frank Buskey to his American neighbors, was of Canadian descent, although born across the border in Michigan. At the age of nineteen he came to Oregon with Samuel Goulet and worked on the farm of Mathias Goulet for two years. He tried mining in Idaho, farming for himself, and again mining. He married Elizabeth Bauer, and after her father's death, bought the rights to the Bauer farm, a level stretch lying between Case and Champoeg Creeks. Their children appear in the St. Louis as well as the St. Paul registers.

Boucher
The name Boucher (Bouché) is so interwoven in the fur trade annals that it is difficult at this late date to trace relationships with much certainty. Two main lines, which may or may not have been fraternal, develop in the Vancouver and French Prairie records. These are Jean Baptiste, born in 1759 and died in 1824, "an honest man", and Jean Baptiste "called Wakan", who would seem also to have been born during the latter part of the 1700's.

Boucher, (Jean) Baptiste "called Wakan"   -1850
The "dit Wakan" serves to identify one line of Boucher descent, for such nicknames were inherited and often came in time to supplant the original surname. Jean Baptiste Boucher (Wakan) was a half-Cree employee of the North West Fur Company as early as 1806, when he was a canoeman with Fraser on the wild rivers of British Columbia. He was interpreter, police-man and steward of supplies under successive post masters, even taking charge of posts himself in the absence of an officer. He was "Wakan the Terrible" in his ruthlessness in dealing with male-factors. Father Morice, in his **History of the Northern Interior of British Columbia**, devoted many words to an appreciation of Boucher's trustworthiness. Wakan's first marriage, which seems to have been brief, was to a Carrier girl; his second, to Nancy McDougal, daughter of

Clerk James McDougal, with whom Wakan had long been associated. Their family is said to have numbered seventeen children. Wakan died of the measles in 1850, "an old man", in the vicinity of Fraser Lake.

Boucher, François (I) (Wakan)
François Boucher and Jean Baptiste the younger may have been brothers, or possibly father and son, from the difference in their ages; both were "Wakan". François is chiefly recorded for his three marriages, to Thérèse Porteuse (probably the same as Costahna), to Henriette Calapooya and to Marianne, native. His known children were Joseph, François II, Isabelle, and an unnamed son who died in infancy.

Boucher, Isabelle (Elizabeth)   1821-
Isabelle married Joseph Barnabé in 1839; nine children are recorded. She was the daughter of "the late Jean Baptiste Boucher, an honest man", who died on the trail in 1824.

Boucher, Isabelle (baby)   1847-
Isabelle was a favorite name in the Boucher family. The baby baptized in these St. Paul records belonged to François Boucher, while the Isabelle Mainville who was her godmother was the wife of Jean Baptiste Boucher II who died in 1852 at Vancouver.

Boucher, James (Jim, Tshem)
James Boucher, son of "the terrible Wakan" in British Columbia, had been of great help to Chief Trader Manson at some of his more difficult northern posts, Manson reported. Good material on this Boucher may be found in Morice: **History of the Northern Interior of British Columbia.**

Boucher, Jean Baptiste   1759-1824
"The late" Jean Baptiste Boucher was past fifty years of age when he came to Fort George as interpreter for the North West Fur Company. He took for his wife Josephte Kanhopitsa (desChaudières) after she had been cast off by John Clarke. Her daughter Josephte Clarke went by the name of her stepfather, Boucher. Jean Baptiste Boucher died while on an expedition to the Snake River country. "This morning, after an illness of 20 days, during which we carried him on a stretcher, died Jean Baptiste Boucher, an honest man." His widow Josephte married Joachim Hubert.

Boucher, Jean Baptiste (II) (Wakan)   1822 c.-1852
Jean Baptiste II was the son of Baptiste "called Wakan" and Nancy McDougal. He was baptized as an adult and shortly married Isabelle Mainville at St. Paul. Isabelle died the following year at the age of twenty-five, and Jean Baptiste in 1852, aged about thirty.

Boucher (Clarke), Josephte   1817 c.-1878
According to her son, George Heron, Josephte was properly Clarke, not Boucher, which was the name of her step-father. His mother was the daughter, he said, of John Clarke of the Pacific Fur Company and Josephte Kanhopitsa (desChaudières). After Clarke left the country, Josephte (Kanhopitsa) took up with Jean Baptiste Boucher and later married Joachim Hubert at St. Paul. Josephte Clarke was the mother of George Heron by Francis Heron. Later she married John McKay ("the McKy Rouge") and was the mother of a large family. Both McKay and Josephte are buried in the Catholic cemetery at Woodburn, Oregon, where they ended their days.

Bourgignon, Julia   1847-1887
Julia (Julie) Bourgignon married John Bayerly in February, 1887, and died in August the same year at Brooks, Oregon. The early records of Brooks are in the Gervais register, as there was no church nor cemetery as yet at Brooks.

Bourgignon, Louis   1845 c.-1887
Louis Bourgignon married Catherine Dépot at St. Louis in 1876. Five children were born to them, two of whom died very young. Louis Bourgignon died at the age of forty-three; his widow Catherine married François Dubreuil. The records of this family are found in the St. Louis and Gervais registers.

Bourgignon, Pierre (Prospere)
Father Cénas, at the marriage of Bourgignon and his country wife in 1852, drew a realistic picture of the trappers' wandering type of life: "In view of the state of cohabitation in which they have found themselves by reason of a natural marriage which they have contracted since several

years in the Indian regions --". Two of the four children made legitimate by the Church ceremony had been baptized in 1847 at Fort John on the Laramie River by Father Brouillet on his way westward. The younger two were baptized at St. Paul. The youngest, Pierre, and his mother Marguerite died within two days in 1853. Pierre, the father, seems to have died not long after, as Rosalie was brought up in the Aplin home, "an orphan", and died at the age of twelve.

Bourjeau (Bourgeau), Hélène   1841-
Hélène, daughter of Sylvain, married Theodore Lacourse in 1856.

Bourjeau (Bourgeau), Jean Baptiste   1837-
Jean Baptiste, son of Sylvain Bourjeau and Josephte Sok, married Geneviève Martineau, daughter of Pierre, not Michel, as written by error in the records. Numerous children were born to the pair.

Bourjeau (Bourgeau), Joseph (I)   1807-1849
Joseph was brother to Sylvain Bourjeau. He joined the service of the Hudson's Bay Company from l'Assomption, Québec, in 1829. He was a boatman at Fort Colvile; he accompanied Tolmie to the north in 1833. Heron had trouble with him for laziness and Tolmie said he was unreliable. He married Angele Lafantaisie, daughter of Jacques Lafantaisie and Susanne Okanogan, who after Bourjeau's death, married Theodore Gervais.

Bourjeau, Joseph (II)   1844-
Young Joseph married Mary Ann Chantell (Quintal). They were the parents of eleven children, born in Douglas County, Oregon, or on the Colvile Reserve. Their marriage ended in separation in 1913.

Bourjeau (Bourgeau), Sylvain   1807-1871
Sylvain and Joseph Bourjeau were early in the West, and as Joseph was in the employ of the Hudson's Bay Company, it may be reasonably supposed that Sylvain was also. His wife Josephte Sok appears sometimes as Josephte Chinook. She died in 1857, after which Sylvain married Angèle Tichailis, widow of Jean Baptiste Perrault. The Sylvain Bourjeau claim lay a few miles north of St. Louis.

Boutin (Bouten)
The name Bouten is recorded in the Tribal Rolls from the 1860's, when one Vasco Bouten married Mary Ann Pickernell, daughter of the well-known pioneer John Pickernell. Vasco Bouten left sons Vasco and Eugene to carry on the name on the Washington coast. Any relationship to Isaac Boutin, husband of Philomene Langlois, is not known.

Bracconnier, Louise
The name "Braconier" appears at Norway House in 1838 (Vancouver Records); Louise was no doubt one of that family. Her husband, Joseph Klyne, was one of the Red River migrants who came to Nisqually in 1841 but left within the year for the better location of the Willamette Valley. Both Klyne and his wife Louise first appear in the records in August, 1842. Klyne died sometime late in the 1840's, and his widow married Charles Demers at St. Louis in 1850.

Brentano, Dr. J. F. J.   1820-1902
On the back of an old photograph in the collection of Mary Bunning, granddaughter of Dr. Brentano, is a concise summary of his life, written by his son: "J. F. J. Brentano, born in Groningen Province, Kingdom of The Netherlands, Mar. 20, 1820. Graduated M.D. in 1843. Married Miss Elizabeth St. J. M. Muller April 17, 1844. Came to the U.S. in the fall of 1857, settled in Dauphin County, Kansas. Moved to California in 1862 (crossed the plains by ox team). Came to Oregon in July, 1863 and settled in St. Paul, Marion County, Oregon, where he died Feb. 10, 1902." He practiced for many years in Marion County; some of his old instruments are stored in a family trunk along with medical papers and a note from Dr. Bailey, another early day physician, asking to borrow "a pair of nippers" (1868).

Brothers, Samuel Thomas   1832-1888
The children of Thomas Brothers and Adolphine Pepin (dit Lachance) born between 1873 and 1888 are found in the Grand Ronde Register and in St. Paul III.

Brouillard, Francois
The record of Brouillard's marriage to Olive Forcier does not appear, being a civil one; it was evidently in 1860 or thereabouts, between the birth of Felicite to Olive Forcier and Charles Petit

in March, 1859, and that of Brouillard's son Gegeon in February, 1861. A daughter Rose was born in 1862. Olive died in 1863, and in 1865 Brouilliard married Aurelie Bonin.

Brouillet, Hypollite -1849
Brouillet first married Elizabeth Finlay, who died in 1845. He then married Angele Gingras, daughter of Jean Gingras, and shortly afterward went to the California gold fields, where he died on August 31, 1849. The gold rush records of Father Delorme are found in the St. Louis Register, as he had accompanied the miners as their chaplain. Brouillet's widow Angele married Cyrille Bertrand the next December.

Brouillet, Jean Baptiste Abraham -1884
Father Brouillet, a secular priest, came west with Father A. M. A. Blanchet, the new Bishop of Walla Walla, and a group of ten other missionary and lay workers in 1847. Among them was David Mongraine, later a settler on French Prairie; he seems to have been a servant to the missionary party. After two months at Fort Walla Walla, Brouillet, Blanchet and LeClaire went to the Umatilla Valley, where Chief Tauitau "relinquished them a house Pambrun had built for him in an attempt to civilize the Cayuse". All the way across the plains the priests had been baptizing and burying the immigrants of the wagon train they accompanied. They were at Umatilla when the massacre at the Whitman Mission took place. Brouillet and a servant or two bathed and buried the victims as best they could. The last five years of Brouillet's life were spent as Director of the Catholic Indian Bureau in Washington, D.C. He died in 1884 and was buried in that city.

Brummer, Henry 1826-
Henry Brummer, born in Prussia, came to Oregon in 1852 by way of New Orleans (1849) and Illinois (1851), in which place he had married Agnes Yonker (Yunker). He took a claim in Muddy Valley, Yamhill County, Oregon, in the foothills behind Bellvue. As there was no church in the valley in 1855, his eldest child was baptized at St. Paul. Later children were baptized at St. Patrick's established in Muddy Valley in 1861, and the records entered at St. Michael's, Grand Ronde, where Father Croquet was resident priest.

Burns, Hugh 1807 (1809?)-1870
Burns was born in Westmeath, Ireland, in 1807, or possibly 1809. He came to Oregon from Missouri in 1842 in the wagon train of Elijah White, and took up a claim across the river from Oregon City with grandiose plans for a rival town, Multnomah City, which never materialized. He sold lots, worked at his trade of blacksmith, took active part in various civic enterprises, and made one ride back to Missouri carrying mail (1846), thus becoming the precurser of the famous Pony Express. He ran a ferry across the Willamette River in competition with that of Robert Moore for some time, but left for California during the 1850's and never returned to Oregon. He died in San Francisco on May 6, 1870.

Caille, Paschal - dit Biscornet 1791-1854
Caille came from Montreal to the Northwest in 1820, settled on a claim north of the later village of Donald in 1845 and became a naturalized citizen. His wife was Louise, a Cowichan from the Fraser River. Their older children, Francois, Henriette and Rose, were baptized at Fort Vancouver, and another child, Moise, died there, although the entry for his death is at St. Paul. A son Joseph was baptized at St. Paul, while for Adelaide, who died at the age of seven, and for Sophie no birth records have been found. Caille died in 1854, aged about 63. His wife Louise outlived him by thirty years, dying at St. Louis on June 8, 1883, "aged about 100 years".

Caillé, Henriette 1834-
Henriette Caillé married Joseph Matte in 1850 at St. Paul and bore him twelve children, recorded at St. Louis.

Caillé, Joseph 1848-1883
Joseph was the youngest son of Paschal Caillé, living south of Butteville. In May, 1875, he married Louise Gagnon at St. Louise; she died in December of the same year. Joseph seems not to have remarried, and died at the home of his sister Henriette Matte of Gervais at the age of thirty-five.

Caillé, Rose 1839-
Rose Caillé married William McKay, son of John McKay, the "McKy Rouge", at St. Louis in 1857 and reared a large family, whose records may be found in the parish register there. William

McKay died at Gervais in 1877; two years later a son Edward, father unknown, was born to his widow at that place.

Caillé, Sophie

Two sisters married two brothers in 1857 when Sophie Caillé, sister of Rose, married John McKay II, brother of William at St. Louis. In the next thirty years Sophie bore fourteen children whose records appear until 1877 in St. Louis, later in Gervais when that parish had been separated.

Calboro, Jean

The name Calboro does not appear elsewhere and may be presumed to be meant for Scarborough, master of the ship at various times. His son John (Jean) was given as seven years old in the census of 1850, and was not living at the time of his father's death in 1855. No other record of the baptism of Jean Scarborough has come to light, although the baptisms of his three brothers appear in Vancouver and Stellamaris records.

Cameron, Edouard

Edouard was the half-breed son of John Cameron and an Algonquin mother in Eastern Canada where various Camerons were active in the fur trade. He married a Walla Walla woman; a son Jean Louis was born May 22, 1846.

Cameron, Luger   -1865

Luger Cameron first appears in the records with his marriage to Marie Ducharme, widow of Joseph Lonetain, in 1861. A son Honoré was born in 1862; between that year and 1865 the Camerons moved to Walla Walla. A daughter Marcelline was born in June of 1865. Two months later Luger Cameron died and was buried in the Walla Walla cemetery.

Camp of Sand (Campment du Sable)

Campment du Sable was the early name for Champoeg because of the sandy nature of the ground there.

Cannon, William   1755-1854

Cannon, who claimed to have been a Revolutionary War soldier at a frontier post, was a member of the overland division of Astor's venture. He was later employed as a miller at Fort Vancouver, and also constructed Tom McKay's mill on Champoeg Creek. During the exceptionally high water of 1843, Cannon was rescued from his perch on a crate in the mill loft by neighbors who ran a canoe directly into the second story window. His age at death is usually given as ninety-nine rather than the ninety-seven in the Church record.

Carefree, Sans Souci, "Sossie"   1809 c.-

Sans Souci, Joseph the Carefree, was mentioned by George Roberts as the man "who settled the wheat bushels" for him at Champoeg, and in 1878 "still living at Champoeg". Numerous San Soucis appear in the Grand Ronde Reserve Register, perhaps sons of old Joseph. One Alcede Sossie, a half-breed, was on the 1850 census in Washington County, Oregon. Payette, the Canadian historian, notes "J. B. Sans Souci, an old North West Company name".

Carpentier, Angélique (Angelica)   1828-1859

The daughters of Charles Carpentier and left motherless, Angélique and her sister Sophie were placed in the Methodist Mission School near Salem for a few years. Sophie married in the Catholic Church, but Angélique seems to have played the field. At the time of her murder at the hand of her current husband, Charles Roe, the **Oregonian** reported, "She had previously lived with a negro and a Kanaka and had children by both." Her former husband, Peter Anderson, may have been the negro Winslow Anderson, who went by a variety of names; the Kanaka is unidentified.

Carpentier, Sophie   1826 c.-

Sophie's father, Charles Carpentier, had placed his motherless daughter in Jason Lee's Methodist Mission school in September, 1835, hence her "abjuration of Methodism" at the time of her marriage. Two years later her sister Angelica was also admitted to the Methodist school. Their teacher, Cyrus Shepard, wrote of them, "Half-breed sisters, with sparkling black eyes and long curling hair". Two sons are recorded to Sophie and Césaire Beaudoin, Joseph (1845-47) and François Xavier, born in 1847 and a daughter Susanne in 1848.

Cascades Tribe
The tribe at the Cascades of the Columbia, wrote Father Blanchet on a mission to that place in September of 1843, was composed mostly of young people, "all the elders having been cut down by the fevers." He was invading territory already under the ministry of the Methodists Daniel Lee and Perkins, but had sanguine hopes of winning the Cascade natives to his own fold, from the willingness of the young Chief Tamakwen to join him. "They leave the summer encampments," he continued, "and move to winter on the Vancouver islands (that is, the river islands above Fort Vancouver), where the cold is less rigorous and hunting more abundant."

Cayuse Tribe
The Cayuse Indians lived in eastern Oregon between the Cascades and the Blue Mountains mainly. They were a stock to themselves, related only to two small groups of Molallas who lived on the west side of the Cascades.

The Cayuse War of 1848 followed the massacre of the Whitman Mission people by members of the tribe who feared they were being systematically exterminated by the whites. Their sturdy little horses, which they raised in large numbers and which may still be found running wild in some remote valleys, take their name from the tribe.

Cemetery, Old, St. Paul   1839-1888
The original cemetery at St. Paul was nominally closed in 1875, and a larger one, still in use, established a short distance to the southeast. The old cemetery was still used by those families whose earlier members had been buried there, one of the last burial to be recorded being that of Adolphe Chamberland in 1888. In all, five hundred thirty-three interments were recorded and 12 removals to the new cemetery. In the overlapping period when both cemeteries were in use, the priest noted "N.C." or "O.C." in the margin of the register. The original plot was perhaps diminished by later roadbuilding and the remaining stones discarded during a clean-up of the neglected cemetery during the 1930's. Nothing now remains but a grassy plot with a central cross and a boulder bearing a bronze plaque.

Chalifou(x), André (I)   (1791) 1789-1851
Chalifou was a steersman on the brigade bringing Fathers Blanchet and Demers west in 1838. He had married Catherine Russie in Canada some years before. She and several of their children came with him on the brigade. Another son was born on the way, Michel, and two sons were drowned in the bateau wreck at the Dalles des Morts, apparently Michel and Charles. Chalifou settled a claim on French Prairie soon after, dying there in 1851, aged sixty-two.

Chalifou, André (II)   1842-1880
Young André married Josette Petre at St. Louis in 1859, when both were seventeen years old. Josette is given as DesRivierès, Peter, Assiniboine, and once, with no explanation, as St. Andre. It is possible the last was a priestly error. She died in 1869, leaving three small sons.

Chalifou, Lucie   1840-1849
Lucie, who died at the age of ten, was buried "in the church". Only 2 others were so recorded, they being another young girl, Louise Boisvert, who died the following May, buried "on the right hand side of the altar towards the middle", and Marguerite Wagner, in 1851.

Chalifou, Rose   1836-1848
Some sort of dispensation or special consideration must have been given to permit the burial of Rose's sister Lucie within the church proper; Rose herself was buried in the cemetery.

Chamberland (Chamberlain), Adolphe   1818-1888
Chamberland was a tinsmith at Fort Vancouver. The Reverend Herbert Beaver, Episcopal chaplain there, called him "Clerk of the French Service" when he gave him a copy of an "Address Delivered to the French Roman Catholics at Fort Vancouver on Good Friday 1838". Chamberland retired to French Prairie, taking a claim on one section lying in the mid-central region on the east side of Mission Creek. His first wife was Julienne Watièce, who bore him five recorded children—Zoë, Joseph, and the three recorded at St. Paul; his second wife was the three-quarter métisse, Louise Humpherville, daughter of Canoté and Marie Machina. Eleven children resulted from this marriage. His burial on March 6, 1888, was one of the last to be made in the Old Cemetery at St. Paul.

Chamberland, Fabian   1852-
After a civil marriage to Léocadie Lachapelle in 1880, the two had their vows renewed in the

Church at St. Louis. Most of their later records are found in the St. Louis and Gervais registers, appearing but once in St. Paul.

Champoeg
Champoeg, "Sand Encampment", was an early center of trade and meeting at the northern end of French Prairie, just upstream from the present hamlet of Butteville and on the south side of the Willamette River. Nothing remains today but a park.

Chehalis
The Chelalis tribes, Upper and Lower, lived in Washington along the river of that name. They were part of the huge Salishan speaking peoples of the Northwest.

Chinook Tribe
"The Chinooks are scattered along the Columbia from this fort (Vancouver) to the Pacific Ocean. Before the year 1830 they formed the most numerous as well as the richest nation of this entire part of the continent . . . proud and haughty . . . but there came a disastrous malady (apparently malaria) which made such terrible ravages among them that it cut down almost nine-tenths. The scourge of God having stricken these unfortunate savages because of their abominable lives . . . "

Father Blanchet

The Chinook language formed the chief Indian basis for the trade jargon used up and down the Pacific coast. Their principal food was salmon, wapato and berries. Their houses were framed buildings of cedar planks and bark, well-made.

Chinook, Cassino (Kinsneau, Casenove), Chief   1790 c.-1848
Cassino was a chief on the lower Columbia as early as 1811, when the Astor men mentioned him. He was friendly to the whites throughout the era of the fur trade, called handsome and intelligent. His portrait was painted by the artist Paul Kane. During an epidemic in 1829 most of his numerous family perished—9 wives, 3 children and 16 slaves, according to Kane. Thereafter he lived near Fort Vancouver, where he was always welcome at table. Just before his death he allowed himself to be baptized under the name of François, though he had resisted until that time.

Chinook, Pierre   1790 c.-1840
Pierre Chinook was one of Father Blanchet's earliest native converts, whose baptism and death were detailed in his letter to the Bishop of Red River as an example of success in the far western field, along with that of Alexis Yamhill. "Natives in large numbers came to the Sunday services," he wrote, "others showed themselves indifferent. Among the latter an old man, after having been present once at divine service, stubbornly kept refusing to return to it, and repelled sharply the entreaties of his relatives: also he refused to listen to the missionary's instructions, which his relatives repeated to him in the hope of bringing him out of his lethargy. He fell dangerously ill. Eternity presented itself to his imagination and he shuddered. He asks for the priest, who instructs and baptizes him. 'I am no longer an Indian', he exclaimed. 'I am a Frenchman and I feel my heart unburdened. The Great Master has recovered His child.' He died in the best state of mind."

Choquette, Amadeé   1840 c.-1908
Amadeé Choquette came to Oregon from Canada during the 1850's and married Marie Bernier at St. Louis in 1859. He bought a farm south of St. Paul, rolling and well-watered, where he raised fine horses for racing, the popular sport of the times. An 1890 photograph shows a large, prosperous looking man, a beautiful wife and a family of fifteen unusually handsome children. Marie Choquette, "Beloved Wife", died in 1892. Amedee Choquette was fatally burned on his way home from town with a can of kerosene in the back of his hack one windy October day. A cigar spark set the straw and kerosene afire. The team dashed madly for home with the blazing equipage while the old man fought to control them until his hands and the leather reins were fused together; he died the next morning. During that last dreadful night his concern was for his scorched horses, which survived.

Choquette, Félix   1888-1970
The younger Choquette children, of whom Félix was next to the last, walked two miles north to the old Four Corners rural school, where it appears the lessons were in French, at least in part. In

his old age Félix once remarked, "I was fifteen years old before I could say 'yes'," and of an American schoolmate he spoke with some disdain, "He couldn't even say 'oui'!"

Clackamas Tribe

The Clackamas Indians were a Chinookan group living along the Clackamas River, a tributary of the Willamette coming in from the east below the falls, and for some distance down the parent stream.

Clatsop Tribe

The Clatsops occupied the south side of the Columbia below Tongue Point and south along the coast to Tillamook Head. They practised head flattening, held slaves, and depended largely upon fish for food. Much intermarriage with the whites occurred, so that although the pure stock has disappeared, the blood remains widely disseminated in the West.

Cloutier, Antoine Joseph   1834 c-1899

Antoine Cloutier's father, also Antoine, seems to have been temporarily at St. Paul during the 1840's, where his 11-year-old son was baptized. Antoine Joseph next appears on the coast, where he married Helene Lattie, daughter of the Columbia River pilot, Alexander Lattie. Cloutier (Cloutrie, Kloutrie) and his wife operated the Summer House at Seaside, well-known for its fine French cuisine. Cloutier acted also as guide for early settlers and timber buyers. On one timber cruising trip to Sugarloaf Mountain, Cloutier and three timbermen died, apparently victims of ptomaine poisoning.

Coffey, Edward   1817-1897

In addition to the Edward Coffey recorded in St. Paul, the registers of Salem and Oregon City record the names of John, George, James and Bartholomew Coffey, who may, as indicated by the dates, have been sons of Edward. Both he and John had claims fronting the river in the big eastward bend above Horseshoe Lake; Coffey's Landing was logged by steamboats as 5.5 miles above Mission Landing. John's land was part of the original claim of Laurent Sauve, the old Hudson's Bay Company dairyman from Sauve Island; Edward's was part of the Michael Coyle claim.

Coleman, James   1821-1911

James Coleman, of Hollander descent, was born in Ohio and lived successively in Indiana and Iowa before joining a wagon train bound for Oregon, accompanied by his wife Frances Murray and their infant daughter. He spent the first winter in the West operating the Mission Mill on Champoeg Creek. The next spring he took a raw, timbered land claim in Muddy Valley, built a log house in which his family was to live for twelve years, and left for the California gold fields. The settlement at Muddy Valley in Yamhill County was composed of Irish Catholic immigrants, who greatly missed the amenities of their church. In November, 1853, a missionary priest visited the settlement, where he was given a glad welcome. His visit resulted in the conversion of James Coleman to the Catholic faith and the baptism of several infants. Coleman became an ardent advocate for the establishment of a parish in Muddy Valley. He gave ten acres of his claim for a church and cemetery, which became known as St. Patrick's and was served by Father Adrian Croquet from the parish of St. Michael's at Grand Ronde, twenty miles to the west. Coleman sold his land claim in 1860 and bought land in St. Paul, where he lived out his long life. His wife Frances Murray died in 1896. Eleven children lived to carry on the Coleman name.

Collet, Octave

The record of Octave Collet on the Prairie is very brief. In August, 1847, he married Marguerite Nesquallie (Skwaleh), who died the next February at St. Louis. Collet the married (1851, St. Louis) Marie, Indian, "raised by Jean Toupin". In 1852 he bought the claim of Pierre Delard (Delore), which lay in the southern part of the Prairie, but not long retain it. Within two years it passed into other hands and Collet is not heard of again.

Colvile Tribe

The Colviles were a Salishan people living between Kettle Falls and the Spokane River. Once they had been a large tribe estimated to have numbered several thousand in 1850, but by 1904 they had been reduced to a few hundred on the Colvile Reserve.

Comartin, Hyacinthe

Comaetin came to Oregon from Montreal, and in 1854 married Catherine Russie, widow of the old boatman Andre Chalifoux I. Two children, Felicite and Francois, are recorded, and the death of Catherine Russie in 1860. The little girl was reared by the T. J. Hubbards in the Pendleton area, where she grew up to marry Perry Knotts in 1876. Francois married Josie Morrissette (LaFave).

Comtois, Jacques Eugene   1829-1918

"Jim" Comtois was the son of Pierre and Angele Comtois of Alecourt in Canada. He was one of five adventurous young men who came to California seeking their fortunes in the gold fields. After some success, they came north to find homes in Oregon. *[For their journey over the mountains, see Jette, Adolphe.]* Three of them married daughters of Louis Pichet, in whose home they first found shelter when they reached Oregon. Comtois married Louise Soulange Pichet and lived for a time on the Prairie, where numerous children are recorded. About 1876 they moved to Cowlitz Prairie, and there are buried, together with twin daughters, born and died in 1888. Soulange died in 1912, James in 1918.

Connor, *[see Hughes]*

Connor, O'Connor

Four original lines of Connor appear in the Register during the latter half of the 1800's:

Connolly (Connelly), Amelia

Amelia was the daughter of Chief Factor William Connolly, British Columbia, and Susanne Cree. She was known as an able and personable woman, a credit to her husband's station as Chief Factor at Fort Vancouver. She and James Douglas had been married in fur trade fashion for nine years when the Reverend Herbert Beaver came to the Fort as Episcopal chaplain in 1836. Beaver considered it a personal triumph when he persuaded them to be united in the Church; not many others followed their example, to the great disappointment of the critical chaplain, who soon left in disgust for England.

Connor, John (1798-1879) and his wife Catherine Bulgar (1800-1869), first recorded in 1863 when their daughter Martha Joanna married Peter Kenrick Murphy. Catherine Bulgar died October 28, 1869, and was buried at St. Louis. John died June 1, 1878, and was buried "next to his departed wife."

Connor, Matthew (1824-1875) "of Minnesota" and his wife Mary Lynch (1825-1905) are first recorded about 1885.

Connor, Patrick Simon (1806-1875) and his wife Elizabeth Dunn first mentioned in 1875, when their daughter Margaret married John Charles McDowell.

Connor, Simon James "of Illinois" and his wife Agnes Scully "of Pennsylvania" first recorded in 1885.

Connor or O'Connor is a common Irish name; any relationship within the above lines is not known.

Cooke, John Joseph   1829-1882

John Joseph Cooke was born in Ireland, coming to Oregon by way of Illinois, as would seem from his marriage entry. His wife, Bridget Lee (1831-1908) was also from Ireland, a sister of Hugh Burns of Westmeath County. No baptismal record has been found for one James L. Cooke, who was perhaps a son of the above John Joseph, whose birth in 1862 (Cemetery record, St. Paul) logically fits between those of Nicholas (1861) and Robert (1864).

Cornoyer, Narcisse   1820-1903

Cornoyer was a quarter-blood from Illinois, son of Narcisse Cornoyer and Marie Anne Bernier. He was intelligent and educated, and acted as sheriff in the early days of government in Oregon. During the Yakima Indian War of the 1850's, he commanded a troop of half-bloods, to whom he was "Corny" and could do no wrong. He was said to be the only officer who could handle the unruly metis. After the war he moved to Athena, Oregon, to spend the rest of days when not acting as agent on the Umatilla Reservation. His wife was Sophie Beleque, daughter of Pierre Beleque I and Genevieve St. Martin.

Cosgrove, Hugh   1802-1901

Cosgrove stated on his Donation Land Claim record that he was born in County Caven, Ireland, married Mary Rossiter in Canada in 1830 or 1832, came to Oregon in 1847 and settled his claim south of Champoeg in 1850. He succeeded in amassing comfortable wealth; his ornate old home still stands. Both he and his wife were influential in the Catholic Church, and their daughters were educated in the Sisters' School in Oregon City in the fashionable manner of the day. The Cosgrove lot in the St. Paul Cemetery is well marked.

Costello, John and family
The Costellos in Oregon are typical of many Irish immigrants to America who progressed westward by degrees, always seeking the promised land. John Costello and his wife, Ellen Burns, came from County Meath. They paused long enough in Baltimore, where Ellen's brother Hugh Burns was then living, to start their family with a son James, born in 1839, or about then. Their next children were born in Fort Wayne, Indiana—John II, Mary Ellen, Mary Ann, Elizabeth and Michael. Here the father, John, died in 1847. A year or two later his widow Ellen Burns married John Gearin, a widower from Cork, Ireland. The family was now beginning to scatter. Daughter Elizabeth died at birth. Son James left for the West with his uncle, Daniel Burns, in the Joseph Miller train of 1848. The rest of the family followed in 1851, including sons Hugh Burns Gearin, aged two years, and John Gearin, "born on the banks of the Umatilla River" as they neared their goal of the Willamette Valley. Mary Ann died within the year, aged ten. Mary Ellen went to Oregon City to attend the Sisters' School, living in the home of her uncle Hugh; she presently married Matthew O'Connell Murphy. James had married Mary Cosgrove and was now a merchant and postmaster at Champoeg. He died in San Francisco, perhaps while on a merchandizing trip, at some time before 1860, when his widow married Jerome Jackson. John— if of the same family—was recorded briefly in Oregon City with a wife Mary Jane Murphy and a son James Henry, born in 1869. Michael, the youngest, died unrecorded, although his stone in the New St. Paul Cemetery reads, "Died in 1866, aged 23 years". As the New Cemetery was not opened until 1875, his body was evidently moved later from elsewhere to the Gearin lot to lie with his mother, sister and step-father. Ellen Burns died in 1879, aged 70; John Gearin in 1893, aged 81.

Cournoille, Joseph I   1803-
The name Cournoille has suffered many mutilations. Joseph Cournoille was born at Sorel, Canada. He joined the North West Fur Company as a youth in 1819, serving in British Columbia until transferred by the Hudson's Bay Company to the Columbia Department in 1826. Chief Trader Samuel Black wrote of him on the rigorous Rocky Mountain Expedition in 1824, " . . . a real rough and tumble . . . he works with hand and foot, tooth and nail at the line". He was one of the crew sent to the Umpqua to recover Jed Smith's furs, and was with Work on the Snake River in 1831-32. Thereafter he was a free trapper, chiefly with Laframboise. Although he had a land claim on which he paid taxes in 1844. he did not live to receive a patent on it. His wife was Therese Spokane, widow of Joseph Grenier who had been drowned at The Dalles in 1830.

Cournoille, Victoire   1832-
Victoire Cournoille, daughter of Joseph I, grew up to marry a Canadian, Felix (Elie) Giguere in 1846. They settled on a claim on French Prairie in 1851, where Giguere died four years later, leaving three children—Sophie, Therese and Pierre. His widow Victoire married Ambroise Gagnon the same year.

Courville, Basile   1822 c-
The records of Basile are few and scattered. He was born in New York State near the Canadian border, apparently a mixed-blood. He came west in 1839, perhaps in the employ of the fur trade, and lived around St. Louis, Oregon, for some years. In 1851 he married Marianne Klickatat, the widow of Honore King, who had died unrecorded at some time between 1848 and 1851, possibly in the gold fields. Courville and his wife went to the South Umpqua River of Douglas County to make their home, where Father Croke, on a tour to Jacksonville in the fall of 1853, baptized their four-month-old son Louis on September 10th, and where Courville acted as godfather or witness at other rites among Indian or metis neighbors. These entries are included in the Immaculate Conception Register (Portland, Oregon), as Father Croke was pastor there. In 1858 Archbishop Blanchet, on a similar tour, baptized Courville's six-months-old son Edouard, and in 1861 the roving Father Poulin baptized four-month Gilbert "on the South Umpqua about 8 miles from Canyonville". These last two entries are recorded in the Oregon City Register. The name Courville is met with in the Willamette Valley today, but relationships are not known. It is interesting to note that "Gilbert and Edward Courville, brothers, hand-hewed the timbers for the beautiful-

ly designed edifice" of St. Claire's Mission on the Muckleshoot Reserve, built by Father Chirouse in 1870. Either an error in dates or a repetition of family names is indicated.

Couturier, Jean Baptiste
The records state only that he married Marie Angelique Pend d' Oreille on February 3, 1845, and that his daughter Marie, born in 1846, died at the age of three.

Couturier, Olivier
This Canadian of Bytown (Ottawa) appears very sketchilly in the records. He married Marguerite, daughter of Chief Cassino (Chinook) in 1839; she had at that time a four-year-old son Pierre Calder.

Cowlitz Tribe
"The natives that live in the neighborhood . . . have a language of their own which does not resemble the Chinook, but as a rule they understand the jargon. They are rather numerous, but poor. They give the missionaries great hopes. After the visit of Mr. Blanchet, they kept saying to the Canadians of Cowlitz, 'The priests are coming to us, too . . . we shall work and do everything they wish.' "

Father Blanchet, 1840

Coyle, James   1847-1898
James Coyle came from the British Isles to Canada at an early age, and in 1835 to Wisconsin, where he engaged in logging for some eighteen years. He had married a Canadian girl, Charlotte Scott, and had a family of four young children when he gave up logging for a new start in the West, setting out with an ox-team in 1853. Cholera broke out in the train, and his wife died not far from Laramie, Wyoming. Coyle and the children continued the journey, settling after a few years on a farm south of Champoeg. He died in Hubbard, Oregon, at the age of eighty-one. Of his four children, one died young, Ellen married Frank Van Wassenhoven, James Jr., married Eliza Henrietta Ray, and Alexander married Helen Everhard.

Crate, William Frederick   -1871 (?)
"About the beginning of 1839 a young London millwright named William Frederick Crate, who had been in the employ of the Hudson's Bay Company for several years, was engaged to construct water mills and to mill flour at Fort Vancouver."

J. Hussey, Fort Vancouver, p 201

William Crate should not be confused with Edouard Crête, often spelled Crate, who was a French Canadian settling at "Crate's Point" a few miles below the Dalles, or long narrows, of the Columbia. The miller, William Crate, is said to have settled at Vancouver after the Company left. The Lewis County, Washington, census lists Sarah Glazebrook, his wife, as having been born in England.

Cree Tribe
The crees originally lived around the west shores of Hudson Bay but gradually spread westward across interior Canada. Many engagés of the fur companies had Cree wives from east of the Rockies.

Crête, Edouard   1821-1894
Edouard Crete, son of Baptiste Crête and Marie Anne Laur of Canada, was a French Canadian voyageur, according to his son. (Edouard Crête is not to be confused with William Frederick Crate, of London, who was in the West at the same time.) Crête came by canoe route across Canada to the West in 1838 and was employed as master of the canoe and bateau "fleet" for the Hudson's Bay Company. He brought the Spalding and Whitman survivors down to Fort Vancouver after the massacre. He worked in connection with Peter Skene Ogden for years. In 1849 he retired to Crate's Point below The Dalles, raising stock and transporting immigrants down river, in partnership with Charles Lefeve, of Pendleton. He married Sophie Boucher and was the father of fourteen children.

Crochière, Joseph   1826 c.-1849
Joseph was the son of one named Chochière and Marguerite Cree, who married André Dubois. Joseph died in the gold fields of California September 12, 1849.

Dalcourt, Esther   1831-1884
Esther Dalcourt, dit Champagne, married Pierre Gauthier in 1844 and became the mother of eleven children, of whom at least five died in infancy. Gauthier died in 1867, and Esther married

François Deschamps (Field). One daughter, Esther, was born to them. Esther Dalcourt died at the age of fifty-five.

Dalcourt, Jean Baptiste - dit Champagne   1804-1856
Dalcourt was in the employ of the Hudson's Bay Company, "a hunter from the prairies of the north", until he retired to French Prairie with his wife, Agathe Khossa (possibly Cayuse), and several children, including her daughter Cécile McDonald by an earlier alliance. When the Methodist missionaries under Jason Lee were looking for a site for their mission, they chose "an eminence about one-half mile south of the place occupied by Baptiste Delcour, near a fountain of living water". A later map of the area shows J. B. Dalcour's claim in the big bend of the river below Fairfield. He had evidently given up his claim by 1846, when one McClane advertised in **The Spectator** of March 19th, "For Sale . . . on Wallace Prairie . . . formerly known as B. Del Cour's claim, having a log cabin and a French barn . . . 200 acres endlosed 3 miles from Salem mills." Dalcourt's wife Agathe died in 1853, and he himself was drowned in 1856.

Dalcourt, Louis   1846-
Louis Dalcourt married Eleanore Plourde in 1867 at St. Louis. The record of his children continues in the register there and in The Dalles.

Davidson, Green C.
The first Davidson on French Prairie, Green C., was the son of an English father who became a captain on the side of the United States in the War of 1812, and a mother descended from a Virginia family. Green was a circus juggler in youth, and met his future wife, Nancy Million, while on circuit in Kentucky. An injury led him to give up juggling for a varied life of farming and storekeeping in Illinois. In 1852 he and his small family crossed the plains to Oregon by horse teams. His life on French Prairie was checkered with success and failure, floods occasionally causing great losses. His wife died, leaving six children, and in 1878 he married Mary Brown in Clackamas County; two children were born of the second marriage. Green Davidson died in Salem at the age of sixty years.

Davidson, William Franklin   1843-1927
William Franklin, called Frank, was the second son of the pioneer Fairfield merchant, Green Davidson. After his marriage to Catherine Ann Coleman he embraced the Catholic faith. Many descendents of their twelve children remain in the St. Paul area today.

DeCraene, Julian   1843-1873
Father DeCraene was a secular priest who came to Oregon in 1869. He died at the age of thirty while serving as pastor at Salem. His body was brought to St. Paul for burial in the right wing of the church, but in 1887 was removed to the new cemetery to be "near Father Blanchet".

Degneau (Daignault), Edouard
Most of the information about Degneau concerns his several marriages. he had come from Canada, apparently in the employ of the Hudson's Bay Company. He married Rosalie Kenoheno at Vancouver in 1846. A son Basile was born and died in 1847, and Rosalie died the following year. Degneau then married Louise Klikatat, "neophyte at this mission" (Vancouver) in 1852; both mother and an infant daughter Rosalie died the same year. In 1856 he married the widow of Etienne Lucier, Marie Marguerite Chinook, and came to the Lucier claim on French Prairie to live very briefly, for the same year she divorced him under the new and liberal divorce laws. A "sister" recalled by Etienne's son Pierre Lucier as having been buried on the farm may have been the child of Degneau, though there is no record of such a child. More probably she was the daughter of Marie Marguerite by a marriage earlier than that to Lucier.

An entry in the Oregon City Church records would seem to refer to the same man, Edward Daigneault, whose daughter Philomena by his wife Marie Boussière was baptized July 14, 1878.

Dégré, Philippe   1739 c.-1847
Dégré was a member of the Lewis and Clark Expedition of 1805, but apparently dropped out along the way, working his way west later, as did François Rivet. As if in amazement at his great age, Father Demers wrote at the bottom of the page in the register, "Mon Dieu, Mon Dieu!" at his death at 108 years.

Deguire, François B.   1818-1909
François was a younger brother of Jean Baptiste Deguire. He was born in Ste. Geneviève,

Missouri, and married Eleanor St. James at that place. In 1855 he joined his brother in Oregon. "At the time F. B. DeGuire arrived at St. Paul, his brother was operating a ferry on the Willamette called DeGuera's Ferry. Afterward it was known as Ray's Landing . . . At this ferry the family found a small, cheaply constructed house they could occupy for the winter . . . and the younger brother operated the ferry during the first winter to help pay their expenses." **Steeves, Book of Remembrance.** Later he became a prosperous settler in the Silverton area. He and several members of his family are buried in the Miller Cemetery near Silverton, the lot marked with a good shaft.

Deguire, Jean Baptiste (I) 1810-1878
Jean Baptiste Deguire was born in Ste. Geneviève, Missouri, of a long-lived family; his grandfather, who is said to have helped build the town, lived to be one hundred and ten, his father to ninety-eight, his brother to ninety-one. He was in the Rocky Mountains with Sublette between 1830 and 1840, after which he retired to the Willamette Valley. He took a claim on the river above St. Paul and ran a ferry at a place later called Ray's Landing. He was the "Batteus De-Guerre" that guided Elijah White during the 1840's; he was spoken of as "a half-breed", (which was incorrect), capable, dexterous, cruel and thoughtless. His young nephew heard eagerly the stories told at the ferry of life in the Rockies, grizzley bears, buffalo and all the rest. Deguire married Marie Anne Perrault. Their recorded children were Jean Baptiste II, Eulalie, Thomas, William, Joseph and a second Eulalie. His wife and three of his children died before 1865; old and bereft, Jean Baptiste died by his own hand in the Marion County Poor House.

Délard (DeLore), Antoine 1838-1898
"Tunish" was the youngest son of Joseph Délard. He was three times married, to Marie Vandale, daughter of Louis Vandale (Vendal of Lake LaBiche); to Marie McKay, daughter of John McKay; and to Esther McKay, daughter of John McKay II. His life was spent in the Willamette Valley and in Vancouver, where he died and is buried.

Délard (DeLore), Augustin 1827 c.-1891
In the customary usage of nicknames to differentiate among repeated common names, Augustin became "Quine", and is so met with in pioneer references as scout and guide. He married Zoë Quintal, daughter of Laurent Quintal, and moved to Wasco County, where they reared a family of eight. He and Zoë later moved to Crook County where they are buried near Suplee.

Délard (DeLore), Basile 1833-1920 c.
Basile DeLore married Rose Poirier, daughter of Toussaint Poirier and Catherine Clatsop. Their married life of sixty-two years was spent at Wapinitia in eastern Oregon, broken by the death of Rose in 1916. Only one of the four children born to this couple left descendants.

Délard, Catherine 1821 c.-1858
Catherine was the eldest child of Joseph Delard and Lisette Shuswap. Of the five sons born to her and Jean Baptiste Lucier dit Gardipie, only Paul seems to have reached maturity. After being widowed in 1851, she married William Lascerte, to whom she bore four children, dying shortly after the birth of the last.

Délard, Joseph 1792-1869
Joseph Délard was the progenitor of a large number of western residents today, having been early in the West. He came from Sorel, Canada, spending many years in the North West and the Hudson's Bay Companies. In 1828 Governor Simpson mentioned him at Kamloop's as "an able good Steersman and an active hand with horses", real praise from the critical governor. Joseph retired in 1832 to a claim near Fairfield on French Prairie. He was one of the eighteen French Canadians signing a petition to the Bishop of Red River for priests to come, and in preparation, built a log chapel for them. As Délard lived close by the chosen site, he was no doubt a consistent workman on the project. He was twice married, first to Lisette Shuswap, then to the métisse daughter of Toussaint Poirier, having children by each. His widow Marie Poirier lived to be very old indeed, dying in 1914, in Portland.

Délard, Marie Anne 1836-1908
Marie Anne Délard was twice widowed, having married successively Louis Vendal, Medard Foisy and Joseph Morell. She seems to have been a mother extraordinary, for at the age of twelve or thirteen she was the step-mother of two of Vendal's children by a former marriage, and in the

twenty-six years that followed, she gave birth to fourteen of her own, six to Vendal and eight to Foisy. She and her third husband are buried, unmarked, in the Gervais Catholic Cemetery.

Délard (DeLore), Pierre 1824 c.-1906
Pierre was born on the trail in the Snake River Country to Joseph Délard and Lisette Shuswap, their eldest son. He took a claim on French Prairie at the site of the later Quinaby Station, where seven of his thirteen children were born. Having lost his farm under the pressure of American immigration, he moved to Wapinitia, then called Oak Grove, and worked for some years as a packer between The Dalles and the mines at Canyon City, "traveling by night and by secret trails to avoid hijackers". By 1882 he moved to Sunflower Flats in eastern Crook County, to raise horses. His wife, Josephte Lapierre, died in 1872, and he presently married Adelaïde Rivet, widow of François Lefevbre.

Delaunois (Delanois), Louis
Although the Delaunois name appears early in the fur trade records, information about any individual is scant. Louis Delaunois is recorded in Vancouver as the husband of Elizabeth Kwoithe and later of Marie Cowlitz, but little more. It would be interesting to know whether he is the same man who married "Isabelle Montour of Umpqua", and whether she was the widow of Tom McKay. The Delaunois name continues in the Roseburg register without shedding much light on Louis or Isabelle.

DeLisle, Félix 1838-1907
Félix DeLisle was one of five footloose young gold-seekers from the East who drifted north from California later to find wives and homes in Oregon, the others being Adolphe Jette, J. B. Piette, James Comtois and Dieudonné Manègre. Three of the five married daughters of Louis Pichet, dit Dupré. DeLisle's wife Marie Pichet died in 1879 at the age of twenty-five; both are buried in St. Paul with her parents and other family members; the graves are well marked.

Delorme, Bartholomew 1825-
Father Delorme came to the West from France as a young secular priest in 1847. He served Prairie parishes for many years, both as priest and vicar general. He had brought with him from France a four volume set of **Maison Rustique,** intended for use in the boys' school known as St. Joseph's College in St. Paul. When that school closed during the California gold rush, he gave the books to Michel Laframboise, one of the few farmers on the Prairie who could read and perhaps profit from them. They remain today a cherished part of the writer's library.

DeMacon, Victor Auguste 1859-1927
Victor DeMacon was a Continental Frenchman who came to Oregon as a young man. His marriage to Marie Clementia Bélèque resulted in a large family, whose records appear in St. Louis and nearby parish registers. In time spared from his work, DeMacon made excellent wooden shoes like those worn in France, which sold readily to truck garden workers in the wet Willamette Valley. A few pairs remain in family keeping as heirlooms.

Demers, Modeste 1809-1871
Demers was born in Québec of a farm family and was ordained to the priesthood in 1837. He was stationed at Red River at the time Father Blanchet was setting out for the Oregon Country to establish missions and was chosen to accompany him. Genial and adaptable, with a facility for learning tribal dialects, Demers worked north of the Columbia among the Indians. He filled Blanchet's place at St. Paul during the absence of the Bishop in Europe, and superintended the building of the brick church there, still in use. Upon the return of his superior, Demers became the Bishop of Vancouver Island, where he died in 1871. The Portland **Catholic Sentinel** of August 12, 1871, carried an appreciation from the Cowlitz Church, where he had labored in the early days of the missions:

> "The deceased prelate, in early days, was pastor of this church for three years, and the first settlers of Cowlitz Prairie have not forgotten, and never will forget, his tender and paternal solicitude for their spiritual welfare."

Dépot, Joseph 1839-
Joseph would seem to have been the son of Pierre Dépot I, and Marguerite Klamak, baptized under the name Pierre at the age of four months in 1839. He married Angélique LaRoc, widow of Martin Bonenfant, at St. Louis in 1858; all later records are found in the Walla Walla (French-town) Registers, closing with the death of his wife and new-born son in January, 1876. One Joe

Dépot, undoubtedly this man, is remembered to have been buried in the abandoned cemetery at Frenchtown, and the name "Despot" is listed on the common monument there.

Dépot, Pierre (I)   1799-1868
Pierre Dépot was an employee of the Hudson's Bay Company who came out from St. Roche in 1820 and was with Ogden on the Snake River in 1824. A son, also Pierre, was born to him and Susanne Tchinouk on February 10, 1833 "in the Rogue River Valley", according to the younger man's statement in his land claim application. Susanne died before the arrival of the priests in 1838. In 1839 Dépot took up the former claim of Nicholas Montour, near the present town of Gervais. His second wife, Marguerite Klamak, died in 1850, "leaving three children, one of whom died". His three recorded children by Marguerite were another Pierre (possibly intended for Joseph who shows up later), Adelaide and Etienne. Adelaïde died at the age of fifteen; Etienne is not heard of again. Dépot married Lizette, "orphan at the home of Louis Vandal" in 1858. to whom two daughters are recorded, Catherine and Marcelline. The latter was not posthumous, as stated in the Vancouver annotations, but born about eight weeks before her father's death.

Dépot, Pierre (II)   1833-
The priest gave young Pierre's age as four years at the time of his baptism in 1839, but by his own count he was more nearly six, having been born on February 10, 1833, to Pierre Depot I and Susanne Tchinouk. (Land Record). In 1851 he married Marie Banak, widow of Louis Brousseau, "deceased in California", and settled near his father's claim in Gervais. He lost the rights to the claim, however, and by 1860 was living in Frenchtown, near Walla Walla. His wife was called Marie Desjarlais in the records at that place, Desjarlais being the name of her step-father. The entries for his children are scattered, those of Rose (who died at the age of seven) and Christine being at St. Louis, his son Louis at St. Paul, and again Esther at St. Louis, Sophie and Mélanie at Frenchtown (Walla Walla Register).

Deschamps, Pierre
At least three Deschamps were employed by the Hudson's Bay Company in the West—Baptiste, Pierre and Antoine. The last two are known to have been half-breed brothers from Red River. Pierre was one of the crew bringing the priests to Vancouver in 1838, and was one of those able to save himself in the upset of the bateau in the rapids. In 1853 he married Marie (daughter of) Louis Oskanha, dit Monique, an Iroquois métisse. Their listed children were Christine, Odile, Chloris, Odile (II), Rosalie, Pierre, Celestine and Jean Ephram. Pierre Deschamps seems to have died between 1866, when his last child was born, and 1869, when his widow Marie married Jean Baptiste Jeaudoin.

Desjarlais, Marguerite
Marguerite was the daughter of Thomas Desjarlais and Marguerite Maskégonne. She married Joseph Gagnon in 1842. Their recorded children were Emerance, who died shortly, Joseph and Félicite. Her husband Joseph died in the gold fields (as did François Gagnon) on September 13, 1849. In 1851 Marguerite married Jean Claude Bellanger. A daughter Catherine was born and died in 1854 at St. Louis, after which Bellanger disappears from view. When his widow Marguerite married a third time, he was not mentioned, she being given as the widow of Joseph Gagnon, as before. The third husband was Jean Baptiste Rondeau, from Fort Wayne, Indiana. The close links between Marguerite Desjarlais and Angélique Marcellais in their three marriages each causes some confusion in the records, but this can be resolved with patience.

Desjarlais, Thomas   -before 1855
Desjarlais was a well-known name in the fur trade in early days in the West. One Desjarlais was drowned with his wife and four children on the Thompson Expedition in Montana, 1808-1810, while two others, François and Joseph, were listed as members of the brigade. Thomas appears to have married in the East, as his wife was Maskégonne (Muskegan).

DeSmet, Pierre-Jean   1801-1873
DeSmet was born in Belgium, came to the United States at the age of twenty, studied for the priesthood in Maryland and Missouri and was ordained in 1827. He spent the next ten years in advanced study in Europe, after which he returned to begin his famous work among the Indians. In 1840 he came to the Northwest to explore the field for missions. He founded St. Mary's Mission among the Flatheads in the Bitterroot region of Montana in 1841, becoming the beloved and saintly "Father of the Rocky Mountain missions". He returned to St. Louis, Missouri, in 1846 to spend the rest of his life in clerical work.

Despard, Joseph Frederic   1788-1875
Despard came early from Montréal and was with the Hudson's Bay Company for many years
before settling on a claim west of Champoeg in the early 1830's. Shards of clay pipes, old blue
Staffordshire earthenware, bits of copper and like artifacts still come to light in the field above
Roth Lake where his cabin once stood. Despard was with Peter Skene Ogden on his Snake River
Expedition of 1825-26. The latter's journal relates this incident: A slave belonging to Finan
McDonald, who was also along on the trip, "had words" with Despard as they were unloading
and packing supplies, evidently at a portage. As Despard neared the top of the bank with his
packload, the Indian slapped his back. Despard slipped off his pack and fought the Indian "for
about five minutes". The latter became ill in camp, vomited blood, and shortly died "in great
pain". Some claimed Despard had kicked him in the stomach, but Ogden could find no evidence
on the body or from Despard. He buried the man, and "since I could not return Despard to
Vancouver", considered the incident closed. He concluded his entry, "The poor man is miserable
and unhappy."
A clipping from an old newspaper mentioned the death of one "Umpqua Joe", an aged Indian,
born near Riddle, "who was taken as a little child by Joseph Despard and George Montour and
raised by them and the Hudson's Bay Company".
Despard died in 1875; his burial was apparently one of the last in the Old St. Paul Cemetery,
where no markers remain.

Despard, Marie   1840-
Marie Despard married François Bernier in 1858, after the death of his first wife, Pélagie Lucier.
Of this marriage were born sons Joseph, Pierre and Sémeon.

Despard, Marie Anne   1834-
Marie Anne was about twelve when she married Joseph Rivet. After his death she married Xavier
Gervais, then Antoine McKay, in Douglas County.

Despard, Victoire   1843-
Victoire grew up to marry Roc Pichet. The pair lived in Douglas County, Oregon, where they
reared a large family and where descendants still live. A faded old picture shows Victoire a small,
sweetly retiring wife seated beside her positive looking husband, surrounded by sons and daughters of all ages. This is one of the most appealing pictures to have come down from the French
Canadian era.

Desrivières, Angélique   1837-
Angelique married Michel Laferté II (dit Placie, Plassée) in 1852. Part of her later life was spent
on the reservation at Grand Ronde, Polk County. Besides the children listed in the St. Paul
volumes, there are recorded at St. Louis, Etienne and Mary Ann, who died at the age of nine
months, and on the reservation a son who died at five years, Mary Angèle, and Agnès, who died
at seven months.

Desrivières, Pierre
As the Indians did not use a two-name system and their native names were almost unpronounce-
able to the whites, they were usually given a name by the priest or brigade leader, the place of
origin or the tribe to which they belonged, which served as a surname for the next generation.
Thus the children of Desrivières were known variously as Des Rivieres, Assiniboine, Sibonne
or Peter.

DeVos, Peter SJ   1797-1859
DeVos was a Belgian priest recruited in the midwest by Father DeSmet in 1843 to come west in
missionary work. He arrived with the Great Migration of Applegate, Burnett and Whitman, and
while DeSmet went on to Europe, DeVos supervised the building of St. John's Church in Oregon
City. The next three years were spent at Colvile, but he was forced by poor health to retire in
1851 and died at Santa Clara College, California, in 1859. He is best remembered as a Jesuit
working amongst the white population.

Dobin, Jean Baptiste   -1849
Dobin was an employee of the Hudson's Bay Company, apparently stationed at Fort Vancouver
during the 1830's, for there he married Nancy, of the Dalles, after her husband Goodrich
(Gaudritche) was drowned at The Dalles. He held land south of Champoeg, where he built a
"big long" log cabin, according to his step-grandson, Thomas Lachance, half on either side of the

line between his claim and that of his wife. Both went to the gold fields, where Jean Baptiste died September 26, 1849, and was buried by Father Delorme, the chaplain of the French Canadian parties, with the simple entry "Dobin" and the date. His wife Nancy returned home but died almost at once, May 23, 1850.

Dompierre, David (I) -1849
Dompierre had married a métisse, Marguerite Soulier (Souillière), in the East, before coming as a carpenter to Fort Vancouver. The Reverend Beaver, who preceded the priest there, had bitter words to say about the Catholics: "The Roman Catholic population is very illiterate. Out of the whole, but one, David Dompier, can read and write . . . He is the person **obliged** by Dr. Mc-Loughlin to teach and read to the others on the Sabbath day, and also to catechise the children **every** day, after four o'clock . . . He is a carpenter, and from his illegal mode of life, unfit for the office to which he is appointed."

Dompierre, David (II) 1837-1858
Young David died at the age of twenty-one at St. Louis.

Dompierre, François Xavier (I) 1845-1911
François Xavier grew up on the Prairie. About 1874 he eloped with Soulange Bergevin, a delicate and educated girl whose father objected to the match. One very old inhabitant of Douglas County still recalls, "You know, my father (Onesime Pelland), he helped "X" Dompier steal dat girl!" Soulange died in a tie-cutting camp along the railroad at Parrish's Gap two years later, leaving a son, also François Xavier. The husband retreated to Douglas County and lived out his life as a trapper.

Dompierre, Julienne 1839-1840
The child baptized as "Julienne" (Vancouver records) died seven months later as "Julien, a son".

Dompierre, Marie 1834-1893
In 1850 Marie Dompierre married Pierre Pariseau, a man much older than she. Most of their married life was spent in the mountain country of Douglas County, where eleven children were born. Many descendants remain there today.

Dompierre, Philomène 1843-1854
Philomène died at St. Louis at the age of ten.

Dorion, Jean Baptiste 1815 c.-1850 c.
The date of the birth of this son of Pierre and Madame Dorion is uncertain; he may have been one of the children accompanying them on the overland trip of the Hunt party. As Pierre Dorion was killed in 1814. Jean Baptiste's birth date must be near or prior to that time. He grew up to marry Josephine Walla Walla (Cayuse) in 1845 and had at least seven recorded children—Denise, Pierre, Geneviève, David, Philomène, Joseph and Marianne. After the death of Dorion about 1850, his six-year-old son David was reared by his father's half-sister, Marguerite Vagnier Gobin, in Montana. Denise married François Laframboise; the remaining children appear to have died young—Geneviève, for instance, is known to have died at St. Louis at the age of twelve.

Dorion, Pierre 1835-1854
This Pierre Dorion was the son of Jean Baptiste and the grandson of the Pierre Dorion who was the guide for the Hunt Party in 1810-1812. He died at St. Louis in 1854.

Douglas, Agnes 1841-
Agnes was the daughter of James Douglas, Chief Factor, and of Amelia Connolly, daughter of another Chief Factor. Douglas was in charge of Fort Vancouver during the absence of John McLoughlin at the time of the priests' arrival in 1838, hence he often appears as sponsor for Company men in the Church records. In 1849 he was sent to Vancouver Island to Fort Victoria, which place he had selected for the new fort there. In 1859 he became governor of British Columbia, was knighted in 1863, and retired in 1864.

Dowd, John 1827 c-1921
John Dowd, of County Kerry, Ireland, married Julie, the eldest daughter of Pierre Pepin (Lachance), at St. Paul where many of their children were baptized; others were baptized at Grand Ronde. Julie died in 1903, John in 1921, at the age of 94. Both are buried at Grand Ronde.

The **Oregonian** of March 16, 1916, carried a lively item concerning the old man, but exaggerated his age by ten years or more. (The Mexican War was a topic of current interest in 1916):

John Dowd, who will celebrate his 104th birthday next Saturday, and who, undoubtedly, is the oldest man in the state, arrived in Portland yesterday from Bend to visit his son, Theodore . . .

Mr. Dowd, whose white beard gives him a patriarchal appearance, made the long railroad trip from Bend without the least discomfort and declared himself in fine condition when he reached the Union Depot here. In one hand he carried a long rifle, carefully wrapped in cloth.

"I have it handy to kill Mexicans with," he said. "It's liable to come in handy any time now. You never can tell when it will be needed and I'm for preparedness."

Mr. Dowd was for many years a soldier. He came to Oregon in 1840, being a member of a detachment of regular Army troops sent out here to allay Indian disturbances.

He settled on a farm near Champoeg, Marion County, and later moved to the Grand Ronde Indian Reservation in Yamhill Co.

Dubois, André 1803-1898
Dubois came west with his Cree wife Marguerite and his step-son Joseph Crochière; perhaps his own son Basile, born in 1829, had also been born in Canada. Dubois settled a claim in 1840, where his wife Marguerite died in 1844. In 1845 Dubois married Josette Marie Quesnel, sometimes called Josette Jeffries, at St. Louis.

Dubois, Basile 1829 c.-1857
Basile, son of André Dubois and Marguerite Cree, married Marguerite Sanders in 1852. Their recorded children, Luce, Marie Magdeleine and André, all died in infancy, and Basile himself died at the age of thirty-two. His widow married Augustin Lambert II in 1860.

Dubois, Pierre
This is the Pierre Below (Bilow) dit Dubois, from St. Cuthbert, Canada, who married Catherine Simipchinó, Spokane, at Vancouver, in 1845. A Below grave in the Pioneer Cemetery at Cathlamet offers interesting speculation as to possible relationships.

Dubois, Susanne
Susanne Dubois married François Plourde, dit Jacques, at Red River about 1820. They came west with the Red River migration of 1841 with several children; others were born in the West. Susanne and Plourde both lived to be very old, it is said, and are buried in the Highland Cemetery, now known as Pioneer, at Mount Angel, Oregon.

Dubreuil, François 1844-
Dubreuil, Thérèse 1846-
François married Marie Madeleine Bourjeau in 1861, but not without a rebuke from Father Malo for his secular disregard of the Church, apparently. His sister Thérèse likewise got a wigging from Father Delorme when she married Jean Baptiste Gobin before a justice of the peace at St. Louis in 1863. "(They) have come, repentant of their fault to implore the benediction of the Church", wrote the priest, who was a kindly man, but decorum must be observed.

Dubreuil, Jean Baptiste -1849
Jean Baptiste Dubreuil, born in Canada, enlisted in the Astor enterprise at St. Louis, Missouri, in 1810 to cross the plains with the Hunt party. At one point near the end of the rigorous journey Dubreuil was left behind, being too exhausted and starved to continue; he was later picked up by another group of the straggling party and brought down to Astoria. He remained in the West in the service of the various fur companies. He married Marguerite Yougleta (Uculet) in 1839; four sons and two daughters are recorded. He died in the California gold fields in the autumn of 1849. Narcisse Cornoyer was appointed guardian of his minor children. His widow married Charles Plante, whom she outlived.

Ducharme, Henriette 1846-1853
Henriette died at St. Louis at the age of seven.

Ducharme, Jean Baptiste 1797/1800-
Jean Baptiste Ducharme was born in Canada about 1800 (he was uncertain as to the year) and came to the United States in 1818, but did not come to Oregon until 1841. A daughter Lucie was

recorded as being born to "a Flathead woman" in 1836, which would indicate he was east of the mountains until the later date. In 1841 he arrived in February, settled on a claim in April and married Catherine Hu (Paul-Hus) in July. Their recorded children were Marie, Henriette, Esther, Jean Baptiste II, Antoine, François and Benjamin, of whom several died in infancy. The family seems to have gone east of the mountains finally, as Jean Baptiste Ducharme received his citizenship at Missoula, Montana, in 1873.

Ducharme, Lucie   1836-1895
Lucie Ducharme was the second wife of Gédéon Sénécal, whom she married in 1850. Their life was spent at St. Louis, Oregon, until about 1880 when they moved to Wapinitia, east of the Cascades, and to nearby Dufur in 1884, where they died and are buried. Many descendants remain.

Ducharme, Marie   1843-
Marie grew up to marry Joseph Lonetain in 1859. He died the same year; Marie bore a post-humous son, Joseph II. Two years later she married Luger Cameron, and still later (1866) Henry Beauvais.

Duchoquette, François   1819-1863
François Duchoquette was the son of another Francois, who had been a member of the Hunt overland party of the Astor enterprises and a blacksmith and steersman at Fort George in 1813-14, but had later "returned east of the mountains". His mother was Marie Marguerite Okanogan, who married André Picard and after his death, Cuthbert Lambert. Dates seem hardly to permit young François to have been a step-son of Joachim Lafleur, as is sometimes claimed, but do not rule out other possible relationships. He helped Lafleur at Fort Okanogan for almost twenty years. When the post closed in 1860, the remaining goods were moved to a new trading post at Similkameen, which Duchoquette ran. He died a few years later. One who knew him wrote that he was intelligent and competent but much addicted to drink. " . . . a short, stout French half-breed, not more than thirty years of age when I first knew him at Fort Okanogan. He died in 1863 and is buried at Shuttleworth Creek about one mile north of Keremeos. Yes, he was educated some, could read and write and was a pretty good bookkeeper."

Dupaté, Agathe   1825 c.-1848
Agathe was the daughter of Jean Baptiste Dupaté (I) by his Calapooia wife. She married Charles Rondeau, widower of "Old Portneuf's daughter", in 1839. She was thirteen, he more than three times her age. After bearing him three children—Jean Baptiste in 1842, Charles in 1844 and Thomas in 1847, she died on the claim near the present Gervais, Oregon, in 1848. Her widower married Elizabeth, Indian, the following year and died in 1855.

Dupaté, Antoine   1841-
Antoine was the son of Jean Baptiste Dupaté and Jany, that is, Eugénie Wanakske (Falls of the Willamette Tribe). He was reared by his step-mother, Catherine Shasta, who married David Vincent after the death of Dupaté, Antoine's father. Antoine was the youngest of Dupaté's children, and a deep affection grew up between him and his kindly, gentle step-mother. It was on the Umpqua River at the home of Antoine and his wife, Marie Anne Despard, that Catherine Shasta died while on a visit there, late in the century.

Dupaté, Françoise   1828-
Françoise Desportes (Depati) McKay was one of the seven children by two wives reported in Jean Baptiste Desportes McKay's "tent" in 1833, this girl by the Calapooia wife. She was placed in the Methodist Mission School in 1837, where she appears to have remained for several years. She married Antoine Bonenfant I at the age of fourteen.
"She lived to be an old lady. She died in the late 1800's and is buried in our old family cemetery on Cavitt Creek. She settled on Cavitt Creek at the time the Indians were being put on the Siletz Reservation. She used to ride across the mountain to visit her brother Antoine Depati McKay and his wife Mary Ann (Despard), who lived on the Umpqua. She would stay overnight at the Pelland home near Sutherlin and then go on her way. She was taking care of Florence Dompier and would take the little girl with her. Florence and Ada (my aunt) had a great time when Françoise visited there. In later years she was known as Grandma Haysoo, as she was living with a Spaniard called Haysoo (Jesus)."

Elsie Pfeiffer, great-granddaughter, 1967

Dupaté, Jean Baptiste (I)   1793 c.-1853
The names Depate, Departy, Dupote and other variants are corruptions of Desportes; the man
was also known as McKay, McKie, McRoy and so on. The multiplicity of names has caused
history no little confusion.
Jean Baptiste Dupaté was a half-breed from Canada whose name was often garbled almost past
recognition. He appears to have been with the North West Company at Fort George by 1812,
and later with the Hudson's Bay Company, but was also called a freeman. He was a noted
marksman, a good hunter, and an employee met at every turn. He retired "to pitch his tent
permanently" along the Willamette above Champoeg with his several wives, children, cats and
dogs, according to John Ball, a teacher turned farmer, who found Dupaté a friend in need and
wrote entertainingly of his experiences with the old hunter. Dupaté was extremely hospitable to
all travelers; he had one of his children buried and another married by the Methodist missionaries
prior to the coming of the priests, and placed some of them in the mission school. His various
descendants gravitated in the main to the Umpqua region; his surviving wife married David
Vincent.

Dupaté, Jean Baptiste (II) (two persons)   1830-
                                                                 1839-1840
The little Jean Baptiste Dupate (II), baptized in the Vancouver records, died at the age of sixteen
months (St. Paul, Vol. I). In St. Louis, Vol. I, another Jean Baptiste (II), son of J-B (I) and
Marguerite, Indian, was baptized in 1847 at the age of seventeen years.

Dupate, John   1836-1910 c.
John (Jonathon) Dupate was the son of Jean Baptiste Dupate (I) by a Calapouya mother. His
marital affairs seem to be somewhat tangled or obscure; he did, however, have two small children by Rosalie Plouffe baptized in Oregon City in 1858, and two more recorded "by his second
wife". The following bits are found in the correspondence of Elsie Pfeiffer: "This man called John
McKay or McKie was well known around Roseburg and here in the mountains. Place of birth—
unknown, but it is thought to be in Southern Oregon. He died about 1910 and is buried at Dead
Man—east of Tiller, He had two children by his second wife—Himan and John. These children
were born on Cavitt Creek and raised by their Aunt Francois." "When John McKay stayed at
their place he always set up his camp some distance from the house and brought his own food.
Occasionally her mother would cook something and take it to him. Naturally when he died they
took care of him and buried him."

Dupaté, Marie Lisette   1823-before 1842
Marie Lisette, aged fourteen, married John Howard at the Methodist Mission, according to the
Mission Record Book:
> Monday 1st May 1837
> Mr. John Hoard was married to Miss Lizette De Portes at the house of Mr. De Portes
> Willamette settlement by Daniel Lee.
The couple was remarried in 1839 by the priest shortly after his arrival. Lisette died a year or two
later, leaving no issue.

Dupré, François   1768 c.-1858
At the age of ninety in 1858, François Dupré must have been one of the earliest born of Prairie
inhabitants. Little can be learned about him other than a name on the North West Company list
as voyageur at English River in 1804-5, which may or may not have been the same man, and
vague references to Louis Pichet as "dit Dupré" in later times. Nazaire Dupré, born in 1808, was
probably his son.

Dupré, Nazaire   1808-1848
Very little can be learned about this man. He may have been the son of old François Dupré
(1768-1858), but there is no proof of their relationship. He married Catherine Lafantaisie,
daughter of Jacques Lafantaisie and Susanne Okanogan, about 1843; their children Geneviève
and Nazaire, Jr., and Nazaire himself all died within one year, May 1848-May, 1849. He was
survived by a son Charles and daughter Angélique, to the best of our knowledge, and by his wife
Catherine, who married David Mongraine.

DuPuis, Edouard   1821-
"Ed" DuPuis was a merchant in Champoeg, a farmer in Muddy Valley, and a stage line
proprietor, apparently all at the same time. His store and stage depot stood at the foot of

Napoleon Avenue in Champoeg close to the ferry landing of Michel Laframboise, from which his lines radiated east to Oregon City on the Old Territorial Road, south to Salem and Marysville (Corvallis), and possibly went to DeGuerre's Ferry across the Willamette River from Dayton. Newspapers of the day carried his notices:

"A stage every hour from Oregon City and Canemah."

The Spectator, 1853

and

"New Stage Line!
Through by Daylight from Champoeg to Salem
E. DuPous has established a line of stages from Champoeg to Salem, which is well stocked with superior American horses. This being the daily line, the stage will leave Champoeg on the arrival of the Washington, and other steamers."

Columbian, Oct. 2, 1852

The Salem line, carrying both passengers and mail, was sold to Ray and Danforth; possibly all DuPuis' lines were sold at the same time. His store at Champoeg burned in 1851, but was rebuilt; all the buildings in the town, save one, were destroyed in the great flood of 1861-62. The site of the store still yields great quantities of burnt crockery shards, mostly heavy ware such as butter crocks and hotel dishes. It is said that DuPuis' wife, Marguerite Ann Dickerson, found life unendurable on the isolated claim on Muddy Creek and used to escape to stay in Lafayette whenever possible. She and Edouard were eventually divorced, the little son Thadeus going with his mother, who later married James Burke. DuPuis is said to have gone to Canada, then California. Thaddeus died in 1898 and is buried in Brookside Cemetery, Dayton, with the spelling of his name Dupuy. The Muddy Valley claim was sold about 1868, but a sign still points to a road winding farther back into the hills, "Dupee Valley".

Durette, Benedict George   1808-1884
Durette and his wife, Louisa J. Warrell, were Huguenots from Louisiana, but in Oregon they espoused the Catholic faith. Durette had a store in Champoeg until his business was ruined by the flood of 1861; thereafter he farmed a place on the river just above Fairfield, a farm that is still in the hands of the family. Both Durette and his wife are buried in St. Louis.

Eldridge, Freeman Edward   1826-
The Eldridge home was the original Donation Land Claim of Joseph Gervais, on the east side of the Willamette River and facing Grand Island. Eldridge was a prosperous farmer and the first postmaster at Parkersville on the Pudding River, from 1852 to 1860. A long list of Eldridge entries appears in the St. Louis Register.

Ernst,

Farron, Dominique   1792-
Farron was a laborer on the Cowlitz Farm under George Roberts during the latter part of his service with the Hudson's Bay Company. He married Josephte Clalam, here given as Sohok, in 1839 at Fort Vancouver, where seven children are recorded. By 1850 he was living in Lewis County, Washington, with five children at home. He appears not to have remarried after the death of his wife Josephte; the final entry in Vancouver, Vol. I, records her death in 1844 at the age of thirty-one. The census list of 1850 does not entirely agree as to the children recorded in the Church Register.

Félix, Antoine (Palaquin, Palanquin) (I)   1805-1861 c.
Félix, also known as Antoine Félix Palaquin or Palanquin, came from Montréal as a canoeman, working out of Colvile after 1829. He retired to French Prairie in 1843, taking a claim near St. Louis, but seems to have died before receiving a patent on it. He had taken Marguerite des-Chaudières as wife "in the Flathead country", probably Colvile, about 1830. She died on the claim in 1848. Félix married Marie Archange Hubert, daughter of Joachim Hubert, the same year. On his land claim application he said he had married "Emelie" early in 1850; he was probably referring to Marie Archange, with a slight error in the date. Besides the four children listed in St. Paul, Emanuel and Guillaume are found in Vancouver, Vol. I, and Narcisse (1830 c.-1848) in St. Louis records.

Félix, Emmanuel (also called Palaquin)   1831-
The record of the children of Antoine Felix I continues in the St. Louis Register, although only two of the recorded six or seven seem to have survived.

Félix, Marguerite (Palaquin)   1841-
Marguerite Palaquin married Alexandre Plourde, son of François Plourde and Susanne Dubois, at St. Louis in 1863.

Feller (Filaire), Francis   1840-
Francis Feller came at the age of fifteen to Illinois from Lorraine, France, when that province was ceded to Germany. Two years later he came by way of the Isthmus of Panama to the Willamette Valley and worked as a hired farm hand or as a miner until he was able to buy land for himself. He developed a large acreage above Butteville for farming and stockraising but in later times mainly for hop growing. He married Rhuama Whitney in 1865; after her death he married Ida Garrett. Ten children in all were born of the two unions. A former railroad station and a road crossing his farmstead recall his name.

Fernandez, Guillaume François (Fernando, William Bailey)   1858-1925
"William Bailey, aged 67 years, one of the finest citizens of South Bend and Pacific County, passed away last Saturday at the family home in Alta Vista.
William Bailey was born in Chinook and spent his early years in Woodburn and Champoeg, Oregon. His father, Julien (José) Fernandez, was a native of Spain, who married a full blood Indian woman. At the age of four years young Bailey was adopted by Dr. (William) Bailey . . . prominent in the territorial history of Oregon." **Willapa Harbor Pilot**, Sept. 4, 1925.
His father seems to have fled the country after a stabbing affray over an Indian woman—probably William's mother—and the child was placed with the Bailey's, whom the mother had known at Champoeg before her marriage. William Fernandez Bailey was a right-of-way foreman for an electric company, fireman and mate on river steamers, and a homesteader. He married Lucy Ramsay. He is buried in the Cemetery at Bay City, Washington.

Fershweiler, John Baptiste and Peter
Almost all the records for the families of these two men are found in the St. Louis Parish Register.

Fitzgerald, Thomas   1820 c.-1860
Fitzgerald came from Cork, Ireland, and married Pamelia Eldridge in Lee County, Iowa, in 1844. She died in 1852, "aged 24", leaving four children, of whom two died young. In 1853 Fitzgerald married Mary O'Loughlin; three sons and one posthumous daughter are recorded. Fitzgerald himself died in 1860. His widow married Jacob Herschberger in 1863. Most of the Fitzgerald records are found in St. Louis records.

Fitzmaurice, Michael   1826-
Michael Fitzmaurice (sometimes Morris) came from Ireland to Baltimore, where he married Mary Ann Garvey, and continued his journey to Oregon. He took a claim in Polk County in 1853. The marriage ended in divorce in 1872, with the "minor children"—the number and names not given—going with their mother.

Flynn, Peter   1786-1873
Peter Flynn and his wife Mary . . . left many descendents, whose records are scattered through St. Louis, Gervais, Grand Ronde and McMinnville.

Foisy, Eulalie   1866-1932
Eulalie was the third daughter of Médard Foisy and Marie Anne Délard whose first husband was Louis Vendal. Eulalie married Eugene Malo and reared a family of nine in the village of Gervais, Oregon. The family lot is in the Catholic Cemetery at that place.

Foisy, Médard Godard   1816-1879
Medard Foisy was born in Québec and educated as a printer. He practiced his trade in the midwest, California and the Oregon country. In the last place, he married Marie Anne Délard and took up farming near Woodburn. The records of his numerous children are found in the St. Louis Register.

Forcier, Louis
Forcier was an early settler on the Prairie about whom little specific is known. He came from St. Hyacinthe, Canada, and by 1829 was listed as a canoeman at Fort Vancouver. He married a Chinook woman, Catherine Canaman, in 1839, having at that time children Louis, Olive and Dominique "by another woman now dead". Later were born to him and Catherine children Alexis, Rose, Gédéon, François (who died) and "a little girl of two years in 1847", who died also. "The wife of Forcier"—doubtless Catherine—died in 1847 at St. Paul.

Forcier, Olive   1834 c.-1863
Olive Forcier was the daughter of Louis Forcier and a "woman now dead". She married Jean
Gingras in 1845 and bore him several children. He died in 1856. Olive gave birth, apparently out
of wedlock, to Felicite in April, 1859, the father of the child being Charles Petit. Olive married
Frank Brouillard in 1861 and died in 1863. The child Felicite was placed with her grandfather,
Amable Petit, Sr., father of Charles.

Forcier, Rose   1840-1850
Rose Forcier died at St. Louis in 1850, "aged eleven".

Fortin
The name Fortin occurs often in the Roseburg Register and at Medical Lake, Washington.

Gagnon, Anne   1846-1874
Anne Gagnon married Pierre Bellique, Jr., in 1869, going with him to the canyons of Douglas
County to live. There she died at the birth of her fourth child. Her husband became a fisherman
at Woods, on the coast; his sister, Genevieve Gregoire, took Marie and Gilbert to rear; the eldest
child had died at six months.

Gagnon, Antoine   1843-1897
Antoine Gagnon, only recorded son of Luc Gagnon and Julie Gregoire, died at St. Louis in 1897.

Gagnon, Emerance   1833-
Emerance (sometimes written Florence), daughter of Luc Gagnon and Julie Gregoire, married
Hubert Petit in 1849. Their children Adelaide, Amable and Josephine are recorded in St. Louis.
Emerance divorced Petit "for cruel treatment, such as dragging her around by the hair". She
presently married Pierre Groslouis "of Umpqua" and the records of their five children are
scattered through St. Louis, Oregon City, Brooks and Roseburg.

Gagnon, Francois I   -1850 c.
Francois Gagnon I and his wife Angelique Marcellais were perhaps married before coming to
Oregon, as their older children are not recorded until the 1850's, when they are in their own
homes. Francois I went to California during the gold rush and died there at some time before
1852, when his widow married Edouard Bellanger. The entry for the baptism of his son Jean
Baptists is evidently in error as to the name of the mother.

Gagnon, Francois II
Francois Gagnon was the son of Francois Gagnon I, "who died in California", and Angelique
Marcellais. The name of young Francois appears only once in the St. Paul Register, at the
baptism of his daughter Florence, born "outside of marriage" to Marie Monique. He did not
marry the mother of the child, but Adelaide Plourde. The record of their family is contained in
the St. Louis Register until 1869, when it shifts to Walla Walla.

Gagnon, Jean Baptiste   1845-
The name of this child's mother is an obvious error by a new priest. Marguerite Desjarlais was not
the wife of Francois Gagnon, and she was already credited in a somewhat garbled account with a
girl baby the same month.

Gagnon, Joseph   -1849
The relationship amongst the Gagnon men, Luc, Joseph and Francois I is not known, but circumstances indicate they may have been brothers. For instance, Luc and Joseph each had a
daughter named Emerance, which would indicate a family name, both Joseph and Francois
went to the gold fields (and died there), and so on. Joseph married Marguerite Desjarlais; their
recorded children were Felicite (probably the "un-named girl" born in 1845 at St. Paul), Joseph
II and Emerance, who died after her father. Gagnon's widow married Jean Claude Bellanger,
then J. B. Rondeau.

Gagnon, Louis   1797-1861
The Hudson's Bay Record Society, Volume I, says that Louis Gagnon was engaged from St. Roch
as a middleman (canoe man) in 1820. He was at Fort Wedderburn on Lake Athabaska for the
winter of 1820-1821, where the officer in charge noted in his report, " . . . not fit for hard work,
but willing to do what he can." This may perhaps be the Louis Gagnon whose son was baptized
at St. Paul in 1851 at the age of eleven years. A Louis Gagnon, again probably the same man,

died April 5, 1861 at the age of eighty years. He would have been less old, however, if the date in the Hudson's Bay Record is correct.

Gagnon, Luc   1807-1872
"Natives of Canada   Requiescat in Pace" So read the stones of Luc Gagnon and his wife, Julie Gregoire, in the rear part of St. Louis Cemetery. The Gagnon claim lay on the Prairie north of St. Louis. The name Gagnon was well-known in the fur trade, appearing in numerous situations.

Gagnon, Marguerite   1835-
Marguerite Gagnon married Antoine Morais (Moret, Murray, Morin, Moreau) at St. Louis in 1856, but soon after the pair moved to Frenchtown, near Walla Walla, where ten or twelve children are recorded. The name is there spelled Morin, as a rule.

Gagnon, Marie Olive Dorilda   1856-
(Not given in St. Paul)
Dorilda Gagnon married Charles LeBrun in 1878 at St. Louis, where all her records may be found. A group picture of much appeal, taken during the 1890's, shows the four surviving daughters of Luc Gagnon and Julie Gervais, only Anne (Beleque) having died on the South Umpqua about 1875 and a baby sister, Sophie, at the age of two.

Galloway, Charles   1798-1884
Charles Galloway was born in Virginia and drifted westward in the common pattern that followed the Revolutionary War—to Illinois, Missouri, Wisconsin and eventually to Oregon, arriving in 1852 with a wife and eight children. He settled in Polk County where he and his wife, Mary Heaney, lived out their lives and died in the same year, 1884. Their son William and grandson Charles V. Galloway were both influential in civil affairs of the time and filled various offices in state government.

Garant, Augustin
Little is found on this man beyond the records of the Church. He married Lucie Cowlitz, and had children Pierre, Thomas, Louis-Marie-Francois, as well as an un-named infant and a daughter Zoe, both of whom died. See St. Paul, St. Louis and Oregon City index.

A newspaper report in the clipping file in the Oregon Historical Society states that T. J. Hubbard (Herbert) was shot and killed by Thomas Garrand "with a pistol" on April 12, 1874. Garrand was found guilty and sentenced to hang; the case was appealed, reversed and remanded. In a second trial Garrand was again found guilty. The outcome was not recorded.

Gardipe, Casimer   1826-
Various Gardipies with various spellings occur in Oregon history; the relationship between Casimer and the others, if any, is not known. Casimer was born in New York State and first appears in the record with his marriage to Genevieve St. Martin, widow of Pierre Belique, Sr., who had died in the California gold rush. Some time after 1862 the couple and their numerous children moved to the eastern part of Oregon, near Athena.

Gauthier, Pierre   1809-1867
Gautier, a Canadian, came to Oregon in Elijah White's party in 1842. Bancroft wrote of this plains crossing: "Before leaving Laramie the company was joined by F. X. Matthieu and half a dozen Canadians, who had been in the service of the fur company east of the mountains and were now going to settle in Oregon . . . Two of the Canadians were Peter Gautier and Paul Ojet (Auger)"
In 1845 he married Esther Dalcour, dit Champagne. The pair were the parents of eleven children, at least five of whom died in infancy: Catherine, Cecile, Joseph, Josephte, Jean Baptiste I, Pierre, Adolphe, Olive, Jean Baptiste II, and two un-named infants. These are chiefly recorded in St. Louis. As they were spaced with consistent regularity, one may be slightly puzzled by Esther's statement written in 1862 " . . . during absence of my husband the undivided half of my husband's land was sold at sheriff's sale". She asked that the remaining land be divided so that her half should have the homestead, or "I would be homeless with my children". A notation added in the Donation Land Claim records implies that the family was being cared for at the time by George LaRoque. Gauthier died in 1867.

Gay, George Kirby   1796-1882
A plaque on a low boulder beside the road fronting his home site on the river near the old landing

at Lincoln reads: "One fourth mile southeast lies the body of George Gay. Born 1796 in Gloucester, England. Died 1882. He built the first brick house west of the Rocky Mountains on his farm one fourth mile west of this spot. He was one of those patriots who, May 2, 1843, founded the Provisional Government at Champoeg." May, 1931. Gay was several times married, always to natives, "who were worth three white wives". He acquired considerable wealth from his cattle herds, but his boundless hospitality to all comers left him poor at his death. Numerous descendants remain today. A replica of his house, built from some of the original bricks which were burned on the farm, stands on the Newell House grounds at Champoeg.

Gay, John   1846-
John was the eldest son of George Gay and his wife Louise St. Claire, or so she was called later—see St. Louis Record, January 27, 1879. As Gay's wife was invariably "Louise", but called Chehalis, Wallis (Worless), Hare, and St. Claire, it is impossible to know whether this is all the same wife, or several. Apparently John and Marguerite Gervais, the mother of his children, had not been married in the Church, for in 1879 there is an entry in the St. Louis records of "Renewal of the consent of marriage, According to the Rites of the Church. John Gay and Marguerite Gervais". Some time later they separate, Marguerite marrying Ulysses Loron.

Gearin, Hugh Burns   1849-1909
Hugh Burns Gearin continued on the farm developed by his father John; it remains in family hands today. For many years he ran the Gearin's Ferry across the Willamette River to Newberg until the construction of a bridge in 1912 made the ferry obsolete. His wife, Mary Cecelia Murphy, outlived her husband by twenty years.

Gearin, John   1808-1893
John Gearin and his wife, whose name is not known, came from Ireland to Indiana in 1834. There his wife died, and in 1848 he married Ellen Burns, the widow of John Costello. She, at this time, had a twelve-year-old daughter, Ellen Costello, a seven-year-old daughter, Mary Ann, who died at the age of ten in Oregon, and three younger sons. Gearin came west in 1851 and developed a large land holding a few miles above Champoeg, the former Gardipe claim for which he paid $500. Two sons, John and Hugh Burns Gearin, were added to the family. Gearin's wife, Ellen Burns Costello, died in 1879.

Geelan, Patrick   1833-1916
Geelan's wife, Eliza Ady, widow of John Goodrich, had been educated in a Methodist school, but embraced the Catholic faith upon her marriage to Geelan. Until the last few years, the old one room Geelan schoolhouse remained on a hill overlooking Little Skookum Lake in the northwest corner of the Prairie.

Geer, Theodore Dwight   1843-1914
The "infidel" who married Philomene Matthieu in the church and was sternly rebuked by the priest (doubtless Father Malo, although the entry is unsigned) was the son of a staunch American pioneer, Joseph Cary Geer, and his first wife, Mary Johnson. The family claim was on the north side of the Willamette River, just across from Butteville. A small, neglected cemetery at the junction of Ladd Hill Road and River Road contain several Geer graves, but Theodore Dwight Geer is buried at Butteville.

Gendron, Edouard   1842-1869
Edouard was the son of Joseph Gendron and Louise Chinook. He married Victoire Vassal at Grand Ronde in 1861; their four children died in infancy, and Edouard himself died at the age of twenty seven. His widow Victoire married Jean Baptiste Bellique and later one Jeffries.

Gendron, Francois
The files on this man are very thin indeed. It is known that he married Marie (Marguerite) Walla Walla and had a son Dominique, born about 1835. Later children recorded at St. Paul include Magdeleine, Lucille, Joseph and Marie (twins), Henriette, and Francois, the last at St. Louis.

Gendron, Jean Baptiste   1846-1888
Jean Baptiste, son of Joseph Gendron and Louise Chinook, married about 1866 on the Grand Ronde Reserve in Polk County. Two sons were born, Charles and Joseph, of whom the latter died; the name of their mother is not known. Gendron married Lucy, a native, in 1875; she died two years later, "aged eighteen". He then married Julia, another native, in 1878. Five daughters

were recorded in the Grand Ronde Register, four of them dying in infancy. Jean Baptiste Gendron died on the reservation in 1888.

Gendron, Joseph (Jandro, etc.)

Joseph Gendron, one of Wyeth's men and later a freeman trapper, was the "convert" who prayed so effectively for supper at the Lee Mission at the Dalles, according to Meek (**River of the West**), reciting in French, which the missionaries did not understand, tales from the Arabian Nights! (1840) Later Chief Factor McLoughlin asked for a repeat performance, when he had heard of the prank, but was too much amused to hear it through. Gendron was paying taxes on a farm on French Prairie in 1844. He had children by three different wives, according to the Church records—Louise (1834) and Pierre (1837) by "another woman", Catherine I and II (1842 and 1844), Edouard (1841), Jean Baptiste (1846) by Louise Chinook, whom he had married in 1839, and Rose (1850) by "Pauly of The Dalles". Rose, Edouard and Jean Baptiste appear later on the rolls of the Grand Ronde Reserve, Polk County.

Gervais, David   1823-1853

David Gervais was the only known son of Joseph Gervais by his un-named Chinook wife. David married Marie Ann Toupin, daughter of Madame Dorion by her third husband. Four children are recorded whose names continue through the records of St. Paul, Roseburg and Grand Ronde. David died at St. Louis, "aged about 34", in 1853. His widow married Francois Robideau, and later George Gay II.

Gervais, Edouard   1836-after 1912

Edouard was a child of four when his mother Yiamust died, and he was reared by a stepmother, Angelique Chinook. He married Nancy Nehalem at the coast, where he lived to great old age, still remembered about Tillamook as a guide, a teller of stories, a master hand at clam bakes, and a general town favorite—"He always had a bunch of kids around him". All three of the younger sons of Joseph Gervais—Isaac, Xavier and Edouard—served in the Indian Wars; Edouard is buried with a military stone in the Legion Cemetery at Nehalem.

Gervais, Francaise (Francoise)   1832 c.-1842

Francaise may have been a twin to Francois Xavier, as their ages are very nearly the same. She died in St. Paul in 1842, "aged 10 years and some months".

Gervais, Francois Xavier   1832-1870 c.

"Zevia" Gervais was a volunteer in the Cayuse war of 1855-56. He married Marianne Despard at St. Louis in 1853. She was the widow of Joseph Rivet, and after Xavier's death, married Antoine (Dupate) McKay. His brother said of him in 1906, "My other brother was named Xavier Gervais, and he died about thirty years ago, aged about 38 or 40 years. He was married but whether his wife is alive I do not know. One son was born of the marriage, but I do not know if he is alive or dead. I have not heard of them for years." There had been an earlier wife, Marie Flathead, who died in 1851. There were at least four children, mostly recorded in St. Louis. Gervais is said to have drowned in the Calapooya River during high water.

Gervais, Isaac   1829-1908

Isaac Gervais, son of Joseph Gervais and Yiamust Coboway (Marguerite) gave the date of his birth as January 15, 1825, and the place as Fort Vancouver on his pension application for service in the Indian wars, his height five feet seven inches, "dark hair, dark eyes, dark complection". He had been baptized by Methodist Jason Lee in 1835: " . . . by the request of Mr. Gervais, baptized his son Isaac, who is sick and apparently near his end." Isaac recovered, however, served in the Indian wars, married Elizabeth Gingras, and lived out his life in Douglas County, where he was a well-known scout and guide.

Gervais, Jean Baptiste   1790-1870

Gervais was born in Canada, a brother to Joseph Gervais. He was one of the partners in the Rocky Mountain Fur Company, with Fitzpatrick, M. Sublette, Bridger and Fraeb in 1830. After the company sold out, Gervais seems to have operated as a freeman in the Rocky Mountains and Great Basin until he retired to a claim near Fairfield, on the Willamette River, in 1850. He became a citizen of the United States in 1850 and sold his claim to Millsaps in 1858. Nothing further is known of his life except that he died at St. Louis November 29, 1870.

His wife was Marie Lucier, daughter of Basile (in all likelihood), who died in 1850 "leaving five children". Of these, Celestine married Louis Lucier and died the same year, Euphrasie (Felicite) married Louis Labonte, Jr., and died two years later.

Gervais, Joseph I   1777-1861
One of the earliest and most influential settlers on French Prairie was Joseph Gervais, brother to Jean Baptiste Gervais of the Rocky Mountain Fur Company. Joseph was a buffalo hunter on the Great Plains when he joined the Hunt party of Astor's venture in 1810. After twenty years' employment in the North West and Hudson's Bay Companies as a free man, he took a claim opposite Grand Island in the Willamette below Fairfield. He was a leader in church and civic affairs, "a quiet person, and one very easy to get along with", wrote Roberts. He had numerous children by his three wives, some not recorded in the Church, but found in contemporary writings. Jason Lee mentioned the death of a child Mary, another was "very ill" when brought by her father to Fort Vancouver to a doctor, and Theodore, "born in Canada", who may or may not have been the son of the un-named Chinook mother. His second wife was Yiamust (Marguerite) Coboway, who died early in 1840 at St. Paul, and his third, married the same year, was Marie Angelique Chinook. Gervais lost his farm through mortgages and died at the home of David Mongraine in 1861. His name is one of the earliest twelve settlers listed on the bronze plaque at the Old Cemetery at St. Paul, where he is buried.

Gervais, Joseph (son of David)   1842-1865
Joseph, son of David Gervais and Marie Ann Toupin, died at St. Louis in 1865.

Gervais, Julie   1820 c.-1845
Julie was the daughter of the un-named Chinook mother and Joseph Gervais. She married a neighbor, Francois Xavier Laderoute, and died at the age of twenty-five, leaving four children.

Gervais, Theodore, Sr.   1829-1902
Theodore Gervais, relationship to Joseph uncertain, was born in Canada in 1829. He settled a claim on the Prairie in 1850 and the same year married Angele Lafantasie, the widow of Joseph Bourjeau, Sr. She died following the birth of their tenth child in 1867. All but two of the other children died before their father, who died in 1902 and was buried in Salem.

Giguere, Helie (Gyere, Felix)   1815 c.-1855
Giguere settled on a French Prairie claim in 1849 and became a citizen in 1851, but died four years later at the age of "about forty". He married Victoire Cornoyer, daughter of Joseph. His recorded children (St. Louis) were Sophie (1847), Therese (-----), Chloris (Clarisse) (1852), who died at the age of seventeen months, and Pierre (1854). Giguere died in 1855 at St. Louis.

Gill, Simeon (Simon)   1823-
Simon Gill first married Marie Chehalis at Vancouver in 1845. A son Simon II was born the same year, and his wife died the next. In 1849 he married a metisse, Marie Pepin, whose mother was a woman of an Eastern Canada tribe. In one place Gill was called a quarter-blood. By 1850 he was listed in the census of Lewis County, a farmer, with wife Marie (Pepin) and son Simon.

Gingras, Angele   1835-
Angele, daughter of Jean Gingras I and Charlotte Okanagan, was born at Fort Okanagan. In May 1848, at the age of thirteen, she married Hypolite Brouillet, widower of Elizabeth Finlay. Brouillet died within the year in the gold fields, and Angele married Cyrille Bertrand in 1849. Several children were born of this union.

Gingras, Calliste   1854-
"Collis" Gingras was the son of Jean Gingras I and his second wife, Olive Forcier. After the death of his mother, the nine-year-old boy went to Douglas County where he grew up. He married Josephine Picard at Roseburg; several children are recorded there.

Gingras, Esther   1845-1845
Esther Gingras, recorded in St. Louis, was seven months old at her death, recorded in St. Paul.

Gingras, Jean (I)   1802-1856
"A handy man," Governor Simpson recorded in 1828, "more interested for the service in the absence than before his superiors." All Gingras's years of service were spent at inland posts between the Rockies and the Cascades. In 1841 he rose to the position of post Master at Fort Okanogan. Within a few years he retired to French Prairie, taking a claim on the river west of the Mission of St. Paul, embracing a part of Horseshoe Lake. After the death of his wife, Charlotte Okanogan, he married Olive Forcier. He is buried in the Old Cemetery at St. Paul, where no markers remain.

The records of his children, Jean (II) and Angele, as well as others who came later, continue through St. Paul, St. Louis and Roseburg registers.

Gingras Jean II   1831-
Jean Gingras II, married Elizabeth (Betsy) Finlay in 1850 at St. Louis. A son Gedeon is recorded in St. Louis, a son Jean III, who died at two months, at St. Paul, and a daughter, Sophie Jean (?) at St. Rose Mission (Frenchtown, near Walla Walla) in 1855, where Gingras may have been living by that time. He does not appear again.

Gingras, Joseph   1829-
Joseph was the eldest son of Jean Gingras I and Charlotte Okanagan. He married Marianne Bastien in 1848, "daughter of Bastien, living in Canada, and Louise Saste". She was fifteen years old, and a pupil in the Methodist Mission School. The marriage was recorded in St. Louis, as was also the birth of two daughters, Esther and Philomene, while a third daughter, Catherine, was recorded in St. Paul.

Gingras, Louis   1842-
Louis Gingras, born in 1842 to Charlotte Okanagan, may have died, as a son Louis Xavier was born to Gingras's second wife, Olive Forcier, in 1846 at St. Louis.

Gingras, Marguerite   1837-1846
Marguerite Gingras died at the age of nine at St. Paul.

Gingras, Narcisse   1833-
Narcisse, the third son of Jean Gingras I and Charlotte Okanagan, married Louise Okanagan; two children, Marcelline and Francois Xavier were born and Louise Okanagan died. Gingras then married Julie Montour in 1867; six months later she too died. Like others of his family, he moved to Douglas County where the Roseburg records pick him up with his marriage to Cecile Dumont and the birth of numerous children.

Glorieux, Alphonse J.   -1917
Father Glorieux was a Belgian priest, ordained in 1867. He came to Idaho in 1885, built up the Church in that state and became Bishop of Idaho.

Gobin, Angelique   1845-1873
Angelique (Angelica) Gobin died at St. Louis in 1873, "aged 29", apparently unmarried.

Gobin, Antoine
Antoine Gobin would seem to have been the cousin mentioned by Jean Baptiste Gobin I in 1886 as having come west earlier than he and having died "some years since". Antoine appears mainly at Vancouver, where a son Jean Baptiste was born to Julie Okanagan in 1838; in 1850 and 1852 sons Joseph and Edouard were born to Angelle "at the mouth of the Cowlitz River". The son, Jean Baptiste, is the one who married Pierre (I) Depot's widow Lisette (Elizabeth) at St. Louis in 1868; the other Jean Baptiste II, son of Jean Baptiste I, had died in 1858, "aged 21".

Gobin, Jean Baptiste I   1805-after 1886
Two early Gobin cousins, Jean Baptiste I and Antoine, are found in Vancouver, St. Louis and St. Paul. The "Gobain" in Vancouver is the same as J. B. Gobin "of Grand Maska". In old age he said that he had come west in 1825 in a large overland Hudson's Bay Company brigade by much the same route as that of Louis and Clark, and that he had worked as builder and trapper for fifteen years. In 1840 he retired to a claim on French Prairie. He had two sons, Jean Baptiste II (1837) and Toussaint (1835) by an un-named "savage woman". In 1841 he married Marguerite Vernier, a daughter of Madam Dorion by her second husband. To them were born Francois Xavier (1842), Angelique (1845), Julie (1849), Isabelle (1851), Antoine (born and died in 1854) and Joseph (1856). Marguerite Vernier died at St. Louis in 1858. Gobin, in 1863, married Therese Dubrueil in a civil marriage, but "who, having been married by a justice of the peace, have come, repentant of their fault to implore the benediction of the Church", wrote Father Delorme reprovingly. Gobin's third set of children were Antoine Arsene (1864-1866), Amadee Nazaire (1866-1870), Josephine (1868-1884)? and Mclacie Jeanne (1869). The doughty old father claimed to have had three wives and eleven children, though the above account numbers twelve. His wives are all accounted for. He outlived all except three children, or so he claimed.

Gobin, Francois Xavier   1842-
Francois Xavier was the eldest son of Marguerite Vernier Gobin, and a grandson of Madame

Dorion. The whole Gobin family lived near St. Louis, where Francois Xavier married Cecile Lafantasie in 1864 and where three children were recorded.

Gobin, Jean Baptiste II 1837-1858
Jean Baptiste II, baptized at Fort Vancouver in 1838, son of Jean Baptiste Gobin I and a native mother whose name is not given, died at the age of 21 at St. Louis, where the family was then living.

Godin, Jean Baptiste -before 1849
The wife "Louise Snake", mother of Madeleine Godin in 1846, would seem to have been the same woman as "Julie, widow of Godin", who is recorded as marrying Charles Beauchemin in the California gold fields in 1849 (September 7), St. Louis Register.

Goemaere, Melanie (Sister Renilde) 1819 c.-1849
Melanie was a member of the second group of Sisters of Notre Dame du Namur that came from Belgium to the mission at St. Paul, called Sainte Marie de Willamette. Always frail, she succumbed to the stern regime of teaching under primitive conditions. She died in Oregon City, but was buried at St. Paul "in the garden of the Sisters". In 1855 her body was transferred to burial within the church. Her name is included with those of the later Sisters of the Holy Names on a common monument at the site of the former mortuary chapel in St. Paul's Cemetery.

Goodrich (Gadritche, Gaudritche) -1831 c.
Goodrich, given name not known, but probably either Silas or John, was one of the American followers that so plagued Peter Skeen Ogden in the Snake River country in the late 1820's. "Two American trappers, Goodrich and Johnson, had joined Ogden the preceding fall." (1827) Disputes over debts to other companies, liquor and so on arose and the pair left. Later they returned to Ogden's company and the episode ended. On the return of the brigade Ogden picked up a wounded Frenchman and an Indian woman carrying a small baby, all near starvation. They had escaped from a Blackfoot massacre beyond the Rockies and were trying to reach Vancouver or some other Hudson's Bay post. Goodrich took the woman, whom he named Nancy, as his wife. He was drowned a year or two later at The Dalles, and was buried on the bench above the town, under an oak tree. His daughter Susanne married Pierre Pepin, dit La-Chance; his widow Nancy married Jean Baptiste Dobin. Dobin died in the gold fields in 1849 and his wife, who had accompanied him, died at St. Paul shortly after her return in 1850.

Goodrich, Susanne 1830 c.-1912
Susanne was the daughter of Nancy of the Dalles and Goodrich; she was but a few days old when her father was drowned. Until her marriage, Susanne lived at Fort Vancouver, where she was lamed for life by a fall from the high porch of Dr. McLoughlin's house while playing with other children there. However she married Pierre Pepin I (LaChance) and reared a large family, every one of whom cherished her memory tenderly. Her stone in the Grand Ronde (Polk County) Cemetery gives her birth date as 1816, an obvious but understandable error in the absence of written family records.

Goyet, Jean Baptiste
Several Goyets appear in the West during the mid-1800's and fade out without much being learned of any of them. One Francois Goyet, "a bachelor" died at St. Louis in 1868, a Francois Xavier married Anna Deloney at St. Paul in 1888, a Joseph Goyette and his wife Perpetua Mercier, "both Canadians", had twin sons Alphonsus Zuisphile and Edmund Stephen, born in Portland in 1860, but only of Jean Baptiste Goyet do we learn his parentage, so that tracing relationships is an idle exercise. Jean Baptiste was at Fort Vancouver as early as 1841. He married an Iroquois-Walla Walla girl, Louise Tawakon, and through his daughter LaRose became the progenitor of a long line of Greer descendants in the West.

Grand Dalles
The Grand Dalles or Long Narrows was the turbulent stretch of water where the Columbia cuts a gorge through the Cascade Mountains at the site of the present city of The Dalles. Farther upstream a few miles were the Little Dalles, or Little Narrows. Both were the scene of many boating tragedies; both are now drowned under quiet pools formed by dams.

Grant, Richard 1794-1862
Grant was a well-known trader and employe of the Hudson's Bay Company, of Scottish and

French ancestry. His first wife, Marie Ann Berland, died in Montreal in 1834. His second wife was Helene McDonald, widow of William Kitson. Grant retired from the service to a cattle ranch in the Beaverhaed region of Montana—"a Falstaff of a man with gray head and beard, portly frame and jovial dignity". Both he and his daughter Helene, aged sixteen, died in a tepee on Mill Creek, near Walla Walla, while returning from The Dalles with a year's supply of provisions for the ranch. Later his grave (possibly that of his daughter as well) was moved to Mountain View Cemetery, Walla Walla, marked in 1923 with a simple stone, "Richard Grant, Chief Trader, H. B. Co."

Gravelle, Gedeon   1827-1883
On his land grant claim, Gravelle said that he had been born in France in 1827. It would seem that his parents, Vincent Gravelle and Adelaide Bellaire, had come to Canada while Gedeon was still young. He came to Oregon before 1845, and married Nancy Pin in 1847, settled a claim on the Prairie in 1850, and became a citizen the next year. He left the Willamette Valley, however, as did many other French Canadians, under the press of American immigration, and took up new land near Walla Walla. Gravelle's claim lay at the eastern edge of Frenchtown, nearest to the Whitman Mission, now abandoned. He and Nancy and their son Gedeon are buried in the old Frenchtown Cemetery, marked only by a cross and a common stone shaft.

Gray, Joseph   1786-1846
Gray was an Iroquois from St. Regis, who had been in the employ of the Company for many years. He was with Work on the Snake River in 1824, with Barnston at Fort Walla Walla, and employed in bringing down horses and doing like errands of the trade. He married Catherine Cayuse in 1841, but at the time of his death his widow was called Marie Walla Walla. They may have been one and the same.

Gregoire, Antoine (Indian)   1825-
Indians often assumed the name of the man they worked for, or in whose homes they lived. Antoine, Indian, is not to be confused with Antoine Gregoire, son of Etienne Gregoire II and Marguerite Souchoube, who was older by a few years. The Indian Antoine is recorded as having a son, Antoine, by "Betzi" in 1850. The son died at the age of twenty-eight. Etienne Gregoire, in dividing his estate in his will, specified "take care of Antoine". As Gregoire died in 1867, his injunction might have referred to either father or son Antoine, Indian.

Gregoire, Antoine   1823-
Antoine, Gregoire, son of Etienne Gregoire I and Marguerite Souchauabe, should not be confused with Antoine Gregoire, Indian; both were about the same age and both appear mainly in the St. Louis records. The above Antoine married Therese Ouvre in 1849; several children are recorded.

Gregoire, Etienne I   1793-1867
Son of an earlier Gregoire of the same name, Etienne I came west about 1839. He took a claim north of St. Louis in 1842. His Kamloops wife Marguerite was born about 1790 and died in 1860. Both are buried at St. Louis under a good stone marker, a somewhat rare circumstance with the earliest settlers on French Prairie. Their children, so far as recorded, were Julie (Luc Gagnon), Sophie (William Porteus, Firmen LeBrun), Antoine (Therese Ouvre), Felix (Genevieve Belique) and Simon Etienne (Victoire McMillan).

Gregoire, Etienne (II)   1834-1892
Etienne Gregoire the Younger, usually called Simon, lived near St. Louis, where the record of his family continues. He married Victoire McMillan, widow of Joseph McLoughlin, and had two recorded children, David and Zenaide. He lost an arm in a sawmill accident, and then his life under the wheels of a train, being handicapped.

Gregoire, Felix   1834 c.-1906
Felix was the son of Etienne Gregoire and Marguerite Kamloops. He and his wife Genevieve Bellique had a prosperous farm south of St. Paul, and having no children of their own, gave a home to Marie and Gilbert, the motherless children of her brother Pierre II, and took Josephine, little daughter of her brother Cyprien, "for company for Marie". After Genevieve's death, Felix married a Wilquet, but died within a few years. He and his first wife are buried at St. Louis and their graves well marked. The date of his birth there is given as 1830.

Gregoire, Julie   1819 c.-1877
Julie Gregoire, wife of Etienne Gregoire II, died at St. Louis in 1877. The date on her stone in the

cemetery there is evidently the stonecutter's error, as 1841 is the date of her marriage to Luc Gagnon, not the date of her birth.

Gregoire, Sophie   1828-1900
Sophie Gregoire married William Porteous in Oregon City in 1842. He was a clerk in the Hudson's Bay Company there, but took a land claim on the Prairie. Sophie remained on the claim when he went to California in the gold rush; he died "at Sawren's Bar" in September of 1849. In 1861 Sophie married Firmin LeBrun. No children were born of either marriage.

Grenier, Marie Ann   1829 c.-1850
Marie Ann Grenier, the first wife of Gedeon Senecal, was the daughter of Pierre Grenier, drowned in 1830 when Marie was an infant. One of the witnesses at her marriage was her step-father, the intrepid Joseph Cournoille. Marie died a few months after the birth of her son Pierre.

Grenier, Pierre   -1830
Grenier was a trapper and boatman, usually with Peter Skene Ogden on the Snake River. Re-turning from the fifth of these trips, Grenier and eight others were drowned when their "crazy boat" was shattered in a whirlpool at The Dalles. Ogden wrote, in part, of that tragedy: "The vortex was rapidly forming, and the air was filled with a confused murmur, high above which might be heard the hoarse voice of the bowman, shouting, "Ramez, ramez, ou nous sommes pais!" . . . The boat glided, at first slowly, into the whirling vortex, its prow rising fearfully as the pitiless waters hurried it round with increasing velocity . . . The spot where the boat had disappeared no longer offered any mark . . . here and there a struggling victim . . . one by one they disappeared." Pierre left one child, Marie Anne, an infant of one year, and his widow, Therese Spokane. She later married Joseph Cournoille.

Groslouis, Charles I   -before 1841
Charles Groslouis was an engage from Canada. He was with Ogden in the Snake River Country during 1824-5-6; possibly he was one of the "freemen" hired. His wife is listed merely as "Flat-head" or Pend d'Oreille. Both were deceased before July 21, 1841, when their son Joseph was baptized. Their children, born between 1821 and 1832, were Ursula, Henriette, Joseph, Pierre, Jean Baptiste (John) and Charles II. At least two of the boys, Pierre and John, seem to have been in school at St. Paul following the death of their parents, both frequent witnesses who signed at baptisms, marriages and deaths. John served in the Cayuse war of 1847-48 in Company D, 7th, First Regiment of Oregon Riflemen. He was also listed on the Census of 1850 in Marion County. "Two Groslouis brothers, half-breeds" are often mentioned in connection with the discovery of gold at Randolph on the Southern Oregon coast and with "lost treasures" of the early 1850's. One of the brothers was probably Pierre, as he appears later in the church records at Roseburg. Ursula married Francois St. Pierre at Vancouver in 1838, dying two years later. Henriette died at the age of eighteen at Vancouver, 1844.

Groslouis, Charles II   1832 c.
Groslouis, Pierre   1827 c.-
"Two Groslouis brothers, half-breeds" are believed to have been the discoverers of the rich gold mines at Randolph on the Oregon coast in the 1840's. A mountain in that region still bears their name. They sold their rights to McNamara for a large sum, and although they buried part of their heavy riches along the trail and were never able to find it again, they were nevertheless wealthy. They went to France to visit relatives, the story goes, and while touring, Charles died in England. Pierre returned to Oregon, where he became the second husband of Emerance Gag-non. Several children are recorded in Douglas County, where the family lived.

Guilbeau, Hilaire   -1849
Hilaire Guilbeau was a middleman in the employ of the Hudson's Bay Company; he was one of those saved in the disaster at The Dalles des Morts with the brigade bringing Fathers Blanchet and Demers to the West in 1838. From 1847 to 1848, at least, he was a laborer at the Cowlitz Farm belonging to the Company. Roberts, manager of the Farm, noted in his journal of September 6, 1847, "Carrier pulling down and carters removing Guilbeaus old house to below the hill where it is to be set up again to answer for a stable this winter". Guilbeau married Louise Walla Walla in 1842, at which time four children, names not given, were recorded. He died June 26, 1849, and was buried at St. Paul. The Francois Gilbeau, aged four, who died at St. Paul on November 8, 1851, was probably his son, for Paul Guilbeau's son Francois was much older.

Guilbeau, Paul (Francois ?) 1800-1849 c.
Paul Guilbeau was a boatman employed by the Hudson's Bay Company, coming from L'Assomption, Quebec. In 1831 he was sent from Fort Walla Walla to join Work's Snake River Country brigade. He had taken as wife Catherine ("Katy") Cayuse, who bore him six children and died in 1848. Guilbeau seems to have been a particular friend of Thomas Tawakon, Iroquois; he was a witness at his death "at the house of Joseph McLoughlin" on the Yamhill (the families were neighbors), and married Tawakon's widow, Francoise Cayuse. Within a year he himself died, possibly in the gold fields, as many did, unrecorded. His widow married Laurent Sauve. Although Guilbeau is listed as proprietor, that is, landowner, at St. Paul, he did not live to patent his claim under the Donation Land Laws. The Francois who died at St. Louis in 1855, "aged twenty-two" was possibly his son, although the father is given as Francois also in the record.

Hare (Worles, Cawchattine)
The name of a tribe living to the west and northwest of Great Bear Lake in Canada. Louise Hare (Worlis) was a wife of George Gay.

Herbert, Thomas 1832-1874
The name of Thomas Herbert is often confused with that of Thomas Jefferson Hubbard, no doubt due to mispronounciation alone. His stone in the St. Paul Cemetery has the correct spelling as well as dates that show him to have been a much younger man than Hubbard. A family photograph is that of a smooth faced, sad eyed young man with a drooping moustache in the fashion of the 1870's. He married Genevieve Longtain in 1858; he was killed by Thomas Garrand in a brawl in 1874. Two years later his widow had his body transferred—"translated", in the notation of the priest—from the old cemetery to the new at St. Paul. She was buried beside him many years later, her second husband, Dan McCann, having been buried in Ireland.

Holy names of Jesus and Mary, Sisters of
In 1861 the Catholic school vacated by the Sisters of Notre Dame du Namur 8 years before was reopened by the Sisters of the Holy Names. They used the same building, which had stood idle, gradually enlarging and improving it. The society still maintains a convent and an elementary school in the parish.

Horagan, Patrick Rowland 1805-1847
An American settler of Irish descent, Rowland came from Montgomery County, North Carolina, to settle finally on a claim in 1845, although he had been in the West some years earlier. His name was written as German, Germain, Patrick, and Paddy, with the surname of Rowland and Horagan or Horrigan being used interchangeably. His death in 1847 brought the item in the **Oregon Spectator:** "The first death from that cause (intoxication) in Oregon, and . . . (let it be) . . . a warning to others." His burial record is equally stark: "February, 1847, has been buried, outside the cemetery and without the presence of a priest, at the age of the woods opposite the Church of St. Paul." (Patrick Rawlind)
Of his children by various native women, "Little Patrick" died three weeks after his father's death, and his daughter Adele grew up to marry Jean Baptiste Jeaudoin and die in childbirth a year later; his other children included David, Catherine, Melanie and Madeleine.

Horan, Michael 1812 c.-
Michael was one of many Irish immigrants that came to America in the late 1840's and early 1850's, following the "potato famine" in their homeland. Horan settled a claim in Yamhill County in 1851. In 1854 he married Catherine Cason, the widow of James Long, who had drowned at Oregon City the previous winter.

Howard, John (Hord)
Howard, Irishman, came up from California with Ewing Young in 1834. He was simultaneously farmer, carpenter and tavern keeper under the locust trees at Champoeg; "Ruth Rover", in **The Grains,** particularly excoriated him as an evil influence. He voted with the Americans at the Provisional Government meeting in 1843. His first wife was Marie Lizette Desportes (Dupate McKay), whom he married in 1839 in the Catholic Church, after an earlier marriage performed by the Methodist Daniel Lee in 1837. After her death less than three years later, he married Catherine Longtain. Three children were recorded before 1849. Little is known about Howard's later life. He was said to be still living in 1858, place unknown; the birth of Catherine, "illegitimate daughter of Catherine Lontain" on March 14, 1855, at St. Paul, raises the question of what had become of Howard.

Hu, Dominique (Ha, Hoe, Hae, Hus)

Hu is difficult to place with certainty. He is mentioned as "a Canadian now deceased" in 1841, who had married a Pend O'Reille woman. A daughter Catherine, born about 1827, married J. B. Ducharme in 1841. At the birth of a daughter Marie in 1843, Catherine was called Paul, not Hu. (It was not unusual to identify children by their fathers' given names in the case of duplicate last names, such as brothers.) Dominique Hoe may well have been a brother to Paul Ha.

Joseph Hae, along with Isaac Ogden, Alex Michel, Joseph Gary and Waccom Umphreville, with two or three small boats, rescued all those marooned in the Prairie region by the great flood of 1861. Joseph was quite surely the son of either Paul or Dominique.

Hubbard, Thomas Jefferson   1803-1877

Thomas Jefferson Hubbard was a little uncertain about his birthplace but "thought" it was New York or Connecticut. He joined Nathaniel Wyeth's second expedition across the plains in 1834, a scheme to establish a fur post and compete with the Hudson's Bay Company trade. The plan failed, and some of the men, including Hubbard, remained in the West to become permanent settlers. He killed a fellow employe in a dispute over a girl on Sauve Island, where Wyeth had built his post. Hubbard was "white and distraught, pacing the beach the next morning", said one report, but he was exonerated by an impromptu jury, there being no organized law at the time, on the grounds of self defense. The girl has not been identified as the same one appearing in Jason Lee's brief record of marriages:

Monday 3d April 1837

Mr. T. J. Hubbard was married to Miss Mary Sommata (St. Martin) at the house of Mr. Billeck Willamette settlement by Jason Lee.

They are not known to have had any children, although Elijah White's census of 1842 lists "one child". Years later they took 4-year-old Felicite Comartin to raise, and "Auntie Hubbard" became a household word in the Birch Creek area, near Pendleton, to which they had moved in 1857. Hubbard died at Birch Creek on the Umatilla Reservation in 1877. His widow Marie outlived him by almost thirty years; she is buried on the Narcisse Cornoyer lot in the Catholic Cemetery in Walla Walla.

Hubert, Archange   1835-

Marie Archange Hubert married Antoine Felix, (Palaquin), a widower much older than she in 1848 at St. Louis.

Hubert, Isabelle   1833 c.-1856

"On February 2, 1846, he (Jean Baptiste Jeaudoin) married Isabelle Hubert at the Mission of the Willamette. She was the eldest daughter of Joachim Hubert and Josephte, an Indian woman. She was born about 1833 . . . They settled down to join the group of young married people including many of their long-time associates and friends . . . The Marion County Census for 1850 records show Jean Baptiste and Isabelle Jeaudom, which is another of the many variations found for the name Jeaudoin. Married four years, having given birth to three children, they are alone. This four year period no doubt brought a life-time of heartache for this young couple with the death of "Grandpa" Charles Jeaudoin and the three young daughters." (Betty J. Jeaudoin, "Jeaudoin Family History", MS, 1962)

Isabelle Hubert married Jean Baptiste Jeaudoin at St. Paul. Of their seven children born in quick succession, only two survived—Charles Jean Baptiste and Joseph.

Hubert, Joachim   1788 c.-1873

This is the "Zuwasha Ubair" that Meek entered on the tax rolls of 1844; the name probably sounded like that to the non-French Meek. Hubert was employed by the Hudson's Bay Company at Fort Colville during the 1830's, three of his children being baptized there when the priests went through on their way to the Willamette Valley in 1838. A few years earlier Hubert had married, fur trade fashion, Josephte Chaudiere. She had borne a daughter, also Josephte or Josette, to John Clarke, an irascible Chief Factor who cast her off; she then bore Jean Baptiste to "old Jean Boucher, an honest man". To Hubert she bore seven more children between 1828 and 1844, two of them named Joseph—a common custom in case the elder had died. Hubert spent forty years in all at Fort Colville before retiring to the Prairie at last.

Since there is some confusion on the scattered records of the various sets of Josephte Chaudiere's children, they are here listed to the best of my research. Josephte (Josette), whose father was John Clarke but who went by the name of her step-father, Boucher; Jean Baptiste (1819), son of "Old Jean Boucher"; Lizette (1826), Andre (1826), Joseph I (1831), Isabelle or Elizabeth (1833), Archange (1835), Adele (1841), Joseph II (1842), and Louis (1844).

Hughes, Andrew
The Hughes-Connor land is part of the St. Francis Xavier claim taken up by the Jesuits as a Provisional Land Claim in 1845. It was recorded in Oregon City under the names of Fathers Accolti and DeVos and Brothers Specht, Claessens and Huysbrecht. Claesenns was a master carpenter, Specht a skilled blacksmith; the first building they put up was a long log shop on the shore of Lake Ignatius, now Connor's Lake. After the gold rush put an end to the Jesuit mission, much of the land passed into the hands of Irish settlers.

Humpherville, Canote   1788-1842
The image of Canote Humpherville has passed into what might be called legend. He was said to be a native, or more probably a metis (for Thomas Humpherville, for one, left numerous mixed-blood offspring in eastern Canada), who joined the North West Company in 1811 or 1813. He was stationed at Fort Colville in 1831-39, possibly longer. His first wife was Pauline Sinpoil, by whom he had three recorded children; after her death he married Marguerite (Marie) Michina, who bore seven or eight children. In 1813 Canote was a canoeman at Fort George, and in May, 1814, steersman of Canoe Number One in the Montreal Express. The Hudson's Bay Company records him as having been drowned in 1842: "One of the boats (in the brigade of Ogden and Manson) was swamped in the Dalles above Okanogan and five men were unfortunately drowned: Canote Umphreville, the Columbia guide, Pierre Martineau, David Flett, Louison Boucher, Andre Areuhoniante. The guide, Umphreville, was a good, faithful servant of 31 years standing in the Columbia." His widow and five small children went to live with her stepson, Pierre (Wakan) Humphreville on French Prairie.

Humpherville, Catherine   1805-1886
Catherine was born at York Factory on Hudson Bay to Thomas Humpherville and his native (or Metisse) wife Anne. She married Pierre Pambrun there, and progressed westward with him from fort to fort over the years. After his death in 1842, she lived at Fort Vancouver, doing fine needle-work to support and educate her children. When they were well along, she went to Oregon City to live with her eldest daughter, Maria, who had married Dr. Forbes Barclay. Her last years were spent with her third daughter, Harriet Harger, at West Chehalem, near Newberg, where she is buried.
"Catherine smoked a pipe, as many pioneer women did. Pierre wanted her to give it up, but she couldn't seem to do so. He made a trip to England, and when he came back he brought a pair of diamond ear-rings. 'These are for you', he said 'if you will give up smoking.' She tried, but the habit was too strong, and the ear-rings were laid aside. After his death they disappeared. The family accused no one, but—so many going in and out at a time like that—. It's just a little family recollection." (Theresa Truchot, 1870)

Humpherville, Felicite   1840-
Felicite was the youngest child of Canote Humpherville and of Marguerite Michina, not Pauline Sinpoil, as might be inferred from her baptismal entry. Marguerite was possibly a Sinpoil as well. (In the St. Louis records she is given as Coeur d'Alene.)

Humpherville, Gregoire   1825-
By 1858 Gregoire had married Isabelle Thomas and was living at St. Louis. A daughter Josette was recorded in that year.

Humpherville, Isabelle   1822 c.-1852
Isabelle, daughter of Canote Humpherville and Pauline Sinpoil married Charles Lafantasie, no record found. Her children were Marie, born and died in 1842; Cecile, born in 1843; Francois, 1845 to 1879; Bibianne, born in 1847 and died a year later; Thomas born in 1849; and Flore, born and died in 1851. Isabelle herself died August 17, 1852, "aged 35", and was buried in the Old St. Louis Cemetery. Her two surviving children were taken into the home of her unmarried brother Pierre (Waccom, Wakan) who was sheltering also their step-mother Marie Machina and five younger half-brothers and sisters.

Humpherville, Josephte   1836-1847
Josephte died at the age of eleven.

Humpherville, Louis   1838-1875
Louis died at St. Paul on May 1, 1875, "aged about 40".

Humpherville, Louise
Louise married Adolphe Chamberlaine, widower of Julienne Watiece, and was the mother of six recorded children.

Humpherville, Louise Canote (Lizette) 1810 c.-1849
Louise was probably the sister of Canote Humpherville. She married Pierre Martineau, whose career closely paralleled that of Canote; both were drowned in 1842 in the same accident. Louise married George Montour and died in 1849 at St. Louis.

Humpherville, Marie Machina
No record of the marriage of Canote Humpherville and his second wife, Marie Machine, has been found, but the baptisms of their five children, the eldest born 1832, appear in the Vancouver Register. After her husband's death in 1842, Marie and the children were sheltered in the home of her step-son Pierre "Waccom" Humphreville on his claim near Waconda. Her later history is not known.

Humpherville, Nancy 1834-1869
Nancy Humpherville married Louis Bellomo in 1858. Their surviving children were Joseph (1866) and Gabrielle (1864), three little girls all having died in the summer of 1863 and a last child, along with the mother, in March, 1869.

Humpherville, Pierre (Wakan) 1817-
Pierre, born in British Columbia, was the eldest recorded son of Canote Humpherville and Pauline Sinpoil, once further identified as "brother to Nancy". After the Donation Land Act of 1850, he tried unsuccessfully to get title to his claim south of St. Louis. He was by this time head of the Humpherville-Martineau families, whose fathers had been drowned in the same accident on the Columbia in 1841. Father Blanchet interceded for him in the land question, writing to the Surveyor General, in part: "I am glad to hear that he never sold his right, that he then be able to keep his claim, because he is and is known by all to be a good, sober, industrious and laborious man, single, 36 years old, supporting since 12 years—a good religious mother, widow from that time; 3 brothers, 2 sisters, by his labours and exertions, besides 2 other orphans of his late sister; altogether 7 orphans and a dear mother. Such is the man called Wakan alias Umphreville. He is certainly deserved, if no favors, at least to enjoy his right in full."
The **Oregon City Argus**, at the time of the 1861 winter flood, reported that "Waccom Umphreville rescued 30 persons between Champoeg and Fairfield, taking fifteen of them from one house, to which they had fled for refuge.

Humpherville, Susanne, Marie Ann 1792-1846
Nowhere is Susanne's father named more specifically than as "Mr. Humphreville", indicating that he was an officer in the Company. It is a safe guess that he may have been Thomas (or his father) at Fort York at the beginning of the nineteenth century. Susanne married Nicholas Montour in 1839 at Vancouver and became the mother of numerous children.

Iroquois, Ignace
Several Iroquois called Ignace appear, but unless another name is added, it seems quite impossible to differentiate them or to trace relationships.
One Ignace was baptized "in danger of death" at St. Paul in 1840, but he seems to have recovered and married Helene Chinook. His daughter Josephine died at the age of six months in 1844 and his wife Helene three months later.

Ignace, Jean Baptiste Shohohanni (Iroquois) 1820-after 1900
Shohohanni was mixed blood Indian, son of the "late" Ignace Iroquois and a Flathead woman. He was born at Missoula in 1820 according to his own statement on his Indian War Pension application in 1895, written "from the foot of Flathead Lake", wherein he described himself as five feet eight inches in height, with black eyes and dark complection, a packer and teamster. He married Marie Pen d'Oreille, widow of J. B. Lajoie, in 1847; she died shortly, whereupon he married Angelique Kalispel, widow of J. B. Couturier, who had died at Ignace's own house. A daughter Marie, born in 1851, died within a few weeks. Ignace seems to have been living near Fairfield until then, when he disappears from Church records. He said himself that he lived in Washington (he was living at Frenchtown, near Walla Walla, in 1855 with a wife and child) and in Montana thereafter.

Iroquois

A great many canoemen were Iroquois recruited in Eastern Canada for the fur company brigades. They were excellent on the water, not so good on the trail, being inclined to desertion, and were generally considered hard to get along with. Many had been exposed to Christianity through the teachings of Father Isaac Joques in Eastern Canada.

Iroquois, Laurent   1798 c-

"Old Laurent" was quite surely Laurent Karonhitchego, as McLoughlin spelled it, or Karatohon, according to Ogden. He was an Iroquois who had been with the Hudson's Bay Company since 1815 as a canoeman, and seems to have been a highly trusted employe, mentioned by Mc-Loughlin as sent to meet the Express, to take charge of a boatload of supplies for Black, and to get back in time "to go to the mountains this fall". His wife was Therese Wahkaikom (Chinook); several children are recorded. He seems to have been loaned as a sort of personal servant or boatman for the priests on their far-flung missions, at hand when needed; on a September mission to the Cascades he was godfather to no less than twenty-nine children and at the Falls of the Willamette to five more. His daughter Cecile, whose mother may have been a later wife than Therese, died at St. Louis in 1859, aged fifteen, "at the house of Senecale". It may be that the William Laurence of Grand Ronde, "born at St. Louis", was his son.

Iroquois, Louis Shaegoskatsta, dit "le frise" (Maranda)

"Tete Frize" was an Indian with David Thompson in the employ of the North West Fur Company in 1808. The above man may be the same.

This Louis Iroquois is called Shaegoskatata in the Vancouver records, the same name as used by Dr. McLoughlin in his Letters, but reappears as Louis Maranda, dit le Frize, "father of the bride, consenting" at the marriage of Marie Anne (aged fourteen) to Joseph Brule at St. Paul in 1848. McLoughlin called him a freeman in 1832; he no doubt had retired to St. Paul, as did many of the Iroquois. A small settlement of them took land on the Yamhill River across from Dayton, for example.

Iroquois, Michel Atenesse

Little beyond Church records can be found on Atenesse, but some good bit may be conjectured. His name appears most often as simply Michel, but in a later volume, with no explanation, as Satacaronty. The latter may be a family name, as a Louis Satacaranta, Iroquois, was on the list of Work's men in the Snake River Country in 1824. Michel's daughter Louise married Fabian Maloin in 1838 and died on the claim near Brooks in 1849. The names Louis, Alex and William Michel are found in the environs of French Prairie during the 1860's. It seems likely that Atenesse settled in the Willamette Valley, along with the Tawakons, Tyikwarhis and Tsetses, and that the next generation drifted to reservations here and there. A Francis Michel, probably Atenesse's son, ("his father an Iroquois, and his mother a full blood Lower Chinook") established the Michel (Michelle) line on the Grand Ronde Reserve, where they and the Norwests formed a sort of Iroquois cluster, witnessing and sponsoring for one another in the Church.

Iroquois, Norwest (Nordouest)

The Ottawa Iroquois from the prairies north of Montreal were called Northwests.

Iroquois, Thomas Canasawarette   -1832

Thomas Canasawarette had been a boatman with the North West Company at Astoria from 1813, when that company took over the post. He was one of those sent to the Willamette Fur Post the first winter to collect meat for the parent fort; the next May he left on the Interior Brigade in the canoe of William Wallace. In due time he transferred to the Hudson's Bay Company and was killed, along with Pierre Kakaraquiron, by the Tillamooks in March, 1832. He is quite probably the father, "the late Thomas Iroquois", of Marie Thomas who married Charlot Tsete in 1839. Marie's mother, wife of Thomas Canasawarette, if the same man, is given as a woman of the Grande Dalles.

Islands of Stones (Iles de Pierres)

Now called Rock Island, ten miles downstream in the Columbia from Wenatchee, Washington. The Iles de Pierres Indians were called Sinkiuse-Columbia by the traders, according to author Swanton.

Isom, James Jefferson   1819-

On his Donation Land Claim application, this man's name is spelled Isham. He was born in 1819 in Tennessee, married Clarissa (Wenn) in Illinois, and settled in Marion County in 1853 (?4). Two years later his wife died at the age of thirty-three.

Jackson, Jerome B. 1824-1885
Jerome B. Jackson, a protestant from New York State, settled a claim in Oregon in 1850. In 1860 he married Mary Cosgrove, the widow of James Costello, at St. Louis. She was a devout Catholic and her children were baptized in the Church; after a time Jackson himself embraced that faith. He died in 1885, at an age nearer sixty than the fifty set down in the record.

Jacquet, Pierre Stanislaus 1813-
"There is at Walamette a young Frenchman . . . Pierre Stanislaus Jacquet, born at Havre de Grace, who left his country at eleven to go to sea. This young man, able to read passably, has been very useful to the missionaries in having prayers recited while the latter were hearing confessions. He is to teach catechism and reading during the absence of the missionary." Father Blanchet, 1840
Jacquet married Victoire Tchinouk in the "big wedding" of January 28, 1839, at the Willamette Mission.

Jeaudoin, Celeste 1825-1899
Celeste was the daughter of Charles Jeaudoin and a Chinook mother. (Jean Baptiste was her brother, a clerical error.) Their mother having died, Celeste and her brother were reared in various homes and both received fair educations, apparently at Fort Vancouver under the Rev. Beaver and later teachers. Celeste married Augustin Rochon. No children were born to them, but they reared some of the children of Jean Baptiste Jeaudoin and various others in need of a home, for the Rochons were particularly devoted to the welfare of children. Most of their married life was spent near Toledo, Washington. Celeste's will provided that her estate, after small bequests, should be given to the Sisters of Charity "for the benefit of the Orphans of the parish."

Jeaudoin, Charles 1800-1848
Charles Jeaudoin was born in Varrenes, Canada, to Louis Jeaudoin and Marie Ann Laverdure. He joined the Hudson's Bay Company in 1818 and was stationed successively at Barens House, Ile-a-la-Crosse, and the Columbia department. He was usually assigned to the southern route under Laframboise or McLeod. Two children were born to him and a Chinook wife—Jean Baptiste and Celeste, who married Augustin Rochon. Charles later married Madeleine Servant, daughter of Jacques Servant and Josephte Okanagan. No children came of this marriage. Charles died in 1845. His widow presently married Louis Bergevin and died in 1863.

Jeaudoin, Charles Baptiste 1851-1921
Only Charles and Joseph, of the children of Jean Baptiste Jeaudoin and Elizabeth Joachim (Hubert), lived to maturity. Following the death of both parents, they were reared in the home of their aunt and uncle, Celeste and Augustin Rochon. Charles married Josephine McKay, daughter of John McKay and Josette Boucher, q.v. Of their eight children, only Lewis lived to maturity. The couple lived at Woodburn, Oregon, kindly and respected, and are buried in the Catholic Cemetery which Charles had cleared for the purpose.

Jeaudoin, Christine 1847-1850
The will of her gentle old grandfather, Charles Jeaudoin, made a few weeks before his death, remembered his only grandchild, " . . . a year old calf and a chicken which I give to my little daughter, the daughter of Baptiste." Christine died at the age of three.

Jeaudoin, Jean Baptiste 1822-1879 c
Jean Baptiste Jeaudoin was the son of Charles, not another Jean Baptiste, as recorded at his baptism at St. Paul in 1840. He was three times married, first to Isabel Hubert, then to Adele Rowland (Horagan), both of whom died early, and last to Marie Monique (Oskanha). Only a few of his numerous children lived to maturity. He himself was drowned in the Elochomin River about 1879, and was buried on a now forgotten site on his farm nearby. He had been somewhat better educated than most servants at the time, and acted as a travelling helper or guide for the early priests in establishing mission sites. His widow married Joseph Lanoutte and died at Cathlamet in 1907 at the age of seventy-four.

Jeffries, Edward (Jeff, Goffers, Jefferson, etc.) 1823-
The name of Jeffries gave as much trouble to the priests as did the name of his wife, Josette

(Susette) Quenel (Cornoyer). Other names for the mother of his children crop up, and may indeed have been those of other women. Jeffries came from England in 1844 and took a claim on the Prairie. The records of his children appear in the registers of St. Paul, St. Louis and Grand Ronde. The name Jeffries continues in Grand Ronde through Edward's son Edmund (1874-1914) to the present time.

Jette, Adolphe   1825-1917
Five young men set sail around the Horn from Eastern Canada about 1850 to seek their fortune in California. The five were Adolphe Jette, Dieudonne Menegre, Felix DeLisle, Jacques Comtois and one known only as Piette, probably John B. P. Piette, q.v. After winning success, they started north to seek homes in Oregon. Apparently they took few precautions against the Rogue River tribes through which they must pass, until they were warned by a young Indian girl stealing to their campfire one night and telling them her people were out to kill them. She guided them north, caught food for them and covered their tracks until they reached the safety of the Willamette Valley.

They found shelter at the log "inn" of Louis Pichet. The question arose about what to do with the girl, whom they called Julia. Old Pichet arranged for them to draw straws, and Jette lost or won, whichever way one chooses to view the outcome. Jette accepted his charge without murmuring, and to show their goodwill, each of the other four handed Julia a little vial of gold from his belt as a wedding gift. She did not know what to do with it, as she placed the vials in Jette's hands, but one may suppose she was moved by wifely submission more than by ignorance. Jette had no cause to regret the short straw. Julia was a quiet little thing who learned to keep house very well in the white man's way, and when her work was done, retired to her own tepee in the back yard. But neither she nor any of her children lived to be very old, falling prey to the omnipresent tuberculosis.

Jette later married Marguerite Liard and reared a second family, some of whose descendants still live on the old home place at Champoeg.

The above romantic tale is one given general credence in the family today and has appeared in print over the years. Although it is not entirely substantiated by recorded facts, it is quite worth repeating for the atmosphere of the gold rush times. The apparent facts are that Jette was born in Canada on June 10, 1825, to Francois Jette and Marie Anne Payette. His westward migration progressed by steps through New York, New Orleans, St. Louis and Fort Laramie to the Rogue River in Oregon. He settled finally in St. Paul as a farmer and merchant, while still keeping in touch with mining interests in Idaho.

Jobin, Sigfroid
A daughter Marie, born at Vancouver, and another Marie, at St. Paul, were children of Sigfroid Jobin. Both died shortly after birth. A son, Joseph Sigfroid, is also recorded at St. Paul. Jobin had married Catherine Pepin in Canada early in the 1840's; they are the people whose story was told by old Thomis Pepin (LaChance) in 1960: "My dad, Pierre Pepin (I) went back to Canada on one of the brigade trips and spent the winter with his parents there. Of course he told them all about the country, how mild it was and what a wonderful place. Then his sister Catherine spoke up, "I'm going back with you!' 'Oh, no, no!' said everyone, 'You can't do that!' They were Catholic, and strict. Dad told her, 'It's a rough, hard trip, no place for a single woman at all.' 'Then I'll get married first,' was her answer. She was the only sister he had, twenty-three years old and not married yet! So he said he'd look around, see what could be done. That evening he met a fellow he knew, told him, 'Why don't you marry my sister Catherine?' and the fellow said, 'I'll go see her!' for he admitted he'd been casting eyes in that direction for some time. So they were married, and she came with the brigade."

Joset, Joseph   1810-1900
Joset was a genial Swiss Jesuit recruited by Father DeSmet to work in the western field of missions. Joset crossed the plains in 1844, and at once began work among the Indians of Idaho and Eastern Washington. He became known as "The Apostle to the Couer d'Alenes".

Joyal, Toussaint and Etienne
Toussaine Joyal was one of the Red River group led by James Sinclair in 1841 as settlers for the Puget Sound Agricultural Farm at Nesquallie. Another Joyal, Etienne, appears as early as 1843 at Fort Vancouver and was employed on the Cowlitz Farm in 1847. The two may have been brothers, or father and son. Etienne Joyal served as a private in the Cowlitz Rangers in the Yakima Indian War of 1855-56.

Kalapoya
The Kalapoyas (Calapooyas) were a linguistic group of several tribes in the Willamette Valley above the Falls. These included the Yamhill, Tualatin, Luckiamute, Santiam, Mary's River and Yoncalla tribes. As few salmon are found in the river above the Falls, the Kalapoyas were considered poor by Indian standards. The Grand Ronde Reserve in Polk County occupies part of the original Kalapoya region.

Kaniseno (Kinsneau, Cassino, Casenove, etc.)   1790 c-1848
Kaseno was a chief on the Lower Columbia as early as 1811 when the Astor party made mention of him. He was friendly to the whites throughout the era of the fur trade. His portrait was painted by the artist Paul Kane. In the epidemic of 1829 most of his family perished—nine wives, three children and sixteen slaves, according to Kane. Thereafter he lived near Fort Vancouver, where he was always welcome at table. Just before his death he allowed himself to be baptized under the name Francois, although he had resisted until that time.

Kavanaugh, Daniel   1831-1903
Daniel Kavanaugh, from Ireland, married Catherine Doyle, also from Ireland, in 1860 in Wisconsin. Immediately after their marriage the young couple started for Oregon by way of the Isthmus of Panama, a journey that lasted eight months. Kavanaugh settled near St. Louis, where for fifty-two years he raised wheat and prospered. His eight children all lived to maturity and became prosperous in their own right, one a doctor, another a judge, and so on. Kavanaugh died in Portland in 1903, his wife in 1918; both were buried in Mount Calvary Cemetery in that city.

Kennedy, Bernard "Barney"   1811-1865
Founder of the Kennedy clan on French Prairie was "Barney" from Blown Rock, County Donegal, in Ireland. He came to Canada as a young man, remained a few years, and moved on to Illinois. There he married a girl from Indiana, Arah Underwood, in 1838. A final move took him across the plains to Oregon in 1847, accompanied by his wife, several children, his brother John and his family. The claim on Champoeg Creek to which he bought the rights from an earlier settler was only slightly improved, but habitable; Kennedy's successful five months in the California mines laid the ground for eventual prosperity. His did at the age of fifty-four; his wife Arah survived him by almost forty years. The Kennedy lot in the Champoeg Cemetery is well filled with family members. His brother John, who had come to Oregon at the same time, settled in the St. Louis parish.

Kil-a-ko-tah, Marguerite   1800 c-1973
Kil-a-ko-tah, daughter of a minor Clatsop chief, Coboway, was the eldest of three sisters to marry white men in the very early days of the fur trade. (See Joseph Gervais for Yiamust and Solomon Smith for Celiast). Kil-a-ko-tah first married William Matthews of the North West Fur Company, to whom a daughter Ellen was born (See George Barnston). Her second union was with James MacMillan, to whom she bore a daughter Victoire (See Joseph McLoughlin). Her third was a marriage in the Church to Louis Labonte, Sr., to whom a daughter Julienne (See Louis Vivet) and a son Louis were born. She seems to have been level-headed and capable, refusing to be crowded off her farm near Dayton, which she had claimed as half of the Labonte Donation Land Claim. Her last days were spent in the home of her daughter Victoire, where she died in 1873.

Killimaux (Tillamook)
Because of the gutteral sound of coastal Indian words, early writers had trouble in getting down some form of written words for them. Killimaux may have been as nearly right as Tillamook. The Tillamook tribe, a Salishan people, lived on the coast between Tillamook and Yaquina Bay.

King, Honore
Little has been learned of King. His wife was Marianne, a son Honore was born to them in 1848, and three years later his widow married Basile Courville.

Kirk, Peter   1830-1897
When Peter Kirk and his wife Margaret Lyons came from Ireland to America, they brought with them Peter's aged father, Thomas Kirk, and Margaret's mother, Helen Lyons, both of whom were to die during the early 1870's. The burial of the latter was the first to be specifically registered in the New Cemetery, with a notation in the Register margin by Father Delorme, "Hereafter N.C. means New Cemetery, O.C. means Old Cemetery", for there was some overlapping

in dates when both were in use. Peter's wife Margaret had died in 1873, her daughter Margaret, aged six, in 1871, and both were buried in the Old Cemetery, but in 1875 both were moved to the New Cemetery to lie beside Helen Lyons. Peter Kirk was married twice more, first to Margaret Gogan (no record found), and after her death in 1893, when her name was given as "Margaret Lynes", to Matilda Dixon. The Kirk land, part of the claim staked out by Father Blanchet in 1839, was acquired by Peter Kirk when the original claim was reduced in conformity with the Donation Land Laws of 1850. The fine old home east of St. Paul is still a family home, built by his son John in 1882. The house of his brother Emmett, built a few years later, is now the museum of the St. Paul Mission Historical Society.

Kittson, Louise Jemima   1836-
Jemima Kittson, daughter of William Kittson and Helene McDonald, married "into the Company". Her husband, William Sinclair III, was a third-generation officer in the Hudson's Bay Company; for some years during the 1860's he was in charge of Fort Shepherd in British Columbia. He committed suicide at Fraser Lake in 1899.

Kittson, Pierre Charles   1832-1915
Pierre Charles was the son of William Kittson and Helene McDonald. Most of his adult life was spent on French Prairie as a logger on the river. He married Angelique Dupre, daughter of Nazaire Dupre and Catherine Lafantaisie, but sometimes called by the name of her step-father Mongraine. The graves of Peter and his wife are well-marked in the St. Paul Cemetery with English spelling of their names. A picture of Pierre shows a rugged face of much determination, a trait still green in local memory of the tough old "river pig".

Kittson (Kitson), William   1793 c-1841
Kittson, born in Canada and a veteran of the War of 1812, was a clerk in the North West Company and the Hudson's Bay Company in various western posts until 1834, when he was sent to Fort Nisquallie to conduct trade and oversee farming activities. His wife Helene was a daughter of the remarkable Finan McDonald and was herself a woman of much courage and resourcefulness. Kittson and his wife formed a considerable buffer between hostile natives of the Puget Sound region and the missionaries. He died in Vancouver "of a long and painful malady" in 1841. His widow married Richard Grant.

Klamak (Clamack), Marguerite   1819 c.-1850
"Margaret", wife of Pierre Depot (I) died in January, 1850, on the claim near the present Gervais, "leaving three children, one of which died", according to Depot's Donation Land Claim record. No church record of her death has come to light.

Klamath Tribe
A tribe of southern Oregon, the Klamath Indians called themselves "people of the lake", after Klamath Lake, about which most of their villages stood. Their food, consisting of fish, water-lily seeds, small game, roots and berries, came mainly from the lake and the surrounding marshes. Slavery was an important feature of their culture.

Klikitats
The Klickitat tribes lived on the north side of the Columbia, west of the Cascade Mountains. They were part of the very large Sahaptin stock. They were active and enterprising traders and from their favorable location served as intermediaries between the coast and the interior tribes. They were famous for their excellent basketry work of coiled manufacture and careful design. After the 1855 treaty, the Klickitats went to the Yakima Reserve.

Kling, Cline - see Klyne

Klyne, Joseph   -before 1850 c.
Joseph Klyne would appear to have been the metis son of Michel Kline, "a jolly old fellow with a large family" in charge of Jasper House during the 1820's. Joseph came with the Red River migration of 1841, first to Nesquallie, then to French Prairie, where he first appears with his wife, Louise Braconnier, in August, 1842. Two children were born to them in Oregon, Joseph, who died at St. Louis at the age of five, and Blandine, born in 1848. Joseph, the father, died before 1850, perhaps in the gold fields; his widow married Charles Demers.

Labonte, Joseph   1844-1864
Joseph Labonte, eldest son of Louis Labonte II and Caroline Montour, died at Walla Walla in 1864, "aged 19".

Labonte, Julienne   1838-1916
Julienne was the only recorded daughter of Louis Labonte and Kil-a-ko-tah Cobway. Her mother had two earlier daughters by officers of the North West Company, Ellen Matthews and Victoire McMillan. Julienne bore a son, evidently outside of marriage, since "legitimate" is omitted in the record, to Alexander Poirior. The son Jacques died in October, 1855, at the age of two and a half. Julienne married Narcisse Vivet in 1858 at St. Paul.

Labonte, Louis (I)   1780 c.-1860
Labonte was one of the four Astor employes to become prominent in the early development of Oregon, the three others being Etienne Lucier, Joseph Gervais and Michel Laframboise. Labonte, from La Prairie, Quebec, had been on the Great Plains in the employ of the American Fur Company since 1808, when he and another Labonte, Jean Baptiste, joined Hunt's overland division of the Astor expedition to found a fur empire in the far west, or so the proprietor hoped. Jean Baptiste Labonte returned to the east, but Louis remained as a carpenter through successive fur companies in the West. When he retired about 1830 he made his celebrated trip "independently" back to Montreal for his discharge, although such a trip was scarcely more than routine, certainly not unique. His wife was Kilakotah, daughter of a minor Clatsop chief, Coboway. His farm across the river from French Prairie was said to be one of the best in the country.

Labonte, Louis (II)   1818-1911
Louis Labonte II was the son of Marguerite Clatsop (Kilakotah) and Louis Labonte I. He was three times married, first to Caroline Montour (from 1843 to 1851), to Euphrasie (Felicite) Gervais (1851 to 1854), and last to Josette Laframboise (1856 to 1879). Of all his children, only Alexander, born to Caroline Montour, and Louis Labonte III, born to Josette Laframboise, are known to have lived to real maturity. (There had been a Louis III born to Caroline Montour in 1850, for whom no death record has been found.) Louis Labonte II lived out his long life with the surviving Louis III after the latter's marriage to Josephine Belique in 1892. He is well remembered from the days he used to trot about St. Paul, an oracular and almost legendary little relic of the very early days of the fur trade in Oregon. He is buried, unmarked, on the lot of a relative in the St. Paul Cemetery.

Labonte, Louis III   1857-1936
Louis was the only one of five sons born to Louis Labonte II and Josette Laframboise to rear a family, all his brothers dying young. Louis lived a mile south of St. Paul on a small holding. He married Josephine Belique, daughter of Cyprien Belique and Julienne Bergevin. Eight children were born to them, some of whom keep the name Louis Labonte alive; currently it has reached the Sixth in direct descent.

Labonte, Nazaire Jeremie   1863-
Nazaire was the son of Louis Labonte, II, and his third wife, Josette Laframboise. Only one of his five brothers lived to establish a family. Nazaire himself died as a young man from burns received in a saloon when someone, for a prank, set fire to spilled liquor.

Labonte, Sara   1848-1848
Sara Labonte, the daughter of Louis Labonte II and Caroline Montour, died at the age of two months.

Labrie, Ferdinand   1829-1866
Ferdinand Labrie, who was a young man of 21 when he witnessed for other young people at St. Paul in 1850, did not linger long on French Prairie, but settled with a group of other Frenchmen in Douglas County at "Garden Bottom", or "The French Settlement". There he married Ann Eliza O'Reilly and had three children baptized by a visiting priest between 1858 and 1862. His grave was blessed by another travelling priest sometime after his death in 1866, "aged 37 years, 10 months, 6 days". Other Labrie records, probably those of a brother, are found in the registers of Roseburg and of Medical Lake, Washington.

Lachapelle, Adrienne   1845-
Adrienne Lachapelle, daughter of Andre Lachapelle, grew up to marry Arthur Grenier, a Portland saloon Keeper. Her daughter Matilda, who lived to the age of 103, had a vast store of recollections of a country and city wherein pioneer region developed into a complex modern state.

Lachapelle, Andre   1802-1881
This Andre Lachapelle should not be confused with the Astor man of the same name who was killed on the Snake River in 1814 in the Reed party. They may possibly have been related, but were not father and son. Andre, the younger, is said to have been employed as a blacksmith (his old portable anvil is still in the family) and boatman by the Hudson's Bay Company from 1817 to 1841, when he retired to a claim just north of St. Louis. He married Adrienne Lucier the same year. He died in 1881 in the newly established St. Vincent's Hospital. His grave in St. Louis Cemetery is marked with a good marble slab, although that of his wife is not. His obituary in **The Oregonian** calls him "the oldest pioneer in Oregon", and credits his age as a full century; however, his tombstone states, no doubt more accurately, that he died at "79 yrs. 1 mo. 29 da".

Lachapelle, Felicite   1842-1872
Felicite, named for her mother's sister, Felicite Lucier Manson, lived and died at St. Louis. She married Amadee Seguin in 1857. Three of her six children died in infancy; she herself died in 1872 at the age of thirty, at St. Louis.

Lacourse, Alexis   1835-1847
Alexis Lacourse, son of Pierre I, died at the age of twelve.

Lacourse, Claude   1832-
During the two years when Claude was witnessing at so many burials, along with Antoine Cloutier, a lad of about the same age, it is likely they were pupils in the new school for boys at St. Paul, always available, and able to sign their names. The second generation was just now becoming literate.

Lacourse, Gilbert   1837-
Gilbert, son of Pierre I is evidently the same as Culbert.

Lacourse, Joseph   1842-1861
Joseph, son of Pierre I died at the age of eighteen.

Lacourse, Marguerite   1840-
Marguerite Lacourse was the daughter of Pierre I. A daughter Agnes was recorded to Marguerite in 1865, no father mentioned. Marguerite married Dominique Pichet in 1856, Elie Pelland in 1863.

Lacourse, Pierre I   1792-1864
Governor Simpson, making a western tour of inspection in 1828, wrote of Lacourse, "A good man- steersman and boat-builder. Is now gone back to Spokan to make boats." After many years at Fort Colville, he retired to French Prairie in 1843, taking a claim along Champoeg Creek and becoming a United States citizen. After the death of his native wife, Archange Tchinouk (also called Skaisis Cree, Skoucisse Chinook and Archange Chehalis), he married Josephte Sinemaule Nez Perce (also called Okanogan), the widow of Jacques Servant. His daughter Marguerite married Dominique Pichet, Elie Pelland.

Lacourse, Pierre II   1828-1861
Young Pierre Lacourse grew up to marry Victoire McMillan, daughter of James McMillan of the North West Company and Chief Coboway's daughter, Kilakotah. Victoire first married Joseph McLoughlin, then Pierre Lacourse. Five of their six children died young, only Claude, one of twins born in 1854, living to maturity.

Lacourse, Rose   1820 c-1845
Rose Lacourse Rivet died "in the night" of August 30, 1845, at St. Paul, leaving several small children.

Laderoute, Francois Xavier   1800-1864
Laderoute, dit Seguin, was an employe of the Hudson's Bay Company. Although land records show him settling on a claim near Fairfield in 1847, he was on the land much earlier, being one of those married by Jason Lee, the Methodist missionary, in 1838 and frequently mentioned by him. The marriage was later redone by the Catholic priest. Laderoute's wife was Julie Gervais, daughter of his neighbor, Joseph Gervais. After Julie's death he married Marie Anne Ouvrie in 1847. He had four recorded children by Julie and eleven by Marie Anne. Through various marriages the Laderoute name became intertwined with many original Prairie names—Gervais, Malouin, Groslouis, Perrault, Lachapelle.

Laderoute, Francois Xavier, Jr. 1844-
Francois, Jr. was the son of Francois, Sr., and Julie Gervais. He died "without issue".

Laderoute, Isadore 1841-
In 1906 Joseph Laderoute testified, "I have one full brother now living, named Isadore Laderoute, now living at Missoula, Montana".

Laderoute, Joseph 1835-
Joseph was the eldest child of F. X. Laderoute and Julie Gervais. He married Rosalie, daughter of the old mountain man Jean Baptiste Gervais and his metisse wife, Marie Lucier. Rosalie died in 1864, "aged 23 years", leaving a three-old son Joseph and an infant daughter, Marie Odile. In 1872 Joseph Laderoute, widower, married Mary Morais at St. Louis. Two more children, Sophie and Isadore were recorded at St. Louis and Gervais. His wife Mary (Marie) died at Gervais in 1881.

Laderoute, Victoire 1838-before 1906
Victoire married Fabien Malouin in 1850; he died five years later, and his widow married Andre Cloutier. Malouin's claim included the present site of Brooks, Oregon.

Lafantasie, Angele 1818 c-1867
Angele, daughter of Jacques Lafantasie and Susanne Okanagan, married Joseph Bourjeau and bore four recorded children. After his death in 1849, Angele married Theodore Gervais I and bore at least nine more children, but of all of both sets, only four or five reached maturity. Many of the later entries for Angele are found in St. Louis.

Lafantasie, Catherine 1825 c-1865
Catherine Lafantasie first married Nazaire Dupre, who died in 1848. Their son, also Nazaire, died the next year. Her second husband was David Mongraine, to whom she bore several children.

Lafantasie, Charles 1816-1861 c.
Charles was born at old Fort Walla Walla, the son of Jacques Lafantasie, who had come on the Tonquin in 1811, and Susanne Okanagan. His wife, Isabel Spokane, was the daughter of Canote Humpherville and his Sinpoil wife, Pauline. The baby Marie, baptized in 1842, died four weeks later. Charles's wife Isabel (Elizabeth) died in 1842, "aged about 35". He then married Genevieve Rondeau, daughter of Charles Rondeau and Lizette Bellaire. Several children were born to each wife and are mostly recorded in St. Louis. His land claim below St. Louis was "relinquished to Delor" (Pierre Delard) about 1850.

Lafantasie, Francois 1845-1879
Francois Lafantasie died at St. Louis at the age of thirty-four, "about 30", according to the entry.

Lafantasie, Jacques
Lafantasie came to Astoria in 1811 on the Tonquin, engaged as a boatman. Simpson wrote of him in 1828, "Interpreter, but not sufficiently resolute with Indians--very thoughtless." Little more is heard of him. "Died a long time ago", was testimony in an Indian land case in later decades; the identification of Susanne Okanagan at her baptism as "the mother of Charles Lafantasie" rather than as the wife of Jacques might imply that he had died before 1848, the date of his wife's baptism.

Laferte, Joseph (Joachim) 1813-Prior to 1905
Joseph Laferte (the name became Lafferty) was born in Canada in 1813. He settled his claim at Butteville in 1847 and became a naturalized citizen in 1851. From his marriage to Sophie Aubichon in 1845, several children were born, but all preceded their mother in death. Sophie died in March, 1905, at the age of seventy-seven.

Laferte, Michel I 1786-1858
Michel Laferte, Montreal, was very early in the West, being on the North West Company roster at Fort George (Astoria) as a boatman in 1813-14. He was with Ogden in the Snake River country in 1824-26, and with Work in the same region in 1831-32. He married Josephte Nez Perce at Fort Vancouver in 1839. Their children, beginning in 1825, are recorded as Antoine, Olivier, Michel II, Marie, Catherine, Madeleine and Pierre. The name gradually took on such forms as Laforte, Lafferty, Placie, Placide and Plassee.

Laferte, Michel II   1831-
Michel II was the son of Michel I and Josephte Nez Perce, Pend d' Oreille or Chimhaney, according to family recollection. For his wife Angelique Sibonne, see Assiniboine or Des Rivieres. Mary Ann Michelle, writing from the Grand Ronde Reserve in her old age, said, "Michel Plassee & his wife, thay were Breeds and thay had three Children, Merie, Peter and Angeline. Thay lived here long time before the last allottment so they got allottment shortly after that the old man died so Mrs. Plassee was left alone Peter left Grand Ronde soon as he was of age the oldest Daughter also died few years later Peter came back to Grand Ronde he was Peter Laferty then." He died at Grand Ronde on Jan. 8, 1889, and was buried in the St. Michael's Cemetery.

Laferte, Pierre   1843-
Pierre Laferte married Ursule Plourde at St. Louis in 1874. A son Olivier was recorded there, and four other children, three of whom died, were born at Gervais.

Laflemme, Edouard   1820-1902
The family of Edouard Laflemme is recorded in the Church Registers of St. Louis, Gervais and Brooks. Additional names and dates can be gleaned from stones in the little hilltop cemetery east of Brooks, where the earlier family members are buried.

Lafleur, Marie   1820-
Marie, daughter of Francois Lafleur and of Marguerite Cree was probably born in Canada. For her later life, see Roi, Thomas.

Lafontaine, Charles
The earliest occurrence of the Lafontaine name on French Prairie seems to be that of Charles Lafontaine on the 1844 Tax Roll, when he paid 89c tax on his horses, cattle and hogs. He does not appear on the 1850 Census Roll.

Peter Lafontaine, "a 22-year-old adventurer from Vermont" was living at Frenchtown, near Walla Walla, in 1855. Relationships, if any, between the two branches of that name are not known.

Laframboise, Abraham   1840-1840
The first son of Michel Laframboise and Emelie Picard was Abraham, who died at the age of six days; the last son, born on Christmas Day, 1856, was also named Abraham. His later life is not known.

Laframboise, Anastasie Louise   1844-1928
Anastasie (Louise in later days) was the second daughter of Michel Laframboise and Emelie Picard. She was a spirited, active little woman, "straight as an arrow, of whom no ill word was ever spoken". She married Henry Hilleary and lived in eastern Clackamas County, where she and her husband donated land from their farm to found the Damascus United Evangelical (now Community) Church, for she had long since left the Catholic Church in which she had been reared. A daughter Pearl and a son John were born to the couple; they also reared Charlotte Larkins, a relative of Hilleary. "The beautiful Lottie" died at the age of fifteen—"The lovely flower has faded." Most, if not all, of Anastasie's family are buried in the churchyard of the church she helped to found, but only the graves of Henry and of Charlotte are marked.

Laframboise, Angelique   1851-
Angelique and her sister Anastasie married brothers, George and Henry Hilleary. George and Angelique ("Anne") lived at Martin's Ferry on the north bank of the Columbia River below St. Helens; only a few of their numerous children were recorded in the Willamette Valley. In old age Angelique became blind. When visiting, should say plaintively, "I can't eat that!" until someone remembered to cut up her meat for her.

Laframboise, Jean (Eugene)   1854-1935
Jean was the last son but one of Michel Labramboise and Emilie Picard. After the death of his first wife, Liza Quintal, he married Nancy White.

Laframboise, Joseph   1841-1855
Joseph, son of Michel, should not be confused with Joseph, son of Francois Laframboise. Michel's son died in 1855 at the age of thirteen.

Laframboise, Josephte   1838-1879
Josephte was the eldest daughter of Michel Laframboise and Emelie Picard. She became the third

wife of Louis Labonte II. Of her six sons, only one survived to carry on the family line. Her one daughter, Josephine, married David Gregoire and died at the age of twenty-one, leaving no children.

Laframboise, Michel I   1790 c-1861
The indomitable Michel was one of the best-known scouts, brigade leaders, emissaries and avengers in the Northwest. He was born near Montreal, sailed on the Tonquin to Astoria, and transferred to successive fur companies. He was literate at a time when many were not, and served as clerk as well as brigade leader. Many of his books are still preserved. His particular "run" was the Umpqua-California route. It was his boast that by having a wife of high rank in every tribe, he was able to travel in safety everywhere. With the arrival of the priests, however, he married Emelie Picard and became a provident, if indulgent, father. Besides the children borne by Emelie, he had two previously recorded—Josette (1831-1837), by a chieftess of the Tsaleel tribe on the Umpqua, and Michel II, by a "Sassete woman". Little Josette died at the age of six while being cared for by the Rev. Herbert Beaver and his wife at Fort Vancouver; a second Josette was born to Emelie in 1839. In appearance he was short and stout, almost anthropoid in face, a big talker and a hearty drinker, but his generosity was boundless and his leadership unquestioned. In his later years he ran a ferry across the Willamette at Champoeg until a stroke forced him to sell his holdings; he seems to have lived with his daughter Josephte until his death two years later.

Laframboise, Michel II   1837-1895 c.
Young Michel was one of several children born to Michel I, the scout and trader, before his formal marriage to Emelie Picard, for Old Michel played the field. Young Michel's mother was said to have been a "Sassete woman, Infidel". He married Margaret McKay, whose father was a Scot, no relation to the other McKays, so far as is known. Young Michel reared several children of his own and one step-daughter, Rose Desrivieres, on a farm west of Vancouver. His step-mother, Emelie, who loved him with devotion, lived out her last years with his family.

Laframboise, Rose   1849-
One of the Laframboise daughters, perhaps Rose, is said to have been sent to the East to study music. She sang "in the opera", the family recalls, and she does not appear again in the West. Pictures sent home from Richmond, Virginia, shows her a woman of poise and excellent taste in dress. Her musical ability was no doubt a gift from her father, Michel I, who had "a good and strong voice, and he knew all kinds of songs; he could sing for hours," his widow Emelie used to recall proudly.

Lahalette, Tekwenton
Lahalette was chief of the Nesquallies near Puget Sound, and served Dr. Tolmie as interpreter during his eighteen months (1833-1834) in that region. He accompanied Tolmie on the ascent of Mt. Rainier and seems to have been a responsible and trusted guide. When the priests arrived six years later, he had three of his children baptized—Etienne, by his wife Tsetsisa, and Charles and Agatha by "a second wife". Artist Paul Kane, touring the West in 1847, painted an excellent portrait of "Lacholette, Nesquallie Chief on the Shores of Puget Sound".

Lajoie, Jean Baptiste   1800-1846
Although the Church record indicates Lajoie was born in 1800, the Hudson's Bay Company record gives 1809. He joined the Company in 1828 as a canoeman and was stationed at Fort Colville. Little else is heard of him beyond the account of his wife's funeral passage by two different eye-witnesses, each starkly told in a few words that picture life and death in a primitive time: *[The sisters of Notre Dame were coming to St. Paul in August, 1844.]*

> "A wagon rolled up; its bed consisted of two beams; a few slats nailed to rough uprights formed its sides; there were no seats; passage must be made by standing. In we climbed, each as best she might. I clung fast to one of the uprights. . . . The corpse of the sacristan's wife, taken on at Oregon City, was placed in front, and off we started."

In Harvest Fields by Sunset Shores, 1926

> "Indian woman carried by in a cart for burial. Her husband and another sitting upon the coffin."

The Grains, Margaret Bailey

[Marie des Chaudiere, wife of Lajoie, had died at Oregon City and was being brought to St. Paul for burial.] Lajoie soon married Marie Pend d'Oreille. He died in 1846, and his widow married an Iroquois, J. B. Ignace Soletroani.

Lajuennesse, Rev. Louis   1853-1880
The mortuary chapel in the New Cemetery at St. Paul, built in 1875, was intended to be the last
resting place of all the Sisters of the Holy Names in Oregon, but it soon became inadequate for
that purpose. Father Lajunnesse, chaplain of St. Mary's Academy in Portland, was interred
therein during the early days of the mortuary.

Lake Wapato
Wapato Lake was a long, shallow body of water on Tualatin Plains, west of the Chehalem
Mountains. It was an excellent ground for the harvest of arrowhead plant, or wapato, the tubers
of which were a staple native food, and for the hunting of wild fowl. It has since been drained to
form rich black onion growing fields. In spring run-off it returns briefly to a show of its former
appearance and is, for a week or two, a haven for migrating wild fowl.

Lambert, Augustin I   1814-1881
Three Lamberts, Cuthbert (1808), Augustin I (1814) and Felix (1822) appear in the West at
about the same time. Their relationship is not known. Augustin I married Catherine Piche,
probably in Canada. Their large family left many descendents on French Prairie, where some
remain today.

Lambert, Cuthbert, dit Robillard   1808-
Father Demers, on a mission to Fort Colville and its environs in the summer of 1839, found the
location of Fort Okanogan forbidding and sterile, but wrote, "For all that, the population there
is eager for the word of God. I had the pleasure of meeting there a Christian by the name of
Robillard, who had taught the prayers to the natives. That unexpected help spared me many
difficulties on that mission." Robillard, more often known as Lambert, retired to a farm on
French Prairie in 1846 and married Marie, the widow of Andre Picard.

Lambert, Isabelle   1833 c-
"Lumbers" *[?]* - see Warfield

Langlois, Rev. Antoine   1812-1892
Father Langlois was a Canadian priest who came to Oregon by sea in 1842 with Father Bolduc.
He had planned to work among the natives, and was alert to learn a few native words from a
ship's passenger, but in the end he served mostly among the French Canadians. In 1849 he was
transferred to California to become the first pastor of St. Francis Church in San Francisco.

Laprate, Alexis   1794-1871
Laprate was an old fur company man, as early as 1813 at Fort George in the employ of the North
West Company. He was in charge of Fort Okanogan "off and on" during the 1830's and 1840's.
In 1842 he took a claim in the southern part of French Prairie. His wife, Nancy Pion, died in
1847, leaving two small children, Alexis and Charlotte. The next year he married Louise
Okanogan at St. Louis, who bore him several more children. He died in St. Louis in 1871.

Laprate, Charlotte   1843-
Charlotte Laprate married Joseph Minor at St. Louis in 1859. The spelling is given also as
Maynard, but he himself signed as Minor.

Larison, John   1794-1860
Larison was one of the old breed of Mountain men, coming from Ohio originally. Robert Newell,
one of the witnesses at his marriage, was well acquainted with him from early days in the
mountains. When he left the mountains, he lived with the DeGuerre's at the ferry near the
mouth of the Yamhill; Reinette Perrault, whom he married when he was nearing fifty, lived just
across the river.

Laroque, Angelique   1838 c-
Angelique, daughter of Joseph Sebastian Laroque, married Martin Bonenfant in 1853. After his
"probable" death she married Joseph Depot in 1868 at St. Louis. A younger Angelique (1843) was
the daughter of Louis Laroque and Marie Toussaint.

Laroque, George I   1820-1877
George Laroque was born in Chambley, Montreal, on April 7, 1820, according to his stone in the
Butteville Cemetery. His father, Joseph Laroque I, was an old Company man, and George
entered the fur trade as a hunter, aged sixteen, at St. Louis, Missouri. He was highly successful in
the California gold fields later, and became a prosperous merchant at Butteville in partnership

with J. B. P. Piette, F. X. Matthieu and Daniel Harvey. His ornate old home "with black marble fireplaces" remained until recently a landmark at the west side of the village. Laroque's marriage to Arsinoe Matilda Clark was civil, and not recorded in the Church, but the baptisms of his four children appear in St. Paul. Laroque died in California (or Colorado), where he had gone for his health; his body was returned for burial, which was recorded in the register at Oregon City on May 1, 1877.

Laroque, Jean Baptiste
Jean Baptiste was apparently the son of Pierre Laroque of Red River, coming west with him in the migration to Nisquallie in 1841. Pierre was listed as "Canadian", Baptiste as "half-breed". In the West he married Therese Makaine, widow of Joseph Plouff, in 1850. A son Pierre was born to them at St. Louis in 1852. Nothing more is heard of them. No doubt John Flett was correct in writing that Baptiste as well as Pierre had returned to Red River.

Laroque, Old Joseph   1787-1866
Although the first Joseph Laroque in the West, called here "the old", this Joseph does not appear in the records of the Church. Yet he seems so interwoven with a host of that name it is the part of reason to give his background as one of the very early North Westers in Oregon. Joseph Laroque is said to have entered the trade at the age of fourteen, about 1800. In 1804 he (or another of the same name, for they were numerous) was a clerk at English River, and in 1813 reached Astoria. Gabriel Franchere, a Pacific Fur Company man at the post, write, "On April 11, two birch bark canoes bearing the British flag arrived at Astoria. They were commanded by Messrs. John G. McTavish and Joseph Laroque, who had nineteen Canadian voyageurs under them. They made camp on a point of land beneath the guns of the Fort. We invited these gentlemen to our quarters and learned from them the object of their visit. They had come to await the arrival of the ship Isaac Todd." The North West Company was preparing to take over the Astor post by purchase, if possible, by force, if not. Laroque is said by Bancroft to have retired in 1837, living fourteen years in France and then returning, wealthy, to Montreal, where he died in 1866. His relationship to the other Laroques in the records is not made clear; he may have been the father of some of them. After his return to Montreal he disbursed generously of his means; St. Joseph's College at St. Paul was one of the chief beneficiaries and bears its name in his honor.

Laroque, Joseph I
(No attempt has here been made to assign generation numerals to the "Old" Joseph Laroque who came to Astoria in 1813, nor to the Joseph Felix Laroque, "an old North wester in charge of Rocky Mountain House" when Governor Simpson passed through in 1825.) Joseph I married Lizette Walla Walla, and is perhaps the Joseph Laroque who was early at Frenchtown and on whose farm the Battle of Walla Walla was waged.

Laroque, Joseph Sebastian
This is not the same man as Joseph Laroque; the distinction is usually made by the inclusion of "Sebastian". The children of Joseph Sebastian are listed as Marie, who married Etienne Biernais at St. Louis in 1852, Angelique, who married Martin Bonenfant in 1853, Joseph Olivier, Basile, Pierre and Genevieve whose records are carried through St. Paul, St. Louis and one loose "insert" page. The mother of them all is given as Marie Flathead (Cayuse). Joseph Sebastian was listed as a middleman at Fort Vancouver in 1830. In that year Chief Factor McLoughlin wrote to Barnston at Fort Walla Walla, "Laroque applies to go back to Walla Walla but as he has not given you reason to approve his conduct he will remain here---"

Laroque, Louis
The name Laroque is one of the oldest in the western fur trade, from Mathurin Laroche, a guide in 1746-47 toward "La Mer de l'Quest" down through Francois A. Laroque, trading with the Mandans on the Missouri in 1804 (where Lewis and Clark saw him), Joseph the "commis", that is, clerk, at English River, Jean Baptiste the interpreter, and Pierre a Voyageur at Upper Red River all in the same year of 1804. Louis Laroque married Marie Toussaint (Savoyard)—she is given both ways—with recorded children Angelique (1843), Marguerite (1846), Louis (1849-50) and Sophie (1851). One Toussaint Savoyard was listed in the North West Fur Company, and it is reasonable to suppose that Marie was his daughter.

Laroque, Pierre
Governor Simpson, in making up the rolls for the Red River migration to Nisquallie in 1841, listed only "the heads of families", one of which was Pierre Laroque. One of the migrants, John

Flett, later wrote a good account of the trip and included others; thus he listed "Pierre Laroque, Canadian" and "Baptiste Laroque, half-breed". He added that both returned to Red River some time around 1850, the inference being that they were father and son. In the West, Pierre's wife Marguerite Cree died, 1847, after which Pierre left the western country and is not heard of again. A different Pierre, perhaps a son of the first, is "late" by 1844. His wife was Genevieve Toussaint "from the other side of the Rockies", probably meaning Red River; neither one appears more than once or twice in the records, and may not have come west at all.

Lattie, Alexander 1802-1849 (?)
Born in Scotland, Lattie took to the sea and became an officer on various Hudson's Bay Company vessels on the Northwest coast. From 1847 to 1849 he was the Factor and bar pilot at the Fort George post. He was drowned while crossing the Columbia near the mouth of the Willamette. The date given in several places varies.

Lattie, Marie 1841-
The baptism of Marie Lattie appears in the St. Paul record, although it took place at Vancouver, December 13, 1841. She married Louis Bernard, and was "deceased before her mother", that is, before 1868.

Lavalle, Pierre 1821-1844
Pierre Lavalle, son of Louis Lavalle and Therese Spokane, was baptized and died in August, 1844.

Lavigueur, Hyacinthe I -1846
Lavigueur was in the West as early as 1831, occasionally appearing as Desloge or Delozhe. He and Marguerite Colville were married in the big wedding of 1839, when the priests made regular many previous unions. He was by trade a farmer and carpenter, "a good one, and he made a good living". He is recalled also as having made pottery utensils as well as kettles and other iron-work articles for the home. Heavy lifting in the brick kiln at the St. Paul church then under construction caused his death. He was the first French Canadian to be buried from the church for which he had given his life; there had been the burial of a little Indian boy and the marriage of Cuthbert Robillard (Lambert) to Marie Okanagan, widow of Andre Picard, earlier in the week.

Lavigueur, Hyacinthe II 1842-
Young Hyacinthe appears as godfather at the baptism of a native at Stella Maris in 1853, though but eleven years old. Both his parents had died, and he and his older brother Joseph were living at the coast, perhaps working as hands in the fisheries there. In his later years he lived and died in an "old folks' home" near Omak, Washington.

Lavigueur, Joseph 1838-
Between 1850 and 1853 Joseph Lavigueur appears as godfather or witness to various rites at Stella Maris at the mouth of the Columbia, at which time he would have been but thirteen years to sixteen years old. His brother Hyacinthe also appears twice, though a mere child. Both their parents were dead, their father Hyacinthe in 1846 and their mother Marguerite Colville in 1848. Joseph married Esther Pichet at St. Louis in 1859; she died a year later. He then married Adelaide Lachapelle in 1865, and reared numerous children.

Lavigueur, Josephte 1840-1931
Both Josephte's parents had died when she was a small child. The four children were scattered about wherever they could find homes; Josephte (Josephine) was placed in the Sisters' School at St. Paul, where she remained until the school closed in 1852. Thereafter she worked in the Newell and Bergevin homes, even after her marriage to Louis Bernier at the age of nineteen. Her lot was harder than that of many pioneer women, hard though the average may have been. She supported her children by any sort of work to be had, including the care of a leprosy patient, a ward of the government. Yet her ability to surmount difficulties with courage and optimism is the trait of character most fondly recalled by her family: "There was one ingredient we cherished worth noting for her descendents—it was her buoyant, happy, loving spirit." She was later married to Cyrille Richter in a union that did not work out well, to Andrew Northern, and lastly to William Moore. She lived out her long life as "Grandma Moore" in Montesano, Washington.

Lawson, Ceceila 1823-1870
Cecelia was a Scottish girl who married James McKay against her parents' will. (She is said to have slid down the fire pole outside her window to elope with him.) The young couple shortly

emigrated to the United States, part of the wave of Irish settlers whose pressure upon the easy-going French Canadians on the Prairie resulted in their widespread dissemination to other parts of the West. Cecelia had previously been Protestant.

LeBas, Leon Achille
Father LeBas was a French priest who came to Oregon in 1847.

LeBlanc
Gratian LeBlanc was from Louisiana, a descendent of the Acadians displaced from Canada in 1755. Gratian and his wife Victoria, two married daughters, Mrs. John B. Lee and Mrs. Thomas (Cleophine) Thornton and a son Eugene LeBlanc (White) came west in a wagon train of other Acadians in the late 1840's to settle in Oregon City. During the next decade the younger families moved to the Battleground area in Washington, where they helped form the St. John's Catholic Mission in 1868.

Leblanc, "wife of the late Pierre"   -1851
Pierre Leblanc had been drowned at the Dalles des Morts of the Columbia while on the brigade that brought Fathers Blanchet and Demers to Fort Vancouver in 1838. His widow, Nancy McKenzie, remained in the West until her death.

LeBreton, George   -1844
LeBreton, an "intelligent, energetic New Englander" was one of the clerks at the Champoeg meeting of May, 1843, and his name appears on the monument as one of the signers in favor of a provisional government. He was killed at Oregon City the following March while attempting to arrest an Indian who was threatening the peace.

LeBrun, Firmin   1825-1910
His relationship, if any, to Hercule is not known. Firmin was the son of Pierre LeBrun and Josette Grenier; he was being educated for the priesthood in the East, but having developed tuberculosis, came to the milder West. He married Sophie Gregoire, widow of William Porteus, q.v. "A most impractical man!" his grandniece recalls fondly, "reading his French books, doctoring the sick and being waited on hand and foot by his wife, while all his fences were falling down. Once my mother and father went away for the day, and mother set out a lunch for Uncle Firmin, but when they returned, they saw it was uneaten. 'You didn't cut any bread for me,' Uncle Firmin complained."

Lebrun, Louis Hercule   1812-before 1858
Hercule Lebrun is one of several Lebruns, relationship unknown, appearing on the Prairie at about the same time. He was literate, and often served as witness or advisor to his neighbors in legal matters, such as wills. His parents were Charles Lebrun and Marie Ann of Maskigonne, Canada. He first appears in 1845; in 1848 he married Marie Anne (Louise) Ouvrie. He took a land claim near the center of the Prairie in 1849 and became a citizen in 1852. His death, for which no record has been found, occurred between 1856 and 1858. Of his five daughters, four died in infancy, three within a space of five weeks in 1858, leaving only four-year-old Melanie, of whose death we have no record. His widow married Adolphe L'Oiseau in 1858.

LeClair (LeClerc), Louis   -before 1877
Very little is recorded of this man. He came from Montreal, and married Susanne Cowlitz in November, 1843; a son Joseph was born in February, and Susanne died the following day, "aged fifteen". The next October LeClerc married Therese Skalle. It is not known whether Louis, Louis Xavier, and Xavier LeClerc are one man or several. Louis LeClair was listed as a laborer and middleman at Cowlitz Farm; he went to Nesquallie Farm in February, 1850, and was fired a few months later. The Louis Xavier LeClair who married Rachel ------- at St. Paul in 1847 appears in 1860 "on the Applegate (River) in southern Oregon with his wife Rachel Hallsa (?) and daughter Zoe." (Oregon City Register)

Lefebre, Francois   -before 1877
Beyond the brief items relating to his marriage to Adelaide Rivet in 1855, little can be learned about Lefebre. His son Joseph Leon (Louis ?) disappears wholly. The son Ephram (Louis ?) born in 1865, was living in the household of his stepfather, Pierre Delard, in Wasco County in 1880. Iva Bernard, a cousin of sorts, remembered hearing, "Adelaide had a son by a former marriage. He was in his early teens (12 years) when his mother married Pierre (Delard). His name was Espram, and he came to San Francisco. No one seems to know what happened to him."

L'Ecuyer, Francois
Francois L'Ecuyer was a middleman at Fort Vancouver as early as 1828, sent here and there to fill out brigade crews as needed.

Leno, Ambroise (David) 1840-1908
David Leno was mixed-blood of Spanish and Indian descent who lived near Grand Ronde, Polk County, a blacksmith. When General Philip Sheridan left Fort Yamhill for the Civil War, he bestowed his household goods, including his common-law wife, Harriet Rogue River, on young Leno. Five years later, Leno left, taking half the house furnishings, to establish a home with Marianne Nipissing (Napassant). After three children had been born, the previous marriages of both Leno and Marianne were declared invalid, as having been made "against their will", and the pair were formally married in 1871. Marianne died two years later, and Leno married Delma (Tilmer) Lachance, who bore him numerous children. The first rising ground beyond Grand Ronde on the road to the coast is still known as Leno's Hill.

Leno, Joseph (Lino) 1819 c-
Leno, the Mexican, disappears from view after the birth of son Joseph in 1842.

Lewis River
The Lewis River, formerly called the Cathlapootl, flows into the Columbia some distance below Vancouver, from the east. "The country between La Center and Martin's Bluff was known as the Lewis River Country. It was so known because of two brothers, Adolphus and Frederick Lee Lewis (Englishmen) who had settled in those parts at an early date." (Clark County History (Washington). 1961, p. 50.) The two were half-breed sons of John Lee Lewes, and educated in England. Adolphus was a surveyor and clerk for the Hudson's Bay Company. He died in 1856.

Liard, Francois Xavier -before 1852
The record of the Liard brothers in the West is brief, beginning in 1843 and ending in 1852. Francois Xavier married Marie Anne Nez Perce; a son Xavier was born and died in 1849; daughters Marie Adeline and Marguerite are also recorded.

Liard, Thomas Stanislaus (Tanis) 1817-1852
Thomas, brother of Francois Xavier, married Nancy Okanagan in 1847, who died two years later. He then married Celeste Rochbrune, who bore him one daughter, Marguerite. Her father died while she was an infant, and the Marion County Court appointed Narcisse Cornoyer her guardian. She grew up to marry widower Adolphe Jette. Her mother Celeste married Henri Picard in 1853.

Lilouais (Liout, Lilioot)
The Lilioots were a western tribe of the Shuswaps.

Longtain, Andre 1793 c.-1879
Longtain was an engage who worked both as boatman and trapper. He seems to have been a consistent member of Work's crew; he was with him when Work was sent to the Fraser River "in a weighty rain"; he was with him in the Rocky Mountains, and to California in 1832. He apparently settled on a Champoeg claim much earlier than the recorded date of 1843, as Jason Lee wrote he had gone to Campment du Sable to baptize a child of "Mr. Longter" in 1837. His claim had originally belonged to Ebberts, the Rocky Mountain man; much of it is now included in Champoeg State Park. After the flood of 1861-1862, when his house was washed away, he built another "down by the creek" on the other side of the river, near the home of his daughter Genevieve Herbert, later McCann.

Longtain, Angelique 1830-1887
Angelique Longtain married Francois Toupin, son of Madame Dorion by her third husband.

Longtain, Catherine 1825-1858
Catherine Longtain married John Howard, a tavern keeper at Champoeg, and died at the age of thirty-three. Howard seems to have left the country, for nothing more is heard of him, and it is hard otherwise to account for the "illegitimate" daughter Ann Catherine, born to Catherine Longtain in 1855.

Longtain, Genevieve 1840-1923
Genevieve married Thomas Herbert in 1858; after his death in a brawl at Champoeg in 1874, she married Dan McCann, an Irishman who ran a ferry boat line across the river.

Lonetain, Henriette   1824-1913
Henriette was born at old Fort Vancouver when it stood on the bluff above the river bottom. She
married Thomas Moisan, an affluent farmer near the present Brooks.

Lonetain, Joseph   1838-1859
Joseph, son of Andre Lonetain and Nancy Okanogan, married Marie Ducharme in 1859 and died
the same year. A son Joseph was born posthumously; and died at the age of two.

Longtain, Luce   1843-
Luce married Joseph Osborn, a carpenter. Scattered through the records occur the names of
children Andre Allen, Nettie Alice, Anna, Jane, Joseph, Thomas, and Violet May.

Longtain, Thomas   1845 c.-1881
No other records for Thomas Longtain than those in the St. Paul Register have come to light. The
graves of Thomas and two young daughters near the rear of the St. Paul Cemetery are marked
with broken stones, all bearing the dates of 1880 or 1881.

Lord, Moise
Moise Lord is an unknown quantity, beyond his marriage to Marie Sanders and the birth of
several children. He was the son of "late" Honore Lord and "late" Marguerite Babin of Montreal.
His wife Marianne Sanders was the daughter of Jean Sanders and "late" Chinook, Catherine. She
was also the granddaughter of the shadowy Tse-Tse, Iroquoise, and his wife Marie. Besides the
children mentioned in St. Paul, additional entries are found in the St. Louis register.

Loyer (Oyer), Charles
Loyer was a North West Company man as early as 1805 at English River in Canada. He spent the
winter of 1813-14 as a canoeman at Fort Flathead. With the union of the fur companies in 1820,
he continued under the Hudson's Bay Company and was one of Peter Skene Ogden's men on the
Snake River brigades of 1824 through 1826. As all his western service seems to have been east of
the Cascade Mountains, it may be assumed that the mother of his daughter Lizette, born about
1818, was a Flathead or Snake woman.

Lucier, Adrienne   1824-1919
Adrienne, second daughter of Etienne Lucier, was born at Fort Vancouver while it still stood on
the bluff above the Columbia. She married Andre Lachapelle in 1841 and was the mother of
twelve children. She seems to have been a woman of much strength of character, fondly
remembered as "Old Grandma", and a midwife, "delivering half the children on the Prairie".
She herself said she had ridden as far as "the foot of the mountains" on such errands. She is
buried, unmarked, beside her husband at St. Louis.

Lucier, Antoine, Sr.   -before 1848
Antoine Lucier, Sr., was a brother to Etienne Lucier, Sr. He was born in Canada and was with
the North West Company in British Columbia, where he married Charlotte Desnoyer.

Lucier, Antoine, Jr.
Antoine Lucier, Jr., was born in British Columbia to Antoine Lucier, Sr., and Charlotte
Desnoyer, apparently the metisse daughter of another engage. His wife was Julie Aubichon,
daughter of Alexis Aubichon and Marianne Chinook, also given as "Wales" and as "Elmermach"
(given name). Of several known children, Marianne (Mary) married Louis Ducheney, Emelie
married one Cashel, and Alexis married Emma Millet. Antoine's widow Julia married twice
more, once to Roberts and once to Price, to whom she bore several children.

Lucier, David (dit Gariessi, Gardipe)   1843-1852
David died at the age of nine and is buried in the old cemetery at St. Louis.

Lucier, Etienne I   1793-1853
Lucier is generally conceded to have been the first farmer in Oregon. He was a member of the
Hunt overland party, having joined at Mackinac in 1810. He remained in the West as a freeman,
and is mentioned throughout the records and journals of the time. About 1828 or 1830 he settled
on a claim adjacent to the old Willamette Fur Post above Champoeg. He became a leader in
church and government affairs, one of two undisputed Canadians who voted affirmatively for
the Provisional Government in 1843. He was twice married to natives, six children being born to
his first wife Josephte Nouite, and two to Marie Marguerite Tchinouk. He is one of twelve
honored by a bronze plaque at Old St. Paul Cemetery, where he lies unmarked.

Lucier, Etienne II   1844-1921
Etienne Lucier, Jr. usually known as Stephen (the English equivalent of Etienne) was the youngest child of Etienne, Sr., and Marie Marguerite. He never married, but lived alone with his little
dog Bismarck in a cabin not far from the home of his brother Pierre. He lost an arm by gunshot in
middle age. The Marion County Census of 1870 mentions that "Steve Lucier, Indian, aged 23"
was working on the farm of B. F. Harding.

Lucier, Felicite   1814 c.-1867
Eldest daughter of Etienne Lucier I and Josephte Nouite, Felicite married Chief Trader Donald
Manson about 1828. As Manson was non-Catholic and since most of their married life was spent
in remote posts, no records are found until her death in 1867 after they had retired to a farm at
Champoeg. She was the mother of eight children. Her grave in Old St. Paul Cemetery is un-
marked, as are all in the old burial ground.

Lucier, Jean Baptiste Gardipe   1815-1850
Jean Baptiste Lucier was the son of Joseph Lucier, who had been in the North West Fur Company in western Canada for many years, and Wewepahawisk, a Cree. Jean Baptiste went by the
name of Gardipe, Garissie, etc., apparently the name of a stepfather. He was a well-known scout
and guide in the Oregon Country until his death at the age of thirty-five. Five recorded sons were
born to him and his wife, Catherine DeLore; only Paul is known to have survived.

Lucier, Joseph
Joseph Lucier, the elder, may have been a brother of the well known Etienne Lucier, as their
family lines seem to intertwine later. Joseph had been a voyageur with the North West Fur
Company at Fort des Prairie on the upper Saskatchewan in 1804. The Henry-Thompson Journals
list him at Fort Vermillion in 1809 with "1 tent, 2 men, 1 woman, 1 child". The child was
probably his daughter Angelique, born about 1803, who married Saloy. He was at White Earth
House in 1810, "1 tent, 2 men, 2 women, 2 children". The mother of Angelique was a Cree
woman called Wewepihawisk, who was probably the same Cree mother of a son Jean Baptiste,
born about 1815, whose true name was Lucier, he himself said, but often called Gardipe or
Garisy. The supposition would be that Joseph Lucier had died and the Cree mother had married
a Gardipe.

Lucier, Joseph   1838-1907
Joseph was the third son of Etienne Lucier and his first wife, Josephte Nouite. He was six months
old at the time of his mother's death. In 1857 he married Louise Martineau, daughter of Pierre
Martineau. Joseph and Louise (Marie) had fourteen children, most of whom reached maturity.
They lived near Woodburn and were influential in bringing the Church to the remote Crooked
Finger region. Both are buried at St. Paul.

Lucier, Louis (Louison)   1832-
Louis was the eldest son of Etienne Lucier and Josephte Nouite. He married Celestine Gervais,
daughter of Jean Baptiste Gervais and his metisse wife, Marie Lucier. He was schooled in the
early church school on the Prairie, to the extent that he wrote French and at least sketchy
English. Celestine died within the year, and Louis himself was given as "deceased" prior to 1860.

Lucier, Michel   1835-
Michel, second son of Etienne Lucier, disappears from the record after 1860. He evidently
attended the Jesuit school at St. Paul as his signature appears "Michel Loucier" on various
documents.

Lucier, Paul   1837-1917
Paul was the eldest son of Jean Baptiste Lucier dit Gardipe, and sometimes Paul went by the
latter name, though he averred his true name was Lucier. He served in the Yakima Indian War,
married Marguerite Pin, widow of Sam Bellman, and spent his last years at the St. Ignatius
Mission, Flathead Reserve. He was an affable, gentle man with a fine sense of humor, and earned
the nickname "July" for some Fourth of July enterprise. He was the father of thirteen children,
the last of whom, Julia Clara Courville, died in 1970.

Lucier, Pelagie   1827-1857
Pelagie married Francois Bernier in 1843. Her home was a farm near Champoeg, which she
managed alone for five months while her husband was in California during the gold rush. She
was the mother of seven children; she is buried, unmarked in Old St. Paul Cemetery.

Lucier, Pierre   1842-1913
Pierre was the son of Etienne Lucier by his second wife, Marie Marguerite. All his life was spent
as a farmer not far from his birthplace on French Prairie. He married Thais Senecal, daughter of
Gideon Senecal and Lucie DuCharme, in 1871, and reared a numerous family. He is remem-
bered by present residents on the Prairie as "a short, very wide" man, fond of smoking Bull
Durham, cards, and swimming.

Lumbers - see Lambert

McCann, Daniel   -1940 c.
"Dan McCann, the Ferryman" was an Irish settler who married Genevieve Longtain after the
death of her first husband, the ill-fated Herbert. They continued living in the fine old home that
Herbert ("Hubbard") had built across the river from Champoeg. The land had once been part of
the Michel Laframboise claim lying in Yamhill County, and Laframboise had plied a ferry across
the river to the foot of Napoleon Avenue. After appearing on the scene, apparently during the
1870's, McCann re-established the ferry line, but made his landing on the south side farther
upstream than the old landing had been. After his wife's death in 1923, McCann returned to
Ireland, where he died about 1940, as nearly as his aged daughter, Mary McMahon, could recall.

McCormick, Matthew   1825-
Matthew McCormick, born in Ireland, was brought by his parents at the age of seven to New
York. His young life was varied, as he was in turn a carriage maker, a soldier in the Mexican
War, a blacksmith and a gold miner in California. By 1850 he had settled down to farming on the
LaRoque land claim, and there lived out his life. Seven children were born to him and his wife
Joanna Clancy, but not all lived to maturity.

McDonald, Cecile   1830 c.-1848
Cecile was the daughter of Clerk Allan McDonald, born in Central Canada. She bore two chil-
dren to Louis Vandale and died in 1848.

McDonald, Helene   1811-1863
Helene was the eldest recorded daughter of Finan McDonald ("ancient clerk"). She was a
capable and staunch friend of the missionaries of the Nisquallie. After the death of her husband,
William Kittson, 1839, she married Richard Grant, commandant at Fort Hall. She is buried at
St. Ignatius Mission, Montana. Her recorded children by Kittson were Pierre Charles, Eloisa
Jemima and Edwin; by Grant they were Helene Wilhelmina, Julia Priscilla, Adelina, and a
somewhat shadowy figure referred to as "Jim", who may have been a son.

McDonald, Miles   1810 c.-1876
Miles McDonald came to Oregon in the wave of immigration that brought a great number from
Ireland during the 1840's. By 1852 he and others had taken claims in Muddy Valley in Yamhill
County, where they established St. Patrick's Church in 1860. Until that time their marriages and
baptisms had been recorded at St. Paul or in Portland; after 1860 they were held in their home
parish and recorded at Grand Ronde, for Father Croquet served both churches. McDonald died
at the age of 66 and was buried in the New Cemetery at St. Paul.

McDougal, Nancy   ---- - ----
Although not stated in the record, Nancy McDougal, metisse, was probably the daughter of
James McDougal or his brother George, who were with the North West Company early in the
1800's in northern posts.

McKarty, Catherine   1846-
Catherine (Kate) McKarty was the daughter of William McKarty and Silsao (Cecelia)
Carcowan, whose father was chief of the Chinooks on the Washington coast. After the death of
William McKarty, Catherine and her mother returned to the tribe of her grandfather at Grays
Harbor. With some difficulty, the white authorities succeeded in getting the "bright, attractive
little girl" into the school at Vancouver. She later married Fred Brown and lived out her life at
Ilwaco on the Washington coast.

McKarty, Charlotte   1808 c.-1842
Charlotte was a Chehalis woman who married William McKarty (McCarty) at Vancouver in
1839. Joseph, who went by the name of McKarty, was her son by a previous alliance.

McKarty, William (McCarty)   -1854
McKarty was known as "Cochon Bill" for his bristly hair, like that of a pig, or "Brandywine" for
a frigate on which he claimed to have sailed. He was born in Ireland, and came up from California with Ewing Young's party in 1834. For a time he lived in the Willamette Valley on a farm
later taken up by William Case. He married Charlotte Chehalis in 1839; she died in 1842. At
about this time he moved down to the Washington coast and took a claim at the Baker's Bay end
of the portage to Shoalwater Bay. He married Silsao, a daughter of Carcowan, and by her had
one daughter, Catherine. He had a "nice zinc house", said Swan, who had many refreshing
stories to tell of him and his family, "where he caught and salted salmon and kept a most hospitable house". He was drowned in the Wallicut by the upsetting of his canoe; his body was recovered
at sea near the entrance to Shoalwater Bay, where it had been carried by coastwise currents.

McKay, Betsy   1834 c-1848
Not the daughter of Tom McKay, whose daughter Elizabeth died in 1849 at the age of three, but
probably the daughter Betsy of Kenneth McKay and Elizabeth. Betsy was baptized at Fort
Vancouver in 1842, "aged six". Her father Kenneth was said to have been a metis Iroquois,
murdered at Pillar Rock about 1840.

McKay, James   1818-1898
James McKay, who was born in Ireland, was reared in Scotland. There he married Cecelia
Lawson, a Scottish girl. During the 1840's they emigrated to America, crossed the plains in a
group of others like themselves, and settled on Champoeg Creek on French Prairie. Their two
eldest children had died in a measles epidemic on the way west, but others soon followed to
compose a large and thriving family. McKay earned enough in the gold rush days in California to
purchase the former Hudson's Bay Company grist mill on Champoeg Creek, built in the early
1840's, and sold to the Catholic Mission in 1845, from which McKay bought it in 1847 for $8000.
He retained the name, "Mission Mills", which was always painted on the flour sacks through a
large brass stencil. After many years the mill fell into disuse and decay; during 1969, while bull-
dozing was being done for a new dam at the site of the old mill, many of the original timbers and
ironwork fittings were brought up from the creek bed. McKay became prosperous in business
affairs, a pillar in the Catholic Church, and active in school affairs. He and many of his family lie
in the St. Paul Cemetery.

McKay, Thomas   1796-1849 c.
Thomas McKay (pronounced McKy) was a somewhat legendary scout and Indian fighter, that is
to say, his deeds were somewhat legendary, for Tom himself was real enough. He was the son of
Alexander McKay and Marguerite Wadin, who became the wife of Dr. John McLoughlin after
Captain McKay's death on the **Tonquin** in 1811. Thomas, aged fourteen, who had accompanied
his father to Astoria, was sent East for a time, returning a few years later as a clerk in the
Hudson's Bay Company. He was lamed from an unattended accident, but the handicap made
little difference in his range of activities. His first wife, who bore him several children, was the
daughter of Chief Concomley of the Chinook tribe; his second was a Nez Perce woman, and his
third was Isabel (Elizabeth) Montour, daughter of Nicholas Montour, by whom he had several
more children. He had both a farm at Scappoose and a grist mill at Champoeg; at the time of his
residence "on an island in the Columbia River", he was probably camped there, running horses
on the island, for Scappoose is just across a deep slough from Sauvie Island.

McKay, William R.   1849-1950.
William McKay ("Uncle Billy"), son of James McKay I, the miller on Champoeg Creek, built a
great yellow house of Victorian splendor on the road south from Champoeg. It was a landmark
for years on the flat Prairie land and finally burned to the ground in 1969. It has sometimes been
mistakenly identified as the home of Tom McKay—an unfortunate error, for Tom had never
lived in half so pretentious a home. McKay built the house in the 1880's, long after Tom's death.

McKinlay, Archibald   1816-1891
McKinlay was a Scotsman long in the employ of the Hudson's Bay Company, first as an ap-
prentice clerk at York Factory, then Clerk in charge at Fort Walla Walla until 1846, when he
took charge of the Company store in Oregon City. He retired in 1851 to go into business with
George T. Allan and Thomas Lowe. Among other establishments, they had a commission house
in the busy river port of Champoeg during the decade of the 1850's, with McKinlay living just
across the river in a fine old home that still stands. The 1860 census lists as living in the house

McKinlay himself, aged 44, his wife Sarah Julia Ogden, 34, their children James, Sarah, Allan, Catherine and Archibald, ranging in age from twelve years to one, his wife's mother Julia Tet Platte Ogden, 60, his wife's defective sister Euretta, 23, and his wife's half-cousins, Therese and Fabian Rivet, 17 and 15. The great flood of 1861-1862 that swept away Champoeg ruined McKinlay financially. He moved to Lac La Hache in British Columbia to spend his declining years in blindness, and died in 1891. His wife followed within a year, having been fatally injured in a runaway carriage accident.

McLoughlin, Dr. John   1784-1857
McLoughlin was born at Riviere-du-Loup, Quebec, of Scottish-Irish-French descent. Educated as a surgeon, he joined the North West Fur Company and later the Hudson's Bay Company. In 1824 he was appointed Chief Factor of the Columbia Department, which post he held until his retirement to a home in Oregon City in 1845. This home is now a National Historic Site. Dr. McLoughlin's hospitality and generosity to pioneer immigrants brought criticism upon him from the Company. The same pioneers later defrauded him of his land claim; he died disheartened and disillusioned, but has since come to be honored as "The Father of Oregon". After two removals, he and his wife now are buried on the grounds of the home he built in Oregon City.

McLoughlin, Joseph   1810 c-1848
Joseph was the son of Chief Factor McLoughlin by a native woman in Eastern Canada. He joined his father in the West, becoming an ordinary engage. He died from the effects of a fall over a cliff in the Umpqua region. He married Victoire McMillan, half-breed daughter of James McMillan, an early official in the fur companies; there were no descendents. His farm near the mouth of the Yamhill River on the north side was later bought by Medorum Crawford, the site of "Crawford's Upper Landing" in steamboat days. "He rode like a centaur," wrote John Dunn, a contemporary.

McLoughlin, Marguerite Wadin McKay   1785 c.-1860
This was the wife of Dr. John McLoughlin. She was of mixed blood, and had previously been the wife of Alexander McKay, who lost his life in the Tonquin disaster. Thomas McKay and several daughters, probably three, were born of their marriage. About 1811 she was married to John McLoughlin in Eastern Canada. Four children were born to them. Both she and her famous husband are buried in Oregon City on the grounds of their former home.

McMullin, Victoire (McMillan)   1822-1898
Victoire was the daughter of James McMillan of the North West Company, who had been stationed in the West for a few years. Her mother was Kilakotah Coboway, who later married Louis Labonte I. Victoire was first married to Joseph McLoughlin, son of Chief Factor McLoughlin by a native woman in Eastern Canada. After the death of Joseph, Victoire married Pierre LaCourse II, and still later Etienne Simon Gregoire. Of her numerous children by LaCourse, only one reached adulthood, two by Gregoire.

McPhail, John   1809-
McPhail was born in Scotland and enlisted in the Hudson's Bay employ as a laborer in 1832. He was also called a middleman, or canoe man, but seems to have spent most of his years as a shepherd at the Company farms at Fort Vancouver, Cowlitz, and Nisquallie. He married Therese Cascade in 1846; she was probably the "native woman" who was the mother of his earlier children, Mary, John, and Catherine. John died at the age of four, Catherine at thirteen at the Sister's School at St. Paul, and Therese Cascade in 1848. McPhail retired to Vancouver Island in 1853. It is interesting to speculate whether he was one of the "early Scottish settlers on the island" who, knitting in the traditional way of Scottish shepherds to pass the time, handed on to the native women the skill that today produces the famous Cowichan sweaters "so well made that they will shed rain".

Mainville, Francois
Francois Mainville was a trader for the Hudson's Bay Company for some time in the 1830's at Basswood Lake, west of Lake Superior. The Saulteaux Indians were from the Great Lakes region.

Makah Tribe
The Makah Indians on the tip of Cape Flattery were seafarers who depended on the open sea for most of their sustenance. They were daring and skillful in cedar dugouts, often going to fishing

banks well out of sight of land. They are called Clallams interchangeably in the old records, but the tribes are distinct.

Makaeno (Makaine), Therese
Therese was the daughter of an Owyhee father and a Chehalis mother. She married Joseph Plouff, blacksmith, and bore seven children, four of whom died in early childhood. Plouff was killed "by a musket ball" under unknown circumstances in Oregon City in 1849. The next year Therese married Baptiste Laroque. The records of this family are scattered through Vancouver, St. Paul, and St. Louis.

Maloin, Fabian (Malouin)   1810-1855
"of the Faubourg St. Joseph, Montreal", says the record, and not a great deal more is known of him. He first married Louise Atenesse, an Iroquois half-blood. After six recorded children, Louise died in 1849. Maloin then married Victoire Laderoute. He lived to prove up on his 1843 claim but died shortly after, in 1855. The claim included the present site of Brooks in the southern part of French Prairie. His widow Victoire married Andre Cloutier.

McPaulin, Rogers (McPoland)   1822-
Rogers McPaulin, or McPoland, was born in Ireland in 1822, married Hannah Hathaway in Missouri in 1851, and settled on a claim in Linn County in 1853. By 1860, however, he seems to have been living on French Prairie, having children baptized at both St. Paul and St. Louis. The name of his wife (if the same woman, and it appears to be) gave some trouble to the various scribes, being written "Hannah Hathaway", "Mary", "Anna", "Ann Ottawa" and "Mary Haner". The McPaulin name last appears on the Prairie in 1882.

Maneigre, Dieudonne   1831-1903
Dieudonne was one of five young men who went from the East to California during the gold rush, somewhat later than the main stream. After making good, they came to Oregon looking for homesites. For the full story, see Jette, Adolphe. Maneigre married Emelie (Amelia) Pichet, deep-voiced and competent. He became a successful business man in St. Paul, where many descendents remain.

Manson, Donald   1798-1880
Manson was born in Scotland and joined the Hudson's Bay Company at the age of 19 as a clerk. In 1825 he was transferred from the eastern side of the Rockies to the western, and there spent the rest of his days, except for a visit to Scotland for a year. "That ramping highlander", as Trader John Tod called him, was a vigorous builder and post master with something of a heavy hand. His posts included Fort Langley, Fort George, Fort McLoughlin, Kamloops, Stikine, and Stuart Lake. In 1857 he retired to a farm at Champoeg, where he died in 1880. He married Felicite, eldest daughter of Etienne Lucier, and reared a family of seven children. His grave is unmarked in the community cemetery at Champoeg.

Maranda, Louis (Iroquois, dit LeFrize)
"Tete Frize" was an Indian with David Thompson in the employ of the North West Fur Company in 1808. The above may be the same man. This Louis Iroquois is called Shaegoskatsta in the Vancouver records, the same name as used by McLoughlin in his Letters, but reappears as Louis Maranda, dit Le Frize, "father of the bride consenting" at the marriage of Marie Anne (aged fourteen) to Joseph Brule at St. Paul in 1848. McLoughlin called him a freeman in 1832; he no doubt had retired to St. Paul, as did many of the Iroquois. A small settlement of them took land on the Yamhill River opposite Dayton, for example.

Marcellais, Angelique   1804-1879
Angelique was the wife of Francois Gagnon I. Their older children are not recorded, being early, until they are married and in homes of their own. Francois Gagnon died in California during the gold rush. In 1852 his widow Angelique married Edouard Bellanger (Blanchey), who was drowned six years later in the Frazer River by the upsetting of a canoe. Her third husband was Charles Derome.

Martineau, Genevieve   1840-
Genevieve, daughter of Pierre Martineau and Lisette Humphreville, married Baptiste Bourjeau in 1858 at St. Paul; other records may be found in the St. Louis Church Register.

Martineau, Louise 1836-1923
Louise Martineau, who married Joseph Lucier the younger, was the mother of fourteen children. Both she and Joseph are buried at St. Paul, well marked with stones.

Martineau, Pierre -1842
Martineau was a native, (probably metis), usually working out of Fort Walla Walla. He had joined the Hudson's Bay Company about 1827; he was not wholly trusted by McLoughlin, who considered him a troublemaker. The lives of Martineau and Canote Humpherville, another native (or metis) engage, were closely parallel. Martineau married Louise, a sister of Canote; the two men witnessed for each other at church rites, and both drowned in the same boating accident on the Columbia in 1842. Martineau's young widow later married George Montour and died in 1849 at the age of thirty. Of Martineau's four recorded children, Pierre II married "Jennie"; Louise married Joseph Lucier, son of Etienne; Xavier married Sophie Chalifoux, daughter of the old boatman Andre; Genevieve married J. B. Bourjeau.

Maskegonne Tribe, Maskegon
The Maskegons were a tribe so closely allied to the Crees that they were known to the traders as Swampy Crees. They inhabited the region of rivers and swamps lying between Hudson Bay and Lake Winnipeg.

Masta, (Mastau) Antoine
Very little is known about this man. He was evidently living on the Despard place in 1850, being included in that census number. He did, however, have a claim of his own near Etienne Lucier in the big bend of the river. A daughter Victoire, aged seven, was given in the same census as living at the Sisters' School at St. Paul.
Joseph St. Amant, a young visitor from France in the late 1840's, left his impressions of the Prairie, and in particular, of a night spent in Masta's cabin. His "Voyages in California en dans l'Oregon" (in French) is unequalled for honesty and clarity of detail.
There had been a half-breed, Raymond Masta, born in 1785, who was an interpreter at Great Slave Lake from 1818 at least until 1821. Any relationship between him and Antoine is not known.

Matte, Louis 1814-
Louis Matte was a blacksmith, presumably with the Hudson's Bay Company. He was born in Lower Canada, according to his land claim deposition, and "came to Oregon in 1851", which may indicate his blacksmithing was in Canada. He married Therese Piedgane (Blackfoot) in 1844, and settled his claim in 1854.

Matthews, William Wallace
Nothing is known of his life before he joined the Tonquin enterprise. He cam as a clerk in the Pacific Fur Company, and remained four and one half years in all on the Columbia. He is several times mentioned by Franchere in his comings and goings to explore or to establish posts. He married Kil-a-kot-ah, one of the daughters of the Clatsop sub-chief Coboway, to whom a daughter Ellen was born in 1815. Matthews returned east the same year. Whether he took the infant Ellen with him, as seems unlikely, or sent for her later is not known, but she is said to have been educated in Montreal and to have married "a wealthy citizen". This was George Barnston, an officer in the Hudson's Bay Company and at one time in charge of Fort Walla Walla.

Matthieu, Charles, Sr. 1834-1918
Charles was a brother to Francois Xavier Matthieu, and had come to Oregon later. Their father also came west (1864). It appears that Charles had married some time before arriving in Oregon, hence the baptism of his daughters in 1862 at St. Paul, the marriage having been "civil". The younger Charles, born to Francois Xavier and Rose Aussant, was his nephew.

Matthieu, Francois Xavier 1818-1914
Francois Xavier Matthieu, Jr., had become involved in the Papineau Rebellion in Canada and left for the United States to escape. He eventually reached Oregon in 1842 and found a home with Etienne Lucier. Matthieu was the last survivor of those who voted for a Provisional Government at the Champoeg meeting of 1843 and came to be regarded as something of an oracle. Rose Aussant, aged about fifteen, was living at the time of Matthieu's arrival in the home of Pierre Belique, just across the fence from the Lucier house on the "knoll" or natural levee south of the river. Presently the young pair married and reared a numerous family. Matthieu became proper-

ous, as farmer, carpenter, and merchant; he plotted the town site of Butteville, along with Alexis Aubichon, from portions of their adjoining claims.

Maxwell Henri
Henry Maxwell had been an officer in the Hudson's Bay Company in northern British Columbia until forced by ill health to retire about 1846 to a better climate. The death of a daughter Charlotte, aged fifteen months, was recorded "near Walla Walla" in October, 1847. By 1882 Maxwell was living in Montana, Roberts wrote, when "I had a letter from him last summer".

Menard, Jean Baptiste   1843-1897
In the Grand Ronde Reserve records of Father Croquet, Jean Baptiste Menard is given as having married Elizabeth Petit on December 11, 1882. She died shortly, and four years later he married Catherine Voutrin. A son Adolphe, born in 1888 and deceased at the age of one year, is the only recorded child. Both Jean Baptiste and his wife Catherine died in 1897, he preceding her by but five months.

Menard, Pierre I   1803 c.-1877
The Menards were early in the western fur trade, one having been with David Thompson in 1808 in Montana. It is not known when Pierre Menard I, born in Canada, came west; he was the son of Louis Menard and Therese Labonte of Berthier. He settled on a claim in the big bend of the river above St. Paul in 1847. His first wife, Josephte Youte, died in 1851, "leaving six children", although only five appear in the records. Pierre then married Marie Blackfoot, who died in 1857, and lastly (now "an old citizen of the parish") he married Therese Saste. Pierre died on the Grand Ronde Reserve June 11, 1877, when his age was given as "80 years".

Menard, Pierre II   1840-1908
Pierre Menard II lived on the Grand Ronde Reserve, where he married Elizabeth Sanagratta, aged fifteen, on July 6, 1869. Twelve children were born to them, six boys and six girls. A photo taken about 1900 shows a handsome old patriarch of poise and intelligence, meticulously groomed.

Menes, Captain Francis   1807 c.-1867
Menes was the captain of l'Etoile du Matin (The Morning Star) that brought the Sisters of Notre Dame du Namur to Oregon in 1844. Several years later he made another voyage to bring merchandise to the coast, but his ship was so badly damaged in crossing the bar at the mouth of the Columbia that she had to be towed to Portland. It was determined then that she was past repair and was burned. Captain Menes removed the cargo to Oregon City and opened what was commonly known as "The French Store", long a landmark on South Main Street. Menes retired to a farm near St. Louis, where he died in 1867.

Merten, Stephen   1852-1928
Stephen Merten's wife was Theresa Gooding (1858-1942). The family were later pioneers, having come to the Willamette Valley from Nevada in the second half of the 1800's. It is still recalled that Clara, who married John Franklin Davidson, as a girl of fourteen had ridden all the way sidesaddle. Her sisters married into other early family lines on French Prairie—Hughes, Kirk, Mullen, McKay.

Michel, Indian   1820 c.-1890
Since he was not on the Reserve, the "Michel, Indian" who died at St. Paul in 1890 was probably the "Michel, Indian of the mountains" whose wife Marguerite Kalapooia was baptized before her death at the age of eighteen, and whose year-old daughter Felicite was baptized shortly afterward, both at St. Louis in 1848. He may also have been the Alex Michel who, with Isaac Ogden, Peter Hae and one other, "using two small row boats, saved all the stranded people in the flood of 1861-1862".

Michina, Marguerite (Marie)   1798 c.-1868
This second wife of Canote Humpherville was called a Coeur d'Alene woman at the time of her daughter Louise's marriage in 1849. At her own baptism in 1843 she was "Marie Sarkina", possibly her native name. She is also given as "Sinpoil". After Canote's death in 1842, she and five small children lived with her stepson Pierre (Wakan) Humpherville near St. Louis—"a good religious mother, widow from that time (twelve years)". At her death in 1868 she was "about 80 years", but was probably more nearly seventy.

Million, Bennett   1812-
Million and his wife Armilda, whom he had married in Wisconsin, came to Oregon in the early
1850's and took a claim in the Jacksonville area. They were the parents of twelve children, and
although the parents do not appear in the Church records of St. Paul, three of their daughters do:
H (Harriet?), wife of G. T. Marshall "of Portland", Nancy, wife of Green Davidson of Fairfield,
and Frances, wife of J. B. P. Piette of St. Paul.

Moisan, Francis Xavier   1845-1926
Francis Xavier was the eldest son of Thomas Moisan and Henriette Longtain. He married Mary
Virginia Manning at St. Louis in 1872; their family was numerous, and many well-known de-
scendents remain today.

Moisan, Thomas   1809-1888
Thomas Moisan was first an engage of the Hudson's Bay Company, then a California miner, and
last a farmer of large holdings in the Lake Labiche region at the southern end of the Prairie.
From his various enterprises he amassed considerable wealth and built a pretentious home with a
third story cupola from which he could observe his cattle herds and watch for the dust of the
approaching Salem stage while reading his French books. His children were Francois Xavier,
Alexandre, Mary and Philomine. He died in 1888; his wife Henriette (Harriet) lived to be very
old, dying in 1913. Both are buried in the Gervais Catholic Cemetery with an imposing stone,
"Of such is the Kingdom of Heaven".

Molala Tribe
The Molalas were a detached band of the Cayuse who had gone to the mountainous region to the
west and there remained. They visited back and forth with their Cayuse relatives in later times,
particularly on hunting or berrying expeditions. One such misunderstood visitation caused the
somewhat disgraceful "Battle of the Abiqua" in 1848 when the white settlers panicked at the
notion of an "invasion". The tribe was removed to the Grand Ronde Reserve in Polk County
in 1855.

Mongraine, David   1806-1882
He was a Canadian that seems to have been a late comer; there is no record of any service in the
fur companies. His claim lay on the Champoeg Creek near the center of the Prairie. In 1849 he
married Catherine Lafantasie, widow of Nazaire Dupre. Old pictures of Mongraine and his wife
are delightful studies of gentle whimsy and humor. Their children included Angelle (born 1850,
married Pierre Charles Kittson, q.v.), David, Jr., Clarisse (born 1855, married Calixte LeBeau),
Clementine (born 1857, married Frank Lambert, q.v.), Josephine (born 1860, married August
Raymond, Jr., q.v.) and Francois Xavier, born in 1864. Many descendents remain among well-
known families of the Prairie today.

Monique   -before 1862
The name Monique appears here and there in Company records, very sketchily as to any one
individual. Thus "Monique, Cowlitz" (1761-1841) died at Vancouver; Joseph Monique, Iroquois
(1790 c-1845) died at the same place; Jose Monique had a Cascade wife and infant son there in
1841; Nicholas Monique was with the Northwest Fur Company at Fort George in 1813. Another
Nicholas Monique—or the same one?—"an old Indian", attempted to carry McTavish's wife on
his back across a bog while Thomas Felix toted the lighter Frances Simpson; the whole crew got
to laughing so hard that Monique "stumbled forward, fell on his face, and gave his unfortunate
rider a summerset into the mud".   (Lady Simpson's Journal)

Monique, Francois Xavier   1821 c-1889
Xavier Monique was the son of Louis Oskhana, dit Monique, an Iroquois employe of the Company, and his Chinook wife Charlotte. Xavier was evidently somewhat older than the children
baptized in 1839 and was not mentioned at that time. He married Madeleine Rowland in 1862 at
St. Louis. Two children, Eleanore and Marie, are recorded. Xavier died "at Champoeg" in 1889
at the approximate age of 68.

Monique, Louis Iroquois, Oskanha   -before 1862
Oskanha seems to have been the tribal name of this Iroquois man, and may be entered so, or
under Iroquois. See all forms of the name. Monique was a boatman, said to be very skillful. His
wife was Charlotte Chinook, apparently the widow of the Antoine Plante whose funeral at Fort
Vancouver was observed by Tolmie the day after his arrival at the fort. There was a seven-year-

old son, Antoine II who became part of the Monique household. The Monique children were Xavier, who appears later in St. Louis, Catherine, who died at the age of about ten, Marie, Ignace and Louis II. Louis, the father, was "late" at the time of Xavier's marriage in 1862 at St. Louis.

Monique, Marie Louise   1835 c-1907

Marie Monique was the daughter of an Iroquois father and a Chinook mother, Louis Oskhana dit Monique, and Charlotte. She was baptized at Vancouver in 1839, aged 3½ years. She is next mentioned in the St. Louis Register as the mother of Florence, "born outside the marriage" to Francois Gagnon, the younger. The child died four years later, by that time called Deschamps, the name of her stepfather. Marie Monique married Pierre Deschamps at St. Louis in 1853. Seven, perhaps eight, children were born before Deschamps disappears from view. Marie then married Jean Baptiste Jeaudoin, to whom she bore five children before his death by drowning in the Elochomin River about 1879. His widow then married Joseph Lanoutte. No church records of her last two marriages have been found at Cathlamet, near which the family lived; the above information was researched by the late Betty Jeaudoin for her **Family History**, including the obituary written at Marie's death in 1907.

> "Tuesday, September 3, 1907 Marie Louise, wife of Joseph Lanoutte, aged 74 years. Mrs. Lanoutte had lived in Cathlamet a great many years, where she had a large circle of friends and acquaintances who deeply mourn her passing away. Her death was not unexpected, as she had been bed ridden and a great sufferer from cancer of the stomach for many months. She was born in Three River, Canada, on July 12, 1833, and was the mother of fifteen children, only three of whom are now living. They are Mrs. R. C. Elliott of Cathlamet, Mrs. O. L. Benedict of Spokane, and John Judway (Jeaudoin), all of whom were present at the funeral. The funeral services were held at the Church conducted by Dr. Peacock and the interment was in the Lower Elokomin Valley."

Montour, Caroline   1825 c.-1851

Caroline was the daughter of Nicholas Montour and Ann Humphreville. She was the first wife of Louis Labonte II. Of her four children, none seems to have reached maturity. However, one Alexandre, who may or may not have been her son and does not appear under that name in the records, lived and reared a large family.

Montour, George

"George Montour", recalled his neighbor, "was a very large man and very powerful; he must have weighed 350 pounds. I have seen him lasso wild cattle and hold them to be branded without any cinch or other thing to hold the saddle on the horse, He did it by mere weight and bodily strength. He would do this for half a day together." His wife was Lizette Canote (Humphreville), widow of Pierre Martineau, who had been drowned in 1842. Lizette died in 1849, "aged about thirty". One daughter, Julie, was recorded in 1846; a son Nicholas was born and died in 1844.

Montour, Julie   1846-1868

Julie was the second wife of Narcisse Gingras. They were married on July 4, 1867; she died the next February, "aged 23".

Montour, Louis   1821 c-1871

Louis Montour was the younger son of Nicholas Montour, half-breed clerk in the Hudson's Bay Company. Louis married Julienne Molalla in 1848, to whom three children were born but only one survived. For this daughter, Appoline, see Winslow, Marc, Grand Ronde. Julienne died following the birth of her third child, in 1854. Some time later Louis Montour moved to the Grand Ronde Reservation, where in 1861 he married another Molalla woman, Anne. Louis died on the reservation in 1871.

Montour, Nicholas   1790-

Nicholas Montour was the half-breed son of a partner in the North West Company, also Nicholas. He was in and out of the employ periodically, being a good clerk, but indolent and unreliable. For a time he held land about where the town of Gervais now stands, but he seems to have relinquished it. His daughter Isabelle was the last wife of Thomas McKay; his daughter Caroline was the first wife of Louis Labonte II. His daughter Maria, baptized "in danger of death" in January, 1841, died in May, "aged 10". His wife Ann Umphreville (Humpherville) died in 1846, "aged 55 years". Montour appears to have had several other wives, as the mothers of his older children are given as Ann Fabeau (mother of Toussaint), Marguerite Crise or Susanne Kuze (mother of Louis Bob), while the rest, if specified at all, are the children of Ann (Susanne) Umphreville.

Morais, Antoine
Antoine Morais (Murray, Moray, Morin) was the son of Francois Morais I and Marie LaRoque. He married Marguerite Gagnon at St. Louis in 1856, but soon afterward moved to Frenchtown, near Walla Walla, where the records of his twelve children continue.

Mullen, Thomas
"Grandfather Thomas Mullen came from Ireland," his grandson Charles related, "and settled here on the river in 1852. My father Patrick (1839-1920) built this old southern-type house before I was born. My mother was Mary Ann Flynn, and I was born in 1882, the second of nine children. The old narrow gauge railroad came up the canyon from Ray's Landing and crossed my father's land. It went north of St. Paul between the Managre and McKillip houses, and then it went pretty straight on to Woodburn. Low trestles took it across Mission and Champoeg Creeks. No, I never rode on the train but I used to hear its whistle as it crossed the field, and I walked the track many a time. The grade was built up pretty well; it took a dozer a day and a half to grade down one fill after the railroad was gone. The rails? They went out of here, except that McKay over at the mill got a lot of them to use for fence posts. Still there, the last time I looked."

Murphy, Daniel   1789-(1800)-1866
Daniel Murphy crossed the continent in early stages. In 1827 in Missouri he married Catherine Dillon, granddaughter of Thomas Hanly, who had been an officer under Wellington in the Spanish campaign. By the 1850's the couple and their sons Matthew O'Connor, Peter Kenrick and Daniel Raphael were settled near St. Paul, Oregon; the mother died in 1864, the father in 1866.

Murphy, Daniel Andrew   1836 (1826)-1896
Daniel Murphy, son of Michael, married Elizabeth Cosgrove in 1856; eight children are recorded. Andrew is said to have done the ornate plasterwork ornamentation when the St. Paul Church was "enlarged and beautified" during the 1890's.

Murphy, James Andrew
(Does not appear in these volumes)
James Andrew Murphy, of County Wexford in Ireland, was the progenitor of two main lines of Murphys on French Prairie. He had come to the United States in 1799 with at least two young sons, Daniel and Michael, whose mother is not named.

Murphy, Matthew O'Connor   1830-1906
Matthew O'Connor Murphy, born in Illinois, came west as a young man and married Ellen Costello. They were the parents of fourteen children. Many descendents keep their memory and the Murphy name alive in the St. Paul area today. He was a civil engineer who surveyed a large part of Oregon and Washington in the early days.

Murphy, Michael
Michael Murphy married Catherine ----- in Illinois; both were deceased by 1856. Their son, Daniel Andrew, appears to have been the only one of Michael's line to come to Oregon.

Murphy, Peter Kenrick   1842-1912
The records of Peter Kenrick Murphy and his wife, Martha Joanna O'Connor, and their seven children are found in the St. Louis Church Registers.

Murray, Frances   1824-1896
"Fanny" Murray, wife of James Coleman, was born in Ireland. She was the daughter of Bernard ("Barney") Murray, who came to America in 1827. The name of her mother is not given. The family seems to have come westward by stages, as Barney Murray became a citizen in Ohio in 1836, Frances married in Iowa, and son Charles came to Oregon in 1852. It is probable that the families came together, for all were settled in Muddy Valley, north of Sheridan, when they first appear in the church records. As there was no church in that area at the time, the records are found in the Immaculate Conception Register, Portland, among the earliest there. Coleman gave land from his claim for a cemetery and church, and Barney Murray was the first to be buried there, November 21, 1859, "aged 80", several years before the church of St. Patricks had become

a reality. His fragmented stone can still be found in the abandoned cemetery in Muddy Valley.

Nancy, of The Dalles   1800 c.-1850
In their old age Nancy's grandsons, Thomas and David Lachance (Pepin) used to relate her story: As a young girl, she married a Frenchman and went with the trappers' party to the Snake River country and to the Rocky Mountains. There the entire party, save one, was killed in camp by the Blackfeet. Nancy, knowing the Blackfoot ways, had slipped away into the woods with her infant Susanne. She travelled westward with much hardship in an effort to get back to her people. After some days she was overtaken by the badly wounded survivor of the massacre, and they struggled on together to a cache she had seen on the way out, where they found food and clothing. While recuperating there, they were picked up by Ogden's brigade, returning from Salt Lake. In the brigade was an American named Goodrich, who had once harassed Ogden and once deserted him, but was now with him again. He took Nancy for his wife, but within a year he was drowned in the Columbia. Nancy later married Jean Baptiste Dobin, and settled on French Prairie. Both went to the California gold fields during the rush, and Dobin died there. Nancy returned, but died a short time after reaching home, May 3, 1850.

Nesqually Tribe (Nisquallie)
The Nesquallies lived along the river of that name south of Puget Sound. Their chief Leschi in 1856 led an unsuccessful attack on the new town of Seattle, for which he was finally executed.

Newell, Robert   1807-1869
Newell, one of the leading citizens of Champoeg, had been a free trapper or "mountain man" in the Rocky Mountains for eleven years, along with John Larison, for whom he was testifying at the latter's marriage. Newell had married Catherine Nez Perce ("Kitty") and was the father of five sons by her. Kitty died in 1845 and was buried on the rise above Champoeg Creek, near the road that in those days crossed the top of the mill dam. The place is still known to a few. Newell then married Rebecca Newman; ten more children followed. With the death of his second wife, Newell left Champoeg, which had been almost ruined by a great flood in 1861, and went to Lewiston, where he married a third time and shortly died.

Nez Perce Tribe
The Nez Perce (Pierced Nose) Indians lived in northeastern Oregon and adjacent parts of Idaho and Washington. They were handsome and able, excellent horsemen, and capable of producing such leaders as Chief Joseph. The Appaloosa horse was a sort of trademark of the tribe. Father Blanchet thought well of them, writing, "The natives known by this name are scattered on the vast plains not far from the Rocky Mountains, extending toward the south. Good by nature, mild and full of respect for everything concerning the Master of Life."

Nez Perce, Catherine   -1845
Catherine (Kitty) was one of three daughters of Chief Kowesote to marry mountain men, the others being Virginia Meek and the wife, name unknown, of Caleb Wilkins. She was buried on the Newell claim on a rise above Champoeg Creek. Newell, it is said, planned a cemetery beside the road that crossed the creek by way of the mill dam and several other burials were made there, but the spot remained unmarked and is now obliterated by park grading.

Nibler (Neibler), John, Joseph and Francis
In 1868, following the closure of the St. Francis Xavier enterprise at St. Paul, their farm land was sold to the three Neibler brothers and Michael Schultheis, all lately come from Bavaria. Their families are recorded in St. Louis, Gervais and St. Paul registers. A member of the 1867 Neibler wagon train wrote of their encounter with the new Mullan Road in northern Idaho that some wagons had broken down, oxen were weak and lame, a number of people were sick, and a young daughter of John Neibler had died and been buried "in the peaceful burial ground at Cataldo Mission". Father J. Caruana, pastor at Sacred Heart Mission recorded in the Mission Burial Book, "November 4, 1867 I the undersigned buried at Sacred Heart Rosa, daughter of Mr. Nibler, from Germany, deceased yesterday."

Nipissing, Chief Louis (Napassant)   1813-1888
Louis Nipissing, an adopted chief of the Umpquas, seems to have been the son of Louis Nipissing, given also as Tom-a-pierre and Lapset, who "died long ago", in other records, and a Chinook woman, whose name was unknown and who also "died long ago". Louis "Chief" Nipissing had been with Father Brouillet at Umatilla during the Whitman massacre, and through various other

associations with the whites was believed to be somewhat knowledgeable in their ways. The Umpqua Tribe adopted him as their treaty chief in 1855, believing he could get them better terms than one of their own number. Later he went to the Grand Ronde Reserve as an Umpqua, where he died in 1888.

His first recorded wife, Louise Nez Perce, died in 1847; her sons, Louis and Joseph, in 1847 and 1850. His second wife was Lizette Klikitat; no record of their marriage has come to light. The entries for their children—LaRose, Pierre, Marianne, Louis (the second), Charles and Henriette —are found in the registers of St. Paul, St. Louis and Grand Ronde.

Nipissing, Marie Anne   1819 c.-
Marie Anne Nipissing (Napassant, Lapset) was the daughter of one called Tom-a-pierre Lapset or Louis Nipissing and a native mother, both of whom died "long ago", the dates unremembered. Her father was "late" in 1839, when Marie Anne was baptized at Vancouver and married Laurent Quintal (Chantell, Cantell). Her later years were spent in Douglas County.

Norwest, Agnes
Agnes Norwest married Augustin Russie II and bore him six children before his death in 1855. What became of Agnes and the children has not come to light, but in the 1890's her sister Cecile (Quintal) and an unmarried son, Sam Quintal, living on the Grand Ronde Reserve, were the guardians of two or more "Russell" children, who appear to have been the orphans of one of Agnes Norwest Russie's sons.

Norwest, Jean Baptiste (Tyikwarhi, Iroquois)   1795-1855
Jean Baptiste Norwest was probably a brother to Thomas Norwest I. Both were Iroquois going by the names of Taikonari, Tyikwarhi, Ottawa, Northwest, Nordouest, Norez, and so forth. Jean Baptiste Norwest's grandson Thomas, son of Thomas Baptiste, wrote in 1897, "About the name, my father had a name in French. They call him Ottawa and sometimes Tommie. But his right name in english is Thomas Norwest. It is impossible that you could not find his name in the record!" Jean Baptiste Norwest married Judith Walla Walla, who was deceased by 1848. She may be the same as Marie Ann Walla Walla, who died early in 1847, when her widower Baptiste married Henriette Pend d'Oreille.

Norwest, (Tyikwarhi), Joseph (Francois)   1846-1940
Joseph Francois, youngest son of Jean Baptiste Norwest and Judith Walla Walla, usually called Frank, "by some means wandered away from home and landed at St. Paul", old Mary Ann Michelle recalled in her reminiscences years later, and was put in school by the Agent there. His parents may have been temporarily in Walla Walla, but his father's death is recorded in St. Paul in 1855, so her recollection may have been somewhat hazy on the point. Frank married Alice Samson, a Rogue River girl on the Reserve, in 1868. After eight children, Alice died, and Frank married Mary Smith, another Rogue River woman. Three more children were born. Their only remaining son, Alpheus, was living in Tacoma in 1967, and writing letters filled with tribal memories of the family origin in Eastern Canada, their French language, and the "civilized" heritage they claimed.

Norwest, Thomas Jean Baptiste   1830-1888
Thomas Baptiste, sometimes called simply Baptiste, as his father had also been called, was the son of Jean Baptiste Norwest or Tyikwarhi, Iroquois, and Judith (Josette, Marie) Walla Walla. He served in the Indian War following the Whitman massacre, then returned to the Willamette Valley, where he spent the remainder of his life, either on his claim on the north side of the Yamhill River near his Iroquois friends, the Tsete's and the Tawakons, or on the Grand Ronde Reserve with his son Thomas and his brother Francois. He married Louise Seguin, called also Assiniboine, St. Andre, Peter or Pierre, in 1856. Infant mortality was high in their large family; by 1897 their son Thomas alone survived. Thomas Jean Baptiste died in 1888 of pneumonia, and was buried in the Reserve cemetery; his widow Louise had gone to live at Oak Grove (Wapinitia), where she died of tuberculosis in 1872.

His old claim on the Yamhill is shown on early maps; it later passed into other hands. Another Norwest, son of his brother Francois Joseph, recalled in 1967, "I can still see the old shack in a grove of brush, one mile north of Dayton." He meant in his memory, for he had known the old homestead from childhood.

Notre Dame du Namur, Sisters of
In the autumn of 1844 six Belgian Sisters of Notre Dame du Namur opened a school for girls at St.

Paul, known as Sainte Marie de Willamette. The school closed in 1853 with the departure of the Sisters for California.

Nouite (Nouette, Newatte, etc.)
The Nouite were a Kwakuitl tribe of northern Vancouver Island, much given to capturing and trading slaves. Like other tribes on Vancouver Island, they were expert canoemen and fishers, warlike and dangerous to their neighbors, and possessed of a distinctive art form developed to a high degree.

Nouite, Josephte   1800 c.-1840
Josephte was early married to Etienne Lucier, one of the Astorians who arrived in 1811 or 1812. She was the mother of six children, Felicite (Manson), Adrienne (Lachapelle), Pelagie (Bernier), Louis, Michel and Joseph, who was a small infant at the time of her death. Her widower remarried during the year; his sons Pierre and Etienne II were from this second marriage.

Ogden, Euretta (Yritta)   1836-
Euretta was the youngest daughter of Peter Skene and Therese Tet Platte. "Her mind was clouded", but not to the extent the other heirs claimed at the time her father's will was read. She was quite capable of handling her share of the estate, her partisan declared, and should not be deprived of it.

Ogden, Isaac   1839-1869
Born June 6, 1839 at Stuart Lake, B.C., Isaac married Anna Manson, daughter of Donald Manson and Felicite Lucier, and lived at Champoeg. He was killed in a brawl on February 10, 1869 at that place, and buried in the Champoeg Cemetery.

Ogden, Peter Skene   1794-1854
Ogden was one of the best known traders and Chief Factors in the West. He was sometimes called "Utah" because of his Snake River expeditions, or 'M'sieu Pete" as a term of regard. He ransomed the survivors of the Whitman massacre and brought them down to Fort Vancouver. After a term of service as Chief Factor he retired to Oregon City, building a good home, "The Cliffs", near the falls. He died in 1854 and is buried in Mountain View Cemetery with a memorial marker erected years later. His wife was a step-daughter of "Old Francois Rivet"; his daughter Julia was the wife of Trader Archibald McKinlay. After Ogden's death, his widow went to live with the McKinlays at Lac La Hache, British Columbia, and there died.

Okanogan, Charlotte Skealks   1805 c.-1845
Charlotte Okanogan was the wife of William Pion, to whom she bore a daughter Nancy in 1824. No record has been found of Pion's death, sometime in the 1820's it appears, for in 1828 Charlotte bore a son Joseph to Jean Gingras. She and Gingras were married in 1841. Various other children are recorded in St. Paul, others in St. Louis.

Okanogan, Therese (Spokane)
Therese Spokane's life was one of tragedy, though perhaps no more so than that of many other native women, were we to know their story as well. Her first husband, Louis Lavallee, was killed by the Blackfeet in 1828 on Ogden's Fourth Snake River Expedition, within a half-mile of camp. "His naked but unscalped body", wrote Ogden, " . . . I had interred. Valuable smart loss. He leaves a wife and three children destitute." These children were Thomas, Martial and Pierre. Therese Spokane's second husband, Pierre Grenier, was drowned in a brigade tragedy at The Dalles in 1828; he left an infant daughter, Marie Ann. Theresa's third husband was the noted steersman, Joseph Cornellier (Cornoyer), who died before receiving the patent to his claim on French Prairie. His children by Therese were Victoire, Joseph and Louis.

Okanogan Tribe
The Okanogans were a Salishan tribe of north-central Washington and southern British Columbia.

O'Kelly, Minrod   1788-
O'Kelly was an American, coming before his wife and children to Oregon. In a dispute with one Mahoney over a land claim he shot and killed the man, by accident, he swore, but nevertheless he was tried, found guilty, and sentenced to be hanged. The case was appealed, lost, and time dragged on. In the meantime his son, having got word of the proceedings, rode on ahead of the wagon train to plead his father's cause. The gallant sheriff turned Nimrod loose, saying that no

woman with several children should be left a widow. During the delay of returning to jail to await execution after the appeal had failed, Nimrod got tired of waiting for the broken-down wagon to be repaired and was allowed to walk on ahead to the jail—"I'll meet you there!" He lived out the remainder of his life peacefully on his farm.

Osborn, Joseph
Joseph Osborn was a carpenter from Baltimore who is said to have worked at building the Mc-Kinlay, McCann (Herbert) and Newell houses at Champoeg. These fine old houses, still standing or restored, are all built to a similar pattern, which Osborn may have learned in the East. They are far above the design of the ordinary cabin or cottage common to the Prairie at the time. Osborn's own home, modest but attractive, stood on a knoll under a grove of fir trees until it was razed in 1971.

Ouvre, Jany   1821 c.-
"Jany" (Genevieve) was a native or possibly metisse, whose name appears variously as Simpson, Tioult, Cowlitz, or Nesquallie. She, as well as her husband, Jean Baptiste Ouvre, was a steadying influence amongst the restless natives at Fort Nesquallie throughout the decade of the eighteen-forties.

Ouvre, Jean Baptiste   1792-1849 c.
Ouvre was a middleman from Montreal who enlisted in the Hunt overland party at Mackinac in 1810 and remained in the West in the employ of succeeding fur companies. He was an invaluable aid to Tolmie on his northward tour in 1833 as messenger, nurse, advisor, and arbiter of Indian quarrels. He seems to have been stationed at Nesquallie later, as in 1840 Dr. Tolman wrote to Kitson at that place regarding medication for his own inflamed arm and "for Ouvre a purgative weekly--a course of blistering to the nape of the neck--interscapular region and sacral region--sponging every morning with sea water and thereafter frictions with a rough towel--". Whether the treatment cured him, or caused him to become "the late J. B. Ouvre" in 1849 is not known.

Owyhee
Many Hawaiians were engaged in the Islands to work on the Hudson's Bay farms or in the saw mill. When their term of service was over, they were to return to Hawaii, but many re-enlisted or simply remained. As a rule, they disliked and mistrusted the Indians, but alliances with native women did occur, as in the entries here. The blood-stream of pioneer Oregon was thus further mixed; one Douglas county resident, a descendent of the Makaine-Plouff line, recalls hearing the word "Owyhee" often in her childhood, but at the time had no idea what it meant.
A surge of Owyhee baptisms early in 1853 leads one to look for the reason. The situation seems to have been that the less employable Kanakas were left behind in "the old slab buildings" as the Company withdrew to Victoria, having no other place to go except to the tribes of their wives. They were poor, unsanitary hangers-on around the barracks and easily picked up the seeds of disease brought up from the Isthmus of Panama by the United States Army, which arrived piece-meal until the close of 1852. Sickness invariably produces a wave of baptisms.

Oyer - see Loyer

Pambrun, Maria   1826-1890
Maria, eldest daughter of Pierre Pambrun and Catherine Humpherville, was born at Fraser Lake, British Columbia, where her father was stationed at the time. Her marriage to the post physician, Forbes Barclay, at Fort Vancouver was one of happiness and fulfillment. She became a figure of importance in the young town of Oregon City; her stone in Mountain View Cemetery there reads, "She hath done what she could."

Pambrun, Pierre Chrysologue   1792-1841
Pambrun was born at Vandreuil, Canada, served in the War of 1812 as a Lieutenant, and became Chief Trader in charge of Fort Walla Walla (Fort Nez Perces) from 1839 to 1841. Previously he had been in the service of the Hudson's Bay Company from 1815 on, beginning at Fort York on Hudson's Bay and proceeding westward by various stages. He went first as clerk at Fort Walla Walla until he was promoted to Chief Trader. He was a most hospitable man, making welcome all travelers by river or trail. He welcomed the Whitman missionaries, helped Whitman establish his post at Waiilatpu, and was attended by Dr. Whitman at the time of his accidental fall from a horse and his death. Buried at Fort Walla Walla, he was later re-interred at Fort Vancouver. His family returned to Fort Vancouver and subsequently to Oregon City, where the children became leaders in various fields of education.

Pariseau, Pierre, Sr.   1796 c.-1892
Pariseau was born in Canada, possibly France, and by his own testimony, came west "while
Jackson was president" for the Hudson's Bay Company. He was employed by J. B. Gagnier in
building and manning Old Fort Umpqua in Douglas County until he retired to a farm south of
Champoeg. His wife was Marie Dompier, much younger than he. Their family numbered eleven
children, most of whom lived to maturity and today form a large segment of population in
Douglas County, to which Pariseau retired in later life. He took a backwoods claim and lived by
hunting mainly, in the primitive way that suited his taste. A fine old picture shows a scraggled
old man "with the look of eagles about him", daring the world to crowd him. The fine old name
Pariseau has now become a phonetic "Parazoo".

Payette, Francois   1795-
This "fat and merry" master at Fort Boise for many years dispensed cheer, food, and information
to all comers. He had come to Astoria on the ship Beaver (not to be confused with the later
steamer Beaver of the Hudson's Bay Company), and remained in the service of successive companies. He and Charles Rondeau had married daughters of Joseph Portneuf, an old Company man.
In 1837, while on a visit to the Willamette Valley to their father Portneuf, both wives died in the
"beautiful death" reported by Jason Lee. Their seventeen-year-old brother Joseph had died at the
Mission shortly before. Payette's son Baptiste went Wast with Wyeth in 1833 for a year's school-
ing. Whether Angelique, born about 1830, was the daughter of the Portneuf wife is not certain,
but she probably was not; the "Spokan woman" was not called "late", as was customary.

Pelissier, Michel
Michel, son of Antoine Pellicier (sic) and Marie St. Germaine of Three Rivers, Canada, came to
Oregon in 1848. He married Catherine Aubichon, daughter of Alexis II and Marianne (Elmermach). Ten children are recorded to the couple. They lived at St. Louis until the middle sixties,
or a little less, then moved to the Walla Walla country to the settlement known as Frenchtown,
where he died at some time after 1870, when his last child was born. He is claimed by a local
historian to have been the first settler at Frenchtown; his claim lay just west of the old Whitman
Mission, with later comers continuing downstream along both sides of the Walla Walla River.
Frenchtown records for the St. Rose of Lima Church are included in the Register at Walla Walla.

Pelland
Numerous Pellands appear in the records, but not a great deal about any one of them.

Alexis Pelland, son of Alexis in Canada, married Emelie, "a neophyte" at Vancouver in 1851; a
daughter Sophie was recorded in 1853. By 1869 he was living at Chinookville, apparently engaged in fishing.
Three brothers, Elie, Onesome and Xavier are said to have "walked from Canada", perhaps in
the Red River Migration of 1841, and settled eventually in Douglas County. A fourth, Octave,
may also have been a brother. **Xavier** ("Zephyr") married Rosalie Plouff, daughter of Joseph
Plouff and Therese Makaine, Owyhee. **Elie** (Helie) married Elizabeth Wagner, daughter of Peter
Wagner, by whom he had children Elie and Pierre. Elizabeth Wagner died in 1863; three weeks
later her widower married Marguerite LaCourse, widow of Dominique Pichet. **Onesime** ("Sim")
married Emma Pichet, daughter of Roc Pichette.

Pelland, Charles Oliver   1840-1904
A later Pelland, Charles Oliver, relationship not known, if any, came from Canada to Oregon
City in 1860, where he worked as a miller. From 1868 he engaged in storekeeping or farming in
Yamhill and Marion Counties to the end of his life. His wife, Mary Coleman, was the daughter of
James Coleman and Frances Murray, early settlers in Muddy Valley north of the present Sheri-
dan. Only the earliest of the eleven children born to the Pellands appear in the St. Paul Registers
here published.

Pelletier, Louise Henriette   1812-
Three Pelletier sisters, daughters of Archbishop Blanchet's sister Rose, came to Vancouver in 1845
with a group of nuns. All three shortly married, Louise to Simon Plamondon, Soulange (Gelan)
to Charles Lucier, and Emelie to Julian Bihan. A fourth sister, Florence, had married Charles
Prevost in Canada. The Prevosts came West by way of Panama in 1853, and Florence died
shortly after arriving.

Pend d' Oreille, Josephte   1800 c.-
Josephte Pend d' Oreille is sometimes recorded as Josephte Nez Perce. In 1893 her daughter,

Catherine Laferte Murray, wrote that her mother's name in the tribe had been Josette Chimhaney.

Pend d' Oreille Tribe
The Pend d' Oreilles ("Ear Drop People") were Kalispels, living around Pend d' Oreille Lake and River in northern Idaho and Washington. Father DeSmet found them receptive and responsive to his teachings, and gave nothing but good reports of his "dear savages".

Pepin, Julius (Jules)   1846-1881
Jules Pepin, second son of Pierre Pepin, Sr., married Elizabeth Yamhill. The record of one daughter, Catherine Marguerite, occurs in the Grand Ronde Register. She was born two weeks after the death of her father. The record of that death in the McMinnville register, reads (in translation): "The 26th of September, 1881, I the undersigned buried the body of Jules LaChance, who died the 24th of this month near Dayton, aged 35. The above burial was made in the cemetery of St. Patrick's. Louis Mitayer, Pr." The cemetery of St. Patrick's in Muddy Valley has been abandoned for many years. Only six or eight stones can be found in the overgrowth, and two iron crosses that possibly mark the graves of Jules and his father Pierre, who died seven years later.

Pepin (dit Lachance), Pierre I   1820-1888
In 1838 Pierre Pepin, against his father's wishes, came to Fort Vancouver at the age of eighteen. He had learned the blacksmith trade from his father, "a good blacksmith in Montreal", and was employed at various posts in the Columbia District. His marriage to Suzanne Goodrich was long and congenial, though beset with poverty. Suzanne had, as a child at play, become lamed by a fall, "so that ever after she walked with a stick, but that didn't prevent her from doing her work, washing and all!" Such was the recollection of her sons, David and Thomas, gentle-minded old men still living in the decade of the 1960's.

Old Mary Ann Michelle wrote "just a memorandum" of the Grand Ronde Reserve, where her life had been spent, and recalled of Pierre Pepin, "Lawshans and his family came to church here from Gopherville. He was a full Frenchman, his wife half breed. They sure had a big family. When old Lachance lost his home in Gopherville he came and lived in Grand Ronde. They had boys and girls that were married, lived in Portland and St. Paul, all with big familys. All landed here in later years."

Pierre Pepin died at Grand Ronde in 1888 and was buried in the St. Patrick's Cemetery, long ago abandoned, in Muddy Valley.

Pepin, Pierre (dit LaChance) II   1845-
Young Pierre was the first child of Pierre Pepin and Suzanne Gaudritche (Goodrich). One of the younger sons of their large and longlived family recalled, more than a century later, a story of earlier, more prosperous times when the second Pierre was an infant at St. Paul: "My father was a blacksmith, as I said. You may have seen the iron cross at the church there? He made that when the church was built. It wasn't cast, he hammered it out on an anvil. Whey they built the church (1846) of course they didn't have much money. Father Blanchet had got hold of a big bell and put it on a framework for people to touch and so on, to raise money. There was an iron bar, and if you struck the bell with that, then that was fifty dollars. My father took my brother in his arms--- he was about a year old---and put the rod in his hands, so the baby struck the bell and my father paid fifty dollars." (1958) The iron cross is now on the rear gable of the church, replaced by a much larger cross when the church was remodelled during the 1890's. The bell is the original.

Pierre, Jr. married Amanda Grimm about 1870. Three daughters, Emilie, Mary Agnes and Josephine, are recorded in the registers of McMinnville and St. Paul. Whether his wife was the same Amanda Grim who had been the wife of Daniel Riley during the 1860's in Muddy Valley is not clear.

Perrault, Jean Baptiste   -before 1857
Perrault came from Riviere du Loup, the home village of Dr. McLoughlin, as a boatman in the early days of the Hudson's Bay Company in the West. He was an early settler on French Prairie, his claim lying on the west side of the Willamette River near the mouth of the Yamhill. One writer (Steeves) states that Perrault's daughter Marie Ann "was a first cousin to Dr. William McKay, son of Tom McKay". If correct, it would thus appear that Perrault's un-named "Tchinouk" wife was a daughter of old Chief Concomley, as Tom McKay's first wife was. Perrault's widow, Angele Tchelis, married Sylvain Bourjeau in 1857.

Perrault, Reine   1820 c.-
It would appear that Reine was stepdaughter to Angele Tchelis; at the time of her marriage her
mother was the un-named Tchinouk who was also the mother of Marie Anne. This un-named
woman may have been a daughter of Chief Concomley, see above entry.

Petit, Amable
Three Amable Petits appear in the records, Amable I, who was the old verger at St. Paul and
whose wife was Susanne Tawakon; Amable II, later a merchant at Ilwaco, Washington, whose
wife was Amelia (Emelie) Aubichon; and Amable III, who died as a child in 1848.

Petit, Amable I   1797-1867
An employe of the Hudson's Bay Company, the elder Petit appears to have left two half-grown
sons in eastern Canada when he came West. His marriage at Fort Vancouver on March 27, 1837,
to Susanne Tawakon is entered on page One of the register kept by the Anglican chaplain,
Herbert Beaver. Petit and Susanne were remarried by the Catholic priests in December of the
following year, very shortly after their arrival. The long list of burials he witnesses is due to his
position as verger at the St. Paul Church. His recorded children by Susanne are Charles, Henri,
Celeste, Marie, Pierre, Francois, Louise, Louise Philomene, and Flavie, dating from 1837 to
1857. He died at the age of seventy at St. Paul and was buried in the old cemetery there.

Petit, Amable II   1817-1890
Amable was the son of the elder Amable Petit and Marianne Baudrie, of Canada. At some unknown time he came west and engaged in various enterprises on French Prairie, such as millwright work and wood hauling by barge, while living in Butteville. He married Emelie
Aubichon in 1846, and took up a land claim in 1850.
"Mr. Petit had moved his family from eastern Washington to Portland during the summer of
1865. There he bought the business of a man who had the contract to furnish cord wood for
certain steamboats using it for fuel. In this deal he got a two-masted schooner in which to carry
wood." (Mildred Colbert, a granddaughter.) The next year he loaded his schooner with supplies
and sailed to Chinookville on the Washington coast. He sold his goods at a profit and thereafter
devoted his time to catching and salting salmon. Ten children were born to him and Emelie
(Amelia), and two others appear to have died in infancy. Both he and his aged wife are buried in
the cemetery at Ilwaco.

Petit, Charles   1837-1873
Charles was the son of Amable Petit, Sr., and Susanne Tawakon. A daughter Felicite was born
out of wedlock, apparently, to him and Olive Forcier Gingras in March, 1859. The following
year he contracted a "civil" (Protestant) marriage with Sophie Gendron, which was validated in
the Catholic Church six months later.

Petit, Felicite   1859-
Felicite was the "natural" daughter of Charles Petit and Olive Forcier born between marriages of
her mother, Jean Gingras having died in 1856 and Francois Brouillard not yet on the scene. At
Olive's death, Felicite was placed in the guardianship of her grandfather, Amable Petit, Sr.; her
stepfather Brouillard was left with a year-old daughter Rose to care for.

Petit, Hubert (Herbert)   1849-1933
Herbert Petit, with his father Amable II and brothers, were fishermen at Ilwaco for many years.
Their descendants are prominent people in the town to the present day. Herbert was three times
married, to sisters Annie and Frances Sweeney and to Mary Greenleaf. The first two are among
the few known to have been buried in the long abandoned cemetery at Chinookville.

Picard, Andre   1781-1846
Andre Picard entered the North West Fur Company from Quebec in 1800. During the 1820's he
advanced to master of the post at Kamloops, where Governor Simpson wrote of him, "Ingenius -
speaks the Okanogan Language well - is weak as a voyageur. 1 woman, 2 girls." (1828) One of
the girls was doubtless Emelie, who became the wife of Michel Laframboise. Picard was one of
the earliest settlers on French Prairie; his claim lay near the center of the plain, not patented. The
earliest twelve settlers are commemorated by a plaque on a boulder at Old St. Paul Cemetery,
their common resting place.

Picard, Emelie   1822-1900 c.
Emelie was the wife of Michel Laframboise when he settled down to having one wife, and that in

the Church. She was spirited and intelligent, literate in both French and English; family tradition claims that Michel himself taught her "in a winter of deep snow". In later life she left the Catholic Church for an evangelical type of Protestant religion, in whose books she instructed her grandchildren with characteristic zeal. After Michel's death, Emelie married Leandre Blain in Douglas County, to whom she bore several children.

Picard, Honore (Henri) I   1829-1892
Honore, or Henri, for he is given both ways, first appears in the Church records with his marriage to Celeste Rochbrune, widow of Thomas Liard, in 1851. So far as is known, he was not related to the earlier Andre Picard. Celina Choquette, who married Henri's son John Adolphe, used to impress this fact upon her granddaughter: "The Picard whose name is on the plaque at the Old Cemetery was a different line altogether. They were short people. We came later, and our people were all tall, remember this." Honore Picard's wife had a daughter Marguerite Liard by her first husband and eleven more by Picard, dying at the birth of the last in 1873. Mother and child were buried together at St. Paul. Honore himself died at Walla Walla in 1892 while visiting his son, Henri II; his body was returned to St. Paul for burial.

Picard, Henri II   1860-1911
Henri Picard II was the first of three brothers to marry three sisters of the Amadee Choquette family, his wife being Mary, the eldest. The couple and their six children moved to Adams, near Pendleton, about 1894. Henri and his daughter Pearl Frances are buried at Athena, but Mary at Arlington, Washington, where she had been living with a son after the death of her husband.

Picard, John Adolphe   1864-1937
John Adolphe Picard, second son of Henri Picard I and Celeste Rochbrune, married Celina Choquette, second daughter of Amadee Choquette and Marie Bernier. A tall, handsome man, he is remembered as the blacksmith who hammered out oilcans to make the weather cock atop the cross on the St. Paul Church. "You can still see the letters," remarked one old resident who had examined the work during repairs on the roof. Besides several children of their own, the Picards reared a granddaughter Delight, who recalls fondly the expeditious precision of her grandmother about her housework, and the old-time autocracy of her grandfather John, "He always cut up my meat for me at the table until I was fifteen years old; then I had to learn to do it for myself."

Picard, Julien Francis   1868-1901
Julien Picard, third son of Henri Picard I and Celeste Rochbrune, married Eleanore, third daughter of Amadee Choquette and Marie Bernier. Marie died in 1901 at the age of twenty-seven, leaving three small children, Julien, Gertrude and Clement.

Pichet, Catherine
Catherine Pichet and Augustin Lambert (I) were already married with several children when they first appear in the records at Fort Walla Walla in 1847. These unrecorded children show up in later records of marriages and deaths. Although Catherine and Augustin Lambert were the parents of at least twelve children, infant mortality kept the number reduced so that the number at home at one time was not very large.

Pichet, Dominique   1837-before 1863
Dominique Pichet served in the Yakima Indian War, married Marguerite Lacourse in 1856, and died before 1863, when his widow married Elie Pellan.

Pichet, Emelie   1845-1919
Emelie, darkly handsome and with a deep contralto voice, was one of the three Pichet sisters who found husbands in three of five adventurous gold hunters coming up from California after the main rush was over. Her husband settled forn to prosperous farming on the Prairie; his sons became merchants.

Pichet, Esther   1839-1860
Esther married Joseph Lavigueur and died at the age of twenty-one.

Pichet, Louis (I)   1797-1876
The historian Bancroft, writing from newspapers of the day, said of Pichet that "he left Canada in 1817 with a company of 25 trappers, and wintered on the plains, losing 7 of the number, and arrived at Astoria in 1818. Pichet roamed about California and Oregon for 12 years in the Hudson's Bay Company. In 1832 he settled on a farm in the Willamette Valley, where he resided for over 40 years."

Pichet, Louis (II)   1832-before 1857
Louis Pichet, the younger, married Genevieve Vandale in 1853 and died shortly, as his widow
married Louis Poirer in 1857. One son, Louis (III) is recorded.

Pichet, Marie   1853-1879
Marie Pichet, daughter of Louis Pichet and Marguerite Bercier, married Felix DeLisle and died
at the age of twenty-five. Both are buried with her parents in St. Paul Cemetery.

Pichet, Roc   1839-1902
Roc Pichet married a neighbor girl, Victoire Despard, lived for a time on the Grand Ronde
Reserve, and moved finally to Douglas County. In late life he suffered from asthma, and on a
visit to eastern Oregon, where he had gone to seek relief in a drier climate, he died rather suddenly. He was buried in the cemetery of St. Andrew's Mission with a white marble slab.
            "Asleep in Jesus, peaceful rest,
            Where waking is supremely blest."

Piette, J. B. P.   1831-1898
John B. P. Piette came to Oregon in 1850 and married Francoise Million in 1860. He served as
legislator for Marion County for a time. Some years after the death of his wife in 1881 he went to
Vancouver "to live with his family" and there died in 1896. He is buried in Vancouver; his wife
Frances in St. Paul, on the lot with or adjacent to the Bellique-Labonte lot. "They were great
friends", explained a Bellique daughter. Piette had later married Amedile Boucher, widow of
Alexis Touzin.

Pillett, Joseph (Pillet)
The Pillets first appear in Oregon Church Registers in 1882, having come from Illinois some time
earlier. Joseph Pillet was of French Canadian descent, his wife Mary Elizabeth Morissette of
French and Canadian. They were the parents of fourteen children, of whom five appear in the
St. Paul records. One great-granddaughter, Sister Marita Rose, S.J.M. (Manning) was for years a
beloved teacher in the Convent school at St. Paul.

Pin, Joseph (Parr, Pain, etc.)   1794-1840 c.
Pin was a Montreal engage of the Hudson's Bay Company from 1813, a boatman. He was with
Ogden in the Snake River Country in 1824 and at Fort Langley in 1829. When his wife,
Marguerite Pend Oreille, died in 1851, her twelve-year-old daughter Marguerite was made a
ward of Dr. McLoughlin, living in his home in Oregon City. She lived to extreme old age and
was able to recall a vast amount of data regarding the old days and customs.

Pin, Joseph (II)   1827 c.-
Joseph Pin was the son of Joseph Pin I and Marguerite Pend d' Oreille, "Born at Spokane House
Dec. 24, 1827. Height 5 feet 6½ inches, complexion gray"—so reads his pension application. The
frustrations of his name (Pain, Parr, Perau, etc.) were explained by Trader Beckwith in a monumental sentence: "His father was French, his mother Indian. He learned to speak both languages,
but he is not now, and never has been able, to pronounce the English language in a proper
manner, and in giving his name his pronunciation of it is so imperfect that it is more often spelled
incorrectly than correctly, and not being able to read or write he is compelled to have others do
this for him, and it has been for the above named reasons that his name appears . . . " His wife
was Adelaide Barnabe, daughter of Francois Barnabe.

Pin, Marguerite   1837-1925
Marguerite Pin, at the age of two months, was having "a hard time surviving, because her
mother had no milk for her. She had to subsist on broth made from the heads of fish, which she
sucked through a goose quill stuck in a whiskey bottle"—thus family recollection. She grew up in
the household of Dr. McLoughlin in Oregon City, and married Sam Bellman, of The Dalles. He
died seven years later, leaving several children. She then married Paul Lucier, dit Gardipe, and
bore six sons and seven daughters to him. She was a handsome woman and an excellent horse-
woman, a fine old tintype in color showing a regal pose in a maroon velvet riding habit.

Pin, Nancy   1830-
Nancy Pin married a Frenchman, Gideon Gravelle, in 1847 and lived out her life at Frenchtown,
near Walla Walla.

Pion, William
Pion appears to have been early in the fur trade, and disappears early. His daughter Nancy was

born about 1824; by 1828 his widow Charlotte Okanogan was bearing children to Jean Gingras I. Another William Pion, probably a son of the elder William, appears on the Marion County Census of 1850. He was mentioned as a half-breed guide sent up from Fort Colville in 1841 to pilot Governor Simpson through the Rocky Mountains. Pion's daughter Nancy married Alexis LaPrate, whose record appears mainly in St. Louis.

Baptiste Peone (properly Pion), for whom Peone Prairie in the Spokane area is named, may have been another son of William Pione the elder. His wife was Catherine Finley, said to have been one of the numerous children of Jacco Finley.

Still another Pion, Louis, was with the North West Fur Company in 1813 as a carpenter. Governor Simpson wrote of him, "A good linguist, tolerable trader, but no clerk. Handy in making tables, chairs and ladies' work boxes . . . but obsequious." Louis was possibly a brother to the first William.

Plamondon, Eusebe Michel   1826-1881

Eusebe Plamondon lived in Salem, where he kept a saloon, but he was married at St. Paul, there being no Catholic church in Salem in 1861. The birth of a son, Eusebe Clifford, is recorded in Salem, but the family record is condensed in a row of large marble slabs in the Salem Pioneer Cemetery:

 Plamondon, Pocahontas, wife of E. M. Plamondon, Born 1832 Died Nov. 17, 1853
 Plamondon, Elizabeth (Illedge) Died Jan. 25, 1862 Aged 19 yrs, 2 mo.
 Plamondon, E. M., of St. Hyacinthe, P. Q. May 27, 1826 Sept. 14, 1881
  "My Husband In life beloved, in death lamented"
 Plamondon, M. A. (Third wife)
 Plamondon, Clifford E. "Our Babe" Feb. 21, 1868, Mar. 30, 1868
 Plamondon, Francois F. ("of Butteville") 1830 - 1871

From the dates and places of birth, one may suppose Francois and Eusebe Plamondon were brothers. Francois is buried on the Eusebe family lot in the Salem Pioneer Cemetery:

 F. F. Plamondon (of St. Hyacinthe, Quebec") June 30, 1830
              April 15, 1871

Plamondon, Simon (I)   1800-1900 c.

Simon Plamondon was one of the original settlers on Cowlitz Prairie. He was born in Quebec in 1800, left home at the age of fifteen, being tall and mature for his years, and journeyed west by way of New Orleans in easy stages. He was employed by the Hudson's Bay Company as a boatman and explored the Cowlitz Valley. He was associated thereafter with the Company Farm at Cowlitz until retiring to a farm of his own. The town of Toledo, Washington, approximate site, was known as Plamondon's Landing. He was several times married, having children by each alliance. His first wife was a native; his second Emelie Finlay, widow of Pierre Bercier; and his third Louise Henriette Pelletier, the niece of Archbishop Blanchet. Simon was a large and handsome man, even in extreme old age; his daughter Marie Ann St. Germaine recalled him fondly as "a very pretty man".

In addition to the above Marie Anne, Plamondon's children by his Cowlitz wife were Sophie (1830) Cottenoir, Therese (1832) Sarault, and Simon II, who said on his pension application that he had married Mary Farron. The full list of his children by his second wife, Emelie Bercier, appears to be Lina (1837), Daniel (1838), Moyse (1840), Angelique (1841), Jean Baptiste (no record found) and Marie Elmina (no record found). The last two, found in **The Plamondon Family**, by George F. Plamondon, were probably recorded in the St. Francis Xavier Register at Cowlitz, which was destroyed by fire in 1874.

Plante, Charles   1784-1854

Charles Plante, from St. Cuthbert, Montreal, is recorded as a trapper on the Snake River expedition of 1830 under John Work, where he was mentioned as "a leading man". He took a land claim a few miles north of St. Paul. His numerous wives are given as Agatha Cayuse, Susanne Cayuse, Elizabeth Chinook, Pelagie Chinook and Marguerite Yougoulta, widow of J. B. Dubrueil, who outlived him. He went to California during the gold rush, being absent from February to June, 1854, while his family remained on the claim. He died shortly after his return, however; having gone to the Surveyor General's office to register his claim, he became too ill to reach his home and died at the home of a neighbor, Charles Rondeau.

Plassee, Placie - see Laferte

Plouff, Antoine   1804-before 1848
Antoine Plouff, from Sorel, Quebec, was a boatman at Fort Colville. The relationship between
Antoine and Joseph Plouff, below, is not known, but they were probably brothers, as the latter
was guardian of Antoine's daughter Rosalie, her father being dead. Note that each man had a
daughter Rosalie, who should not be confused. Antoine's daughter Rosalie married James
Boucher at St. Paul in 1848.

Plouff, Joseph (Carillon)   -1849
Joseph Plouff, from Berthier, Canada, was a blacksmith at Fort Vancouver. He was "killed by a
musket ball" in Oregon City in 1849, leaving his wife, Therese Makaine, and seven children. His
widow married Baptiste LaRoc the following year. Plouff had settled on a farm on French
Prairie prior to 1844, and his daughter Rosalie, aged ten, was enrolled in the Sisters' School by
1850. Therese Makaine, Plouf's wife, was the daughter of an Owyhee and a Chehalis mother.
Note that both Joseph and his brother (?) Antoine had a daughter Rosalie, and that Joseph was
guardian of Antoine's Rosalie after her father's death before 1848.

Plouff, Rosalie   1834-
As James Boucher, Rosalie's husband, was employed "in the country of the Carriers" well to the
north, this Rosalie disappears from the record, so far as is known. Any further references are to
Rosalie, daughter of Joseph, so far as can be learned.

Plouff, Rosalie   1840-
Rosalie Plouff, daughter of Joseph, was a ten-year-old pupil in the Sisters' School at St. Paul in
1850, her father being dead. She later lived in Douglas County, where she was allied or married
to P. O. Riley, John Desportes McKay, and Xavier Pelland. Her mixed heritage combined
harmoniously to make a handsome woman of soft and kindly face.

Plourde, Francois (dit Jacques)   1793 c.-1906 c.
Plourde, or Jacques, was one of the "heads of families" who signed up with the Red River Migration of 1841, seeking a better home in the West. The group was dissatisfied with the Nesquallie
area, where they were first sent, and shortly most if not all went to the Willamette Valley.
Plourde was nearly fifty at the time he undertook the long trek across the Canadian plains, with a
middle-aged wife and several children, among whom were Andre and Monique. More were born
on the French Prairie farm near St. Louis. Plourde died at the reputed age of 108; both he and his
wife Susanne Dubois are buried in the "Highland Cemetery", not located, according to an
undated newspaper clipping. The record of his sons, Alexandre, Andre and Basile appear in the
St. Louis Register.

Poirier, Alexandre   1825-
Alexandre was the eldest son of Basile Poirier and Celiast Coboway, and he himself gave his birth
date as January 4, 1825. His application for a pension late in life continues, both he and his
brother Francois as well as their cousin Louis, served in the Indian War of 1855-56, he in
southern Oregon. He was five feet 6½ inches tall, with brown eyes, black hair, and dark complection; by occupation he was a miner, working in Oregon, Idaho and Montana. In 1853 he had
a son Jacques by Julienne Labonte, apparently outside of marriage; the child died at the age of
two. In 1873 Alexandre married Susanne Finlay, "widow of Ignace". He became a farmer and
ended his days on the Flathead Reservation.

Poirier, Basile   1774-1844
Basile Poirier was a baker for the fort at Vancouver, coming originally from Montreal. His wife,
Celiast Clatsop, left him to make her home with her sister, Mrs. Joseph Gervais, when it was
learned that Poirier had a wife living in Canada. The children that Celiast took with her were
later returned to their father. By 1838 it was learned that his Canadian wife was deceased, and
he was permitted to marry Louise Moatwas. By each wife he had three recorded sons. He died
suddenly on his farm, which is claimed by some to have been the old Lucier claim in Portland,
early abandoned.

Poirier, Etienne (Xavier)   1823-6 c.-
Etienne is possibly the same as Xavier (Vancouver Register). He died, according to G. B. Roberts
of leprosy—"It usually takes some years to carry them off. I knew of many cases of this disease.
Our medical men treated it with arsenic--this was only a temporary stimulant". Whether the
leprosy referred to in the West was Oriental leprosy or a form of venereal disease is in dispute.

Poirier, Joseph   1836 c.-1906
Joseph Poirier, son of Basile Poirier and Louise Moatwas, has little recorded beyond his tomb-stone and that of his family in the cemetery at Vancouver. His wife C. (Catherine?) Therese died in 1876, aged forty, and a Francis Poirier, who died in 1892, aged thirty-four, may have been a second wife and the mother of children George and Sidney, both of whom died also in 1892. The Catherine Poirier who witnessed at the burial of an infant in 1851 (Vancouver II, page 116, S-4) may have been the first wife of Joseph.

Poirier, Marie   1826-1914
Marie was the daughter of Toussaint Poirier and Catherine Clatsop. She became the second wife of Joseph Delard, an older man with a large family. She bore him several more children and outlived him by many years, dying in Portland at an advanced age in 1914.

Poirier, Toussaint   1782-1850
The brothers Poirior came from Montreal to Fort Vancouver, Basile as a baker and Toussaint as a cooper, sometimes given also as a miller. He married Catherine Clatsop in 1839, their children at the time being Marie, Antoine and Louison. Later came Rose and Joseph. By 1844 Poirior was living on French Prairie, "blind, invalid", exempt from paying taxes. Both he and his wife died in 1850, she first. The records of their deaths are found in the St. Louis Register. His daughter Marie became the second wife of Joseph Delore and his daughter Rose, the wife of Joseph's son, Basile; the relationships resulting were no more complicated than many of the time.

Pomeroy, Walter   1802-
Pomeroy, from Hamshire County, Massachusetts, came west in the wagon train of Elijah White in 1842. He took up a Champoeg claim briefly, which later became that of Robert Newell, but mainly devoted himself to wheat growing on Tualatin Plains and to various constructional and promotional projects in Oregon City.

Porteurs (or Staotin)
The word is the native term for those living in the region of Fort Alexandria in New Caledonia. "The men are rather remarkable for their tall stature and by the grace of their bearing. The women are tall and have a kind of corpulence or plumpness that is not noticed among those of the Columbia River tribes . . . These wretched natives do not distinguish themselves from animals; on this account as well as by their low intelligence they are degraded and entirely subject to the slavery of the senses."   Father Demers

Porteus, William   1820-1849
The Porteus name was well known in the North West Fur Company from early days of the firm, and William Porteus had married in British Columbia. He was Commissioner in Charge of the Hudson's Bay Company affairs in Oregon City until leaving for the California mines in 1849 with a group of French Prairie gold-seekers. Upon reaching the diggings, the group scattered, but later reported that they had heard Porteus had died in September "at Peter Sawrens".

Porteuse, (Nankaselais)
NanKaselais may be a village or tribe of the Carrier Indians in northern British Columbia, inas-much as Catherine is listed elsewhere as Huat, Porteuse (Carrier). The name Carrier, according to Ogden, derived from the custom of requiring a widow to carry the ashes of her husband on her back for a period of time, months or perhaps years.

Porteuse, Unat   1800 c.-1866
At the time of her baptism and her marriage to Louis Vandal of Lac la Biche at St. Paul in 1841, Unat's name was given as "Catherine, born of infidel Indians of the country of Nankaselias to the north". She died at St. Louis on May 8, 1866, and was buried in the old parish cemetery there.

Portier, Nicholar Jean
Nicholas Jean Portier is mentioned only briefly as being from Bordeaux, France, as having mar-ried "Marie, coming from California", and as having a daughter Magdeleine, born in 1843.

Nicholas Portier, of Havre, France, appears only as the husband of Marie Laroque and as the father of two sons, Francois (1847) and Narcisse (1850). The two Portiers may well be the same man.

Poujade, Jean Pierre   1790-1875
Poujade was a doctor, born in France, who had lived for some time in eastern parts of the United

States before coming with his half-grown family to Oregon, where he settled on a claim in Gervais in 1847. His first wife, the mother of his sons, (Mary Noble) had died in Louisiana. He married Marie Ann Sable in Perry County, Ohio, in 1839. This is surely the wife "Ann" buried beside him at St. Louis, aged 93.

Prevost, Charles I   1811-1895
"He came with his family from St. Charles, Quebec, about 1853. My recollection is that my father told me she (Grandmother, Florence Peltier) died while crossing the Isthmus of Panama on the way from Canada to Oregon. However, my cousin Louise seems to feel that while she was taken ill on the trip or voyage, she made it to Oregon and died shortly afterwards." From a letter by grandson, Charles Prevost, about 1962. The entry indicates "Cousin Louise" was correct. (Charles Prevost, III)

Prevost, Charles II   -1854
Charles.Prevost had come to Oregon from Quebec with his parents, Charles Prevost, Sr., and Florence Peltier in 1853, a year before the tragic explosion of the steamer Gazelle at Canemah. A marker, somewhat obscured, on the bluff above the Falls at Oregon City points out the site of the accident, in which nineteen persons were killed.

Prevost, Louis   1836-1917
"Louis Prevost, my uncle, was the oldest son of Charles Prevost (and Florence Pelletier). He had a hardware store in Woodburn for years. Next to him is his wife Pauline LeFaure. She came from St. Malo, France." Letter from Charles Prevost, III.

PREVOST BROS. MERCANTILE COMPANY
Dealers in

Hardware and Crockery	Fine Groceries	Tinware and Graniteware
Fine Cutlery	Cigars and Tobacco	Lubricating Oils
	WOODBURN, OREGON	(1902)

Provost, Julien
Provost had come around the Horn in the forties with Father Delorme to teach in the St. Joseph's School for boys. The gold rush shortly closed the school, and Provost, who was no farmer, kept the post office and a store at Bellvue for many years. His old account book is complete, well-written, and filled with the names of the old French families on the Prairie. His picture shows a scholar's face with grave eyes and a conservative beard; his wife Caroline was plump, dressed in buttons and bows, pleasingly coy. Provost became the first mayor of St. Paul, which he had platted as a town, so say the family.

Quesnel, Francois   1789 c.-1844
Three by the name of Francois Quesnel carry on the name, no doubt in direct descent. "Old" Quesnel was early in the fur trade employ; there were several at the same time. He was living on the Prairie at the time of his wife's death, noted by Margaret Baily ("Ruth Rover") in characteristically acid words:
"May, 1841 An Indian woman, wife of a neighbor, buried today, her corpse being carried to the grave on a cart, and followed by six men on horseback. When passing the wheatfield, two of the men left the procession to look at the wheat! an evidence of what is the ruling passion."
"Old" Quesnel died three years later. "Young Quesnel", (1836-   ) orphaned, found a home on the Grand Ronde Reserve in time, where he married Rose Nipissing in 1869. Their son, Francois Fabien, called Captain Frank from his position on the Native Police on the Reserve, was a farmer and a musician in the Grand Ronde Band. (1880-1913).

Quinny
Possibly Quinault or Yaquina, both on the seacoast.

Quintal, Laurent   1800-1860 c.
The name Quintal occurs also as Coutrell, Cantrel, and Kantal. Laurent was "that sly dog, Laurent" to his leader, Alexander Ross, on the Snake River in 1824; "our steward or waiting man" to Dr. Tolmie at Nesquallie, and "an old man, a Frenchman, named Louis Coutrell" to a neighbor in Douglas County, where Quintal lived after leaving the Prairie. The same neighbor recalled, "The old man had a presentiment one morning in harvest that he would never see the sun rise again, and he did not, for when binding wheat in his field he was bitten by a rattlesnake and died in a few hours". (George Abdill) His daughter Zoe married Augustin "Quine" DeLore. His wife was Marianne Nipissing.

Quintal, Louis 1835-
Louis, son of Laurent Quintal, married Cecile Norwest at St. Louis in 1853. His record continues through St. Paul, Oregon City and Roseburg.

Raboin, Louis 1782 (?)-1865 c
One writer says that Louis Raboin was an American Fur Company trapper in the Bitterroot Mountains who left to get away from the Blackfeet, another that he was from Illinois of French descent; both may be correct. Raboin settled on the Tucannon River of southeastern Washington in 1853, having at that time a Flathead wife and six children. At the time of the Cayuse Indian War a year or two later, Governor Stevens saw him at his homestead in the canyon, calling him "a very experienced and kind-hearted mountaineer", who had already amassed about fifty horses and many cattle and was raising good potatoes and wheat. Raboin was small and active, and for that reason, it was said, was called "Maringouin" by the Indians, meaning Mosquito, a name usually shortened to Marengo by the settlers. A town of that name grew up at his homestead where the trail to Pomeroy crossed the Tucannon, a stage stop between two steep grades. Nothing now remains of the town, though Raboin's farm is still occupied. An unconfirmed account says that Raboin died at the hands of one of his sons at a forgotten date.

Ray, Charles 1831-19--
Charles Ray was a man of varied enterprises, having a stage line to Salem, a livery stable, and a farm as well as a landing and ferry across the Willamette River at the former DeGuire site.

Raymond, Augustin (Remon) 1811-1873
Augustin Raymond, Canadian, was in Oregon by the early 1840's, or perhaps earlier; no record has come to light that he was ever employed by the Hudson's Bay Company. He was well educated and bore a scholarly appearance; when his old house was dismantled following his death, a great mass of old papers and books were burned in a bonfire, the excuse being that they were all in French anyway. He had a prosperous farm just south of St. Paul, gave three hundred dollars to the new brick church in 1846, and was successful in the California gold fields in 1849. A large family was reared by him and his little metisse wife, Marie Servant. Large oil paintings of both are in the stacks of the Oregon Historical Society in Portland.

Raymond, Salome 1860-1912
Salome was the youngest of the Augustin Raymond family. She grew up to marry Eusebe Fortier, commonly called Alex. He had come West much later than the old Company men, by rail from Montreal. After numerous children, a frail little son was born, and in order to leave the mother free to take care of the ailing infant, a six-year-old daughter went to live with her aunt, Caroline Raymond, and uncle Julien Provost. She was made much of, as the Provosts were childless, so that although the infant at home at length died, little Ouida remained permanently at the Provost home.

Ravalli, Anthony 1812-(Oct. 2)1884
Father Ravalli was an Italian Jesuit, recruited in 1844 for the missions of eastern Washington and Montana, where he labored for twenty-six years. He was trained in medicine as well as theology, a selfless and dedicated man, well-loved. In the spring of 1845, when the entries over his name were made at St. Paul, he was apparently on his way to the stations farther east.

Richter, Cyrille 1827-1898
Richter left his wife, Josephte Lavigueur and went to the Walla Walla country, where he died on June 17, 1898. He was buried in the Mountain View Catholic Cemetery there.

Rivet, Adelaide 1840-1909
Adelaide, daughter of Joseph Rivet and Rose LaCourse, was orphaned during childhood. She married Francois Lefebre at the age of eighteen, but he died within a few years, leaving at least one son. Adelaide married Pierre Delore in 1877, becoming stepmother to his brood by a previous marriage. In old age she lost her sight, and was affectionately known as "Blind Grandma" to these children's children, who cherished her. She is buried in the Catholic Cemetery at The Dalles.

Rivet, Antoine 1809 (?)-1886
Antoine, son of Francois Rivet, was born in Montana and was employed by the Hudson's Bay Company along with his father. He settled on the Prairie a short distance south of St. Paul. When the Sisters' School closed out in 1852, Antoine rented their farm and raised a good crop, they

reported. During the Yakima Indian War of 1855 he served with some distinction, being chosen by his fellow soldiers as First Lieutenant in Captain Narcisse Cornoyer's First Regiment of Oregon Mounted Volunteers. He retired to the Flathead Reservation in Montana, where he died in 1886. His widow Emelie long survived him; she was still applying for his Indian War pension in 1903.

Rivet, Francois   1759-1852
Rivet was a Canadian hunter and trapper who had been on the Great Plains of the United States for twenty years before joining the Lewis and Clark expedition in 1804. He dropped off in the Rocky Mountains to fend for himself, but came to the Oregon country a few years later as an interpreter for the Hudson's Bay Company, brigade member, and "kind of a hedge blacksmith" at Fort Colville. He took a claim south of St. Paul late in 1839, became a United States citizen in 1852 and died the same year, aged about ninety-four years. His wife, Therese Flathead, had a daughter by a previous alliance, generally called "Princess Julia", who became the wife of Peter Skene Ogden. Two sons of Rivet, Antoine and Joseph, lived nearby in Oregon; at least one older son remained in the basin east of the Cascades.

Rivet, Joseph   1816-1852
Joseph, son of Francois Rivet, was born in the country east of the Cascades. He farmed with his father and his brother Antoine near St. Paul. His wife, Rose LaCourse, died in 1845, after which he married Marie Ann Despard. He died of alcoholism in 1852. His widow married Xavier Gervais and still later Antoine (Desportes, Departy) McKay. Peter Skene Ogden, writing to Archibald McKinlay, said, "--the tiding of Joe's death. Poor Fabian is now without Father or Mother, in every sense of the word an orphan. Joe accelerated his death by drink, nor did the intelligence surprise me. I hope the Old Lady (Mrs. Ogden, Fabian's step-aunt) will take care of his property. I allude to his cattle and horses, if any be remaining."

Robillard - see Lambert

Rocbrune (Rochbrune, Rocquebrune), Joseph, Antoine, Thomas
Names of all three engages appear in the Hudson's Bay Records, but little information is given beyond that Antoine, boatman, the son of Antoine, also boatman, had been born in 1810 and had joined the service in 1828.

Joseph Rocbrune married Lisette Walla Walla in 1839. At the time they had a newborn son, also named Joseph. They had at least one elder daughter, Celeste, who married Thomas Liard in 1849. Later children included Olivier, Helene (married William Duke) and Roch, who died at the age of five. After the death of Lisette, Rocbrune married the widow of David Dompierre, Marguerite Souilliere. Two more sons were born, one named Olivier for the earlier son who had died at the age of six.

Rochon, Augustin   1817-1898
Augustin Rochon came overland with Fathers Blanchet and Demers by way of Canada, a sort of lay servant. He witnessed at many ceremonies and constructed the "Wolf's Head Chapel" at Cowlitz. In 1842 he married Celeste Jeaudoin, daughter of Charles Jeaudoin and Walalikas Chinook. Soon after their marriage, the young couple moved to a claim at Cowlitz, where the rest of their lives were spent. Unusually fond of children, they had none of their own, but reared various nephews and other orphans, and left their money to an orphanage at their deaths. Celeste lived but one year longer than Augustin; they are buried under an arched stone in Cowlitz Cemetery.

Rondeau, Angelique   1827 c.-1850
Angelique's mother ("another woman" in the record) was Lizette Bellaire, daughter of Register Bellaire, who had been with David Thompson in Montana in 1808-11, and was a freeman and hunter in the Willamette in 1813-14. Angelique married Etienne Bernais in 1846 and died four years later.

Rondeau, Charles   1792-1855
Two or more Rondeaus appear in early records of the fur trade in the Northwest. Charles Rondeau was born in Sorel, Quebec. He was with Work in the Rocky Mountains in 1831, and seems to have been mainly in the Snake River country until he retired during the 1840's. His land claim lay near Gervais, where his aging father-in-law (who was actually the same age as Charles himself), Jean Baptiste Desportes McKay, lived with or near him. The three eldest children of

Charles Rondeau were born to Lizette Bellaire, daughter of Register Bellaire, an early fur trade man. After her death he married a daughter of "Old Portneuf", another fur trader. In 1837 he and his family came to the Willamette Valley to visit Portneuf, now retired; while on the Prairie, Rondeau's wife died "the happy death" hopefully recorded by Jason Lee, Methodist missionary. The following year Rondeau married Agatha Depatie (McKay), who died in 1848; he next married Elizabeth "Indian, living at the house of Baptiste Aubichon".

Rondeau, Thomas   1847-after 1927
Thomas Rondeau married Clementine Groslouis. Their family numbered fifteen or sixteen children, including several sets of twins. From about 1880 their records are found in the Roseburg Register, for the couple made their home in Douglas County from that time. His children attended the log school he had helped to build, and later his grandchildren went to the same place. He lived by farming and hunting, or as guide during the summer. In old age he could recount endless tales of early days, in particular the plentitude of game on every hand. Many names in Douglas County today recall Thomas Rondeau.

Rousseau, Louis   -1851
Rousseau was a seminarian who came west with Magloire Blanchet in 1847. He founded St. Peter's Mission at The Dalles the same year, building there a log cabin church that served also as his rectory. It was recalled by pioneers as a pleasant little church with a dirt floor and matting-hung walls. A few years later it was burned when the matting caught fire, but Father Rousseau was no longer there. He had labored among the Indians for three years, when his failing health sent him home to Canada; he died on board ship en route.

Roussin, Joseph   1831-
Joseph Roussin was the son of Sieur Roussin of Lake Superior and Marguerite Souilliere, who later married David Dompierre. The boy remained with his mother; in 1855 he married Adelaide Barnabe at St. Louise. Years later, the family recalls, "Joe Rosa" appeared at the funeral of "Grandma Pariseau" (Marie Dompierre) saying he would pay the funeral expenses, since "he was her half-brother, and had never done anything for her".

Roy, Thomas (Roi) I   1794-1852
Thomas Roy was born in Canada in 1794, according to his own statement. He married Marie Lafleur in 1838; the record of his marriage and children continue through St. Louis until his death in 1852. He held two parcels of land near Gervais, but died before his wishes about granting a strip from one of them to Jean Paradis could be carried out. His wife endeavored to do as Roy had wished, but she, too, died with the grant unfulfilled. The resulting land contest is a matter of record. F. X. Matthieu was appointed guardian of the minor children at their mother's death.

Russie (Russil), Augustin, Sr.   -prior to 1844
Since the name is spelled variously, it would appear that Russie, "old servant of the Hudson's Bay Company", is probably the same Augustin Roussil that came west on the Tonquin as a blacksmith and was listed as a smith at Fort George in 1813-1814. He had left a daughter Catherine in Canada, who married Andre Chalifoux and came west herself in 1838, q.v. Russie married again in Oregon, his wife being Rose Cayuse, who was the mother of Augustin, Jr.

Russie, Augustin, Jr. (Augustin Paul)   1825-1855
Augustin, Jr., was the son of Augustin, Sr., and Rose Chinook, and half-sister to Catherine Russie Chalifoux who took the place of guardian after their father's death. He married Agnes (Anne) Norwest (Tyikwari) in 1844. He was the father of Joseph, Paul, Marie (died at 8 mo.), and Marguerite. A son Hyacinthe was born posthumously two weeks after Augustin's death. Agnes Russie, widow, married William Tison, q.v.

Russie, Catherine   -1860
Catherine Russie was born in Canada to Augustin Russie I. She married Andre Chalifoux I, the noted steersman, in 1834 and accompanied him to the West in 1838 on the brigade that brought Fathers Blanchet and Demers. A son Michel was born en route the last of September; two other children were lost in the wreck of the bateau at the Dalles des Morts on the Columbia. Catherine acted as godmother at baptisms along the way and very often after reaching the West. After the death of Chalifoux in 1851 she married Hyacinthe Comartin. She had nine recorded children by Chalifoux, two by Comartin.

St. Andre, Ellen Helene 1841-
Helene was a boarding pupil at the Sisters' School at St. Paul in 1850. She married Alexander Davies and was living at Vancouver, apparently, where her son Peter was born, (and died) in 1856.

St. Martin, Andre 1810-1886
Andre St. Martin, son of Pierre St. Martin and Francoise Peloquin, came from Sorel, Canada, as an engage of the Hudson's Bay Company. He married Catherine Tawakan in 1839 at Fort Vancouver. She had at the time a two-year-old daughter, Catherine Davis, who was baptized under the name Francoise. (See Thomas Davis) Born to St. Martin and Catherine were Pierre (1839), Isadore (1841), Andre (1846), and Francois (1848). There may have been others. The family lived in Lewis County, Washington, after St. Martin retired from the Company. Andre and Joseph were probably brothers; Andre was godfather to Marie, daughter of Joseph, who was deceased.

St. Martin, Genevieve 1824-
Genevieve St. Martin married Pierre Beleque (I), and had numerous children. After his death on the return journey from the California gold fields, she married Casimer Gardipe and continued to bear children. The later part of her life was spent in the Walla Walla country.

St. Martin, Isadore 1841-1910
Isadore was born and reared in Lewis County, Washington, son of Andre St. Martin and Catherine Tawakan. During the Indian War of 1855-56 he served in Captain Warbass' Mounted Volunteers along with his father and elder brother Pierre, although scarcely fifteen years old. For a time after the war he ran a string of packhorses from The Dalles to the mines at Canyon City, then took up a homestead on Wind River and developed a resort known as St. Martin Hot Springs, still operative. His wife was Marguerite Arcouet, daughter of Amable Arcouet, who was a capable helpmeet. In applying for his Indian War pension many years later, he described himself as "five feet, seven inches tall, with bronze complexion, red hair, and velvet gray eyes." According to a newspaper account of the day, St. Martin met death at the hands of a disgruntled patient at the hot springs, who claimed the springs were worthless, inasmuch as they had not helped him. When he became abusive, St. Martin ordered him to leave, but as he mounted his horse, the patient stabbed him fatally. "Too bad", philosophized the newspaper, "a man with one foot in the grave should have done such a thing at the last."

St. Martin, Joseph -before 1839
" . . . the guide, a powerful man" was mentioned by Alexander Ross about 1814. He was probably the man with David Thompson in Montana in 1808 who was "impudent; I dislocated my right thumb in thrashing him". He was listed as a devant with the North West Company at Fort George in 1813. His daughter Genevieve by a Chinook woman married Pierre Belleque, I. Another daughter, Marie, was born in 1821. Joseph was probably a brother to Andre.

St. Martin, Marie 1821 c-1907
Marie, daughter of Joseph St. Martin, was possibly the femme fatale in the shooting of one Thornburg on Sauvie Island in 1834, before the days of any organized government and outside the scope of the Hudson's Bay Company. An impromptu court exonerated the slayer, T. J. Hubbard, who afterward married the girl "at the house of Mr. Belleck", whose wife Genevieve was Marie's elder sister. Jason Lee, the Methodist missionary, performed the ceremony. Their later life was spent in the Pendleton area, where Hubbard is buried, but Marie, who lived to be very old, is buried on the Narcisse Cornoyer lot in Walla Walla.

Sand, Camp of
An early name for Champoeg, also Sand Encampment, Campement du Sable, and variants.

Sanders, John Alexandre 1801-1874
Little except the marriages of Sanders and those of his children is found in the church records. His Donation Land Claim statement gives his birth date as 1800 at Montreal, and his arrival in Oregon as 1828. He seems to have married successively Catherine Chinook, Susanne Tkope and Lizette of The Dalles, having children by each.

Sanpoil, Marie
This second wife of Canote Humphreville is usually called Marie Michina, Couer d'Alene.

Sauteuse, Sauteux
The Sauteux Indians lived north of the Great Lakes and the area around the Red River. They are also called Chippewa.

Sauve Island
Sauve Island, now generally spelled Sauvies, is a large and fertile island silted in at the juncture of the Willamette River with the Columbia. It was formerly ill-drained, and was known as Wapato Island by the early explorers from the wapato plants that furnished them and the natives with a great deal of their sustenance. Laurent Sauve managed the Hudson's Bay Company dairy on the island for many years.

Sauve, Laurent - dit LaPlante   1784-1858
"Sauvies Island was called after an old Canadian by the name of Sauve, dit Laplante", wrote George B. Roberts, master of Cowlitz Farm. Sauve was a dairyman and cowherd for the Hudson's Bay Company on the island that bears his name, misspelled, in the Columbia at the mouth of the Willamette. He had been in the service for about twenty years, and spent perhaps ten more at the dairy at the approximate site of Wyeth's old Fort William before retiring to French Prairie in 1844, where he took a claim just north of Horseshoe Lake. He was twice married to natives. His wife Josephte having died in 1848, he married Francoise Walla Walla, widow successively of Thomas Tawakon (Iroquois) and of Paul Guilbeau. Two children of his first wife died young; one daughter by the same wife married Joseph Champagne and died within a few months.

Scarborough, James   1805-1855
Scarborough was an English sea-faring man. He joined the Hudson's Bay Company in 1829 as an officer on the **Isabella**, and later served on the **Lama** and the **Beaver**, and as captain on the **Cadboro** and the **Mary Dare**. After 1843, when he married a native, Anne Elizabeth, and took a claim at Chinook Point at the mouth of the Columbia, he was bar pilot until his sudden death in 1855. His farm running up the slope of Scarborough Head was noted by all comers and goers, for the Head was a conspicuous landmark and a lookout for approaching vessels. One visitor wrote that his wife cultivated the land; another that "the captain had a fine farm with excellent fruit trees and a large herd of cattle." Many tales about his lost grave and "buried treasure" still circulate. After his death, his two surviving sons, Edwin and Robert, were reared by James Birnie.

Schultheis, Michael
Michael Schultheis was one of four German immigrants who bought the Jesuit farm at St. Francis Xavier after the gold rush had subsided and St. Joseph's College had closed. Three Neibler brothers joined Schultheis in the enterprise.

Senecal, Gideon   1812-1896
Senecal came relatively late, 1840, to the Prairie. He may have been with the Company much earlier, however, for he retired in 1842 to a claim on the road south of Butteville. After the death of his wife Marie Grenier in 1850, he married Lucie DuCharme. He moved to Wasco County about 1880, where he died in 1896, leaving many descendents.

Servant, Jacques   1795-1854
Believed by some historians to have come from Canada about 1816, as he may have, but the family firmly believe "A few years earlier, with Lucier and Labonte", that is, with Astor's overland party under Hunt. He was a boatman on brigades out of Fort Colville. Of the three children baptized at the Fort of the Nez Perces, Marguerite married Cyrille Bertrand, Antoine married Louise Gingras, and Angelique died at the age of eleven. Marguerite, wife of Bertrand, died in the same year, 1848. The Servant record continues on French Prairie, where he had taken a centrally located claim. At St. Paul he formally married Josephte Sinemaule Nez Perce (also called Okanogan), mother of the three above children as well as others both older and younger. Jacques Servant died at St. Paul in 1854; his widow married Pierre Lacourse.

Servant, Marie   1830 c.-
Marie, daughter of Jacques Servant and Josette Okanogan, married Augustin Raymond. She is still recalled by elder people as a small, delicate looking woman, renowned on the Prairie for her stories and legends and her singing of hymns in Chinook jargon. A tape recording of her songs is said to have been made. Large oil paintings of her and her husband are in the Oregon Historical Society, Portland.

Shasta Tribe (Saste)
The Shastas lived in northern California and into southern Oregon. The California trail of the brigades passed through their country, and Shasta Indians often found their way to the French settlement, many of them as slaves of other tribes.

Sheil, James Dr. 1829-1853
Dr. James Sheil was one of the first practising physicians on the Prairie, preceded by Dr. William Bailey and contemporary with him. Sheil was born in Ireland, and came as a young man to New Orleans, where he married Julia Noble. He came to San Francisco, then Portland, and finally established himself on the Prairie, where his wife and children joined him. He died three years later. His widow married Dr. Bailey; all three lie buried together in St. Paul with a shaft that notes of Julia, "She passed doing good". The body of Sheil was one of several moved from the old cemetery to the new when it was established in 1875. Cemetery records show Dr. Bailey bought the first lot in the new place a month before his own death.

Shohoanni, Sotshohanni, etc. - see Ignace, Jean Baptiste, Iroquois.

Simon, Louis Henry 1827-1904
Simon was born at St. Servan in northern France, as was his wife. He came to America in 1853 and took a claim the following year. His wife Anne died in 1907; both are buried in St. Paul.

Sinpoel (San poil, Simpoil, etc.)
The Sinpoels were one of the five tribes called by Father Blanchet "Gens des Lacs," who lived in the Okanogan-Colville area.

Smith, Thomas 1808 c.-
Smith was the half-breed son of an un-named Smith and a Cree. He was listed merely as a trapper in the Columbia District in 1830. He had been in the Walla Walla country in 1831, and was to be sent back to Vancouver with the next boat that came by, "to go a-trapping," we read in McLoughlin's letters. His wife was Marguerite Nesquallie, whom he married and who died in the space of one year, 1844. A daughter Marie was baptized at St. Louis two weeks later, her mother being given as Marguerite Walla Walla. It seems likely a slight mixup in details accounts for the discrepancy.

Snake Tribe
The Snake (Serpent) Tribe lived in the basin of the Snake River, chiefly in Idaho. They were in the main non-aggressive and on good terms with the whites. Although commonly called Flatheads, they did not practise head-flattening, which was a custom of the coastal tribes.

Soderini, Tiberius
Soderini was a priest recruited in Rome by Father De Smet in 1843. It appears he may have been from a minor noble family to account for the "ex-bus" in his signature.

Souchouabe
Souchouabe, Shuswap, She-waps and Okanogan are tribal names used almost interchangeably in the old records. The Shuswaps lived in southern British Columbia, where a large lake bears their name.
The marker at Lake Shuswap: "This beautiful lake takes its name from the Shuswap Indians, northernmost of the great Salishan family and the largest tribe in Interior B. C. Once numbering over 5000, these people were fishermen and hunters. They roamed in bands through a vast land of lakes and forest stretching 150 miles to the west, north and east."
The famous "shovel nose" or "sturgeon nose" canoe of the Kootenais was used by many of the tribes, for Sinpoil, Kalispel, Okanogan, Atnans and Colvilles are all related branches of the great Salishan group.

Souchouable (Shuswap), Lisette 1870 c.-1841
Lisette Shuswap married Joseph Delard in the "Big Wedding" at the Willamette Mission in 1839. Her surviving children were Catherine, Pierre, Augustin, Basile, Marie Ann and Antoine.

Souliere, Marguerite
Souliere and Soulier are the same name, well known in Montreal. One William Soulliere was an engage at Norway House where his little daughter Catherine was baptized when the priests passed through in 1838.
Marguerite Souliere was the daughter of Basile Souliere and a Cree woman. (Vancouver records)

The son Joseph mentioned at the marriage of Marguerite to David Dompierre was Joseph Roussin, from an earlier alliance. After Dompierre's death in 1849, Marguerite married Joseph Rochbrune.

Spokane, Isabelle (Elizabeth Canote)   1827 c.-1852
Isabelle was the eldest recorded daughter of Canote Humphreville and Pauline Sinpoil. Of her six known children, only two survived childhood; these were taken into the home of her brother Pierre (Waccom, Wakan) Humphreville, who was unmarried, along with his stepmother Marie Michina and five younger half-brothers and sisters. The family record continues through the St. Louis Register.

Spokane, Therese
Therese was a Spokane woman who had married Louis Lavalle, one of the men who had come with Hunt overland in 1811, and had remained through successive fur companies. Her sons, Martial and Pierre, were born during the 1820's. After Lavalle's death she married Pierre Grenier, and was again widowed by his death by drowning at The Dalles in 1830. Therese then married Joseph Corneille (Cornoyer). Her recorded children thus were Pierre and Martial Lavalle, Marie Ann Grenier, and Victoire, Joseph and Louis Cornellier.

Spokane Tribe
The Spokans were one of the five tribes in the upper Columbia region called by Father Blanchet "Gens des Lacs" in his reports.

Silvestre, Joseph (Sylvestre)   1826 c.-1854
Joseph Silvertre's appearance on the Prairie was brief and he died at the age of twenty-eight. The St. Louis Church Register gives his birthplace as St. Thomas in the Antilles. The birth and death of a daughter Genevieve in 1851 at St. Paul is the first we hear of him. The register entry gives the child's mother as "Rosalie, widow of Plouff", which is evidently an error for Therese, widow of Plouff, whose daughter Rosalie was but eleven years old. In 1852 Silvestre married Rose Poirier, daughter of Toussaint Poirier, at St. Louis. Two years later it is recorded that he died at Salem and was buried "without ceremony" at St. Louis on May 1, 1854. His widow Rose shortly married Bazile Delore.

Staatz, John (Staats)
The record of John Staatz is unfortunately incomplete. It is known that two Staats men, Stephen and Isaac, probably brothers, came from New York State in 1851 and settled in Polk County. John was no doubt the son of one of them. His wife, Marie Toupin, was the granddaughter of Madame Dorion and also of Andre Longtain.

Stikine
Stikine river and fort are in northern British Columbia.

Sylvestre, Jean Baptiste   1811 c.-1851
The name Sylvestre appears very sketchily in the records, though it is known several of that name were in the West. Jean Baptiste occurs only as a witness and as "deceased" September 21, 1851, aged 40 years, both in St. Paul records.

Tawakon, Thomas   -before 1854
The Tawakons were an Iroquois family living on the north side of the Yamhill River in a little cluster of their friends and countrymen, including the Tsetes and the Tyikwarhis. During his days of employment with the Hudson's Bay Company, Thomas Tawakon had as his wife "a woman of the country, a Chinook", and had two recorded daughters, Catherine and Susanne, born about 1820 and 1821. Catherine married Andre St. Martin and Susanne married Amable Petit I at about the same time their father married Francaise Walla Walla, or Cayuse, all in 1839 or late 1838. Three old Iroquois friends were married together, perhaps just having returned from a brigade, or merely because of their deep friendship, on July eighth, 1839—Louis Monique, Jean Baptiste Tyikwarhi and Thomas Tawakon, along with Alexis Aubichon, an employe of long standing in the Company. The same witnesses signed for all, Jean Baptiste Jeaudoin and Joseph McLoughlin. The Joseph McLoughlin home, where young Thomas died (quite surely a son of Thomas Tawakon) was near the cluster of Iroquois. Joseph himself was to die a few months later. Two children were recorded to Thomas Tawakon and Francoise Walla Walla, born in the late 1830's, Pierre and Louise. At the age of fourteen Louise married J. B.

Goyet (1854), at which time her father was deceased. The later Tawakon records are found in the St. Paul register. Tawakon's widow Francaise married in turn Paul Guilbeau and Laurent Sauve.

Tawakon, Thomas I -before 1839
The Tawakons were Iroquois, the family so confusing that it seems best to differentiate the two Thomases at the start. Several "Thomas Iroquois" were on the rolls of the Hudson's Bay Company, some of which can not now be identified. Three daughters are recorded to the elder Thomas Tawakon, Iroquois, the mother (if all the same woman) being given as "a Chinook", (of Catherine born about 1818), as "a woman of the country", (of Susanne, born about 1820) and as "a woman of the Grand Dalles (of Marie Anne, born about 1823). Catherine married Andre St. Martin in 1839, Susanne married Amable Petit I in 1838, and Marie Anne married Charlot Iroquois in 1839, at which time Father Thomas Tawakon was deceased.

Tawakon, Thomas II 1820 c.-1848
The younger Thomas was quite surely a son of Thomas Tawakon I, though not specifically so identified. Each may appear merely as "Thomas". The younger Thomas married Francoise Walla Walla (Cayuse) in 1839, with two small children at the time. There may have been others later, unrecorded. Thomas died at the home of Joseph McLoughlin on the Yamhill River on May 7, 1848, aged 28. His widow Francoise married Thomas's old friend, Paul Guilbeau, who died very shortly, possibly in the gold fields, and in 1850 she married Laurent Sauve. Tawakon's daughter Louise married Baptiste Goyet in 1855.

Tellier, Louis
Louis Tellier, who appears briefly in the St. Paul register, was a Hudson's Bay Company employe who seems to have settled for a time on French Prairie, but by 1855 was living at Frenchtown, near Walla Walla, with a native wife (Angelique Pend d'Oreille) and six children. His claim lay a short distance to the west of the old Whitman Mission, next to that of Michel Pelissier; their families intermarried; later records are carried in the Walla Walla register, which included Frenchtown as a mission.

Thomas - see Tawakon

Tkope, Susanne 1814 c.-1842
Susanne Tkope was the second recorded wife of Jean Alexander Sanders. She died March 21, 1842, "aged 21", at St. Paul and was buried in the old parish cemetery. At the baptism of her daughter Veronica at St. Louis in 1845, she was given as Susanne Yamhill.

Toupin, Francois 1825-1862
Francois Toupin was half-brother to Pierre Dorion, the Younger, their mother being Madame Dorion. Francois married Angelique Longtain in 1847. Their children included Marie (Staats), Francois II, who died at the age of one year, and an unrecorded "James", (Jacques) "who married a Davidson of Wheatland". Francois died in a snowstorm while packing supplies from Lewiston to the mines in 1862. The Jean Baptiste born in 1852 may be the Jacques mentioned as "unrecorded". The first child of the marriage, 1847, was born and died un-named.

Toupin, Jean Baptiste 1792 c.-1862
Toupin was the third husband of Madame Dorion; he outlived her by twelve years. Besides his children Francois and Marie Anne, he seems to have had other children by another woman, as Jean Toupin, Jr., was godfather to a relative in 1871. According to one historian, Toupin had been an interpreter at Fort Nez Perce since 1821, a man of Work's crew, "quarrelsome, unreliable". He was a messenger "back and forth" following the Whitman massacre.

Toupin, Marie Anne 1826-
Marie Anne was the daughter of Madame Dorion by her third husband, J. B. Toupin. After the death of David Gervais at the age of 34 (1853), Marie Anne married Francois Robideau (1857). Four children were born to Gervais, one to Robideau.

Toussaint, Marie (Savoyard)
One Toussaint Savoyard is listed with the North West Company at Fon du Lac in 1805; it is reasonable to suppose that Marie and Genevieve Toussaint "from the other side of the Rockie Mountains" (St. Paul Register), both of whom married Laroque men, were his daughters. Marie and Louis Laroque, the parents of Sophie here baptized about 1850, had earlier recorded chil-

dren in the Willamette Valley—Angelique (1843), Marguerite (1846), at St. Paul, and Louis (1849-1850) at St. Louis.

Tsalile Tribe
The Tsaliles were a tribe on the lower Umpqua River, called savage in the extreme.

Tse-te, Charlot Iroquois
The Tsete name was most difficult to spell, appearing on land records even as Schegte. This man may have been the "Iroquois Charles" with David Thompson in 1808-1810 in Montana, or the "Old Indian Charlie" with Work in the Rocky Mountains in 1831-1832, but the latter is doubtful, as in April of 1832 he was a member of Laframboise's crew sent to avenge the murder of two trappers, Thomas Canasawarette and Pierre Kakawaquiron, by the Tillamooks, then to proceed to California. At that time he was listed as a freeman. Before 1840, probably by the mid-1830's, he had retired to French Prairie and was one of those signing two petitions to the Bishop of Red River asking for priests to be sent to the West. Here his name was written as Charlo Chata. "We have begun to build," they wrote, meaning a log chapel, adding a list of eighteen "Willammeth Settelers" who were doing the work. By 1844 Tsete was living on a land claim on the north side of the Yamhill River, opposite the present Dayton, in a little Iroquois community of the Tawakon and Tyikwarhi families. Partial records of three wives appear: Charlotte Pend d' Oreille, the mother of Agatha, Marie Thomas (Canasawarette ?) and a Calapooya woman usually mentioned as Therese. Charlot had 100 acres enclosed, mostly in cultivation, when his claim was recorded in 1847. The next year he sold his claim to a newcomer, James Martin, and no more is heard of him.

Tualatin Plain
The Tualatin River lies between the Coast Range and the Chehalem Mountains, joining the Willamette shortly above the Falls.

Tualatin Tribe
The Tualatins were a small branch of the Calapooian Tribe. When the Treaty of 1855 absorbed their range in the valley of the Tualatin River, the remnants of the tribe were placed on the Grand Ronde Reserve in Polk County.

Tumwater (Tomwata) Tribe
Tomwata or tumwater is the Chinook jargon word for waterfall, and here refers to the Cascades of the Columbia. The tribe is also called Mathlomat.

Turner, John   -1847
John Turner, American, said to have been a large and powerful man, was the survivor of three Indian massacres, two while on expeditions with Jedediah Smith and one with Ewing Young. He lived for a time a few miles north of Salem on the river, later going to California. He was accidentally killed in 1847 by the discharge of his own gun.

Tyikwarhi - see Norwest

Umpqua Tribes
These people occupying the basin of that river in Southwestern Oregon, were divided by language differences into the Upper and Lower Umpquas. Both were generally truculent enemies of the whites; even the fur traders had trouble with them. One Catholic Father wrote, "The natives of that area are wicked and little civilized. One sees there immense meadows where missionaries could establish themselves to spread the gospel."

Vassal, Louis   1828 c.-1898 c.
Louis Vassal was a Red River mixed blood; his wife was Catherine, a Lower Chinook from Baker's Bay. Although "dangerously ill" and baptized at St. Paul in 1848, "aged about 25 years", he recovered and lived to the age of seventy. He and Catherine were married at St. Paul shortly after both were baptized in 1848. At the time her name was given as Atalo; Charles McChesney, in making up the Rolls in 1906, put it down as Ki-yah-tol and called her half Chinook and half Clatsop. She died in 1853 at the age of thirty-five. (Rolls)

The infant Isadore evidently did not survive, as at the time of his parents marriage four years after his birth, only two children, Victoire and Flore, were "recognized." It seems that later children, as well as Flore, also died, as Victoire deposed in 1906 that "I had two brothers, who died in infancy; I never had any sisters." The births of Adelaide and Moyse were both recorded at St. Louis.

Vassal, Victoire 1846-
Victoire Vassal, daughter of Louis Vassal and Catherine Chinook, married Edouard Gendron at the age of fifteen. Their four children all died in infancy, and Gendron himself in 1869 at the age of twenty-five, all on the Grand Ronde Reserve. Two years after Gendron's death, his widow married Jean Baptiste (Francois) Belique. This marriage did not work out; she left him, and later married one Jeffries, still on the Reserve.

Vendal, Genevieve 1839 c.-1875
Genevieve was the daughter of Louis Vendal "of Lake Labiche", at the southern end of French Prairie, and a Carrier woman. She married Louis Pichet in 1853 and Louis Poirier in 1857.

Vendal, Jean Baptiste 1845-1908
Jean Baptiste Vendal, son of Louis B. Vendal ("the younger") and Cecile McDonald, lived out his life on French Prairie. He first married Marcellina Senecal, daughter of Gedeon; she died at the birth of her second child. Vendal then married Clementia LaChapelle, daughter of Andre, by whom she had fourteen children. He is recalled as a big, handsome man with sandy hair and ruddy complexion. He and his family are buried in the St. Louis Cemetery, well marked.

Vendal, Louis A. 1798 c.-1862
The presence of two Louis Vendals on the Prairie at the same time leads to some confusion. Louis A. is often called "the elder" or "of Lac Labiche" to distinguish the two. The elder was perhaps the father of the younger Vendal. The elder came from Sorel, Canada, took a claim in the swampy southern part of the Prairie, and became a naturalized citizen in 1851.

Vendal, Louis B. 1819-1859
Louis B. is sometimes identified as "the younger" to distinguish him from Louis A. "of lac Labiche", who was possibly his father. Louis B. was en engage of the Hudson's Bay Company until his retirement to a claim on French Prairie a short distance west of Woodburn. He first married Cecile McDonald, metisse daughter of Chief Trader Allen McDonald. She died in 1848, leaving two living children. He then married Marie Anne Delard, daughter of Joseph Delard, aged about thirteen. She bore him six children. Vendal was stabbed to death in an argument with Tobias Marchetti in 1859. His widow married Medard Foisy, and still later Joseph Morrel.

Vernier, Louis Joseph
Little is known of this man beyond the fact that he was the second husband of Madame Dorion between the years 1814 and 1821, approximately. One daughter, Marguerite (Gobin), is recorded.

Vernier, Marguerite 1821-1858
Marguerite was the daughter of Madame Dorion by her second husband, Louis Joseph Vernier. She bore several children to Jean Baptiste Gobin, and reared at least one of her deceased brother's sons. She died in May, 1858. The new cemetery at St. Louis was blessed four days later "in the presence of all the inhabitants of the Parish", and Marguerite Vernier Gobin may possibly have been interred there.

Vertefeuille, Jude
Besides the children listed in the St. Paul volumes, a daughter Celine was baptized at St. Louis on July 16, 1865.

Vercruysse, Aloysius
Father Vercruysse was one of the priests recruited in Europe by Father DeSmet in 1844. He worked mainly with the Canadian farmers at French Prairie, establishing a mission at St. Louis that grew into a parish in 1845. During the late 1850's he was at Colville, where the Church flourished under his leadership.

Veyret, Francois 1812-1879
Father Veyret came from France on the Etoile du Matin to work at the Willamette mission. By 1850 he was in Oregon City, where he and Father Blanchet ministered to the last hour to the five condemned Cayuse who were executed there for the Whitman massacre. He later went to serve on the faculty of Santa Clara College in California.

Vivet, Louis   1797 c.-1844
Vivet was an employe of the Hudson's Bay Company from about 1821, said to be a tinsmith at
Fort Vancouver. However, he was mentioned by Tolmie in 1833 as coming and going with furs
to Fort Nesquallie, a voyageur. His Chinook wife died at some unrecorded time, leaving Henriette and Narcisse. Louis himself died at the age of forty-seven "at the home of Etienne Lucier of
a short illness." Henriette married Louis Bercier, Narcisse married Julienne Labonte, daughter of
Louis Labonte, Sr.

Vivet, Narcisse   1830-1870
Narcisse Vivet married Julienne Labonte, daughter of Louis Labonte I and Kilokatah, in 1858.
Five children are recorded.

Wagner, Peter   1796 -.-1865
Wagner was a Canadian who entered the service of the Hudson's Bay Company as a butcher in
1820. He married Marie Stomis Chinook upon the arrival of the priests, and had his children
baptized. After his retirement, he took a claim in the big bend of the Willamette, to the south of
Etienne Lucier. His wife Marie died on the farm in March, 1865, at the age of sixty; three months
later Peter himself died, aged seventy-five.

Wales - see Marianne Chinook, Aubichon

Walla Walla Tribe
The Walla Wallas (Little River) lived along the stream of that name and along the Columbia
from the Snake to the Umatilla. By the 1855 treaty they were removed to the Umatilla Reserve.
Their diet was mainly roots, berries, and fish which they caught by nets and weirs. They were a
handsome people, related to the Nez Perce.

Walla Walla, Francoise (Cayuse)   1814 c.-
Francoise Walla Walla, or Cayuse was three times married, according to the records: to Thomas
Tawakon in 1839, to Paul Guilbault in 1848 at St. Paul, and to Laurent Sauve of St. Paul in 1850.

Wapeto, Lake
Lake Wapeto was a shallow and marshy lake in the basin of the Tualatin River. The arum plant
called wappeto by the natives grew abundantly in the shallow water and was a great source of
food to the Yamhill tribe. The lake has now been drained and is used for onion raising, but it
sometimes fills briefly in the spring run-off and is visited by flocks of migrating waterfowl to
recall for a moment the old days.

Warfield, James   1811-1840 c.
James Warfield, from Tennessee, was a convert to Catholicism at the time of his marriage to
Lizette Oyer in 1840. He died on the California Trail, and Lizette married Henry Black on
August 7, 1842: "-by J. S. Griffith, at the house of Robert Newell before the congregation assem-
bled for Divine Service." She died on the claim in 1846, "leaving four children". (By Warfield
these were Marie and Betsy. Warfield was also the guardian of 7-year-old Isabelle Lumbers.)
(Lambert?)

Wassenhove (Van Wessenhove), Francois   1841-
Francois (Frank) Wassenhove was born in Belgium in 1841, coming with his parents to America
at the age of three years. He lived in Michigan until grown, then came West in 1859, where he
farmed in Oregon or tried mining in Idaho. His wife, Mary Helen Coyle, died in 1898. His
second wife was Ellen Walsh, the widow successively of Patrick Ferguson and Edward Ramsey.
The farm home near Champoeg was a well-known stock and hop raising center for many years.

Watiece, George
Two Watiece men, George and Thomas I, who may have been father and son, appear in the
Vancouver and St. Paul records. The wife of George is given merely as "a native woman", with a
daughter Julienne born about 1820. Thomas I married Marie, a Snake woman, in 1846. His
parents are given as "Iroquois" (father) and Chinook mother. The above George may well have
been an Iroquois, lacking evidence to the contrary.

Weremus, Chief
Weremus was a wily old chief at the Falls of the Willamette who acted as interpreter for the
priests there in the early days of their mission and played them against the Methodist Waller for

all he could get from either side. He seems to have spent a great deal of time sulking when the gifts did not please him. He does not appear to have been solidly committed to any religion finally. "He caused me to be answered that I could go visit some other place," wrote Father Blanchet, "that as for him and his, their mind was made up and that they could do without me." He seems to have left no children of his own at his death; his niece, Anne, who married Benjamin Williams, was the beneficiary in a will, dated May 9, 1844, that came to light in the Clackamas County Court House more than one hundred twenty years later (filed in 1934) which reads: "Be it known that whereas Wasamus (sic) Chief of the Tribe of Indians living at the falls of the Willhamet do give and bequeathe to my Neice Ann, wife of Benjamin Williams and to her heirs forever all my right, interest and title of, in and to a certain piece of land lying and being at the falls of the Willhamet River, bounded as follows: viz:
"Beginning at the mouth of a small spring branch about three hundred yards below the falls and on the west of the Willhamet thence west 140 chs. to the Talatine River thence down and with the meanders of the stream to its mouth, thence down and with the meanders of the Willhamet to the place of Beginning."
The will was signed by Chief Wasamus and witnessed by James Force and Thomas Davis.

Weston, David   1820-1876
David Weston was an 1842 immigrant from Indiana. He was a blacksmith at Champoeg until the devastating flood of 1861 washed away the town. He married Marie Sinclair, daughter of Thomas Sinclair and a native woman, the daughter of Chief Cowhicales, (Chinook?) Seven children were recorded. For many years his house stood under a hill near a creek east of Champoeg; Weston and members of his family are buried in an unmarked sliver of woods at the edge of his claim.

Williams, Benjamin
Benjamin Williams appears in Elijah White's census list of 1842 as married and the father of two children at that time. He owned horses, cattle and hogs, but had no land under cultivation. For his wife's inheritance, see Weremus, Chief.

Winslow, George (Anderson)
Winslow, though he changed his name so often one is uncertain what to call him, was a negro who came up from California with Ewing Young in 1834. He settled on the Willamette near present Clackamas, married a Clackamas Indian, and fathered several children. He was involved in the Cockstock affair, having quarreled with the irascible Indian, and was also involved in the manufacture of "blue ruin" whiskey along the Clackamas River. He claimed to be a doctor—for he was given to wild stories—and complained to emigrants that Dr. Barclay had come along and had "bust out" his trade.

Yamhill, Alexis   1825 c.-1840
The death of Alexis Yamhill "in his hut" was cited by Father Blanchet as one of the first fruits of his Willamette Mission, as he wrote to his superior in Red River (apparently) in his third Notice: "A young native of fifteen years, sick with consumption, asked for the missionary, who explained the Christian truths to him. At the second visit his joy burst forth; he was raptured at the sweet thought that baptism would inscribe him among the number of God's children. 'Thanks, thanks, Father,' he repeated oftenwhile listening to the words of consolation addressed to him. He received baptism and died predestined."

Yamhill Tribe
The Yamhill Indians were the northernmost tribe of the Calapooias, inhabiting the region of French Prairie and the valley of the Yamhill River.

Yogalta Tribe (Yougleta, Uculet, etc.)
"The Yougletas, a fierce and barbarous nation, live on the large Vancouver Island . . . All (the other) nations have to defend themselves against the cruel Yougletas, who occasionally surprise them and carry away slaves for use in traffic." So wrote Father Blanchet after visiting the island on a mission.

Yougleta, Marguerite   1814 c.-1893
Following the death of her first husband, Jean Baptiste Dubreuil, in the gold fields, Marguerite Yougleta married Charles Plante. She outlived him by forty years, as she is recorded as dying in 1893 at the reputed age of 90 years.

Youte Tribe
More often spelled Ute; a group of tribes to the southeast, as in Utah and Nevada; also called Paiutes.

OLD ST. PAUL CEMETERY

The Old Cemetery at St. Paul was blessed by Father F. N. Blanchet on his second mission to the Willamette Valley in May-June, 1839.

"This 10 June, 1839, we priest Vicar General of the Columbia have blessed, following the custom, a plot of ground 33 paces on the front and of 25 of depth, surrounded by an enclosure of upright stakes, having in the center a large consecrated cross, to serve, the said ground, for burials and to be the cemetery of the Catholic Mission of Saint Paul of the Wallamette. This benediction has been made in presence of Joseph Gervais, of Etienne Lucier and of a great number of others who have not known how to sign, and of Sieur Nicolas Montour who has signed with us.

Nicolas Montour
F. N. Blanchet, priest, V.G.

* * *

Burials recorded in Vancouver Register, Book I

1839

Marie Indian, slave at house of Joseph Delard	Jan. 16	20 years	page	29
Un-Named	June 10	-		43
Jacot	" 10	-		43
Un-named	" 10	-		43

St. Paul, Book I

Catherine Kalapoya	Dec. 2	9 years	page	2
Joseph McKarty	" 22	14 "		3

1840

Josephte Nouette [Lucier]	Jan. 12	40 years	4
Julien Dompierre	26	7 mo.	4
Marguerite Clatsop [Gervais]	29	28 years	5
Alexis Tamhile	Feb. 12	15 "	6
Pierre Tchinouk	21	50 "	6
Abraham Laframboise	Mar. 5	6 days	7
Jacques, at house of Gervais	Summer	33 years	7
Betsy Calapoya, house of Delard	"	15 "	7
Jean Baptiste Depati	July 6	16 mo.	13
Paul Kalapoya, dit Captain	Oct. 1	20 years	17
Son of Roy	Nov. 11	- days	20

1841

Adelaide Gervais	Jan. 31	3 years	21a
Lisette Souchouabe	Feb. 20	36 "	21b
Ignace, at house of Labonte	Mar. 9	25 "	22
Marie Tchailis	May 16	30 "	25
Maria Montour	" 21	12 "	25
Tchinouk man	July 29	50 "	30

1842

Marie Indian	Jan. 1	-	page	40
Agathe Plante	6	22 years		40
Gregoire Patetis	22	15 days		42
Pierre Dalcour	Feb. 24	15 mo.		43
Marie Indian	Mar. 13	30 years		45
Susanne Sanders	22	21 "		46
Charlotte McCarty	May 25	34 "		50
Madeleine Joseph Okanogan	June 18	-		50
Madeleine Laferte	July 3	2 "		50
Jacob Indian	Oct. 3	-		60
Catherine Indian	8	7 "		61
Andree Indian	8	3 "		61
Marie Indian	Nov. 27	-		63
Laurent Quintal	Dec. 5	10 days		64
Marie Lafantaisie	5	1 mo.		64
Francois Gervais	10	10 years		64

1843

Susanne Plante	Jan. 10	20 "	65
Agathe Indian, house of Plante	27	10 "	66
Alexis Indian	Feb. 23	-	69
Basile Picard	Mar. 30	11 "	70
James [unknown]	Apr. 10	2 "	70
Alexis Indian, house of Lucier	23	18 "	71
Baptiste Plante	May 25	16 "	73
Xavier Barnabe	June 2	3 mo.	73
Barthelimi Martineau	July 19	12 years	75
Amable Koose	20	20 "	75
Leon Arquaite	Oct. 3	-	79
Romain gagnon	14	1 mo	82
Marie Indian	18	20 years	82
Elizabeth Plante	23	14 "	83
Francois Tlakes	Nov. 11	15 days	84
Marie Indian, house of Despard	21	18 years	86
Frederic Indian, house of Perrault	Dec. 2	60 "	88
Unknown	4	-	88
Amable Indian	15	3 mo.	88
Ignace Indian, house of J. B. Aubichon	21	-	89

1844

Michel Indian	Jan. 16	10 years	90
Jacques Gagnon	Feb. 12	5 "	90
Marguerite Dubois	Mar. 13	-	91
Toussaint Racine	19	8 "	93
Josephine Ignace	26	4 mo.	93
Adele Rivet	Apr. 10	2 "	93
Child Indian	May 29	3 "	97
Joseph Indian	30	5 years	98
Child Indian	June 4	3 "	99
Helene Ignace	11	-	99

1846

Esther Lefebre	Jan. 13	-	Page 129
Child	Feb. 16	-	135
Child of Nashke	17	-	131
Joseph Indian	15	20 years	131
Little girl	24	-	131
Cecile Indian	Apr. 18	17 mo.	132
Henriette Yogalta	26	-	132
Susanne Humphreville Montour	May 20	55 years	133
Francois Chaudiere	24	-	133
Jacques Calapoya	19	18 years	133
Andre Picard	11	65	134
Son of Felix	June 3	1 "	136
Francois Felix	Jul. 22	9 "	138
Child of Senecal	Aug. 2	"	140
Jean Baptiste Lajoie	18	46 years	140
Thomas Waticie	20	-	140
Marie Kalapoya	30	-	141
Charlotte Walla Walla	Sep. 12	36 years	142
Rose Chalifoux	Oct. 12	12 "	143
Joseph Lilouais	Nov. 4	9 "	144
Hyacinthe Lavigueur	12	-	144
Marie Jobin	Dec. 2	3 years	145
Paul Garant	23	12 days	145
Marguerite Gingras	27	2 years	146
Child of Rivet	27	-	146
Joseph, at the College	Nov. 4	8 years	146

1847

Mary Smith McGinnis	Jan. 8	27 years	147
Isabelle Kalapoya	12	3 "	147
Henriette Plouff	14	6 "	148
Patrick Rowland Horigan	Feb. 11	-	149
Alexis Lacourse	24	12 years	150
Philippe Degre	29	108 "	150
Child of Thos. Watiece	Mar. 8	-	151
Francois Labonte	11	0 days	151
Jean Baptiste Lavigueur	11	15 years	151
Angelique Payet	26	17 "	151
Charles Brouillet	27	8 "	151
Thomas Indian	Apr. 9	30 "	153
Joseph Beaudoin	9	2 "	153
Michel Saste	27	12 days	153
Indian, house of Plante	same week	-	153
Wife of Aubichon	16	-	153
Joseph Bellique	May 27	5 years	153
Marguerite Laroque	June 20	-	153
Isabelle Mainville Boucher	July 5	25 years	156
Josette Hunphreville	22	10 "	156
Louise Nez Perce	Aug. 1	23 "	157
Louis Nipissing	5	18 mo.	157
Child of Peletier	Dec. 5	-	171
Child of Vandale	8	-	171
Charles Hord [Howard]	June 21	15 mo.	99
Janotte Indian	22	4 years	99
Louis Vivet	26	47 "	99
Pierre Laroque	29	9 "	100
Benjamin Indian, at house of Despard	July 8	12 "	100
Marie Descbaudiere Lajoie	Aug. 17	24 "	102
Virginia Chamberland	Sep. 5	1 "	102
Spanish ----	5	-	102
Louis Youte	Oct. 15	-	103
Michel Indian	Dec. 8	-	104
Louise Indian	18	9 years	105
Boy Indian	24	-	105
Emelie Indian	24	-	105
Marguerite Smith Indian	24	-	105
Boy Indian	29	-	105
Francois Quesnel	29	65 years	106

1845

Philomene Tetreau	Jan. 5	5 years	106
Marie Smith	Feb. 2	-	107
Marie	5	2 days	109
Marie Rose Chamberland	5	21 days	109
Elizabeth Servant	15	2 years	109
Marie Indian	Mar. 8	-	110
Jeanne, house of J. B. Aubichon	12	12 years	111
Child, unknown	May 7	-	113
Louise Gingras	9	-	114
Nicolas Montour	27	9 days	114
Marie Indian	June 26	-	118
Joseph Dalcourt	27	2 years	118
Susanne Molelis	July 1	-	118
Emelie Indian	8	-	119
Julie Gervais	11	-	119
Marie Senecal	Aug. 20	-	121
Rose Lacourse	Sep. 1	-	121

Marie Laderoute	2	-	121
Woman, house of Forcier	15	-	122
Esther Gingras	17	-	122
Charlotte, house of J. McLoughlin	23	-	123
Philomene Dorion	Oct. 20	4 mo.	124
---- Lafantaisie	Nov. 7	7 years	124
Joseph des Dalles, ho. of Vandale	9	-	125
Two children, unknown Chinook	9	-	125
Marie Tchinouk	10	-	126
Toussaint Molelis	15	-	126
Indian Molelis	22	-	126
Joseph des Dalles, ho. Gervais	23	-	126
Elizabeth Brouillet	Dec. 31	-	128
Man, Unknown Tchinouk	31	-	128
house of Despard			
Joseph Focolino	31	6 mo.	128
Wife of Boucher	Dec. 9	-	171
Son of Boucher	15	-	171
Nicolas Okanogan	20	-	171
Child of Benon	20	-	171
Wife of Peletier	21	-	171
Dau. of Joseph Spokane	22	-	171
Wife of Guilbeau	29	-	171
1848			
Boy of Rossi	Jan. 1	-	171
Marguerite Indian, house of Lacourse	4	-	171
Boy of Dubois	7	-	171
Marie Indian, ho. of Arquet	8	-	171
Wife of Liard	10	-	171
Boy Indian, ho of Plante	11	-	171
Boy of Liard	11	1 day	171
Wife of Forcier	12	-	171
Son of Cosgrove	12	-	171
Xavier Liard	14	-	171
Susanne Godin	16	-	172
Indian boy, ho. of Thomas	20	-	172
Gai-hord	21	-	172
Daughter of Arquet	21	-	172
Daughter of Forcier	31	2 years	172
Kopper, boy	31	-	172
John Sauve	Feb. 1	-	172
Noel Lavigueur	17	-	172
Indian girl, ho. of Arquet	14	-	172
Patrick Rowling	Mar. 1	-	172
Indian man, ho. of Forcier	9	-	172
Child of Saste	27	9 years	172
Elizabeth Mongo	31	2 or 5 years	172
Wife of Lavigueur	Apr. 1	-	172
Louis Indian, ho. of Bernier	21	-	173

Total recorded burials in Book I, St. Paul — 200

St. Paul, Book II

1847

Jean Laprade	Sep. 31	7 mo.	page	1
Marie Indian, ho. Aubichon	23	12 years		2
1848				
Marie Indian	Feb. 3	-		2
Charles Jeaudoin	May 2	-		4
Indian, ho of Aubichon	5	-		4
Thomas	7	28 years		4

Child of Thomas	9	-	5
Elizabet McKay	16	14 years	5
Sara Labonte	20	2 mo.	5
Josephte Sauve	-	-	6
Indian woman	Jul. 6	-	8
Jean Indian, ho of Belique	Oct. 28	30 years	13
Celeste Jeaudoin	Nov. 16	2 mo.	14
Marie Indian, ho Plante	18	-	14
Son of Senecal	20	-	14
Margueriete Servant	30	-	15
Joseph McLoughlin	Dec. 23	28 years	15
Amable Petit	26	-	15
1849			
Angelique Servant	Jan. 7	11 years	15
Pierre Indian	13	2 "	16
Marie Couturier	14	3 "	16
Thomas Spokane, ho Laframbpose	20	20 "	16
Child of Bourgeau	Feb. 8	-	17
Cyrille Bertrand	19	3 mo.	17
Xavier Liard	Apr. 12	2 days	19
Marianne Bourgeau	May 1	1 year	19
Olivier Rochbrune	22	6 "	20
Hilaire Gilgeau	Jun. 26	-	21
Therese Tchinouk	28	8 years	21
Rosalie Kalispel	Aug. 11	-	22
Catherine McPhael	Oct. 13	13 Years	23
David Dompierre	19	-	23
Rose Fenlay	Nov. 11	-	23
Luce Chalifoux, in church	Dec. 31	11 years	24
1850			
Zoe Garant	Jan. 8	6 weeks	24
F. Xavier Lavigueur	8	-	25
Marie Gilbeau	Feb. 9	9 years	25
Celeste Jeaudoin	Mar. 3	6 mo.	26
Marie Indian	30	1 year	26
Marie Pichet	Apr. 8	-	26
Augustin Sephio	10	1 mo.	26
Joseph Sotshohoanni	22	-	26
Louise Boisvert, in church	May 2	-	26a
Nancy Dobin	23	-	26a
Moise Bergevin	27	3 mo.	26a
Marie Indian, ho of Maxwell	June 11	-	26a
Christine Jeaudoin	July 12	3 years	27
Marie Indian	Aug. 19	-	28
Joseph Nipissing	Sep. 14	7 years	29
Rosalie Indian	27	6 "	29
Jean Baptiste Saste	Oct. 21	3 "	30
Joseph Laframboise	24	3 years	30
Emelie Quesnel	Nov. 5	12 "	30
Jean Baptiste Saste	Dec. 9	·15 "	31
1851			
Laurent Iroquois	Jan. 8	-	33
Marie Flathead Gervais	8		33
Flavie LeBrun	19	3 mo.	33
Susanne	25	4 years	33
Isabelle Pelletier	Feb. 9	-	33
Joseph Pend d'Orielle	Mar. 6	1 year	35
Jean Baptiste Indian	15	10 days	35
Magdeleine Indian	26	11 years	35

Marguerite Wagner	Apr. 13	8 "	36
Catherine Laurent	19	8 "	36
Marie Despard	29	43 "	36
Susanne Pieriche	June 3	1 "	37
Genevieve Sylvestre	19	1 mo	38
Antoine Norwest	20	7 years	38
Calixte Chamberland	July 6	15 days	39
Archange Plouff	29	8 years	39
Caroline Montour Labonte	Aug. 3	26 "	39
Catherine Monique	12	9 "	40
Marguerite Pin	17	48 "	40
Joseph Lecuyer	Sep. 20	6 days	40
Jean Baptiste Sylvestre	21	40 years	40
Pelagie Plant	23	60 "	41
Josette Menard	24	50 "	41
Andre Chalifoux	26	62 "	41
Marie Ignace	Oct. 3	8 mo.	42
Rose Saste	6	33 years	43
Joseph Jacques	31	26 "	43
Francois Gilbeau	Nov. 8	4 "	43
Laurent Sede	Dec. 26	4 "	45
Charles Saste	31	25 mo.	45
1852			
Eusebe Norwest	Jan. 4	6 years	page 46
Joachim Fennely	13	15 "	46
Xavier Menard	Feb. 14	4 "	46a
Henriette Norwest	23	38 "	46a
Joseph Rivet	Mar. 16	40 "	46b
Joseph Menard	17	15 "	46b
Stanislaus Liard	18	35 "	46b
Marie Russi	Apr. 2	8 mo.	46b
Julie Beauchemin	May 9	30 years	46b
Catherine Sauve Champagne	17	13 "	46b
Marie Indian	June 29	79 "	48
Acadie Bernier	July 5	5 "	48
Marie Attalon	24	25 "	48
Marie Florence Prevost	Oct. 1	43 "	49 inset
John Weston	Sept. 27	14 "	50
Francois Rivet	27	95 "	50
Catherine	Oct. 7	32 "	50
Therese Rivet	13	97 "	51
Jean Gingras	15	2 mo.	51
Marie Costello	Nov. 19	10 years	51
Olivier Laferte	23	23 "	51
Celestine Gervais Lucier	25	20 "	52
1853			
*James Sheil	Jan. 4	35 years	52
Charles Indian	10	35 "	52
Jean Indian	27	15 "	53
Child of Gervais	Feb. 6	0 days	53
Etienne Lucier	Mar. 9	60 years	55
Pierre Bourgignon	24	3 "	55
Marguerite Bourgignon	25	30 "	55
Agathe Delcour	May 4	40 "	55
Antoine Rivet	4	5 "	55
Rosalie Perrault	Aug. 29	16 "	57
Jerome Rivet	Nov. 4	10 mo.	58
Thomas Deguire	Dec. 7	2 years	59

	1854		
Joseph Jacques	Jan. 13	2 years	60
Cuthbert Lacourse	21	16 "	60
Marguerite Kalapoya	Mar. 3	2 "	62
Louis Lacourse	11	1 "	62
Edouard Rivet	Apr. 6	2 "	62
Charles Prevost	11	-	63
Jacques Servant	June 4	-	63
Boy of Pichet	19	0 days	64
Louise Petit	Aug. 8	1 year	65
William Cannon	30	97 "	65
Felicite Lucier Gervais	Oct. 22	16 years	67
Archange Lacourse	Nov. 3	50 "	67
Eloi Ducheneau	Dec. 4	26 "	68
Catherine Weston	11	20 mo.	68
Francois Pascal Biscornet	23	63 years	69
	1855		
Euphreme Jeaudoin	Jan. 16	4 mo.	70
Moise Rivet	31	4 mo.	70
John Indian, ho of Lacourse	Feb. 8	23 years	70a
Joseph Laframboise	15	13 "	70a
Michel Laferte	Mar. 15	18 mo.	70a
Therese Delcourt	23	18 years	70b
Augustin Russie	Apr. 6	30 "	70b
James Robinson	17	41 "	70b
Baptiste Norwest	Apr. 25	60 "	71
Sarah Lacourse	June 11	6 mo.	72
Anders Norwest	23	3 years	72
Clarissa Isom	Oct. 7	33 "	74
Lizette Indian, ho of Laferte.	28	60 "	74
Jacques Poirier	29	2 "	75
	1856		
Marie Okanogan	Jan. 20	4 years	76
Francois Indian	Feb. 3	4 "	77
Luce Gardipe	20	2 "	77
Clarisse Montour	27	1 "	78
William Gladman, ho. of Longtain	Mar. 7	24 "	78
Elizabeth Jeaudoin	-	-	78
Maxime Moise	Apr. 24	4 years	79
Rose Baptiste, ho. of Arquet	May 3	11 "	79
Pierre Baptiste Norwest	June 7	2 "	80
Pelagie Lucier Bernier	10	-	80
Baptiste Delcourt	July 8	55 years	80
Jean Gingras	Oct. 7	-	82
Madeliene Pend d'Oreille	11	2 years	82
Francois Rivet	31	17 "	82
	1857		
Marie Menard	Jan. 8	30 years	84
Caroline Gardipe	Feb. 2	2 "	84
Josette Bourgeau	May 10	-	86
Elizabeth Boisverd	Sep. 23	-	88
Josette Servant	24	12 years	88
	1858		
Virginia Lebrun	Jan. 2	9 mo.	page 90
Celeste Petit	2	14 years	90
Catherine Longtain Howard	19	30 "	91
Charles Norwest	24	-	91
Philomene Lebrun	Feb. 28	10 years	92
Charles Gingras	Mar. 1	18 mo.	92

Esther Lebrun	8	2 years	92
Lucy Indian, ho. of Wagner	24	15 "	93
Son of Laderoute	Apr. 18	0 days	93
Laurent Sauve	Aug. 3	-	97
Michael Laferte	22	-	97
Francois Dupre	Dec. 13	90 Years	99
Kennedy	31	-	100
1859			
Catherine Petit	Jan. 3	11 years	100
Son of Aplin	23	0 days	100
Hyacinthe Russie	Mar. 15	6 years	101
Marie Blanche Franconi	Apr. 8	6 "	101
Joseph Langtain	Sep. 2	21 "	101
Antoine Laferte	Oct. 19	2 "	101
Marguerite Pariseau	Dec. 29	-	102
1860			
Margaret Fraley	Feb. 16	2 days	104
Child of Norwest	23	4 "	104
Agnes Lacourse	Mar. 10	3 years	105
Amable Arcouette	27	2 "	106
Rosalie Bourgignon, ho. of Aplin	May 4	12 "	107
Catherine Comartin	July 13	30 "	107
Louis Labonte	Sep. 13	80 "	110
Adele Rowland	Nov. 7	10 "	113
Esther Lavigueur	8	21 "	113
Joseph Jerome Jackson	-	4 days	114
Marie Vivet	Dec. 19	11 mo.	113
Louis Lacourse	24	14 Years	113
1861			
Michel Laframboise	Jan. 28	75 years	115
Thomas Smith	Feb. 17	-	116
Hilaire Gardipe	Mar. 19	1 year	117
Pierre Lacourse	Apr. 18	33 "	118
Joseph Lacourse	26	18 "	118
Joseph Gervais	Jul. 15	84 "	119
1862			
Joseph Deguire	Jan. 17	2 years	Page 124
*Joseph Longtain	31	2 "	124
Henri Clovis Matthieu	Feb. 21	15 mo.	125
Helene Laroque	Jun. 25	6 years	130
Gideon Brouillard	July 13	18 mo.	130
Marie Magdeleine Bergevin	13	1 mo.	131
James McKay	16	2 years	131
Cyrille Richter	21	3 weeks	131
1863			
David Boucher	Feb. 4	33 years	134
*James Cosgrove	4	26 "	134
Elizabeth Pellan	May 21	23 "	135
Mary Howard	July 6	12 "	136
Nettie Alice Osborn	Aug. 26	10 days	137
Charles Choquette	Sep. 14	18 mo.	138
Madeleine Servant Bergevin	Oct. 5	40 years	139
Narcisse Pichet	19	3 "	139
Matilde Jette	Nov. 6	8 "	140
Olive Forcier	30	34 "	140
1864			
Rosalie Gervais	June 21	23 years	143
Marianne Perrault Deguire	Aug. 19	30 "	145
Nazaire Dubreuil	20	10 mo.	145

Jeanne Laferte	Oct. 6	5 years	145
Pierre Lacourse	17	70 "	146
Xavier Laderoute	Dec. 19	50 "	146
*Catherine Murphy	24	50 "	147

Total recorded burials in Book II, St. Paul — 227

St. Paul, Book III

1865

Anne Norwest	Jan. 16	5 weeks	Page 1
Julie Jette	Feb. 25	25 years	2
Marie Bastien	Mar. 18	20 "	3
Joseph F. Bertrand	18	12 days	3
Marie Wagner	24	60 years	3
Pierre Wagner	June 16	75 "	4
Catherine Lafantaisie Mongrain	Aug. 7	40 "	5

1866

*Daniel Murphy	Jan. 25	66 years	7

1867

Pierre Gauthier	Apr. 27	58 years	14
Francois Banget	May 4	58 "	14
Felicite Lucier Manson	June 12	53 "	14
Amable Petit	July 18	70 "	14
Charles Norwest	Aug. 21	2 mo.	15
Adolphe Manson	Sep. 13	-	15
Michael Coyle	23	60 years	16
Alexis Aubichon	30	80 "	16

1868

Julie Gingras	Feb. 3	23 years	21
Son of Hirsch	11	3 "	21
Simeon Bernier	June 18	2 mo.	23
Catherine Horan	Sept. -	58 years	24
Theodore Raymond	Dec. 29	2 "	26

1869

Angelique Longtain	Aug. 4	3 mo.	29
Josette Chalifoux	24	23 years	30
*Theodore Aplin	Sep. 16	2 mo.	30
Son of Noress	Oct. 26	9 days	30
Peter Fitzgerald	31	-	31
Theresia Schultheis	Nov. 18	8 mo.	31
Adelaide Lambert	28	10 years	32

1870

Eleanor Pepin	Mar. 2	-	34
Narcisse Vivet	7	39 years	34
Francois St. Martin	Apr. 14	1 "	35
Robert Daly	May 27	40 "	36
*Cecelia Lawson McKay	June 15	50 "	37
Marguerite Waponte Arquet	Oct. 5	72 "	39
Euphrosene Kitson	Aug. 18	8 years	40
John Nibler	Sep. 22	1 "	40
Mary Ellen Horan	22	-	41
Margaret Kerr	Oct. 12	-	41

1871

*Margaret Kirk	Jan. 16	6 years	43
Margaret Fleishman	25	71 "	44
Philomene Raymond	29	1 mo.	44
Veronica Rochbrune Richter	May 5	-	46
Sylvain Bourgeau	June 13	70 years	47
Mary R. Coffey	July 28	54 "	49
Mary Jane Pichet	6	9 "	49
Margaret Nibler	Sep. 12	81 "	50

Mary Flynn	23	71 "	51
F. X. Nibler	Oct. 28	5 mo.	51
Boy of Chamberland	Dec. 10	1 "	51
1872			
Marcelline Pepin	May 5	4 mo.	53
Peter Fleishman	July 8	73 years	56
Peter Bourgeau	Aug. 17	2 "	56
Charles Roch Pichet	17	1 mo.	56
Elizabeth Flynn	Sep. 14	2 years	58
1873			
Celina Brouillard	Mar. 17	2 years	61
Eulalie Deguire	May 17	18 "	62
Peter Flynn	20	87 "	63
Mary Petit Picard	June 15	35 "	64
Charles Petit	21	39 "	64
Clementine Dubreuil	21	12 "	64
Mary Jane Bourgeau	July 11	7 "	65
Margaret Coboway Labonte	20	80 "	66
*Margaret Kirk	Sep. 2	42 "	67
Mary Jane Pichet	15	2 mo.	67
*Mary Rossiter Cosgrove	17	65 years	68
Augustine Raymond	Oct. 14	-	68
Josette Servant Lacourse	Nov. 4	76 years	69
1874			
Jean Baptiste Chamberland	Feb. 6	6 mo.	71
Louis Bernier	Mar. 7	2 "	72
James Picard	26	4 "	72
Alfred Lucier	Apr. 8	7 weeks	73
*Thomas Herbert	22	-	73
Henry Joseph Langlois	June 9	-	74
Andrew Chalifoux	20	10 mo.	75
Adelaide Lambert	July 11	6 years	76
Victoire Charlebois Rochbrune	Sep. 22	30 "	77
Louis Clement Raymond	Oct. 9	7 mo.	78
Priscilla Matthieu	Nov. 9	20 years	78
Francois Dubreuil	Dec. 1	3 "	78
Josephine Bourgeau	23	14 days	79
1875			
Pascal Pariseau	Mar. 12	8 years	81
Adeline Josephine Belique	Apr. 30	10 mo.	83
Joseph Frederic Despard	May 11	87 years	83
Frances Rose Lavigueur	Sep. 17	3 mo.	87
Thomas Alex. McLaughlin	29	4 "	88
1876			
Charles Gaston Dueuron	Jan. 13	24 years	93
Joseph Pichet	14	-	93
Louise Chamberland	Apr. 17	50 years	95
Soulange Bergevin Dompierre	June 13	20 "	98
1877			
Francois Bernier	Jan. 12	70 years	102
Mary Genevieve Bellanger	Apr. 10	8 mo.	104
Son of Roch Pichet	Aug. 21	8 days	109
Archange Kitson	Oct. 28	10 years	110
Catherine Kitson	28	6 "	110
Rose Junstine Kitson	29	4 "	110
Child of Denoiple	Nov. 17	-	111
Edouard Kitson	Dec. 14	5 weeks	112

	1878		
Narcisse Chamberland	Mar. 31	17 years	114
Flavie Petit	Sep. 25	25 "	117
Susanne Petit	Nov. 26	-	118
	1879		
Josette Laframbois Labonte	Jan. 15	40 years	119
Moses Servant	Apr. 3	29 "	123
	1880		
Charles Hilaire Chalifoux	Feb. 9	4 mo.	129
Francois Augustin Bernier	Mar. 28	2 years	129
Child of J. Jackson	Apr. 6	0 days	130
Amable Arcouet	July 8	81 years	131
Sara Julia Bernier	23	3 "	132
	1881		
Sara Magdelen Raymond	Oct. 12	10 days	142
	1882		
Francis Labonte	Apr. 17	3 years	144
Alexandre Louis Raymond	Dec. 23	1 mo.	149
	1883		
Jean Baptiste Labonte	Mar. 30	20 years	151
Nathan August Raymond	Sep. 25	6 mo.	153
August Crete	Oct. 24	4 years	154
Virginia Crete	29	5 "	154
Charles Kitson	Nov. 6	13 "	155
	1884		
Anthony Labonte	Apr. 3	17 years	157
Charles Galloway	Oct. 2	86 "	St. James, McMinnville
	1888		
F. Adolphe Chamberland	Mar. 6	70 years	179
	1891		
Julien C. Provost	Nov. 12	1 day	206

Total recorded burials in Book III, St. Paul — 119
Total recorded burials in Old Cemetery — 546
*Recorded removals to New Cemetery — 11
                                       535

B-1

BIBLIOGRAPHY

General:
Allen, A. J. *Ten Years in Oregon: Travels . . . of Dr. E. White and Lady, West of the Rocky Mountains . . .* Ithaca, N. Y., 1850.
Bagley, Clarence B., ed. *Early Catholic Missions in Old Oregon.* 2 vols. Seattle, Washington, 1932.
Bailey, Margaret Jewett. *The Grains, or Passages in the Life of Ruth Rover, with Occasional Pictures of Oregon, Natural and Moral.* 2 vols. Portland, Oregon, 1854.
Ball, John. *Autobiography of John Ball, Compiled by his Daughters, Kate Ball Powers, Flora Ball Hopkins, Lucy Ball.* Grand Rapids, Michigan, 1925.
Bancroft, Hubert Howe. *History of Oregon.* 2 vols. San Francisco, 1888.
Baker, Burt Brown, ed. *Letters of Dr. John McLoughlin, Written at Fort Vancouver, 1829-1832.* Portland, Oregon, 1948.
----- *The Financial Papers of Dr. John McLoughlin.* Oregon Historical Society, Portland, Oregon, 1949.
Blanchet, Francis Norbert. *Historical Sketches of the Catholic Church in Oregon, During the Past Forty Years.* Portland, Oregon, 1878.
British and American Joint Commission for the Final Settlement of the Claims of the Hudson's Bay and Puget's Sound Agricultural Companies. 14 vols. Washington; Montreal, 1865-1869.
Vol. I. *Memorials Presented to the Commissioner, under the Treaty of July 1, 1863 . . .* Washington: Government Printing Office, 1865.
Vol. II. *Evidence on the Part of the Hudson's Bay Company.* Montreal: John Lovell, 1868.
Vol. III. *Evidence on the Part of the Puget's Sound Agricultural Company.* Montreal: John Lovell, 1868.
Caywood, Louis R. *Final Report, Fort Vancouver Excavations.* Mimeographed report, issued by the United States Department of the Interior, National Park Service, San Francisco, 1955.
Chittenden, Hiram Martin. *The American Fur Trade of the Far West.* 2 vols. New York, 1935.
Clarke, Samuel, A. *Pioneer Days of Oregon History.* 2 vols. Portland, Oregon, 1905.
Colvocoressis, Lt. George M. *Four Years in a Government Expedition.* New York, 1852.
Cox, Ross. *Adventures on the Columbia River.* London, 1832.
DeSmet, Pierre-Jean. *Origin, Progress and Prospects of the Catholic Mission to the Rocky Mountains.* Philadelphia, Pennsylvania, 1843.
Douglas, David. *Journal Kept by David Douglas During his Travels in North America, 1823-1827.* New York, 1959.
Dugger, Sister Anne Clare, F.C.S.P. *Catholic Institutions of the Walla Walla Valley, 1847-1950.* A Thesis Presented to the Department of History of Seattle University, 1953. Mimeographed.
Dunn, John. *History of the Oregon Territory and British North-American Fur Trade.* London, 1844.
Ermatinger, Edward. *Edward Ermatinger's York Factory Express Journal, Being a Record of Journeys Made Between Fort Vancouver and Hudson's Bay in the Years 1827-1828.* From Transactions of the Royal Society of Canada, Vol. VI. Ottawa, 1912.
Farnham, Thomas Jefferson. *Travels in the Great Western Prairies, the Anahuac and Rocky Mountains, and in the Oregon Territory.* Poughkeepsie, N.Y., 1841.
Field, Col. Virgil F. *Official History of the Washington National Guard.* 7 vols. Office of the Adjutant General, Tacoma, Washington, 1961. Mimeographed.
Franchère, Gabriel. *Narrative of a Voyage to the Northwest Coast of America.* New York, 1854.
Genealogical Forum of Portland, Oregon. *Genealogical Material in Oregon Donation Land Claims.* 4 vols. Portland, Oregon, 1957, 1959, 1962, 1967. Multilithed.
Gilbert, Frank T. *Historic Sketches of Walla Walla, Whitman, Columbia and Garfield Counties, Washington Territory.* Portland, Oregon, 1882.
Gray, William Henry. *A History of Oregon, 1742-1849, Drawn from Personal Observation and Authentic Information.* Portland, Oregon; and New York, 1870.
Hafen, LeRoy R. and Ann W., eds. *Mountain Men and the Fur Trade of the Far West.* 10 vols. Glendale, California.
Hargraves, Letitia. *Letters of Letitia Hargraves.* Edited by Margaret A. McLeod, Champlain Society, Vol. 28, 1947.
Henry, Alexander. *New Light on the Early History of the Greater Northwest; The Manuscript Journals of Alexander Henry . . . and of David Thompson . . .* edited by Elliot Coues, 3 vols. New York, 1897.

Hodge, Frederick W. *Handbook of American Indians.* Smithsonian Institutions, Bureau of American Ethnology, Bulletin No. 30. 2 vols. New York, 1959.

House of Representatives, 59th Congress, 2nd Session, Document No. 133, *Rolls of Certain Indian Tribes in Oregon and Washington.* Washington, D.C., 1906.

Hussey, John A. *Champoeg: Place of Transition.* Portland, Oregon, 1967.

-----*Chinook Point and the Story of Fort Columbia.* Olympia, Washington, 1957.

-----*The History of Fort Vancouver and its Physical Structure.* Portland, Oregon, 1957.

Innis, Harold A. *The Fur Trade in Canada.* New Haven, 1962.

Irving, Washington. *Adventures of Captain Bonneville.* New York, undated.

----- *Astoria.* New York, undated.

Jessett, Thomas E., ed. *Reports and Letters of Herbert Beaver, 1836-1838.* Portland, Oregon, 1959.

Kowrach, Edward J. *Big Bend Missions and Medical Lake.* Medical Lake, Washington, 1963.

Landerholm, Carl, trans. and ed. *Notices and Voyages of the Famed Quebec Mission to the Pacific Northwest.* Portland, Oregon, 1956.

Lang. H. O., ed. *History of the Willamette Valley, Being a Description of the Valley and Its Resources . . . Together with Personal Reminiscences of Its Early Pioneers.* Portland, Oregon, 1885.

Lee, D. and Frost, J. H. *Ten Years in Oregon.* New York, 1844.

Leonard, Zenas. *Adventures of Zenas Leonard, Fur Trader and Trapper, 1831-1836.* Edited by W. F. Wagner. Cleveland, Ohio, 1904.

Lockley, Fred. *History of the Columbia River Valley from The Dalles to the Sea.* Chicago, 1928.

McArthur, Lewis A. *Oregon Geographic Names.* Portland, Oregon, 1952.

McCrossin, Sister Mary of the Blessed Sacrament. *The Bell and the River.* Palo Alto, California, 1957.

McNamee, Sister Mary Dominica, S.N.D. de N. *Williamette Interlude.* Palo Alto, California, 1959.

McNeal, William H. *History of the Centennial Churches of The Dalles, Oregon.* Mimeographed. The Dalles, Oregon 1969.

Michelle, Mary Ann. *Just a Memorandum.* Bulletin of the Genealogical Forum of Portland, Oregon, Vol. X, numbers 8, 9, 10.

Mitchell, Howard T. *The Journals of William Fraser Tolmie, Physician and Fur Trader.* Vancouver, Canada, 1963.

Morice, Adrian Gabriel, O.M.I. *The History of the Northern Interior of British Columbia.* Fairfield, Washington, 1971.

O'Hara, Edwin V. *Pioneer Catholic History of Oregon.* Portland, Oregon, 1911.

Parish Registers of:
    Church of the Assumption, Brooks, Oregon.
    Church of St. Gervais and St. Protais, Gervais, Ore.
    Immaculate Conception, Portland, Oregon.
    Stellamaris (Star of the Sea), Chinookville, Wash.
    St. James, Vancouver, Washington.
    St. John the Evangelist, Salem, Oregon.
    St. John's, Oregon City, Oregon.
    St. Louis of the Willamette, St. Louis, Oregon.
    St. Michael's, Grand Ronde, Oregon.
    St. Patrick's, Walla Walla, Washington.
    St. Paul of the Willamette, St. Paul, Oregon.
    St. Stephen's, Roseburg, Oregon.
    Ste. Rose of the Cayuse, Walla Walla, Washington.

Parker, Samuel. *Journal of an Exploring Tour Beyond the Rocky Mountains.* Auburn, N.Y., 1846.

Pash, Rev. Joseph J. *History of the Immaculate Conception Parish in the Colville Valley.* Colville, Wash., 1962.

Payette, B.C. *The Oregon Country Under the Union Jack.* Montreal, 1964.

Publications of the Hudson's Bay Record Society. (A continuing series). Toronto and London.

Ross, Alexander. *The Fur Hunters of the Far West; a Narrative of Advantures in the Oregon and Rocky Mountains.* 2 vols. London, 1855.

Russell, Osborne. *Journal of a Trapper*, edited by Aubrey L. Haines. Lincoln, Nebraska, 1955.

Schoenberg, Wilfred P., S.J. *A Chronicle of Catholic History of the Pacific Northwest, 1743-1960*. Portland, Oregon, 1962.

----- *Jesuits in Montana, 1840-1960*. Portland, Ore., 1960.

----- *Jesuits in Oregon, 1844-1959*. Portland, 1959.

Scott, Harvey W. *History of the Oregon Country*. 6 vols. Cambridge, Mass., 1924.

Sheridan, Philip H. *Personal Memoirs*. 2 vols. New York, 1888.

Sisters of the Holy Names of Jesus and Mary. *Gleanings of Fifty Years.* .Portland, Oregon, 1909.

Spencer, Omar C. *The Story of Sauvies Island*. Portland, Oregon, 1950.

Steeves, Sarah Hunt. *Book of Remembrance of Marion County, Oregon, Pioneers 1840-1860*. Portland, Oregon, 1927.

St. John's Church, Oregon City. *St. John's Parish, Oregon City, 1844-1957*. Portland, Oregon, 1957.

Strong, Thomas Nelson. *Cathlamet on the Columbia*. Portland, Oregon, 1906.

Swan, James Gilchrist. *The Northwest Coast*. Fairfield, Washington, 1966.

Swanton, John R. *The Indian Tribes of North America*. Smithsonian Institution, Bureau of American Ethnology, Bulletin No. 145. Washington, D.C., 1952.

Thomas, Edward Harper. *Chinook, a History and Dictionary*. Portland, Oregon, 1935.

Thwaites, Reuben Gold, ed. *Early Western Travels*. 32 vols. Cleveland, Ohio, 1904-1907.

Victor, Frances Fuller. *Early Indian Wars of Oregon*. Salem, Oregon, 1894.

----- *The River of the West*. Hartford, Conn. and Toledo, Ohio, 1870.

Wilkes, Charles. *Narrative of the United States Exploring Expedition during the years 1838, 1839, 1840, 1841, 1842*. 5 vols. Philadelphia, 1845.

Williams, Edgar and Co. *Historical Atlas Map of Marion and Linn Counties, Oregon*. San Francisco, 1878.

Williams, Lewis R. *Chinook by the Sea*. Portland, Oregon, 1924.

----- *Our Pacific County*. Raymond, Washington, 1930.

Wright, E. W., ed. *Lewis and Dryden's Marine History of the Pacific Northwest*. Portland, Oregon, 1895.

Writers' Program, Washington. *Washington, a Guide to the Evergreen State, Compiled by Workers of the Writers' Program of the Work Projects Administration in the State of Washington*. Portland, Oregon, 1941.

Newspaper Files:

Oregon City Enterprise, Oregon City, Oregon

Oregon Journal, Portland, Oregon

Oregon Spectator, Oregon City, Oregon

Oregon Statesman, Salem, Oregon

Oregonian, The, Portland, Oregon

Union Bulletin, The, Walla Walla, Washington

Periodicals:

British Columbia Historical Quarterly (Vancouver, B.C.)

Catholic Sentinel (Portland, Oregon)

Clackamas County Historical (Oregon City, Oregon)

Clark County History (Vancouver, Washington)

Cowlitz County Historical Quarterly (Kelso, Washington)

Marion County History (Salem, Oregon)

Oregon Historical Quarterly (Portland, Oregon)

Pacific Northwest Quarterly (Seattle, Washington)

Pioneer Days in Canyonville (Canyonville, Oregon)

St. Joseph's Magazine (Mount Angel, Oregon)

The Beaver (Winnipeg, Canada)

The Sou'wester (South Bend, Washington)

The Umpqua Trapper (Roseburg, Oregon)

Transactions of the Oregon Pioneer Association (Portland, Oregon)

Washington Historical Quarterly (Seattle, Washington)

Other Sources:

Jeaudoin, Betty Jean. *Jeaudoin Family History*. (Mimeo.)

Oregon State Archives, Bulletin No. 3. *Pioneer Families of the Oregon Territory*.

Plamondon, George H. *The Plamondon Family*. (Mimeo.)

Warner, Mikell De Lores. *De Lore Family History*. (Xerox)

Cemetery Records.

Correspondence and interviews with descendants.

Land Office maps, State Census Lists, and various official records on file in the State Capitol, State Library, and County Courthouses.

Personal Scrapbooks.